LEARNING TO WRITE
IN COLLEGE

By

REED SMITH

University of South Carolina
Columbia, South Carolina

D. C. HEATH AND COMPANY

BOSTON

D. C. HEATH AND COMPANY

Offices: BOSTON   NEW YORK   CHICAGO   DALLAS

ATLANTA   SAN FRANCISCO   LONDON

LEARNING TO WRITE IN COLLEGE

I am convinced more and more, every day, that fine writing is, next to fine doing, the top thing in the world.

— JOHN KEATS

Three fourths of writing well consists in giving definite, well-chosen details and plenty of them. The other fourth doesn't matter.

Learning to write is a serious business, but it need not be a solemn one.

Acknowledgments

Detailed acknowledgments of copyright permissions are made throughout the text, but it is fitting that general acknowledgments also be made here as follows : —

The American Scholar, for an article by William A. Shimer.

D. Appleton-Century Company, for selections from Thomas Huxley and Frederick Adams Woods.

The Atlantic Monthly Press.

The Bell Syndicate, Inc., for a selection from James J. Montague.

Chicago Tribune.

The China Inland Mission, for a quotation from Elisabeth Scott Stam.

The Clarendon Press.

Coward-McCann, Inc.

Reginald C. Dingle and Allen Upward's sister.

Dodd, Mead and Company, Inc.

Doubleday, Doran and Company, for material from Kipling.

E. P. Dutton and Company.

Famous Features Syndicate.

Funk & Wagnalls Company, for a selection from W. W. Ellsworth's *Creative Composition*.

Ginn and Company.

Harcourt, Brace and Company, for selections from Sinclair Lewis, John Dos Passos, and Stuart Chase.

Harper and Brothers, for selections from Mark Twain, Mary Wilkins Freeman, Philip Wylie, and *Harper's Magazine*.

D. C. Heath and Company, for a selection from John Dewey.

Henry Holt and Company, for a selection from William Beebe.

Houghton Mifflin Company, for selections from Holmes, Emerson, Aldrich, Meredith, Wren, and Anna Hempstead Branch.

Institute for Propaganda Analysis, for a selection from *Propaganda Analysis*.

Alfred A. Knopf, Inc., for a selection from H. L. Mencken.

J. B. Lippincott Company, for a selection from W. H. Prescott.

Little, Brown and Company.

Longmans, Green and Company.

New York Evening Post.

New Yorker.

W. W. Norton and Company, Inc., for "Invocation to the Muse" by Celima Roi Leonard and for "Carnival" by Rowe Morrell.

Publishers Syndicate.

The Reader's Digest, for the pro-and-con argument, "Abolish Intercollegiate Football?"

Charles Scribner's Sons, for selections from Joel Chandler Harris, F. Hopkinson Smith, Robert Louis Stevenson, George Washington Cable, Thomas Wolfe, and Conrad Aiken.

The Viking Press, Inc., for selections from *Boners* and *More Boners.*

The Writer's Digest, for material on revision.

The Yale Review, for an article by Raphael Demos.

Sincere appreciation goes also to the various professors of English who have generously allowed the use of the large amount of student writing which is employed for illustrative purposes throughout this volume. Specific acknowledgment is made in each instance to author and institution.

Individual acknowledgments also go to Mrs. Eliza London Shepard for a paragraph from Jack London's story, "All Gold Cañon"; to Mrs. Rudyard Kipling for the Kipling material from *Captains Courageous;* to Christopher Morley for a paragraph from his "Travels in Philadelphia."

Special thanks are due also to the editor and publishers of the *English Journal* for the many devices and suggestions taken from that publication; and also to the editor and publishers of the *Atlantic Monthly* for the use of four essays from the Atlantic Contests for College Students.

Personal gratitude and acknowledgment go to the following friends and fellow teachers who have generously given their time and assistance in many different ways: first, in the order of time, to Miss Lois Hentz, Secretary of the Graduate School, University of South Carolina; Dr. George Armstrong Wauchope, former head of the English Department, University of South Carolina, for the symbols of graphical analysis suggested in Chapter IV, "The Analysis of Sentences"; to Dr. Havilah Babcock, head of the Department of English Literature, University of South Carolina, Professor Henry C. Davis, head of the Department of English Language and Rhetoric, and the following members of the department, Dr. Robert Duncan Bass, Mrs. Maude M. Hawkins, and Mr. W. Yeaton Wagener, all of whom read the manuscript before publication and made helpful suggestions.

Preface

This book is the outgrowth of twenty-five years' experience in teaching composition. Its method throughout is threefold: first, the definite statement and clear explanation of the general principles and techniques underlying all effective writing; second, the illustration of these principles and techniques from the work of both students and successful authors; third, the discussion and application of these principles and techniques by means of an abundant variety of exercises, questions, Round-Table discussion hints, and assignments.

In addition to rich and abundant quotation of the best author material both of the past and of the present, particular attention has been given to including specimens of the best student writing in all the various fields. Among the institutions represented are colleges and universities in Arkansas, California, Illinois, Iowa, Massachusetts, Michigan, Missouri, Nebraska, Ohio, New Hampshire, and South Carolina. This cross-section of the best college writing that is being done at present throughout the United States is very stimulating and suggestive. It would probably never occur to a college student that he has it in him to parallel such acknowledged masterpieces as George Herbert Palmer's "Self-Cultivation in English," Kipling's "They," Stevenson's "Markheim," Edna Ferber's "A Gay Old Dog," John Galsworthy's "Quality," or Logan Pearsall Smith's "Silvia Doria"; but a delightful essay or thrilling story by another college student who is no older or better taught than he, but who yet has caught the trick and has succeeded highly where he himself may never have risen above mediocrity, is another matter entirely. It is both an open invitation and a constant challenge. And the last step before doing a thing oneself is the feeling that one is able to do it.

The numerous Round-Table discussions have been prepared with special care. Taken together they constitute a complete practical work-book covering the entire field of grammar, analysis, and composition. Their purpose is, first, to appeal to the student's reason and make him really think about himself and his environment as well as about the processes of learning to write; and, second, to stimulate interesting class discussion. More questions are suggested than could always be used with profit. The training and ability of composition classes vary not only in different colleges, but also in the same college. Knowing the class as the instructor will do, he can select wisely among the various questions. So important does the author deem them that he would advise any instructor, rather than study the text and slight the exercises, to emphasize the exercises and the Round Tables and to slight the text.

The arrangement of the book into parts will enable each instructor to adapt it to the needs of his particular class. A poorly prepared class may need careful and detailed drill in Part I, Fundamentals; a better-prepared group may need only a rapid review and check-up of this material, with primary emphasis on analysis rather than on grammar; a particularly bright and advanced group might conceivably be ready to go to Part II as soon as they have finished the opening chapter, "Writing the Paragraph."

To all subjects pertaining to composition, but especially to the three important ones of punctuation, sentence usage, and the study of words, the approach is entirely fresh and modern. Both language and literature are alive and growing, and the usage of today is in many particulars not that of yesterday. Through the use of such sources as the new Merriam-Webster *International Dictionary, Current English Usage, An Experience Curriculum in English,* and *A Correlated Curriculum,* three recent monographs of the National Council of Teachers of English, the files of the *English Journal,* and other publications listed throughout the text, the results of the latest and best research scholarship have been utilized.

The author has tried to keep three guiding ideas constantly before him: (1) teaching students to write is largely a matter of teaching them to think; (2) the secret of all good writing is the secret of going into details; and (3) humor should have a part both in writing and in the teaching thereof.

REED SMITH

January 16, 1939

Contents

PART THREE

WORD STUDY AND VOCABULARY BUILDING

PART FOUR

IMAGINATIVE WRITING

PART ONE
FUNDAMENTALS

CHAPTER I

Writing the Paragraph

(Logically this chapter should open Part II, Writing for Practical Purposes. It is put here, however, in order that practice in actual writing may begin at once.)

1. The Importance of the Paragraph in Writing

We think in sentences and we talk in sentences; or, to express the same idea differently, the sentence is the unit both of thought and of speech. Conversation is usually a give-and-take affair, each person contributing a remark in turn, and often expressing himself in fragments of sentences, in exclamations, or by gestures and facial expressions, instead of in complete and connected sentences. An accurate shorthand report of our conversations would usually read more like a parody than a word-for-word record.

While we are actually talking, however, we are not aware of how much we are leaving unsaid, for the very good reason that our interest in other people, the warmth of argument, the glow of friendship, or possibly merely the pleasure of expressing our own opinions, serves to color and cement our words into seemingly satisfactory units of thought. Without the interplay of personality, however, and the opportunity to watch the faces and gestures of our companions, our words themselves, if we could read them over later in cold type, would seem strangely disconnected and inadequate.

That is one reason why to write well is much harder than to talk well, and it explains why many a bright, entertaining talker becomes dull and commonplace when he takes pen in hand and tries to express himself on paper. All the vitality and charm somehow seem to evaporate, and to leave only a dry, gray shell of our real meaning and of our true selves, struggling and straggling in awkward sentences across the pages of our manuscript.

Hence it comes about that our written sentences, since we are not present to interpret and emphasize them with voice, manner, and bearing, have a double duty to perform. Not only must each sentence be correct and clear in and by itself, but also, taken together, the sentences must as a group express our meaning completely, each successive sentence growing naturally out of the preceding sentence and helping forward our meaning somewhat as the successive steps of a staircase lead uninterruptedly upward, or as the links of a chain are connected each with the other. That is to say, each sentence not only must be satisfactory in itself, but must also act in partnership with the other sentences toward a common purpose. Teamwork is just as necessary in the paragraph as it is in baseball or football.

Because of this fact, the paragraph becomes of first importance in learning to write. In fact, little real progress can be made until the paragraph has become thoroughly familiar both in theory, through studying the writing of others, and also in practice, through writing done by ourselves.

2. Independent Paragraphs

As a practical matter in writing, paragraphs may be divided into two classes: (1) independent or unrelated paragraphs, and (2) chain or related paragraphs. Their names suggest the difference between them.

An independent paragraph is one whose meaning is distinct and complete in and by itself. It is not connected with or related to any other paragraph. It stands alone, like a one-room cabin or like a single freight car on a sidetrack. It has its own subject, or topic, which it develops by means of as many particulars and details as the writer may need to give in order to drive home his idea. His purpose may be to explain or to make clear; he may wish to prove or to disprove; he may be trying to depict a sense impression or a mood; or he may be interested in relating an incident or telling a story. But whether expository, argumentative, descriptive, or narrative, when the paragraph ends, if it has been successfully written, it leaves nothing more to be said on that subject at that time. The circle of thought has been fully rounded out and is complete within itself.

Independent paragraphs have many uses. They have increased greatly in numbers and variety as modern life has speeded up, and as the demand has grown for things that take less time and space than formerly. Long, detailed arguments and explanations have given place to succinct, one-paragraph articles which say keenly and convincingly all that need be said on some current topic. Contrast, for example, the heavy one-column or even two-column editorials of a former day with the brief, pointed editorials and articles in many present-day newspapers and in such widely differing magazines as *Collier's*, *Time*, the *New Yorker*, and the *Saturday Evening Post*. The independent paragraph, both of explanation and of argument as well as of incident and of description, has come to stay. Brevity, point, and pungency are keynotes of the modern spirit and the modern style.

Thus, in the light of the present and growing demands for paragraphs of this kind, but chiefly because ability to compose paragraphs forms a most important step in learning to write, a great deal of practice in independent paragraphs is necessary. Every day during the next month that the composition class meets, every student should write an independent paragraph either in class or on assignment. The more, the better. There is no way to learn to write except by writing, and the independent paragraph is the best place to start.

Chain, or connected, paragraphs are dealt with in Chapter VII, pages 141–177 below.

3. Writing from Topic Sentences

In order to keep definitely on the track of the paragraph idea, the first ten or twelve paragraphs should be written not from topics but from actual topic sentences. At the end of this chapter, pages 16–18, are eighty topic sentences, which can be worked up into satisfactory independent paragraphs. They are divided, though not equally, between exposition, argument, description, and narration.

Look over the list carefully, and, as preparation for class, do the following three things : —

1. From the list choose one sentence from each of the groups — exposition, argument, description, and narration — which you feel that you can best expand into a paragraph. The paragraph is to be not less than half a page long, nor more than a page and a quarter.

2. From these four sentences choose the one you feel you can develop most easily.

3. Think up some of the particulars and details that seem to belong to it. Try to think of at least five details. This may not be as easy as it sounds, for before you can write, you must think. Count the details on your fingers as you think of them, without writing any of them down on paper. Shut your eyes if you feel like it, and *force* your mind to *realize* or *see* the topic unfolding, or unraveling, into a series of details and related sentence thoughts. Time yourself, and see how long it takes you to think up the five details. Do not stop with five if you can think of more.

Next day let the instructor run through the list of topic sentences with the class and let the class as a whole do what each member did the evening before; that is, first select the best topic sentence from each of the four groups, and secondly, vote on the one topic sentence that the class is to write on. If either the instructor or the class can suggest a better topic sentence, select that one instead of one from the list.

4. The Need for Details

The instructor will then write the chosen sentence on the board, and ask everybody to think about it. To take a very obvious and easy example, suppose that the sentence selected is this one : —

> I recently visited a friend's room that showed many signs of carelessness and untidiness.

Before even such a simple paragraph topic as this can be developed, it is necessary to think up and think over the various details and particulars that serve to give a room an untidy appearance.

(1) AN UNTIDY ROOM

One class carried out the following plan. After writing the sentence on the board, the instructor asked the students to suggest details of untidiness. As different students named different details, he wrote each detail down in sentence form, numbering them in order. After giving every student a chance to express himself, the list of numbered sentences on the board read after the fashion given on the next page.[1]

[1] C. J. Thompson, "Thought-Building in the Paragraph," *English Journal*, Vol. 5, 1916, pp. 610–619.

Details of an Untidy Room

1. The soiled, tattered curtains hung crookedly.
2. The air was close and stale.
3. To one side there was a bookcase, in the wide-open door of which dangled a bunch of keys.
4. The window shades were faded.
5. Books and magazines were lying on a chair.
6. The table in the middle of the room was rickety.
7. Over the arm of a Morris chair was hanging a red sweater.
8. On the table were a baseball, a glove, a broken package of cigarettes, some ends of burned matches.
9. On the floor were an open shoe box, a pair of old shoes, and a soiled collar.
10. The bed was rumpled and littered with newspapers and clothes.
11. The walls were papered in ugly yellow.
12. There were no pictures on the walls.
13. There were no school or college pennants in the room.

"Now," said the instructor, "there are the details with which we are to build the paragraph. Shall we use them all, or are there some which we should leave out as having no bearing on the topic?"

After some discussion, it was decided to omit the last three details, because while yellow wallpaper and the lack of pictures and pennants might make the room look ugly and bare, they were not really signs of carelessness or untidiness.

Each student was then instructed to take the remaining ten details and work them into a paragraph, changing the sentences or the order in which they came as he saw fit.

One of the paragraphs that were written in this way follows. It is not a masterpiece, but it is a fair paragraph of elementary description, having a clear topic sentence and seven sentences of details that bear directly on the topic.

An Untidy Room

1. Last spring I visited a student's room in which there were many evidences of carelessness and untidiness. 2. The faded window shades and soiled, tattered curtains had been carelessly adjusted, as if with no thought of their appearance. 3. Old and used smells filled the room. 4. To the left there stood a bookcase, in the wide-open door of which dangled a bunch of rusty keys. 5. Near the middle of the room, but against the farther wall, stood a rickety old table, on the bare surface of which there

were a baseball and a glove, a broken package of cigarettes, some ends of burned matches, a checkered cap, a shaving set, and a brush and comb. 6. On one arm of a Morris chair near the table dangled a wrinkled red sweater.   7. On the bare floor, in front of the chair, near the table, lay an open shoe box, two discarded shoes, and a soiled collar.   8. To the right stood a once well-made bed, littered with sections of a Sunday newspaper and with clothes.

An Unsuccessful Night Hunt

(Original Version)

Once when an instructor left the choice of a subject to the class, a student handed in the following theme : —

On a cold wintry night last year, a few boys and I went possum hunting. While in the woods we built a large fire, and sat there to warm our cold bodies. After about an hour had passed we heard one of the dogs bark, and then after a few moments all of them began barking as fast as they could. We left the fire, and ran down through the woods where the dogs were, or at least, where we thought they were, but we did not find the dogs anywhere. We looked and listened for about an hour but could not find the dogs anywhere. Finally we left the woods, and went home. On our way we saw the dogs, and found out that they just had a fit instead of trailing a possum.

Notice how flat and tame this account is. The details, which are the only means by which we can realize the incident, are not only few but are also generalized and uninteresting. In fact the only details given are these : —

Incident : An Unsuccessful Night Hunt
Details to make the reader realize the incident : —

1. A cold night in winter.
2. A few boys went possum hunting.
3. We built a large fire in the woods.
4. At the fire we warmed our cold bodies.
5. After an hour one of the dogs barked.
6. Shortly afterwards all the dogs joined in.
7. We left the fire.
8. We ran through the woods to where we thought the dogs were.
9. We did not find them.
10. After an hour's looking and listening we still did not find them.
11. At last we went home.

12. On the way we met the dogs.
13. They had had a fit instead of trailing a possum.

The instructor read the theme aloud to the class the next day, and called attention to three things: (1) that the details were few and commonplace; (2) that there was an unfortunate instance of repetition in the second and third sentences from the end; and (3) that though correct in spelling, punctuation, and sentence structure, the theme did not deserve a passing grade.

Then the instructor assigned the same subject for a paragraph to be written in class that day, cautioning the class to be sure to give enough definite details to enable the reader to see and realize what happened.

Among the paragraphs written in thirty minutes was the following. Contrast it, as to both the number and the interest of the details, with the original version on page 8.

An Unsuccessful Night Hunt

(*Improved Version*)

On a cold night last winter, a few boys and I went possum hunting. In hunting possums there is not much for the hunters to do until the dogs locate a trail. Walking along slowly, we began to grow cold, and when we came to a little hill with plenty of dry, dead pine branches on the ground, we stopped and built a fire. The warm blaze felt so good that we decided to stop there for a while. We were sitting around telling stories when we heard one of the dogs barking somewhere down by the foot of the hill. "Listen!" said Fred. All talking halted at once. In a few moments, all four of the dogs joined in, and it seemed to us as though they were going away from us. With a cry of "Possum!" we all ran as fast as we could down the hill. Jack stumbled over a log and fell, but was up again in a second. We reached the spot where we thought the dogs had been, but there was no sign of them. We listened for their barking. It had stopped. We looked for them for perhaps half an hour. By that time it was nearly midnight, so we started home. At the edge of the woods we met the dogs, tired out and panting. We all agreed that one of them had had a fit. When a dog is attacked with one of these fits, he usually starts running, with no evident aim or purpose. If there are other dogs around, they will join in after him and run until they are worn out. Our possum hunt had been a failure so far as hunting was concerned, but we all said that our little talk around the warm fire made up for the lack of possums. Then, too, we got plenty of exercise!

An analysis of the details in the preceding paragraph gives the following result: —

Details to make the reader realize the incident: —

1. A cold night in winter.
2. A few boys went possum hunting.
3. Not much for possum hunters to do till the dogs strike a trail.
4. Walking slowly, we grew cold.
5. We came to a little hill covered with dry pine branches.
6. We stopped and built a fire.
7. We stayed by the fire warming.
8. We sat down and began to tell stories.
9. We heard one of the dogs bark near the foot of the hill.
10. "Listen!" said Fred.
11. We all stopped talking.
12. All four dogs joined in the barking.
13. They seemed to be going away from us.
14. We cried "Possum" and ran down the hill.
15. Jack fell over a log but was up again at once.
16. We reached the place where we thought the dogs were.
17. There was no sign of the dogs.
18. We listened for their barking.
19. They had all stopped barking.
20. We looked for them for half an hour.
21. By that time it was nearly midnight.
22. We started home.
23. We met the dogs at the edge of the woods.
24. They were tired out and panting.
25. We agreed that one of them had had a fit.
26. When a dog has a running fit, he starts running without aim or purpose.
27. Any other dogs near will join in.
28. They will run till they are tired out.
29. Our possum hunt had failed.
30. We had enjoyed our talk around the fire.
31. We had had plenty of exercise.

Here are thirty-one details instead of the original thirteen, and there are touches of interest here and there. Though the theme hardly deserves more than a B, it is a great improvement on the original; and this improvement is due almost entirely to the more successful use of details.

5. The Need for Details Again

The way in which the paragraphs on "An Untidy Room" and "An Unsuccessful Night Hunt" were written has been described at length because it makes clear how essential it is to think up details and particulars before the topic sentence can be developed. That is the chief purpose of all paragraphs — to give details and particulars.

Recall the maxim on page v: "Three fourths of writing well consists in giving definite, well-chosen details, and plenty of them; the other fourth doesn't matter." In fact, from one point of view the whole problem of writing resolves itself into the process of presenting a procession of minute details.

Every paragraph normally consists of a topic idea (often definitely stated in a topic sentence) which is developed in a series of connected details something like the fingers of the hand, the spokes in a wheel, the twigs on a limb, the leaves on a twig, the galaxy of stars from a bursting skyrocket, or, to grow anatomical, like the legs of a spider or the tentacles of an octopus. This branching, ramifying structure from the topic as a center is characteristic of most forms of paragraph development,[1] though sometimes the paragraph structure resembles rather a chain, wherein each link proceeds from and is connected with a preceding link. In any event, however, each sentence link or branch consists of a single detail or particular of the topic idea, and the sum of these details and particulars constitutes the topic idea in so far as the writer has succeeded in putting it before the reader.

6. Methods of Paragraph Development

The way in which a paragraph is developed depends largely upon what use it is being put to: that is, whether the writer's purpose is to explain, to prove, to narrate, or to describe. As the objective varies, so too do the length and nature of the paragraphs vary in order to carry out the different purposes. A typical expository paragraph differs from a typical narrative paragraph; likewise, a paragraph of argument is built up differently from a paragraph of description.

[1] See page 12.

The following table gives the simpler, more important ways in which paragraphs are developed. Often, of course, several forms of development are used together in the same paragraph; as, for example, definition and repetition, or examples and details, or comparison and contrast.

TABLE OF PARAGRAPH DEVELOPMENT

Types	Purpose	Method of Development
I EXPOSITION (Topic sentence usually given)	to explain or to make clear	1. **Definition** (plus repetition in other words) 2. **Details and particulars** (when the topic is concrete and specific) 3. **Examples and specific instances** (when the topic is a general statement, principle, or law) 4. **Comparison or contrast**
II ARGUMENT (Topic sentence usually given — sometimes put last)	to prove or to disprove	1. **Positive proof** (causes and reasons for) 2. **Negative proof — refutation** (causes and reasons against)
III DESCRIPTION (Topic sentence sometimes given)	to depict a sense impression or a mood	1. **Details and particulars** (1) Grouped by location in space (2) Chosen and grouped for emotional effect
IV NARRATION (Topic sentence rarely given)	to relate an incident or to tell a story	1. **Details and particulars** (of incidents in time order) 2. **Conversation and dialogue** (a new paragraph each time the speaker changes)

7. A Good End-Sentence

To have a clear topic sentence, and to give enough examples and details to develop it, are generally unfailing guarantees of a good paragraph; of a *good* paragraph, yes, but not of the *best* paragraph. One other thing is needed to raise "good" to "best."

This is to sum up, drive home, apply, or give the result or effect of the paragraph topic in a short, striking **end-sentence**. The closing sentence is to the rest of the paragraph what the snapper is to the whip.

Consider the excellence of the following italicized end-sentence which closes an article by Bruce Barton on automobiles: "The modern motor car has become intimately woven into our social and economic fabric. It has enriched the lives of our people. *It has transformed a nation into a neighborhood.*"

We may not be able to write as good end-sentences as that, but we can at least keep from ending our paragraphs with sentences that are feeble, stringy, and sprawly.

You will notice that the last sentence of the paragraph on "An Untidy Room," page 8, merely adds one further detail — the untidy bed. There is no final sentence giving either a summary or a general impression, or any application of the paragraph as a whole. No such sentence is essential here, but a good end-sentence would certainly do no harm and might serve to give a more finished effect — for instance, one of the following: —

> All in all, it was not the kind of room I should choose to live in.
> Taken as a whole, it was about as unattractive a room as I ever saw.
> If the room had been mine I should have hated to have my mother or father see it in its present condition.

Three Suggestions for the Paragraph

To sum up, in your practice work in writing independent paragraphs, make each of your paragraphs measure up to the following triple test: —

1. Does the opening sentence state the paragraph idea simply and definitely?

2. Are there enough details and particulars to make the paragraph idea clear and interesting?

3. Is the closing sentence good enough to deserve the place of honor at the end?

If you consider the paragraph a somewhat limited and restrictive instrument of expression, remember this: The paragraph is an exceedingly subtle and elastic unit. Like a mirror it reflects faithfully whatever we hold up to it; and like our skins it grows and develops with us and will always be able to hold everything that we have the wherewithal to put into it.

Paragraphs by Students Showing
Use of Details

Here are six paragraphs by students — three of exposition, two of description, and one of narration.

Each paragraph consists of details and particulars — that is, is built up in the same way that nine tenths of all the paragraphs which you write this year will be built up.

1. You and Your Dog

It is no disgrace to be afraid of a dog, but it is a disgrace for a dog to be afraid of you. Cruelty to animals is the most depraved form of cowardice. It is one of the surest symptoms of an inferiority complex. The man who kicks a dog cannot hold his own in an equal struggle, so he chooses this means of venting his spleen. It has been said that a person's character may be judged by the kind of magazines he reads, the subjects of his conversation, and the behavior of his dog. A better statement would be that a man's intelligence may be judged by his magazines and his conversation, but his character is best judged by the behavior of his dog.

2. Writing and Talking

RAYMOND POLLARD

(*University of Illinois*)

Conversation is keen and flickering like a rapier; writing, its companion, is slow and unwieldy as a pikestaff. Where conversation nimbly pirouettes, thrusting and feinting, writing plods mechanically, lunging and lurching. Because of intimacy of contact, conversation is much more impressive than writing. Eloquent speakers often spellbind their audiences so completely that they may produce at will tears, scowls, or laughter. It is seldom that a printed word can induce any such effects as this, no matter what depth of feeling is intended. A talker can gesture, he can laugh, he can snarl, he can shout, he can prance; a writer can only wield his pen patiently and pray that his words may in a small way produce the desired effect.

3. Birds

CHARLES LEE

(*University of South Carolina*)

Birds are very interesting. Living in the air above us, they make the back of the wind their road and the clouds their milestones. Yet how differently each of them travels this ethereal highway! The hummingbird, like a prism-cast beam of sunlight, darts no higher than the blossoms which he robs; the turkey buzzard, wing-stretched on top of an air current, glides high over valleys and up the sides of mountains. Like a pursued buccaneer the hawk flashes silently through the tree trunks of the forest; the heron, his long legs trailing, flies openly over the tidal marsh. Over the breakers of the Atlantic the pelican moves ponderously, his heavy head weighting him forward; near him the white gull stops his flight, and, like a weight cut from a plumb line, drops into the sea. These are the solitary ones. Who has not seen their cousins moving in great companies? A covey of quail whirring out of a field of yellow broom-sedge; bull bats, with white-tipped wings, flitting through the dusk; crows cawing over the cornfields on a misty spring morning. Over sea and lowland and misty mountain top the birds move and have their being; how earth-bound and immovable we, their watchers, seem!

4. Landing in the Surf

DORIS VIVIAN

(University of New Hampshire)

Close to the shore, where the water was shallow, a narrow line of breakers thundered and roared. They came sliding in — cool, green, smooth rollers, breaking into smothering, frothy suds, swishing up the beach to lick the gleaming white sand, and sucking it back to meet the endless procession of charging, churning surf. The tender came riding in on the crest of a huge smashing wave that rushed it far up on the beach, dropped it reluctantly, and slithered back to mingle with the tempestuous onslaught of the next comber. The crew scrambled out of the tender, dragged it over the scrunching sand above high-water mark, put out a kedge anchor still farther up toward the low, rolling dunes above the beach, and set out along the shore.

5. Walking in the Rain at Night

The sharpest twinkle of a star or the brightest ray of the moon could not have penetrated the heavy clouds that night; it was only by the friendly but fragile beams the street light cast from under its little tin umbrella that I could see the rain dancing on the walk like a thousand-thousand diamonds which then ran together and made a shimmering, wrinkling, transparent sheet. Everything was very quiet and peaceful. I could almost count the sounds, the rain dripping from leaves and roofs, the merry gurgling of the water racing down the gutter, Paul's chatter, the splashing of our feet, and the sticky, pulling noise of tires on the wet pavement. I liked to see the cars pass because they always flung back a red streamer in a trembling zigzag down the street.

6. DAD

LOIS G. MAXON

(Ward-Belmont College)

Every July for five years Dad and I have gone fishing together in Canada. I remember one time especially when we paddled on a windy blue day across to a cove in the shelter of a steep, pine-clad island. The white-capped waves slapped the sides of the canoe, rocked us across the bay, swished their spray into our eyes as we paddled back, then gently rocked us across again. I can see Dad yet, his sandy red hair ruffled in the wind, the collar of his old blue flannel fishing shirt flopping against his sunburned face, as he carefully selected a feather fly from the ribbon of his green felt hat. With one long *zing* he cast the line out, gave a quick backward jerk of the wrist, and started calling out, "Ride him, cowboy! How old Mr. Bass can rear and charge! Ride him, cowboy!" However, I enjoyed most our fishing toward evening, when Dad's face wrinkled up in a quiet smile about his blue eyes as he watched his bobber sail out over the sun-crested waves. Then we talked of those infinite things: of life after death, of unborn children, of the reason we were put in the world. And all his answers seemed right.

TOPIC SENTENCES FOR WRITING INDEPENDENT PARAGRAPHS

I. Exposition

1. Swimming is excellent exercise for boys and girls.
2. Literary societies are beneficial to college students.
3. Everybody has a natural desire to be somebody else.
4. Birds are very interesting.
5. The eye sees easily and quickly what it is interested in.
6. Nicknames are earned in many ways.
7. Regular exercise is essential to health.
8. Everyone should have a hobby.
9. Other people have had several ambitions for me.
10. In my opinion, the greatest invention is _____.
11. Believe it or not, the dictionary is an interesting book.
12. My father is a (give business or profession).
13. An invention I hope for but never expect is _____.
14. I think the finest human quality is _____.
15. Fashions in clothes (slang) change rapidly from year to year.
16. Boys gossip as much as girls do.
17. Campus slang is something to marvel at.
18. I think _____ is used oftener than any other word in the English language.

19. If I were teaching this class, there is one change I should certainly make.
20. My hobby is ____.
21. A good bird dog is probably the most intelligent of all animals.
22. Any intelligent person is bound to feel discontented over certain things in life.
23. Radio is a most interesting hobby.
24. A hard question to answer is, "Where do all the smart babies go?"
25. I had rather have a dog (cat) than a cat (dog) for a pet.
26. Man never stops in his search for more speed.
27. The more man learns about preserving life, the more he learns about destroying it.

II. Argument

1. The greatest need of our college is ____. (Or exposition)
2. Although a dead language, Latin should not be dropped from the curriculum.
3. Boys should be required to study music.
4. All grades should be posted.
5. People disagree as to whether dogs can reason. (Or exposition)
6. A course in practical cookery would help most boys.
7. Children should (not) be told the truth about Santa Claus.
8. It helps us to debate occasionally on the side to which we are opposed.
9. It is wrong to keep animals in captivity.
10. It should be against the law to wear fur or feathers as ornament.
11. Students making a grade of A should be exempted from examination.
12. The study you like least may be doing you the most good.
13. Every person should be taught to swim.

III. Description

1. One could tell it was Easter morning.
2. The two boys were arguing furiously.
3. His (Her) costume was the most original at the party.
4. Spring is here at last.
5. The baby lost his temper the other day.
6. I'd hate to have you see my top bureau drawer.
7. The queerest pet I ever had was ____.
8. Down the street dashed the runaway horse.
9. Not long ago I happened to be passing the engine house when the fire alarm sounded.
10. I still remember my first visit to the dentist's.
11. I barely escaped getting drenched in the hard shower yesterday afternoon.

12. The flower bed was a thing of beauty.
13. He was the queerest person I had ever seen.
14. It was a perfect autumn day.
15. It is very hard to be stern with a baby.
16. It would be hard to imagine two people differing more widely in looks and disposition than A and B.
17. Yesterday was winter in her roughest mood.
18. My first night in the open was a delightful (not a delightful) experience.
19. When its nest is in danger, a mockingbird will attack a cat (dog).
20. Look at the two pictures on pages 520 and 521. Discuss the pictures in class, calling attention to different details. Describe one, or the contrast between the two, as vividly as you can in a paragraph.

IV. Narration

1. On account of the darkness and the rain I mistook the girl (boy) for my sister (brother).
2. Hurrying does not always save time.
3. It was the cleverest trick I ever saw played.
4. I had a very narrow escape the other day.
5. Practical jokes do not always have funny endings.
6. I think the meanest thing I ever did was this.
7. Did you ever try to get into the house without making a noise?
8. I overheard an interesting conversation yesterday on the streetcar.
9. The party was a great success.
10. If a girl ever asks you to teach her how to drive a car, don't accept.
11. It was my shoestring that caused the trouble.
12. I've had lots of hard luck lately.
13. It is the unexpected that frequently happens.
14. Taking the cook's place for a day is no fun.
15. Everything went wrong that morning.
16. The neighbors were very curious to learn the cause of the screams at our house last night.
17. A soft answer turneth away wrath.
18. She fell back terrified as she opened the door.
19. I might have known that little brother could not keep a secret.
20. Look at the two baseball pictures on pages 520 and 521. Discuss the pictures in class, calling attention to different details. Tell the story which the pictures suggest to you.

CHAPTER II

The Parts of Speech

In general, grammar may be described as a great observational science, dealing with the facts and laws of language, just as botany deals with plant life and geography deals with the earth's surface. The facts and laws of language are manifold and complicated. Anything that aids us to understand them properly is worth while, for to write and to speak our mother tongue effectively are both the hardest and the finest tasks that face us in college and in life. Grammar and analysis — parsing words and analyzing sentences — are helpful preparatory steps toward success. They lay the foundation for a more rapid and intelligent progress in the art of writing.

There are hundreds of thousands of words in the English language. The latest dictionary contains 600,000.[1] In spite of their tremendous numbers, however, all words can be put into eight classes or groups, according to the way they are used in sentences. These eight family groups are called "parts of speech" and are termed, respectively, (1) Nouns, (2) Pronouns, (3) Adjectives, (4) Verbs, (5) Adverbs, (6) Prepositions, (7) Conjunctions, (8) Interjections.

These are all of the parts of speech. No matter how often we speak, no matter how often we write, no matter how often we read, every word we come in contact with from the cradle to the grave is either a noun, a pronoun, an adjective, a verb, an adverb, a preposition, a conjunction, or an interjection.

The **eight parts of speech** may be grouped as follows: —

1. The **Verb** (usually the action word), always the key word in the sentence
2. The Two Modifiers or Qualifiers
   Adjectives, modifying nouns and pronouns
   Adverbs, modifying verbs, adjectives, or other adverbs

[1] The new Merriam-Webster, 1935.

3. The Two Name Words, or Substantives
    Nouns
    Pronouns, substitutes or place-takers for nouns
4. The Two Link Words or Connectives
    Conjunctions
    Prepositions, which govern objects as well as connect
5. **Interjections,** exclamations expressing feeling, which have no connection with the other words in the sentence

A word does not really become a part of speech till it is used in a sentence and enters into relationship with other words in the sentence. In short, it is not what a word looks like, but what it does that settles what part of speech it belongs to. To express it more formally, it is function, not form, that determines.

We cannot tell what part of speech a word is unless we can see how it is behaving in company with other words in a sentence. We should not ask, for example, "What part of speech is the word *fast* or *steel?*" *Fast* might be any of four parts of speech, according to the work it does: —

1. When the siege was lifted, the soldiers broke their long *fast.* (A noun, because it names)
2. Many people *fast* during Lent. (A verb, because it asserts action)
3. Only a very *fast* runner can do the hundred-yard dash in ten seconds. (An adjective, because it modifies a noun)
4. Greyhounds can run very *fast.* (An adverb, because it modifies a verb)

Similarly, *steel* is three different parts of speech in the three following sentences: —

1. *Steel* is used all over the world.
2. Trains run on *steel* rails.
3. Hard-hearted men *steel* themselves against the requests of the needy.

Consider the sudden exchange made by *pipe* and *clay* in the two sentences: —

1. He has a valuable deposit of *pipe clay* on his land.
2. He is smoking a *clay pipe.*

In fact, words in a sentence are very much like members of a baseball or a football squad. When a baseball team comes out on the field, it is impossible at first to tell what position the members will play. The catcher and the first baseman can usually be identified by the kinds of mitt they are carrying, but no one can at sight single out the shortstop from the third baseman or the left fielder from the right fielder. It is only when the team takes the field that we can distinguish the different players. In fact it is only because he pitches, for example, that a player becomes a pitcher, and so on for the other positions on the team. Sometimes, too, when a substitution is made, the players on the same team shift positions. Let the pitcher lose control, for instance, and if he is a good batter he may be transferred to center field, the third baseman may be put in to pitch, and the center fielder be placed on third. Thus, in a moment, three members of the team change places and by virtue of the change, while remaining the same persons, play different positions. Again, it is function, not form, that determines.

So, in the sentence, it is what each word does, the part it plays, that makes it what it is. Recognizing the parts of speech is thus a mild kind of detective game, in which we first have to find out what any given word is up to, and thereby assign it to its proper class or group.

Ability to recognize the parts of speech is fundamental in grammar. Enough practice, both oral and written, should be given to bring the class up to the desired average in accuracy and speed.

Exercises in the Parts of Speech

I

What parts of speech are the two *first's* and the four *that's* in these sentences : —

1. Put *first* things *first*.
2. He said *that that that that* you used was unnecessary.

II

Tell what part of speech the italicized words are : —

1. (*a*) Cheap things don't *last* long.
   (*b*) Her shoes are made on a narrow *last*.
   (*c*) *Last* came the Pilot of the Galilean Lake.
   (*d*) The *last* time I saw him was day before yesterday.
2. (*a*) And Jill came tumbling *after*.
   (*b*) We left immediately *after* dinner.
   (*c*) *After* we got home, we rang you up.

3. (a) We broke *camp* soon after daybreak.
   (b) Please hand me the green *camp* stool.
   (c) We shall probably *camp* near the bend of the river.
4. (a) Put the money back in the *till*.
   (b) Can you stay *till* bedtime?
   (c) Please don't go *till* I get back.
   (d) If you *till* the ground carefully, you will raise a good crop
5. (a) He said *that* you told him about me.
   (b) *That* is not true.
   (c) *That* time she guessed wrong.
   (d) The last book *that* you lent me is certainly interesting.
6. (a) He looks *like* his father.
   (b) Do you *like* olives?
   (c) There is an old proverb, *Like* master, *like* man.
   (d) I shall not look upon his *like* again.

III

Write sentences using the italicized words as directed: —

1. *Since* as a conjunction, a preposition, and an adverb.
2. *Light* as a noun, an adjective, and a verb.
3. *Second* as a noun, an adjective, a verb, and an adverb.
4. *Iron* as a noun, an adjective, and a verb.
5. *Still* as a noun, a verb, an adjective, and an adverb.
6. *Clear* as a verb, an adjective, and an adverb.

IV

Using the sentences on pages 67–68 and pages 85–87, continue practice on the parts of speech as long as needed.

For written parsing either of the following forms is convenient: —

1. The chief pleasure in using a taxi is the carefree feeling you have when the fenders crumple.
2. A detour is the roughest distance between two points.

FIRST FORM

1. The = definite article   carefree = adjective
   chief = adjective   feeling = noun
   pleasure = noun   you = pronoun
   in = preposition   have = verb
   using = verb   when = conjunction
   a = indefinite article   the = definite article
   taxi = noun   fenders = noun
   is = verb   crumple = verb
   the = definite article

2. A = indefinite article   distance = noun
   detour = noun   between = preposition
   is = verb   two = adjective
   the = definite article   points = noun
   roughest = adjective

SECOND FORM

Noun	Pro-noun	Adjective	Verb	Adverb	Prepo-sition	Con-junction	Interjec-tion
1. pleasure	you	the	using		in	when	
taxi		chief	is				
feeling		a	have				
fenders		the	crumple				
		carefree					
		the					
2. detour		A	is			between	
distance		the					
points		roughest					
		two					

CHAPTER III

Parsing and Review of Grammar

When operating together to form a sentence, the parts of speech have various contacts with or relations to the other parts of speech. They stretch forth, as it were, one or more hands to some other part of speech which stretches out an answering hand in return.

Sometimes these relationships between words are shown by changes in the form of the word itself. We can recognize them with the eye. For example, there is the difference in number between *dollar* and *dollars*, one *tooth* and a set of *teeth*, one *ox* and a yoke of *oxen*; there is the difference in case between *boy* (nominative or objective) and *boy's* (possessive singular) and *boys'* (possessive plural), or between *I* and *me*; or in tense between *come* and *came*, or between *go* and *have gone*. Such changes take place in nouns, pronouns, verbs, adjectives, and adverbs, and help to make clear exactly what the word is doing in the sentence.

Just as often, however, the way a word looks gives no clue to its relationships. Then we have both to consider the sentence as a whole and also to examine each part in order to tell what any given word is doing in that particular place at that particular moment. For example, *The dog bit the boy* means one thing, and *The boy bit the dog* means something entirely different, although the forms of the words *boy* and *dog* have not changed in any way. In the following sentences the word *man* is used in six different constructions without the slightest corresponding change in form.

> The *man* came. (Subject of a verb)
> The lion killed the *man*. (Object of a verb)
> She gave the *man* a dollar. (Indirect object of a verb)
> The tree fell on the *man*. (Object of a preposition)
> Mr. X, the *man* in question, has gone away. (In apposition with a noun in the nominative case)
> She failed to find Mr. X, the *man* she was looking for. (In apposition with a noun in the objective case)

To parse a sentence is to tell first what part of speech every word in it is, and then by means of either form or function to discover exactly what each word is doing in the sentence. Sometimes this is easy. Again it may be hard, calling for no little logical ingenuity and skill.

The chief functions of the various parts of speech and their most important sentence contacts are indicated in the following charts, together with a review of the more definitely practical usages of grammar and examples of detailed written parsing.

The study of grammar and practice in parsing can be carried out with as much thoroughness and detail as may be desired. The sentences on pages 67–68 and pages 85–87 contain abundant material for both parsing and analysis.

1. The Noun

Kind   Gender   Number   Case [*and why*]

2   3

1   **NOUN**   4

(1) KINDS OF NOUNS

There are two chief kinds or classes of nouns: —

1. **Proper nouns, or the particular names of individual persons, places, and things,** such as *America, London, Napoleon, Mary, John, Amazon, California*, etc.

Each proper noun names an individual belonging to a class designated by a corresponding common noun. Thus, "America" is a *country*, "London" a *city*, and so forth.

2. **Common nouns, or the names of classes or groups of objects,** such as *country, city, man, girl, boy, river, dog, cat, flowers*, etc.

The practical point of difference between proper and common nouns is that, in writing, proper nouns begin with a capital and common nouns with a small letter.

In addition to common nouns, many grammars recognize also (3) collective nouns and (4) abstract nouns and verbals.

3. **Collective nouns are the names of collections or special groups of persons, animals, and objects,** such as *army, flock, mob, jury, herd, troop, band, company, family, covey, brood, audience, choir, drove, squadron, swarm, team, fleet, regiment, committee.*

The important thing about collective nouns is the fact that they may take either the singular or the plural verb according as they are thought of as a unit (the collection or group taken as a whole) or thought of as individuals making up the group or collection. For this reason, collective nouns take either a singular or a plural verb and can be referred to by either a singular or a plural pronoun. Consider the following sentences, all of which are correct : —

1. The mob was dispersed.
2. The public are often deceived by appearances.
3. The board are of the opinion (*or* The board is of the opinion).
4. After a long meeting of the committee, its decision was announced.
5. After a long meeting of the committee, they went home.
6. The jury has reached a decision.
7. The jury are eating their dinner.
8. The public is cordially invited to attend.
9. The public are cordially invited to attend.

4. **Abstract nouns are names of qualities, actions, and conditions.** Examples are *swiftness, grace, courage, pride, rejoicing, height, dancing, faith, friendship, beauty, fragrance, redness, blackness,* and so on.

The qualities that they name are thought of as apart from or *abstracted from* the actual objects or concrete nouns that possess them. Thus, flowers are *beautiful*, pictures are *beautiful*, mountains are *beautiful*, and so are stars, women, the moon, sunrise, sunset, the sea, and a host of other things in nature. We can, therefore, by an intellectual process, *abstract* or distill this quality of *beauty* from the flowers, pictures, mountains, stars, and thus think of it and speak of it as if it had an actual objective existence, though it has none. And so for all abstract nouns. To put it epigrammatically, "There is no such thing as disease ; there are only sick men and women." [1]

(2) GENDER

There are three genders, corresponding exactly to the facts of sex in life and in nature.

[1] See the threefold division of nouns ("labels as names for things") that is proposed on page 138 below as an aid to clear thinking.

1. **Names of males are masculine,** such as *man, father, son, uncle, brother, prince, king, Joseph, Francis, cock, gander, drake, bull, stallion.*

2. **Names of females are feminine,** such as *girl, woman, actress, waitress, aunt, sister, princess, queen, Josephine, Frances, hen, goose, duck, cow, mare.*

3. **Names applying to neither males nor females — in other words, to things without life — are neuter.** *Neuter* is a Latin word that means "neither." For example, *tree, house, car, street, window, courage, moon.*

4. **Names applying to either males or females are sometimes considered to be of common gender,** such as *parent, child, person, chicken, sheep, bird.*

(3) NUMBER

There are two numbers, the singular applying to one, and the plural applying to more than one.

This distinction offers little difficulty either theoretically in parsing, or practically in writing and speaking, except in two instances: (1) nouns with foreign plurals, and (2) nouns ending in *-ics.*

1. Nouns with Foreign Plurals

Singular	Plural	Singular	Plural
addendum	addenda	focus	foci
alumna	alumnae		(or focuses)
alumnus	alumni	formula	formulas
analysis	analyses		(or formulae)
antithesis	antitheses	fungus	fungi
axis	axes		(or funguses)
bandit	bandits	genie	genii
	(or banditti)	genus	genera
beau	beaux	oasis	oases
	(or beaus)	parenthesis	parentheses
cherub	cherubs	phenomenon	phenomena
	(or cherubim)	radius	radii
crisis	crises		(or radiuses)
curriculum	curricula	stratum	strata
datum	data	terminus	termini
		thesis	theses

2. Nouns Ending in -*ics*

There is a small but important group of words ending in -*ics* which are puzzling in practical use because they sometimes take a singular and sometimes a plural verb. Examples are : —

acoustics	gymnastics	politics
athletics	mathematics	statistics
economics	phonetics	tactics
ethics	physics	

When such words denote a scientific subject or study, or a book about it, they are construed as singular.

> Mathematics (or economics, or ethics, or phonetics, or physics) *is* an important branch of learning.

When such words denote matters of practice or procedure, they may be construed as plurals.

1. Gymnastics are of many kinds and varieties.
2. The tactics employed by Stonewall Jackson in his valley campaign are highly regarded in Europe.

Like collective nouns (see above, page 26), which these words resemble, they may be used in either the singular or the plural sense according to the idea to be conveyed : —

1. Acoustics is a branch of physics.
2. The acoustics of this building are bad.
3. Athletics has come to be an important feature of modern education.
4. Athletics [in the sense of athletic sports and exercises] often take up too much of a student's time.
5. Politics makes strange bedfellows.
6. Politics of that kind [in the sense of political tricks and intrigues] are on a low level.
7. Statistics is not yet an exact science.
8. His statistics [that is, tabulated facts and figures] were incorrect.

(4) CASE

There are three cases in English grammar, nominative, possessive, and objective.

1. NOMINATIVE CASE

(1) The chief use of the nominative case is as the subject of a verb. Other uses are these : —

(2) In apposition with a noun or pronoun in the nominative case.

(3) Complement (predicate nominative) after an intransitive verb.

(4) Nominative of address.

(5) Nominative absolute.

2. POSSESSIVE CASE

As its name implies, the possessive case indicates possession or ownership. In regularly inflected nouns, the possessive singular case can be recognized by the *apostrophe s* ('s) and the possessive plural by the *s apostrophe* (s').

3. OBJECTIVE CASE

In nouns there is no difference in form between the nominative and the objective case.

(1) As the name indicates, the objective case is the case of the direct object of a transitive verb. This is its chief use. Other uses of the objective case are these : —

(2) Object of a preposition.

(3) Indirect object of a verb. Instead of being called the objective case, this use is usually known as the case of the indirect object or the dative case.

(4) In apposition with another noun or pronoun in the objective case.

(5) To indicate weight, number, age, value, measure, and direction, such as duration of time and extent of space. This use is called the adverbial objective, for the nouns so used act as adverbs to modify verbs, adjectives, or adverbs.

> The river is a mile wide at this point. (*Mile* modifies the adjective *wide*)
> This fishing pole is twenty *feet* long. (*Feet* modifies the adjective *long*)
> That picture cost ten *dollars*.
> The meeting lasted two *hours*.
> The live oak is green all *winter*.
> You should have come a *day* earlier.

(5) THE FOUR TESTS FOR A NOUN

There are four chief constructions, or uses in the sentence, that only a noun is capable of (only a noun and, of course, a pronoun, which both in purpose and in effect is a substitute noun). The four uses are these : —

(1) The subject of a verb.
(2) The object of a verb.
(3) The object of a preposition.
(4) Being modified by an adjective.

If a word or a group of words is used in any of these four ways, it automatically and invariably is a noun. These four tests also determine whether or not a phrase or a clause is a noun phrase or a noun clause. The four tests are thus of great practical importance in parsing and analyzing.

(6) NOUN PHRASES

Over the fence is out. (Subject of a verb)
It's no use *to cry over spilt milk*. (Logical subject of a verb)
Cats hate *getting their feet wet*. (Object of a verb)
Nearly everyone dislikes *being corrected*. (Object of a verb)
You can depend upon *his keeping his word*. (Object of a preposition)
I never heard of *a girl's kissing her own elbow*. (Object of a preposition)
They were afraid of *being late*. (Object of a preposition)

(7) NOUN CLAUSES

How the cat got into the room is still a mystery. (Subject of a verb)
Whether you go or stay will make little difference in the long run. (Subject of a verb)
I fear *that you are mistaken*. (Object of a verb)
He denied positively *that he had said it*. (Object of a verb)
Don't count too heavily on *what he promised you last month*. (Object of a preposition)
I judge by *what I see and hear*. (Object of a preposition)
What you do makes so much noise I can't hear *what you say*. (First clause, subject of a verb; second clause, object of a verb)

(8) PARSING NOUNS

To parse nouns in detail means to tell their

(1) Kind,   (2) Gender,   (3) Number,   (4) Case, and Why.

WRITTEN PARSING OF NOUNS

1. A friend is one who sees your point of view and who laughs at your jokes.
2. Courage is grace under pressure.

Noun	Kind	Gender	No.	Case	Construction
1. *friend*	common	common	sing.	nom.	subject of verb *is*
point	common	neuter	sing.	obj.	object of verb *sees*
view	common	neuter	sing.	obj.	object of preposition *of*
jokes	common	neuter	plur.	obj.	object of preposition *at*
2. *courage*	common (abstract)	neuter	sing.	nom.	subject of *is*
grace	common (abstract)	neuter	sing.	nom.	predicate nominative after intransitive verb *is*
pressure	common (abstract)	neuter	sing.	obj.	object of preposition *under*

Exercises

Parse the nouns in any group of five successive sentences on pages 67–68 or 85–87 (*a*) orally in class; or (*b*) written in class; or (*c*) as assigned work to be handed in in class.

In class the students may exchange papers and correct them as the instructor calls out the correct answers.

Such practice should be continued in the case of the class as a whole until a high average of both accuracy and speed is attained. If any member falls much below the average, additional exercises and practice work, with advisory coaching by a well-informed student, should be assigned.

2. The Pronoun

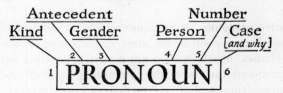

The word **pronoun** means a **for-noun**. **Pronouns are substitutes, or place-takers, for nouns,** and came into use to avoid the awkward and tiresome repetition of nouns.

Being substitutes for nouns, pronouns have the same sentence uses and obey the same sentence laws as nouns do. They have, for example, the same gender, number, and case functions, and likewise answer to the four chief tests of a noun, in that they are used as (1) the subject of a verb, (2) the object of a verb, (3) the object of a preposition, and (4) are modified by adjectives.

In addition to their noun uses, pronouns (except indefinite pronouns) refer to a noun or other pronoun, which is called their antecedent, since it usually comes before or *antecedes* the pronoun that refers to it.

One special class of pronouns, moreover, the personal pronouns, distinguish between the person speaking, the person spoken of, and the person spoken to. In addition, therefore, to telling the kind, gender, number, case, and why of pronouns, at need we should tell also their antecedent and person.

(1) KINDS OF PRONOUNS

1. **Personal pronouns** are called personal because they show by their form whether they refer to the person speaking, the person spoken to, or the person or thing spoken of : —

First person (person speaking)	*I*	*we*
Second person (person spoken to)	*you (thou)*	*you (ye)*
Third person (person or thing spoken of)	*he, she, it*	*they*

2. **Interrogative pronouns,** or pronouns used to ask questions : —

who?   *which?*   *what?*

3. **Demonstrative pronouns,** or pronouns used to point out (*demonstrate*) or to direct emphatic and definite attention to : —

this   *these*   *that*   *those*

When these words are used with nouns, they become demonstrative adjectives.

4. **Relative pronouns,** or pronouns which (*a*) refer or relate to a noun or another pronoun in the same sentence and (*b*) also connect adjective clauses, of which they are a part, with their antecedents. Relative pronouns thus have the combined powers of pronouns (to refer to antecedents) and of conjunctions (to join clauses).

who   *which*   *what*(= *that which*)   *that*

5. **Indefinite pronouns.** Besides the five personal, the four relative, the three interrogative, and the two demonstrative pronouns, there

is a large group of indefinite pronouns, between forty and fifty in number. As their name indicates, they do not refer to any particular individual or definite antecedent. Most of them can be used as adjectives also, to modify a noun. They are about halfway between real pronouns on the one hand, and nouns and adjectives on the other.

Among the most important are *one, anyone, anything, everyone, everything, someone, no one, none, one another, each other, anybody, nothing, somebody, something, each, any, all, some, other, either, neither, several, few, many, both, such.*

With the exception of *none,* which can be either singular or plural, nearly all the others are singular in both form and function.

(2) ANTECEDENT

An antecedent is the noun or noun equivalent to which a personal or relative pronoun refers. *Antecedent* means "going before, preceding." The term comes from the fact that the antecedent usually comes before or precedes the pronoun that refers to it.

(3) GENDER

Pronouns have the same gender uses as nouns do. When pronouns refer to definite antecedents, they of course take their gender from their antecedents. *They,* for example, is masculine if it refers to a word like *men* or *boys;* feminine if it refers to *women* or *girls;* neuter if it refers to *trees* or *stones;* and common if it refers to *people* or *children.*

The third personal pronoun is unusual in showing three gender forms in the singular, *he, she, it.* It is the only word in English that does this.

(4) PERSON

As has been said, personal pronouns are the only pronouns which have the power to indicate person by means of their forms.

First person	*I*	*we*
Second person	*you (thou)*	*you (ye)*
Third person	*he, she, it*	*they*

Other pronouns derive their person, as they also do their gender, from their antecedents. All nouns are in the third person except those in apposition with pronouns in the first or second person and those indicating someone directly spoken to, as "John, come here."

(5) NUMBER

As with gender and person, so too do **pronouns derive their number from their antecedents.** If the antecedent is singular, the pronoun is singular; if the antecedent is plural, the pronoun is plural.

1. He *who* comes is a friend. (Singular)
2. They *who* come are friends. (Plural)
3. All *that* believe this hold up their hands. (Plural)
4. Everything *that* lives must die. (Singular)

Only the personal and demonstrative pronouns and a few of the indefinite pronouns have different forms for singular and plural.

Personal

Singular	*Plural*
I	we
thou	ye
he	
she	they
it	

Demonstrative

Singular	*Plural*
this	these
that	those

Indefinite

Singular	*Plural*
one	ones
other	others
somebody	somebodies

(6) CASE

Of all the words in the English language only the personal, relative, and interrogative pronouns have different case forms for the nominative and objective cases.

Personal

Nominative	*Objective*
I, we	me, us
he, they	him, them
she, they	her, them

Interrogative

Nominative	*Objective*
who?	whom?

Relative

Nominative	*Objective*
who	whom

This unusual richness in objective case forms makes it easier to parse pronouns in grammar but harder to use them correctly in speaking and in writing.

In determining the case of a pronoun, its own use in the sentence or clause is the controlling factor, not that of its antecedent. Pronouns derive their gender, person, and number from their antecedents, but their cases are, as it were, their own private affair, with which their antecedents have nothing to do. For example, in the three following sentences the relative pronoun *that* is in three different constructions, while the construction of its antecedent, *man*, remains unchanged : —

1. He is the man *that* came yesterday. (Subject of a verb)
2. He is the man *that* I saw yesterday. (Object of a verb)
3. He is the man *that* I spoke to yesterday. (Object of a preposition)

Consider, too, the cases of the pronouns in these paired sentences : —

1. (*a*) I don't know *what* you are. (Nominative case)
   (*b*) I don't know *what* you mean. (Objective case)
2. (*a*) I know *who* he is. (Nominative case)
   (*b*) I know *whom* I can trust. (Objective case)

THREE SPECIAL USES OF *IT*

The pronoun *it* has three special, or idiomatic, uses : —

1. **As an expletive;** that is, as the anticipatory subject of a verb, to take the place of the phrase or clause which is the real, or logical, subject, and which then follows the verb.

> It is hard to acknowledge a mistake.
> It is useless to ask him again.
> It is not true that he has confessed.
> It is doubtful whether she will agree.

This use of *it* is very similar to the corresponding use of *there* as an expletive (page 59). Compare, for instance : —

> It is no use to cry over spilt milk.
> There's no use crying over spilt milk.

2. **As the subject of a few intransitive verbs that refer chiefly to the weather.** These verbs cannot have a person for their subject, and are therefore called **impersonal verbs.**

> It will probably rain tonight.
> It was cold yesterday but it is warmer today.
> It is snowing hard. It grew dark rapidly.
> Is it far to the next town?

3. **As a vague impersonal object after certain verbs that usually take no object at all.**

> Come, and trip it as you go
> On the light fantastic toe.
>   — MILTON'S "L'Allegro"

> The entire party footed it carefully over the ice.
> You can't put it over me that way.
> She lords it over her servants as if she were a queen.

PARSING PRONOUNS

Fully **to parse pronouns** means to tell their (1) Kind; (2) Antecedent (if there is one); (3) Gender; (4) Person (if needed); (5) Number; (6) Case and Why.

WRITTEN PARSING OF PRONOUNS

These are some of the books which your father lent me from his library.

Pron.	Kind	Ante-cedent	Gender	Pers.	No.	Case	Construction
These	demon.		neuter	third	plur.	nom.	subject of verb *are*
some	indef.		neuter	third	plur.	nom.	pred. nom. after intran. verb *are*
which	rel.	books	neuter	third	plur.	obj.	object of verb *lent*
your	pers.		common	second	sing.	poss.	showing possession of *father*
me	pers.		common	first	sing.	obj.	ind. obj. of verb *lent*

Exercises in Parsing Pronouns

Parse the pronouns in any group of five or ten successive sentences, pages 67–68 or 85–87, (*a*) orally in class; (*b*) written in class; (*c*) or as assigned work to be handed in.

Have the written parsing corrected in class by interchanging papers and marking them according to the instructor's directions.

Continue practice till the class reaches the desired level of speed and accuracy (and so on for the other parts of speech).

3. The Adjective

Adjectives are words that modify a noun or pronoun. Any word that modifies a noun or pronoun is an adjective; any word that doesn't, isn't.

(1) KIND

Adjectives are of two kinds or classes: descriptive and non-descriptive.

1. **Descriptive adjectives** are those which name qualities or characteristics of the object described so that we can see, hear, smell, taste, or feel it more definitely and vividly. Examples are adjectives like *tall, short, white, red, happy, loud, smooth, ugly, sweet, cold.*

Proper adjectives, which are derived from proper nouns, can be considered loosely as belonging to the descriptive group.

Only descriptive adjectives can be compared — that is, used in the positive, the comparative, and the superlative degree.

Positive	*Comparative*	*Superlative*
tall	taller	tallest
cold	colder	coldest
ugly	uglier	ugliest
soft	softer	softest
beautiful	more beautiful	most beautiful

2. **Non-descriptive adjectives** are those which merely point out or indicate number or amount, without describing the object they modify. Non-descriptive adjectives are of several subgroups or classes, such as adjectives of quantity, amount, and number, like *little, few, many, some, all, much, five, ten, first, second,* etc.; the articles; the numerals; and the pronominal adjectives, which consist of the pronouns listed on pages 32 and 33 (personal, interrogative, demonstrative, relative, and indefinite pronouns), when these words turn into adjectives by virtue of modifying a noun or pronoun.

The definite article *the* and the indefinite articles *a, an,* belong to this non-descriptive group.

(2) TEST OF AN ADJECTIVE

In parsing adjectives there is only one test, but it must be strictly and literally applied: Does the word in question modify a noun or a pronoun?

Most nouns, particularly nouns of material, can be used as adjectives: an *oak* tree, a *silver* watch, *childhood* years, the *head* waiter, a *clay* pipe, *pipe* clay, a *gold* chain.

Conversely, adjectives easily become nouns when they are used in place of a noun instead of to modify a noun.

1. The *bravest* are the *tenderest*.
2. The *loving* are the *daring*.
3. To the *pure* all things are pure.
4. The *good*, the *true*, the *beautiful*.

Occasionally, too, the difference between adjectives and adverbs, which is usually clear and definite, becomes hazy, and keen thinking is needed to keep them apart. Such is the case with the use of the predicate adjectives, where adverbs would naturally be expected, in such phrases as *turn pale* or *turn sour*, *shine bright*, *stand firm and sure*, *smell sweet*, *taste sour*, *ring clear*.

Again, *well* and *badly* look like adverbs and usually are, but are correctly used as adjectives in the following sentences: —

1. I felt *well* yesterday, but I am feeling *badly* today.
2. You looked *badly* after your operation, but you are looking *well* now.

(3) PARSING ADJECTIVES

To parse an adjective is to tell (1) the kind (descriptive or non-descriptive) ; (2) the noun or pronoun it modifies.

Since non-descriptive adjectives cannot be compared, and since an overwhelmingly large proportion of even descriptive adjectives are in the positive degree, no reference need be made to the degree of comparison an adjective is in, unless it is in the comparative or the superlative degree, when this fact should be pointed out.

WRITTEN PARSING OF ADJECTIVES

Soon o'er the yellow fields, in silent and mournful procession,
Came from the neighboring hamlets and farms the Acadian women,
Driving in ponderous wains their household goods to the seashore.

Adjective	Kind	Noun or Pronoun It Modifies
the	definite article	*fields*
yellow	descriptive	*fields*
silent	descriptive	*procession*
mournful	descriptive	*procession*
the	definite article	*hamlets* and *farms*

Adjective	Kind	Noun or Pronoun It Modifies
neighboring	descriptive (participle)	*hamlets* and *farms*
the	definite article	*women*
Acadian	descriptive (proper)	*women*
ponderous	descriptive	*wains*
their	non-descriptive (pronominal)	*goods*
household	descriptive	*goods*
the	definite article	*seashore*

4. The Verb

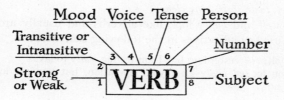

The verb is the most important and many-sided of all the parts of speech. It is always necessary to a sentence. No verb; no sentence.

1. ACTION VERBS

Verbs are prevailingly the action words of a sentence, and can almost be defined as words that express action. To answer the question *Who does what?* is usually to put your finger on (1) the subject (the *who*), (2) the verb (the *does*), and (3) the complement or object (the *what*).

Action words of this kind affirm or deny; they tell, declare, or assert something about their subject.

2. LINK, OR COPULATIVE, VERBS

There are, however, in addition to the large number of action verbs, a small but important group that do not assert action, but serve merely to join the subject to the predicate; in other words, they are verbs that assert being instead of action. Such verbs are really links, joining the subject to the complement. They are prevailingly intransitive, except when taking a cognate object. (See page 47.)

The most important and commonest of these is the verb *to be*, which in its various forms, either as an independent or as an auxiliary verb, is the commonest verb in the language.   Other important copulative verbs are *seem, remain, become.*   Many other verbs are capable of being used in a copulative or link fashion, thus being followed by an adjective instead of an adverb.   Examples are *sound, feel, taste, smell, grow, look.*

(1) STRONG (IRREGULAR, OLD) AND WEAK (REGULAR, NEW) VERBS

The principal parts of a verb are the first person singular, present tense; the first person singular, past tense; and the past participle. These three parts are called "principal" because from them is built up the whole conjugation of the verb in all its tenses and forms.   To arrive at the principal parts of any verb, all that is necessary is to think of the verb forms that go with (1) *now*, (2) *yesterday*, (3) and *have*.   Thus : —

Present	[I] *sing* [now]
Past	[I] *sang* [yesterday]
Past participle	[I have] *sung.*

Both historically and actually verbs are divided into two great classes according to the way they form their past tense and past participle.

1. Strong, or Irregular, Conjugation

Verbs that belong to this class form their past tense (*a*) without adding any letter and (*b*) usually by changing their vowels; and form their past participle (*a*) by adding -*n* or -*en* and (*b*) usually by also changing their vowels.

STRONG VERBS

Following are the principal parts of seventy-seven of the leading strong, or irregular, verbs.   The fourteen that cause the most trouble in speaking and writing are starred and italicized.   Devote particular attention to them.

Present Tense	Past Tense	Past Participle
abide	abode	abode
am	was	been
bear	bore	born, borne
beat	beat	beaten (beat, *colloq.*)
* *begin*	*began*	*begun*
bid	bade, bid	bidden, bid
bind	bound	bound
bite	bit	bitten (bit, *colloq.*)
blow	blew	blown
* *break*	*broke*	*broken*
chide	chid	chidden, chid
choose	chose	chosen
cling	clung	clung
* *come*	*came*	*come*
dig [1]	dug	dug
* *do*	*did*	*done*
draw	drew	drawn
drink	drank	drunk
drive	drove	driven
* *eat*	*ate*	*eaten*
fall	fell	fallen
fight	fought	fought
find	found	found
fling	flung	flung
fly	flew	flown
forget	forgot	forgotten, forgot
forsake	forsook	forsaken
freeze	froze	frozen
get	got	got (*gotten*, authorized in the United States)
* *give*	*gave*	*given*
* *go*	*went*	*gone*
grind	ground	ground
grow	grew	grown
hang	hung (*hanged*, only of the death penalty)	hung (*hanged*, only of the death penalty)
hide	hid	hidden, hid
hold	held	held
know	knew	known
* *lie* (*i.e.* lie down)	*lay*	*lain*
ride	rode	ridden
* *ring* [2]	*rang, rung*	*rung*

[1] Also weak: *dig, digged, digged.*
[2] Weak in the sense of "to surround with a ring": *ring, ringed, ringed.*

Present Tense	Past Tense	Past Participle
rise	rose	risen
* *run*	*ran*	*run*
* *see*	*saw*	*seen*
shine [1]	shone	shone
shrink	shrank, shrunk	shrunk
sing	sang, sung	sung
sink	sank, sunk	sunk
* *sit*	*sat*	*sat*
slay	slew	slain
slide	slid	slid, slidden
slink	slunk	slunk
smite	smote	smitten
speak	spoke	spoken
spin	spun	spun
spring	sprang, sprung	sprung
stand	stood	stood
steal	stole	stolen
stick	stuck	stuck
sting	stung	stung
stink	stank, stunk	stunk
string	strung	strung
strive	strove	striven
swear	swore	sworn
swim	swam (swum, *dial.*)	swum
swing	swung	swung
* *take*	*took*	*taken*
tear	tore	torn
thrive [2]	throve	thriven
throw	threw	thrown
tread	trod	trodden, trod
wake	woke, waked	waked
wear	wore	worn
weave	wove	woven
win	won	won
wind	wound	wound
wring	wrung	wrung
* *write*	*wrote*	*written*

2. WEAK, OR REGULAR, CONJUGATION

Verbs in this group form their past tense and past participle (*a*) without changing their vowels and (*b*) by adding -*d*, -*ed*, or -*t* to the

---

[1] Weak in the transitive sense of "to shine shoes": *shine, shined, shined.*
[2] Also weak: *thrive, thrived, thrived.*

present tense. All new verbs which come into English follow this conjugation.

Examples are as follows : —

Present Tense	Past Tense	Past Participle
love	loved	loved
decide	decided	decided
finish	finished	finished
die	died	died
dye	dyed	dyed
volplane	volplaned	volplaned
electrocute	electrocuted	electrocuted
phone	phoned	phoned

3. Special Class of Weak Verbs

The distinction between strong (irregular) and weak (regular) verbs is in the main easy to apply. There are, however, about sixty common verbs that are puzzling because they seem to show both strong and weak characteristics. Close attention, however, will reveal that they belong to the weak group.

In general, the test of a weak verb is whether it adds a *d* or a *t* to form the past tense. If it does, even if it also changes its vowel, it is a weak verb. Contrast in this particular the strong verbs *bind, bound; fight, fought; find, found;* and *wind, wound,* with the weak verbs *bring, brought; catch, caught; sell, sold.*

SPECIAL CLASS OF WEAK VERBS

Present Tense	Past Tense	Past Participle
bend	bent	bent
bereave	bereft	bereft
beseech	besought	besought
bet	bet	bet
bleed	bled	bled
breed	bred	bred
bring	brought	brought
burst	burst	burst
buy	bought	bought
cast	cast	cast
catch	caught	caught
cleave (*to split*)	cleft	cleft
cost	cost	cost

Present Tense	Past Tense	Past Participle
creep	crept	crept
cut	cut	cut
feed	fed	fed
feel	felt	felt
flee	fled	fled
have	had	had
hear	heard	heard
hit	hit	hit
hurt	hurt	hurt
keep	kept	kept
kneel	knelt	knelt
lay [1]	laid	laid
lead	led	led
leave	left	left
lend	lent	lent
let	let	let
lose	lost	lost
make	made	made
meet	met	met
pay	paid	paid
put	put	put
quit	quit	quit
read	read	read
rend	rent	rent
rid	rid	rid
say	said	said
seek	sought	sought
sell	sold	sold
send	sent	sent
set [2]	set	set
shed	shed	shed
shoe	shod	shod
shoot	shot	shot
shut [3]	shut	shut

[1] This verb is always transitive and means *to place* or *to set* something in a certain position.

[2] This verb must not be confounded with *sit*, which is always intransitive, except in the phrase "to sit a horse." It is, of course, proper to say "The sun sets" and to speak of the "setting sun." As to a "setting hen," good usage has long ago justified the expression. Those who raise hens are not going to talk about "sitting hens."

[3] The student should beware of the expression "to get shut of," which appears more often as "shet of" or "shed of." It is commonly derived from the verb "shut," but was doubtless influenced by the verb "shed." At any rate, it is a vulgarism for which "to get rid of" may always be substituted.

Present Tense	Past Tense	Past Participle
sleep	slept	slept
slit	slit	slit
spend	spent	spent
spit	spit	spit
split	split	split
spread	spread	spread
sweep	swept	swept
teach	taught	taught
tell	told	told
think	thought	thought
thrust	thrust	thrust
weep	wept	wept
wet	wet	wet

(2) TRANSITIVE AND INTRANSITIVE VERBS

Transitive verbs are those which take objects. The action passes over (*transits*) from the subject and lands upon the object.

> The dog *bit* → the man.
> The horse *ate* → the hay.
> Children *love* → their mother.
> This is the dog that *worried* → the cat that *killed* → the rat that *ate* → the malt.

Intransitive verbs are those which do not take an object.

> Hey, diddle, diddle! The cat and the fiddle!
> The cow *jumped* over the moon;
> The little boy *laughed* to see such sport
> And the dish *ran* away with the spoon.

Verbs are prevailingly transitive or intransitive. Even when they are not used in sentences, a genuine difference can be felt between such words, on the one hand, as *give, strike, throw, bear, see, set, lay,* and, on the other, *run, rise, live, go, come, wander, shine,* and *lie,* to say nothing of such non-action or link verbs as *be, seem, appear,* and *become.* In reality, however, as need arises, any transitive verb can be used intransitively and the intransitive verbs (except the verb *to be* and its equivalents) can be used transitively. When an intransitive verb is used transitively, it (1) either takes a cognate object, or (2) is used in a causative sense.

1. COGNATE OBJECT

Even a verb like *sleep, dream, live, run, fight,* can take as its object a noun with the same meaning as the verb, as, for example, *to sleep our last sleep, to dream a bad dream, to live a useful life, to die a hard death, to run a winning race, to fight a good fight.* This construction, in which the object is born from the verb itself, is called the **cognate object,** cognate meaning "born with," "akin."

2. CAUSATIVE VERBS

Again, certain intransitive verbs can become transitive when they are used in the **causative sense** of causing or producing the action which they name. Examples are to *fly* a kite (to make a kite fly); to *walk* a horse (to make a horse walk); to *work* an employee hard; to *float* a raft down the river, etc.

(3) MOOD

Verbs have three moods, or manners, in which they can make assertions and form sentences. They are the **indicative,** the **imperative,** and the **subjunctive.** The first two of these offer little difficulty.

1. INDICATIVE MOOD

The indicative mood is the mood of all direct statements of fact and direct questions. More than nine tenths of all the verbs in both speech and writing are in this mood.

2. IMPERATIVE MOOD

The imperative mood is the mood of command. It has only one tense, the present, and only one person, the second. The subject is always *you,* either singular or plural, and since this fact is so well known, the pronoun is nearly always omitted.

3. SUBJUNCTIVE MOOD

The subjunctive mood, both in theory and in practice, is puzzling and subtle. It is the mood of indirectness, of unreality, and of doubt. It has been suggestively termed "the wabbling mood." Although comparatively rare, it is too interesting and important to be ignored. The three most important present-day uses of the subjunctive are these: —

(1) Uncertainty

The subjunctive is used in uncertain conditions in order to emphasize their doubt much more strongly than the indicative mood would do. For example: —

1. If it *turn* out as we hope, it will be a miracle.
2. If he *come*, I shall try to see him.
3. If it *rain* tomorrow, nobody could come.
4. If he *be* a man of his word, he will do what he promised.

In each of these sentences the indicative could be used, and its only effect would be to lessen the doubt and uncertainty suggested by the subjunctive. Incidentally, this use of the subjunctive is rapidly disappearing except on the part of the nicest speakers and writers.

(2) Conditions Contrary to Fact

A second use of the subjunctive is to express a condition contrary to fact: —

1. If he *were* here, all would be well (but he isn't here).
2. If I *were* you, I wouldn't do that (but I am not you).
3. If it *were* in my power, I'd come to your aid (but it isn't in my power).
4. *Hadst* thou *been* here, my brother *had* not *died* (but thou wast not here).

This use of the subjunctive in unreal conditions is still both standard and necessary, and gives no signs of disappearing.

(3) Wish

The third use of the subjunctive is to express a wish: —

1. Oh, that I had the power to help you!
2. God bless you!
3. Peace be with him!
4. Long live the king!
5. Hallowed be thy name!
6. Plague take it!
7. The devil take the hindmost!
8. God be with you! (The original form of "good-by")

(4) *As It Were* and *Had Rather*

Two unrelated uses of the subjunctive are to be seen in the phrases *as it were* and *had rather*. *As it were* suggests that the statement with which it is used is not to be taken fully and literally at its face value.

1. He seemed, as it were, in a kind of mental fog.
2. He behaved, as it were, more like the child's mother than its father.
3. The very heavens, as it were, opened and flooded the earth.

The *had* of the phrases *had rather*, *had better*, *had as lief*, and *had as soon* is in the past subjunctive. These phrases have been in good use for hundreds of years and are still standard. *I had rather go* means *I should have* (or *hold*) *it more agreeable to go*. *Had* has the same meaning in the other phrases.

4. THE TWO VERBALS: INFINITIVES AND PARTICIPLES

(1) The Infinitive

The infinitive is sometimes spoken of as a mood, although it does not have the power of asserting action as do the other moods. The infinitive is the noun form of the verb and is called a verbal. It can be used like other nouns as the subject of a verb, the object of a verb, the object of a preposition, and so forth.

The infinitive has two forms, the root infinitive with *to* and the infinitive in *-ing* or the gerund.

Root Infinitive	*Infinitive in "-ing" (Gerund)*
to go	going
to come	coming
to see	seeing
to believe	believing

Such words are double-natured: they have at the same time the uses of both verbs and nouns.

On the verb side they are modified by adverbs; if transitive, they take objects; if intransitive, they are followed by predicate nouns or adjectives. On the noun side they can be used as the subject of a verb, the object of a verb, the object of a preposition, and can even be modified by adjectives.

Consider their double nature as revealed in the following sentences: —

1. *Rowing* a heavy boat against the current is hard work.

   (As a verb, *rowing* governs the object *boat* and is modified by the adverb phrase *against the current;* as a noun, *rowing* is the subject of the verb *is.*)

2. It is hard to avoid *hating* one's enemies.

   (As a verb, *hating* governs the object *enemies;* as a noun, *hating* is the object of the infinitive *to avoid.*)

3. Everyone dislikes *being* sick.

   (As a verb, *being* is completed by the predicate adjective [attribute complement] *sick;* as a noun, *being* is the object of *dislikes.*)

4. You can depend upon his *keeping* his word strictly.

   (As a verb, *keeping* governs the object *word* and is modified by the adverb *strictly;* as a noun, *keeping* is the object of the preposition *upon* and is modified by the pronominal adjective *his.*)

(2) The Participle

The participle is the adjective form of the verb, and like the infinitive is called a verbal. At the same time, it shares in the uses of both adjectives and verbs.

1. *Lifting* his hat politely, he bowed to the lady.

   (As a verb, *lifting* governs the object *hat*, and is modified by the adverb *politely;* as an adjective, *lifting* modifies the pronoun *he.*)

2. *Being* the richest man in town, Mr. X subscribed largely to the new library.

   (As a verb, *being* is followed by the predicate nominative [attribute complement] *man;* as an adjective, *being* modifies the noun *Mr. X.*)

3. *Turning* pale with fright, the child burst into tears.

   (As a verb, *turning* is completed by the predicate adjective *pale;* as an adjective, *turning* modifies the noun *child.*)

4. He is *doing* the best he can.

   (*Doing* after the verb *is* forms the present progressive tense of the verb *to do.*)

The present participle, ending in *-ing*, has the same form as the infinitive in *-ing*, or gerund. Being thus identical in form, they are apt to be confused with each other. The only way to keep them apart is this: If a verb form in *-ing* modifies a noun or pronoun, it is an adjective — that is, a *participle*. If the verb form in *-ing* is the subject of a verb, the object of a verb, the object of a preposition, or a predicate nominative (attribute complement), it is a noun — that is, the **infinitive** or **gerund**.

Exercises in Distinguishing Participles and Infinitives

Are the italicized forms participles (adjectives) or infinitives (nouns)?

1. *Forgetting* the past is sometimes a virtue.
2. *Laughing* at the funny expression, I turned to my sketch and began *working* in earnest.
3. The boy *standing* at the head of his class is my brother.
4. I am very proud of him for *standing* first.
5. And Arthur, *passing* thence, rode to the wood.
6. This is good only for *passing* the time.
7. He enjoyed *reading* your letter.
8. She always sings while *doing* her work.
9. Genius is an infinite capacity for *taking* pains.
10. The children stood *watching* them out of town.
11. By *praising* a man we sometimes injure him.
12. *Playing* baseball or football for money prevents a student from *representing* his school in athletics.
13. Again *thanking* you for your kindness, and *hoping* to hear from you soon, I am, etc.
14. *Making* promises is not *keeping* them.
15. "*Moving* pictures is a great nuisance."
    "You should say, '*Moving* pictures are a great nuisance,' shouldn't you?"
    "Say, you never cleaned house, did you?"
16. While I nodded, nearly *napping*, suddenly there came a *tapping*,
    As of some one gently *rapping, rapping* on my chamber door.

(4) VOICE

Transitive verbs, or verbs that take objects, have two voices, the active and the passive.

The active voice of a transitive verb represents the subject as acting upon, or doing something to, the object. The line of action points from subject to object.

1. Heavy clouds hid → the sun.
2. Two people saw → him fall into the water.
3. Lightning struck → the house.

The passive voice reverses this situation. The line of action, instead of pointing forward from subject to object, points backward from object to subject.   The subject receives the action, and is acted upon. The former object becomes the present subject.

    1. The sun ← was obscured by heavy clouds.
    2. He ← was seen to fall into the water by two people.
    3. The house ← was struck by lightning.

(5) TENSE

Tense means time.   There are only three possible times — present, past, and future.   In the conjugation of the verb, however, there are six tenses instead of three.   Tense in a verb, therefore, shows not only time but the state or kind of action as well — that is, whether or not it is ended or complete (perfected or perfect).

Present	*Present Perfect*
I write	I have written
Past	*Past Perfect*
I wrote	I had written
Future	*Future Perfect*
I shall write	I shall have written

(6) AUXILIARY VERBS

Much of the force and variety of the English verb come from its free use of verb phrases.   With the exception of two tenses only, the simple present and simple past of the active voice, every tense in both voices is composed of a verb phrase — that is, of a principal verb preceded by an auxiliary, or assisting, verb.

These helping, or auxiliary, verbs are the following.   Notice that they are all words of one syllable and that most of them are defective, or lacking, in one or more of their principal parts.

Present Tense	*Past Tense*	*Past Participle*
be (am)	was	been
have	had	had
do	did	done
may	might	
can	could	
must		
ought		
shall	should	
will	would	

Notice, too, that the past tenses *might, could, should,* and *would* are past *only in form, not in use* or function. "I might go" and "I could go" are no more past in meaning than "I may go" or "I can go." In fact, any of these four forms (*may, might, can, could*) can even refer to the future and can be modified by either the adverb *now* (present) or the adverb *tomorrow* (future), but not by *yesterday* (past).

Let As an Auxiliary Verb

Let, followed by the root infinitive without *to,* has one important auxiliary use today. This is to form a verb phrase expressing a strong wish or a command in the third person.

> Let us go at once.
> Don't let him hurt me.
> When I ope my mouth, let no dog bark.
> Just let him say that again.
> Let me go, I tell you.
> Let's not quarrel any more.

In addition to this auxiliary use, *let* is also a notional, or independent, verb, meaning "to permit, to allow."

> I will give him $5 if you will let him have an equal amount.
> The cashier will not let us borrow the money at 5 per cent.

SYNOPSIS OF THE COMPLETE CONJUGATION OF
GIVE

PRINCIPAL PARTS

Present	*Past*	*Past Participle*
give	gave	given

ACTIVE VOICE

INDICATIVE MOOD

Present	*Present Emphatic*	*Present Progressive*
He gives	He does give	He is giving
Past	*Past Emphatic*	*Past Progressive*
He gave	He did give	He was giving
Future		*Future Progressive*
He will give		He will be giving

INDICATIVE MOOD — *Continued*

Present Perfect	*Present Perfect Progressive*
He has given	He has been giving
Past Perfect	*Past Perfect Progressive*
He had given	He had been giving
Future Perfect	*Future Perfect Progressive*
He will have given	He will have been giving

SUBJUNCTIVE MOOD [1]

(Often preceded by *if*)

Present	*Present Emphatic*	*Present Progressive*
He give	He do give	He be giving
Past	*Past Emphatic*	*Past Progressive*
He gave	He did give	He were giving
Present Perfect		*Past Perfect Progressive*
He have given		He have been giving
Past Perfect		*Past Perfect Progressive*
He had given		He had been giving

IMPERATIVE MOOD

Present	*Present Emphatic*	*Present Progressive*
give	do give	be giving, do be giving

INFINITIVE

Root Infinitives

Present	*Present Progressive*
to give	to be giving
Perfect	*Perfect Progressive*
to have given	to have been giving

Infinitives in *-ing*

Present	*Present Progressive*
giving	
Perfect	*Perfect Progressive*
having given	having been giving

[1] The verb phrases formed by means of the auxiliary verbs *may, might, could,* and *should* also have the effect of the subjunctive (sometimes called the "conditional") mood.

PARTICIPLES

Present	*Present Progressive*
giving	
Perfect	*Perfect Progressive*
having given	having been giving

PASSIVE VOICE

INDICATIVE MOOD

Present	*Present Progressive*
He is given	He is being given
Past	*Past Progressive*
He was given	He was being given
Future	
He will be given	
Present Perfect	
He has been given	
Past Perfect	
He had been given	
Future Perfect	
He will have been given	

SUBJUNCTIVE MOOD

(Often preceded by *if*)

Present	
He be given	
Past	*Past Progressive*
He were given	He were being given
Present Perfect	
He have been given	
Past Perfect	
He had been given	

IMPERATIVE MOOD

Present	*Present Emphatic*
be given	do be given

INFINITIVES

Root Infinitives

Present
to be given

Perfect
to have been given

Infinitives in -*ing*

Present
being given

Perfect
having been given

PARTICIPLES

Present
being given

Past
given

Perfect
having been given

(7) AND (8) PERSON AND NUMBER

There are three persons of the verb, first, second, and third, corresponding to the three persons of the personal pronouns.

There are two numbers of the verb, singular and plural, corresponding to the two numbers of nouns and pronouns.

The verb takes both its person and its number from its subject, or, in other words, is said to agree with its subject in person and number.

(9) PARSING VERBS

Fully **to parse a verb** is to tell these facts about it: (1) Strong or Weak Conjugation; (2) Transitive or Intransitive; (3) Mood (Indicative, Subjunctive, or Imperative); (4) Voice (if Transitive, Active or Passive); (5) Tense (Present, Past, Future, Present Perfect, Past Perfect, Future Perfect); (6) Person (First, Second, or Third); (7) Number (Singular or Plural); (8) Subject (which determines its Person and Number).

Written Parsing of Verbs

1. **Never** cross a bridge until you come to it.
2.   He who fights and runs away
                May live to fight another day;
                But he who is in battle slain
                Can never rise and fight again.

Verb	*Strong or Weak*	*Trans. or Intrans.*	*Mood*	*Voice*	*Tense*	*Pers.*	*No.*	*Subj.*
1. *cross*	weak	trans.	imper.	act.	pres.	second	sing.	*you* [1]
come	strong	intrans.	indic.		pres.	second	sing.	*you*
2. *fights*	strong	intrans.	indic.		pres.	third	sing.	*who*
runs	strong	intrans.	indic.		pres.	third	sing.	*who*
may live	weak	intrans.	indic.		pres.	third	sing.	*he*
to fight	strong	intrans.	infin.		pres.			
is slain	strong	trans.	indic.	pass.	pres.	third	sing.	*who*
can rise	strong	intrans.	indic.		pres.	third	sing.	*he*
(can) *fight*	strong	intrans.	indic.		pres.	third	sing.	*he*

Exercises

Using the sentences on pages 67–68 and 85–87 below, the class should be given enough practice in both the oral and the written parsing of verbs to insure reasonable familiarity with them.

5. The Adverb

Verb, Adjective, or Adverb that it modifies

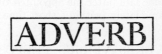

ADVERB

Together with the adjective, the adverb is one of the two parts of speech that modify. The difference between them consists in what they modify: adjectives modify nouns and pronouns; adverbs modify verbs, adjectives, and other adverbs. This is the sole test for an adverb, and is to be applied invariably to any adverb element — word, phrase, or clause.

[1] Understood.

The most conspicuous use of the adverb is to modify a verb, and from this fact it got its name, *adverb* — that is, something added to (*ad* = to) a verb.

Like adjectives, though to a less extent, adverbs are compared. In parsing an adverb, however, its degree can be taken for granted as positive, unless it is in the comparative or superlative, in which case it should be commented on.

(1) ADVERBS VERSUS ADJECTIVES

As was noted in connection with adjectives, **to tell adverbs from adjectives sometimes calls for careful watching.** The ending *-ly* usually marks off the adverb from the adjective, but not every descriptive word ending in *-ly* is an adverb, as is shown by the fact that a number of common adjectives end in *-ly*, such as *cowardly, friendly, manly, womanly, silly, kindly* (also an adverb), *cleanly* (klĕn´-lĭ, not klēn´-lĭ), *lowly, sickly, timely, lovely, lonely, mannerly*, and so on.

Examine and discuss the shifting adverb or adjective tinge in the italicized words: —

> To play *safe;* to drink *deep* and to drink *deeply;* to stand *erect;* to look *good* and to look *well;* to feel *warm* and to feel *warmly;* to arrive *safe* and to arrive *safely.*
> That house looks *good* (*well*).
> We found the road *easy* (*easily*).

1. Still water runs *deep.*
2. The sun shines *bright* on my old Kentucky home.
3. Velvet feels *smooth* and looks *rich* and *glossy.*
4. She grew *tall.* She grew *rapidly.*
5. (*a*) He came late (after the appointed time).
   (*b*) He came lately (within a short time ago).

(2) ADVERBS VERSUS PREPOSITIONS

A preposition without its object becomes an adverb. Constant care, therefore, is needed to tell whether words like *in, up, out, within, without,* modify verbs and are therefore adverbs, or whether they take objects and are therefore prepositions. If they are prepositions, the phrase which they introduce may modify a verb and hence be an adverb phrase. See the section, The Preposition and Its Object, page 61 below.

(3) ADVERBS VERSUS CONJUNCTIONS

Many adverbs, such as *after, before, how, why, where, wherever, when, whenever, as, while,* and so forth, can be used either as simple adverbs to modify a verb or as both adverb and conjunction. This double function of modifying and connecting is evident in such sentences as these : —

1. Tell me how you did it.
2. Come whenever you can.
3. I don't know where you are.
4. We reached the station after the train had. gone.

When thus used as both an adverb and a conjunction such words are sometimes called "conjunctive adverbs." In effect, however, they are subordinating conjunctions, and this term seems preferable. See below, pages 63–65.

(4) *THERE* EXPLETIVE, OR ANTICIPATORY

The word *there* has one important, idiomatic use. This is to act as a kind of introductory subject, occupying the rightful place of the subject before the verb, and thus letting the real subject come after the verb in a more prominent position for the sake of emphasis. When used in this way, *there* has little or no idea of place.

1. There is no telling when he will come.
2. There is no use crying over spilt milk.
3. There was no way to tell them apart.

In this convenient construction *there* is known not as an adverb but as an expletive, because it fills out the sentence while waiting for the subject. (The word *expletive* means "a filling up.") The pronoun *it* is used likewise in much the same way. Then *it* is an expletive rather than a pronoun. See page 36 (1).

(5) ADVERBIAL OBJECTIVE

There should be recalled at this point the adverbial use of a noun in the objective case to indicate length, measure, amount, etc. See above, page 29 (5).

(6) PARSING ADVERBS

To parse adverbs is to point out the verbs, adjectives, or other adverbs which they modify, and thus show their adverbial use.

WRITTEN PARSING OF ADVERBS

1. Never have I seen so much power so easily controlled.
2. If I were running the world I would have it rain only between two and five A.M.   Anyone who was out then ought to get wet.

	Adverb	Verb, Adjective, or Adverb It Modifies
1.	never	· have seen (verb)
	so	much (adjective)
	so	easily (adverb)
	easily	controlled (adjective)
2.	only	between two and five A.M. (adverb phrase)
	out	was (verb)
	then	was (verb)

6. The Preposition

Word modified
by the Prepositional phrase

Object of the Preposition		Kind of phrase (Adjective or Adverb)
1	2	3

PREPOSITION

There are two essentials to be remembered in dealing with prepositions: (1) Prepositions always take an object; and (2) prepositions introduce and form a part of a small group of words, called a phrase, which modifies some other word in the sentence.   If the phrase modifies a noun or a pronoun, it is an **adjective phrase.**   If it modifies a verb, adjective, or adverb, it is an **adverb phrase.**

The commonest prepositions are these: *about, above, across, after, against, along, among, around, at, before, behind, below, beneath, besides, between, by, concerning, down, during, except, for, from, in, into, off, on, out, over, to, under, until, upon, up, with, within, without.*

The commonest prepositional phrases are: *out of, from out, as to, on this side of, in front of, in spite of, because of, instead of, in regard to, for the sake of, according to, apart from, by means of, on account of, in place of.*

(1) THE PREPOSITION AND ITS OBJECT

A preposition always takes an object. In fact, a preposition has been loosely but aptly described as "a little word that always takes an object."

Remove the object from a preposition, and the preposition turns into an adverb.

1. Come *in* the house.   (Preposition)
2. You may come *in*.   (Adverb)
3. The dog ran *down* the street.   (Preposition)
4. The ladder fell *down*.   (Adverb)
5. "Get *off* the steps, I tell you.   Get *off*."   (First *off*, preposition; second *off*, adverb)
6. The wagon went *up* the hill.   (Preposition)
7. We got *up*.   (Adverb)

(2) PHRASES INTRODUCED BY PREPOSITIONS

The group of words introduced by a preposition always acts together as a unit to modify some other part of the sentence; in short, the phrase does the work of either an adjective or an adverb.   Hence, a good definition of a preposition is that it is a word placed before (*preposed*) a noun or its equivalent to make up an adjective or an adverb phrase.   This is the chief purpose of prepositions: to enable a noun or pronoun to modify another word.

(1) Adjective Phrases, Modifying Nouns or Pronouns

1. The house *by the side of the road* _____.
2. The face *on the barroom floor* _____.
3. The tree *by the gate* _____.
4. The man *on the bay horse* _____.
5. The girl *with the red hair* _____.

(2) Adverb Phrases, Modifying Verbs or Adjectives

1. _____ rode *at a rapid pace*.
2. Come *in a hurry*.
3. _____ stumbled *over the chair*.
4. _____ slipped *on the floor*.
5. _____ shining *in the sky*.

The only way to tell whether a phrase is an adjective phrase or an adverb phrase is thus to see what it modifies.   What the phrase does in the sentence determines its nature.

For further examples of prepositional phrases, see the sections on Phrases and Recognizing Phrases, pages 72–75 below.

To the large number of prepositions and their common use the English language owes much of its elasticity and expressiveness.

(3) PARSING PREPOSITIONS

To parse a preposition is (1) to name its object; (2) to give the full phrase which the preposition introduces; (3) to point out the word which the phrase modifies and thus determine whether the phrase is an adjective or an adverb phrase.

WRITTEN PARSING OF PREPOSITIONS

1. Above all things be pleasant to those around you.
2. The house on the corner belongs to the man with the stick in his hand.

Preposition	Object	Word Modified by the Phrase	Kind of Phrase
1. *above*	*things*	*be* (verb)	adverb
to	*those*	*pleasant* (adjective)	adverb
around	*you*	*those* (pronoun)	adjective
2. *on*	*corner*	*house* (noun)	adjective
to	*man*	*belongs* (verb)	adverb
with	*stick*	*man* (noun)	adjective
in	*hand*	*stick* (noun)	adjective

7. Conjunction

Whether coördinating or subordinating	If subordinating the kind of clause it introduces (Noun, adjective, or adverb)
1	2

CONJUNCTION

Conjunctions are words that connect words, phrases, and clauses. They are the coupling pins, as it were, of the train of thought, which hold it together, and enable it to add modifier after modifier and thought after thought until we have thoroughly and satisfactorily rounded out our meaning.

Conjunctions are of two classes: co-ordinating and subordinating.

(1) CO–ORDINATING CONJUNCTIONS

To co-ordinate means "to make or to keep equal"; thus co-ordinating conjunctions connect words, phrases, and clauses that are equal in rank.

There are four chief co-ordinating conjunctions, each of which has several synonyms: —

1. *And (also, likewise, moreover, besides, too)*
2. *But (however, still, nevertheless, yet, notwithstanding)*
3. *Or (either, neither, nor, else)*
4. *Therefore (for, hence, then, accordingly)*

Co-ordinating conjunctions offer little difficulty either theoretically in parsing or practically in writing and speaking. All that is needed is to be able to recognize them on sight and, if they connect clauses, to be sure that the clauses are of equal rank.

(2) SUBORDINATING CONJUNCTIONS

Subordinating conjunctions are both numerous and troublesome. They differ from co-ordinating conjunctions in several important ways.

1. As their name indicates, they introduce clauses of subordinate rank — in other words, clauses that depend for their full meaning upon the clause to which they are attached by the conjunction.

Consider how incomplete is the meaning of the following clauses, each a dependent clause introduced by a subordinating conjunction and left hanging in space without any main clause to depend from (and to depend on): —

(1) If it doesn't rain soon _____.
(2) Although he promised to come _____.
(3) When I heard her sing _____.
(4) Because I wanted to read it too _____.
(5) Where the road crosses the creek _____.

2. Unlike co-ordinating conjunctions, subordinating conjunctions do not merely connect, but also form a part of the clause which they introduce. See also conjunctive adverbs (Adverbs versus Conjunctions, page 59).

3. Subordinating conjunctions properly introduce clauses, and rarely connect phrase with phrase or word with word as co-ordinating conjunctions do.

There are ten subclasses of subordinating conjunctions. It is troublesome to list them and learn them, but it is more troublesome not to do so, so frequent and important are they in speech and writing.

(1) Time
> *when, whenever, while, as, until, before, since, after, as soon as, as long as*
> I'll be ready when you come.

(2) Place
> *where, whence, wherever*
> Let's go where you saw the deer yesterday.

(3) Manner
> *as, just as, as if*
> Please do as I say.

(4) Degree and Comparison
> *as much as, so far as, as, than*
> He has known you longer than me = (he has known me).
> He has known you longer than I = (I have known you).

(5) Cause or Reason
> *because, since, whereas, as, for*
> I believe it because you said it.

(6) Result
> *that, so that*
> He worked so hard that he saved a large sum for old age.

(7) Condition
> *if, unless, as if*
> I know you will help her if you can.

(8) Concession
> *though, although, even if*
> Though they are very rich, they do not put on airs.

(9) Purpose
> *that, so that, in order that, lest*
> He worked hard so that he would have enough for old age.

(**10**) *That* to Introduce a Noun Clause

 That you don't agree is clear. (Subject)

 I see that you don't agree. (Object)

 The fact that you don't agree is clear. (Apposition with a noun in the nominative case)

 I regret the fact that you don't agree. (Apposition with a noun in the objective case)

 The reason is that you don't agree. (Predicate nominative)

(3) PARSING CONJUNCTIONS

There are two points of importance in parsing conjunctions : (1) to determine whether they are co-ordinating or subordinating ; and (2) if subordinating, what kind of dependent clause they introduce — whether a noun, adjective, or adverb clause. It is not necessary to name the subclass to which subordinating conjunctions belong, as time, place, manner, degree, etc.

WRITTEN PARSING OF CONJUNCTIONS

1. Knowledge comes but wisdom lingers.
2. Either you are mistaken or I am.
3. God made the country, and man made the town. (COWPER)
4. When I heard it, I was much surprised.
5. This is the place where he told us to come.
6. If you think so, you are mistaken.
7. He promised her that he would never leave her.
8. He ran so fast that he got out of breath.
9. Unless you go, we can't go either.
10. Though he is not rich, he is generous.

Conjunction	Kind	Kind of Clause It Introduces
1. *but*	co-ordinating	
2. *or*	co-ordinating	
3. *and*	co-ordinating	
4. *when*	subordinating	adverb
5. *where*	subordinating	adjective
6. *if*	subordinating	adverb
7. *that*	subordinating	noun
8. *that*	subordinating	adverb
9. *unless*	subordinating	adverb
10. *though*	subordinating	adverb

8. The Interjection

INTERJECTION

The interjection is the only part of speech that has no contacts with or relations to the other words in a sentence. Strictly speaking, therefore, interjections are hardly a part of speech at all. They are merely exclamations, expressing deep or sudden feeling. Examples are words like *oh, ah, bah, pooh, bravo, alas, hurrah, pshaw, hush, hello, amen*. Much profanity and some slang are also exclamatory in nature, and might properly be ranked as interjections.

Many words and phrases can be used as exclamations and interjections; for example, *Horrors! Good work! Mercy on us! For shame! Oh dear me!*

It is only a step from phrases like these to longer exclamatory expressions such as

> What a shame!
> What a pity!
> How very beautiful!
> What a beautiful night!

The next step is the complete exclamatory sentence punctuated with an exclamation point instead of a question mark: —

> Isn't he a superb driver!
> Did you ever see such a black cloud!
> Wasn't that an exciting game!

PARSING INTERJECTIONS

Interjections need only to be recognized and pointed out. Since they have no grammatical connection with the rest of the sentence, no further parsing is possible.

Sentences for Parsing and Analysis

I

1. No bird soars too high if he soars with his own wing.

2. The guide pulled him from his blankets at dawn, and led him westward toward the distant line of foothills.

3. Such was the extremity of distress that the rats, who came to feast in those hideous dens, were eagerly hunted.

4.
> So nigh is grandeur to our dust,
> So near is God to man,
> When Duty whispers low, Thou must,
> The youth replies, I can!

5.
> I strove with none; for none was worth my strife,
> Nature I loved, and next to Nature, Art;
> I warmed both hands before the fire of life,
> It sinks, and I am ready to depart.

6.
> There was a young lady of Lynn,
> Who was so uncommonly thin
> That when she essayed
> To drink lemonade,
> She slipped through the straw and fell in.

II

1.
> The mossy marbles rest
> On the lips that he has prest
> In their bloom;
> And the names he loved to hear
> Have been carved for many a year
> On the tomb.

2.
> Whither, midst falling dew,
> While glow the heavens with the last steps of day,
> Far through their rosy depths, dost thou pursue
> Thy solitary way?

3.
> He who, from zone to zone,
> Guides through the boundless air thy certain flight,
> In the long way that I must tread alone,
> Will lead my steps aright.

4.
> He prayeth best who loveth best
> All things both great and small;
> For the dear God who loveth us,
> He made and loveth all.

5.   "Aha!" cried the egg,
            As it splashed a bit.
            "I was cast for the villain
            And made a hit."

6.   I hear in the chamber above me
            The patter of little feet,
            The sound of a door that is opened,
            And voices soft and sweet.

7.   I had a little doggy who went and bit a calf,
        And though he did it jokingly, I really couldn't laugh;
        I cut a little birch rod and took him down a peg:
        Because, you see, the calf he bit was one that's on my leg.

8. He that cannot think is a fool; he that will not think is a bigot; he
    that dare not think is a slave.

9.   My neck was sore in front before
            And also sore behind before. — Burma-Shave Jingle

CHAPTER IV

The Analysis of Sentences

Analysis versus Parsing

Parsing is concerned with the parts of speech and deals with words separately. **Analysis is concerned with the parts of sentences,** and deals with sentences as units. Parsing concentrates upon nouns, pronouns, adjectives, verbs, adverbs, prepositions, conjunctions, and interjections. Analysis concentrates upon subject, predicate, object or complement, and their modifiers, whether word, phrase, or clause.

Because analysis treats of matters like the kinds of sentences, modifiers of all kinds, and phrases and clauses as such, it is of direct use in learning to write. Especially is this true when it becomes necessary either to improve vague, weak sentences or to correct the scores of errors that will creep in despite our best efforts. Analysis thus conveniently bridges the gap between grammar and composition. Sentences are stubborn and tricky things, as every writer knows, and skill in analyzing them helps us handle them with greater ease and sureness.

SENTENCE ELEMENTS

Practically every element of sentence analysis is included in the tables on the following page. To know what these terms mean and to be able to recognize the sentence functions which they name is to know the essentials of sentence analysis.

ELEMENTS OF SENTENCE ANALYSIS

Sentence = subject plus predicate

Subject = $\left\{ \begin{array}{l} \text{noun or its equivalent} \\ \text{(word, phrase, or clause)} \end{array} \right\}$ plus adjective modifiers $\left\{ \begin{array}{l} \text{word,} \\ \text{phrase,} \\ \text{or clause} \end{array} \right.$

Predicate = $\left\{ \begin{array}{l} \text{(1) transitive verb} \\ \quad \text{plus adverb modifiers} \left\{ \begin{array}{l} \text{word,} \\ \text{phrase,} \\ \text{or clause} \end{array} \right\} \text{plus object} \\ \qquad\qquad\quad \text{or} \\ \text{(2) intransitive verb} \\ \quad \text{plus adverb modifiers} \left\{ \begin{array}{l} \text{word,} \\ \text{phrase,} \\ \text{or clause} \end{array} \right\} \text{plus complement} \end{array} \right.$

Object = $\left\{ \begin{array}{l} \text{noun or its} \\ \text{equivalent} \end{array} \right\}$ plus adjective modifiers $\left\{ \begin{array}{l} \text{word,} \\ \text{phrase,} \\ \text{or clause} \end{array} \right.$

Complement = $\left\{ \begin{array}{l} \text{(1) noun or its equivalent} \\ \quad \text{(word, phrase, or clause)} \end{array} \right\} \begin{array}{l} \text{plus adjective} \\ \text{modifiers} \end{array} \left\{ \begin{array}{l} \text{word,} \\ \text{phrase,} \\ \text{or clause} \end{array} \right. \\ \qquad\qquad\quad \text{or} \\ \text{(2) adjective or its equivalent} \left| \begin{array}{l} \text{plus adverb} \\ \text{modifiers} \end{array} \right\} \left\{ \begin{array}{l} \text{word,} \\ \text{phrase,} \\ \text{or clause} \end{array} \right.$

NEEDED GRAMMATICAL KNOWLEDGE

1. The Three Kinds of Sentences: Simple, Complex, and Compound.

2. The Difference between Phrases and Clauses.

3. The Three Kinds of Phrases: Noun, Adjective, and Adverb.

4. Dependent Clauses and Independent Clauses.

5. The Three Kinds of Dependent Clauses: Noun, Adjective, and Adverb.

1. Simple Sentences

A simple sentence is one that contains one subject and one predicate.

To analyze a simple sentence is to point out (1) the subject and the predicate; (2) their modifiers; and (3) the object or complement and its modifiers.

(1) SYMBOLS FOR WRITTEN ANALYSIS OF SIMPLE SENTENCES

Bare Subject, underlined once

Bare Verb, underlined twice

Bare Object, underlined three times

Adjective Modifiers (words or phrases), underlined with a wavy line

Adverb Modifiers (words or phrases), underlined with a broken line

Predicate Nominative or Noun Complement, not underlined

1. Fine feathers do not make fine birds.

2. The girl on the corner is a friend of my sister's.

3. There hath passed away a glory from the earth.

4. At Christmas he always sent all the sick people in the hospital beautiful flowers.

5. After a brief discussion the committee unanimously elected Mr. Glenn chairman.

6. Full many a gem of purest ray serene
   The dark unfathomed caves of ocean bear.

7. Up and down the dreary camp,
   In great boots of Spanish leather,
   Striding with a measured tramp,
   The Hidalgos, dull and damp,
   Cursed the Frenchmen.

(2) COMMENTS ON THE USE OF THE SYMBOLS

Long experience has shown that these five symbols are the ideal number. They could easily be increased, but only with a loss in ease and effectiveness.

Both the indirect object and the objective complement, when a noun (see sentences 4 and 5), are to be underlined with three lines, just as the direct object is.

The predicate nominative (or noun complement after an intransitive verb — see sentence 2) is not underlined, thus distinguishing it from (1) the direct object, which is underlined three times, and (2) the predicate adjective (or adjective complement), which is underlined with a wavy line.

In underlining phrases, as distinguished from separate adjectives and adverbs, care should be taken to extend the line under the whole phrase, instead of breaking it up under each word.

> The big, bad wolf is here.   (Separate adjectives)
> Who's afraid of the big, bad wolf?   (Adverb phrase)
> The cowboy was wearing a big, handsome, black hat.   (Separate adjectives)
> The man in the big, handsome, black hat is a cowboy.   (Adjective phrase)

(3) PHRASES

The chief trouble in analyzing simple sentences comes in handling phrases. **A phrase is a group of words (1) containing no subject or predicate and (2) performing the work of a single part of speech,** usually a noun, an adjective, or an adverb.

1. Noun Phrases

A noun phrase is a phrase that is used like a noun. Its four commonest uses are the following : —

1. The subject of a verb

   (*a*) *To give cheerfully* increases the pleasure of giving.
   (*b*) *Your calling him a coward* doesn't make him one.
   (*c*) *To see a dumb animal abused* always made him angry.

2. The object of a verb

   (a) No one likes *being a loser*.
   (b) I hate *having to resort to trickery*.
   (c) They refused *to accept charity*.
   (d) Everyone wants *to be happy*.

3. In apposition with a noun

   (a) The phrase *"On your toes"* was often used by our coach.
   (b) His first ambition, *to be the richest man in town*, was realized.
   (c) The verdict *"Not guilty"* was most pleasing to the prisoner.

4. Predicate nominative

   (a) Her chief fear was *losing her hair*.
   (b) My brother's hobby is *collecting postage stamps*.
   (c) It is not easy *to keep on good terms with all your neighbors*.

Exercises in Noun Phrases

Point out the noun phrases in the following sentences, and tell how they are used.

   1. Sitting around a campfire and telling stories is great fun.
   2. What confused me was your forgetting to bring the manuscript.
   3. It is hard to teach an old dog new tricks.
   4. The dog's barking in the house frightened the burglars away.
   5. To give money is not always the best form of charity.
   6. Your standing first in the class caused your parents great pleasure.
   7. There is no use crying over spilt milk.
   8. Writing an interesting story is a hard thing to do.
   9. To win over such able opponents made me happy.
  10. He resolved never to give up.
  11. To jump across the ditch was impossible.
  12. Your being late made us miss the train.
  13. Everyone must learn to control himself.
  14. Dr. Johnson said that being on shipboard is like being in jail.

2. ADJECTIVE AND ADVERB PHRASES

Phrases introduced by prepositions are the most numerous and troublesome. Practically all such phrases modify either (1) a noun or pronoun and are hence adjective phrases, or modify (2) a verb, adjective, or adverb, and are hence adverb phrases. To find what they modify is the only way to tell them apart. The same phrase that is an adjective phrase in one sentence, because it modifies a noun or pronoun, may be an adverb phrase in another sentence because it modifies a verb, adjective, or adverb.

Adjective Phrases	*Adverb Phrases*
1. The hat on the table is mine.	1. Please put my hat on the table.
2. The house by the side of the road belongs to a friend of mine.	2. He got out of the car and stood by the side of the road.
3. The man on the white horse is a good rider.	3. He was mounted on a white horse.
4. The stick in the corner fell down.	4. The stick standing in the corner fell down.

See also the section on Phrases Introduced by Prepositions, page 61 above.

Exercises in Recognizing Phrases

I

Tell what the italicized phrases modify and thus determine whether they are adjective or adverb phrases.

1. Just put your coat *in the hall.*
2. You will find the book *on the table in the parlor.*
3. Come *at the first possible moment.*
4. You will find us *waiting for you.*
5. You will find us waiting *for you.*
6. We once considered buying the house *with the green roof.*
7. A man of your standing should not stoop *to such tricks.*
8. There is always room *at the top for the best.*
9. Let's start *on our trip* early *in the morning.*
10. Failure *to convict* is no proof *of innocence.*

II

Point out the phrases introduced by prepositions and show them to be adjective or adverb phrases by telling what they modify.

If this exercise is assigned as written work, copy these sentences and underline adjective phrases with a wavy line and adverb phrases with a broken or dotted line.

1. A bird in the hand is worth two in the bush.
2. Under no circumstances will I agree to your proposal.
3. After supper we went to the best show in town.
4. One of the forts was laid in ruins.

5. A thing of beauty is a joy forever.
6. He is not for an age, but for all time.
7.   Full well they laughed with counterfeited glee
      At all his jokes, for many a joke had he.
8.   Man's inhumanity to man
        Makes countless thousands mourn.
9. There came to the beach a poor exile of Erin.
10. A clock of brass ticked on the mantel.

Simple Sentences for Analysis

Analyze the following sentences, using the symbols suggested on page 71.

1. A rolling stone gathers no moss.
2. Take things always by their smooth handle.
3. The weak in courage is strong in cunning.
4. The early bird catches the worm.
5. One man in his time plays many parts.
6. Shook's snapshot shop shall show some sharp snapshots soon.
7. A highbrow is a person educated beyond his intelligence.
8. Drenched with rain, he rode at a gallop through the gate of the castle.
9. My heart is in the coffin there with Caesar.
10. Columbus crossed the Atlantic in 1492 with ninety men, and landed at San Salvador.
11. They wash, iron, cook, eat, and sleep in the same room.
12. The child ran into the room, and kissed its mother affectionately.

2. Complex Sentences

A complex sentence is one that contains one or more dependent clauses.

A dependent clause is one which does not make complete sense in and by itself, but which depends upon another clause for its full meaning.

Consider, for example, the incomplete, unfinished meaning of the following dependent clauses which have been cut away from their independent clauses and left hanging in the air.

1. Unless you will help me _____.
2. _____ that you have been sick.
3. If you don't believe it _____.
4. _____ who sold it to me.
5. Although it is widely advertised _____.
6. _____ because he looked so hungry.

Now match these dangling dependent clauses with the following independent clauses to which they belong and both the meaning and the grammatical construction are complete.

1. ____ I have no one to turn to.
2. I am sorry ____.
3. ____ ask your father.
4. I can't remember now the clerk ____.
5. ____ I have never liked that brand of tooth paste.
6. I gave the tramp some food ____.

A great deal of time and attention should be devoted to dependent clauses. Just as the phrase is the trouble spot of the simple sentence, so the dependent clause is the trouble spot of the complex sentence. To master dependent clauses is to go a long way toward mastering the analysis of sentences, and, by the same token, to be able to use dependent clauses properly in writing is to go far toward achieving an accurate and flexible style.

In written analysis the three different kinds of clauses may be indicated as follows: —

Noun Clauses: enclosed in pointed brackets   **< >**

Adjective Clauses: enclosed in round brackets   **( )**

Adverb Clauses: enclosed in square brackets   **[ ]**

(1) PHRASES VERSUS CLAUSES

In **distinguishing phrases from clauses** there is one important point of likeness and one important point of unlikeness. The point of likeness is that both phrases and clauses are used as a single part of speech — either as noun, adjective, or adverb. The point of unlikeness is that the clause has a subject and predicate and that the phrase has none. Consider the difference as regards subject and predicate in the following parallel examples: —

Phrases	*Clauses*
1. The man on the corner is my friend.	1. The man (that is standing on the corner) is my friend.
2. Please come at the first possible moment.	2. Please come [as soon as you possibly can].
3. Upon the arrival of the train the band struck up a lively tune.	3. [When the train arrived] the band struck up a lively tune.

Phrases	*Clauses*
4. After winding the clock she turned out the light and went upstairs.	4. [After she had wound the clock] she turned out the light and went upstairs.
5. We must be on our way before sunrise.	5. We must be on our way [before the sun rises].

(2) DEPENDENT CLAUSES

1. How Introduced

So important and varied are dependent clauses that it is advisable to notice in detail the ways in which they are introduced. **Dependent clauses are usually introduced by either (*a*) subordinating conjunctions, or (*b*) relative pronouns.**

(*a*) Subordinating Conjunctions   (See Review of Grammar, pages 63–65, above.)

1. Time : *when, whenever, while, as, until, before, since, after, as soon as.*
2. Place : *where, whence, wherever.*
3. Manner : *as, just as, as if.*
4. Degree and Comparison : *as much as, so far as, as, than.*
5. Cause or Reason : *because, since, whereas, as, for.*
6. Result : *that, so that.*
7. Condition : *if, unless.*
8. Concession : *though, although, even if.*
9. Purpose : *that, so that, in order that, lest.*
10. The conjunction *that* introducing a noun clause.

(*b*) Relative Pronouns

Relative pronouns are *who, which, what, that.*
They usually introduce adjective clauses.

2. Kinds of Dependent Clauses

Whether introduced by subordinating conjunctions, by relative pronouns, or in whatsoever way, **dependent clauses are of three kinds : —**

(*a*) Noun Clauses
(*b*) Adjective Clauses
(*c*) Adverb Clauses

The way to distinguish them is the same as the way to distinguish (*a*) the parts of speech and (*b*) phrases: namely, to see what work they do in the sentence.

(*a*) Noun Clauses

A noun clause is a clause that is used like a noun — that is, in any of the six following ways: —

1. The subject of a verb

   <That he is mistaken> is evident.
   <Whether you go or stay> makes no difference.

2. The object of a verb

   They promised <that they would come>.
   I heard <that you are going to leave town>.

3. The object of a preposition

   Do you still agree with <what you said yesterday>?
   The decision will depend upon <whether you vote aye or no>.

4. In apposition with a noun

   The fact <that you agree> pleases all your friends.
   I hate to believe the cynical old saying <that every man has his price>.

5. Predicate nominative

   The question is <whether he has really been convinced>.
   The point at issue is <where you got the information>.

6. After certain adjectives like *sure, certain, glad, sorry,* and so forth.

After certain adjectives like *sure, certain, positive, glad, sorry, afraid,* and so forth, an interesting grammatical situation arises in connection with the *that* clause following them.   For example: —

   I am sure that I paid him.
   I'm certain you're wrong.
   I'm glad that you can come.
   We are all sorry that you have to go.
   She's afraid her mother won't let her.

Are the *that* clauses noun clauses or adverb clauses?

Many grammarians consider them adverb clauses, because they complete the meaning of the adjectives *sure, certain,* and so on, and thus may be loosely held to modify them.   Other grammarians consider *I am sure* and *I am certain* to be the equivalent of *I know; I am sorry* to equal *I regret;* and *I am afraid* to equal *I fear.* These few adjectives, therefore, seem to require the objective relationship after them, and hence the clauses are noun clauses. This is the view of the author of this book. Discuss this point in class with the instructor.

(b) Adjective Clauses

An adjective clause is one that modifies a noun or a pronoun.

1. Your opinion is the only thing (that matters).
   (Modifies the noun *thing*)
2. The book (which you lent me yesterday) is most interesting.
   (Modifies the noun *book*)
3. Will you (who have always been his friend) turn against him now?
   (Modifies the pronoun *you*)
4. They were out of town during the time (you refer to).
   (Modifies the noun *time*, the relative pronoun being omitted)
5. This is not the book (I wanted).
   (Modifies the noun *book*, the relative pronoun being omitted)

(c) Adverb Clauses

An adverb clause is one that modifies a verb, adjective, or adverb.

1. He came [when you called].
2. We waited [where you told us to].
3. [If you think so], go ahead.
4. We can't afford a new car [unless we get a good exchange price for the old one].
5. [Just as he reached for the rail], his foot slipped.
6. [Although my hours have been shortened], I still have too much to do.
7. We ran so fast [that we got out of breath].
8. The situation is not as bad [as we had feared].
9. His condition is better [than we had even dared to hope].

See also the section on Subordinating Conjunctions, pages 63–65 above.

(3) RECOGNIZING CLAUSES

Using the pointed brackets **< >** for noun clauses, the round brackets **( )** for adjective clauses, and the square brackets **[ ]** for adverb clauses, point out the dependent clauses in the following sentences.

1. She learned to play the piano when she was still a little girl.
2. If you will come with me, I will take you to your room.

3. Although the boys were very tired, they kept working until they had finished the shack.
4. All things come to him who waits.
5. The fact that he believes it does not make it true.
6. He also serves who only stands and waits.
7. June is the month when days are longest.
8. He jests at scars who never felt a wound.
9. Although trifles make perfection, perfection is no trifle.
10. There was never yet a philosopher that could endure the toothache patiently.
11. We asked what the price of the house was, but the owner said that it was not for sale.
12. I don't know what to tell her when she comes.

(4) ANALYSIS OF COMPLEX SENTENCES

After marking the dependent clauses as noun, adjective, or adverb clauses by means of the different brackets, further analysis of both the independent and the dependent clauses proceeds as in the simple sentence. That is, each clause is taken separately, and the subject, verb, object, or complement, and all modifying words and phrases, are marked as indicated on page 71.

1. Never put off till tomorrow <what you can do today>.

2. Have a heart (that never hardens), a temper (that never tires), and a touch (that never hurts).

3. No statue has ever yet been erected to a man (who was afraid of <what people might say>).

4. [If you would realize the state of the ant under your foot] think of your condition [were you under the foot of an elephant].

— PERSIAN PROVERB

5. Breathes there the man with soul so dead (Who never to himself hath said, <This is my own, my native land!>)

6.   There was an old man of Tarentum,
(Who gnashed his false teeth [till he bent 'em]).
[When they asked him the cost
    Of <what he had lost,>]
He replied, <"I can't say, [for I rent 'em"]>.

(5) COMMENTS ON THE USE OF THE SYMBOLS

It will be noticed that neither co-ordinating nor subordinating conjunctions are marked. This in itself serves to distinguish them from other parts of speech which might be confused with them.

Notice, too, the use of the brackets, if there is more than one dependent clause in the sentence. There are several possibilities.

1. The dependent clauses may all be dependent on the same independent clause, in which case the brackets marking them off will neither overlap nor even partly coincide. For example: —

(1) Tell me [when you can come] [if you don't mind].
(2) Have a heart (that never hardens), a temper (that never tires), and a touch (that never hurts).

2. One dependent clause may be dependent on another dependent clause, in which case the brackets of the inner clause will be included within the brackets of the clause on which it depends.

(1) They wired <that they could not stay [as long as they had expected]>.
(2) Here is the clerk (that promised us <that he would sell us the chairs at a 50 per cent reduction>).
(3) This is the cat (that killed the rat (that ate the malt (that lay in the house (that Jack built)))).

Complex Sentences for Analysis

I

1. If a man empties his purse into his head, no man can take it away from him.
2. Never cross a bridge till you come to it.
3. A critic is a legless man who teaches running.

— CHANNING POLLOCK

4. I wonder why London cannot keep its own fools at home.

— GOLDSMITH

5. A specialist is a man who knows more and more about less and less.
— DR. WILLIAM J. MAYO

6.   Lives of great men all remind us,
We can make our lives sublime.
— LONGFELLOW

II

1. The world is a comedy to those who think, a tragedy to those who feel.
2. A fool is one who is intelligent at the wrong time.
3. Nothing is particularly hard if you divide it into small jobs.
— HENRY FORD
4. The measure of a man's real character is what he would do if he knew he would never be found out. — MACAULAY
5. Music is the only language in which you cannot say a mean or sarcastic thing. — JOHN ERSKINE
6. An old-fashioned girl blushes when she is embarrassed; a modern girl is embarrassed when she blushes.
7. The town was so small that when the train stopped, the engine was out in the country.
8. The man who cannot put fire into his speeches should put his speeches into the fire.

III

1. It was easy to teach the dog that he must come to me when I whistled.
2. We regret to inform you that we have no more straw hats in stock and that we shall not buy any others till next spring.
3. That is the desk where lost and found articles are restored to their owners.
4. Father said as he patted my shoulder, "Don't feel so discouraged because you failed."
5. He who knows only his side of the case knows little of that.
6. The smallest dewdrop that lies on the meadow at night has a star sleeping in its bosom.
7.   Then let us say you are sad
Because you are not merry.
— SHAKESPEARE

3. Compound Sentences

A compound sentence is one that contains two or more independent clauses.

Independent clauses are joined by co-ordinating conjunctions, chief of which are these: —

1. *And* (*also, likewise, moreover*)
2. *But* (*however, still, nevertheless*)
3. *Or* (*either, neither, nor*)
4. *Therefore* (*for, hence, then, accordingly*)

(See Conjunctions, Review of Grammar, page 63, above.)

(1) ANALYSIS OF COMPOUND SENTENCES

If none of the independent clauses of a compound sentence contains a dependent clause, such a compound sentence consists in effect of several simple sentences linked together by co-ordinating conjunctions. Analysis then proceeds as in the simple sentence: —

1. The heavens declare the glory of God, and the firmament showeth his handiwork.

2. The rat, the mouse, the fox, the rabbit, watch the roots; the lion, the tiger, the horse, the elephant, watch the fruits.

(2) COMPLEX–COMPOUND SENTENCES

If one or more of the independent clauses of a compound sentence contain a dependent clause, such a compound sentence is in effect a linking of a simple sentence with a complex sentence or a linking of several complex sentences with one another. In order to distinguish this type of compound sentence from the preceding type, many grammarians use the term "complex-compound sentence." In either case, such sentences offer no difficulties in analysis which have not already been touched on.

Examples of the analysis of complex-compound sentences are these : —

1. Men must work, and women must weep,
   [Though storms be sudden and waters deep],
   And [the harbour bar be moaning].

2. He (who fights and runs away)
   May live to fight another day;
   But he (who is in battle slain)
   Can never rise and fight again.

3. One soldier [when the fight was red],
   Threw down his broken sword and fled;
   Another snatched it, won the day
   With <what his comrade threw away>.

— EDWIN MARKHAM

Compound Sentences for Analysis

1. Cowards die many times before their deaths;
   The valiant never taste of death but once.

2. The hours of folly are measured by time, but the hours of wisdom no clock can measure.

3. Straws float upon the surface, but gold lies at the bottom of the stream.

4. Some are born great, some achieve greatness, and some have greatness thrust upon them.

5. Faithful are the wounds of a friend, but the kisses of an enemy are deceitful.

6. The fair breeze blew, the white foam flew,
   The furrow followed free.

7. A thing of beauty is a joy forever;
   Its loveliness increases; it will never
   Pass into nothingness.

   — KEATS

8. The curfew tolls the knell of parting day,
   The lowing herd winds slowly o'er the lea,
   The ploughman homeward plods his weary way
   And leaves the world to darkness and to me.

   — GRAY

Sentences for Parsing and Analysis

I

1. From Clive's second visit to India dates the political ascendancy of the English in that country.

2. I play a musical instrument some, but only for my own amazement.
   — FRED ALLEN

3. The egg is smooth and very pale;
   It has no nose, it has no tail;
   It has no ears that one can see;
   It has no wit, no repartee.

4. When wicked witches whisk switches, which witch whisks switches swiftest?

5. The Night has a thousand eyes,
   And the Day but one;
   Yet the light of the bright world dies
   With the dying sun.

6. You never know what is enough unless you know what is more than enough.

II

1. I may disapprove of what you say, but will defend to the death your right to say it. — VOLTAIRE

2. They say that the first time a Scotchman used free air he blew out four tires. — *Atlanta* (Ga.) *Journal*

3. Heredity is an omnibus in which all our ancestors ride, and every now and then one of them sticks his head out and embarrasses us.
   — OLIVER WENDELL HOLMES

4. Some men would look more spic if they didn't have so much span.
   — *Chicago Daily Tribune*

5. If your hair isn't becoming to you, you should be coming to us.
   — Beauty Shop Ad

6. You are never fully dressed until you wear a smile.
   — Sign in an elevator in a Duluth hotel

III

1. The only difference between a rut and a grave is in their dimensions.
   — ELLEN GLASGOW

2. A newspaper is a portable screen behind which a man hides from the woman who is standing on a streetcar.
   — *Los Angeles Times*

3. Too many parents are not on spanking terms with their children.

4. Nothing is really work unless you would rather be doing something else. — SIR JAMES BARRIE

5. The most appropriate dressing for some heads is not hair tonic but furniture polish.

6. When a man doesn't care a whoop what people think of him, he has likely reached either the top or the bottom.

7.
> Week-old beard so masked his face
> His bulldog chased him off the place.
>> — Burma-Shave Jingle

IV

1.
> Far in a wilderness obscure
> The lonely mansion lay.

2. If it is not right, do not do it ; if it is not true, do not say it.

3. He that is good at making excuses is seldom good at anything else.

4. He who loses wealth loses much ; he who loses a friend loses more ; but he who loses courage loses all. — CERVANTES

5.
> There was a young maid who said, "Why
> Can't I look in my ear with my eye?
> If I give my mind to it,
> I'm sure I can do it,
> You never can tell till you try."

V

1. With only two minutes to play, Colgate's rangy left end speared a forty-yard forward pass with one hand, stiff-armed one Amherst tackler, sidestepped another, and raced ten yards for the winning touchdown.

2.
> 'Most any golfer, poor or rich,
> Would never count the cost,
> Could he but buy a golf ball which
> Would bark when it is lost.

3.
> Ah, yes, I wrote the Purple Cow —
> I'm sorry, now, I wrote it!
> But I can tell you, anyhow,
> I'll kill you if you quote it.
>> — GELETT BURGESS

4. There are poor people in the mountains who live in such dilapidated shacks that every time it rains they have to go out and get in the sedan. -— *The Literary Digest*

5. I usually get my stuff from an awful lot of people — who promised somebody else that they would keep it a secret.

— WALTER WINCHELL

6. "I can't decide whether I should go to a palmist or to a mindreader." "By all means go to a palmist. It's evident that you have a palm."

7. Here lie one hundred roses dead,
That Alice may smell nice to Fred.

— AL KLEIN, "Perfume"

8. *Etc.* is a sign used to make others believe that you know more than you do.

VI

1. What this country needs is a zipper olive bottle.
2. Be not merely good; be good for something.
3. I am an old man, and have known a great many troubles, but most of them never happened. — MARK TWAIN
4. Nature never did betray the heart
That loved her.

— WORDSWORTH

5. It has been proved that pictures can be transmitted by radio.
6. When she opened those ruby lips of hers she spoke pure spearmint.

— *Dinner at Eight*

CHAPTER V

Punctuation

A lot of punctuation is simply grammar made graphic.
— WILSON FOLLETT

(1) THE IDEAL IN PUNCTUATION

Punctuation is both reasonable and logical. The system was not imposed upon writers by former pedants, who wished to make writing more difficult, but it was slowly evolved by the leading printers and publishers to make writing clear and easy to read, in somewhat the same way and with somewhat the same purpose that every state and city has established highway markers and traffic signals in order to guide and to aid traffic.

Punctuation is as much a part of your writing as the letters with which you spell words.

It is easy to punctuate a good sentence which you understand thoroughly. What makes punctuation hard is either (*a*) lack of a clear understanding of the structure of the sentence to be punctuated or (*b*) the fact that the sentence itself is obscurely or awkwardly put together. If we write good clear sentences, punctuation is a comfort instead of an encumbrance. In the words of Professor Charles Sears Baldwin, "No one can punctuate with his hand until he has punctuated with his head."

The writer's aim is always "Clearness first!" Communicating our thoughts and feelings to others is an uncertain business at best, and to keep from being misunderstood will tax all our ingenuity and effort. As the reader's eye races from word to word, he needs every particle of help we can give him. Of all aids to clearness, intelligent punctuation is one of the best.

(2) END PUNCTUATION

The two most important items of punctuation are the **use of a capital letter to mark the beginning of a sentence and a period to mark the end.** The capital and the period are, as it were, the headlight and the taillight of the sentence, and without them a sentence would run wild in the dark. No other forms of punctuation can compare in importance with this use of the capital and period to mark the limits of the sentence. Sometimes, of course, one of the other two forms of end punctuation — the question mark or the exclamation mark — takes the place of the period. In fact, the same sentence, if given different end punctuation, will change its meaning : —

> You don't believe me.
> You don't believe me?
> You don't believe me!

Here the period, the question mark, and the exclamation point each give a different turn to the thought. In all three cases, however, the principle is the same : The first and greatest law of the sentence is a capital to start it off and a period to bring it to a close.

(3) INTERNAL PUNCTUATION

In addition to the capital-period combination for end punctuation, there are several marks which are used to make clear the relation of phrases and clauses within the limits of the sentence itself. Chief among these internal marks of punctuation are **the colon, the semicolon, and the comma.** As we read, the eye and the mind working together absorb the meaning not all at once but in little jets or spurts, as it were. Our progress is not by means of one sustained rush, like the flight of an arrow or a bullet, but is a kind of hop, skip, and a jump movement. Take the following simple example : —

> About one o'clock today, on the way home to lunch, I saw the new fire engine come tearing by.

The way most people get the full meaning of this sentence is by four steps or stages : (1) about one o'clock today (2) on the way home to lunch (3) I saw the new fire engine (4) come tearing by. When the sentence is read in this way, there is no confusion or misunderstanding. All the details stand off clearly from one another, each detail following the preceding one logically and distinctly.

To bring about this desirable situation in every sentence is the purpose of all internal punctuation. By the use of comma and semicolon, that which is distinct in thought must be separated so that the reader can instantly grasp the separation, and at the same time what belongs together must be grouped so that the reader can easily grasp the grouped idea. Consider the following examples.

(4) FAILURE TO SEPARATE

> As the frightened animals rushed by the people on the corner shrank back in fear.

Printed thus, this sentence trips the reader up, for he has to read it twice to see that *people* is not the object of *by* but is the subject of *shrank*. A comma to separate these ideas makes all clear : —

> As the frightened animals rushed by, the people on the corner shrank back in fear.

DIFFERENCE OF MEANING

A change in punctuation changes the entire meaning of the following sentences : —

1.   Soldiers do not complain of hardships.
1 (a)   Soldiers, do not complain of hardships.
2.   Mr. Green, your next-door neighbor sent you these apples.
2 (a)   Mr. Green, your next-door neighbor, sent you these apples.
3.   Who said our guide is the best shot in the state?
3 (a)   "Who," said our guide, "is the best shot in the state?"
4.   Please phone Tom and say we can't come.
4 (a)   Please phone, Tom, and say we can't come.
5.   No price is too high.
5 (a)   No. Price is too high.
6.   Slow! Men working.
6 (a)   Slow men working.

Then there are the four following instances of the great difference punctuation may make.

I

Woman! Without her, man would be a savage.
Woman without her man would be a savage.

II

A teacher who was on very good terms with her class came into the room one day a little late and found this sentence on the board : —

This class thinks its teacher is the best in the whole school.

With a smile she added two commas and gracefully returned the compliment : —

This class, thinks its teacher, is the best in the whole school.

Incidentally, the semicolon gives another meaning still : —

This class thinks ; its teacher is the best in the whole school.

III

The United States once suffered heavily through the wrongful placing of a comma. Congress had drafted a tariff bill and, in enumerating the articles to be admitted free, had included "all foreign fruit-plants, etc." When copying this clause, however, a clerk omitted the hyphen and placed a comma after *fruit*, so that the clause read "all foreign fruit, plants, etc." As the mistake could not be rectified for about a year, all kinds of foreign fruits, such as lemons, oranges, grapes, and bananas, entered free of duty, and the Government lost a large sum of money. — *Word Study*

IV

A woman living in a small seaport town sent the following notice up to the pulpit to be read aloud at the morning service : —

A husband going to sea, his wife desires the prayers of the congregation.

Unfortunately, not being versed in the art of punctuation, she did not put the comma between *sea* and *his*. The congregation, therefore, much to its surprise, heard the minister solemnly say : —

A husband going to see his wife desires the prayers of the congregation.

THE TENDENCY TODAY TOWARD LIGHT PUNCTUATION

The trend in punctuation today is away from the heavy, close system of the past, with its complicated sentences and thick sprinkling of commas and semicolons, toward a simpler sentence structure with only the necessary punctuation marks to make the meaning clear.

(5) FREQUENCY OF THE DIFFERENT MARKS

Here is a table prepared from examining 10,000 words in magazines, newspapers, and letters, and averaging the number of times the different marks were used.[1] It shows that the period and the comma are each used from three to four times as often as all the other marks put together.

Mark	Number of Times Used	Mark	Number of Times Used
Comma	556	Semicolon	22
Period	535	Dash	21
Quotation Marks . .	44	Question Mark . . .	14
Apostrophe . . .	40	Colon	11

This is an interesting table, and its results will apply with a fair degree of accuracy to your own writing.

CAPITALS

The use of capital letters was not included in the investigation, but since every sentence must begin with a capital letter, besides occasionally containing proper names and proper adjectives, which also begin with capitals, it is safe to say that we use at least as many capitals as we do commas or periods — about ten or twelve to every page.

(6) PRESENT–DAY USAGE OUR GOAL

In learning how to use these marks correctly and confidently, it is important to know not the practice of the past, but the standard usage of today. A recent important investigation[2] has made the actual facts of current usage available. A questionnaire on punctuation was sent to fifty-four leading book publishers, sixty-seven influential newspapers, and twenty-three important magazines. Their replies represent an authoritative cross-section of the standard usage of today. On this basis the following simplified treatment of punctuation has been put together. It represents the minimum requirements of standard modern punctuation. Even including the sections

[1] Helen Ruhlen and S. L. Pressey, "A Statistical Study of Current Usage in Punctuation," *English Journal*, Vol. 13, 1924, p. 327.

[2] Sterling Andrus Leonard, *Current English Usage*, published for the National Council of Teachers of English, 1932.

on the apostrophe (pages 338–341 below) and the use of capital letters (pages 114–119 below), the rules are neither too complicated nor too difficult to be thoroughly mastered. They number only forty-four in all. They are less than half as long and half as hard as the multiplication table, and there is no guesswork in our knowledge of and use of that. Naturally we cannot expect to punctuate as accurately and exactly as we multiply, but except in the case of a few uses of the comma we can come near doing so. Nothing less than that should satisfy us.

(7) FREAKS OF PUNCTUATION

Try your hand on the following freaks of punctuation : —

1. Every lady in this land
    Hath twenty nails upon each hand ;
    Five and twenty on hands and feet ;
    And this is true without deceit.

2. A funny little man told this to me :
    I fell in a snowdrift in June said he ;
    I went to a ball game out in the sea ;
    I saw a jellyfish float up in a tree ;
    I found some gum in a cup of tea ;
    I stirred my milk with a big brass key ;
    I opened my door on my bended knee ;
    I beg your pardon for this, said he,
    But 'tis true when told as it ought to be.

3. that that is is that that is not is not that that
    is not is not that that is that that is is not
    that that is not is not that it it is

4. It was and I said not but.

5. A Latin Example

The Oracle of Apollo at Delphi in ancient Greece was frequently consulted by kings and warriors as to the outcome of future events. Often cleverly worded, ambiguous answers were given. On one occasion a well-known Roman general sent to ask his fate in a war which he was about to undertake. He received the answer : *Ibis, redibus. Nunquam in bello peribis.* (You will go, you will return. Never in war will you perish.) He embarked confidently for the war, only to fall in the first battle. His indignant widow reproached the oracle bitterly. The reply was that she had misread the message. The period was meant to come after *nunquam*, not after *redibus*.

PUNCTUATION TABLE
All Uses
(Starred uses are explained on the pages indicated.)

I. THE PERIOD
(*Two Uses*)

*1. To mark the end of every sentence that is not a question or an exclamation (page 97).
2. After abbreviations.

II. THE COMMA
(*Fourteen Uses*)

1. Between city and state.
2. Between the date and the year.
3. Before *but* and *for* in compound sentences.
*4. To separate members of a series (page 98).
5. To set off a word in direct address.
6. To set off appositives.
7. To set off absolute phrases.
8. After *Yes* and *No* and mild exclamations.
9. To set off parenthetical sentence modifiers like *however, in fact, of course.*
*10. To set off nonrestrictive clauses (page 102).
11. After the greeting in friendly letters.
12. Before short quotations.
*13. To wedge apart words or phrases which if read together would give a wrong meaning (page 105).
*14. After a long, dependent adverbial clause coming first in the sentence (page 106).

III. THE SEMICOLON
(*Three Uses*)

*1. Between co-ordinate clauses not joined by *and, but,* or *for* (page 108).
*2. Before *however* and certain other conjunctive adverbs when a complete independent statement is added to another complete independent statement (page 109).
*3. Between long independent statements when either statement is punctuated with commas (page 110).

IV. QUOTATION MARKS
(Two Uses)

1. Before and after a direct quotation.
*2. To indicate the titles of articles, chapters, short stories, and single poems — but not the titles of books, magazines, and newspapers, which should be underlined (page 112).

V. THE APOSTROPHE
(Three Uses)

*1. To indicate the omission of a letter or a syllable (page 338).
*2. To help form the plural of letters, figures, and words used without reference to their meaning (page 339).
*3. To help form the possessive case of nouns and indefinite pronouns (pages 339–341).

VI. THE DASH
(Three Uses)

1. To mark a sudden change or an abrupt break in the thought.
2. Instead of commas, to enclose parenthetical expressions less closely connected with the thought.
3. Instead of the colon, before an informal list or enumeration.

VII. THE QUESTION MARK

1. After every direct question, whether quoted or not.

VIII. THE COLON
(Three Uses)

1. After the greeting in a formal or business letter.
*2. After such expressions as *these, the following, as follows*, to give notice of a list of particulars or examples (page 113).
3. To give notice of a formal quotation several sentences long.

IX. UNDERLINING (ITALICS)
(Three Uses)

*1. To indicate the titles of books, magazines, and newspapers (page 113).
2. To indicate foreign words and phrases not yet felt to be a part of the language.
3. To indicate words taken out of their context and used without regard to their meaning.

X. EXCLAMATION POINT

(One Use)

1. To indicate strong feeling after interjections and words or phrases meant to be understood as highly emotional.

XI. PARENTHESES

(One Use)

1. To enclose and separate interpolated material which is unexpectedly introduced and not grammatically connected with the rest of the sentence.

XII. CAPITAL LETTERS

(Eight Uses)

*1. The first word in every sentence (page 115).
*2. In the title of themes, stories, and books, the first word and all other words except the articles, prepositions, and conjunctions (page 115).
3. The first word of every direct quotation (*a*) which is introduced by *say* or its equivalent, and (*b*) which makes complete sense in and by itself.
*4. Proper names (page 116).
5. Titles, degrees, and terms of family relationship when used with the names of persons.
6. Adjectives derived from proper names.
7. The first word of every line of poetry.
8. The pronoun *I* and the vocative interjection *O*.

SPECIAL TROUBLE SPOTS IN PUNCTUATION

Of the forty-four usages in punctuation listed in the Punctuation Table, the following seventeen need special attention either because of their unusual importance or because of difficulty in mastering.

1. The period at the end of a sentence, page 97.
2. The comma to set off members of a series, page 98.
3. Restrictive and nonrestrictive clauses, pages 100–105.
4. The comma to wedge apart words or phrases which if read together would give a wrong meaning, page 105.
5. The comma after a long dependent adverbial clause coming first in the sentence, page 106.
6. The semicolon between co-ordinate clauses not joined by *and*, *but*, or *for*, pages 108–109.

7. The semicolon before *however* and certain other conjunctive adverbs when a complete independent statement is added to another independent statement, page 109.
8. The semicolon between long independent statements when either statement is punctuated with commas, page 110.
9. Quotation marks to indicate titles of articles, chapter and section headings, short stories, and single poems, but not the titles of books, magazines, and newspapers (see usage number 12, Underlining), page 112.
10. The apostrophe in all three of its uses. See Spelling, pages 338–341.
11. The colon after such expressions as *these, the following, as follows,* to give notice of a list of particulars or examples, page 113.
12. Underlining the titles of books, magazines, and newspapers, page 113.
13. Capitalizing the first word in every sentence, page 115.
14. In the titles of themes, stories, and books, capitalizing the first word and all other words except the articles (*a, an, the*), prepositions, and conjunctions unless standing first, page 115.
15. Capitalizing proper names and proper adjectives of various kinds, page 116.
16. Three don't's in capitalizing, page 118.
17. For the punctuation of footnotes, bibliographies, and so forth, see The Research Paper, pages 274–280.

1. The period at the end of a sentence.

A period marks the end of every sentence that is not a question or an exclamation.

This is the most important single rule in punctuation, and is too familiar to need illustration. It is neither debatable nor optional. It is final and essential: put a period at the end of every declarative and imperative sentence.

Failure to do so is the gravest error in writing, and can be explained only in one of two ways: (1) ignorance of what constitutes a sentence or (2) haste and carelessness. Neither explanation is an excuse.

Two Danger Spots

The two chief violations of this rule, which are always considered serious, are these: (1) Punctuating a phrase or clause as if it were a sentence. See "The No-Sentence, or the Period Fault," pages 190–193, below. (2) "The Run-Together Sentence or the Comma Splice." See pages 194–196, below.

These two offenses against sentence unity should have been entirely weeded out of your writing by this time.   As a test try the following ten sentences, and if you leave a single mistake uncorrected, glance through the two sections just referred to, pages 190–196.

Test on the Period Fault and the Comma Splice

Name and correct the mistakes in these sentences : —

1. It was a good many years ago, as men figure time.   The place, an old, dilapidated shack near the rim of the desert.
2. My speech was over, I felt that I had failed.
3. This is still a good car, it can make sixty miles an hour on a paved road.
4. The sun's shining down so exceedingly hot causing me to faint.
5. His preparations for the night were very simple.   The removal of his shoes and coat, in fact.
6. Last week we visited Tampa and St. Petersburg, they're on the gulf.
7. Notwithstanding the fact that it is doubtful whether a poet named Homer ever lived.
8. His desk was piled high with papers, before him were reports on three different cases.
9. "Watch the fullback," a man said, "he is going to try for a field goal."
10. The cornerstone of the building which had been put into place with elaborate ceremonies.

2. The comma to separate the members of a series.

A series is three or more words, phrases, or clauses in the same construction.   (Sometimes called *the red, white, and blue* construction)

Words in Series

1. The colors of the American flag are red, white, and blue.
2. She was tall, graceful, and charming.
3. A narrow, winding, slippery road is doubly dangerous at night.
4. The whole family cooked, ate, and slept in one small room.

Phrases in Series

1. The stage setting for this scene consists of a piano and stool, a tall floor lamp, a leather sofa, and a small revolving bookcase.
2. In a large city you have your choice of traveling on the elevated, in a surface car, or on the subway.

3. The airplane, the high-powered automobile, and the streamlined train were all developed in answer to man's demand for more speed.

4. George Washington was first in war, first in peace, and first in the hearts of his countrymen.

CLAUSES IN SERIES

1. It was evident that he had heard the rumor, that it had made him very angry, and that he was determined to learn the truth.

2. What you hear, what you read, and what you think all help to form your mental background.

3. If you eat prudently, take enough exercise, and get enough sleep, you ought to keep your health for many years to come.

4. Our three greatest moments are when we are born, when we are married, and when we die.

THE COMMA BEFORE *and* IN A SIMPLE SERIES

The comma before *and* in a simple series is preferred by a large majority of the leading publishers of books and magazines, although newspaper usage is against it. So far as the best practice is concerned, therefore, we should continue to use it.

Preferred: Red, white, and blue are colors.
Permitted: Red, white and blue are colors.
Preferred: She was tall, graceful, and charming.
Permitted: She was tall, graceful and charming.

An important exception to this rule is the names of business firms and book publishers ending in *& Co.* or *and Company*. Usually no comma is used before the *and*. For example: —

Sears, Roebuck and Co.
Harcourt, Brace and Company
Doubleday, Doran & Company
Scott, Foresman and Company
Little, Brown & Company

3. Restrictive and nonrestrictive clauses.

In order to understand nonrestrictive clauses, we must first know what a restrictive clause is.

A. Restrictive Clauses

Modifying clauses are of two kinds, restrictive and nonrestrictive. **A restrictive clause gets its name from the fact that it restricts or limits the meaning to one particular person, group, place, or thing.** Take, for example, the sentence : —

The hat that you bought yesterday is very becoming to you.

The clause *that you bought yesterday* restricts the meaning of *hat* to one particular hat out of all the hats in the world, and is hence a restrictive clause.

The man who just spoke to me is our doctor.

Again, the clause *who just spoke to me* limits the idea *man* to one particular man out of all the men in town, and is hence restrictive.

Where is the book I left on the piano last night?

Here, too, the clause [*which*] *I left on the piano last night* singles out one particular book from all the books in the house, and is hence a restrictive clause.

Read the following sentences thoughtfully and notice how the clauses, all of which are restrictive, limit the idea to one particular person or thing out of all the possible persons or things in existence.

1. She borrowed a pencil from the boy who sat in front of her.
2. An amateur athlete is one who contests for pleasure, not for money.
3. The plumber who fixed the pipes this time is not the one that we had before.
4. A restrictive clause is one that restricts the meaning to one particular person, group, place, or thing.
5. "A man admires the woman who makes him think, but he keeps away from her ; he likes the woman who makes him laugh ; he loves the girl who hurts him ; but he marries the woman who flatters him." — NELLIE B. STULL
6. The Community Chest is an organization that puts all its begs in one ask-it. — *Reader's Digest*

We might thus represent a restrictive clause as a pointing finger that singles out one individual from all other similar persons or things and in this way particularizes and identifies it.

The hat
that you bought
yesterday

is very becoming to you.

The man
who just spoke
to me

is our doctor.

Where is the book
I left on the
piano last night?

Let all
who favor
the motion

make it known by rising.

Or we might represent a restrictive clause by a sharp-pointed wedge which narrows the idea to one alone out of the many possibilities.

This is not the knife < which I lent you yesterday.

Is that the house < which was struck by lightning?

Not all clauses, either restrictive or nonrestrictive, are introduced by the relative pronouns *who*, *which*, and *that*. Many are introduced by subordinating conjunctions like *when, while, where, as, since, because, if, unless, although*.

Here are a few restrictive clauses introduced in this way. Notice that they are not set off by commas.

Restrictive Adverbial Clauses

1. He came when you called.
2. She listened to the radio while she was waiting for him.
3. We waited where you told us to.
4. Fold the paper just as I did.
5. I have never seen him since he left town.
6. The machine won't run till you fix it.
7. I can't go unless you go too.

Restrictive clauses, whether adjectival or adverbial, are so closely connected with the rest of the sentence that they cannot be cut away from it by any form of punctuation, not even commas.

B. NONRESTRICTIVE CLAUSES

Nonrestrictive clauses do not restrict or limit the thought to any particular person or thing, but merely add another fact or idea to the one expressed in the main part of the sentence.

Examples

1. I am studying Latin, which is a hard subject.

Here the clause *which is a hard subject* does not single out any particular kind of Latin, but applies to Latin in general, to all Latin. It is hence a nonrestrictive clause.

2. Texas, which was once a part of Mexico, is the largest state in the Union.

Here again, the clause *which was once a part of Mexico* applies to Texas as a whole, and does not restrict the meaning in any way, merely adding another fact concerning it, namely, that it was once a part of Mexico.

3. Printing, which is man's most important invention, was introduced into England in 1476.

Again, the clause *which is man's most important invention* does not limit the term *printing* to any particular kind, but applies to the idea of *printing* as a whole, adding the thought that it is man's most important invention. It is thus a nonrestrictive clause and is set off by commas.

Think over the following sentences, and note how the clauses do not restrict or limit the nouns they modify, but merely give an additional fact concerning them. Each clause thus being nonrestrictive is set off by commas.

1. The mayor's son, who has been away at college for four years, has just returned to town.
2. We started at once for the clubhouse, which was only six miles away.
3. My father, who was a minister, was both a scholar and a gentleman.
4. Water, which is composed of two atoms of hydrogen to one of oxygen, is one of the most useful substances in the world.

If we were to try to represent what these and all other nonrestrictive clauses do in a sentence, we should have to use not a sharp wedge or a pointing finger, but a parallelogram of equal width at both ends.

Taking the three sentences above, we should have something like this : —

I am studying Latin, | which is a hard subject | .

Texas, | which was once a part of Mexico | , is the largest state in the Union.

Printing, | which is man's most important invention | , was introduced into England in 1476.

The boxed-in, nonrestrictive clauses could all be omitted from the sentences, and the meaning would still be complete and largely unchanged. Read the sentences without them. They are not essential to the meaning.

Restrictive clauses, however, are usually essential to the meaning, and cannot be omitted without falsifying or destroying it.

In the light of what has been said of restrictive clauses study the following paired sentences. The clauses in them have been made as much alike as possible in order to emphasize the difference.

Nonrestrictive	*Restrictive*
1. Unfortunately she has lost her handbag, which contained her diamond ring. (She had only one handbag.)	1. Fortunately she did not lose the handbag that contained her diamond ring. (She had several handbags.)
2. Jane Farley, who just went by, lives across the street from us.	2. The girl who just went by lives across the street from us.
3. Bread, which has been called the staff of life, is good to eat.	3. Bread which has begun to mold is not good to eat.
4. Bill Gray, who failed to pass on four subjects, has been ruled ineligible for football.	4. No student who fails to pass on four subjects will be allowed to play football.
5. Alice Bryce, who made a daily average of 90, was excused from examination.	5. All students who make a daily average of 90 will be excused from examination.

It is probable that most of the clauses which you write will be restrictive, not requiring commas. Before setting off a clause with commas, therefore, be sure that it is nonrestrictive and hence needs to be set off.

THE ROUND TABLE

Recognizing Restrictive and Nonrestrictive Clauses

In the following sentences distinguish between restrictive and nonrestrictive clauses. In order not to reveal the nonrestrictive clauses, the commas which should set them off have been omitted. Indicate where the necessary commas would come.

1. Jane Wilson who was elected May Queen this year is my best friend.
2. This is the best theme that you ever wrote.
3. Everybody who knows her was surprised at her sudden decision to become a trained nurse.
4. Chaucer who has been called the Morning Star of English poetry was a contemporary of Dante.
5. Some pupils never read a single book which they do not get from the school library.
6. Every duty which is put off returns with seven fresh duties on its back.
7. This man who is a stranger in the city wants to be directed to the best hotel.
8. Anyone who has ever tried to edit a school paper knows how much trouble it is.
9. Madame Curie who discovered radium is a Frenchwoman.
10. I shall never forget the man who sold me my first long trousers.

11. My older brother who has just turned twenty-one weighs only ten pounds more than I do.

12. The friends that we make in school and college last all through life.

13. Have a heart that never hardens, a temper that never tires, and a touch that never hurts.

14. He hurried home to see his brother who had been badly hurt in an automobile accident. (He had only one brother.)

15. He hurried home to see his brother who had been badly hurt in an automobile accident. (He had four brothers.)

16. The world is a comedy to those who think, and a tragedy to those who feel.

17. A specialist is a man who knows more and more about less and less.

18. He who cannot think is a fool; he who dare not think is a slave.

19. The Congressional Library which is located in Washington City is the largest in the United States.

20. She's still wearing the dress she bought last summer.

21. All the people who had been injured in the wreck were given first aid on the spot.

22. The highway which followed the river was crowded with automobiles last Sunday. (Several highways in that neighborhood.)

23. The highway which followed the river was crowded with automobiles last Sunday. (Only one highway in that neighborhood.)

24. The books which help us the most are those which make us think the most.

4. The comma to wedge apart words or phrases which if read together would give a wrong meaning.

This use of the comma is a general rather than a particular one, but is sometimes necessary unless we recast the entire sentence and remove the trouble in that way.

Refer to the example quoted on page 90 above : —

As the frightened animals rushed by, the people on the corner shrank back in alarm.

As we have seen, without the comma, *people* would seem to be the object of *by* instead of the subject of *shrank*.

Exactly the same confusion is avoided by the comma in the following sentence : —

Near by, an old oak lifted its gaunt limbs to the skies.

The comma is needed to keep us from getting the wrong meaning, *Near by an old oak, etc.*

Read the following sentences rapidly and see what a difference a few commas make : —

Without : 1. I like to go to the mountains and to go to the seacoast is delightful too.

With : 1. I like to go to the mountains, and to go to the seacoast is delightful too.

Without : 2. She was always a little sentimental sister.
With : 2. She was always a little sentimental, sister.

Without : 3. Don't crowd ladies.
With : 3. Don't crowd, ladies.

Without : 4. For many a day spent in bed would be a perfect heaven of rest.

With : 4. For many, a day spent in bed would be a perfect heaven of rest.

Without : 5. When the picnickers are ready to eat their lunch will be ready for them.

With : 5. When the picnickers are ready to eat, their.lunch will be ready for them.

Without : 6. A few minutes before the first boat had started.
With : 6. A few minutes before, the first boat had started.

5. The comma after a long dependent adverbial clause coming first in the sentence.

Adverbial clauses are of many kinds. Read again at this point the sections on Adverbial Clauses, pages 77 and 79 above, and on Subordinating Conjunctions, pages 63–65 above.

When such clauses come first in the sentence the rule is as follows : (a) with short clauses no comma is required, though it is permitted ; (b) with long clauses the comma is strongly preferred in order to make the reading easier and simpler.

Short Introductory Clauses : Comma Permitted but Not Required

Permitted : 1. When Father gave an order, we always obeyed.
Also Permitted : 1. When Father gave an order we always obeyed.

Permitted : 2. While the sun was shining, we took several excellent pictures.
Also Permitted : 2. While the sun was shining we took several excellent pictures.

Permitted: 3. Unless you will help me, I don't see how I can
                     possibly finish this afternoon.
Also Permitted: 3. Unless you will help me I don't see how I can
                     possibly finish this afternoon.

The former rule required the comma after short, introductory, adverbial clauses like these.   Recent usage, however, is against requiring the comma.   In fact, out of thirty leading book publishers and magazine publishers, only 43 per cent prefer the comma, while 57 per cent prefer not to use the comma.   Newspaper usage, which is much less authoritative, is strongly against the comma in the ratio of six to one.

LONG INTRODUCTORY CLAUSES: COMMA PREFERRED

After long introductory clauses, however, the comma is still so overwhelmingly preferred that it may fairly be said to be required.

Preferred: 1. When I learned that the train was a local and took
               nearly all day to make the trip, I decided to go by
               bus instead.
Preferred: 2. While we were rushing around frenziedly trying our best
               to get the job finished before dark, Mother called to
               us that supper was ready.
Preferred: 3. Since he had never showed any signs of improvement
               during the whole school year from September to June,
               his parents decided to put him to work.

The Semicolon
(*Three Uses*)

Ability to use the semicolon adds considerably to a writer's resources.
                    — GEORGE L. SUMMEY, *Modern Punctuation*

The semicolon has three established uses, none of which gives any sign of losing ground, for the semicolon fills a place that no other mark does.   Its use is a sign of a varied and usually a satisfactory sentence structure.   Look through several of your back themes, and if you fail to find several semicolons to each theme, the chances are that your sentence structure will be choppy and monotonous, verging on the type called "Baby Sentences" and discussed below, pages 211–215.

6. Use the semicolon between co-ordinate clauses not joined by *and*, *but*, or *for*.

Remember that the only time the comma can be used to join the parts of a compound sentence consisting of two statements is when the parts are relatively short and are joined by a pure conjunction like *and*, *but*, or *for*.

In all other cases the clauses must be separated either by a period or, if short and closely connected in thought, by a semicolon. This use of the semicolon has been suggestively called the "half-period."

For and Comma

Right: He sat down by the side of the road, for he was very tired.

Period

Right: He sat down by the side of the road.   He was very tired.

Semicolon

Right: He sat down by the side of the road; he was very tired.

And and Comma

Right: The violence of the wind blew the front door open, and the butler ran into the hall to close it.

Period

Right: The violence of the wind blew the front door open.   The butler ran into the hall to close it.

Semicolon

Right: The violence of the wind blew the front door open; the butler ran into the hall to close it.

Semicolon

1. The wind died down; the leaves fell silently through the still air to the earth.
2. The train jolted to an unexpected stop; the passengers sat up in their seats and looked questioningly at one another.
3. Night came down quickly over the little valley; here and there lights began to spring up in the cabins.
4. The flight of duck circled closer and bowed their wings for the long glide to the pond; Fred crouched down lower in the blind and slipped the safety catch up.

(Note that while the semicolon is correctly used in these four sentences, either the period or the *and*-comma could be substituted. The comma by itself, however, could not be used in place of the semicolon. This would turn the sentences into comma splices.)

7. Use the semicolon before *however* and certain other conjunctive adverbs when a complete independent statement is added to another complete independent statement.

Other common conjunctive adverbs requiring the semicolon when one complete independent statement is added to another are *hence*, *moreover*, *nevertheless*, *otherwise*, and *therefore*.

Examples

1. He had worked hard all his life and had invested wisely; however, the bank failure swept his savings away.
2. She has frequently deceived me before; hence I cannot altogether believe her now.
3. The school which we beat in the championship game has a much larger student body; moreover it has a more highly paid coaching staff.
4. My father listened patiently to my argument for letting me hitchhike to California; nevertheless he was not persuaded and refused to give his permission.
5. You had better get a new tire for your left front wheel or have the old one retreaded; otherwise you will have a bad blowout some day.

This same principle of punctuation that requires the semicolon with *however* formerly required it with *yet* and *then*. Now, however, usage is divided; and although the semicolon is to be preferred, the comma is permissible. With *so*, on the other hand, the comma is preferred.

Yet and *Then*

Preferred: 1. The rain began to fall faster and faster; yet the children did not come in.
Permitted: 1. The rain began to fall faster and faster, yet the children did not come in.

Preferred: 2. The boat began to leak worse and worse; then it turned over and sank.
Permitted: 2. The boat began to leak worse and worse, then it turned over and sank.

So

Preferred : 1 Just then the bell rang, so we all went in to dinner.
Permitted : 1. Just then the bell rang; so we all went in to dinner.

8. Use the semicolon between long independent statements when either statement is punctuated with commas.

The logic of this use of the semicolon is clear : it is to enable the reader to see instantly the relationship of the independent statements and to distinguish them from phrases or words within the statements themselves which are set off by commas. This use has been called the "double comma."

Take, for example, the following sentence : —

The road was winding, slippery, and steep, and the car we were driving was old, shaky, and none too powerful.

With only the comma after *steep* to divide the two independent clauses, the meaning is not clear till the end is reached ; but if a semicolon is used instead, both relationship and meaning are instantly clear.

The road was winding, slippery, and steep ; and the car we were driving was old, shaky, and none too powerful.

Examples

1. (The sentence in the text, six lines above, beginning "With only the comma after steep," etc.)
2. The town had never been large, and of late years had lost instead of gained in population ; but the climate was delightful, the people were both cultured and kind, and all in all it was a pleasant place to live in.
3. The result of his long exposure to the African sun was, as is usually the case, a serious illness ; and when in this weakened condition he contracted a serious case of flu, we all feared the worst.
4. The man who first said, "Look before you leap," was wise ; but for my part I had rather take as my motto, "Nothing risked, nothing gained."

Exercises in All Uses of the Semicolon

Supply semicolons wherever needed : —

1. The men were kept busy carrying buckets of water to the newly planted cedars and Carolina cherry trees shrubbery must be kept alive at all costs.

2. We felt almost unnecessarily conscientious when we read the telegram for the fourth time however we all wanted to be sure to send it in the best form.

3. We thoroughly enjoyed the barbecue we had never eaten crisply browned pork with mustard sauce that tasted so delicious, or potato salad with such a subtle blending of onions and vinegar and celery, or tomatoes so perfectly sun-ripened — in short, no meal we could remember had been so good as this one.

4. The letter startled me and made me tremble with joy I had been willed ten thousand dollars.

5. The big stone fireplace in the sunroom was beautiful and convenient consequently we had our steak dinners in this porch with the many windows.

6. The sandwich was difficult to eat it had been toasted until it was as hard and slippery as a ballroom floor.

7. On the old man's face was a beard, and on his son's, another the boy was a football player under a vow.

8. Gene's father told him never to try to start his car when it was rolling backward yet Gene, failing to follow good advice, tried anyway.

9. He had missed his streetcar, and it was raining so hard that he did not like the prospect of waiting on the corner he was therefore delighted when a friend invited him to ride in an automobile.

10. The driver of the car had once been sandbagged as he repaired an automobile tire in the open road hence he always drove with his car filled with friends.

11. Through the open door we could see a picture the old woman in the dark little house wore a brilliant pink dress and a bright green shawl.

12. She had read none of Glasgow's novels however she decided it was not too late to start, and said to the librarian, *"Vein of Iron,* please."

13. Brass andirons, a gleaming fender, a brass-bound fire screen, all made the fireplace look ready for a hospitable blaze we were proud of our hearth.

14. The small green worm stood on end and waved itself in the air the white tablecloth on which it rested seemed to annoy it.

15. Molly always said, sentimentally, "I do love an open fire," and smiled dreamily when winter was mentioned moreover she seemed to be taking credit for inventing open fires, for her air was smug.

16. The rug on the floor was dyed a soft gray-blue all the curtains were made of gray linen.

17. Five terraces, each built by a generation that has lived in the old house, lead down toward the river moreover a sixth is under construction.

18. Dahlias, Michaelmas daisies, and goldenrod were combined in the blue vase I thought how brightly the dahlias, which were of a rich crimson, glowed in contrast to the blue and gold.
19. We did not know trees could be fed therefore ours starved.

9. Use quotation marks to indicate titles of articles, chapters, sections, short stories, and single poems, but not titles of books, magazines, and newspapers, which should preferably be underlined instead of quoted. (See Underlining, number 12, page 113.)

Examples

1. Have you ever read Thomas Nelson Page's pathetic Negro story, "Marse Chan"?
2. Gray's "Elegy" and Poe's "The Raven" have been called the best-known poems in English and American literature.
3. Huxley's "A Piece of Chalk," Lowell's "Democracy," and Emerson's "The American Scholar," all of which we consider essays, were first delivered as speeches.
4. "Punctuation" is the title of the chapter in this book which we are studying at present.
5. Bret Harte's three greatest short stories are "The Luck of Roaring Camp," "The Outcasts of Poker Flat," and "Tennessee's Partner."

Exercises in the Use of Quotation Marks

Supply quotation marks wherever needed: —

1. As children the two girls had written, or rather had begun, a romantic tale entitled Romona, Heiress of Gonzales Court, but the story was never published.
2. I should like to write an article called Exciting Themes I Never Had a Chance to Read.
3. The class enjoyed My Great, Wide, Beautiful World, a group of letters by a Negro maid, published in the *Atlantic.*
4. Would you read any story with such a title as Little May? asked Virginia scornfully.
5. The Revolt of Mother by Mary E. Wilkins Freeman is a well-known realistic story.
6. Did you believe every word of Mark Twain's Baker's Blue-Jay Yarn?

10. For the three uses of the apostrophe see Spelling, pages 338–341.

11. Use the colon after such expressions as *these, the following, as follows*, to give notice of a list of particulars or examples.

Examples

1. Last month the kinds of books most in demand at the public library were these: adventure stories, detective stories, love stories, biographies, and plays.
2. At most American colleges the required studies in the freshman and sophomore years are the following: English, history, mathematics, a foreign language, and a laboratory science.
3. A recent article in a sporting magazine listed the leading game birds of America as follows: the wild turkey, the wild duck, the bob-white or partridge, and the dove.

For other examples see the section on the sentence of announcement in developing a jointed subject, page 157 below.

Recall also, as is noted there, that if no such expression as *these, the following*, or *as follows* is used, no punctuation mark at all should come between the verb and the list that it introduces. For example, in the first sentence given above, if the word *these* is omitted the colon should be omitted too. Then the sentence would read: —

Last month the kinds of books most in demand at the public library were adventure stories, detective stories, love stories, biographies, and plays.

Recently, however, there has become evident a distinct tendency to use the colon to announce a list whether or not any term like *these* or *as follows* is employed. Watch for this usage in your reading of current magazines and books.

Note finally that in introducing a list, whether or not *these, the following*, or *as follows* is used, in no case can either the comma or the semicolon be employed.

12. Underlining a word in writing is a sign to the printer to set that word in italics. Since it will probably be some years before your work will appear in print, the term *underlining* will be used here instead of *italics*.

Underline the titles of books, magazines, and newspapers.

Notice the difference in usage between quotation marks and underlining as indicated both in this rule and in section 9 under Quotation

Marks, page 112 above. The titles of books, magazines, and newspapers are preferably underlined, while the individual parts or sections of a book, such as chapter headings, individual stories, individual poems, and so on, are put in quotation marks.

Examples

1. The leading story in George Washington Cable's *Old Creole Days* is "Madame Delphine."
2. One of the best articles in the *Encyclopaedia Britannica* is by Theodore Watts-Dunton on "Poetry."
3. Did you read the editorial "What Are We Coming To?" in a recent issue of the *New York Times?*
4. Three of the most interesting novels ever written are Stevenson's *Treasure Island*, Conan Doyle's *The White Company*, and Dumas's *The Three Musketeers.*
5. One of the most discussed stories of the year was Erskine Caldwell's powerful but dismal "Kneel to the Rising Sun," which appeared in *Scribner's Magazine* for February, 1935.

Two thirds of the book publishers and magazines favor underlining (that is, italics) for titles of books, magazines, and newspapers as exemplified in these sentences. One third of the book publishers and magazines, however, together with newspapers in general, prefer quotation marks to italics. It seems decidedly best to follow conservative usage on this point, and use italics.

Capital Letters

Capital letters have eight uses. Investigation shows that the most frequent of these are the following.[1]

		Times Used in 10,000 Words
1. The first word of every sentence		368
2. Names of places		123
3. Names of persons		98
4. Titles with names		67
5. Names of organizations		61
6. Commercial trade names		42

[1] S. L. Pressey, "A Statistical Study of Usage and of Children's Errors in Capitalization," *English Journal*, Vol. 13, 1924, p. 729.

Some of the eight uses are easy, and mistakes in them seldom occur. The pronoun *I*, for example, and the names of persons are practically always capitalized correctly. Other uses have a much higher frequency of error. Following is a table showing the five uses that are responsible for three fourths of all errors in capitalization.

		Percentage of All Mistakes
1.	First word in every sentence	42 per cent
2.	Title of book	12 per cent
3.	First word in a quotation	9 per cent
4.	Names of places	8 per cent
5.	Names of organizations	5 per cent

13. Capitalize the first word in every sentence.

Beginning the first word in every sentence with a capital letter is by all odds both the most important and the most frequent use of capitals. In fact, it is *the* basic rule of capitalization, just as putting a period at the end of every declarative and imperative sentence is *the* basic rule of punctuation. Whatever else is or is not done, these two rules must be unfailingly observed.

14. In the titles of themes, stories, and books, capitalize the first word and all other words except the articles (*a, an, the*), prepositions, and conjunctions.

(1) THEME TITLES

Center the title of the theme on the first line of the paper. Put no punctuation mark after it, unless the title is a question or an exclamation, when of course a question mark or an exclamation point will be necessary. Do not put quotation marks around the title. Begin the title with a capital and, as was said, capitalize all the words in it except the articles *a*, *an*, and *the* and prepositions and conjunctions. This is the usual rule, although some writers capitalize long prepositions like *concerning, underneath, notwithstanding*, and so on, and long conjunctions like *nevertheless, consequently, accordingly*, and *moreover*. Follow the instructor's directions on this point.

Leave one line vacant between the title and the beginning of the theme.

Here is a list of titles for themes. Write them out, (*a*) capitalizing them correctly and (*b*) centering them on the page. Leave a line between each title and the next, and make as attractive a display page as you can.

1. The most beautiful object I ever saw
2. Do animals think
3. A dog's love of motoring
4. What I have found out about tires
5. The first friend I made in college
6. Some things which the modern child has never seen
7. A scene I remember from the talking pictures
8. Matters on which I am forced to disagree with my parents
9. Getting acquainted with the neighbor's dog
10. Sources of vitamin B and the diseases caused by a lack of this vitamin

(2) BOOK TITLES

Following is a list of well-known books and short stories illustrating the use of capitals in titles. Read them carefully until you see clearly the reason for each capital and each lower-case letter.

Mark Twain	*The Adventures of Huckleberry Finn*
Captain Mayne Reid	*The Boy Hunters of the Mississippi*
James Willard Schultz	*With the Indians in the Rockies*
Thomas Bailey Aldrich	*The Story of a Bad Boy*
R. H. Dana	*Two Years before the Mast*
Zane Grey	*Riders of the Purple Sage*
Cleveland Moffett	*Careers of Danger and Daring*
Rudyard Kipling	*The Man Who Would Be King*

15. Capitalize all proper names, such as the names of persons, places, countries, races, languages, organizations, and so forth, including the names and the titles of God.

Second only to beginning the first word of every sentence with a capital, this is the most important use of capital letters. Most proper nouns are the names either of persons or of places. The names of persons give no trouble. Practically everybody capitalizes them correctly, initials included. Curiously enough, however, an appreciable percentage of error crops up in writing the names of places and organizations.

(1) GEOGRAPHICAL NAMES

The names of all continents, oceans, countries, states, counties, cities, streets, rivers, lakes, and so forth, should be capitalized.

Europe	Texas	Mississippi River
Atlantic Ocean	Cook County	Lake Erie
France	Mecklenburg County	State Street
United States	Boston	Pennsylvania Avenue

(2) MAIN STREET VS. MAIN STREET

In regard to capitalizing such words as *county, river, street, college,* and so forth, when they are a part of proper names, usage is sharply divided between books and magazines on the one hand and newspapers on the other. About five out of every six publishers of books and magazines prefer to capitalize; about two out of three newspapers prefer not to capitalize.

Book and Magazine Usage	*Newspaper Usage*
Cook County	Cook county
Mississippi River	Mississippi river
State Street	State street
Swarthmore College	Swarthmore college

The usage for us to follow is clearly that of the best books and magazines. Capitalize, therefore, both parts of geographical names.

(3) NORTH, SOUTH, EAST, AND WEST

A special situation exists in regard to the words *north, south, east,* and *west.* When used to mean simply the points of the compass, or to indicate direction, they are common nouns and take a small letter.

Examples

1. The farther north you go, the colder it gets; the farther south you go, the warmer it gets.
2. The coast is a hundred and fifty miles due east from here.

When, however, these words refer to particular sections, or well-defined areas of this country, they are capitalized.

Examples

1. Although they have lived in the North all their lives, they have many friends and relatives in the South.
2. The Middle West is a rich and populous section of this country.

(4) NAMES OF ORGANIZATIONS, BUSINESS FIRMS, AND TRADE NAMES

Troublesome varieties of proper names are the organizations, business firms, and copyrighted trade names which have sprung up in such large numbers and which form no small part of the national advertising and national correspondence in this country. All such names are the property of the particular organization, industry, or business which has adopted them, and we must take care to spell, punctuate, and capitalize them exactly as they are given in the advertisement or on the official stationery.

Examples

Organizations	*Business Firms*
The Rotary Club	Parke, Davis and Co.
The Boy Scouts of America	Western Clock Company
The Society for the Prevention	Houghton Mifflin Company
of Cruelty to Animals	The Macmillan Company
The National Council of	G. & C. Merriam Co.
Teachers of English	

Trade Names

Deerfoot Farm Sausages	Gem Safety Razor	Ivory Soap
Eversharp Pencils	Phoenix Hosiery	Beech-Nut Gum

Likewise capitalize adjectives derived from proper nouns like those just listed on pages 116-117.

16. Three *don't's*.

Do not capitalize the names of (1) the seasons, (2) classes in school or college, or (3) studies, except the languages.

(*a*) SEASONS

The days of the week and the months of the year are capitalized, but not the seasons — spring, summer, autumn or fall, winter.

1. July is usually the hottest month of summer, and January is the coldest month of winter.
2. March, April, and May are usually considered the spring months.
3. Thanksgiving Day is the last Thursday in November, thus coming between the end of autumn and the beginning of winter.
4. Nuts do not ripen till after the first heavy frost in the fall.

(b) CLASSES

School and college classes are not capitalized.

1. My sister is a sophomore at teachers' college, my brother a senior at medical college, and I am a freshman at the state university.
2. Her younger brother is in the fourth grade.
3. One of my cousins is in first year at junior high, and another of them is in third year at senior high.

(c) STUDIES

Among the studies and courses at school and college only the languages are capitalized.

1. Most girls find mathematics hard.
2. Shall you take physics or chemistry next year?
3. I studied Latin in high school and expect to take up French in college.
4. One subject that is required during all four years in high school and during the first two years of college is English

THE ROUND TABLE

1. Copy the following titles of books, short stories, and plays, supplying capital letters wherever needed : —

Howard Pyle	The merry adventures of robin hood
Archibald Rutledge	Tom and i on the old plantation
Ernest Thompson Seton	wild animals i have known
Mark Twain	Life on the mississippi
Harold Bell Wright	The shepherd of the hills
John Fox, Jr.	The little shepherd of kingdom come
Hamlin Garland	A daughter of the middle border
Alice Hegan Rice	Mrs. wiggs of the cabbage patch
John Buchan	Book of escapes and hurried journeys
C. Alphonso Smith	What can literature do for me?
Mark Twain	The celebrated jumping frog of calaveras county
Edgar Allan Poe	The murders in the rue morgue
	The fall of the house of usher

2. Copy and bring to class the names and addresses of five national advertising firms. Be sure to get both spelling and capitalization correct.

General Exercises in Punctuation

Take the following sentences ten or twenty at a time as the instructor directs, either as written exercises to be handed in or as dictation in class. Supply all needed punctuation marks. Some of the sentences are correct as they stand. Exchange papers and correct them in class under the direction of the instructor.

I

1. I beg your pardon sir
2. The librarian has just ordered the following books Scott's *Ivanhoe* Dickens's *A Tale of Two Cities* and Thackeray's *Henry Esmond*
3. I do not think she is at home however I shall phone her anyway
4. There are three things we can do keep on with the same plan give it up or make a new one.
5. It was hard pulling for the hill was long and steep
6. Mr. Stone the proprietor of the store ran to the window and shouted police.
7. Remember if you lose the bet will have to be paid.
8. Inside the rooms were painted a cool gray.
9. The road is steep for most of the route lies in the mountains.
10. It is very easy to confuse affect and effect.

II

11. Up above the big rock towered over us.
12. The chief forms of amusement are tennis golf and swimming.
13. You would enjoy meeting my mother who plays beautifully on the piano.
14. Before we could move the vase toppled over
15. The bible is the book of books.
16. He is our chief therefore we should loyally follow his wishes.
17. We were on the lookout for a place that was high dry and sheltered.
18. Benjamin Franklin who was a friend of Thomas Jefferson was one of the most versatile men that this country ever produced.
19. When I was fifteen years old my father gave me three pure-bred Red Leghorn hens which were the start of my flock
20. When I was fifteen years old my father gave me the three pure-bred Leghorn hens which were the start of my flock.

III

21. Run here Mary your kitten has fallen into the bathtub
22. Dr. Welborne our family physician is one of the most popular men in town.

23. Why didn't you tell me that your brother was sick
24. The question of expenses however is not what is bothering me.
25. We had better go at once hadn't we
26. At daybreak he woke us up and said its time to start if we expect to get to town in time to meet the bus
27. The following club members have resigned Mr. Wilton Mr James Mr Simms and Mr. Anderson
28. Inside the piano was going at full blast.
29. A pupil who does not really study hard misses much that is of permanent value in after life.
30. General Lee who was an ideal gentleman was made president of Washington College after the Civil War

IV

31. I liked all the fellows but one in particular was the nicest chap I ever met
32. As soon as the bus comes in the station takes on new life.
33. Well if you can't I can
34. My favorite fruits are peaches grapes and cantaloupes
35. The six most important cereals are wheat corn oats rye barley and rice
36. Next year I shall begin the study of French, geometry, and Shakespeare.
37. It rained hard all the morning otherwise I should certainly have come
38. Our modern language teacher can speak three languages French Italian and Spanish
39. He was the best athlete in school in fact he made his letter in baseball, football, basketball, and track.
40. Two of the greatest bars to success are these fear of ridicule and fear of making a mistake.

V

41. Two of the greatest bars to success are fear of ridicule and fear of making a mistake.
42. Mark twains huck finn is a very interesting book it tells the story of a boys life on the mississippi river
43. When the coach told me I want you to play fullback tomorrow I could hardly keep from yelling for joy.
44. Pat our Irish setter was lying on the porch.
45. Poe who died at the age of forty is one of the most famous of American poets
46. "Come around to the back door," said the woman and I'll give you some food.

47. Three very desirable qualities are accuracy, promptness and dependability.
48. Everybody began to run down the street shouting stop thief
49. Tennis, golf, and swimming, are my favorite sports.

VI

50. The Union Station quick said the sheriff as he jumped into the taxi. "I've got to make the 12.20 train sure."
51. The policeman on the corner who had been watching the quarrel somewhat uneasily, now stepped forward and held up his hand.
52. There are as many is as ss in Mississippi.
53. The most useful tools are a screwdriver, a pair of pliers, a lug wrench and a jack.
54. No said the teacher you havent got it right yet.
55. "What has become of the library copy of Who's who in America?"
56. He was a manly little fellow.
57. My schedule is as follows: on Monday, Wednesday, and Friday, Math, History, and English on Tuesday, Thursday, and Saturday, French, Chemistry, and Bible.
58. The boy obligingly said, "No, father let me get it for you then he ran quickly out to the car and brought back the missing package.
59. Having called the meeting to order the chairman asked someone to state the object of the meeting.

VII

60. Salt which chemically is sodium chloride is a most important article of diet.
61. The book that I enjoyed most last summer was Margaret Mitchell's Gone with the Wind.
62. Ever since he has been coming to Myrtle Beach so much does he like it.
63. My visitor who turned out to be the son of an old friend was utterly unlike his father.
64. Genius it has been well said is only the infinite capacity for taking pains.
65. Sink or swim, live or die survive or perish I give my hand and my heart to this vote.
66. There are three kinds of sentences namely simple compound and complex.
67. My father used to say to me Pay as you go and if you can't pay don't go.
68. The building in which father has his office is on State Street.
69. My father has his office in the Medical Building which is on State Street.

VIII

70. The boy who was elected president of the senior class is working his way through school.
71. William Simpson who is working his way through school was elected president of the senior class.
72. I had to run for the train.
73. I had to run for the train was already in motion.
74. "Why blame me" he asked indignantly
75. "Help help" she called loudly
76. He knocked at the bronze door which opened on the front porch.
77. He knocked at the door that opened on the front porch.
78. Memphis where I was born is on the Mississippi River.
79. I say porter watch where you are going can't you?

IX

80. I thought there was no one at home but Tom simply had not heard the bell.
81. There was no one at home but Tom and he was asleep.
82. However uninteresting this book may seem at first it is really thrilling after you get fairly started.
83. However uninteresting as this book may seem at first it is really thrilling after you get fairly started.

THE ROUND TABLE

1. Dictation is a sovereign aid to attaining skill in punctuation. Every day that this chapter is being studied, a short passage from a story or essay selected from the class text in literature or from a current magazine might well be dictated in class.

2. In the next question it is suggested that you analyze your own powers (and weaknesses!) of punctuation. Guard specifically against the following six trouble spots : —

   (1) Avoid the comma splice (see pages 194–196).
   (2) Avoid the no-sentence fault (see pages 190–193).
   (3) Do not put either a colon, a semicolon, or a comma between the verb *are* or *were* and a following list of details and examples (see page 157).
   (4) Do not put a comma between the last adjective in a series and the noun.
       Right : Red, white, and blue colors.
       Wrong : Red, white, and blue, colors.
   (5) Do not put anything, even a comma, between the subject and the verb.
   (6) Do not put anything, even a comma, between a verb and its complement.

3. Remember that in punctuating you are your own doctor, nurse, and druggist. That is, analyze and study your own weaknesses in punctuation. Look over your back themes, get the instructor to help you, and ask yourself two questions: (a) Is there any principle of punctuation that I do not understand or that I feel uncertain about? (b) What seem to be my weak points or prevailing errors in punctuation? The answers to those two questions are of more importance to you than to anybody else.

4. Take a page of this textbook assigned by the instructor and explain all the punctuation marks on it, including paragraphing.

5. Do the same thing with a page from the *Atlantic Monthly* or *Harper's Magazine*.

6. For your own interest try to estimate the number of words of writing that all your college work requires during one month. Then, applying the frequency table given on page 92, estimate how many of the different punctuation marks you will probably have need of (a) during the month, (b) during the term, (c) during the college year.

7. In your last two themes draw a ring around every punctuation mark and capital letter and account for its use by stating the rule concerned.

8. Glance back through your last month's (or two months') themes to see what mistakes you made in punctuation. Ask for class discussion on any usage you do not feel certain about.

9. Take as a class project the making of a style book on punctuation and capitalization. Adopt this as the class standard, and if the project makes a good showing, have it typed or mimeographed for use in the other departments. Why should not your class help raise the standard of written work in the entire college?

ANSWERS TO FREAKS OF PUNCTUATION, PAGE 93

1.   Every lady in this land
    Hath twenty nails; upon each hand
    Five; and twenty on hands and feet;
    And this is true without deceit.

2.   A funny little man told this to me:
    "I fell in a snowdrift; in June," said he,
    "I went to a ball game; out in the sea
    I saw a jellyfish float; up in a tree
    I found some gum; in a cup of tea
    I stirred my milk; with a big brass key
    I opened my door; on my bended knee
    I beg your pardon for this," said he,
    "But 'tis true when told as it ought to be."

3. That that is, is; that that is not, is not; that that is not, is not that that is; that that is, is not that that is not. Is not that it? It is.

4. (a) It was "and" I said, not "but."
   (b) It was *and* I said, not *but*.

PART TWO

WRITING FOR PRACTICAL PURPOSES

CHAPTER VI

Definition

Language is primarily the thing we think with; it is more than mere communication.

—HAROLD E. PALMER

Of all the aids to clear thinking and hence to clear expression two of the most unfailingly valuable are the twin processes of (1) definition of terms and (2) analysis of idea. We may call them "twin processes" because they aid and supplement each other as do the right and the left hand or the two blades of a pair of shears. They are complementary in the sense in which that word is used in geometry.

Definition is one of the highest functions of the human intellect. The term *define* comes from two Latin words, *de*, meaning "from," and *finire*, meaning "to bound, to mark off the boundaries or limits of." Thus, **to define a word or an idea** means to mark off its boundaries, to tell exactly what it includes and what it excludes, to put it into its proper class and at the same time to indicate the distinctive qualities that set it apart from all other objects in that class.

1. Receptive Definition in Reading

For you as a reader, writer, and thinker, whether in the classroom or in the world outside, the process of definition has two practical and permanent contacts. The first of these is receptive and passive — namely, **definition in reading.** This is done for us, chiefly by the makers of dictionaries, encyclopedias, and textbooks. The second is **productive and active** — namely, making your own definitions in thinking and writing. This we do for ourselves with such aid from other sources as we can obtain.

Definition for the sake of increasing our speaking, writing, and reading vocabularies is discussed in the section on The Word, pages 319–325. Take a few minutes at this point to glance through that section and see what topics it covers.

2. Active Definition in Thinking and Writing

In active or productive definition we examine a term, an object, or an idea, and frame our own definition.

To do this is far from easy. It requires mature powers of straight thinking. In fact, to define a hazy, murky idea accurately and completely calls for as much mental skill as performing a delicate operation requires of a surgeon. The analogy between thinker and surgeon is closer than might be at first supposed. Both mind and scalpel must be keen and polished, and both must be guided unerringly in dividing the false from the true.

3. How to Define

(1) SYNONYMS

One of the simplest and most familiar ways to define is by means of synonyms. This is the usual method of the dictionary. The word to be defined is explained by the aid of a number of other words which mean almost or nearly the same thing. Each of the synonyms illuminates one phase or facet of the term in question, or throws, as it were, a loop of explanation around it until the term is surrounded on all sides by its closest synonyms and is thus taken captive by the understanding.

Take, for example, the three following words, all of which are in common use, but which are literary rather than colloquial in character: *acrimony*, *fell* (adjective), *importune*. By means of groups of synonyms their meaning can be made clear for all practical purposes, though not with scientific exactness.

acrimony: bitterness, sharpness, tartness, asperity, rancor

fell (adjective): fierce, cruel, brutal, inhuman, ruthless, unfeeling, ferocious, savage

importune: beg, ply with requests, urge, beseech, entreat, implore, supplicate

The general subject of synonyms is treated in more detail under Exactness, pages 389–393. Glance briefly at this section, particularly at the assignments in the Round Table and the additional list of synonyms in number 4, page 392.

(2) SCIENTIFIC DEFINITION

The most exact form of definition, when it can be applied, is logical definition by means of genus and differentia. This method first puts the term to be defined into its genus or class, and then gives the differentia or essential difference which marks off or sets apart that particular term from all other members of its class or genus. In this sense, "defining means determining exact significance by general classification and specific differentiation." This method is indispensable in the sciences.

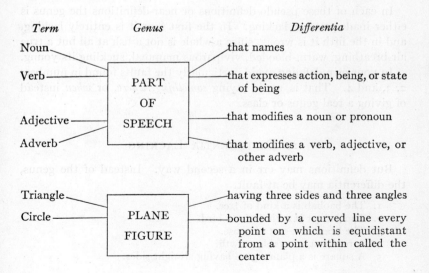

Term	Genus	Differentia
Noun		that names
Verb	PART OF SPEECH	that expresses action, being, or state of being
Adjective		that modifies a noun or pronoun
Adverb		that modifies a verb, adjective, or other adverb
Triangle		having three sides and three angles
Circle	PLANE FIGURE	bounded by a curved line every point on which is equidistant from a point within called the center

Logical definition is thus a double process of inclusion and exclusion: first inclusion into a larger class (genus) and then exclusion from every other member of that class (differentia). A satisfactory logical definition, therefore, must conform to a fourfold requirement.

(1) It must be true of the thing or term in question.

(2) It must not be true of any other thing or term.

(3) It must be clear and simple.

(4) It must not repeat in the definition the word or a derivative of the word to be defined.

All of the examples given thus far conform to all four of these requirements. Consider, however, partial definitions like these: —

1. INADEQUATE GENUS

1. A knife is to cut with.
2. Soap is something to wash with.
3. A store is where you buy things.
4. Cowardice is when you are afraid.
5. A whale is a big fish.
6. Heresy is where a child looks like his father.

— *Boners*

In each of these pseudo-definitions or near-definitions the genus is either inadequate or lacking. In the first four it is entirely lacking, and in the fifth it is wrong, since a whale is not a fish at all but a true air-breathing, warm-blooded, viviparous mammal, suckling its young.

In your own defining avoid particularly the faults found in numbers 2, 3, and 4. That is, avoid saying *something*, *where*, or *when* instead of giving a real genus or class.

2. DIFFERENTIA LACKING

But definitions may err in a second way. Instead of the genus, the differentia may be at fault.

1. The baobab is a kind of tree.
2. The gannet is a kind of sea bird.
3. The brant is a sort of goose.
4. A reed is a vegetable growth.
5. A square is a plane figure having straight sides.

Each of those definitions is all right as far as it goes, but it doesn't go far enough. The genus is given, and that is of some help. We know, for instance, that if a baobab is a kind of tree it is not a strange animal, fish, or mineral. But the identifying differentia which would set the baobab off from all other trees, or the gannet off from all other sea birds, is lacking. Not until the proper differentiae are supplied can these definitions be considered complete.

(3) APPROXIMATE OR LITERARY DEFINITIONS

Sometimes the purpose of a writer or speaker may be not to give a logical definition true to the facts but to offer a *suggestive definition* which will be true to the spirit or mood of the moment and which will contain a touch of humor, sentiment, or unexpectedness. Some definitions of this kind are very effective. Here are a few particularly good ones.

1. Poetry is the journal of a sea animal living on land, wanting to fly the air. — CARL SANDBURG
2. A baby is the latest edition of humanity, of which every couple think they possess the finest copy.
3. Man is the only animal that can be skinned more than once.
4. Education is a gradual adjustment to the spiritual possessions of the race. — BUTLER
5. A fanatic is a man who redoubles his efforts after he has forgotten his aim. — GEORGE SANTAYANA
6. A cynic is a man who knows the price of everything and the value of nothing. — *The Importance of Being Earnest*
7. A fool is one who is intelligent at the wrong time.
8. A critic is a legless man who teaches running.
   — CHANNING POLLOCK
9. An adult is a man who has stopped growing at both ends but not in the middle. — *Boners*
10. A highbrow is a person educated beyond his intelligence.
11. Home is the place where, when you have to go there, they have to take you in. — ROBERT FROST
12. Music is love in search of a word. — SIDNEY LANIER
13. Bunk is the treasure chest of the advertising man, the bugaboo of the scientist, and the limbo to which the average man consigns everything that he doesn't understand.
    — ANDRÉ DORYNOFF

DEFINING CONCEPTS AND IDEAS

Leaving the domain of facts and things and entering the higher, harder one of abstractions and ideas, we encounter such terms as

fiction	socialism
atheism	communism
education	evolution
poetry	faith
culture	honor
patriotism	realism
democracy	romanticism

and a host of others.

These concepts, most of which are abstractions, do not exist in the world of nature, but lead their entire existence in the mind of man.

Stuart Chase, in a recent interesting book on words,[1] describes as follows the essential difficulty that faces all of us when we try to define or even to use terms like these, which he calls "labels for essences or qualities" : —

Years ago I read a little book by Allen Upward, called *The New Word*. It was an attempt to get at the meaning of "idealism" as used in the terms of the Nobel Prize award — an award for "the most distinguished work of an idealist tendency." Upward began his quest — which was ultimately to lead him over the living world and back to the dawn of written history — by asking a number of friends to give a personal interpretation of the term "idealism." He received the following replies : —

fanatical	poetical	what cannot be proved
altruistic	intangible	opposite of materialism
not practical	sentimental	something to do with imaginative
exact	true	powers

This gave me pause. I thought I knew what "idealism" meant and had used it many times with confidence. Obviously, on the basis of Upward's study, what I meant was rarely, if at all, communicated to the hearer. Indeed, on examining my own mental processes, I had some difficulty in determining what I did mean by this lofty word. Thereafter I was unable to escape an uneasy feeling, slight but persistent, like a mouse heard in the wall of a room, that something was wrong.

(4) LONGER, EXPLANATORY DEFINITION

Once off the limited ground of definition by genus and differentia, the process of defining spreads out in several directions and tends to

[1] *The Tyranny of Words*, Harcourt, Brace and Company, 1938, pp. 3–4.

shade off into exposition in general, even becoming expository description or expository narration. Such explanatory definitions may increase in length from a sentence or two to a paragraph, a page, or a whole chapter. They make use of any or all of such aids to explanation as these.

1. **Derivation, or etymology, and history of the term as it has developed during the years.**

In a limited way the second paragraph on page 127 thus gives the derivation of the term *definition* as the first step in defining it.

2. **Examples or instances.**

This method is used when, instead of, or in addition to explaining the concept or process in general terms, an example of what it is or of how it works is given. Thus if asked what a gyroscope is, the best possible explanation would be to show a toy model in action, and, while it is actually spinning before you, to explain its principle and curious behavior.

Again, the abstract idea of reciprocity is clearly illustrated by citing the following example of how it operates between the United States and Brazil.

> Its principle, rightly understood, is axiomatic. Brazil grows coffee and makes no machinery. We make machinery and grow no coffee. She needs the fabrics of our forges and factories, we need the fruit of her tropical soil. We agree to concessions for her coffee and she agrees to concessions for our machinery. This is reciprocity.
> — CHARLES EMORY SMITH

And one of the best explanations ever offered of *tact* is the following given by a colored bellboy in a large hotel when he was asked the difference between tact and politeness. "Well," he said, "suppose I busts into a lady's room without knocking and she is undressed. I bows, backs out, and says, 'Please excuse me, suh.' Now, when I says, 'Please excuse me,' that's politeness. But when I says, 'Please excuse me, *suh*,' dat's tact."

3. **Comparison (or contrast) with something known and familiar.**

This is one of the commonest and most helpful methods of defining and explaining. Even when used loosely and inaccurately it helps clear the ground, as when we describe a zebra to a child as "a striped mule," or speak of a giraffe as "a barberpole on four legs." One of the most familiar examples is Victor Hugo's comparison of the ground plan of the Battle of Waterloo to a gigantic A, with the sunken road which finally checked the charge of the Old Guard forming the cross bar of the A.[1]

4. Division or analysis into parts, with a brief explanation or exemplification of each part.

As has been said, together with definition, and on a parity with it, the process of division or analysis of ideas is the second sovereign aid to complete comprehension and satisfactory understanding. So important is it that it is discussed in detail in the next chapter, pages 142–148. Let us here simply note its great importance as an intellectual process, and underline the fact that definition and analysis together are the twin blades of the mental shears by means of which the thinkers among mankind divide, cut, trim, fashion, and perfect the world's storehouse of ideas.

A single example may be given. Let us take the complex subject of the *forms* or *types of literature*, using definition, division, and exemplification to explain them.

A. Definition

Literary forms are modes of self-expression and communion, through spoken or written language, characterized by relative stability and relative universality.

B. Division   C. Exemplification

LITERARY FORMS

I *Poetry*
- (1) Epic   *The Iliad; Beowulf; Paradise Lost*
- (2) Lyric   Gray's "Elegy"; Tennyson's "Crossing the Bar"; Kilmer's "Trees"
- (3) Dramatic   *As You Like It; Macbeth; Hamlet;* Rostand's *Cyrano de Bergerac*

---

[1] See *Les Misérables*, Cosette, IV, A, opening paragraph.

B. Division	C. Exemplification
LITERARY FORMS	

II *Prose*
  (1) Essay
    (*a*) Formal Essay   Huxley's "A Piece of Chalk"; George Herbert Palmer's "Self-Cultivation in English"

    (*b*) Informal, Personal   Lamb's "Dream Children"; Christopher Morley's "Syntax for Cynics"

  (2) Biography, Autobiography   Plutarch's *Lives;* Franklin's *Autobiography;* Boswell's *Life of Johnson*

  (3) Speech   Burke's *On Conciliation with the American Colonies;* Lincoln's "Gettysburg Address"

  (4) Novel   Hugo's *Les Misérables;* Dickens's *David Copperfield;* Stevenson's *Treasure Island*

  (5) Short Story   de Maupassant's "The Necklace"; Poe's "Gold Bug"; Harte's "Outcasts of Poker Flat"; Ferber's "Gay Old Dog"

  (6) One-Act and Longer Plays   Zona Gale's *Neighbors;* Barrie's *The Admirable Crichton;* Ibsen's *A Doll's House*

(5) EXAMPLES OF LONGER, EXPLANATORY DEFINITIONS

The chief purpose of expository definition is to be accurate, but it need not on that account be dull. Here are three selections by widely different writers, each of which is both suggestive and interesting.

1. THE ROMANTIC [1]

H. L. MENCKEN

There is a variety of man whose eye inevitably exaggerates, whose ear inevitably hears more than the band plays, whose imagination inevitably doubles and triples the news brought in by his five senses. He is the enthusiast, the believer, the romantic. He is the sort of fellow who, if he were a bacteriologist, would report the streptococcus pyogenes to be as large as a

[1] *Prejudices*, III, p. 266. Alfred A. Knopf, Inc. By permission of the publishers.

St. Bernard dog, as intelligent as Socrates, as beautiful as Beauvais Cathedral and as respectable as a Yale professor.

2. TWO KINDS OF THINKING [1]

JOHN DEWEY

(1) Active, persistent, and careful consideration of any belief or supposed form of knowledge in the light of the grounds that support it, and the further conclusions to which it tends, constitutes reflective thought.

(2) In its loosest sense, thinking signifies everything that, as we say, is "in our heads" or that "goes through our minds." He who offers "a penny for your thoughts" does not expect to drive any great bargain. In calling the object of his demand *thoughts*, he does not intend to ascribe to them dignity, consecutiveness, or truth. Any idle fancy, trivial recollection, or flitting impression will satisfy his demand. Daydreaming, building of castles in the air, that loose flux of casual and disconnected material that floats through our minds in relaxed moments are, in this random sense, *thinking*. More of our waking life than we should care to admit, even to ourselves, is likely to be whiled away in this inconsequential trifling with idle fancy and unsubstantial hope.

3. THE SARGASSO WEED [2]

WILLIAM BEEBE

An amazing amount of fiction and nonsense has been written about the sargasso weed, but the truth is actually more unbelievable. Though we see it in such immense patches, and although for days the ocean may be flecked with the scattered heads of the weed, yet it is no more at home in mid-ocean than the falling leaves in autumn may claim as their place of abode the breeze which whirls them about, or the moss upon which at last they come to rest. Along the coast of Central America the sargasso weed grows, clinging, as is the way with seaweeds, to coral and rock and shell, and flowering and fruiting after its lowly fashion. The berry-like bladders with which the stems are strung are filled with gas and enable the plants to maintain their position regardless of the state of the tide. Vast quantities are torn away by the waves and drift out to sea, and these stray masses are what we see on every trip south, and which, caught in the great mid-ocean eddy, form the so-called Sargasso Sea. Just as the unfailing fall of dead leaves has brought about a

---

[1] "What Is Thought," *How We Think*, D. C. Heath and Company. By permission of the publishers.
[2] *Jungle Peace*, pp. 16–20, Henry Holt and Company. By permission of the publishers.

forest-loving clique of brown and russet-colored small folk — frogs, crickets, lizards, birds, and mammals which spend much of their life hiding beneath or living upon the brown dead leaves, so this never-ending drift of weed has evolved about it a little world of life, a microcosmos of great intimacy, striving by imitation of frond and berry and color to avoid some of the host of enemies forever on the lookout.

It is possible to place a bit of weed in a tumbler of salt water and have a dozen people examine it without seeing anything but a yellowish brown frond with many long, narrow leaves and a number of berry-like structures. Here and there are patches of thin ivory-white shells — tiny whorls glued closely to the surface of the leaves. Yet on this same small piece of weed there may be several good-sized crabs, slug-like creatures, shrimps, and a fish two or three inches in length. Until they move, the eye is powerless to detach them. No two are alike; the little frog-fish is mottled and striped, with many small flabby filaments, and apparently ragged fins, with curious hand-like fore limbs which clutch the fronds closely. The pipe-fish and sea-horses are draped and ragged, and splashed with yellow and brown, the slugs are simply flaccid stems or leaves, and the crabs are beyond belief, living bits of weed. Some are clear yellow, others are mottled, others again have white enameled spots like the small masses of tiny shells. The little shrimps are mere ghosts of life, transparent, yielding to every movement of the water — altogether marvelous. Then there are other beings, blue like the sea, white like the foam, or translucent bits of disembodied organs. This is all absorbingly wonderful, but the unreality of this little world's existence, the remembrance of its instability, is always present, and the tragedy of the immediate future looms large.

The weed along the coast is honest growth, with promise of permanence. The great floating Sargasso Sea is permanent only in appearance, and when finally the big masses drift, with all their lesser, attendant freight, into the gulf stream, then life becomes a sham. There can be no more fruiting or sustained development of gas-filled berries. No eggs of fish or crabs will hatch, no new generation of seahorses or mollusks appear among the stems. Bravely the fronds float along, day by day the hundred little lives breathe and feed and cling to their drifting home. But soon the gas berries decay and the fronds sink lower and lower. As the current flows northward, and the water becomes colder, the crabs move less rapidly, the fish nibble less eagerly at the bits of passing food. Soon a sea-horse lets go and falls slowly downward, to be snapped up at once or to sink steadily into the eternal dusk and black night of deeper fathoms. Soon the plant follows and, like all its chilled pensioners, dies. The supply from the Sargasso Sea seems unfailing, but one's sympathies are touched by these little assemblages, so teeming with the hope of life, all doomed by the current which is at once their support, their breath, and their kismet.

THE ROUND TABLE

1. Following is a statement by the English philosopher John Locke which seems at first extreme, but which seems less so as we ponder its implications : "For he that well considers the errors and obscurity, the mistakes and confusion, that are spread in the world by an ill use of words, will find some reason to doubt whether language, as it has been employed, has contributed more to the improvement or hindrance of knowledge among mankind."

2. Stuart Chase's book on the same subject as the passage quoted on page 132 suggests the following threefold classification of words on an ascending scale of difficulty in defining : —

Labels as names for things may be roughly divided into three classes on an ascending scale : —

(1) Labels for common objects, such as "dog," "chair," "pencil." Here difficulty is at a minimum.

(2) Labels for clusters and collections of things, such as "mankind," "consumers' goods," "Germany," "the white race," "the courts." These are abstractions of a higher order, and confusion in their use is widespread. There is no entity "white race" in the world outside our heads, but only some millions of individuals with skins of an obvious or dubious whiteness.

(3) Labels for essences and qualities, such as "the sublime," "freedom," "individualism," "truth." For such terms, there are no discoverable referents [1] in the outside world, and by mistaking them for substantial entities somewhere at large in the environment we create a fantastic wonderland. This zone is the special domain of philosophy, politics, and economics.

3. If you have never trained your mind to define, and are hence inclined to underestimate either the importance or the difficulty of defining, suppose that a foreign student has brought you the six following common words and has asked you to explain exactly what they mean : —

vitamin	glass	muscle
a county	tree	wheel

Of course everyone knows what they mean, but *can you define them?* If you think you can, write out your definitions of any three, and then compare your definitions with those in a large dictionary. You will probably be surprised at the inherent stubbornness that lurks in even the commonest terms.

4. Consider next three common non-literary terms that you have been hearing and using almost every day : *graft, racket, hazing.* Exactly what do they mean? And, lastly, if you are still in a hopeful mood, discuss with yourself — or better with a friend — the difference (!) between a fruit and a

[1] *Referent:* the object or situation in the real world to which the word or label refers.

vegetable. It took a Supreme Court decision in 1893 to decide to which class the tomato belongs. The court ruled that it is legally a vegetable.

5. As directed by the instructor, be prepared to explain any of the following common terms, from business and finance: —

money	bill of lading	passport
currency	sinking fund	fire insurance
specie	stock company	life insurance
check	stock market	copyright
bank draft	bonus	royalty
promissory note	bond	taxes
mortgage	bulls and bears	primary election
lien		

6. With the use of a sketch or diagram write a brief explanation of one of the following objects as if for a small encyclopedia: —

siphon	pair of scissors
safety razor	door hinge
fountain pen	candle
flashlight	umbrella
can opener	box camera
pulley	single-action pump
microscope	periscope

7. First distinguish the following paired terms from each other by defining them in contrasting definitions, and then use them correctly in sentences. In several instances try framing a literary or humorous definition instead of a literal, exact one.

(1)	canoe	boat	(11)	college	university
(2)	boot	shoe	(12)	illusion	delusion
(3)	game	sport	(13)	optimist	pessimist
(4)	fact	opinion	(14)	denotation	connotation
(5)	stock	bond	(15)	courage	fortitude
(6)	salary	wages	(16)	fable	parable
(7)	safety	touchback	(17)	metaphor	simile
(8)	trade	profession	(18)	vocation	avocation
(9)	immigration	emigration	(19)	ingenious	ingenuous
(10)	incredible	incredulous	(20)	majority	plurality

8. Criticize and discuss in class the following definitions, supplying deficiencies where needed. Not all the definitions are faulty.

(1) An okapi is an African animal.

(2) A mine is a hole in the ground.

(3) A mine is a hole in the ground owned by a liar. (Attributed to Mark Twain)

(4) A simile is an expression in which two objects are compared.

(5) A lawmaker is one who makes laws.

(6) Description is when you describe a person or thing.

(7) A cause is that which produces an effect.

(8) Philosophy is the science of principles.

(9) Opium is a vegetable product which produces sleep.

(10) Mad call I it; for, to define true madness,
What is't but to be nothing else but mad?
— *Hamlet*, II, iii, 93–94

(11) Table salt is sodium chloride.

(12) Network: anything reticulated or decussated at equal distances, with interstices between the intersections.
— JOHNSON'S *Dictionary*, 1755

(13) Dirt is matter in the wrong place.

(14) Hazing is any form of pain or embarrassment inflicted by upperclassmen on a first-year student because he is a first-year student.

(15) Graft is illicit spoils in connection with politics or municipal business.

(16) Graft is the abuse of a public trust or fiduciary relationship to secure something of value for which no adequate service has been rendered.

(17) Art is nature seen through a personality.

(18) A racket is any scheme for exploiting the industry of others maintained by intimidation, terrorism, or political favoritism.

(19) Culture "implies enjoyment of things that the world has agreed are beautiful, interest in knowledge that mankind has found valuable, comprehension of the principles that the race has accepted as true." — A. LAWRENCE LOWELL

9. As directed by the instructor, explain the meaning of any of the following proverbs, first in general terms and then, if possible, by means of a short anecdote or incident somewhat after the fashion of *Aesop's Fables*.

(1) Do not burn the candle at both ends.

(2) Those who dance must pay the fiddler.

(3) Beware of the man with an axe to grind.

(4) Every time a sheep bleats it loses a mouthful.

(5) He that will eat the kernel must crack the nut.

(6) Beware of jumping from the fireplace into the fire.

(7) Do not put all your eggs in one basket.

(8) A rolling stone gathers no moss.

(9) Never cross a bridge before you come to it.

(10) A small leak will sink a great ship.

(11) You must take the fat with the lean.

(12) It is hard for an empty sack to stand upright.

10. For suggestive definitions of more than two score difficult ideas and concepts, see the Forum Definition Contest which was a feature of the *Forum* from 1926 to 1931. Consult the *Forum* index for specific examples.

CHAPTER VII

Extended Explanation: Chain Paragraphs and Jointed Subjects

A composition is an oral or written proof of clear thinking.

— RACHEL SALISBURY

CHAIN PARAGRAPHS

The only real difference between independent paragraphs and chain paragraphs is that, as their names indicate, **chain paragraphs are connected while independent paragraphs stand alone.** As stated in Chapter I, an independent paragraph is one whose meaning is complete in and by itself. Whether its underlying purpose is to explain, to argue, to describe, or to narrate, it deals with a single topic, and develops that topic in as much detail as seems advisable to the writer at that time. The end sentence of an independent paragraph serves only to round out, sum up, and drive home the paragraph idea, clenching the nail securely as it were.

A chain paragraph, however, has a double function to perform. Its first purpose, like that of the independent paragraph, is to develop a single topic, but it does not stop there. It is only one link in the chain of thought, and prepares the way for and leads on to the next related topic, which in turn is developed in the next paragraph. Chain paragraphs may be likened to different rooms in the same house connected with one another by halls and doors, or to freight cars in the same train joined together by couplings and coupling pins. Or, to change the figure, an independent paragraph stands alone with its arms folded; a chain paragraph places its hands on the shoulder of the paragraph in front of it, and they all march in the same direction.

WRITING ON JOINTED SUBJECTS

As was stated in Chapter I, the first fundamental in writing is ability to compose independent paragraphs. But we cannot stop there. Much of the writing that we shall be called upon to do both in college and afterwards in the world will consist not of single paragraphs but of a series of paragraphs dealing consecutively and progressively with the same subject and linked each to each.

So far as exposition and argument are concerned, the way to proceed is very definite and clear. For example, consider the following prescription for writing a four-paragraph theme of explanation. It has almost the value of an exact formula.

There are five necessary steps. To omit any one of them not only will keep you from doing your best work but will almost certainly result in weakness and failure. There is nothing magical in the five steps. They are simply the result of applying to the task of writing the same kind of intelligence and common sense that a farmer uses in planting his crop, that an architect uses in building a house, or that an engineer uses in planning a bridge.

THE FIVE STEPS IN EXPLAINING

(Before Beginning to Write)

The First Step: Analyzing the Subject into Paragraph Ideas
The Second Step: Choosing the Paragraph Ideas to Be Developed
The Third Step: Arranging the Paragraph Ideas

(After Beginning to Write)

The Fourth Step: Announcing the Paragraph Ideas
The Fifth Step: Connecting the Paragraph Ideas

1. The First Step: Analyzing the Subject

(Before Beginning to Write)

Granted a suitable subject, **the first thing to do is to divide the subject up into its parts or elements or points.** Henry Ford stated a highly useful principle when he said, "Nothing is particularly hard if you divide it up into small jobs." He was not thinking of writing when he said it, but it holds good for writing themes as well as for making automobiles.

(1) SIZING UP A SITUATION

This first step of analyzing the subject is absolutely imperative. Nor is it just one more troublesome process invented by college professors and textbook writers to take the joy out of life. The power to analyze, to get at the bottom of things, to size up a situation, to leave no essential factor out of account, to be able to tell the difference between the important, the unimportant, and the most important — this is a demand that the world of business makes on every successful man. The merchant, the banker, the lawyer, the head of any business or important department, must have this ability to a marked degree or he will not go far or last long. Under the name of judgment it is the chief factor in business efficiency and material success in life.

Not only this — it is impossible for anyone to live a day in college or at home without having constantly to exercise his powers of analysis on dozens of matters of all kinds, both large and small, both trivial and important. In fact, we do it every time we have to choose, or, as we say, have to make up our mind about anything.

The daily situations calling for analysis and decision are so common that we are hardly aware of how frequent they are. Is our next pair of shoes to be tan or to be black? Which moving-picture show shall we go to tonight — a comedy, a Western, or a tragic drama? Do we want our father to buy a large, heavy car or to buy a smaller, lighter car and put the difference in price into new living-room furniture? Do we wish the family to go this summer to the beach or to the mountains? Which team will you try for in the spring — track or baseball? Which of the two fraternities that have given you a bid will you join? Shall you change from the A.B. to the B.S. degree or possibly enter one of the professional schools? Are you considering whether to stop college and go to work instead of continuing your course? Are you satisfied with your choice of a profession, or after all should you be planning for something else? If you were your mother, would you, at some personal inconvenience, for the sake of economy, buy food from the cash-and-carry, or would you pay higher prices at a store where you could run a charge account and have things delivered? If you were your father, with $10,000 to invest, would you buy business property or residence property, or would you put it in low-interest bonds or in high-interest stocks?

Whether we are aware of it or not, we spend many of our waking moments analyzing and deciding such matters as these.   Thus when we analyze a subject before beginning to write, what we are really doing is simply utilizing in our writing whatever powers of analysis, decision, and judgment we are fortunate enough to possess.

(2) ANALYZING THE SUBJECT

Analyzing the subject is not only the first step in point of time, but it is also the first step in point of importance.   You cannot do anything with a subject until you have taken it apart and can thus consider each point individually.   Of all the five steps it is the one most generally neglected by inexperienced writers, and to its neglect are due more weak themes than to any other single cause.   If "Look before you leap" is a good rule, "Think before you write" is a better one.

. Consider the six following subjects.   They are all good ones, and every student in class will have some ideas about them.

1. Causes of Student Failure in College
2. Qualities of Ideal Manhood
3. Bars to Success in Life
4. Leading Causes of Automobile Wrecks
5. The Advantages of Being a Man (or a Woman)
6. Why People Tell Falsehoods

Let us suppose that the first subject is the one assigned — Causes of Student Failure in College.   Now the causes of failure are varied and numerous.   Some are important, some are unimportant; some affect many students, some affect only a few students.   It is clearly out of the question to write a short theme on all of the causes or even on any large number of them.   To try to do so would end only in naming the causes over without discussing them.   In other words the result would be a list instead of a composition.

Let it be agreed, therefore, that we shall deal with only the four or five leading causes of failure.

In order to do this intelligently, however, we shall have first to list all the causes that we can think of and weigh them with one another to decide which are the most important.   Suppose that the instructor calls for suggestions on this point from individual students.

As the various causes are named, they are written down on the board for all to see.

If the class is really in earnest and everybody tries to think, the resulting list may take some such shape as the following, which was put together by a class of twenty-two students in twelve minutes' time.

Causes of Student Failure in College

1. Not enough study
2. Lack of interest in subject
3. Sickness
4. Too much participation in student activities
5. Worry
6. Too many outside social activities
7. Poor preparation in previous years
8. Having to do outside work to earn money
9. Carelessness
10. Mentally deficient
11. Inattention in class
12. Not knowing how to study
13. Inability to concentrate
14. Misbehavior
15. Ill favor of instructor
16. Indifference as to passing
17. Bad companions
18. Dissipation
19. Timidity
20. Poor teaching
21. No ambition
22. Discouragement

In looking over the list, notice that each topic has been jotted down exactly as it was called out by the student. No effort was made by the instructor to improve the wording or to avoid duplication. For example, topics 2, 11, 16, and 21 are more or less alike — Lack of interest in subject, Inattention in class, Indifference as to passing, No ambition; as are also numbers 12 and 13 — Not knowing how to study, and Inability to concentrate. Never mind how helter-skelter or ragged the list of topics looks when you first jot it down. Order and smoothness will come with the second step of choosing and arranging the most suitable topics. The first essential is to get down on paper as long and as varied a list of related topics as you can possibly think up.

Nobody can build a house without materials, and at this stage your only building materials are topic ideas.

Again, suppose we take the second subject on page 144, Qualities of Ideal Manhood. Immediately the question arises, "What *are* the qualities of ideal manhood?" Not much thinking will be needed in order to draw up some such list as the following: —

QUALITIES OF IDEAL MANHOOD

1. Courage	9. Generosity
2. Morality	10. Sympathy
3. Enthusiasm	11. Courtesy
4. Unselfishness	12. Self-reliance
5. A Sense of Humor	13. Good Sportsmanship
6. Sincerity (Honesty)	14. Ambition
7. Determination	15. Intelligence
8. Loyalty	16. Tact

This is by no means a complete list, though it does name sixteen outstanding qualities. Again it is at once evident that to develop all of these topic ideas would require too much time and space. Therefore, again we find it necessary to take the second step of choosing and arranging the key qualities which we wish to develop.

This we leave till the next section.

Exercises in the Analysis of Ideas

Review at this point the example of analysis and division given in the chapter on Definition, pages 134–135.

1. Divide and classify several of the following terms. If possible, suggest more than one basis or principle of division. List the subdivisions in what seems to you the most logical order, either with or without further definition and explanation as the instructor directs.

college degrees	trees
types of government	holidays
religious denominations	taxes
education	dogs
automobiles	parts of a book
social sciences	parts of a magazine
laboratory sciences	parts of a newspaper
winter sports	college athletics
summer sports	

2. In answer to a questionnaire, 1158 alumni of Purdue University recently named as the most desirable qualities in a teacher the eight following ones. Consider them carefully, discuss them in class, and suggest any important addition that occurs to you.

(1) A wholesome attitude and a balanced philosophy of life
(2) Alertness
(3) Fair-mindedness
(4) Courtesy
(5) Humor
(6) Sincerity
(7) Tolerance
(8) Neatness

3. Name three causes for the decrease in passenger travel on the railroads.

4. What are the chief causes for the present decrease in church attendance?

5. What are some of the essential elements in the following qualities?

good temper	real patience
a high sense of honor	loyalty

6. Suppose you were running for mayor of your town. What needed improvements as to buildings, paving, sewerage, parks, and so forth, would you advocate in your platform? Remember to make no recommendations that you would not be willing to defend and justify before the voters and taxpayers.

7. Suppose that the trustees of your college have $500,000 available for improvements and have appointed you to represent the student body as their adviser. What would you recommend that they should do with the money?

8. Glance again through the list of the Causes of Student Failure on page 145, and the list of Qualities of Ideal Manhood on page 146, and see whether you can make any important additions to either list.

9. Either individually or with the whole class thinking together, and the instructor at the board, take the following two of the remaining four subjects suggested on page 144 and analyze them fully in class: —

Bars to Success in Life
Leading Causes of Automobile Wrecks

10. Analyze the two remaining subjects of those given on page 144: —

The Advantages of Being a Man (or a Woman)
Why People Tell Falsehoods

Try treating the man and woman subject humorously.

11. For other opportunities for analysis, see the list of Jointed Subjects, pages 166–169.

12. The following table was prepared by Easley S. Jones and printed in a bulletin of the Illinois Association of English Teachers. It includes nearly everything it is possible to do in exposition, or the explaining of ideas. The

methods of the first column are best suited to formal essays.   The next time ideas are slow in coming, glance over this table for suggestions.

SUGGESTIONS FOR ANALYZING AND DEVELOPING A SUBJECT

1. *Define*
2. *Classify*
3. Seek *Origin*
4. Discuss *Changes*
5. Treat *Historically*
6. Show *Cause and Effect*
7. Make a *Comparison* or a *Contrast*
8. *Illustrate* by examples
9. Make a *Hypothesis* (suppose conditions were otherwise)
10. Describe *Uses*
11. Describe your *Feeling toward the Subject*
12. *Criticize*, or go further, and
13. Assign a *Value*
14. Treat as a *Symbol*
15. Think of it as *Evolving, Growing, Having a Future*

2. The Second Step: Choosing the Paragraph Ideas

(*Before Beginning to Write*)

Analysis provides the working materials, and is thus the first step toward writing.   **The second step consists in looking through the suggested points and choosing the best of them for development into paragraphs.**   To do this is much easier than to provide the materials in the first place through analysis.

Consider the twenty-two Causes of Student Failure in College which were listed on page 145.   They are of various kinds.   Some are large, some small; some important, some unimportant; some duplicate others.   Let us limit our choice to four, and let us try to choose wisely. After some discussion and argument the composition class that originally proposed the twenty-two topics decided that these four are the most important : —

> Not enough study
> Too many outside social activities
> Poor preparation in previous years
> Not knowing how to study

This is a fairly satisfactory choice, though not everyone would agree on exactly these four.   Other good topics that might well have been chosen are these : —

Lack of interest in subject
Too much participation in student activities (with special reference to athletics)
Discouragement

These two groups of topics taken together, however, include the cream of the list and would satisfy nearly everybody.

Turn next to the sixteen Qualities of Ideal Manhood named on page 146. It is hard to limit ourselves to only four of these, for all sixteen are admirable characteristics. From the sixteen, one composition class which was working with this subject selected the following four : —

Courage
Enthusiasm
Sincerity
Determination

The same students were assigned the allied subject, Qualities of Ideal Womanhood. After listing twelve or fifteen desirable feminine traits, this class, which was composed of boys, selected the following : —

Charm (including good looks)
Good character
Sincerity
Patience

In a large girls' school the girls were asked to vote on the qualities they thought the Ideal or Model Husband should possess. The majority declared that he should be (1) good-looking, (2) courteous, (3) clean, (4) temperate, and (5) religious.

(1) UNITY

Such examples as these illustrate the value of weighing and choosing our topics from a large list of mixed possibilities. If we have analyzed thoroughly and chosen wisely, there is no doubt or guesswork about the result. We can feel sure that we have the best possible selection of paragraph ideas. We can also feel sure that every idea which we have selected in this way vitally belongs to the subject. No alien or foreign topic can creep in. In other words, so far as paragraph topics are concerned, what we write will have clear and complete unity. Our chosen ideas will bear directly upon our subject and upon nothing but our subject.

3. The Third Step: Arranging the Paragraph Ideas

(Before Beginning to Write)

The arranging of the topic ideas in the clearest and strongest order is the next step. As soon as we have selected the three, or four, or five best topics, the next thing to do is to arrange them. Remember that the order of topics is important. It always makes some difference, and sometimes makes a great deal of difference, which idea comes first, which comes second and third, and, above all, which comes last.

The safest working rule is to open with the next most important idea, to close with the most important idea, and to put the other ideas in between. If we let the index figures on the letter A indicate the relative importance of the topic ideas, the formula for arrangement will be something like this : —

First Paragraph	A^3
Second Paragraph	A^1
Third Paragraph	A^2
Fourth Paragraph	A^4

This same order should be followed whether the development calls for four paragraphs or for twelve : open with the next most important, save the most important for the end, and arrange the others in between in the order of climax, or of increasing importance.

(1) ARRANGING PARAGRAPH IDEAS

As a result of this plan, the same classes which analyzed the subjects as explained on pages 145–146, and which selected the four most important topic ideas as indicated on page 148, next proceeded to decide upon their relative importance. There was considerable discussion, and no unanimous agreement was reached. Majority opinion, however, settled upon the following order as the most satisfactory.

CAUSES OF STUDENT FAILURE IN COLLEGE

A^3	Poor preparation in previous years
A^1	Not knowing how to study
A^2	Too many outside social activities
A^4	Indifference and laziness

QUALITIES OF IDEAL MANHOOD

A³ Courage
A¹ Enthusiasm
A² Determination
A⁴ Sincerity

QUALITIES OF IDEAL WOMANHOOD

A³ Good character
A¹ Charm (including good looks)
A² Patience
A⁴ Sincerity

(2) SPACING PARAGRAPH IDEAS

Along with planning the order of the paragraph ideas goes **the need of devoting enough space to each idea in order to develop it properly.** We must avoid at all costs writing ourselves out on the first two or three paragraphs, and then, since the theme has reached the required length, dismissing our last idea, important as it is, in a hurried sentence or two. That is almost exactly how *not* to write a good theme. Yet it is a danger we are all likely to fall into unless we do a little intelligent planning as to paragraph length at the same time that we plan the paragraph order.

This is very easy. All that we have to do in a short four- or five-paragraph theme is to reserve enough space for the all-important last paragraph, at least as much as we give to the first paragraph and probably a little more. Nor is it a bad plan to write the last paragraph first. Try it sometime. An average four-paragraph theme, of the type we are considering here, will probably run to not much less than two pages or to not much more than four pages. That means that the average length of the paragraphs will come somewhere between one half and two thirds of a page, or between two thirds of a page and a page each.

While it is neither desirable nor possible to limit too strictly the length either of the theme as a whole or of the individual paragraphs, a little definite planning as to space will be found necessary. A safe rule of thumb in exposition, if not followed too closely, is to make no paragraph less than half a page or more than a page long.

Keeping in mind this requirement of paragraph length as well as that of paragraph order, and applying both of them to the topics already chosen, we get some such results as these : —

FOUR LEADING CAUSES OF STUDENT FAILURE

First Paragraph . . . . Poor preparation in previous years
  (Length : three quarters to a full page)
Second Paragraph . . . Not knowing how to study
  (Length : one half to three quarters of a page)
Third Paragraph . . . Too many outside social activities
  (Length : one half to three quarters of a page)
Fourth Paragraph . . . Indifference and laziness
  (Length : three quarters to a full page)

QUALITIES OF IDEAL MANHOOD

First Paragraph . . . . Courage (three-quarters to a full page)
Second Paragraph . . . Enthusiasm (one-half to three-quarters of
  a page?)
Third Paragraph . . . Determination (one-half to three-quarters
  of a page?)
Fourth Paragraph . . . Sincerity (three-quarters to a full page)

QUALITIES OF IDEAL WOMANHOOD

First Paragraph . . . . Good character
Second Paragraph . . . Charm (including good looks)
Third Paragraph . . . Patience
Fourth Paragraph . . . Sincerity

Never mind for the moment whether you agree with the relative value of the different paragraph ideas as revealed by the way they are arranged in these four topic outlines. The two essential things here are (1) that these topics were thoughtfully chosen as the best topics from a number of other possible topics and (2) that they were weighed one with another and the most important put last and the next most important put first.

(3) CLEARNESS AND EMPHASIS

Choosing the topic ideas, as already noted, secures unity. **Arranging the topic ideas before beginning to write secures both clearness and emphasis.** It secures clearness, for when the topic ideas are thus weighed and considered in advance and as a consequence are arranged in the most suitable order, their clearness is assured, since the inner essential of clearness *is* effective order.

Arranging the topic ideas according to the plan suggested likewise secures emphasis, for one half of emphasis consists in putting important ideas in emphatic positions, and we have agreed to put the most important topic idea last (which is the most emphatic place) and the next most important topic idea first (which is the next most emphatic place). The other half of emphasis consists in giving sufficient space (or time) to the proper development of important ideas instead of letting them straggle along and tail off into nothingness after we have exhausted our energy in the first couple of paragraphs. By planning in advance, therefore, to make the last paragraph at least as long as the first paragraph, we avoid sacrificing our most important idea and thus give it emphasis by space as well as emphasis by position.

Exercises in Choosing and Arranging Topics

1. According to the method suggested, choose and arrange the four (or three, or five) best topic ideas from the class list made up in Exercise no. 9, page 147, on

Bars to Success in Life
Leading Causes of Automobile Wrecks

2. Choose and arrange the best topic ideas resulting from Exercise no. 10, page 147, on

The Advantages of Being a Man (or a Woman)
Why People Tell Falsehoods

3. Discuss in class and arrange the five most desirable qualities in a teacher as indicated in Exercise 2, page 147.

4. Read over the following suggested list of the "Ten Marks of an Educated Man," from an article by Albert Edward Wiggam in the *American Magazine*. Choose and arrange the four or five marks you think most important. Be prepared to defend your opinions if necessary.

THE TEN MARKS OF AN EDUCATED MAN

(1) He keeps his mind open on every question until the evidence is all in.
(2) He listens to the man who knows.
(3) He never laughs at new ideas.
(4) He cross-examines his daydreams.
(5) He knows his strong point and plays it.

(6) He knows the value of good habits and how to form them.

(7) He knows when not to think and when to call in the expert to think for him.

(8) You can't sell him magic.

(9) He lives the forward-looking, outward-looking life.

(10) He cultivates a love of the beautiful.

5. Following is a list of America's Twelve Greatest Inventors, recently chosen by a secret committee of prominent men.   Select and arrange the five you consider most important.

(1) Robert Fulton (steamboat)

(2) Eli Whitney (cotton gin)

(3) Samuel F. B. Morse (telegraph)

(4) Charles Goodyear (vulcanizing rubber)

(5) Cyrus Hall McCormick (grain reaper)

(6) Elias Howe (sewing machine)

(7) George Westinghouse (air brake)

(8) Alexander Graham Bell (telephone)

(9) Thomas Alva Edison (electric lamp, phonograph, motion pictures, and many other devices)

(10) Ottmar Mergenthaler (linotype)

(11) Charles Martin Hall (process for making cheap aluminum)

(12) Wilbur Wright (co-inventor with his brother, Orville, of the airplane)

6. What, *in addition to his classroom courses*, should the college graduate get from college?   Here is a suggestive list of ten achievements or objectives that was drawn up by a college president.[1]   Discuss in class their relative importance.

TEN OBJECTIVES OF A COLLEGE TRAINING

(1) A reasonable facility and correctness in the use of one's mother tongue.

(2) A decent ability to speak in public.

(3) A familiarity with the major social, economic, literary, and philosophical problems of one's day, with some understanding of their historical antecedents.

(4) A broad acquaintance with the findings of science in its larger fields and some first-hand acquaintance with the scientific method.

(5) A mastery of a chosen field of knowledge wherein one shall dig deep and well.

---

[1] "Sitting Through College," President Kenneth Irving Brown of Hiram College, *The Journal of Higher Education*, December, 1937, pp. 457–463.

(6) An enthusiasm for books, a knowledge of where they are to be found, experience in using them, and assistance in enjoying them.

(7) A thoughtful determination of one's vocation after a sound and impersonal appraisal of one's capacities.

(8) A beginning of a philosophy of life which shall tend to afford a single-directional vitality to living.

(9) An acquaintance with certain daily routines, the importance of which lies in their commonness. (Examples: elementary banking practices; accepted forms of social correspondence; an understanding of the consumer's rights; practices of budgeting, both personal and family; the art of conversation; a layman's introduction to legal procedure.)

(10) An introduction to certain areas of activity and appreciation which may serve as happy occupations for the leisure periods of life. (Examples: music, art, literature, writing, photography, handicraft, sports, and so forth.)

7. Why Highway Accidents Happen. Here are four authoritative lists indicating the leading causes of automobile wrecks, or what a leading accident insurance company calls "America's shameful automobile accident record." Compare them and study them. (a) Which do you think is the best list? (b) Weighing all these together and adding others from your own experience and observation, draw up your own list of the ten leading causes of automobile accidents.

List I [1]

1. Exceeding the speed limit
2. Reckless driving
3. Driving on the wrong side of the road
4. Driving off the highway
5. Losing control of the car
6. Disregarding signals
7. Not having the right of way
8. Passing on a curve or a hill
9. Cutting in
10. Skidding

List II [2]

1. Driving too fast for conditions
2. On the wrong side of the road, cutting in, passing on hills, curves, etc.
3. Failure to grant the right of way

4. Carelessness in approaching pedestrians
5. Turning left improperly
6. Following too closely

List III [3]

1. Driving too fast for conditions
2. Passing on hills and curves
3. Passing on the straightaway without sufficient clear distance ahead
4. Driving on the wrong side of the road
5. Refusing to give the right of way to an overtaking vehicle
6. Failing to slow down at intersections
7. Failing to slow down on approaching the crest of a hill

[1] From *Popular Government*, University of North Carolina, Chapel Hill, N. C.
[2] State Department of Motor Vehicles, Connecticut.
[3] Michigan State Police.

8. Failing to slow down on approach to pedestrians at night in the glare of oncoming headlights
9. Making improper turns and failing to signal
10. Violation of traffic control devices
11. Dangerous and unlawful parking on rural highways

LIST IV [1]

1. Exceeding the speed limit
2. On the wrong side of the road
3. Not having the right of way
4. Cutting in
5. Passing on a curve or on a hill
6. Passing on the wrong side
7. Failure to signal and improper signaling
8. Driving off the roadway
9. Reckless driving

4. The Fourth Step: Announcing the Paragraph Ideas in the First Sentence

(*After Beginning to Write*)

The most important part of skyscrapers and of railroad bridges is underground. In these structures, what we see depends for both its efficiency and its safety upon what we do not see. So it is with writing. The three important steps described in the last fourteen pages must all be taken before we begin to write at all. A thoughtful mental foundation must be laid.

After we have (1) analyzed the subject, (2) chosen the best topic ideas, and (3) arranged them in the proper order, we are then ready to begin to write — and not till then. Since clearness and definiteness are our principal aims in this type of theme, **the best way to start is with a sentence of enumeration,** as it is called, which names over for the reader the topic ideas to be discussed. In this way the writer lets the reader know at the start (1) exactly what aspects of the subject are to be considered and (2) in what order they will be taken up. The value of an opening sentence of this kind in a theme of explanation is evident.

To illustrate exactly what is meant, glance back at the first topic outline of the Causes of Student Failure in College, on page 148, and let us suppose we are starting to write a four-paragraph theme based on it. The opening sentence might take some such form as this: —

[1] The Travelers Insurance Company, Hartford, Connecticut.

The four leading causes of student failure in school are poor preparation in previous years, not knowing how to study, too much indulgence in outside social activities, and downright laziness.

In regard to this sentence you will note (1) that it is simply, almost barely phrased, and (2) that there is no punctuation mark after the verb *are*.

In case we wished to begin with a somewhat more elaborate sentence, we might open in this way : —

The reasons why students fail in school are both numerous and varied, but probably the four most important ones are these: students are poorly prepared in previous years, they do not know how to study, they indulge too much in social activities, and they do not spend enough time on their studies.

The first sentence of a theme on the Model Husband, the topics of which are given on page 149, might read as follows : —

The five traits that a model husband should possess are temperance, good looks, cleanliness, courtesy, and religious feeling.

Another, less formal beginning would be this : —

I don't know what kind of man other girls would choose for a husband, but I want mine to be temperate, good-looking, clean, courteous, and religious.

From these examples it will be seen that the opening sentence of enumeration can be either matter-of-fact and formal in tone, or more personal and informal if desired. In either case, attention should be paid to two particulars : (1) the sentence must name the topic ideas in exactly the order in which they will be developed later in the theme ; and (2) there are only two correct ways to punctuate : (*a*) Use no punctuation mark at all after *are* if the topic ideas follow directly, as in all but the second of the four illustrative sentences given above ; (*b*) use the colon after such expressions as " —— *are these*"; or " —— *are as follows*"; or " —— *are the following*" — as in the second of the illustrative sentences on the Causes of Student Failure in College. In no case use either the comma or the semicolon after *are* or whatever verb it is that takes the place of *are*.

Exercises in Naming the Paragraph Ideas in the First Sentence

Write two opening sentences of enumeration, one simple and formal and one more informal and personal, on several of the following subjects. Be sure to punctuate as directed in the preceding paragraph.

1. Qualities of Ideal Manhood (see topics on page 149).
2. Qualities of Ideal Womanhood (see topics on page 149).
3. Bars to Success in Life (see Exercise 1, page 153).
4. Leading Causes of Automobile Wrecks (see Exercise 7, page 155).
5. The Advantages of Being a Man (or a Woman) (see Exercise 2, page 153).
6. Why People Tell Falsehoods (see Exercise 2, page 153).
7. The Most Desirable Qualities in a Teacher (see Exercise 3, page 153).
8. The Ten Marks of an Educated Man (see Exercise 4, page 153).
9. The Four (Five) Greatest Inventors (see Exercise 5, page 154).
10. Ten Objectives of a College Training (see Exercise 6, page 154).
11. In accordance with this plan, be sure that the first sentence of every theme written on any of the jointed subjects suggested on pages 166–169 below announces the topic ideas in the order in which you will develop them. In spite of the definiteness of the form of these opening sentences, try to make them as varied and original as possible.

(1) WRITING THE THEME

After the four preceding steps have been taken, with the subject analyzed and the topic ideas chosen, arranged, and named in the opening sentence, the actual writing of the theme begins in earnest. Each paragraph in turn, from the first to the last, is to be developed in detail as was explained in the chapter on the Independent Paragraph, pages 3–13 above. Remember that there is no essential difference between the independent paragraph and the chain paragraph except that the former stands by itself and the latter belongs to a group. Each needs a topic sentence, or at least a definite topic idea; each must have enough definite details to make the topic idea clear or vivid to the reader; and each is the better for a short striking end-sentence which drives home and clinches the topic idea.

To each of our chain paragraphs, therefore, we must apply the same three questions as were applied to the independent paragraph : —

1. Does the opening sentence state the paragraph idea simply and definitely?

2. Are there enough details and particulars to make the paragraph idea clear and interesting?

3. Is the closing sentence good enough to deserve the place of honor at the end?

There is, however, one important additional requirement that the chain paragraph must fulfill: it must be connected with what goes before, and must lead up to what comes after.

To meet this requirement is the purpose of the fifth and last step.

5. The Fifth Step: Connecting the Paragraph Ideas

(1) TRANSITION WORDS AND PHRASES

The word "transition" comes from the Latin, and means a "going over" or a "passing across." In a mental sense it means exactly what the Anglo-Saxon word "bridge" means in a physical sense. Both are means of getting from one thing to another thing. By the aid of bridges we pass over gaps in the ground, and **by the aid of transition words and phrases we pass over gaps in the thought and follow easily the writer's ideas from paragraph to paragraph.**

Transition words and phrases not only are bridges but are guide-posts and road signs as well. They not only show the way but also carry us over. Thus in their double duty of directing mental traffic and of furnishing a bridge for it, transition words and phrases are of the greatest possible service in exposition and argument. They are thought signals. The careful writer makes constant use of them. They are sovereign aids both to clearness of expression and to ease in reading.

As is the case with many other useful things, however, we are likely not to notice them, but to take them for granted, as we do the nails in a box or the screws in a watch, which, whether they are noticed or not, are necessary in order to hold the box and the watch together.

It will help us to realize the importance of connectives to recall what the great English poet Coleridge said of them. In his "Essay on Method" Coleridge asks: "What is that which first strikes us, and strikes us at once, in a man of education, and which among educated men so instantly distinguishes the man of superior mind, that . . . 'we cannot stand under the same archway during a shower of rain, without finding him out'?" His striking answer to this question is, "That man's use of English connectives."

A necessary step, therefore, in writing chain paragraphs is first to become keenly aware of the value and necessity of the various kinds of transition, and secondly to train ourselves to make regular and increasing use of them in writing.

Although our language has a great variety of transition expressions, their number is after all not so large that we cannot become thoroughly familiar with most of the good ones. The following list contains the commonest and best. Consider it carefully, for it is a most useful collection.

(2) TRANSITION TABLE

1. DEMONSTRATIVES: **this, that, these, those**
2. NUMERALS AND SYNONYMS FOR NUMERALS (to imply a series): **first, in the first place, to begin with, secondly, in the second place, lastly**
3. "AND" AND ITS SYNONYMS (continuing the same line of thought): **again, also, in the next place, once more, furthermore, moreover, likewise, besides, similarly, for example, for instance, in fact**
4. "BUT" AND ITS SYNONYMS (introducing opposed or contrasting thoughts): **but, then, nevertheless, still, however, at the same time, yet, in spite of that, on the other hand, on the contrary**
5. DEGREES OF CERTAINTY: **certainly, surely, doubtless, indeed, perhaps, possibly, probably, anyhow, anyway, in all probability, in all likelihood, at all events, in any case**
6. CONSEQUENCE OR RESULT: **therefore, consequently, accordingly, hence, then, thus, as a result, in consequence of this, as might be expected, so**

Study this list until you know by heart its six divisions, and can name at least half the transition words in each of the six groups. All of them, except two, are satisfactory bridge words and should be used in your writing just as often as you can make a place for them. The trouble with the writing of most of us, and the weakness that we shall have to fight against continually, is that we use transition words far too seldom, and thus leave our sentences and paragraphs standing helplessly alone instead of taking firm hold on each other as they should do. For this negligence on our part it is our readers that pay the penalty.

In the second sentence of the preceding paragraph, it was said, "All of them, except two, are satisfactory bridge words." Did you wonder, as you read it, which two were meant? They are the two commonest connectives of all — *and* and *so*. The trouble with both *and* and *so* is that they have been worn out through being overworked. They have almost become examples of the old saying, "So good as to be good for nothing." In regard to *and* we should (1) cut down our use of it so far as possible by substituting other more exact connectives for it, and (2) should never, except in the most chatty and informal style, begin a sentence with it. In regard to *so* the best rule is, except in informal conversation, not to use it as a connective at all. It has been worked to death by countless inexperienced writers and should be given a good long rest.

(3) TRANSITION AND CLEARNESS

Clearness (1) not only means putting things in the best order; it (2) also means making the reader see this order and the reasons for it. The arranging of the topic ideas as advised in the Third Step in writing secures clearness of the first sort — that is, the best order. Using transition words and phrases to call the attention of the reader to this order and to guide him definitely from detail to detail and from paragraph to paragraph secures clearness of the second sort — showing and proving the order to the reader.

(4) LINKING CHAIN PARAGRAPHS

As each paragraph idea is reached in turn, from the first one to the last one, we must make clear to the reader exactly how and in what order our paragraphs are being developed. In fact, we must not only make this so clear that our readers can easily follow the development, but we must make it so clear that our readers cannot possibly *fail* to follow the development. This sounds like a hard requirement, but in a theme of explanation or argument it is a just one. We have at our disposal the means to do it if we will use them.

Two things are necessary: **(1) at the beginning of each paragraph the paragraph idea should be clearly stated in the topic sentence, and**

(2) *some definite transition word or phrase* should be used to link the paragraph with what has gone before.

The first of these two necessities, that of the topic sentence, has been dealt with in detail in the section on Independent Paragraphs, pages 5–12. To state the paragraph topic clearly and definitely is always helpful in explaining and arguing; it is more than helpful in the type of explanatory theme we are considering here — it is essential. Each chain paragraph deals with a different topic. Each chain paragraph thus constitutes an additional step in the development of the thought. Unless, therefore, the writer is both intelligent enough and considerate enough to state in a topic sentence the different steps in his treatment of his subject, the reader is left in the dark as to where he is going and how he is to get there. Be sure, therefore, that the opening sentence of each paragraph states the paragraph idea simply and unmistakably.

The second necessity is definitely to link each paragraph with the preceding paragraph by means of a transition word or phrase like one of those suggested in the list on page 160. Theoretically this is an easy thing to do, but for some reason it is hard to form the habit of doing it regularly. All experienced writers know the value of it, and instinctively use transition words to guide and assist their readers from paragraph to paragraph. Inexperienced writers, however, go ahead blindly from topic to topic, and leave the reader to flounder along as best he can. There was once a student who could write satisfactory independent paragraphs but who continued to have trouble with transition words and phrases. He just could not seem to remember that he owed it to his readers to put transitions in. He finally cured himself by means of this simple remedy. He imagined that each paragraph that he wrote was a little box to hold his thoughts, but that the box would fall to pieces unless he took care to nail it together. The nails were transition words. When he began to write a paragraph, he would say to himself, "Don't forget the nails." When he had finished a paragraph he would read it over again and ask himself, "Have I put in enough nails?" In this way he soon learned to handle connectives so satisfactorily that he became one of the clearest and most reliable writers in the class.

This definite linking of paragraph with paragraph is the fifth and last of the five steps in writing. If we now apply it to the illustrative outlines of the themes on the Causes of Student Failure and The Model Husband, the final result will be something like this. Transition words are italicized in order to call attention to them.

THE FOUR CHIEF CAUSES OF STUDENT FAILURE

First Paragraph The four leading causes of student failure in college are poor preparation in previous years, not knowing how to study, too much indulgence in outside social activities, and not studying hard enough. *In the first place,* poor preparation in previous years often brings about failures in such continuing subjects as English, history, mathematics, and the languages.

(This cause of poor preparation is developed in the rest of the first paragraph, about three quarters of a page or a page long.)

Second Paragraph *In the second place,* no small number of students fail because they spend too much time on outside social activities and pleasures.

(This cause is developed in the second paragraph, about one half to three quarters of a page long.)

Third Paragraph *A third important cause* of student failure is not knowing how to study.

(This cause is developed in the third paragraph, about one half to three quarters of a page long.)

Fourth Paragraph *The fourth and probably the chief reason why students fail* is simply that they do not study hard enough to pass.

(This cause is developed in the fourth and last paragraph, about three quarters of a page or a page long.)

THE MODEL HUSBAND

First Paragraph I don't know what kind of man other girls would choose for a husband, but I want mine to be temperate, good-looking, clean, courteous, and religious. *To begin with,* I want him to be temperate in all things, in eating as well as in drinking, in play as well as in work.

(This idea of temperance is developed in the rest of the first paragraph.)

Second   *Of course, too,* like every girl, I want the man of my
Paragraph   choice to be good-looking.

(This trait is developed in the second paragraph.)

Third   *Not only should he be temperate and good-looking,* he
Paragraph   should be thoroughly clean in both mind and body as
              well.

(This trait is developed in the third paragraph.)

Fourth   *Besides having the traits I've already mentioned,* a really
Paragraph   good husband should be instinctively and always courte-
              ous.

(This trait is developed in the fourth paragraph.)

Fifth   *Above all else,* and the more you think about it the less
Paragraph   surprised you will be, I want the man with whom I have
              to live all the rest of my life to be deeply reverent and
              spiritual.

(This trait is developed in the fifth paragraph.)

Note how exactly these two skeleton outlines illustrate the five
steps that have been dealt with in this chapter. They definitely
accomplish the following results : —

1. Before they could be put into their present shape, real preliminary thinking had to be done in (a) analyzing the subject, (b) choosing and (c) arranging the topic ideas to be
   developed.
2. The opening sentence of enumeration names over the topics
   to be discussed.
3. The first sentence of each paragraph
   (a) states clearly the topic idea of the paragraph and
   (b) by means of definite transition words links its paragraph
       with the preceding paragraph and advances the develop-
       ment of the thought one distinct stage.

To sum up, in the five sentences of these skeleton outlines there is
present every necessary element for writing an adequate explanation
of the proposed subject. In addition, they meet all the demands of
unity, clearness, and emphasis. Moreover, they have the clearness of
an architect's plan and the efficiency that comes only from intelligent thinking. In short, they offer an ideal pattern for explaining.

THE ROUND TABLE

1. If you do not agree with Coleridge's opinion that what instantly distinguishes the man of superior mind is his use of English connectives, try to disprove it.

2. Point out all the transition words and phrases in the last paragraph of the text, page 164.

3. The aim of this whole chapter on Chain Paragraphs and Jointed Subjects is to give the ability to accomplish the five steps in writing, in the order named, and consequently to enable the student to draw up complete skeleton outlines like those quoted on pages 163 and 164.

With those two outlines as guides, prepare similar outlines, one or two at a time as the instructor may direct, on the six remaining subjects which have been analyzed in the previous sections of this chapter.

The Qualities of Ideal Manhood (Womanhood)
Causes of Automobile Wrecks
Bars to Success in Life
The Advantages of Being a Man (Woman)
Why People Tell Falsehoods
The Most Desirable Qualities in a Teacher
Ten Marks of an Educated Man (see page 153)
The Four (Five) Greatest Inventors (see page 154)
Ten Objectives of a College Training (see page 154)

4. Using the subjects in the list on pages 166–169 below, the instructor should assign as many (a) skeleton outlines and (b) complete themes as may be needed in order to give the whole class almost automatic ease in handling jointed subjects.

5. Note the fact that the proof of a satisfactory theme is the ability of anyone to get a clear understanding of the development of the thought from hearing the five key sentences read aloud (that is, the first two sentences of the first paragraph, and the first sentence of the second, third, and fourth paragraphs). Each day themes are to be handed in, several students should be asked to read the five key sentences to the class. Pay particular heed to clearness and definiteness both of language and of transition.

6. The instructor should read aloud the best skeleton outline and the best theme in each assignment, and post an honor roll of themes graded B and above. If there are several sections of the English class, the best themes should be exchanged occasionally for purposes of comparison.

7. The students themselves should correct one another's themes occasionally. The following plan has been found to work well: —

(a) Redistribute the themes when they are handed in so that each student will have someone else's theme.

(b) Ask that each student (1) try to correct all mistakes in spelling, punctuation, grammar, paragraphing, and sentence structure; (2) write a general comment or opinion on the theme as a whole;

(3) give the theme a grade and sign and date it. If desired, this can be done in class the day the themes are handed in.

(c) Redistribute the themes again, and have a second student do the same three things that were done by the first student.

(d) The instructor will then glance over the themes finally, correcting them in red pencil or ink, grade them, and hand them back to be looked over again by the writer and the two students who corrected them

This plan has large possibilities in helping the student to cultivate an intelligent critical attitude.

JOINTED SUBJECTS FOR THEMES

Many of these subjects should be treated in a less formal way than is advocated in this chapter. (See the chapter on The Personal Essay, pages 537–559, for suggestions.)

COLLEGE LIFE

1. Pros and Cons of Hazing
2. How to Develop a Vocabulary
3. What We Can Learn from the Dictionary
4. Traits of a Good Athlete
5. Why Go to College?
6. Pros and Cons of Examinations
7. Advantages (Disadvantages) of a Large College
8. Advantages (Disadvantages) of a Small College
9. Pros and Cons of Intercollegiate Athletics
10. Interesting College Traditions
11. Holidays

FAMILY LIFE

1. A Good Time Today versus a Good Time in My Grandfather's (Grandmother's) Day
2. Sounds That Keep Me Awake at Night
3. Guests I Have Insulted
4. My Faults According to My Family
5. Practical Ways College Students Can Economize
6. The Essentials of a Good Living Room
7. Trials of an Only Daughter (Son)
8. Tragedies of My Childhood

COMMUNITY LIFE

1. Causes of Decrease in Local Church Attendance
2. The Chief Needs of Our Community

3. The Chief Causes of Fires
4. What Our City (or County or State) Taxes Buy for Us ✓
5. The Prevention of Unnecessary Noises
6. The Chief Amusements of Our Locality
7. Some Interesting Local Superstitions
8. The Three (Four) Most Beautiful Spots near _____
9. What Laws Affect Me Directly

OUT-OF-DOORS LIFE

1. Native Wild Flowers
2. How Animals Protect Themselves
3. Useful Trees of My Locality
4. Poisonous and Harmless Snakes of My Locality
5. Useful and Harmful Birds
6. Bird Enemies
7. How Seeds Are Scattered
8. Fish That Are Found in My Locality
9. Hunting versus Fishing As a Sport
10. How to Train a Dog
11. Habits of My Neighbor's Dog
12. Interesting Seeds
13. The More Intelligent Insects
14. Instances of Memory in Animals
15. How Animals Prepare for Winter
16. What Flowers Bloom First, and Where
17. Tricks of Horses (Dogs)
18. Birds I Have Studied
19. Pets of Which My Family Did Not Approve
20. Pets I Have Loved and Lost

MISCELLANEOUS

1. Why Some Girls Are So Popular (Unpopular)
2. Why People Buy the _____ Automobile
3. Four Great Leaders
4. The Elements of Friendship
5. The Essential Qualities of a Good Farmer
6. Advantages (Disadvantages) of Farm Life
7. Qualifications for Leadership
8. Traits of Character I Most Admire
9. Summer versus Winter
10. What Made Lincoln (Lee) a Great Man
11. Traits of Good Sportsmanship
12. The Beach versus the Mountains
13. Reading a Newspaper and Reading a Magazine
14. Things in Modern Life That I Am Dissatisfied With

15. People I Have Copied
16. Ghosts I Should Like to Meet
17. Some Uses of Electricity
18. My Debts — Other Than Financial
19. Winter Sports
20. The Work of the S.P.C.A.
21. The Causes of the Seasons
22. My Favorite Magazine — and Why
23. Introducing Myself
24. Four Wonders of the Modern World
25. Reasons against (or for) Sunday Movies
26. Moving Pictures Are a Benefit (Detriment) to the Social Life of Today
27. The Greatest Influences of My Life
28. Collecting Stamps (or Picture Post Cards)
29. The Art of Hitch-Hiking
30. Things I Like to Eat
31. Careers Others Have Chosen for Me
32. My Boyhood (Girlhood) Ambitions Five Years Ago
33. What I Have Learned from People Who Dislike Me
34. Things I Get the Greatest Kick From
35. If I Had Three Wishes
36. Things I Hate to Do
37. Things I Should Like to Forget
38. Things about Girls (Boys) That Irritate Me
39. My Favorite Boyhood (Girlhood) Heroes (Heroines)
40. Picking a Football Team from the Heroes of History (or of Fiction)
41. The Five Books I Would Take with Me if I Were to Live Alone on a Desert Island
42. How to Drive Safely
43. Living Men and Women Who Are Doing Things That Are Worth While
44. Heroes of the Sport Page
45. People Who Bore Me
46. How to Use a Dictionary
47. Making Up a Book List of My Own Favorites
48. The Parts of a Book
49. Radio Entertainers I Like Best
50. Animal Traits in Human Beings
51. Human Traits in Animals
52. Flivver Wit
53. The Three Foot Faults in Tennis
54. Advertising Signs Seen on a Trip
55. Forms of Stinginess
56. Things I Have Lost

57. My Pet Superstitions
58. Hobbies That Are Worth While
59. The People Who Come into a Drugstore
60. Three Books I Want to Own, and Why
61. Characteristics of the Days of the Week
62. Harmful Recent Inventions
63. How the Days of the Week Got Their Names
64. The Cleverest Ads I've Noticed Lately
65. Famous Fallacies Concerning Women
66. Ambitions That Others Have Had for Me
67. Things Which No Longer Shock the Public
68. An Accident As Seen by the Driver of One Car, the Driver of the Other Car, and a Man on the Sidewalk
69. Kinds of Candy I Bought As a Child
70. The Disadvantages of Having Ears
71. Bugaboos
72. Things I Consider Nonsense
73. Nicknames of History
74. A Study of Advertisements
75. What Some Outsiders Think of College
76. Poisons in Common Use Today
77. The Best Cartoon I Remember
78. Sounds and Odors That Arouse Memories
79. My Seven Wonders of the World

Student Essays

Here are four essays by students, the last two, incidentally, by freshmen. As you read them, compare their method and technique. Taken together they illustrate interestingly the whole range of exposition — from formal to informal in successive steps. The first essay, "The Four Essentials of Greatness," is formal, and was put together in accordance with the directions for The Five Steps in Explaining given in this chapter; the second essay, "The Red Blanket," is less strict in structure but is still a formal essay; number three, "Schick Tests," is explanatory, but uses the much less formal and very effective method of explanation by means of narration and description; number four, "Night Cargo," is so prevailingly narrative that it can hardly be called explanatory at all and should accordingly be ranked as a narrative sketch rather than an expository essay.

Discuss in class the method, technique, and effect of these four essays.

The next step from "Night Cargo," page 175, takes us frankly into the realm of the personal informal essay. See pages 548-559.

(1) STRICTLY FORMAL

THE FOUR ESSENTIALS OF GREATNESS

(The way this theme was put together offers an interesting exercise both in independent paragraphs and in jointed subjects. Each of the four paragraphs was written by a different student, the first and last by girls, as it happens, and the second and third by boys. The paragraphs were written independently of each other as supposed editorials for the college paper. The following week the instructor and the class put them together, chose the title, and wrote the part of the theme that is printed in italics, namely, the sentence of enumeration and the transition phrases connecting the paragraphs. Thus four independent paragraphs on kindred subjects were linked into one connected treatment.)

No man can be considered truly great who lacks courage, enthusiasm, determination, or sincerity. To begin with, courage is such a simple word and yet such a necessary quality. Are you courageous? Have you, as a college boy or girl, the spirit to overcome your obstacles both in your college and outside activities without help? Have you, as a businessman, the moral courage to be strictly honest with all your competitors and your clients? Are you, the parents of the nation, strong enough to raise your children to be worth-while citizens by allowing them to make their own decisions when necessary or do you choose the easier way and decide for them? Have you, as a Christian, the fearlessness that is necessary to do what you know is right? Courage is bravery in both the physical and moral sense; it is that quality of mind which meets danger and opposition with firmness and intrepidity. Without it one loses everything; with it one conquers his world.

In the next place, enthusiasm is necessary for one's complete success in any undertaking. Under its powerful influence men often accomplish astounding things in many fields of endeavor. It is human nature for people to be enthusiastic over things not in their line of duty rather than over things which they must do, but there are a few people who are more fortunate in this respect. These few usually are brilliant successes in their particular vocations. Without enthusiasm all progress in the scientific field, in religion, in civilization, would be greatly retarded if not stopped altogether. Without enthusiasm there can be no great athletes, no great writers, no great scientists, no great nation.

In addition to courage and enthusiasm, determination is also necessary.
To hang on although believing you are beaten, to keep trying because you
don't want to admit defeat — these are two elements of determination.
Nothing succeeds like success and nothing fails like failure. No man has
probably ever scaled the heights who has not had the sickening feeling
that his work was all in vain and wondered why he kept struggling when
the odds were so much against him. I read something once which particularly impressed me — "What is a failure?"

> "It is only a spur to the man who receives it right
> To go in and fight once more.
> If you've never failed, it's an even guess
> You never have won a high success."

The grit to come back and lick the thing that licked you — that's determination.

The last and most important characteristic of all is sincerity. Sincerity is
one of the most beautiful words in the English language. It carries with
it a multiplicity of associations: nobility of spiritual qualities, genuine-
ness, steadfastness, and permanence. It is the pure gold ingredient of
friendship, the bed rock upon which friendship is built. The man who has
a reputation for sincerity is indeed fortunate. His opinions are valid, his
advice is sought, and he is highly esteemed. As a friend he is without
parallel. His frankness may hurt, but he is genuinely interested in you,
and his advice is worth twice that of an obsequious flatterer. His sincerity
includes not only meaning what he says but being honest in behavior. His
business life is beyond reproach, and he is honest in all dealings with his
fellow men. His character rings true and mellow like an old Chinese gong
which has stood the test of ages.

(2) LESS FORMAL

THE RED BLANKET [1]

BERNARD LIVINGSTON

(*Antioch College*)

It is early morning on the great ore docks at Cleveland, and a towering,
gaunt freighter wearily leans her weatherbeaten side against the rough
supporting shoulder of the dock. Her taut lines are singing to the tension
produced by the rough pushing and shoving of the five giant Hewlitts which,
with a deafening roar of clanging bells, grinding cogs, whirring cables, and
the screech and whine of steel plate against steel plate, are scooping out of
her hold twenty-ton mouthfuls of ore in a frantic effort to get her unloaded
by daybreak. The glare of many electric lights and the shifting eyes of

---

[1] From Atlantic Monthly Essay Contest, 1925–1926.

giant searchlights show up the dirty, weary faces of the men, while over all the silently shifting ore dust lays down a thin red blanket.

How many people have witnessed this sight? How many people realize the vast workings of this enterprise? How many people know and understand the great continuous movement of the ore over its aquatic route? Very, very few. The average layman knows that the ore comes to the furnaces in a dump car, and is vaguely aware that it has its source up north "some place" on Lake Something-or-other. But the average layman's failure to know is his loss, for it is a great story — this shipping of ore.

Those who live along the Detroit River see the slowly moving freighters pick their way surely up its long course ; they see their foamy wakes, white in the sun, lead out of sight across the rippling surfaces of Lake St. Clair and Lake Huron ; or perhaps at night they hear the deep note of their whistles echo and re-echo across the flats. Yet they do not realize that they are seeing and hearing the greatest cog in the vast machinery of ore transit : the freighter. Pounding the ice in the winter, the steel decks hot under the sun in the summer, the big boats carry the ore from the far-off and forsaken North to the Bessemer furnaces and the coal. It is this great fleet of boats and their hardened crews that make possible the immense steel production of the nation.

The amount of shipped ore is astounding. A greater tonnage goes through the locks of Sault Sainte Marie in one year than goes in and out of the harbor of New York City over the same span of time. This fact may seem surprising at first thought, but, when it is taken into consideration that practically all the ore used in this country comes from the western end of Lake Superior, it loses its aspect of strangeness and gives to us a better realization of the immensity of the machinery that moves the ore. Duluth, Minnesota, is the terminal for most of the product that is shipped from the ranges in that section. Two harbors, Ashland and Superior, also in Minnesota, and close by Duluth, ship out nearly as much. Escanaba, Michigan, is another in the group of terminals that handles ninety-nine per cent of the total output. From these terminals the ore moves downward to Michigan, Illinois, Indiana, and Ohio, where it is loaded into cars for the short haul to the furnaces. And so, considering the vast tonnage of the ore, it can easily be seen why shipment by rail is impracticable and shipment by water imperative.

From the ore ranges, some of which are several hundred miles from the terminal centers, the ore journeys to the boat by rail. This end of the voyage is the easiest from the actual labor point of view and the hardest from the mechanical and technical point of view. Every range has a certain grade of ore and every ore has a different percentage of iron deposit. This fact necessitates long and careful grading of the ore and much shifting and switching of the cars to separate the different grades for loading. The loading itself is a very simple process. The docks are the height of an average seven- or eight-story building and extend several thousand feet out over the water. The trains are run out on the top of the dock and their contents dumped into pockets according to grade. Long chutes are lowered from these pockets, and by means of the chutes the ore slides into the hold. Oftentimes two or three different kinds of ore must come in one boat. This causes endless shifting of the boat from one end of the dock to the other with the exasperating slowness of just one or two pockets being dumped after several long shifts. But every attempt is made to load the ore as quickly as possible, and usually the hatches are closed and the boat is well under way before three or four hours have elapsed.

As I mentioned in a preceding paragraph, bulk shipment is the big necessity in handling iron ore. The more ore brought down, the greater the profits, and every extra hour taken to load or unload the cargo is an hour lost on the ship's time and bears directly upon the profits of the company. Therefore every possible preparation is made before docking to hasten the movement of the ore. Just as soon as the boat noses into the breakwater the hatches are "jerked," the lines made ready to go over; the crew are at their stations for a quick tie-up, and on the dock are the big Hewlitts, lined up to get at the cargo. Car after car is loaded and moved off. Several freight trains at a time are filled and sent on their way to the furnaces. Every man works at top speed, and when the last ton of ore is taken out and the last thud of the Hewlitts is felt, the lines are thrown off and a dirty boat with a dirty crew is off — to get another load.

It is a fascinating tale of hardships, of luxuries, of sorrow, of excitement, of all those things that enter into the great business of creation and production. It is a mighty enterprise, full of interest from the time the first ton slides into the hold until the last ton leaves the clean-swept ship to go on its way to the furnaces. The red blanket, for all its dirt and grime, symbolizes one of the most interesting and romantic of enterprises — the shipping of the ore down the Lakes.

(3) EXPOSITION BY MEANS OF NARRATION AND DESCRIPTION

SCHICK TESTS [1]

HELEN CHURCH

(University of Illinois)

Four hundred Schick tests in one day! This is an accomplishment that I look back upon with pride but hope never to look forward to again. Four hundred alcohol swabs, four hundred sterilized hypodermic needles, four hundred frightened kids, and last but not least, four hundred arms. Plump arms, scrawny arms, dirty arms, hairy arms — every variety under the sun!

[1] From *Green Caldron*, A Magazine of Freshman Writing, University of Illinois.

A Schick test, if anyone still does not know, is a very particular sort of inoculation given to determine whether or not a previous serum injection has successfully immunized an individual from diphtheria. It is usually made with a peculiar-looking hypodermic needle about half an inch long, the squarish base of which has been beveled off on one side, to allow just the proper slant into the skin. It is very different from the ordinary hypodermic injection or "shot," which is usually nothing more than a quick jab into the thick part of the arm, an equally quick withdrawal of the needle, and it's all over. With this test, however, arms have to be held jerkingly; the needle must be pressed against the forearm at a slanting angle and forced gently but firmly between the two layers of skin. The progress of the needle can easily be seen beneath the skin, and when the proper length has been reached, the fluid is released from the syringe and leaves a tiny bump on the arm about as large as a bee sting. Altogether the process is so painful that most people, especially children, are not fond of it.

The doctor and I were to give these tests mostly in country schools within a radius of fifteen or twenty miles, and in order to get around to all of them we left the office at eight o'clock. Schoolteachers had been asked to have their pupils come at eight o'clock instead of the usual nine, so that when we drove into the first school yard, there was a throng of wary-eyed children watching from doors and windows. The doctor advised me to smile hugely as I went in so they wouldn't know what they were in for. So smile we did, although I have often thought since that we must have looked extremely silly and probably fooled no one.

The first thing we did, of course, was get into surgeon's caps and gowns. Then we washed our hands in a basin of lukewarm water that had been placed on the stove by a thoughtful teacher. Applicators, tipped with cotton, we placed on a handy desk; the doctor filled the syringes while I sterilized extra needles, and we were ready to go to work. But getting something to work on was a little different matter. Those children knew what was coming and had decided, one and all, that they weren't having any! It took all manner of coaxing from the teacher before one husky twelve-year-old boy strutted up, assuring us that he'd "be darned if he was scared of that old needle!" After we had finished with him and he was going around proudly displaying his "bump" among his fellows, it was a little easier to get customers, but we had to do many a child whose screaming and struggling forced us to resort to two or three pairs of hands to hold him. Several times it took the teacher, one of the child's parents if they happened to be at hand, the doctor with one hand, and me with both, to keep the arm in the proper position. Hour after hour this went on; school after school was visited, and we had many different types of children to deal with. There was, for instance, the plucky four-year-old who, although his father was holding him, jerked his arm at the wrong time and had to be done all over — this time on the other arm. He did not even whimper and when we were through, he held up his arms for his father's inspection and said,

"Look, Pop. I dot bumps on bofe of mine!" Then there was the other type, the fourteen- and fifteen-year-old "big" girls in school who held out their arms flinchingly, turned their faces delicately away, and managed to cry quite successfully during the process. It didn't take long to get out of patience with this kind, and toward evening I'm afraid the doctor and I both became quite harsh as we grew more and more tired.

Finally, however, we were through and went back to town. With the exception of a trip to check the results within forty-eight hours, the doctor was finished with the job. But was I? Oh no. There were four hundred inoculation certificates to be made out and each had to be signed with the doctor's name in two places. But did the doctor sign them? He did not! I did it, and after I'd forged his name eight hundred times, I really became very good at it. Some day, when he has practiced a long time and has become very rich, I may take advantage of that fact. One never knows.

(4) A NARRATIVE SKETCH VERGING ON EXPLANATION

NIGHT CARGO [1]

F. SCHURECHT

(University of Illinois)

The trip began at the Chicago terminal. Fred Weppner, the driver, was painting the big chains on Truck 100 as I crossed to the end of the long shed. Behind us a dozen men toiled in the glare of the loading platform. Boxes, barrels, crates, bundles were being packed into the huge trucks and trailers. Tailboards slammed. Motors barked and roared. Machines lumbered away into the darkness, heading north, south, east. The night fleet of the Chicago Transport Express was beginning to roll.

Fred finished his last-minute job, carefully hung his brush on a hook under the truck, stowed his pail of oil, looking like black molasses, in a rack on the running board, and we both climbed into the cab.

Our load was ready. The "tickets" covering the consignments were handed up in an oilcloth pouch. Fifteen tons, including ten thousand nickel cigars, two dozen guinea pigs, wallpaper piled like cords of stovewood, and a crate of yelping collie pups, were riding on the eighteen balloon tires of our truck and trailer.

With a load more than a fifth of a block long, Fred carefully pulled out of the shed, rolled down a dark alley, and turned into a glittering main street of Chicago. I looked at my watch; it was nine P.M.

[1] From *Green Caldron*.

For five minutes we worked our way through traffic along residence streets, past factories, out to the suburbs. Then we settled down to the long grind, the roar and clatter of the engine filling the cab.

Fred, who was driving one of his father's trucks for the summer, had invited me to ride on the night-haul to watch a motor transport in operation. Outside our cab a cold wind rushed past. But we were snug and warm, for the heat is automatically regulated in these large trucks.

At the toll house of the Cairo bridge, we pulled up with a hiss of released air from the brakes. Fred fished the three-dollar toll from his pocket. Off again, we cut around a furniture van with five red lights strung across its back, and then bowled along for a mile and a quarter over the white concrete spanning the river.

Beyond Cairo we began to climb out of the valley, and now there were hills all the way. We labored up one side and plunged down the other. The trailer, more heavily loaded than the truck, butted us as we slowed down and jerked back when we speeded up. "When the trailer is full and the truck is almost empty," Fred said, "you need spurs to stay on."

"Do you know why truck drivers wear suspenders?" Fred asked. I made a guess, but it was the wrong one. "It's to keep their shirts in. If you wear a belt on a pitching truck, your shirt tails keep coming out all the time."

At this time of night the cities are dead. We roar through canyons between high buildings, past a huge red-brick factory with twin towers, and out into the open country again. A cold mist is closing in. Telephone wires, white silos, and mailboxes are covered with moisture and have a silvery sheen in the beams of our headlights.

From our seats, high in the cabs, the lights of approaching cars seem to pass under us. At Runk's Road Fred throttles down and eases over to the curb, across from an electric sign suggesting food. Inside the restaurant a group of truck drivers are being served. Over the coffee percolator is the cheerful greeting, "Use less sugar and stir like the devil. We don't mind the noise."

When we leave the diner, the fog has thickened. Fred snaps out the dash light so that he can see better. A pale greenish glow enters the cab windows, coming from the high clearance lights running along the top of the truck. Fred explains that our truck is a good fog machine. Its headlights are set low, illuminating the concrete.

A long, gray bus flashes past and disappears in the mist. Suddenly, high in the sky ahead of us we see two dim, close-set lights dropping steadily toward the ground as though in a descending balloon. They brighten and out of the mist comes a car which has descended the invisible road down a long hill.

On this forty-five per cent incline the truck loses headway rapidly. Fred shifts gears five times on the way up. "Now watch her lay back her ears and dig in!" he says as he shifts the last time. Slowly the thundering engine drags the fifteen-ton load up the last hundred yards of the hill and over "the peak." On the other side the fog is even worse. It is billowing up the slope like rolls of cotton. Fred knows every inch of the road and plunges down the hill for the long toboggan to the bottom.

Cars are thinning out on the roads. On the downward grade we meet a slow truck climbing the hill with the headlights of three impatient passenger machines peering like eyes from around the rear. Then miles go by without a car in sight.

Fred's watch shows five forty-five when we reach the outskirts of Memphis. We emerge into bare, deserted streets, wind through half a dozen blocks between dark warehouses and then back to the terminal. It is a few minutes after six A.M. We have pulled a fifteen-ton load approximately four hundred miles in nine hours.

CHAPTER VIII

Revising and Rewriting

1. The Necessity for Revising

When I say writing, O, believe me, it is rewriting that I have chiefly in mind.

—ROBERT LOUIS STEVENSON

Weigh well these wise words spoken by the gifted author of *Treasure Island*. They form the motto for this chapter and are a sure guide to better writing.

Nearly all writers, except those who earn their living by their pen, overestimate tremendously the value of the first draft or the first copy of their work; or rather, to put the emphasis where it belongs, they underestimate tremendously the necessity of revising and re-revising. The first copy of every writer, experienced and inexperienced alike, is sure to contain blunders, omissions, and weaknesses of various kinds. From long experience, the trained writer knows this, allows for it in planning his day's stint, and revises carefully and frequently everything that he writes. The untrained writer, on the other hand, is likely to put all his time on his first draft, or at most to glance through it hastily as soon as he has finished it, and never look at it again. Thus his work is submitted (and abandoned!) with most of its imperfections still on its head.

The sooner each beginning writer realizes that there is nothing sacred about his first draft, that, in fact, the first draft exists for the purpose of being torn to pieces and then put carefully back together in clearer, stronger shape — the sooner he realizes this, the nearer he is to success. Like it or not, that is the only way.

(1) WHAT SUCCESSFUL WRITERS SAY ABOUT REVISING

Among all writers who have made a conspicuous success the testimony concerning the need of revision and the way to set about it is practically unanimous.

Benjamin Franklin in composing his *Autobiography* wrote on only one half of each sheet of paper and left the other half for additions and corrections. Thomas Huxley, the English scientist and trained thinker, said, "Sometimes I write essays half a dozen times before I can get them into the proper shape." Cardinal Newman, the great English prelate and essayist, testified: "It is simply the fact that I have been obliged to take great pains with everything I have written, and I often write chapters over and over again, besides innumerable corrections and interlinear additions."

The enormous pains the brilliant essayist and historian Macaulay took with his writing have been set forth in detail by his nephew: —

> The main secret of Macaulay's success lay in this, that to extraordinary fluency and facility he united patient, minute, and persistent diligence. . . . He never allowed a sentence to pass muster until it was as good as he could make it. He thought little of recasting a chapter in order to obtain a more lucid arrangement, and nothing whatever of reconstructing a paragraph for the sake of one happy stroke or apt illustration. . . . When at length, after repeated revisions, he had satisfied himself that his writing was as good as he could make it, he would submit it to the severest of all tests, that of being read aloud to others. . . . He could not rest until the lines were level to a hair's breadth, and the punctuation correct to a comma; until every paragraph concluded with a telling sentence, and every sentence flowed like running water.

Robert Louis Stevenson once spent two days on a page and wished afterward that he had made it three. Lafcadio Hearn, in describing a dragon-fly darting about in the sunny air over a swamp, rewrote a short paragraph of ten lines seventeen times before he was satisfied with it. As Charles Fox, the English statesman and orator, once trenchantly remarked, "Easy writing makes d—— hard reading."

The American fiction writer F. Hopkinson Smith has interestingly described the trouble he took with his stories. "The only inspiration I know of in writing," he said, "is days and nights of the labor called thought.   I wrote the first chapter of *Colonel Carter of Cartersville* nine times and corrected the proofs until the printer refused to send any more.

"I am conscious that I cannot do very much, but the little I do is done the very best I know how.   I write very large and heavy, and when the words necessary to make the proper swing or rhythm will not come, I make dashes representing the length of the missing words, and fill them in when revising.   And I never rise from my chair until the work I have laid out is done."

What recent writers have to say concerning the imperative need for revising and rewriting is equally impressive.   "I revise a great deal, and have always done so.   Nothing comes easy to me," said one professional writer.   "I generally revise every serious thing I write two or three times ; everything I put in book covers, four or five times," stated a second professional.   Said a third, "Everything I have published has been written from four to eight times."   John Bennett, the author of *Master Skylark*, said that he frequently rewrote a page as many as thirty times before he was satisfied that he could not improve it further.   In the words of Mary Raymond Shipman Andrews, "The germ of the germ is wanting to do it hard enough.   *Hard enough*." Or, to sum it all up in the trenchant phrasing of Mary Heaton Vorse : "The art of writing is the art of applying the seat of the trousers to the seat of the chair."

The effect of the combined testimony of these thirteen writers should be irresistible.   Among them are two notable writers of fiction, several famous essayists, a great scientist, a well-known historian, and America's most versatile man of affairs.

If after a lifetime of thinking and writing, such men as these still found it necessary to rewrite and to revise, the lesson for us is unmistakable : without vigorous and repeated revision, we cannot even hope to do our best work.   The first draft of what we write is not the end of the job but merely a more or less promising beginning.   For some time to come the destination of our first drafts should be not the instructor, but the wastebasket.   To repeat the striking statement of Stevenson, "When I say writing, O, believe me, it is rewriting that I have chiefly in mind."

There is a Latin motto that was anciently phrased to meet the situation : *Nulla dies sine linea* — no day without its line.   It is the golden rule of all determined writers. Hear Barrett Wendell: "The only way to learn to write so that anyone will read you is to write: *nulla dies sine linea.*" Charles Reade, the author of *The Cloister and the Hearth*, called *nulla dies sine linea* "the eleventh commandment." In practical application of this idea William Webster Ellsworth, author and editor, makes this suggestion: "If I were . . . a young man in college, with the idea in the back of my mind that I would like to write . . . I think I would start what we used to call a 'Commonplace Book' — only, I would honor mine by calling it an 'Uncommonplace Book' — and I would put on the title page the motto, '*Nulla dies sine linea*,' and I would try to make it come true — no day without a line." This is excellent advice. As Stevenson said in another connection, "That, like it or not, is the way to learn to write."

2. The Way to Revise

In revising longer, assigned themes, there is a fairly definite procedure to follow which long experience has proved to be best.

(1) LET YOUR WORK GET COLD

For one thing, be sure to let at least one night go by between the first writing and the final revision. By all means correct and revise as soon as you have finished your first draft. In this way, you will find many mistakes. But do not stop there. Explain it as you will, you cannot then catch all of the blunders. Still less, while the glow of the effort of writing is yet upon you, can you improve and strengthen your sentences to top pitch. In this condition the mind of every writer tends to project upon his pages ideas that really exist only in his mind and which his pen has never transferred to paper at all. He cannot tell his good work from his bad. Let a night pass, however, and he sees everything in the clear cold light of the morning after, and mistakes and weaknesses fairly leap to the eye. That is why some themes that may seem impressive when we first write them dwindle to a strange level of dullness when we get them back from the teacher, so that we wonder at ourselves for ever having thought them good.

Once on theme day an instructor tried this experiment. He received the themes from the class as usual, spent a short time in discussing the day's lesson, and then gave each student back his theme with the direction, "For the next fifteen minutes imagine that you are the teacher of this course and that I have written this theme on the subject I assigned you. Correct and criticize it." Then he collected the themes again. When he looked them over that night, he found that on the average the students had found and corrected two out of three of all misspelled words and nine out of ten of all other mistakes. The reason was that each writer was looking at his own work with a new viewpoint and with critical eyes.

The ideal way to write is to start a theme three days before it is due. On the first day write out the first copy and revise it as best you can. On the second day revise it again more thoroughly. As the final and severest test, read it aloud to yourself and listen to it carefully. Your ear will catch monotony of sentence structure and weaknesses in punctuation and phrasing that your eye missed. Then write out your final copy carefully. Make it look as inviting as you can. On the next day, before you hand it in, glance through it once again as a final precaution. Many a ridiculous mistake has been caught and set right at the last minute.

To revise thus properly takes both time and trouble, but the effort is richly worth while. Some writers allow regularly one third of their time for revising. Out of every hour they spend in writing, twenty minutes goes to correcting and rewriting. An experienced writer once gave this advice to a class in writing: "We must be ready to go back over our work not only once but a half-dozen times, if the sixth time will uncover one bad error, will bring out one of our chief ideas more clearly, or will result in giving any paragraph a more striking end-sentence."

(2) WHAT TO LOOK FOR

The mistakes that we make in writing are countless, but most of them can be classified under six heads. Look over the list carefully, for it is an important one.

1. Spelling and Capitalization
2. Punctuation
3. Grammar
4. Choice of Words
5. Sentence Structure
6. Paragraphing

Nine tenths of all the errors that you will ever make from the time you start your next theme until you sign your last will and testament will fall under one or the other of these six classes.

As to the frequency of the different kinds of mistakes, careful tabulation of many hundreds of themes shows that, excluding paragraphing, the mistakes of the average untrained writer are distributed as follows: Punctuation, 30 per cent; Choice of Words, 19 per cent; Sentence Structure, 19 per cent; Spelling, 18 per cent; Grammar, 14 per cent. In other words, the chances are that of every ten mistakes you make three will be errors in punctuation, two in the choice of words, two in sentence structure, two in spelling, and one in grammar. Detailed instruction and practice in correcting these various types of errors are given in later chapters, particularly in the chapters on Punctuation, pages 88–124 above, and on the Sentence, pages 188–235 below.

(3) REVISE THREE TIMES, EACH TIME FOR A DEFINITE PURPOSE

Most people have single-track minds — that is, they can accommodate only one train of thought at a time.

The application of this singleness of aim to revising is the practical one that you can't do it all the first time, or even the second time. Even a short theme is as complicated in its way as, say, a watch, and you can't be on the lookout for everything at the same time. At least three readings are necessary to give you a fair chance to correct and tighten your work.

1. **Read first for what are called mechanical or elementary mistakes.** Have your mind only upon blunders in (*a*) spelling and capitalization; (*b*) punctuation; (*c*) grammar; and (*d*) sentence structure, with definite reference to the two worst sentence faults, the No-Sentence fault (see page 190) and the Comma Splice (see page 194). These four classes of errors belong together, and can be discovered and corrected at the same reading, though it will take every bit of care and concentration that you can muster.

2. **Look rapidly once again through the theme to see that the paragraphing is correct.** Should you combine several short paragraphs into one? Should you divide any of your longer paragraphs? The

subject of paragraphing is discussed at length in Chapters I and VII. A fairly safe general rule is to be suspicious of any page you write that has more than two paragraphs (unless you are writing conversation), and to be equally suspicious of any page that contains no paragraph indentation at all. Of course sometimes you may have three or more legitimate paragraphs to the page or may have a page and a half to one paragraph, but in most themes the odds will be against either chance.

3. These first two readings are concerned with correctness. Next comes effectiveness. After having revised for surface errors and paragraphing, **read the theme in order to judge what effect it will have on others.** If someone else had written it, how would it impress you? If it is argument, would it convince you? If it is exposition, does it seem complete and entirely clear? If it is description, is it vivid? If it is an incident, would it interest you? In the last analysis those are the qualities which make all written work good or bad and which, surface errors having been taken care of, determine whether or not you will amount to anything as a writer, either now or hereafter. Weigh your work well in this regard, and with the aid of the instructor's corrections and grades learn how to estimate your work fairly and squarely.

(4) READ YOUR WORK ONCE ALOUD

The last and severest test to which you should put your work is to read it aloud, listening critically the while. Listen for both faults and defects. A fault may be loosely defined as "something there which is wrong," and a defect as "something which ought to be there but isn't." Errors of both these kinds abound in writing, and strange to say the ear will detect many which the eye has overlooked. By reading aloud you can better test the flavor of such things as the beginnings and ends of your paragraphs and the quality of your sentence structure. Monotonous or babyish sentences entirely escape notice if read silently. By reading aloud, many a B theme has been turned into an A theme. It is one of the best ways to acquire efficient self-criticism.

3. The Importance of Outside Form

Do not underestimate the importance of the physical appearance of written work. How a theme looks as it is lifted from the pile, before even the first sentence is read, makes a great deal of difference. First impressions are strong. An attractive, careful piece of work starts off with everything in its favor, the instructor included. A slovenly, hasty, careless-looking theme has everything against it from the first word to the last, and must be of exceptional value or charm to overcome its physical handicap. The clothes our thoughts wear are as important as the clothes we ourselves wear. We should not clothe a soldier like a tramp, or dress a princess like the ragpicker's daughter.

There are three qualities which should unfailingly characterize every piece of assigned work you hand in during the college year: (1) Attractiveness, (2) Promptness, and (3) Correct Form.

Take real pride in every paper you sign your name to, and make it just as neat and just as attractive as lies within your power. After all, what you write is as much a part of you as your smile or your voice, and reflects your personality with astonishing intimacy. Next only to meeting a person and hearing that person talk, you can get the truest impression of what he is inside from reading what he writes. When you finish your next theme and have it ready to hand in, look at it critically and ask yourself, "What impression would this make on a cultured foreigner who does not know a word of English?"

To come to a lower but very practical motive, without neatness your theme will almost certainly fail to receive a good grade. A few years ago a director of education made a careful investigation in order to find out exactly what influence handwriting has upon the grading of themes. A few carefully selected themes were sent to forty-three successful English teachers to be graded. The themes were the same in each instance, and were sent at intervals of several months in three different kinds of handwriting — good, fair, and bad. The average difference in grade between the themes in good handwriting and the same themes in bad handwriting was $8\frac{1}{3}$ points. The moral of this is plain: No time is wasted that is spent on making your themes neat and attractive. The easiest way to raise a grade from a D to a C or from a C to a B is to devote an extra fifteen minutes to recopying it in your best handwriting.

As a final word on revision, think over the bearing of these two statements on your own career: (1) Nine out of ten of all the people who, since the world began, have learned to write well have done so by learning first how to revise their own work. The universal law is "Write, revise, rewrite." (2) No one who always has a thing done for him by someone else will ever learn to do that thing himself. If you rely on the instructor to find and correct your mistakes, you will never learn to correct them yourself, and will be in a parlous state after graduation. If you can form in college the habit of intelligent self-criticism, you will have a lifelong ally to call on at need.

THE ROUND TABLE

1. After reading this chapter are you prepared to agree with the following statement of an experienced teacher: "In the last analysis the quality of a student's written work will depend upon his attitude toward revision"?

2. Thinking back over your written work of the last term, what proportion of your errors that the instructor found and corrected were due to real ignorance on your part and what proportion to haste and carelessness?

3. A good way to begin the habit of self-criticism is to ask the instructor to return one theme with the number and kind of mistakes indicated on the outside but not where the mistakes occur. Then try to find and correct every mistake thus made known. Suggest that this be done with an early group of themes.

4. As an interesting variation of revising your theme by reading it aloud to yourself, try this plan with a classmate: Let him read your theme to you and you read his theme to him. Wherever either of you halts or stumbles in his reading, there is likely to be need for revision, particularly in punctuation.

5. Have you heard or read of any incident concerning a writer's taking unusual time and care to perfect his work?

6. In your own writing, (a) How much time do you spend, on the average, on a page (theme)? (b) What proportion of this is devoted to correcting and revising?

7. Does the testimony of successful writers concerning revising seem encouraging or discouraging? It should be encouraging. You may think you have really tried to write and have probably been disappointed over the result; but did you ever *try hard enough?*

8. Some writers, who are very much in earnest about their work, advise the following plan for beginners who really wish to learn: "Write out a first draft as well as you can. Then tear it up. Write out a second draft from memory and start your revising on that." As a variation of this, try the following plan in class, if the instructor approves: On some theme

day, without previous notice to the class, let the instructor collect the themes as usual, and then have the class rewrite them from memory and revise them during the class period. Return the two versions for purposes of study and comparison. To repay the extra trouble, the instructor can either record the higher of the two grades or give a double grade averaged between the two.

9. For once copy a theme in your very best handwriting, as if competing for a $1000 prize, and compare it with your average written work.

10. Ask the instructor to pass around the class the two best-looking and the two worst-looking themes in the next set he corrects. Glance through them without reading them and file the difference away in your memory.

11. Ask the instructor about your individual handwriting. Has it any peculiarities that you should correct? Is it better or worse than the average for the class?

12. For further interesting testimony as to the importance that the best-known writers of the present attach to revising and rewriting, see Josephine K. Piercy's *Modern Writers at Work* (Macmillan).

CHAPTER IX

The Sentence: Making Sentences Unified

A sentence is easier to twist and turn than a rubber band.
— J. W. LINN

Said a wise author, "Do not have too much respect for a sentence the first time you write it."

Think carefully over the two foregoing statements. To realize what each of them implies is to take at the outset the proper attitude toward those tricky, stubborn, disobedient, and yet eloquent and mighty groups of words called sentences.

As was said in Chapter I above, pages 3–18, the paragraph is such an important unit in writing that with it practice in writing should begin. Correct paragraphing can come only from thoughtful planning. In other words, good paragraphs are the result of foresight or prevision.

On the other hand, the sentence, which is the unit of both thought and speech, is in a very special sense the unit for revision. Most writers have the habit of driving ahead with their first draft as fast as they can. If the right word or the right phrase will not come promptly, many do as F. Hopkinson Smith explained on page 180 that he did — namely, leave a blank space and go ahead anyhow. The chief thing is not to lose motion, but to keep on putting ideas and details down as rapidly and as long as they come into the mind. As was noted in the chapter on Revision, pages 178 to 187, the result is that sentences are frequently both faulty and fragmentary. After we have finished a paragraph or a theme comes the need of going back over it and correcting and tightening it. In this process the sentence is emphatically the strategic point of attack. Each sentence must be read over carefully to see first that it *is* a sentence [1] and then

[1] On the growing popularity of the fragment-sentence, see page 192.

to see whether it is doing the work it is supposed to do. Is it unified? Is it clear? Is it emphatic? Are there too many sentences of the same length and pattern? Are there mistakes in grammar? These and a hundred other questions crowd in upon any writer who is really trying to improve his writing and bring it up to the highest level of correctness and effectiveness within his present powers.

The ways in which a sentence can go wrong are almost as numerous as the sands of the sea. Nine tenths of the violations of both correctness and effectiveness, however, fall under a dozen or so patterns. This and the following chapters describe these patterns and give directions for correcting the commonest mistakes. Learn to recognize these main sentence sins and how to remedy each.

Following is an outline of this and the next three important chapters. The outline is not as complicated as it seems at first. Familiarize yourself with it at the outset and refer to it often by way of review.

BETTER-SENTENCE TABLE

CHAPTER IX

Making Sentences Unified
  Avoiding the Two Worst Offenses
    (1) The No-Sentence, or the Period Fault
    (2) The Run-Together Sentence, or the Comma Splice

CHAPTER X

Making Sentences Clear
  1. Getting the Main Thought into the Main Clause
  2. The Proper Placing of Modifiers
  3. The Proper Use of Reference Words
    (1) Pronouns
      (a) Wrong Reference
      (b) Ambiguous Reference
      (c) No Reference
    (2) Participles (Hanging)
  4. Avoiding Faulty Change in Grammatical Construction
    (Parallel Structure for Parallel Ideas)

Making Sentences Unified

Unity in the sentence requires (1) that each sentence shall be a complete statement, with a subject and a predicate, instead of being a fragment or a part of a sentence; (2) that there shall not be too many ideas crowded into any one sentence; and (3) that the ideas in the same sentence shall be akin to and consistent with each other.

1. The Two Worst Offenses

Of the many sins against the sentence, by far the two worst are (1) the No-Sentence, or the Period Fault, and (2) the Run-Together Sentence, or the Comma Splice. The No-Sentence violates a fundamental rule of grammar. Both the No-Sentence and the Comma Splice violate unity, the No-Sentence because it has too little and the Comma Splice because it has too much.

(1) THE NO–SENTENCE, OR THE PERIOD FAULT

Both grammar and unity require that a sentence shall be a complete statement, with a subject and a predicate, instead of being a fragment of a sentence like a phrase or a clause.

A Phrase Used As a Sentence

Wrong: 1. He formed the habit of reading a great deal. Thus storing his mind with much valuable information.

Right: 1. He formed the habit of reading a great deal, thus storing his mind with much valuable information.

Wrong: 2. Most pupils go to high school and live at home. In this way combining the unusual advantages of both school and home.

Right: 2. Most pupils go to high school and live at home, in this way combining the unusual advantages of both school and home.

Also Right: 2. Most pupils go to high school and live at home. In this way they combine the unusual advantages of both school and home.

A Clause Used As a Sentence

Wrong: 3. There is a teacher I shall always remember. Because she had a sweet voice and a pleasant smile.

Right: 3. There is a teacher I shall always remember, because she had a sweet voice and a pleasant smile.

Wrong: 4. The accused declared that he was not guilty. That if given a chance he could prove an alibi.

Right: 4. The accused declared that he was not guilty, and that if given a chance he could prove an alibi.

In order to avoid the No-Sentence fault, or to correct it if it somehow slips in among respectable sentences, one needs the following knowledge gained from grammar and analysis: —

(1) Clear understanding of what constitutes a subject and what constitutes a predicate.

(2) Clear understanding of the asserting power of the finite verb as distinguished from infinitives and participles.

(3) Clear understanding of (a) the incompleteness of thought in dependent clauses such as "because she had a sweet voice and a pleasant smile" (sentence 3 above) and "that if given a chance he could prove an alibi" (sentence 4 above); (b) the incompleteness of thought in phrases such as "thus storing his mind with much valuable information " (sentence 1 above) and "in this way combining the unusual advantages of both school and home" (sentence 2 above).

Review the definitions and examples of phrases and clauses in the section on Analysis, pages 76–77.   If you do not feel sure of these distinctions, ask for class practice and discussion of doubtful points.

To correct the No-Sentence fault, all that is usually necessary is to employ a comma instead of the offending period that shuts the helpless clause or phrase off from the rest of the sentence on which it depends.   This is the case with most of the examples given above. Notice, however, that sometimes other steps are advisable.   Sentence 2, for example, can be split into two sentences by substituting the finite verb *combine* for the participle *combining*.

Among recent writers there is a growing tendency to use fragmentary sentences, especially in building up the details of a descriptive or impressionistic paragraph.   Sinclair Lewis, for example, in *Main Street* describes a house by means of the following phrases, which he punctuates as sentences : —

> A concrete sidewalk with a "parking" of grass and mud.   A square smug brown house, rather damp.   A narrow concrete walk up to it. Sickly yellow leaves in a window with dried wings of box-elder seeds and snags of wool from the cotton-woods.   A screened porch with pillars of thin painted pine surmounted by scrolls and brackets and bumps of jigsawed wood.   No shrubbery to shut off the public gaze. A lugubrious bay-window to the right of the porch.   Window curtains of starched cheap lace revealing a pink marble table with a conch shell and a Family Bible.

Likewise Percival Christopher Wren uses periods instead of dashes or semicolons to set off the words and clauses in the following paragraph from *The Desert Heritage:* —

> Life's an amazing thing.   Life.   Fate.   Destiny.   The Providence that shapes our ends.   God's will.   Whatever you choose to call it.

Both Mr. Lewis and Mr. Wren are successful and distinguished fiction writers, and have as much right as anyone else to take liberties with sentences.   The reason they can afford to do so is that they know words and their ways.   Entirely different, both in motive and in effect, is such an accumulation of sentence fragments and miscapitalizations as the following, which was written by a college freshman who ought not to have been passed out of high-school English : —

> A four story structure surrounded by an Athletic field, tennis court, and Gymnasium.   The Riverside Park on the banks of the James,

an ideal amusement. Consisting of a club house, bathing beach, ball grounds and a large lawn covered with trees and flowers; The Public Library, and Various Churches.

Compare these three paragraphs, and if you find yourself leaning toward a fragmentary style, adopt this working rule: Write only complete sentences with obvious subjects and predicates, until you have your first book published. Then let your conscience be your guide.

Exercises in the No-Sentence Fault

1. In the passages quoted from Mr. Lewis and Mr. Wren on page 192, how many of the word groups punctuated with periods are (*a*) complete sentences, (*b*) clauses, (*c*) phrases, (*d*) words?

2. One teacher uses the following plan in dealing with the fragmentary style in themes. She allows the students to write an occasional impressionistic paragraph composed of the shreds and patches of sentences, but only on condition that the writer put a star (*) after each incomplete sentence to show that he is writing no-sentences from choice, not from ignorance.

3. Copy and correct the following sentences. Do not limit yourself merely to changing the period to a comma if you can find a better way.

   (1) It was a good many years ago, as men figure time. The place, an old, dilapidated shack near the rim of the desert.

   (2) The sun's shining down so exceedingly hot causing me to faint.

   (3) The boys, Philip Ray, a miller's son and Enoch Arden, a poor, rough sailor lad.

   (4) His preparations for the night were very simple. The removal of his shoes and coat, in fact.

   (5) Notwithstanding the fact that it is doubtful whether a poet named Homer ever really lived at all.

   (6) The cornerstone of the building which had been put in place with elaborate ceremonies.

   (7) The final score being nothing to nothing, much to the sorrow of the crowd.

   (8) Making both incisions a fourth of an inch long and one inch broad, thus enabling the wound to bleed freely.

   (9) Until the scout pronounced that he believed it would be safe once more to land.

   (10) At this point, where their footsteps might be expected to be no longer visible.

How would you punctuate the following extract from a recent editorial in a prominent newspaper?

"As regarded by its devotees, mathematics is considered not only as the essence of fidelity, but as possessing an unending charm of grace and symmetry. An elegance that is clear, warmless, exact. So unyielding and precise as to arouse one's awe. So relentless in its virtue of universal and indomitable accuracy as to challenge every one's admiration.''

(2) THE RUN–TOGETHER SENTENCE, OR THE COMMA SPLICE

The second grave sentence fault is the **Run–Together Sentence, or the Comma Splice.** It consists of joining (splicing) two sentences by means of a comma. Examples of the comma splice abound not only in the writing of high-school and college students, but also, unless they are very careful workmen, in the work of professional writers as well. The comma is the trickiest of all punctuation marks, and seems to have a special knack of slipping in between two sentences, where it has no right to be.

Wrong: 1. I do not care for any more fruit, I have had enough.
Wrong: 2. I felt sure that he would come, I never knew him to break a promise.
Wrong: 3. I took my watch to the jeweler's to be fixed, he found a good deal of dust in it.
Wrong: 4. He put the little bird on a twig in the cedar tree, it just stood there without trying to fly.

There are four ways of correcting the comma splice, any of which will do the work. Which one is best in any given case will depend upon the closeness or kinship of the ideas expressed in the two spliced sentences. The four ways are these : —

I. Make two sentences, using a period instead of a comma.
II. Use a semicolon instead of a comma.
III. Add a conjunction between the sentences.
IV. Reduce one of the sentences (usually the first) to the level of (*a*) a phrase or (*b*) a clause.

If we apply these remedies in turn to the four offending sentences quoted above, we get the following results. The starred sentences are best.

Right: 1. I do not care for any more fruit. I have had enough. (I)
Also Right: 1. *I do not care for any more fruit; I have had enough. (II)

Also Right: 1. *I do not care for any more fruit, for I have had enough. (III)

Also Right: 1. I do not care for any more fruit, having had enough. (IV *a:* second sentence reduced to a phrase)

Also Right: 1. I do not care for any more fruit, because I have had enough. (IV *b:* second sentence reduced to a clause)

Right: 2. *I felt sure that he would come. I never knew him to break a promise. (I)

Also Right: 2. I felt sure that he would come; I never knew him to break a promise. (II)

Also Right: 2. *I felt sure that he would come, for I never knew him to break a promise. (III)

Also Right: 2. I felt sure that he would come, never having known him to break a promise. (IV *a:* second sentence reduced to a phrase)

Also Right: 2. I felt sure that he would come, because I never knew him to break a promise. (IV *b:* second sentence reduced to a clause)

It will be noted that in these first two type sentences any one of the four methods of correction can be used, though not with equal effectiveness. In the third and fourth sentences, however, not all the methods can be applied.

Right: 3. I took my watch to the jeweler's to be fixed. He found a good deal of dust in it. (I)

Also Right: 3. I took my watch to the jeweler's to be fixed, and he found a good deal of dust in it. (III)

Also Right: 3. *When I took my watch to the jeweler's to be fixed, he found a good deal of dust in it. (IV *b:* first sentence reduced to the rank of a clause)

Right: 4. He put the little bird on a twig in the cedar tree. It just stood there without trying to fly. (I)

Also Right: 4. *He put the little bird on a twig in the cedar tree, but it just stood there without trying to fly. (III)

Also Right: 4. *When he put the little bird on a twig in the cedar tree, it just stood there without trying to fly. (IV *b:* first sentence reduced to a clause)

These four sentences clearly illustrate the comma splice and the four ways of curing it. With four right ways of connecting two sentences and only one wrong way, the odds would seem to be in favor of correctness. Both human nature and the comma being what they are, however, careful writers regard their commas with just suspicion. The comma fault is so definite that it can be readily detected, and the cure is so simple that it can be easily applied, but to do so will require watchfulness in revision.

An instructor who was trying especially hard to help his class root out both the period fault and the comma splice from their sentences made a series of tests by having his students correct their own themes with these two errors particularly in mind. He found that while the pupils themselves discovered and corrected only about one third of the period faults, they discovered and corrected nine tenths of the comma splices. From this he concluded that the comma splice is due to carelessness and the no-sentence to ignorance.

A word to the wise is sufficient.

Exercises in the Comma-Splice Fault

Try each of the four methods of correcting the following comma splices and choose the one best suited to each sentence: —

1. My speech was over, I felt that I had failed.
2. Some of the children were well-dressed, others were wearing old, ragged clothes.
3. This is still a good car, it can make sixty miles an hour on a paved road.
4. There we can visit the prisoners, we know how to get permission.
5. The sky is blue, between the leaves of the chestnuts rises the green spire of St. Margaret's Church.
6. After they have left school they will not go through life chaperoned, they must learn to stand on their own legs.
7. The bird dogs are the staunchest allies to the hunters, they not only locate the birds but also retrieve them after the killing.
8. We had that experience once, we don't want it again.
9. "It must be murder," the detective pointed out, "a man can't shoot himself twice through the heart either by accident or on purpose."
10. His desk was piled high with papers, before him were reports on three different cases.
11. He was always rather harsh to her, too, they were never like some fathers and daughters are.
12. "Watch the fullback," a man said, "he is going to try for a field goal."
13. When I bought the radio I paid $25.00 down, the rest is to be paid in monthly installments.
14. A pig is like a person, it must have fresh air and exercise to develop properly.
15. Last week we visited Chicago and Milwaukee, they're on Lake Michigan.

CHAPTER X

Making Sentences Clear

After unity, or rather hand in hand with it, goes coherence, or clearness. Clearness within the sentence depends upon many things, but chiefly upon position, or the order of words. If the word order is right, clearness usually follows as a matter of course.

Clearness will be discussed under the four following heads: —

1. Getting the Main Thought into the Main Clauses
2. The Proper Placing of Modifiers
3. The Proper Use of Reference Words
   (1) Pronouns
   (2) Participles
4. Avoiding Faulty Change in Grammatical Construction

1. Getting the Main Thought into the Main Clause

One of the ever-present problems in writing clear-cut sentences is putting the main thought in the main clause. A complex sentence (see pages 75–82) consists of one independent clause and one or more dependent clauses. The laws not only of good writing but of common sense as well require that the leading idea shall be carried by the independent clause. To do this is not hard if two conditions are met: (1) if the sentence is relatively short, consisting, say, of only two clauses; and (2) if we take time to think the sentence through before beginning to speak it or to write it down.

For example, the relative importance of the main thought and of the secondary or modifying thought in the following four sentences is clear. In each, the modifying thought is in the dependent clause and the main thought is in the independent clause. The main thought is capitalized in order to call attention to it.

Correct: 1. When I look upon the tombs of the great, EVERY EMO-
TION OF ENVY DIES IN ME.

Correct: 2. If a man empties his purse into his head, NO MAN
CAN TAKE IT AWAY FROM HIM.

Correct: 3. Before I ask you to be my friend, I WILL BE OPEN
AND SINCERE WITH YOU.

Correct: 4. Although Greece is a small country, IT HAS PRO-
DUCED MANY GREAT MEN.

The trouble comes when we begin a sentence without knowing how
it will end, and therefore slip into the fault of putting the secondary or
modifying thought in the independent clause and tacking on the main
thought in a trailing dependent clause or phrase.   As one student
who was guilty of a number of errors of this kind explained to the
instructor: "I just kept writing on without stopping to think."   In the
following sentences, for example, the main thought, which is again
capitalized, is banished to the dependent clause or phrase.

Faulty: 1. I had acquired a liking for the law, SO I DECIDED TO
GO TO COLLEGE.

Faulty: 2. They were just turning the corner, WHEN THEY
HEARD THE NOISE OF A SHOT.

Faulty: 3. It was a cool, shady place, SO WE DECIDED TO EAT
LUNCH THERE.

Faulty: 4. The distinguished visitor advanced to the front of the
platform WHEN THE WHOLE AUDIENCE ROSE
AND CHEERED.

Faulty: 5. He was weakened by age and disease, DYING BEFORE
ANY OF THE OTHERS.

The remedy in all such cases is simple: reverse the situation and put
the secondary or modifying thought in the dependent clause, and give
the main thought to the main clause: —

Correct: 1. As I had acquired a liking for the law, I DECIDED
TO GO TO COLLEGE.

Correct: 2. Just as they were turning the corner, THEY HEARD
THE NOISE OF A SHOT.

Correct: 3. Since it was a cool, shady place, WE DECIDED TO
EAT LUNCH THERE.

Correct: 4. When the distinguished visitor advanced to the front
of the platform, THE WHOLE AUDIENCE ROSE
AND CHEERED.

Correct: 5. Weakened by age and disease, HE DIED BEFORE
ANY OF THE OTHERS.

Exercises in Getting the Main Thought into the Main Clause

Improve the following sentences by putting the main thought in the independent clause and the secondary or modifying thought in a dependent clause : —

1. We were driving slowly down a little side road in the woods when we saw a deer with a lovely little fawn.
2. I was about to enter the house when I heard someone cry, "Fire!"
3. She was looking at the new car with great interest when the salesman came up and asked what she thought of it.
4. I was walking down the street when I heard the firebell ring.
5. Tom was hurrying to school yesterday, when he suddenly met an old friend.
6. It is raining hard, and I can't see how to drive.
7. He was talking to me in the drugstore when we heard a tremendous thunderclap.
8. The proprietor was closing up the store last night when he was held up by a burglar.

2. The Proper Placing of Modifiers

Between the time of King Alfred and that of Chaucer, the English language lost most of its inflections — that is, lost those word changes which show such functions as number, case, person, tense, and so forth. In particular, except in pronouns, the ending that showed the objective case was worn off, so that no way remains of telling from how a noun looks whether it is the subject or the object of a verb. Adjectives likewise lost all outward indications of whether they modify a singular or a plural noun and whether that noun is masculine, feminine, or neuter. For all genders and both numbers only one form remains.

As a result of such changes as these, the order of words in an English sentence has become of the greatest importance. There is an old legal saying, "Possession is nine points of the law." In English, position is nine points of the sentence. As was indicated in the section on Parsing, page 24, *The dog bit the boy* means one thing, while *The boy bit the dog* means something entirely different, though no change in the words themselves has taken place, but only a change in their position. And to continue the illustration, no living person could tell the meaning of such word orders as those on the following page.

> Bit the dog the boy.
> Bit the boy the dog.
> The dog the boy bit.
> The boy the dog bit.

Thus out of the six possible combinations, those five words can be arranged in one way only in order to bring out the desired meaning unmistakably, namely, *The dog bit the boy.*

The same principle is particularly true of modifiers. For both clearness and effectiveness, the position of all modifiers must be carefully attended to. It usually makes a big difference where they are put.

KINDS OF MODIFIERS

On the basis of complexity, **modifiers are of three degrees: words, phrases, and clauses.** Whether a modifier is a word, a phrase, or a clause, however, it does the same work in the sentence and should be *put as close as possible* to that which it modifies.

Examine the following four sentences. They illustrate both the two kinds of modifiers, adjective and adverb, and the three degrees of modification, word, phrase, and clause.

Adjective Modifiers

Word	*Phrase*	*Clause*
1. The *corner* house is mine.	The house *on the corner* is mine.	The house *that is on the corner* is mine.
2. The *long-haired* dog is a setter.	The dog *with the long hair* is a setter.	The dog *that has long hair* is a setter.

Adverb Modifiers

3. He came *unwillingly.*	He came *against his will.*	He came *although he was unwilling.*
4. The dog ran *fast.*	The dog ran *at a rapid rate.*	The dog ran *as fast as he could.*

The trouble with all modifiers, whether word, phrase, or clause, is that they have no discretion. They do not seem to care in the least what they modify. You may have seen a live crab in a bucket. It scuttles around waving its claws wildly and clutches desperately at everything in reach. Sticks, fingers, toes, forks, even another crab —

everything that comes within reach it instinctively seizes. Modifiers are like that; they attach themselves to the thing nearest them, with no regard to either logic or meaning.

Notice the following absurdities. They are all due to the fondness that modifiers always display toward their nearest neighbors: —

1. Only he lost his hat (nobody else did).
   He only lost his hat (nobody stole it).
   He lost only his hat (and nobody else's).
   He lost his only hat (he never had but one).
   He lost his hat only (but saved his shoes and clothes).
2. Lost: A silk umbrella by an old gentleman with a carved ivory head.
3. Wanted: Gentleman wishes room and board with garage space for wife in refined private home.
4. Wanted: Double bed wanted cheap by an elderly lady with wooden head and foot, wire springs, and mattress.
5. The captain's wife wore a diamond pin in her hair which had been bought in Paris.
6. He struck the goldfish bowl with his head, which was fortunately empty.

In such extreme cases as these the error is both clear and easy to correct. The misplaced modifier must be moved and put in the right place, immediately touching what it modifies, so that nothing can come between them and divorce them.

Exercises in the Proper Placing of Modifiers

1. She lived in the fear of being permanently discharged for two years.
2. I have read the diary that my sister wrote many times.
3. I almost caught ten fish last week.
4. I neither like history nor mathematics.
5. He not only is dishonest but a coward as well.
6. He invited us either to come on Friday or on Saturday.
7. The child tried to swallow the pill three times.
8. The blaze was extinguished before much danger had been done to the house by the firemen.
9. His father told him to never do that.
10. He said on New Year's he would turn over a new leaf.
11. Pompey wished to go home to see his wife and children whom he loved once in a while. — *Boners*
12. As I approached the front door I glimpsed a man carrying a heavy package who resembled my father very much. — *Boners*

3. The Proper Use of Reference Words

(Pronouns and Participles)

(1) PRONOUNS

In the previous section, a modifier was compared to a crab, fastening upon everything within reach. By the same token, a pronoun is like a mirror. A mirror reflects whatever is nearest it regardless of everything except the nearness of what it reflects. So, too, a pronoun insists on referring to whatever noun is nearest it, regardless of logic or meaning. To pronouns, provided that the number and gender are satisfactory, all antecedents look alike. Of all the parts of speech, therefore, pronouns are among the hardest to manage. Loosely handled, they cause a large number of errors.

Mistakes in pronouns fall under three classes: (1) wrong reference, (2) ambiguous reference, and (3) no reference. (1) In wrong reference, the pronoun refers to the wrong antecedent; (2) in ambiguous reference, the pronoun refers to too many antecedents; and (3) in no reference, the pronoun has no antecedent to refer to.

1. WRONG REFERENCE

In instances of wrong reference, the pronoun refers to the wrong antecedent, usually because the wrong antecedent stands between the pronoun and its rightful antecedent. Amusing results often follow mistakes of this kind.

1. He pulled out an old handkerchief, blew his nose, and then put it in his pocket.
2. The captain of the ship swam ashore, and so did the cook. She was insured for fifty thousand dollars, and was heavily loaded with pig-iron.
3. The Woman's Missionary Society met Wednesday evening with Mrs. ____. Miss Minerva ____ read a paper on "Personal Devils." Sixteen were present. (*From a county newspaper*)
4. Last night I lay in a gondola on the Grand Canal at Venice, drinking it all in, and life never seemed so full before.
5. If fresh milk disagrees with the baby, it should be boiled.
6. In the statue, "The End of the Trail," the Indian is on horseback with his tail between his legs.

Anyone, Anybody, Everyone, Everybody — THEY!

An important variety of wrong reference is the use of a plural pronoun to refer to a singular antecedent. The four worst trouble makers are *anyone, anybody, everyone,* and *everybody.* Each of these is definitely singular in form, and should therefore be referred to by a singular pronoun. Thus, *If anybody calls, ask him to wait* is right, while *If anybody calls, ask them to wait* is wrong. For two reasons, however, it is very hard to keep from using a plural pronoun to refer to *anyone, anybody, everyone,* and *everybody.* In the first place, all four of these words, although singular in form, are plural in effect. *Everyone* and *everybody* are equivalent to *all;* and *anyone* and *anybody* likewise mean any possible one, hence every possible one, hence all. In the second place all four words are of common gender — that is, they refer indifferently to males and females alike. There is, however, no common singular personal pronoun in English, but only *he, she,* and *it.* When, therefore, we refer to *anyone* or *everyone* by a singular personal pronoun, we have to choose between the sexes, and say either *he* or *she,* although in the first instance *anyone* or *everyone* may be thought of as neither masculine nor feminine but as both. These two reasons make it much easier and more natural to say *anyone — they* or *everyone — they* than to say *everyone — he* or *anyone — he.* Everybody, authors and teachers included, would like to use *they, their,* and *them* to refer to these words instead of using *he, his, him,* or *she, her, her.* It may be that the two reasons mentioned above will gradually establish the plural pronoun reference as correct. In fact, in loose, colloquial usage the plural pronoun seems already fairly well established. So far as we are concerned, however, we should in serious writing continue to use the inconvenient, but correct, singular.

Loose: 1. Every member of the camping party must bring their own bedding.

Better: 1. Every member of the camping party must bring his own bedding.

Loose: 2. Anybody can do this if they try.

Better: 2. Anybody can do this if he tries.

Loose: 3. If everybody has finished their work, they can go home.

Better: 3. Whoever has finished his work can go home.

Also Better: 3. All who have finished their work can go home.

Loose: 4. If anybody thinks it is an easy job to manage a school
              paper, they will change their minds if they ever
              try it.

Better: 4. If anybody thinks it is an easy job to manage a school
              paper, he will change his mind if he ever tries it.

2. AMBIGUOUS REFERENCE

Ambiguous means "doubtful," "uncertain," and comes from a
Latin word that means to "wander around." **In cases of ambiguous
reference the pronoun refers not to one antecedent but to several
antecedents, and confusion results.**

1. When anyone passed he gave him a kick.
2. The man was driving an old ox when he became angry and kicked
   him, hitting his jawbone with such force as to break his leg.
3. When Will saw his father he asked him to go to the bank and cash
   a check for him, but he said he was too busy.
4. One woman, meeting another, said to her that her children were
   playing in her yard among her flowers, and that they were nearly
   ruined, and she had better look after them.

The confusion among pronouns and antecedents in sentences 3 and
4 is so great that such sentences have been called the Who's Who
sentences. In sentences of this kind the surest remedy is to quote
directly what was said.

Sentence 3 would thus read : —

When Will saw his father he said, "Please go to the bank and cash a
check for me," but his father said that he was too busy.
Also clear : When Will saw his father Will asked him to go to the bank
and cash a check for him, but his father said he was too busy.

Likewise, according to either of its two most probable meanings,
sentence 4 could be changed to read as follows : —

One woman, meeting another, said to her : "Your children are playing
in my yard among my flowers. My flowers are nearly ruined, and
you had better look after your children."
One woman, meeting another, said to her : "Your children are playing
in your yard among your flowers. Your flowers are nearly ruined,
and you had better look after them."

3. No Reference

In cases of no reference, the pronoun has no antecedent to refer to, but is loosely used to refer to a whole clause or to a preceding idea. This type of error, although very common, is both hard to detect and hard to correct. It is already winning its way in colloquial usage.

Loose: 1. We do not tear your clothes with machinery.
We do it carefully by hand. (*Laundry advertisement*)
(Grammatically, the only word in the sentence that could correctly serve as the antecedent of *it* is *machinery*. Such reference is absurd. Equally absurd is the loose reference of *it* to the idea of tearing your clothes. The sentence should read: —

Better: 1. We do not tear your clothes with machinery. We do our work carefully by hand.

Loose: 2. A crowd of us went deer hunting last week and killed four of them.

Better: 2. A crowd of us went deer hunting last week and killed four deer.

Loose: 3. He demanded too much of his workmen, and discharged them because they couldn't come up to it.

Better: 3. He demanded too much of his workmen, and discharged them because they couldn't come up to his demands.

The Orphan "Which"

The worst offender in the no-reference type of pronoun errors is the relative *which*. It is so easy to add a final clause to a sentence by means of a *which* that does not refer to any definite antecedent but to the general idea or action conveyed in the sentence. Though this usage is not only highly convenient but also frequent in colloquial speech,[1] it is slipshod, and is usually a sign of loose thinking. It is permissible in informal conversation, but not in serious writing.

[1] The rulings of *Current English Usage*, a monograph of the National Council of Teachers of English, 1932, on *everybody . . . they* and the orphan *which*, are as follows: —
1. Everyone was here, but *they* all went home early. (Established in colloquial use.)
2. Everybody brought *their* own ticket. (Disputable.)
3. I went immediately into the banquet room, *which* was, I found later, a technical error. (Established in colloquial use.)
Not all authorities would agree to these rulings.

Loose: 1. I stuck my head out of the window, which was a foolish thing to do.

Better: 1. I foolishly stuck my head out of the window.

Also Better: 1. Sticking my head out of the window was foolish.

Also Better: 1. It was foolish of me to stick my head out of the window.

Loose: 2. He yelled at his dog as it was crossing the street, which confused it and caused it to get run over.

Better: 2. His yelling at his dog as it was crossing the street confused it and caused it to get run over.

Also Better: 2. The fact that he yelled at his dog as it was crossing the street confused it and caused it to get run over.

Loose: 3. As I was crossing the street I heard an auto horn blare right behind me, which gave me a bad fright.

Better: 3. As I was crossing the street, the blaring of an auto horn right behind me gave me a bad fright.

Also Better: 3. As I was crossing the street, I was badly frightened by the blaring of an auto horn right behind me.

Loose: 4. Her father was one of the meanest and most influential men in town, which made the policemen unwilling to summons her for breaking traffic laws.

Better: 4. The fact that her father was one of the meanest and most influential men in town made the policemen unwilling to summons her for breaking traffic laws.

Also Better: 4. Her father was one of the meanest and most influential men in town, and this fact made the policemen unwilling to summons her for breaking traffic laws.

(2) PARTICIPLES

Along with pronouns, another part of speech which gives constant trouble is the participle. This is because **a participle is two parts of speech at the same time.** For illustrations and examples, see the chapter on the Review of Grammar, pages 50–51 above. On one side the participle is a verb, and (a) if transitive takes an object; (b) if intransitive, it may take a complement; (c) it is modified by adverbs. At the same time, a participle is an adjective, and since it is an adjective *must have a noun or a pronoun to modify.* In connection with this last necessity trouble comes. We start a sentence off with a participial phrase, but when we come to the independent clause we do not provide the participle with anything to modify, and thus leave it hanging or dangling helplessly in space. For this reason this error is known as the hanging or the dangling participle.

The error can be most clearly seen in such humorous instances as the following, in which the participle, having nothing to modify, lays fast hold on the nearest noun and thus makes merry with the meaning.

HANGING PARTICIPLES

1. Entering the churchyard, a large white tombstone is seen.
2. Crossing the field, a deep ditch is seen.
3. Having eaten our lunch, the steamboat departed.
4. Wearing a pale blue skirt and white suède shoes, Father looked at her in admiration.

If the error is as ridiculous as these, it can be easily detected and remedied. When, however, there is nothing funny or unusual about the hanging participle, it often escapes notice.

Faulty	1.	Being always a good student, the teacher felt sure he would pass.
Better:	1.	Since he was always a good student, the teacher felt sure he would pass.
Faulty:	2.	Riding rapidly along the highway, it was impossible for us to tell much about the surrounding country.
Better:	2.	Riding rapidly along the highway, we could not tell much about the surrounding country.
Faulty:	3.	Listening intently, a faint groan was heard.
Better:	3.	Listening intently, I heard a faint groan.
Faulty:	4.	Having very little to do, there was a good chance to read as much as we wanted to.
Better:	4.	Having very little to do, we had a good chance to read as much as we wanted to.
Also Better:	4.	Since we had very little to do, we had a good chance to read as much as we wanted to.

From these and the foregoing examples it is easy to see that both pronouns and participles are natural trouble makers. In revising our work we should look upon them both with constant suspicion, in order to see to it that every pronoun is provided with a definite antecedent and that every participle has a definite noun or pronoun to modify. Unattached pronouns and unattached participles have the habit of messing up the best of sentences.

Exercises in the Proper Use of Reference Words

Classify the mistakes in the following sentences as (1) wrong reference; (2) ambiguous reference; (3) no reference; (4) hanging participle. Then correct the mistakes: —

1. After bolting my sandwich the train pulled out.
2. The men went deer hunting, but were unable to find any.
3. There go the Joneses in their new car; she is driving as usual.
4. She often became angry, but it was soon over.
5. Hunting takes one outdoors, and you soon learn to know the different kinds of birds.
6. When you read very hard, it makes your eyes smart by bedtime.
7. If a fact does not fit your theory, discard it.
8. After his father finished scolding him, he grew angrier and angrier.
9. Upon going to bed the light should be turned off.
10. I didn't sleep well the night before, which made me late for breakfast.
11. You must be very careful in handling a pistol. They are very dangerous to fool with.
12. When you fill the coffee cup, be very sure not to spill any of it on the tablecloth.
13. It was a rule of the camp that everyone had to be in their room by ten o'clock.
14. The man told his neighbor that he had caught his boy in his strawberry patch the day before and that if he did it again he thought he ought to punish him.
15. If anyone in the audience has lost a gold fountain pen they can get it by going to the ticket window and identifying it.
16. Standing on my front porch, a big silvery Zeppelin came into view in the western sky.
17. The popcorn came in a paper bag and we ate it.
18. Each play on the football field is called out on the radio just as they are made.
19. Having worked so hard it was a pity he failed.
20. Mary asked Lucy where her tennis racket was.

4. Avoiding Faulty Change in Grammatical Construction

(*Parallel Structure for Parallel Ideas*)

One prevalent danger in writing is an unconscious tendency to change constructions midway in a sentence. A famous piece of advice given by Lincoln was, "Don't swap horses in the middle of a stream."

An equally good rule in writing is, "Don't change constructions in the middle of a sentence." If there are two or three ideas of parallel rank in one sentence, these parallel ideas should be expressed in parallel form. Such sentences as the following show various shades of this type of error : —

Faulty : 1. He said that he would return soon and for us to work hard while he was away. (Two parallel ideas, the first expressed in a *that* clause and the second in a *for to* phrase)

Faulty : 2. Football teaches a boy quickness, courage, and what to do in an emergency. (Three parallel ideas, the first two expressed as nouns and the third in a *what* clause)

Faulty : 3. I like taking a long walk in the country and also to ride in a good automobile. (Two parallel ideas, the first expressed in a gerund, or infinitive in *ing*, and the second in the infinitive with *to*)

Faulty : 4. When we finally reached the beach, a beautiful sunset was seen. (Faulty change from the active voice of the first clause to the passive voice of the second clause)

The remedy in all such cases is to give parallel forms to the parallel ideas. There are usually two ways of doing this : (1) change the wording of the first idea so as to make it like the wording of the second idea; or (2) change the wording of the second idea so as to make it like the wording of the first idea. Thus the four sentences above can be improved as follows : —

Better : 1. He said that he would return soon and that we must work hard while he was away. (Both parallel ideas in parallel *that* clauses)

Better : 2. Football teaches a boy quickness, courage, and resourcefulness. (Three parallel ideas in parallel noun form)

Better : 3. I like taking a long walk in the country and also riding in a good automobile. (Both parallel ideas in parallel gerund phrases)

Also Better : 3. I like to take a long walk in the country and also to ride in a good automobile. (Both parallel ideas in parallel infinitive phrases)

Better : 4. When we finally reached the beach, we saw a beautiful sunset. (The active voice of the first clause correctly continued in the second clause)

We should make every effort carefully to avoid such unnecessary shifts in construction as are illustrated in the four original sentences.

Rather, as it is impossible always to compose correct sentences in the rush of getting our first draft on paper, we should in revising watch for all such faulty shifts and make them similar in form.

To put the matter negatively, avoid the following pitfalls : —

(1) Don't pair a clause with a phrase (sentence 1, page 209).

(2) Don't pair a noun with a phrase or a clause (sentence 2, page 209).

(3) Don't. pair an infinitive in *ing* (gerund) with a *to* infinitive (sentence 3, page 209).

(4) Don't change from the active voice to the passive voice (sentence 4, page 209).

In short, express all parallel ideas in similar form.

Exercises in Correcting Faulty Change in Grammatical Construction

In the following examples of mixed structure, try making (1) the first idea similar in form to the second; and (2) the second idea similar in form to the first.   Choose the better form.

1. He decided to go west this summer and on going to Europe next winter.

2. His high grades were due partly to his own hard work and partly because he had a quick mind.

3. At first he thought that she was proud, conceited, and that she had a hard heart.

4. He had trained himself in writing correctly and to speak as correctly as he wrote.

5. The audience are requested to be in their seats when the curtain rises and that they should not interrupt a number by applauding.

6. In the fair grounds was a big crowd, some blowing horns, some throwing confetti, and others walked up and down the midway.

7. In the engineering course students learn the use of a transit and how to survey land.

8. The standing of a student depends both upon his mind and how hard he studies.

9. Although we had fixed the tents and the beds very carefully, an uncomfortable night was spent by all of us.

10. Anyone who wishes to learn the violin must begin young, for you cannot really master it after you are grown.

11. From my window I could look out on the valley, and in the distance beautiful blue mountains could be seen.

12. The army and the navy teach men instant obedience, not to make excuses, and how to control themselves.

CHAPTER XI

Making Sentences Emphatic

As compared with the whole composition or the paragraph the sentence is a very small unit. **Sentence emphasis, therefore, resolves itself chiefly into a question of emphasis by position rather than by space.** The different sentence elements such as subject, verb, object, and the various modifying words and phrases must be shifted around till the unimportant ones are tucked away in the middle of the sentence, and the important word or phrase is placed at the end.

Violations of sentence emphasis will be dealt with under three heads:

1. Baby Sentences
2. Wordy Sentences
3. Something before the Subject
    (1) Putting the Important Idea Last
    (2) Out-of-the-Natural-Order Emphasis
    (3) Loose and Periodic Sentences
    (4) Putting Something before the Subject

1. The Baby Sentence

You will remember that back in first-grade days all the sentences in your primer consisted of tiny, simple statements, one to each sentence. The sentence order was always the same, Subject, Verb, Complement, like this: —

I have a dog. My dog's name is Don. Don sees me. Don runs to
meet me.

We may smile at these baby sentences, but even college students in weaker moments have been known to revert to earlier habits and hand in a paragraph that reads after this fashion: —

Ellen was a beautiful maid. Her cheeks were tinged by the sun. She
lived on an island. This island was in Loch Katrine. It was a very
beautiful island.

In such exaggerated sentences as these the childishness and weakness of the sentence structure can be readily seen. The remedy, likewise, is simple: combine the short, monotonous, simple sentences into larger complex sentences. The four statements about the dog could be put together thus: —

> When my dog Don sees me, he runs to meet me.

The four statements about Ellen and her island might be combined in either of the two following ways: —

> Ellen was a beautiful maid who lived on a lonely island in Loch Katrine; or, On a beautiful island in Loch Katrine lived a lovely maid whose name was Ellen.

Even after being properly combined, the two sentences are not world-beaters, but they clearly mark a tremendous advance in maturity over the two sets of separate kindergarten statements.

Consciously, as we write and revise, we should try to keep from writing too many short simple sentences or too many compound sentences held together by *and's* and *but's* and *so's*. It is a sign of growing maturity and mental development to increase our average of complex sentences wisely linked together by such connectives as *when, where, since, because, although, if, unless, so that,* and so forth.

In particular, two childish sentence patterns are to be avoided, the *and* habit and the *so* habit.

(1) THE *AND* HABIT

Just one step removed from the kindergarten stage of "I have a dog," "My dog's name is Don," comes the practice of linking simple sentences in twos and threes by means of the much overworked *and*.

Faulty:	1.	I have a dog, and he is a setter.
Better:	1.	I have a dog. He is a setter.
Also Better:	1.	I have a setter dog.
Also Better:	1.	My dog is a setter.
Faulty:	2.	The lifeguard was a big, fine-looking fellow, and his name was William.
Better:	2.	The lifeguard, whose name was William, was a big, fine-looking fellow.
Also Better:	2.	The lifeguard was a big, fine-looking fellow named William.

Faulty: 3. "Thanatopsis" is a beautiful poem about death and it was written by Bryant.

Better: 3. "Thanatopsis," a beautiful poem about death, was written by Bryant.

Also Better: 3. "Thanatopsis," a poem by Bryant, is a beautiful treatment of death.

The trouble with such sentences as these is that the two ideas linked by *and* are not equal in value — in other words, are not co-ordinate. One of the two ideas is distinctly secondary to the other and therefore should not be joined to the main idea by *and*, which shows equality of value. Instead, the secondary idea should be expressed in a modifying word, phrase, or clause which gives the exact relationship and the relative importance of the two ideas expressed. Thus, in the sentences quoted, "I have a dog and he is a setter," the two ideas (1) that I own a dog and (2) that this dog is a setter are wrongly co-ordinated. If the fact that I own a dog is uppermost in the writer's mind, the best way to put it is, "I own a setter dog," while if the fact that this dog is a setter is uppermost, the best way to put it is, "My dog is a setter."

Thus at bottom the *and* sentence is the result of loose thinking. In order to avoid it or, if it is found, to correct it, the exact relationship between the ideas must first become clear to the writer and then be made clear to the reader by the way the secondary idea is subordinated to the main idea. The problem of breaking the *and* habit, therefore, is much the same as that of getting the main thought into the main clause, discussed on pages 197 to 199 above.

(2) THE *SO* HABIT

Equally prevalent and equally slipshod with the *and* habit is the *so* habit.

Faulty: 1. The cook is sick, so we shall either have to go out for dinner or cook it ourselves.

Better: 1. The cook is sick; consequently we shall either have to go out for dinner or cook it ourselves.

Also Better: 1. Since the cook is sick, we shall either have to go out for dinner or cook it ourselves.

Faulty: 2. She was very tired after her long trip, so she went to bed early.

Better :   2. She was so tired after her long trip that she went to
                   bed early.
Also Better : 2. Because she was very tired after her long trip, she
                   went to bed early.
Faulty :   3. She wanted to create a good impression, so she wore
                   her prettiest dress.
Better :   3. Because she wanted to create a good impression, she
                   wore her prettiest dress.
Also Better : 3. She wanted to create a good impression; therefore she
                   wore her prettiest dress.

While the *and* and *so* habits are very similar, the *so* habit is easier
to correct than the *and* habit for the following reason : almost any
relationship between ideas may be loosely expressed by *and*, and hence
the exact relationship must be discovered before the weakness is corrected. On the other hand, *so* expresses only two relationships :
(1) usually cause or reason ; (2) sometimes result. To correct the
loose use of *so*, therefore, is simple. There are three ways of doing
it : —

(1) Instead of *so* use *consequently*, *therefore*, or *hence* preceded by a
semicolon.

(2) Begin the sentence with *since* or *because* and omit *so*.

(3) If the relationship is result, use *so* in the first clause as a modifier followed by *that* to introduce the second clause. For example : —

Faulty   We were tired by the time we reached Richmond, so we decided
            to spend the night there.
Better : We were so tired by the time we reached Richmond that we
            decided to spend the night there.

Let it be noted that there is nothing inherently or grammatically
wrong with either the *and* or the *so* habit. Both are natural and
convenient ways of expressing our random thoughts. They are permissible in conversation and in informal personal letters. They are
as easy-going as a pair of old shoes. In themes, however, and in
serious writing they should not be used. Avoid them whenever it is
possible. No one would think of wearing bedroom slippers to a party.
As host or hostess to our readers we should treat them — and our
thoughts — with equal respect.

Exercises in Correcting the "And" and the "So" Habit

Find other and better connectives for the *and's* and *so's:* —

1. Everyone was nice to us, so we enjoyed our visit very much.
2. John came home and the dog was dead.
3. The visitor arrived promptly at six o'clock and then he went to his room.
4. Our auto broke a rear spring under the heavy load, so we had to postpone our trip till later.
5. I have a dog, and it is partly white and partly black.
6. The tire was almost entirely worn out, so we decided not to have it vulcanized.
7. The Thomsons didn't have enough money to pay cash for their new radio, so they bought it on the installment plan.
8. These negro boatmen are very skillful, and launch their boat through the surf with little difficulty.
9. He was getting angry at her teasing, so she decided to stop.
10. At the end of the midway is a small grandstand, and this is always crowded at night.
11. It began to rain at breakfast time, and by dinner time it was raining harder than ever, so we decided to put off the trip.
12. The foundation is next put into place, and it may consist of either brick or concrete.

2. Wordy Sentences

Probably the greatest bar to clean, firm sentences is wordiness. Using too many words will make even good ideas waver and stumble along instead of forging straight ahead. There is a proverb to the effect, Blessed is the man who makes two blades of grass grow where one grew before. The reverse of this should be the writer's aim — to make one word grow where two grew before. Wordiness is the foe both of emphasis and of effectiveness. No sentence can be either striking or pleasing that is rambling and wordy.

The habit of using too many words is the besetting sin of all beginning writers. Experienced critics estimate that 30 per cent of the words in the average freshman theme could profitably be omitted. Think that statement over. If true, it means that every C theme you write could be greatly improved by being compressed into two thirds of its original length. That is, if you average two hundred words to the page and the completed theme is two and a half pages long, at least a hundred and fifty words could profitably be cut out, approximately three fourths of a page. This is a serious charge against freshman theme work, and you should test out its personal application to your own writing. The instructor's criticism and help will be very valuable here.

One trouble with detecting and remedying this quality of wordiness is that it is a general rather than a specific fault. The No-Sentence blunder, for example, described on page 190, and the Proper Placing of Modifiers, dealt with on pages 199–201, are both very definite errors, and can be spotted almost as clearly as a mistake in multiplication. Wordiness, however, is vague and pervasive. Unless it is very flagrant it is hard to put your finger upon it and say, "Here lies the fault." It is often accompanied by repetition of word and phrase, and sometimes by the use of big words and a general clumsiness of expression. Consider the fuzzy, confused effect of such writing as this : —

> I think one's home town should be very closely connected with one's self. It should be something, which, as we grow older, we will look back upon the pleasant memories connected with our home town.
> (35 words)

There is more the matter with this passage than wordiness. If, however, we cut down the number of words as much as we can, we shall find that we have cut out the confusion and the repetition at the same time : —

> Our home town should be so closely connected with us that, as we grow older, we will look back upon it with pleasant memories. (24 words)

Wordy : 1. It was with great difficulty and effort that I wrote my theme last night. (14 words)
Better : 1. I had great difficulty in writing my theme last night.
(10 words)
Wordy : 2. There is quite a good bit of labor and expenditure of money involved in the laying out and keeping up of a golf course.
(24 words)
Better : 2. It takes lots of labor and money to lay out and keep up a golf course. (16 words)
Wordy : 3. She spoke to me when we met each other yesterday in a very cool way. (15 words)
Better : 3. She greeted me yesterday very coolly. (6 words)

Wordy: 4. As regards the methods whereby Benjamin Franklin became eminent and famous, there are several good reasons.
(16 words)

Better: 4. There are several good reasons why Benjamin Franklin became famous. (10 words)

Exercises in Improving Wordy Sentences

Trim and tighten the following sentences into as few words as possible: —

1. There is nothing which is more refreshing than a drink of iced lemonade.
2. In the English room is a small reference library containing books to be used in connection with the parallel reading of this course.
3. Without a single opposing vote she was unanimously selected as the prettiest girl in school.
4. He succeeded in landing the fish in a way that was really skillful.
5. The main and principal purpose is to increase the general health of the state as a whole.
6. The far-famed and world-renowned mountains of Switzerland are very beautiful.
7. May I have the pleasure of having an interview with you?
8. There were two great universities which were developed in England during the Middle Ages.
9. In making chocolate cake, the first thing to do is to get your ingredients gathered together.
10. There are many purposes that the radio is used for at the present time.
11. The old, worn-out, thin, trembling horse plodded slowly and wearily along.
12. The boy who was tallest was asked to hang the holly over the mantelpiece.
13. A night that is lighted by the moon is best for rowing on the lake.
14. When the mayor went out of office, he was made the recipient of a beautiful silver pitcher.
15. There were over ten thousand people who attended the Thanksgiving game.
16. The wonderful choice of words in "The Raven" is unsurpassed in its superb selection of diction.
17. To read too many books that are sad and depressing is not good for the mind.
18. There are a good many reasons why we should have a new athletic field, and among them the three most important are these:
19. This kind, which is of a deep purple shade, is much more rarely found.
20. There is another story which is very interesting in this collection.

3. Something before the Subject

As was pointed out in the section on the Proper Placing of Modifiers, page 199, the paramount thing in an English sentence is the order of words. For a thousand years the established order has been Subject — Verb — Object or Complement. This order is drilled into us from childhood to old age hundreds of times every day, until it becomes a fixed part of our speech consciousness.

Any change, therefore, from the Subject-Verb-Complement order is unusual and attracts attention to itself. The surest way, then, to emphasize a word or a phrase is to take it out of its expected place and put it somewhere else, just as a plowshare, which attracts little attention in a hardware window, causes a great deal of curiosity on a blue velvet cushion in a jeweler's window. This art of taking words from their expected places and putting them somewhere else has many and important bearings not only on sentence structure but on style in general as well. Remember, as was said on page 188 above, that a sentence is easier to twist and turn than a rubber band. Remember also that to change the order of words is always to change the emphasis on ideas.

The two most important places in the sentence are the beginning and the end, with the end far outranking the beginning. The problem, therefore, of calling attention to an important idea usually resolves itself into how the word or phrase carrying the important idea may be put at the end of the sentence. You have seen how the spotlight in a theater follows the star actress from place to place around the stage, focusing brilliantly upon her. The emphasis of the sentence is focused on the close. That is the place for the important idea.

The effect of this simple fact upon sentence structure is fundamental. Granting that you write with a fair degree of grammatical correctness, nothing will improve your style as much as wise attention to the way your sentences end. The influence of the order of words in the sentence will be discussed in these divisions : —

    (1) Putting the Important Idea Last
    (2) Out-of-the-Natural-Order Emphasis
    (3) The Periodic Sentence
    (4) Putting Something before the Subject

(1) PUTTING THE IMPORTANT IDEA LAST

Read the following paired sentences carefully and notice how the emphasis each time focuses on the end idea.

1. (a) The United States made a momentous decision on April 6, 1917, in declaring a state of war to exist with Germany.

1. (b) In declaring on April 6, 1917, a state of war to exist with Germany, the United States made a momentous decision.

2. (a) What we really are depends on our heart, not on our head.

2. (b) What we really are depends not on our head, but on our heart.

3. (a) And my heart shall nevermore be lifted from out that shadow
   That lies floating on the floor.

3. (b) And my heart from out that shadow that lies floating on the floor
   Shall be lifted — nevermore.

4. (a) But these three, faith, hope, love, now abide; and love is the greatest of these.

4. (b) But now abideth faith, hope, love, these three; and the greatest of these is love.   (Revised Version)

5. (a) I think that you are mistaken, however.

5. (b) However, you are mistaken, I think.

5. (c) I think, however, that you are mistaken.

As we read these sentences, we see the distinct change in emphasis produced by changes in the word order.   Under, or rather within, each word there is an idea, and altering the order of words alters the order of ideas.   Always remember that the end of the sentence is the place for the important idea.   **Specifically, avoid closing with a weak qualifying phrase like *I suppose, however, in my opinion, it seems to me.***

Exercises in Sentence Emphasis

Try the effect of putting some other idea in the end position.

1. A pupil should feel that to hand in dishonest work is beneath him.

2. Professor X is the most popular teacher on the faculty, according to the student opinion.

3. Bottle tops or buttons may be used if checker men are not available.

4. However, I believe I can graduate if I can pass geometry.

5. The thing that people fear most is being laughed at.

6. He might have passed the course if he had studied harder during the term.

7. Most of the workmen are foreign born, I am told.

8. I must have jumped ten feet when I heard the snake hiss.
9. The Washington Monument has become famous throughout the world because of its height and graceful proportions.
10. He could never be guilty of dishonesty, even when it was to his own advantage.
11. I shall go on without him if he does not come soon.
12. I have never been accused of lack of frankness, whatever other faults I may have.
13. The car hit an oily patch and skidded badly as we made a sharp turn around the corner.
14. Anything is worth doing well if it is worth doing at all.
15. Dickens, Mark Twain, and Zane Grey are my favorite authors.

(2) OUT–OF–THE–NATURAL–ORDER EMPHASIS

EMPHASIS BY INVERSION

One striking way to secure emphasis is to invert the usual word order — that is, to turn the sentence exactly around and begin with the object or modifier of the verb and end with the subject. It is as easy to invert a sentence as it is to invert a fraction. The only difference is that in inverting a fraction you turn it upside down, and in inverting a sentence you turn it hind part before. The keynote of the inverted sentence is, The last shall be first.

Read the following sentences in the inverted order, then turn them around to the natural order, and notice how their emphasis evaporates.

1. Blessed are the peacemakers. — MATTHEW V. 9
2. Never again will you catch me doing that.
3. How great a matter a little fire kindleth.
4. How are the mighty fallen!
5. Now is the accepted time.
6. Gone are the days when my heart was young and gay.
7. Silver and gold have I none; but what I have, that give I thee.
— ACTS iii. 6

The publishers of a recent detective story made good use of the inverted order in an advertisement on the book's cover. The capitals are theirs.

A half-smoked cigarette, and the dead woman didn't smoke; a strand torn from her dress, caught on a floor splinter far from the place she died; a finger print on the space bar of the typewriter on which she had written a suicide note — and the finger print not hers!

THESE THREE THINGS young Scotland Yard Inspector P. C. Richardson found when assigned to the sensational case of Naomi Clynes.

The inverted sentence is an unusual way of securing emphasis. It differs from the more common method of putting the most important idea last in that it gives special stress not to the sentence end but to the sentence beginning. Instead of a spotlight in the rear, it carries, as it were, a headlight in front. On this account it is sometimes called the Display Sentence.

Most exclamatory sentences are cast in the inverted order. We say "What a beautiful day!" or "What a sad death!" instead of saying, "The day is very beautiful" or "The death is very sad." Some writers fall into the trick of using too many inverted and too many exclamatory sentences. The tendency of beginning writers, however, is all the other way: they are apt to use none at all. It is a good rule to have at least one inverted or one exclamatory sentence to every page. Form the habit of doing this and you will add to your style a touch of both vividness and variety.

(3) LOOSE AND PERIODIC SENTENCES

For the third time in this chapter let us remind ourselves that the normal order of words in the English sentence is Subject — Verb — Object or Complement. According to whether (*a*) this order is kept, or (*b*) the verb is withheld until the end, sentences are classified as (1) Loose and (2) Periodic.

1. LOOSE SENTENCES

A loose sentence is one which unfolds in the natural order of Subject, Verb, Complement, adding one detail after another until the meaning is complete. A loose sentence can be stopped in one or more places before the end is reached and still make sense. Loose sentences are natural, easy, and effective, if they are not used to the exclusion of other kinds of sentences such as the periodic, the exclamatory, and the inverted forms.

Following are two typical loose sentences. The figure in parentheses after each sentence gives the number of places at which the sentence could be stopped before the end. Find these places and verify the fact that the sentences could be stopped there.

1. The ship finally crept into port, with her crew utterly worn out, her rigging caked with ice, and her hull leaking in several places after her long battle with November gales. (4)
2. The car nearly turned over, after sideswiping the wagon and skidding across the road into the bank. (3)

2. PERIODIC SENTENCES

A periodic sentence is one which, instead of unfolding its meaning as it goes, withholds its meaning until the end is reached. It cannot be stopped before the close and still make sense. It accomplishes this by withholding the verb, always the key word of the sentence, as long as possible, usually till just before the end. An easy way to remember the periodic sentence is to remember that its meaning is not complete until the period is reached.

In order either to write periodic sentences or to make loose sentences periodic, all that is needed is to put the modifying phrases and clauses first and thus save the end place for the verb. For example, the two loose sentences quoted above can be turned into periodic sentences as follows: —

1. With her crew utterly worn out, her rigging caked with ice, and her hull leaking in several places after her long battle with November gales, the ship finally crept into port. (The four prepositional phrases put first; the meaning incomplete till the end)
2. After sideswiping the wagon and skidding across the road into the bank, the car nearly turned over. (The three prepositional phrases put first; the meaning incomplete till the end)

Read carefully the six following sentences and compare them. The first three are loose and the second three periodic. All six are by established writers, and are effective instances of good sentence craft.

Loose Sentences

1. On the other side he looked down into a deep mountain glen, wild, lonely, and shagged, the bottom filled with fragments from the impending cliffs, and scarcely lighted by the reflected ray of the setting sun. — IRVING, "Rip van Winkle"

2. And the little pale, round-shouldered dealer stood almost on tiptoe, looking over the top of his gold spectacles, and nodding his head with every mark of disbelief. — STEVENSON, "Markheim"

3. The old philosopher is still among us in the brown coat with the metal buttons and the shirt which ought to be at wash, blinking, puffing, rolling his head, drumming with his fingers, tearing his meat like a tiger, and swallowing his tea in oceans.
— MACAULAY on Johnson

Periodic Sentences

1. When all the preparations were done and the holy evening come, a sweet enchantment would sink down over them.
— SELMA LAGERLÖF, "A Christmas Guest"

2. Past the mocking bareness of the benches, past the blackboard where the flag, loosed from three of its tacks, hung limp and dispirited, he made his way to the shaky little pulpit.
— BARRET WILLOUGHBY, "The Devil Drum"

3. And pulseless and cold, with a Derringer by his side and a bullet in his heart, though still calm as in life, beneath the snow lay he who was at once the strongest and yet the weakest of the outcasts of Poker Flat.
— BRET HARTE, "The Outcasts of Poker Flat"

All six of these sentences are good. Each accomplishes effectively what the author wished it to accomplish. The loose sentences are easy, natural, and vivid. Vivid too are the periodic sentences, which give the impression of more care and thought than do the loose sentences and which, since they suspend their full meaning till the end, produce a definite effect of focused emphasis.

Two important principles follow from these facts: (1) either the loose or the periodic sentence is good if it is well written; (2) neither the loose nor the periodic sentence is good if it is used to the exclusion of the other. To get the best effect they should be mixed. Too many loose sentences give the impression of careless, slipshod thinking; too many periodic sentences give the opposite effect of an over-careful, artificial style. Since, however, the universal tendency of beginning writers is to use only loose sentences, the point for us to work on consciously and carefully is how to increase our use of periodic sentences.

There is only one way to do this, but it is both easy and effective: *Put something before the subject.*

(4) PUTTING SOMETHING BEFORE THE SUBJECT

Unless we watch our sentences very carefully, we are likely to begin ten out of ten of them with the subject. This results in a monotonous, childish style that reminds the thoughtful reader of rompers, hobbyhorses, dolls, and other accompaniments of the nursery.

Now it is almost impossible for an inexperienced writer to begin a sufficient number of his sentences with something other than subject when he is writing his first draft. In revising, however, anyone can notice whether too many sentences begin with the subject.

The best general rule is to begin from at least a third to a half of your sentences with something other than the subject. After your first draft has been corrected for such elementary errors as grammar, spelling, punctuation, and so on, read each paragraph over carefully to see how your sentences begin. By transferring modifying words, phrases, and clauses to the front of the sentence, you can increase the proportion of something-before-the-subject sentences, greatly to the benefit of the variety and vividness of your style.

Consider the following paragraph from one of the best known of American stories, "Rip van Winkle." It has five sentences, only two of which begin with the subject. Of the other three sentences two begin with adverbial phrases and one with an adjective phrase. These before-the-subject phrases are italicized in order to emphasize them. If you will change them to positions after the verb (indicated in the text by carets), you will notice a decrease in effectiveness.

> *In a long ramble of the kind on a fine autumnal day*, Rip had unconsciously scrambled ∧ to one of the highest parts of the Kaatskill Mountains. He was after his favorite sport of squirrel shooting, and the still solitudes had echoed and re-echoed with the reports of his gun. *Panting and fatigued*, he threw himself, ∧ late in the afternoon, on a green knoll, covered with mountain herbage, that crowned the brow of a precipice. *From an opening between the trees* he could overlook ∧ all the lower country for many a mile of rich woodland. He saw at a distance, the lordly Hudson, far, far below him, moving on its silent but majestic course, with the reflection of a purple cloud, or the sail of a lagging bark, here and there sleeping on its glassy bosom, and at last losing itself in the blue highlands.

This paragraph was written over a hundred years ago. Here is a paragraph from "The Talk of the Town" taken from the October, 1934,

New Yorker. Of its ten sentences five begin with something before the subject. All good writing, whether past or present, avoids the monotony of beginning too many sentences with their subjects. As you read, notice the monotony that would follow from taking the italicized expressions and putting them in the places indicated by carets.

FIELD TRIALS FOR SPANIELS

At intervals after Labor Day every year, about thirty-five hundred pheasants are set loose ∧ on the island in batches of five hundred by the English Springer Spaniel Field Trial Association. *By the time of the trials,* the birds are presumably sufficiently acclimated ∧ to behave naturally. The dogs compete in pairs, and each dog has two men with him, a "handler" (sometimes the owner and sometimes a trainer) and a "gun." The gun does nothing but shoot the bird when the dog locates and flushes it. He remains as unobtrusive as possible while the handler, who wears his dog's number on an armband, gives all the orders. *Behind the dogs and men are* two judges ∧. *To their rear* are the steward of the beat (a sort of general manager), a man with a big sign bearing the dogs' names and numbers, and the gallery, generally numbering about a hundred and fifty ∧. The dogs start off together on parallel courses and one of them usually flushes a bird in fifteen or twenty minutes. His gun shoots it, his handler gives orders, the dog retrieves it, and his judge takes notes. *When each entrant has got a bird,* the "series" is over ∧.

An examination of the work of most careful writers such as Macaulay, Carlyle, Stevenson, and others, will show that a large proportion of their sentences do not begin with the subject. Recent writers, too, vary their sentences skillfully between putting the subject first and putting something before the subject. An interesting, mature style cannot be attained in any other way.

Exercises in Putting Something before the Subject

Try several arrangements of the following sentences, in each case putting something before the subject : —

1. The man behind the gun is in the last analysis the one who wins the war.
2. He crept downstairs very early in the morning and lighted the fires.
3. The regiment proudly marched into the cheering city with flags flying and drums beating.

4. Pluck is better than luck, say what you will.
5. Don't let him argue you into signing the petition whatever you do.
6. Determination is better than brilliance in the long run.
7. The piping call of a curlew came faintly from the chilly gray sky.
8. The last of these reasons is undoubtedly the strongest.
9. I knew we were going to be good friends as soon as I saw him smile.
10. A truck ran into a new Rolls-Royce not five minutes before you got here.
11. The soldiers continued to file by one after another in never-ending procession.
12. The mountains rise far ahead on the southern horizon. They look like a blue mist from this distance.
13. My friend gave up duck hunting in disgust, after nearly freezing in the cold wind and bogging down several times in the sticky marsh mud.
14. Mr. Milton has to catch the 7.55 train every morning, no matter how late breakfast is or how sleepy he feels.
15. The doctor at last decided reluctantly to operate after having tried every other remedy.

CHAPTER XII

Making Sentences Pleasing

Thus far we have considered the correcting of mistakes and the tightening of sentences up to an average level of respectability. There now enters the problem of cultivating a pleasing and varied sentence structure and possibly of developing an effective style of our own.

Making sentences Unified and Clear is a duty: *You must.*

Making sentences Emphatic is a responsibility: *You ought.*

Making sentences Pleasing is an ideal: *You will if you can.*

Making sentences pleasing depends upon a multitude of things. As much as anything else it depends upon the choice of words. Words and their ways form the subject of Part III, pages 319–424. So far as structure is concerned, however, sentence effectiveness may be considered under three heads: —

1. Variety
2. The Short, Memorable Sentence
3. The Balanced Sentence

1. Variety

Sentences may be divided according to three principles: —

I. According to Grammar
   (1) Simple
   (2) Complex
   (3) Compound
       (See pages 71–84.)
II. According to the Order of Words
   (1) Loose
   (2) Periodic
       (See pages 221–223.)

III. According to the Number of Words
    (1) Long
    (2) Short

Of course these divisions are not exclusive, but overlap each other. We may have, for example, a short, loose, simple sentence or a long, periodic, complex sentence, and so on.

The important point is that although there are many kinds of sentences and although each kind is good in itself, no kind is good if it is used too much. Variety is necessary. We must not write too many simple sentences one after the other, or too many compound sentences, or too many of any kind whatsoever. Emerson's lines in "Each and All" describe the situation exactly : —

> All are needed by each one ;
> Nothing is fair or good alone.

Both simple and compound sentences need a fair proportion of complex sentences to set them off to the best advantage ; short sentences should be varied with long, and loose sentences should be interspersed with periodic. In fact, writing a paragraph is not unlike making a cake : good materials are of course necessary, but it is equally necessary to blend the materials in the right proportion.

In seeking for sentence variety, therefore, each writer must revise his work with that particular purpose in view. He should take as a basis the threefold division suggested above : namely, the kinds of sentences according to (1) grammar, (2) the order of words, and (3) the number of words. With this in mind as he revises, he should look over his work a paragraph at a time, and ask himself such questions as these : —

1. What is my favorite kind of sentence? (The answer will probably be the short simple or the short compound.)

2. Do I use this kind of sentence too much, and thus exclude other and possibly better sentence forms?

3. Has my sentence structure enough variety to avoid monotony and poverty of thought?

4. What is my average sentence length?

As regards sentence length, it is interesting to note how widely the practice of different writers varies. Some of the best of the older essayists, like Carlyle, Ruskin, and Stevenson, have an average sentence length of something like thirty words; Macaulay averages from twenty to twenty-five; Emerson, close to twenty; college freshmen, around fourteen. Your own average will probably not be far from fifteen words, or say, roughly, a line and a half to two lines. If this is true, and you find that you are prone to write too many two-line sentences, vary them by an occasional one-line sentence, and a more than occasional three- or four-line sentence.

Drawing together the different sections of the chapter which touch on this matter of sentence variety, we may summarize them in a series of directions. To form the habit of following these directions as you revise will go far toward helping you to acquire a varied, pleasing style.

(1) FOR THE SAKE OF VARIETY

1. Diagnose your own sentence structure and find what kind of sentence you use too much and what kinds you use too little. The instructor's aid on this point will be most helpful.

2. Something before the subject. On the average, see to it that from a third to a half of your sentences begin with something before the subject. (See pages 218–220.)

3. The inverted sentence. Of your something-before-the-subject sentences, put at least one on every page in the inverted order, that is, Complement — Verb — Subject. (See pages 220–221.)

4. Try the effect of having at least (a) one exclamatory sentence and (b) one interrogative sentence on every page.

5. Vary your sentence length purposely. On the average, for every five sentences that are two lines long, have one sentence that is one line long and two sentences that are three or four lines long.

2. The Short, Memorable Sentence

"An epigram," said Arlo Bates, "is a notion rounded like a snowball for throwing." This both defines and illustrates what a short, memorable sentence should be.

In our writing we should try our best to make an occasional sentence like that — pithy, pungent, striking. The ideal place for such a sentence is either at the beginning of the theme, in order to attract the reader at the outset, or at the end of each paragraph, in order to round off and drive home the paragraph idea.

In the October, 1934, issue of *Outdoor Life*, Douglas Marsh has an article on snakes which begins as follows: "People have more fool ideas about snakes than about any other subject, not excluding love and money." Though highly informal, this is a good opening sentence, for it puts an idea strikingly and makes us want to read further to find out which of our notions about snakes are foolish. Think how many more people will read the article than if it had opened thus: "There is a great deal of ignorance and mistaken information about snakes prevalent in the minds of most people."

The need for good end-sentences was pointed out on page 12 above. Each paragraph, so far as it is within your power, should close firmly and crisply. No matter how good — or how poor — a paragraph may be, it is helped by a striking close, and hurt by a stringy, sprawly close. Nothing but the best sentence you can possibly write is worthy of the place of honor at the end of a paragraph, or, for an even better reason, at the end of a theme. First impressions are strong, but last impressions are stronger. Incidentally, do not forget the value of brevity. Rarely should your end-sentence be more than a line and a half or two lines long.

Here are interesting examples of pungent, striking sentences, "notions rounded like snowballs for throwing."

1. Good libraries are not made; they grow.
2. A fool is a man who is intelligent at the wrong time.
3. Education is the cheap defence of nations.
4. Unto the pure all things are pure.
5. A sword, a spade, and a thought should never be allowed to rust.
   — JAMES STEPHENS
6. You can't tell whether an author is alive until he is dead.
   — WALTER RALEIGH
7. There never was a good war or a bad peace.
8. Poetry is the record of the best and happiest moments of the happiest and best minds. — SHELLEY
9. A smart man is one who hasn't let a woman pin anything on him since he was a baby. — *Cokesbury Pi*

Bring in two similar examples that you have found in your reading, and comment on them in class.

3. The Balanced Sentence

Often sentences gain point and pungency if they are balanced. A balanced sentence is one which sets similar or contrasted ideas over against one another in matched and paired clauses and phrases. The paired clauses and phrases not only match each other in thought but are parallel in structure as well. This similarity of structure gives tremendous emphasis to the parallel ideas. A good balanced sentence is hard to write, but is exceedingly effective. Experiment with trying to make at least one good balanced sentence in your next theme.

Read the following balanced sentences more than once, noticing how the thought is paired and the expression is parallel.

1. If you call a man friend, do not doubt him; if you doubt him, do not call him friend.
2. When reason is against a man, he will be against reason.
3. Character is what we are; reputation is what people think we are.
4. As we account for every idle word, so must we account for every idle silence. — BENJAMIN FRANKLIN
5. A gentleman is unselfish because he never remembers himself, and courteous because he never forgets himself.
6. Some books are to be tasted, others to be swallowed, and some few to be chewed and digested. — FRANCIS BACON
7. The notice which you have pleased to take of my labors, had it been early, had been kind; but it has been delayed till I am indifferent, and cannot enjoy it; till I am solitary, and cannot impart it; till I am known, and do not want it.
   — SAMUEL JOHNSON TO THE EARL OF CHESTERFIELD
8. There were gentlemen and there were seamen in the navy of Charles II; but the seamen were not gentlemen and the gentlemen were not seamen. — MACAULAY
9. A cynic is one who never sees a good quality in a man, and never fails to see a bad one. — HENRY WARD BEECHER
10. Parents spend half their time worrying how a child will turn out, and the rest of the time wondering when a child will turn in.
11. Imagination was given to man to compensate him for what he is not; a sense of humor to console him for what he is.

THE ROUND TABLE

(Based on the four preceding chapters)

1. (*a*) Take your last theme and draw a ring around every *and* and every *so* which connects clauses. Revise the sentences so as to substitute other and more exact connectives. Then notice the improvement. (*b*) Write at least one theme without using a single *and* or a single *so* to connect clauses.

2. Take any of your themes with a grade of C and condense it into two thirds of its present length.

3. Examine your last two themes for the proportion of loose and periodic sentences. Be prepared to give the figures in class, and to discuss them in the light of what other students are doing in this regard.

4. Look over your last two themes and see whether you have used a single (*a*) inverted, (*b*) exclamatory, or (*c*) interrogative sentence.

5. Count the sentences in your last theme and see how many begin with the subject and how many with something other than the subject.

6. Examine at least two of your themes for the proportion of sentences (*a*) under two lines long and (*b*) over two lines long.

7. Ask the instructor to assign to the class five older authors and five more recent authors to discover their average sentence length. Divide the passages up among the class so that no assignment will be too long.

8. As a class exercise write an independent paragraph on one of the subjects suggested on pages 16–18 above. Let the paragraph consist wholly of short, simple sentences of the Subject-Verb-Complement type. Next day rewrite the paragraphs using as many kinds of sentences as possible, such as the exclamatory, the interrogative, and the inverted. Do not leave a single sentence that begins with the subject. Compare the versions.

9. From your reading find short, memorable sentences and striking balanced sentences to bring to class and read aloud.

10. What do you consider the best two or three sentences you have written thus far this term?

11. What is the most beautiful prose passage you have ever read? Bring it to class and read it aloud. Start making a short collection of beautiful prose passages to be compared with your favorite poetic passages.

12. Here is an amusing take-off on a certain type of sentence which may be called the men-may-come-and-men-may-go-but-I-go-on-forever sentence. In passing, note that it is a good character sketch as well as a clever parody.

My dear Miss Price,

How awfully sweet of you to ask me to stay with you for a few days but how can you think I may have forgotten you for of course I think of you so very often and of the three ears I spent in your school because it is such a joy not to be there any longer and if one is at all down it bucks one up derectly to remember that thats all over atanyrate and that one has enough food to nurrish one and not that awful monottany of life and not the petty fogging daily tirrany you went in for and I can imagine no greater thrill and luxury in a way than to come and see the whole dismal grind still going on but without me being in it but this would be rather beastly of me wouldnt it so please dear Miss Price dont expect me and do excuse mistakes of English Composition and etcetra in your affectionate old pupil,

EMILY THERESE LYNN-ROYSTON

ps, I often rite to people telling them where I was educated and highly reckomending you.[1]

Miscellaneous Sentence Errors
for Correction
(Based on the four preceding chapters)

Name and correct the errors in the following sentences.

1. If you will turn to the appendix, the example I quoted will be found.
2. I am sure everyone had a good time and enjoyed themselves all day.
3. He borrowed the clothes with which he disguised himself from a friend.
4. If one will study hard in high school and college the chances are they will amount to something in later life.
5. He was not strong, so he refused to work in the mines.
6. If you told someone that you lived in a cubicle, they might not know what you meant.
7. The art of chewing gracefully the lips held closely together in my mind is a cultivated man.
8. Playing tennis is more fun than to play golf.
9. He was kind, likable, and had a generous nature.
10. I have only heard from her once this summer.
11. The judge sentenced him to jail for having been helplessly drunk for ten days.
12. Everyone expressed their regret at having to leave so early.
13. When the war was over, each state had a celebration to welcome their home regiments.
14. No man would work hard to make a living if they could get one in any other way.
15. After some discussion we decided not to drive any further that night. The road being slippery and dangerous when it strikes the mountains.
16. Last year I had four classes a day. Each being forty-five minutes in length.

[1] Taken from *And Even Now* by Max Beerbohm, published and copyrighted by E. P. Dutton and Company, Inc., New York.

17. There are three subjects that give me a great deal of trouble, they are Latin, History, and English.
18. I was watching a large three-master sailing down the coast through my father's field glasses.
19. I thank you for your prompt reply, and wishing you a pleasant holiday, I am,

> Yours sincerely,
> TOM WILSON

20. Conan Doyle is the author of *The White Company*, this is an exciting historical novel.
21. If there is any student in the class who can answer this question, I wish they would do so.
22. Not one of the girls would tell their age.
23. The private saluted the lieutenant, which he returned.
24. The schoolhouse needs to be painted badly. Its lack is an eyesore.
25. Everyone should do their own thinking.
26. It seemed as if every time he looked at a donkey he brayed.
27. All the children worked hard picking up the trash, including Mary Wilson.
28. It felt cold when I went out, which led me to wear my overcoat.
29. Every pupil in school is asked to come to the meeting if they possibly can.
30. If you fail in college it will not be because the course is too hard but will be due to your lack of study.
31. Saturday can either be used for work or for recreation.
32. The librarian then gave us some idea of the book. What sort of book it is and who wrote it.
33. At eighteen we are told that Keats was already a great lyric poet.
34. While sitting in class yesterday an English sparrow flew in at the window.
35. While the burglar stole the silver, the family was asleep upstairs.
36. After wandering around for an hour, the right road was found.
37. Everybody thought he would become a great writer ten years ago.
38. A tortoise is a kind of turtle, I have seen one at Hampton Park.
39. In September the bathing is at its best. Particularly at sunset when everyone is at supper.
40. Being very costly, I do not own many first editions.
41. One cannot remember everything the teacher tells you.
42. Every student came to the game feeling sure that their team would win.
43. Whenever he met the president he always greeted him cordially.
44. Robert's father died when he was six years old.
45. Strikes are responsible for disorder, loss of wages, and they stir up trouble and hard feelings.

46. In my opinion, Reeves was a tricky sort of customer, in spite of the high opinion that Norman had of him.   And unscrupulous at that.

47. All women are not free and all men are not equal.

48. The mills refused to raise wages, which is why they struck.

49. The president told the dean that he was right.

50. The doctor saw the minister going into his house.

51. The customer bought the car, but it was sold by him soon afterwards.

52. A general course is somewhat different you may choose any two subjects besides History and English, these are required.

53. In gym it teaches you to march in correct time and to hold yourself erect.

54. Whether raining, snowing, or hailing, every person in the audience stands, faces the flag, and if it is a man, he removes his hat.

CHAPTER XIII

Letters

The ninety-and-nine will write letters throughout life, and they will write nothing else.

— THOMAS C. BLAISDELL

The Importance of Letter Writing

Next only to conversation, **letters are both the most universal and the most personal form of communication.** In school and college we get useful practice in many varieties of writing — usually in the story and in both kinds of essay, the expository and the informal, as well as in verse and plays. After graduation, however, not more than one person out of a thousand develops sufficient talent to have his work accepted for publication, and thus embark upon the career of an author. There is, however, one kind of writing which the other $99\frac{9}{10}$ per cent will have to do as long as they live — everyone at least once a month, many probably every week, and a few possibly every day. That kind of writing is letters.

Along with the universality of letter writing, and in large measure because of it, goes its importance. The ability to write a good letter means far more than we are apt to realize. For example, it frequently makes the difference between an average and an exceptional business-man; and, what is more important, it often makes the difference between a commonplace acquaintance and a lifelong friend. On the dollar-and-cents side the business world has no time to waste on a firm that conducts its correspondence in a careless, slipshod way; and on the human side as we grow older we come to set increasing store by those among our friends and families who can — and do — write bright, attractive, sincere letters.

Universal and important as letter writing is, it is something more besides: it is the most personal and intimate form of writing. A letter from you is as much a part of you as your voice, your smile, your frown. It represents and reflects you with unforgiving faithfulness: it is you who have chosen the kind of ink and paper; it is you who have selected the person to whom the letter goes; what you say and how you say it depend upon you and you alone. From the stamp affixed on the front to the flap sealing the back, no hand but yours and the postman's has touched it. It is a tiny little book, composed, published, and distributed by one person, proclaiming as it is opened and read: "Mark me well. I come to you as the personal representative of my sender. From me you can tell much of the kind of person he is and what he thinks of you. I only hope that if I look hasty, careless, and inaccurate, you will not judge my sender by me alone, but will let your past and future face-to-face dealings with him remedy my own imperfections."

Too often when writing home we dash off a few scrappy details and close with a request for money or some article that we forgot to take with us — a request that forms the real motive for the letter. This style of letter was once humorously parodied by a father who had a son playing summer baseball in a near-by town and who was not hearing from him as often as he wished. He sent his son a batch of stamped, self-addressed envelopes with a dozen typewritten copies of the following: —

DEAR DAD,
     We played today against ____ and won (lost) by the score of ____ to ____. I went to bat ____ times and got ____ hits (doubles ——, triples ____, home runs ____). I struck out ____ times and walked ____ times. I am feeling ____. Please send me check for $____.

                                                                    Love,
                                                                    ____

Kinds of Letters

In general there are three kinds of letters, the forms of which are to be carefully distinguished and mastered. They are as follows: —

1. Business Letters
2. Formal Invitations and Their Replies
3. Friendly Letters

Since both (1) the business letter and (2) formal invitations have a fixed, definite form, they will be taken up first and explained briefly.

1. Business Letters

The history of business everywhere has been the history of an ever-widening circle of contacts and sales. Modern methods of communication and transportation cross and recross this country like the meshes of a vast web. Orders pour in by mail, telegraph, or long-distance telephone, and are filled by freight, express, parcel post, or truck lines. National advertising in magazines, on billboards, and over the radio creates a nation-wide demand. Mail-order houses do a tremendous business. Tens and hundreds of thousands of customers transact business with firms and factories which they never visit or even see a personal representative of. We have become a nation of long-distance shoppers.

One of the factors that have helped largely to bring about this state of affairs is the business letter, which has been developed to a high degree of efficiency. Every large business house maintains a corps of highly trained correspondents and expert stenographers whose sole function is to write letters: attractive letters on attractive stationery; letters that will result in satisfied customers; letters that will both hold present business and win new business.

As the first requirement, **a business letter must present a pleasing impression while the envelope is being opened and the letter taken out.** Good taste should be evident in every detail: neatness; quality and color of the paper; kind, color, and arrangement of the type in which the firm's name is stamped on the letter sheet; the care with which the letter itself is centered on the page, with ample margins on each side and equal spacing at the top and the bottom, whether the letter is long or short. All such details, which go to make up what is called the letter picture, must be above reproach in dignity and refinement. A letter must please the eye before it pleases the mind.

Most business letters are a combination of exposition and persuasion — that is, they explain and they urge. Prevailingly, however, they explain, for clear explanation is itself an argument, and too much urging usually defeats its own purpose. We sometimes listen to an importunate agent merely because we dislike to ask him to leave, but an overurgent sales letter always finds a ready home in the wastebasket.

The commoner kinds of business letters are six in number, the first three dealing with the financial and the last three with the personal side of business.

1. Letter ordering goods
2. Letter acknowledging order
3. Sales letter
4. Letter of introduction
5. Letter of application
6. Letter of recommendation

Being largely explanatory, **a business letter must strictly observe the general principles of all writing.** It must be perfect in spelling and punctuation. Above all it must be paragraphed with careful strictness, each different item of information being carefully set off by itself in its own separate paragraph, so that the reader can instantly grasp and as easily answer each different point.

(1) THE FIVE C'S

In addition to such general requirements, to reach its highest effectiveness a business letter must have five qualities pre-eminently. **It must be (1) clear, (2) correct, (3) complete, (4) concise, and (5) courteous.** Each of these five adjectives obviously justifies itself, and doesn't need further elaboration. We might call them the Five C's of Good Business Correspondence. They should unfailingly characterize every business communication.

(2) SPECIAL FORM

The business letter is a strictly utilitarian document. It exists for business, not for pleasure, and its object is to convey information as clearly, accurately, completely, concisely, and courteously as possible. For this purpose the long experience of the business world has developed a fixed, definite form. This form consists of six distinct parts. There's a good reason for each part, and hence little cause to alter the arrangement and no excuse for making a mistake.

Its six parts are these: —

(1) Heading
(2) Inside Address
(3) Greeting
(4) Body of the Letter
(5) Complimentary Close
(6) Signature

So far as the letter sheet is concerned, these six parts are distributed and grouped as follows: —

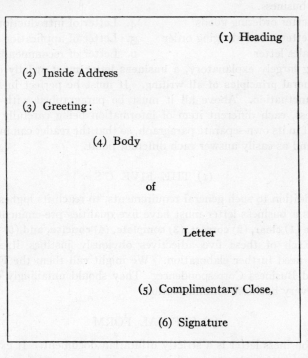

(1) Heading

(2) Inside Address

(3) Greeting:

(4) Body

of

Letter

(5) Complimentary Close,

(6) Signature

(Note that there are only two compulsory punctuation marks: the colon after the greeting and the comma after the complimentary close. See the next section.)

1. THE TWO ARRANGEMENTS OF LINES AND THE TWO SYSTEMS OF PUNCTUATION

With special reference to parts one and two, the heading and the inside address, and likewise the outside address on the envelope, two arrangements of lines are permissible. The older method, which is still standard and indeed recommended by the Post Office Department, is **the indented or slanting order.** In this order, each successive line is set back or indented like the first line of a paragraph, in this fashion : —

_____

_____

_____

The other method, which is newer, and is now the overwhelming favorite for typewritten business letters, is **the block system.** In this, the successive lines are not indented, but begin flush with the same margin, in this fashion : —

_____

_____

_____

Either of these arrangements, as was said, is permissible. The indented arrangement is still usually followed by those who write a letter by hand. The block system is almost unanimous among those who use typewriters.

2. THE TWO SYSTEMS OF PUNCTUATION : CLOSED AND OPEN

There are two prevailing ways of punctuating the heading, the inside address, and the outside address on the envelope. **The older method is the closed, in which commas are used after each line except the last, and a period after the last line.** Closed punctuation can be used with either the indented or the block arrangement of lines. **In the open system no commas or final periods are used,** unless of course a line ends with an abbreviation; then it is followed by a period.

CLOSED PUNCTUATION

Indented Arrangement   *Block System*

_____,   _____,

_____;   _____;

_____.   _____.

OPEN PUNCTUATION

Indented Arrangement   *Block System*

_____   _____

_____   _____

_____   _____

Again, either the closed or the open system of punctuation is correct. The closed system is the older, is still recommended by the Post Office Department, and is usually followed by those who use the indented arrangement of lines and write their letters by hand. The open system is overwhelmingly preferred by those who use the block system and typewrite their letters.

(3) THE BODY OF THE LETTER

The body of the letter is the main thing. All the other parts are merely incidental or preliminary to it. To the Five *C*'s mentioned on page 239 should be added the sixth golden essential of business efficiency — namely, promptness. If possible, all business houses try to answer every letter either the day or the day after it is received. "A clear desk at the end of the day" is a maxim in most offices.

As to form, a large majority of business concerns (*a*) indent each paragraph and (*b*) double space the lines throughout the entire letter. This is known as **the modified block style.** Possibly a fourth of the business houses, however, (*a*) do not indent the paragraphs but leave a double space between paragraphs, and (*b*) single space the lines throughout each paragraph. This is known as **the strict block style.**

The best usage today is away from the stereotyped short cuts, abbreviations, and rubber-stamp expressions of the past, such as the following : —

ult. (for ultimo), the last month
inst. (for instant), the present month
prox. (for proximo), the next month
Yours of the 15th inst. received and contents duly noted. Will say in reply, etc.
I beg to advise
Your esteemed favor
Your valued order
10/12/35 (instead of October 12, 1935)

Likewise the somewhat complicated participial close, which used to be in favor, is losing its hold. Most correspondents avoid such expressions as

> Thanking you for past favors and hoping for a continuation of the same, I remain,
> Thanking you in advance for your kindness in attending to this matter, I am,
> Hoping to be favored with an early order, I am

(4) THE ENVELOPE

The envelope should contain the two following items clearly and correctly given: —

1. The name and address of the sender, in the upper left-hand corner of the envelope or on the back.
2. The name and address of the recipient neatly spaced across the main part of the envelope.

These two addresses (1) may be in either the indented or the block form, and (2) may use either the closed or the open system of punctuation. Both are already contained in the letter itself in the heading and in the inside address. Their form and punctuation on the envelope will of course follow the style used in the letter.

THE ROUND TABLE

1. "Zero for an Error." So clear and definite is the form of the business letter that, once learned, no errors should be permitted. After reading this section and writing two specimen business letters, are you willing to agree that no business letter will receive a passing grade that contains a single mistake in any of the six parts? This means an error in form, not in the body of the letter.

2. If possible, bring to class any actual business letters that you can courteously and legitimately secure. Call attention to any unusual features.

3. Choose the business or profession you prefer and draw up your own letterhead. What color of paper and kind of type will you select?

4. Among the six following assignments in the strictly business letter, write at least one in the indented style with closed punctuation and one in the block style with open punctuation.

(1) Address two envelopes (or slips of paper cut to envelope size, usually $3\frac{5}{8}'' \times 6\frac{1}{2}''$) to advertisers in a national magazine.

(2) Write the inside address and greeting only to two of the following: the President; the Secretary of the Interior; one of your national Senators; your Governor. Consult a large dictionary for the proper form of salutation. In the new Merriam-Webster Dictionary this information is found under the heading "Forms of Address," pages 3012–3014.

(3) Answer an advertisement in the *Saturday Evening Post* or the *Ladies' Home Journal* requesting a catalogue.

(4) Write a letter subscribing for your favorite magazine. Mention how you are sending the money.

(5) Write a business letter ordering several items from a store or factory advertising in a local paper.

(6) Write to a school principal or superintendent in your state applying for a position to teach. Be definite as to what grade or subject you feel best fitted to deal with. State your qualifications fairly and fully.

5. Find in a daily paper an advertisement in the "Help Wanted" column which you think you could fill. Imagine that getting this place is very important to you just now. Apply for it.

6. Appoint a small class committee to represent the employer, and (a) let them judge the letters of application written in Exercise 5 on looks only, on paper, handwriting, margins, neatness, etc. — rejecting all that fail to come up to a high standard; (b) then let the committee read over the accepted letters, and on the score of correctness and effectiveness appoint personal interviews for those who deserve them.

7. Write as secretary, in the name of your class, inviting a prominent man or woman of your state to deliver the commencement address. Remember that this is asking a good deal of a busy person. Give some details as to why you wish this particular person to speak for you, and state whether a fee or simply expenses will be paid, and where and how entertainment will be provided.

8. A friend whom you both know and like is applying for a position in the nearest large city. Having in mind an actual friend and a position he (she) is fitted to fill, write a letter of recommendation.

9. You are business manager of your college annual or paper. Write a letter soliciting an advertisement from some national or state business firm. Try to write a logical, persuasive letter.

10. Write to the dean asking permission to make a canvass in the college in behalf of the Society for Prevention of Cruelty to Animals. Go into some detail.

11. Write a sales letter boosting some product that is either manufactured or grown in your community. You will have to know the product thoroughly and believe in it before you can convince others. An effective sales letter is the hardest of all business letters to write well.

12. Write a letter to the proper college authority, applying for a scholarship. State your qualifications, based upon your school and college record,

both in and out of the classroom.   Give references and ask for a printed application blank.

13. Decide what single improvement the college needs most and write a letter to the trustees through the chairman petitioning for this improvement.

14. Order from a Sears, Roebuck catalogue or some other large mail-order house five dollars' worth of musical supplies, sporting goods, or automobile accessories.

15. You do not approve of a recent article or editorial which appeared in the college weekly.   Write a formal letter to the editor stating your objections and the reasons for them.

16. You are attracted by a contest in which a prize is offered for the best advertisement of a certain make of shoes.   Write for particulars.

2. Formal Invitations and Replies

A special form of social communication, as fixed in its form and conventions as the business letter itself, is the formal invitation and its reply.   **The formal invitation has neither heading, inside address, greeting, complimentary close, nor signature.**   All necessary information as to time, place, person, and purpose is given in one brief paragraph.   It is written throughout in the third person.   It is usually either written by hand or engraved.   It is never typewritten or mimeographed and should not be printed if this can possibly be avoided.   It is usually centered upon a correspondence card or upon very heavy white paper approximately $3\frac{1}{2}$ by $5\frac{1}{4}$ inches, or slightly larger than regular note paper folded.   So far as possible all abbreviations are avoided and even figures are written out in full, for both abbreviations and figures suggest business and lack of leisure.   Everything about a formal invitation savors of formality, dignity, good taste, and the avoidance of the cheap and the commonplace.

If the invitation is engraved, the company that does the engraving will have sample forms and styles to go by.   These forms have been carefully established, and they are kept up to standard by the National Association of Steel and Copper Plate Engravers.   The language is highly formal, but the lines may either be arranged in the block style or separated according to the different items of the invitation, each line being centered exactly on the page.   If this latter style is followed, the name of the person or organization occupies the first line, the invitation itself the second line, the purpose the third line, the date the fourth line, the hour the fifth line, and the place the sixth line. If an answer is expected, there are placed in the lower left-hand corner the letters R. S. V. P. or R. s. v. p., standing for the French phrase *Répondez, s'il vous plaît* (Reply, if you please). Or the simple English expression may be used, *Please reply* or *Please respond*.

If written out by hand, the invitation either may follow the group arrangement of lines described above or may be in block style, centered on the card, with no indentations.

REPLIES

Replies to formal invitations follow exactly the style of the invitation itself, rewording every item except the hour.

3. Friendly Letters

Do you find the real inside of him in his letters? . . . This is a pretty sure test. — JAMES RUSSELL LOWELL

(1) THE FORM OF FRIENDLY LETTERS

The **friendly letter** is different in both form and purpose from the business letter and the formal invitation. The only part of the friendly letter that is strict in form is the address on the envelope. Since this address guides the letter to its destination, it should of course be as accurate and as complete as the address on a business envelope. Friendly letters are usually written by hand, and the address can follow either the indented or the block system of arranging the lines, and either the closed or the open style of punctuation. Unless you are sure that the person to whom you are writing is at the address you give, and unless you are also sure that the address itself is clear and complete, it is well to put your own return address on the upper left-hand corner of the envelope as is regularly done in business correspondence. The Post Office Department advises this in all cases.

Notice that the greeting in friendly letters is punctuated with a comma instead of with a colon as in business letters.

One final word as to paper and handwriting. When writing to very intimate friends and to members of our immediate families, we have a tendency to dash off a few hurriedly scrawled lines on any old piece of note paper we happen to have at hand. Of course affectionate informality between loved ones is not only proper but even desirable. No one would write to his father or sister in the terms in which he would address a school superintendent in asking for a recommendation or the president of a bank in applying for a position. We should not, however, go too far and let intimacy degenerate into illegibility, and informality into sloppiness. Take a little extra time and trouble to make your intimate letters attractive in looks as well as affectionate in tone.

As was said on page 237, each letter you write is really a little part of yourself. Make the messenger worthy of its message.

The note paper itself should be of first-class quality and in perfect taste. White, cream, or pale gray is preferable to the gaudier colors. **The ink should be black or blue-black,** not red, green, or violet. Strongly perfumed paper should be avoided. Everything about the letter should suggest refinement and good taste.

(2) THE LETTER ITSELF

Friendship is an intensely personal thing; and as our friends and our relations with them vary, so too do our letters differ in tone and purpose. There is the letter of congratulation in which we express our pleasure in a friend's success, promotion, or good fortune. And there is the opposite, the letter of condolence, in which we convey our sympathy for a friend's sickness, loss of a loved one, or misfortune. Then there is the note of invitation, in which we ask someone to visit us at home or to come to a house party or to spend a week-end with us at the beach or in the mountains. There is the bread-and-butter or guest letter, in which we express our thanks and appreciation for having been entertained in our hostess's home. There is the note of acknowledgment conveying our gratitude for a gift or for a favor. There is the letter of intimate, newsy details between close friends which is really a chat by mail instead of in person. Then there is the letter home in which we tell our father or mother something of our experiences in school or college, or how much we are enjoying ourselves on our trip or on a visit to a friend.

So various in tone and purpose are our manifold friendly letters that no single prescription will cover them all. Perhaps the best is the beautiful sentiment from Proverbs: "A man that hath friends must shew himself friendly." That is, friendship carries its own obligation; if we have friends, we must show ourselves worthy of them by carrying out the obligations of friendship and affection. Not the least of these is, in absence, to keep alive and cherish the friendly feeling by means of bright, attractive letters, as intimate and affectionate as the mutual relationship warrants. Whatever other qualities such letters should have, they should above all be natural, sympathetic, and as interesting as we can make them.

To tell anyone to be interesting sounds like bidding him to be rich or wise or happy: it is a counsel of perfection. Everybody agrees it is a highly desirable quality, but how attain it? So far as friendly letters are concerned, being interesting resolves itself largely into taking the time and trouble to go into details. No one can dash off a bright, interesting letter in five minutes, in a hundred words. When we read letters like those quoted on pages 250–253, we are surprised at their charm, their care, and their detail. They are really little artistic personal essays, and as much time and effort went into them as went into the personal essays of the same length quoted on pages 548–559. Their writers put into them all they had of brightness, sympathy, vividness, and friendship. You can pour out of a cup only what has first been poured into it, and it is a stubborn law of life that everything worth while seems to take both time and trouble. Our letters are faithful examples of this principle. Everything that this book has to say about the importance of the detail applies directly to friendly letters. See above in the sections on the independent paragraph, pages 6–11; on the concrete, specific word, pages 398–403; on narration, pages 431–435; and on description, pages 508–513. Take time to give details. One experience, one scene, one person, described in detail is vastly better than a longer list which merely mentions experiences, scenes, and people in general terms like items in a card catalogue or a shopping list.

THE ROUND TABLE

1. Name all the different kinds of friendly letters (a) that you have had occasion to write during the past twelve months, and (b) that you think you may have occasion to write during the next twelve.

2. A former schoolmate now in another college has recently won state-

wide distinction in athletics, oratory, debating, scholarship, or writing. Write him (her) a cordial note of greeting and congratulation telling him (her) how proud you are of him (her).

3. Write to a close personal friend of your family asking permission to use his name as reference in applying for a position you are seeking in the capital of your state.

4. Write a note to the mother of a friend who has entertained you at their cottage in the mountains (or at the seashore) for a week-end.

5. Write a note acknowledging an unexpected Christmas gift of five dollars from an uncle who lives in a distant city and whom you see but seldom.

6. Write a note to an elderly woman friend of your family who sent you some flowers during your recent illness.

7. Write to a friend in a near-by town who entertained another friend of yours at dinner when he (she) was visiting in that town last week.

8. Write a cheerful letter to a friend (boy or girl) who has had a bad automobile accident and is laid up in bed with a broken leg.

9. The family of one of your classmates (boy or girl) is moving to a distant city. You have a first cousin there whom you wish your classmate to meet. Write your cousin an informal letter of introduction about your friend.

10. There is usually an elderly person in every community who is an authority on the history of the community or county. Write this person a note introducing a friend from another state who wishes certain information about the past.

11. You and your next-door neighbor are on good terms, but his family is a little peculiar and apt to take offense. Write him a tactful, friendly letter on one of the following delicate situations: —

(1) His dog barks at night and keeps you awake.

(2) His chickens come into your yard and scratch up your flower beds.

(3) The radio at his house is played by the open window with the loud-speaker on and keeps you from studying and sleeping.

(4) His son, who delivers newspapers on a motorcycle, warms up the motor with the muffler cut out and wakes up your whole family every morning at five o'clock.

(5) His cat has eaten several of your little chickens.

12. Write a letter to your favorite character in fiction telling why you would like to meet him (or her).

13. You are sending some flowers to a sick friend. Write a cheerful little note to accompany them.

14. An unexpected automobile trip out of town with friends has made you forget an engagement to be present at a friend's party. Write a note of explanation and apology.

15. Write a letter to amuse a child in a hospital. If you can draw, put in a few humorous sketches by way of illustration even if you can make only

rudimentary figures like Little Jets, or match-stick men. These letters could be sent.

16. A classmate has made a failing grade in English, and has been taken out of college by his (her) indignant parents, who think it is all the instructor's fault. You know that it is your friend's fault. Write the father (or mother) a kind, frank letter explaining the facts and urging that the boy (or girl) be sent back to college, and offering to help him (her) with his (her) work.

17. Write a note of congratulation to a classmate who has won a contest or tournament in which you were a contestant.

18. Write a letter to an old friend of your family's telling him of the two professions you are debating entering, and asking his advice as to which to follow.

19. Write to the minister of your church telling him of a new member of his denomination who has just moved to town, and suggesting that he call.

20. Write to a classmate who stopped school last year and went to work in a neighboring town, telling him about your studies this year and giving him some interesting class news.

21. From biographies and autobiographies you have access to, bring in examples of well-written letters which reveal the mood or personality of their writers.

22. Write a good long letter home at least once a week. Many grown sons and daughters write to their father or mother unfailingly every Sunday. Only when you are in the place your parents occupy now will you see the inestimable value of doing this. It is something you will never be sorry for.

Effective Letters

1. **Thomas Bailey Aldrich, the author of** *Marjorie Daw*, **writes a guest letter to William Dean Howells, the novelist:** —

PONKAPOG, MASS.

Dec. 13, 1875 [1]

DEAR HOWELLS, —

We had so charming a visit at your house that I have about made up my mind to reside with you permanently. I am tired of writing. I would like to settle down in just such a comfortable home as yours, with a man who can work regularly four or five hours a day, thereby relieving one of all painful apprehensions in respect to clothes and pocket-money. I am

[1] From *Letters of Thomas Bailey Aldrich*, Houghton Mifflin Company. By permission of the publishers.

easy to get along with. I have few unreasonable wants and never complain when they are constantly supplied. I think I could depend on you.

Ever yours,

T. B. A.

P. S. I should want to bring my two mothers, my two boys (I seem to have everything in twos), my wife, and her sister.

2. **Robert Louis Stevenson to his friend W. H. Low:** —

CHALET LA SOLITUDE, HYÈRES

October 23, 1883

MY DEAR LOW, —

I am now a person with an established ill-health — a wife — a dog possessed with an evil, a Gadarene spirit — a chalet on a hill, looking out over the Mediterranean — a certain reputation — and very obscure finances. Otherwise, very much the same, I guess; and were a bottle of Fleury a thing to be obtained, capable of developing theories along with a fit spirit even as of yore. Yet I now draw near to the Middle Ages; nearly three years ago, that fatal Thirty struck; and yet the great work is not yet done — not yet even conceived. But so, as one goes on, the wood seems to thicken, the footpath to narrow, and the House Beautiful on the hill's summit to draw further and further away. We learn, indeed, to use our means; but only to learn, along with it, the paralysing knowledge that these means are only applicable to two or three poor commonplace motives. Eight years ago, if I could have slung ink as I can now, I should have thought myself well on the road after Shakespeare; and now — I find I have only got a pair of walking-shoes and not yet begun to travel. And art is still away there on the mountain summit. But I need not continue; for, of course, this is your story just as much as it is mine; and, strange to think, it was Shakespeare's too, and Beethoven's, and Phidias's. It is a blessed thing that, in this forest of art, we can pursue our wood-lice and sparrows, *and not catch them*, with almost the same fervour of exhilaration as that with which Sophocles hunted and brought down the Mastodon.

Tell me something of your work, and your wife. — My dear fellow, I am yours ever,

R. L. STEVENSON

My wife begs to be remembered to both of you; I cannot say as much for my dog, who has never seen you, but he would like, on general principles, to bite you.

---

[1] By permission of the publishers, Charles Scribner's Sons.

3. An unexcelled example of the hardest of all kinds of letters to write: —

JAMES MEMORIAL UNIVERSITY

JAMESON, TENNESSEE

October 11, 19— [1]

MRS. E. P. WATERS
RICHMOND, VIRGINIA

MY DEAR MRS. WATERS:

Something happened here this morning that I want you to know.

About nine o'clock a young fellow swung on to the campus with a long-legged stride that would have been astonishing anywhere else. He had come a hundred miles from his home in the mountains of North Carolina.

I turned him over to Dean Stuart, but I listened to the conversation. He had brought with him the sum of just $10, — no more, — all he had on earth. The dean told him that it was hard to know what to do with him, and explained as kindly as he could that all our rooms were occupied.

I looked at the young man; he never flinched; he smiled, confidently faced us both, clear-eyed and steady, and this is what he said: "Dean, I didn't come here to get a room or to get a bed; I came to get an education. I can sleep on the floor."

There was no answer to that. At least, neither the dean nor I could think of one, and we simply made a place for him; we had to. We cannot refuse this sort, and we will not do it as long as there is a dollar in sight.

These boys are the salt of the earth — big, strong, upstanding fellows; old Revolutionary stock, most of them; mountain-born; fearless, quiet, loyal, high-principled, and clean. They must have help. They need it and they deserve it. The sum of $25,000 is required at once for the actual current expenses of the year. We must have that amount at hand or in prospect at an early day.

We are asking not only because the money is needed for the great work that we are doing but because it is right that you should have an opportunity to give if you can. Your gift may make the difference between a life of ignorance and a life of knowledge, to some mountain boy.

Sincerely yours,

(*Signed*) SHERIDAN P. EDWARDS,

President

DCM

---

[1] From Roy Davis and C. H. Lingham, *Business Letter-Writing*, Ginn and Company. By permission of the publishers.

4. From *Letters from a Bald-Headed Dad to His Red-Headed Daughter*, by Robert Quillen: —

September 19th [1]

My Dear Louise:

This letter isn't prompted by the fact that you live in a small town. Human nature is changed very little by population statistics, and a large community is merely a collection of small ones.

In all communities of which I have knowledge, the people are divided into two classes — those who talk about things and those who talk about people. Of course the classes aren't wholly distinct. Those who talk about things — about politics, books, current events, music, law — these may at times discuss their friends and their servants; but the other class, composed of those who talk about people, is incapable of talking or listening unless the topic of conversation is a neighbor.

You are now forming the social habits that will stay with you through life. The next five years will determine which class is yours. Environment will decide the matter for you if you make no effort to do anything for yourself. You will develop the habit of making conversation as your daily companions do.

Don't fool yourself by assuming that you can spend your youth in discussion of your neighbors and then blossom out overnight and become a charming conversationalist capable of discussing anything under the sun. Habit isn't formed that way. Your future way of life won't be decided upon next year or the next. You are cutting the pattern now.

Do you wish to be a common scold? That is the ultimate fate of every woman who talks about nothing but people. You can't make conversation about your neighbors' virtues and triumphs. Ordinary things aren't interesting. If you make it a practice to talk about people, you will talk about their faults and their sins, their mistakes and their failures. And after a few years of that your mind will travel in a rut and you won't be able to open your mouth without saying something uncomplimentary about somebody.

You can't change after the habit jells. Once you become a confirmed neighbor discusser, you will be happy only among others of your kind. When chance places you in a group that talks of other things, you will be as dumb as an oyster.

Talk of many things, Honey. Otherwise you'll be tongue-tied when you meet a stranger who doesn't know the Joneses.

Love,
Dad

5. Read again the letter of "Emily Therese Lynn-Royston" to "Miss Price," by Max Beerbohm, pages 232–233 above.

[1] By permission of the author and of Publishers Syndicate, 30 N. La Salle St., Chicago, Ill.

CHAPTER XIV

The Library

Knowledge is of two kinds: we know a subject ourselves, or we know where we can find information about it. — SAMUEL JOHNSON

The difference between the trained and the untrained mind lies not so much in the amount of information possessed by each as in the ability of the trained mind to get, without difficulty and without delay, information desired at any moment.
— JOHN MATTHEWS MANLY AND EDITH RICKERT

The focal point of a college is the library. On it, as on a great hub, the curriculum centers and turns. One of the first things to do on entering college is to learn the system and the resources of this great treasure house wherein is stored the accumulated learning of the ages. To do this is not as easy as it may seem, for a large library is a marvel of complex organization. To become acquainted with its chief features and their location, however, is not only an interesting experience in itself, but a labor-saving necessity for your four years' residence within college walls. Well did President Kenneth Irving Brown of Hiram College set as one of the major objectives of a college course "an enthusiasm for books, a knowledge of where they are to be found, experience in using them, and assistance in enjoying them." [1]

What to Look For

Go to the library on an early and intelligent inspection tour with somewhat the same interested expectancy that you would feel in visiting a famous historical building, a trades display, an automobile show, or a museum, for a great library is truly the first wonder of the intellectual world. Learn both (1) *what* and (2) *where* — that is, become

[1] "Sitting One's Way through College," *The Journal of Higher Education*, December, 1937, p. 461.

acquainted with the leading features of the library and where they are located. Look specifically for these four: the card catalogue, the reference room, the periodical room (for both bound and current magazines), and special departments or departmental libraries.

(1) THE CARD CATALOGUE

First comes the **card index, or card catalogue** of the general library.

Here, arranged alphabetically, are to be found three cards for every book in the library, arranged alphabetically, one card for the author's name, another card for the book's title, and a third card under the general subject with which the book deals, such as Agriculture, Amusements, Biography, Geology, Law, Medicine, Poetry, Sacred Art, Theology, Useful Arts, and so on.

You will note from these cards the fact that library usage differs from standard usage in capitalization, only the first word and proper nouns and proper adjectives being capitalized on the library cards.

(2) THE DEWEY–DECIMAL SYSTEM

The leading system of library classification in the United States is known as the **Dewey-Decimal** after its propounder, Melvil Dewey. This system divides the entire field of knowledge into nine main classes numbered 100 to 900, and places general works of reference in the preliminary class numbered zero to 99, as follows: —

CLASSES

0–99	General Works	500–599	Natural Science
100–199	Philosophy	600–699	Useful Arts
200–299	Religion	700–799	Fine Arts
300–399	Sociology	800–899	Literature
400–499	Philology	900–999	History, Biography, Travel

Each class is in turn divided into ten divisions, including the first, which is general. Take, for example, Fine Arts, numbered 700–799.

700–709	Fine Arts	750–759	Painting
710–719	Landscape Gardening	760–769	Engraving
720–729	Architecture	770–779	Photography
730–739	Sculpture	780–789	Music
740–749	Drawing, Decoration, Design	790–799	Amusements

Each of these divisions is, in turn, divided into ten subdivisions or sections, as, for example : —

790	Amusements	795	Games of Chance
791	Public Entertainments	796	Outdoor Sports
792	Theater, Pantomime,	797	Boating and Ball
	Opera	798	Horsemanship and Racing
793	Indoor Amusements	799	Fishing, Hunting, Target
794	Games of Skill		Shooting

The figures on the library card that follow the first three classification figures usually indicate the wing, the floor, the alcove, and the shelf number where each individual book may be found in the stacks. Familiarize yourself with this local reference part of the call number as well as with the Dewey-Decimal classification system.

(3) THE REFERENCE ROOM

Make the rounds next of the **reference room,** where are stored on easily accessible tables and shelves the standard collections of reference books, both general and special — the encyclopedias, dictionaries, bibliographies, atlases, gazetteers, and various handbooks and compendiums of knowledge. Here is the first place to go for any needed information and here every term paper and research article has its logical start.

Examine and estimate the resources of this surprising microcosm of human learning, for the further you proceed on the great adventure of being educated — or rather of educating yourself — the oftener will you find it advisable to resort to this spot.

In your preliminary survey first look for and then learn to avail yourself of the advantages of such standard works as these : —

BIBLIOGRAPHY IN GENERAL

Library of Congress. (A card catalogue of all books copyrighted in the United States.)

The United States Catalog imprint by years in the United States. (Three volumes, with supplements; authors, titles, subjects, publishers, dates, and prices of books.)

American Library Association ("*A. L. A.*") *Index.* (A subject index to nonfiction books and government publications.)

Book Review Digest, 1906–.

Hutchings, Margaret, Johnson, Alice S., and Williams, Margaret S.,
Guide to the Use of Libraries, 1922.
Mudge, Isadore G., *New Guide to Reference Books*.

ENCYCLOPEDIAS

The Encyclopedia Americana, latest edition, 1932.
The Encyclopaedia Britannica, fourteenth edition, 1932.
The New International Encyclopedia, 1922, with supplements in 1925,
1930.

DICTIONARIES [1]

American Standard Dictionary. (Its largest abridgment is known both
as the *Practical Standard Dictionary* and as the *College Standard
Dictionary*.)
Century Dictionary and Cyclopedia, 12 vols.
New English Dictionary or the *Oxford English Dictionary*, 10 vols.
(The great authoritative historical dictionary of English giving the
etymology, meaning, and spellings of 414,825 words by means of
1,827,306 dated quotations showing their earliest form and later
changes.)
Webster's Collegiate Dictionary, 1935. (The largest abridgment of
the *New International*, almost indispensable for desk use.)
Webster's New International Dictionary, 1935. (Contains a greater
number of words than any other dictionary.)

COMMON QUOTATIONS, PROVERBS, ALLUSIONS

Bartlett, John, *Familiar Quotations*.
Brewer, E. C., *Dictionary of Phrase and Fable*.
————, *Reader's Handbook of Famous Names in Fiction, Allusions,
References, Proverbs, Plots, Stories and Poems*, 1898.
Hoyt's *New Cyclopedia of Practical Quotations*.

PROPER NAMES [2]

Century Dictionary and Cyclopedia of Proper Names.
Gayley, C. M., *Classic Myths in English Literature*.
Lippincott's Biographical Dictionary.
Lippincott's Gazetteer.

SPECIAL ENCYCLOPEDIAS AND REFERENCE BOOKS

Agriculture
Agricultural Index, 1916–
Bailey, L. H., *Cyclopedia of American Agriculture*, 4 vols.

[1] On the use of the dictionary, see below, pages 322–324.
[2] See below, pages 355–356.

Biography

Dictionary of American Biography, 20 vols.
Dictionary of National Biography (British), 63 vols. with supplements.
Who's Who. (Annual, living British subjects.)
Who's Who in America. (Annual, living Americans.)

Education

Education Index, 1929–.
McLaughlin, A. C., and Hart, A. B., *Cyclopedia of American Government*, 3 vols.
Monroe, Paul, *Cyclopedia of Education*, 5 vols.
Watson, Foster, *Encyclopedia and Dictionary of Education*, 4 vols.

History

A History of All Nations from the Earliest Times, 24 vols.
Allison, William H., etc., *A Guide to Historical Literature.*
Cambridge Ancient History, 7 vols.
Cambridge Medieval History, 6 vols.
Cambridge Modern History, 13 vols.
Channing, Edward, and others, *Guide to the Study and Reading of American History.*
New Larned History for Ready Reference, 12 vols.
Ploetz's *Manual of Universal History.*

Literature, English

Baker, Blanche M., *Dramatic Bibliography.*
Cambridge History of American Literature, 4 vols.
Cambridge History of English Literature, 15 vols.
Manly, John M., and Rickert, Edith, *Contemporary American Literature*, with Bibliographies and Study Outlines.
——, *Contemporary British Literature*, with Bibliographies and Study Outlines.

Religion

Catholic Encyclopedia, 17 vols.
Frazer, Sir James G., *The Golden Bough*, 12 vols.   (One-volume abridgment, 1922.)
Hastings, James, *The Encyclopedia of Religion and Ethics*, 13 vols.
——, *Dictionary of the Bible.*
New Jewish Encyclopedia, 12 vols.
The New Schaff-Herzog Encyclopedia of Religious Knowledge, 13 vols.

Science

Cambridge Natural History, 10 vols.
Cattell, J. McK., ed., *American Men of Science.*
Popular Books of Science (a reading list prepared by the American Library Association).

Sarton, George, *Introduction to the History of Science* (in process of publication).

Thomson, J. S., *The Outline of Science*, 2 vols.

Social Science

Seligman, Edwin R. A., ed., *Encyclopedia of Social Sciences*, 1930– (in process of publication).

INDEX TO PERIODICALS [1]

Book Review Digest, 1905–
International Index to Periodicals, 1920–
The New York Times Index, 1913–
The Official Index to The Times (London), 1906–
Poole's Index to Periodical Literature, 1802–1906.
Readers' Guide to Periodical Literature, 1900–

YEAR BOOKS

(Statistics and facts for individual years)
American Annual.
American Labor Year Book.
Chicago Daily News Almanac.
Commerce Year Book.
New International Year Book.
Statesman's Year Book (chiefly English).
Statistical Abstract of the United States.
Whitaker's Almanac (chiefly English).
World Almanac (inexpensive and useful).
Year Book of Agriculture.

(4) PERIODICALS

1. CURRENT PERIODICALS

Pay an early visit to the **periodical room,** walk slowly past the shelves and tables on a preliminary tour of inspection to see just what magazines and newspapers are available. Among the more reliable and influential magazines are these. Form at least a bowing acquaintance with them: —

American Mercury	*Nation*
American Scholar	*New Republic*
Atlantic Monthly	*Saturday Evening Post*
Foreign Affairs	*Scribner's*
Harper's	*Time*
Life	*Yale Review*

[1] See also pages 259–260.

Here, too, you will find your favorite magazine or magazines for recreational reading. For a knowledge of current events and current ideas cultivate the habit of skimming *Time, The Reader's Digest*, and one good scientific magazine, possibly *Science Service* or *Popular Science*. In this way you can easily and pleasantly keep abreast of the times while you devote most of your intellectual energy to the serious and varied courses of the college curriculum.

2. BOUND MAGAZINES, GOVERNMENT REPORTS, ETC.

Indispensable for most investigations is the information stored in the bound volumes of magazines, newspapers, and the reports of the government and of various sectional and national organizations. Pay particular heed to this feature of the library, and acquaint yourself with what it contains. You will often be able to obtain information from this source that you could get in no other way. Locate and learn to use the essential guides to this varied and scattered body of material, which have already been referred to on page 259.

International Index to Periodicals, 1920–
The New York Times Index, 1913–
The Official Index to The Times (London), 1906–
Poole's Index to Periodical Literature, 1802–1906
Readers' Guide to Periodical Literature, 1900–

(5) SPECIAL AND DEPARTMENTAL LIBRARIES

Sometimes a department or a school of the university will maintain a highly specialized library apart from the general library. The School of Law uniformly and the School of Education frequently do this. Occasionally also a department such as Chemistry or Modern Languages will do likewise. Ask about such special, individual libraries and find out their scope and value. It may well be that at some crowded moment in the future the exact bit of information essential to your investigation will be available only in one of the special libraries.

To sum up, as early as possible after entering college, *learn your library and how to use it*. This is not only one of the most important possibilities that face you in your whole college course, but also one of the most interesting. Reflect on the following thoughtful passage : —

The study of bibliography and of the scientific methods of using books should have an assured place in the university curriculum . . . and . . . all who go forth into the world as graduates should have such an intelligent and practical knowledge of books as will aid them in their studies through life. . . . I do not mean that the university student should learn the contents of the most useful books; but I do mean that he should know of their existence, what they treat of, and what they will do for him. He should know what are the most important reference books. . . . If a question arises as to the existence, authorship, or subject of a book, an educated man should know the catalogues or bibliographies by which he can readily clear up the doubt. . . . He should know the standard writers on a large variety of subjects. He should be familiar with the best method by which the original investigation of any topic may be carried on. . . . No person has any claim to be a scholar until he can conduct such an original investigation with ease and pleasure. — WILLIAM FREDERICK POOLE

As a final word add what the English essayist Carlyle has to say on the subject: "In books lies the soul of the whole Past Time: the articulate audible voice of the Past, when the body and material substance of it has altogether vanished like a dream. . . . All that the university or final highest school can do for us is to teach us to read."

THE ROUND TABLE

1. As assigned by the instructor, let a small selected group of students make brief oral reports on interesting or unusual facts they have discovered about the college library.

2. Does the library have a special Treasure Room where rare or valuable books are displayed? If so, give some account of it.

3. What special or departmental libraries are maintained apart from the general library?

4. Ask the instructor to discuss with the class the resources of the library, with special reference to its strong points, its weak points, and its comparative standing among other college libraries in your state and section.

5. What system of classifying books does your library use?

6. If you have difficulty in learning the significance of the various numbers on the cards in the library catalogue, ask the instructor to discuss and explain in class several typical call numbers.

7. Find the author, title, and subject cards for two books that you have read or are interested in.

8. Look up two recent books you are familiar with in the *United States Catalog.*

9. Find the title and date of issue of four periodicals which carried reviews of *Anthony Adverse* or *Gone with the Wind*.

10. Glance at the articles on "Ballads," "Fine Arts," and "Poetry" in the *Britannica*, *Americana*, and *New International* encyclopedias, and note differences in style and method of treatment.

11. Look up the words "(to) be," "enough," and "who" in the *Century*, *Webster's*, *Standard*, and *New English* dictionaries and observe styles and differences in the treatment of spelling, pronunciation, derivation, and meanings.

12. Find the source, including author, book, and date, of the following quotations : —

(1) We are advertised by our loving friends.

(2) God tempers the wind to the shorn lamb.

(3) Where ignorance is bliss,
'Tis folly to be wise.

(4) Facts are stubborn things.

(5) And fools, who came to scoff, remained to pray.

(6) The ruling ideas of each age have ever been the ideas of its ruling class.

(7) Every man takes the limits of his own field of vision for the limits of the world.

(8) Provided a man is not mad, he can be cured of every folly but vanity.

(9) I disapprove of what you say, but I will defend to the death your right to say it.

(10) (*a*) Few men have been admired by their domestics.
(*b*) No man is a hero to his *valet-de-chambre*.

(11) (*a*) The end justifies the means.
(*b*) The end must justify the means.

(12) There'll be a hot time in the old town tonight.

(13) There is no cure for birth and death save to enjoy the interval.

(14)   God gives all men all earth to love,
But since man's heart is small,
Ordains for each one spot shall prove
Beloved over all.

(15) What I like in a good author is not what he says, but what he whispers.

(16) She'd fight a rattlesnake and give it the first two bites.

(17) Rose is a rose is a rose is a rose.

13. In *Who's Who* and *Who's Who in America* respectively, glance at the sketches of well-known contemporary Englishmen and Americans, and report on the kind of information given.

14. In J. M. Manly and Edith Rickert, *Contemporary American Literature*, count the references to the life and works of two of the following : Amy Lowell, Carl Sandburg, Edwin Arlington Robinson, William Beebe, H. L. Mencken, Sinclair Lewis, Booth Tarkington, and Eugene O'Neill.

15. In *Contemporary British Literature* by the same authors count the references to two of the following: Rudyard Kipling, John Galsworthy, Thomas Hardy, J. M. Barrie, John Masefield, Joseph Conrad, and George Bernard Shaw.

16. Glance through what the *Encyclopaedia Britannica,* the *Catholic* and the *Jewish* encyclopedias have to say about (*a*) Peter and (*b*) Paul. Comment on the differences of treatment.

17. Spend five minutes turning the pages of a late volume of *Readers' Guide to Periodical Literature* and learn its system of reference, abbreviations for the titles of magazines, and so forth.

18. How many contemporary current periodicals does your library subscribe to?

19. How many periodicals are represented in the bound volumes in your library?

CHAPTER XV

The Term Paper

Preparing a term paper is becoming a requirement in an increasing number of college courses. **A term paper,** sometimes called a research theme, consists of two distinct forms of endeavor: (1) the thorough and intelligent investigation of a definite phase of some subject, or limited field of knowledge, and (2) the presentation of the results in an accurate and orderly way. Long experience on the part of scholars and investigators has developed a fairly definite technique for the research article, of which the two most obvious formal features are (1) the use of footnotes throughout the text in order to give exact and complete references to the sources of information, and (2) a final bibliography, arranged alphabetically by authors, in order to show in a single orderly grouping the scope and variety of the sources consulted.

This chapter is devoted to explaining the technique of the term paper, a technique that remains the same, though it advances in thoroughness and delicacy, for the master's thesis and the doctoral dissertation.

1. Gathering Material, or Investigating Sources

The use of footnotes and the inclusion of a bibliography are, as was said, two outward essentials of the research article. Its chief inner feature, however, as its name indicates, is **research** — that is, the intelligent, critical, and thorough investigation of available sources of information concerning the subject chosen. It is the amount and quality of the research, the time and care spent upon investigating sources, that largely determine both the nature and the value of the finished article. Herein lie both the danger and the opportunity of this kind of work.

Most of the writing that college students are called on to do grows out of their personal observation and experience. Specifically is this true of the more imaginative forms of writing such as verse, the personal essay, and the short story. See, for example, the attractive specimens of student writing in two of these fields on pages 485–497 and 548–559. All such writing is an illustration of Philip Sidney's imperative advice to himself : —

> Biting my truant pen, beating myself for spite;
> "Fool," said my Muse to me, "look in thy heart and write."

The research article, however, while still owing its general tone and individuality to the personality and purpose of the writer, depends for its material upon the findings of other men, largely as these findings are recorded in magazines and books. Writing a term paper, therefore, is not unlike building a house : the first and most important step is assembling the materials. You may think of your research article as a Gothic cathedral, a Greek temple, a dwelling, a barn, a garage, or only a dog house, but think of it as *a definite structure requiring definite building material*. Each fact or opinion that you glean from the library and record upon your cards is as actually a bit of needed material as if it were a brick, a plank, a beam, or a sack of cement. Only when enough fit material has been accumulated can an actual beginning be made toward erecting the finished structure.

(1) THE TIME ELEMENT

In planning a term paper, therefore, this necessity of spending much time and effort in gathering material must be taken into account and definitely allowed for. Instead of considering the actual writing of the paper as the most important part of the process, consider it as secondary in both time and effort to the first essential of gathering material. Definite apportioning of time is perhaps not possible, but the following ratios have proved useful in many cases and will at least be suggestive : —

Finding and recording material . . . . . . $\frac{5}{10}$ of the total time
Organizing and writing the article . . . . $\frac{3}{10}$ of the total time
Footnotes and bibliography . . . . $\frac{1}{10}$ of the total time
Revising and polishing . . . . $\frac{1}{10}$ of the total time

Note particularly the amount of time assigned to gathering material. It will, of course, vary greatly with the character and grade of the investigation. In laboratory or experimental research in the sciences, and in such subjects as sociology and education, finding the facts may take anywhere from three fourths to nine tenths of the total time and energy, but for most pieces of undergraduate library research, one half of the total time is a fair approximation.

1. REGULAR AND REPEATED EFFORTS

Two other very practical observations should be made. Gathering material can rarely be done in one concerted rush or uninterrupted drive. The necessities of the college routine do not allow it. **Material must be gathered in frequent and repeated spurts of effort,** by patient and gradual accumulation. The theme song of the investigator is the old refrain,

> Every little bit added to what you've got
> Makes just a little bit more.

While preparing the article, therefore, allow deliberately and unalterably for daily or at least tri-weekly visits to the library. Schedule your time as carefully as if you were a crack passenger train and had to make all the speed the law allows. To your daily schedule of meals and recitations, add a regular visit to the library at a definite time, and see to it that nothing is allowed to interfere with it. Plan for as much time as you possibly can, but set the minimum at six hours a week.

2. THE VALUE OF LITTLE UNITS OF TIME

In the last place, do not underestimate the value of little units of time, even fifteen-minute or half-hour attacks. Scholarly and authoritative books have been written by busy men who were engulfed in the flood tide of pressing routine duties but who knew how to discover and regularly utilize the little vacant spaces in the day's schedule that the ordinary worker would dismiss with a shrug of the shoulders and a careless "What's the use?" It is truly amazing how much anyone can accomplish in little recurrent units of idle time if he will only look for them and use them unfailingly and enthusiastically.

If you work thus by the incremental method of little-drops-of-water-and-little-grains-of-sand, you will not only make the mighty ocean and the pleasant land, but best of all will have a surprisingly good time while doing it.

2. Recording Material

An intelligent use of the sources for finding information available to you through the card index, the reference room, and *Readers' Guide* will normally result in a flood of material, consisting of both facts and opinions, of varying kinds and values. In order to save trouble later on and to keep the raw material of the research paper from burying both you and your subject under an avalanche of unorganized information, **a fairly definite technique for taking notes has been developed.** Long experience has proved the following method to be the easiest and simplest in the long run. Note its four steps.

1. Use separate cards three by six inches.

This is approximately the size of a business envelope. If desired, paper cut into this size and shape will serve. A sheet of regulation theme paper measures $10\frac{1}{2}$ by 8 inches, and will thus conveniently make three such slips either with or without the margin.

2. Take down fully and accurately the complete details of the source of the information.

To do this is essential. It will seem a little troublesome at first, but do not neglect it on that account. *And do it all the first time.* That is, make the reference both full and accurate, for you will later have to use the information concerning that source both in a footnote and in your general bibliography. One of the most annoying of the minor trials of life is, after having carefully collected enough excellent material and while actually engaged in putting your article together, to find that, owing to haste and carelessness weeks before, you did not record the reference satisfactorily and now have to interrupt your work, go to the library, and supply the omitted information. Nor does it cheer one up to find then that someone else has taken that particular book out in the meantime and that it is hence unavailable for several weeks. As a labor-saving device the proverbial stitch in time does not compare with the wisdom of making each reference full and accurate the first time you come into contact with it.

To be both full and accurate, a reference should contain the following items of information : —

Book Reference

(1) Author's name
(2) Title of book, underlined
(3) Name of publishing firm
(4) Place of publication (unless the publishing firm is a well-known standard one)
(5) Date of publication
(6) Page or pages on which the information is contained

Since these references are for your own personal use, the exact form in which they are recorded makes little difference, provided, of course, that all the needed information is taken down accurately and fully. One convenient form is as follows : —

Hunt, Independence of

Chard Powers Smith
Annals of the Poets
Charles Scribner's Sons, New York, 1935, p. 353.

To save space, however, all the information concerning the book or the magazine may be given continuously on the same line, punctuated by commas as it will appear in the footnotes and the bibliography Following are three such typical reference cards : —

Book Reference

Hunt, Independence of

Chard Powers Smith, *Annals of the Poets*, Charles Scribner's Sons, New York, 1935, p. 353.

Hunt was fined £1000 for calling the Prince Regent a "fat Adonis of fifty." When Shelley started to raise his fine by subscription, Hunt had the independence to refuse the kindness.

Book Reference

Corporal Punishment, Johnson on

M. Dorothy George, *England in Johnson's Day*, Harcourt, Brace and Company, 1928, Intro., XIV.

While Johnson was in advance of his time in regard to the ferocities of criminal law, he was conservative in the matter of school discipline. "There is now less flogging in our great schools," he said in 1775, "but then less is learned there; so that what the boys get at one end they lose at the other."

Magazine Reference

Flexner's *Universities, etc.*, Significance of

W. H. Cowley, "The University and the Individual," *The Journal of Higher Education*, October, 1931, p. 390.

Because Mr. Flexner's book, *Universities: American, English, German*, has been the most provocative volume published upon the problems of higher education in many a year, his doctrine must needs be critically appraised by conservatives and liberals alike.

If more than one reference is made to a book or to an article, only the first reference need contain full bibliographical details. For example, later notes from the second book referred to on page 269 can be abbreviated something like this : —

George, *Eng. in Johnson's Day*

Be sure, however, that your first reference contains every single item of needed bibliographical information and contains it fully and exactly.

3. To quote, cite, or summarize?

Two questions must be decided each time a note is taken: first, how much to include, and secondly, in what form; in other words, whether to quote, cite, or summarize. No satisfactory general answer to these questions can be given here, for both the "how much" and the "how" will depend upon the kind and scope of the subject being investigated and also upon the kind of material being recorded. Certain suggestions, however, can be made.

If while taking notes you are in doubt as to how much to record, it is better to take down too much than too little. It is always easy to discard material or to delete it if you have a superfluity, but it is next to impossible at the last moment to go back over your references and record information that you should have taken down the first time.

As to the form in which you record material, each of the three possibilities mentioned has its advantages.

To quote is of course to give the exact words of your source. Quotation is advisable when the information in question is very subtly or delicately put and might easily be misunderstood if paraphrased in your own words; or when the authority being quoted is so famous or important that his exact words will carry weight on that account; or when the phrasing or choice of words of the passage in question is so beautiful, or striking, or unexpected, that it should not be spoiled by being altered. In general, however, actual word-by-word quotation should be made to justify itself by some real reason and should be limited to reasonably short passages. Some research students find it convenient to copy a great deal of quotation in their notes and then, when writing the article out, either to retain the quoted form or to transfer it into citation as proves preferable.

To cite is to state the fact or opinion not in the writer's words but in your own language. This is the form in which much of your material will be recorded, for citations can be made as short and definite as you desire, and can also be worked up more easily into the text as you put your article together.

To summarize is to make a synopsis of; to give in concise, unabridged form the substance or chief ideas of a longer treatment. A summary is useful in handling a large block of material which would be impossible to quote and unsatisfactory to cite. Thus it is often possible to state in a few sentences or in a couple of paragraphs the essential point of contact between your subject and a whole chapter or section or even book.

Notice, however, that whether you are quoting, citing, or summarizing, you must give full and accurate reference to the source of your material.

4. Put only one fact on each card.

Put only one item of information on each card. There is always a temptation to crowd your note slips with several miscellaneous facts jotted down in the order in which they are given in the book or article that you are consulting. This is a great hindrance to ease and elasticity of handling later when you begin to organize your article, for the order of your own presentation is sure to differ from that of your sources, and two items that come together on the same card may be separated by several pages in your finished paper. Therefore, record only one note to the slip; put a key word or phrase in the upper left-hand corner; and put the library call number in the upper right-hand corner so that if necessary you can again consult your source with a minimum of time and trouble.

An even stronger reason for recording only one item on each card is that this allows you to rearrange and regroup your cards at stated intervals as your work proceeds. Such elasticity of organization is necessary, for you will find that often your subject will take a new direction or an altered emphasis while being investigated. Nothing in research is more surprising and interesting than this highly independent way an investigation has of taking the bit in its teeth and turning down a road of whose existence you had previously not known. You set out to prove one thing, and end by proving something entirely different. So much the better. By being able easily to reshuffle and rearrange your cards, you are in a position to give up a preconceived theory and to follow your facts instead of forcing them.

3. Weighing Material

Both while you are consulting sources and also while you are putting your article together, you should make an intelligent effort to evaluate the material you are gathering, particularly, as so often happens, where authorities disagree. There is a wide diversity both in accuracy and in authoritativeness among the writers in any given field or on any debatable subject. The suggestions for weighing evidence and detecting propaganda which are given in the next chapter will be found most useful in this regard. Refer to these frequently and form the habit of applying them instinctively not only to your serious investigations but to your current day-by-day reading and thinking as well. As Burns so truly says in a different connection: —

> It wad from monie a blunder free us,
> An' foolish notion.

In particular, test your source material by these three important and easily applied standards: —

1. Is your source a judge or an advocate? That is, does it seem to have a fair, unbiased attitude toward the subject or is it special pleading, with a thesis to maintain, a point to prove, or an intellectual axe to grind?

2. Does the particular item of information you are considering consist of fact or of opinion? See pages 286–287 for this important criterion.

3. Is the author of the book or article you are quoting (in other words, the witness who is testifying) a standard authority in his field?

This point is of great importance in the case of contradictory opinions. In all such instances follow the best and latest authorities. If you have difficulty in determining this matter for yourself, ask your instructor's opinion or the opinion of one of the professors in the field of knowledge concerned.

THE ROUND TABLE

Using all the sources and references available in your library, record the evidence and form an opinion on one of the seven following points as the instructor directs: (1) John James Audubon was born in (a) San Domingo in 1875, or (b) in Louisiana in 1780. (2) Edward C. Pinckney's middle name is properly spelled (a) Coate, (b) Coote. (3) Francis O. Ticknor's middle name is properly spelled (a) Orreray, (b) Orray. (4) Bret Harte was born in (a) 1836, (b) 1839. (5) The correct title of Hamlin Garland's leading collection of stories is (a) *Main Traveled Roads, Main Travelled Roads, Main-Traveled Roads*, or *Main-Travelled Roads*, and (b) it was published in 1890, or 1891. (6) John B. Tabb's middle name is properly spelled (a) Bannister, (b) Banister. (7) James Whitcomb Riley was born in (a) 1849, (b) 1853.

4. Footnotes

(1) THE PURPOSE OF FOOTNOTES

The footnotes in a research paper serve two purposes. The first and most important is to afford exact and full references to the sources of the material used. In all investigations and research work such reference is necessary. It accomplishes three things : (a) it establishes the validity of the evidence ; (b) it acknowledges indebtedness to the sources ; and (c) it directs other investigators to pertinent material. It is easy to see the reason for each of these. First, without knowing your sources, no one could estimate the value of your material. Secondly, common honesty requires anyone who uses another's work to acknowledge indebtedness. Plagiarism is an ugly word, and we all recognize that another's phrase should be as private as his purse. The same situation exists, however, whether you are quoting, citing, or summarizing, and whether you are borrowing facts or opinions. In each instance, give full ascription of indebtedness. To do so will strengthen, not weaken, your conclusions. Thirdly, by means of your references you tell others who are interested in the subject where to go for material which without your assistance they might never learn of. The most valuable parts of many a research paper are the footnotes and the bibliography. Many subscribers to technical and learned journals read little else in an article except the opening and closing paragraphs and the footnotes.

In addition to giving exact and full reference, footnotes also afford the investigator a chance to develop certain points or sidelights without interrupting the momentum and the continuity of the text itself. If you have a bit of information which does not concern the main development of your article directly, but which is yet too interesting or significant to throw away, put it in a footnote. There it is available but not obtrusive.

(2) THE PLACING OF FOOTNOTES

The three most convenient ways of handling footnotes are these : —

1. Number all footnotes consecutively, 1, 2, 3, etc., and put them at the end of the paper with corresponding references throughout the text.

2. Put the footnotes at the bottom of the page to which they refer, either numbering them consecutively throughout or beginning over again (1, 2, 3, etc.) for each page.

3. Put each footnote in the line immediately following the word or passage to which it refers, using double spacing for the text and single spacing for the footnotes; and when the footnote is complete continuing with the text exactly as if there had been no interruption.

Of these three methods the second is best if you have an experienced typist; otherwise, the first.

(3) THE PUNCTUATION OF FOOTNOTES

Remember that the following five (or six) items are necessary to make a complete, exact reference : —

1. Name of the author exactly as it is given on the title page, followed by a comma.
2. Title of the book, (a) underlined, and (b) followed by a comma.
3. Name of the firm publishing the book, followed by a comma.
   (a) Place of publication, followed by a comma (unless the publisher is one of the well-known, standard firms).
4. Year of publication, followed by a comma.
5. Exact page or pages in the book where the information referred to is to be found, followed by a period.

BOOKS

The most workmanlike way to make a reference to a footnote is to put a small figure in an inverted caret ($\overset{1}{\vee}$) at the place in the text where the reference is made and then to repeat the figure at the bottom of the page or at the end of the article, wherever the notes are to be placed, and follow it with the complete reference.   For example : —

As a prominent teacher and writer once said, "There is no reason why a scholarly piece of research work should be dull, heavy, and unreadable." [1]

[1] André Morize, *Problems and Methods of Literary Criticism*, Ginn and Company, Boston, 1922, p. 298.

MAGAZINES

A reference to a magazine follows the same form except that while the name of the magazine is underlined, the title of the article is put in quotation marks. For example: —

> A contemporary critic and novelist recently made this striking observation on the relation between grammar and punctuation: "A lot of punctuation is simply grammar made graphic." [1]

THE USE OF COMMAS

Notice that the system of punctuating footnotes that is advocated here is to set off each item by means of commas. This practice is simple, clear, and logical, and has the sanction of many of the leading colleges, universities, and publishing houses. Another system, which is also widely used, is to employ periods between the different items of the reference, but to put a colon between the place of publication and the name of the publishing firm. For example, according to this system, the reference to André Morize would take this form: —

[1] André Morize. *Problems and Methods of Literary Criticism.* Boston: Ginn and Co., 1922, p. 298.

There are other styles of reference, but these two are the leading ones. Of the two the use of commas throughout seems preferable. In this matter, however, follow the custom of your college or the wishes of your instructor.

(4) THREE CONVENIENT ABBREVIATIONS

To save time and space in footnoting, three abbreviations will be found useful: *ibid., op. cit.,* and *loc. cit.* Each requires some care in handling.

Ibid. is an abbreviation of the Latin adverb *ibidem,* meaning "in the same place." If you give a reference, and then refer again to the same source, whether book or magazine, *with no other reference intervening,* use *ibid.,* which in this respect serves as a kind of bibliographical ditto mark.

[1] Wilson Follett, "On Doing without Grammar," *The Saturday Review of Literature,* October 30. 1937, pp. 3–4.

Op. cit. is an abbreviation of the Latin phrase *opere citato*, and means "in the work (or book) quoted." If your investigation makes use of only one book by an author, after giving the full reference the first time, in referring to the same book you need not repeat the title of the book, but give only the author's surname, followed by *op. cit.* and the page number.

Loc. cit. comes from the Latin phrase *loco citato*, and means "in the place cited." Its use is exactly like that of *op. cit.*, except that *op. cit.* is used in referring to books and *loc. cit.* in referring to magazine articles.

To illustrate these uses, if you wished to make another reference to Morize's *Problems and Methods of Literary Criticism* on the same or an adjacent page of your article, and if no other reference intervened, *ibid.* could be used, thus : —

[1] *Ibid.*, p. —.

If you wished to make another reference to Morize's *Problems and Methods of Literary Criticism* somewhere further on in your article, and if no other book by Morize were referred to, *op. cit.*, with the name of the author to identify it, could be used, thus : —

[2] Morize, *op. cit.*, p. —.

If you wished to make another reference to Wilson Follett's article on grammar, and if no other article by Follett were referred to, *loc. cit.*, with the name of the author to identify it, could be used, thus : —

[3] Follett, *loc. cit.*, p. —.

(5) THREE PERIODS TO MARK OMITTED MATTER

When matter is omitted in quoting, the sign of omission is three dots, or periods, in a row. Since, however, a period is the end punctuation for every sentence that is not a question or an exclamation, this means that usually four periods will be necessary, one for the sentence and three for the omitted matter. For example : —

> An English critic has made the following striking observation concerning Coleridge : "His best work is but little, but unique of its kind. . . . All that he did excellently might be bound up in twenty pages, but it should be bound in pure gold." [1]

[1] Stopford A. Brooke, *English Literature*, The Macmillan Company, 1898, pp. 229–230.

For the further use of three periods to indicate omitted matter, see the quotation from William Frederick Poole, page 261, first paragraph.

THE ROUND TABLE

1. Glance through the footnotes in several issues of *The English Journal*, *The Journal of American Folk-Lore*, *The Journal of Social Forces*, *Modern Language Notes*, *Modern Philology*, *Publications of the Modern Language Association*, and any other periodical the instructor assigns, and ascertain (*a*) the exact style of punctuation, and so on, and (*b*) the general function the footnotes perform in the development of the article.

2. Write out three full and exact references as follows : —
   (1) A brief quotation or citation from a book (not one of your text-books) ;
   (2) A brief quotation or citation from a bound volume of a magazine in the library ;
   (3) A brief quotation or citation from a current magazine in the periodical room.

5. The Bibliography

At the end of the research article comes the complete bibliography — that is, an alphabetical list of all the sources used.   If the references that were made in recording material are accurate and full, preparing the bibliography is an easy task.   There are only two differences between the references in footnotes and in a bibliography : —

1. In a footnote a definite page reference is given, but not in the bibliography.

2. .In a footnote the last name of the author is usually put last, but in the bibliography the last name is given first in order to make the alphabetical arrangement possible.   Sometimes, also, as an indication to the reader of the length and hence of the general scope of treatment in a book or article, the total number of pages of the book or the article is given after the date of publication.   Sometimes, too, if the introduction to a book is of sufficient length and importance, the number of pages in the introduction, in Roman numerals, followed by a plus sign, precedes the number of pages in the book proper.

Following is a bibliography of books and pamphlets dealing with the subject of research papers and theses.   Examine it carefully, first for the purpose of noting the exact style of making such references, and secondly for seeing what material is available on this subject.

BIBLIOGRAPHY ON METHODS OF RESEARCH

BOOKS

Almack, John C., *Research and Thesis Writing*, Houghton Mifflin Company, 1930, xiii + 310 pages.

Cross, T. P., *Bibliographical Guide to English Studies*, University of Chicago Press, 7th edition, 1938, 123 pages.

Funkhouser, W. D., *Suggestions for Thesis Writing*, University of Kentucky, Lexington, Ky., 1931, 43 pages.

Manly, J. M., and Rickert, Edith, *The Writers' Index*, Henry Holt and Company, 1923, pp. 3-37.

Morize, André, *Problems and Methods of Literary History*, Ginn and Company, 1922, x + 314 pages.

Morrow, Paul Reed, and Willard Oral Mishoff, *A Guide to Thesis Writing*, University of Georgia, Athens, Ga., 1932, 16 pages.

Reeder, Ward G., *How to Write a Thesis*, rev. and enlarged, Public School Publishing Company, Bloomington, Ill., 1930, 136 pages.

Rudler, Gustave, *Les techniques de la critique et de l'histoire littéraires en littérature française moderne*, Oxford University Press, 1923, xv + 204 pages.

Schluter, W. C., *How to Do Research Work*, Prentice-Hall, Inc., 1927, 137 pages.

Schmitz, R. Morrell, *Preparing the Research Paper*, Richard R. Smith, Inc., 1931, 94 pages.

SeBoyar, Gerald E., *Manual for Report and Thesis Writing*, F. S. Crofts and Company, 1930, 57 pages.

Wann, Louis, *The Preparation of Course Papers in the Field of Literature*, rev. ed., Jesse Ray Miller, 3566 University Avenue, Los Angeles, Calif., 1928, 67 pages.

Following is a brief sample bibliography of magazine articles on the subject of ballads and folksongs.

MAGAZINES

Barry, Phillips, "The Origin of Folk-Melodies," *Journal of American Folk-Lore*, vol. xxiii (1910), No. 90, pp. 440-445.

Gerould, G. H., "The Making of Ballads," *Modern Philology*, vol. xxi (1923), pp. 15-28.

Gordon, G. W., "Old Songs That Men Have Sung," *Adventure*, December 20, 1925.

Kittredge, G. L., "Ballads and Songs," *Journal of American Folk-Lore*, vol. xxx (1927), no. 117, pp. 283–369.
Moore, John Robert, "The Influence of Transmission on the English Ballads," *Modern Language Review*, vol. xi (1916), pp. 385–405.
Smith, C. Alphonso, "Ballads Surviving in the United States," *Musical Quarterly*, January, 1916, pp. 109–129.
Tolman, Albert H., "The Group-Authorship of Ballads," *Publications of the Modern Language Association*, vol. xlii (1927), pp. 428–432.

6. Final Revision

It is an inconvenient but fundamental fact that no one is born accurate and scholarly. The price of safety in those regards is always eternal vigilance. So far as the text or the main body of a research paper is concerned, therefore, careful revision and rewriting are as necessary as in any other kind of writing. Refer again to the chapter dealing with this subject, pages 178–187. Over and above the usual besetting sins of composition, the research article, on account of the presence of numerous footnotes and the bibliography, needs special care and watchfulness. In addition, therefore, to (1) letting your work get cold before finally revising it, and (2) reading it for mechanical blunders in (a) spelling and capitalization, (b) punctuation, (c) grammar, (d) sentence structure, and (e) paragraphing, you must also read it through carefully several times to check on the numbering, punctuation, and general accuracy of the footnotes and the bibliography. Everyone who has ever had to deal with footnotes and bibliographical details knows the incredible amount of innate depravity that lurks beneath their simple-seeming exterior. They are the most contrary things in the whole field of composition. If you can achieve correctness here, you can achieve it anywhere.

7. Form and Style in General

Do not forget what was said on page 185 about the importance of the physical appearance of all written work. This applies of course to the research article. Make it as attractive a piece of work as lies within your power. If possible, have it neatly typewritten, double spaced of course, and with wide generous margins on both sides and at the top and bottom. Every particle of time and care that you expend in this way will bring gratifying results.

The three qualities in a term paper which have been stressed thus far are the three essentials — **accuracy, thoroughness, and clearness.** Remember, however, André Morize's significant statement, "There is no reason why a scholarly piece of research work should be dull, heavy, and unreadable." We should consciously strive to write as interestingly and attractively as we can. To the *musts* of accuracy, thoroughness, and clearness let us add if possible the *shoulds* of **warmth and color.** In gathering material, watch for incidents, opinions, facts, and phrases which will add a little lightness, humor, or at least unexpectedness. If you have a touch of sparkle in your make-up, do not put the damper on when you sort out your cards and begin to write the research article. A research article is not a personal essay, but any touch of originality in approach or in treatment that you can muster is greatly to be desired. Scholarship and literary charm are not necessarily incompatible. As one teacher and writer surprisingly but logically remarked to an audience of college students : —

> "It is time to reverse the question 'Why should I write this?' . . . and ask instead 'Why should anyone read this?'" [1]

In conclusion, as an example of the point of view that is expressed in the preceding paragraph, consider this beginning of an interesting and scholarly term paper on Nicholas Vachel Lindsay. The complete paper was twenty-four manuscript pages long. Only the two opening paragraphs are given.

NICHOLAS VACHEL LINDSAY

There is something deadly about term-papers — they are always disagreeable things to write, and assuredly, disagreeable things to read. Their different materials, gathered together from such diverse sources : books, magazines, lectures, conversations, etc., and patched together by the cerebration of an undergraduate, must unavoidably suggest to the reader the Confusion of Babel. It is likely that such a conglomeration of incoherent fact and opinion will remind him of the old-fashioned crazy-quilt — serviceable as covering, but aimless in design.

[1] John Rothwell Slater, *Freshman Rhetoric*, D. C. Heath and Company, 1922, p. 150. By permission of the publishers.

The crazy-quilt motif, luckily, is not incompatible with the life of Nicholas Vachel Lindsay, the subject of this term-paper. Now a term-paper is a formal composition, and only interesting within certain limits, but Vachel Lindsay is a human being and a poet too, so he has a right to his manifold facets and seeming inconsistencies. "I refuse," he says, "to be put into uniform paraffin packages, like Uneeda Biscuit." And he can be forgiven for being poet, politician, artist, pamphleteer, Egyptologist, prohibitionist, scholar, beggar, hero-worshiper, democrat, universalist, pacifist, and several other things at the same and at different times. A queer combination, but (to borrow a phrase from Havelock Ellis) perhaps the diversities of the Many are made up for in the higher consistency of the One. For despite his rambling interests, Lindsay's outstanding characteristic is his absolute sincerity and simplicity. No one, unless he were fortified by an intense sincerity, could openly expose himself to ridicule as he has done. He sees the world with the eye of a child, however erudite and civilized he may seem. And whether he is airing his theories of art, supporting the Anti-Saloon League, deciphering Egyptian hieroglyphics, or praising William Jennings Bryan, he remains childlike in his viewpoint. A precocious child, to be sure, but a child nevertheless. His whimsy, his seriousness with details, his flamboyance, his idealism and optimism, all bespeak a childlike nature. It is likely that he will always remain the white-headed boy. . . .

CHAPTER XVI

Clear Reasoning and Straight Thinking

The trouble with most people is that they think with their hopes or fears or wishes rather than with their minds.

— WALTER DURANTY

The Importance and Prevalence of Argument

Most of the arguing that we do in college is informal, though it may be none the less heated for all that. We argue formally only when we are put on debate in literary society or in an intercollegiate contest. Others argue with us as much as we argue with others. Our minds and wills are constantly being joggled and pushed and pulled about at home, in college, at church, from the lecture platform, on the streets, on the athletic field, by radio addresses, by newspapers, magazines, and books — by everybody, it seems, and everywhere.

It therefore becomes a matter of the utmost practical importance to us throughout life to be able to think straight, to tell good argument from bad, to form the ability of deciding wisely when to change our minds either on questions of fact or on questions of procedure — in short, to train ourselves in the desirable but difficult art of knowing (1) what to believe and (2) what to do.

This objective is of importance under all conditions and in every circumstance, but it is of critical importance to all who, like us, live in a democracy, and thus carry on the complicated business of government largely by popular election and public debate. Almost may the United States be called a "government by public discussion." Each of us dwells within a fourfold political circle — city (or district), county, state, and nation.   We are taxed by, and required to obey the laws of, each of these four political divisions.   We elect our officials, from coroner to president; and also elect our lawmakers, from town councilmen or county commissioners to United States Senators. Frequently important or highly controversial questions such as prohibition or large bond issues are submitted to the direct vote of the people.   Surely if light and wisdom were ever needed, they are needed by the citizens of today, living as we do in a nation-wide welter of conflicting arguments, opposing policies, organized aggressive selfishness, and open and subtle propaganda.

(1) SIX DOORS TO ERROR

Useful as is the power to convince others, more useful still to most of us, because much more in demand, is the power to be convinced intelligently — *intelligently*.   Following are six of the most prevalent dangers we must guard against in weighing evidence and testing reasoning : —

1. Not Distinguishing Fact from Opinion
2. Insufficient or Unreliable Evidence
3. Overhasty Generalization
4. Faulty Analogy
5. Ignoring the Question, or Evading the Issue
6. Begging the Question : Calling Names

Remember, finally, that a mistake in reasoning and the consequent reaching of a wrong conclusion mean more to the person who makes the mistake than to anyone else in the world.   If sheer bluster or shrewd deceit prevails instead of reason and intelligence, in the long run it is you who will pay the penalty.

THE ROUND TABLE

1. To ask an important and highly personal question, do you continue to read an argumentative article if it attacks the view or opinion that you hold?   Face this question fairly, and consider its bearing on your mental condition twenty years from now.

2. Do you remember ever having been convinced by an argument that you were in the wrong?   If so, did it take effect immediately or later?

3. In what respects would you say that you were a conservative?   A progressive?   A radical?

4. The reasoning powers of the human race are not highly regarded by the world's thinkers. Here are two opinions on the subject, one more than three hundred years old and the other contemporary. Read them carefully and try to refute them if you disagree with them.

    (a) Doth any man doubt, that if there were taken out of men's minds vain opinions, flattering hopes, false valuation, imaginations as one would, and the like, but it would leave the minds of a number of men poor shrunken things, full of melancholy and indisposition, and unpleasing to themselves?

                    — FRANCIS BACON, "Of Truth"

    (b) The so-called "opinions" of the ordinary man are usually a mixture of the veriest smattering of information and misinformation, with a large injection of his favorite newspaper's attitude and the influence of his personal environment.

          — JAMES TRUSLOW ADAMS, "The Voter: His Rights and Duties," *Yale Review*, autumn, 1932

5. Find and bring to class a brief argument that seems convincing to you.

6. What is the best paragraph or short example of persuasion you have ever come across?

7. Describe the methods of persuasion used by the most attractive public speaker you have heard.

8. Study Henry Ward Beecher's "Speech at Liverpool" as a masterly example of conciliation of a hostile audience.

9. In Shakespeare's *Julius Caesar* contrast Brutus's speech (III, ii. 13–66) and Antony's speech (III, ii. 78–266) as examples, respectively, of conviction and persuasion. Antony took over the mob just where Brutus delivered it to him — enthusiastic over Brutus, vaguely approving or at least not disapproving of Caesar's death, not understanding the great issues involved, and mildly wondering what it was all about anyway. A short while afterward Antony's eloquent and incredibly adroit oration had welded them into a white-hot unit, seething with rage and bent upon destruction.

10. Think over the implications of the following definition of a controversy: "A controversy is normally an exploitation of a set of misunderstandings for warlike purposes." — I. A. RICHARDS

11. Concerning what two or three subjects have you heard the most arguing this term?

12. As a famous instance of the power of logic read and report on Jonathan Swift's humorous "Predictions for the Year 1708," in which he proved (?) to everybody's satisfaction that the almanac maker, Dr. Partridge, would "infallibly die upon the 29th day of March, about eleven at night of a raging fever." On the thirtieth of March Dr. Partridge stated in the newspapers that he was still alive. Then Swift replied in "A Vindication of Isaac Bickerstaff," again proving that Dr. Partridge had really died as prophesied. The whole incident illustrates Swift's sense of humor, and has added perceptibly to the gayety of nations.

13. Explain the logic upon which Oliver Wendell Holmes's "The Deacon's Masterpiece, or The Wonderful 'One-Hoss Shay'" is based.

1. Not Distinguishing Fact from Opinion

One of the first distinctions we should learn to make is the difference between fact and opinion. The two are as unlike as chalk and cheese. **A fact is something that has actual existence;** it is an actual happening in time or space; it is based on actuality and reality. As such, it can be definitely proved or disproved, provided only that enough evidence is available.

Opinion, on the other hand, is an inference drawn from facts. It is a belief, a notion, or a judgment which exists in someone's mind. It is not what is or was, but what we think and believe. Opinion may be right or wrong; it may be based on ignorance, prejudice, or desire. Obviously, opinion has no value other than that given by (1) the facts behind it and (2) the judgment of the person expressing the opinion.

No speaker or writer separates fact and opinion as he argues with us. Each hearer or reader has to do that for himself. In *The House of Fame* Chaucer relates how, in order to reach the ears of mankind, a lie and a truth sometimes happened to struggle out of the same opening at the same time, and consequently became so closely intermingled that no one from that time forth could tell them apart. That is the way fact and opinion come to us, woven together into the warp and woof of argument. Wise is the man who can tell one from the other and, honestly and intelligently, use each for what it is worth.

Read the following examples and unwind facts from opinions. The difference is fairly obvious because of the brevity of the intertwined statements.

1. Edgar Allan Poe, who died in 1849, is America's most gifted poet.
2. Automobile accidents have been steadily increasing of late years. A national law should be passed requiring all manufacturers to install a governor on each engine that would prevent its being run at over fifty miles an hour.
3. The greatest invention of our day is wireless. It was invented by Marconi in 1902.
4. *Hamlet*, the greatest of Shakespeare's plays, was probably written in 1601.

5. The English failed at Gallipoli, but their heroic attack on the strongly entrenched Turkish forces there was the most daring exploit of the World War.

6. (a) The Prohibition Amendment was passed in 1919. It did more to curb drinking than any other step this country ever took, and its repeal in 1933 was a sad blow to American civilization.

   (b) The Prohibition Amendment was passed in 1919. Its tendency was greatly to increase drinking, especially among young people. Its repeal in 1933 was a most constructive step.

7. Granted that the face of Helen of Troy launched a thousand ships, neither she nor the famed Venus of Milo can hold a candle to some of today's reigning beauties of the screen and stage.

8. No wonder Euclid's name is still famous, for geometry, of which he is called the father, is the most important branch of mathematics.

9. Jim Jeffries, who held the world's heavyweight championship from 1906 to 1908, was the most formidable fighter in ring history.

THE ROUND TABLE

1. Bring to class a short selection from a contemporary newspaper or magazine that mingles fact and opinion. Read it to the class, and point out where one ends and the other begins.

2. Write a brief argumentative passage on some question about which you are well informed. Read it to the class and distinguish for them between your statements of fact and your assertions of opinion.

2. Insufficient or Unreliable Evidence

Evidence consists of those facts which bear upon the question under discussion. Evidence is the material from which the argument is constructed; or, to carry out in detail this figure of building, evidence is the material, reasoning is the architect, and proof is the structure.

Evidence is of two kinds: (1) **testimonial or direct evidence** — that is, the testimony of human witnesses; and (2) **circumstantial or indirect evidence** — that is, the evidence not of human witnesses but of facts or incidents which afford a basis for a reasonable inference concerning the point at issue.

Huxley has clearly distinguished these two kinds of evidence as follows: —

Suppose that a man tells you he saw a person strike another man and kill him; that is testimonial evidence of the fact of murder. But it is possible to have circumstantial evidence of the fact of murder; that is to say, you may find a man dying with a wound upon his head having exactly the form and character of a wound which is made by an axe, and, with due care in taking surrounding circumstances into account, you may conclude with the utmost certainty that the man has been murdered; that his death is the consequence of a blow inflicted by another man with that implement. We are very much in the habit of considering circumstantial evidence as of less value than testimonial evidence, and it may be that, where the circumstances are not perfectly clear and intelligible, it is a dangerous and unsafe kind of evidence; but it must not be forgotten that, in many cases, circumstantial is quite as conclusive as testimonial evidence.[1]

Of these two kinds of evidence — testimonial and circumstantial — we are here mainly concerned with testimonial. The scientist in the laboratory and the lawyer in the courtroom deal with the circumstances of life and the facts of nature, and both scientist and lawyer undergo a long and careful training for the task. You and I, however, in the world of government, business, and society, are chiefly guided by what we hear and read. The evidence with which we deal consists of the spoken and written word. It is testimonial evidence then that we must train ourselves to weigh and evaluate.

(1) TESTIMONIAL OR DIRECT EVIDENCE

The source of all testimonial evidence is a human witness. This is true whether the witness testifies in person by word of mouth, as in the law courts, or whether he testifies in writing by means of a letter, a newspaper editorial, a magazine article, or a book. Obviously, the only value that human testimony possesses comes from the character and the competence of the witness himself — the man behind the testimony.

We are all familiar with the process of trial by jury, in which the witnesses are examined and cross-examined by the prosecution and the defense, and every shred of evidence is subjected to critical scrutiny. Oral testimony thus has to fight for its very existence in a court of law. Written testimony, however, frequently lulls our doubts and questionings to sleep through the dignity of print or the prestige of the organization or person responsible for the article. Always remember, however, that whether spoken or written, human testimony can rise no higher than the intelligence and honesty of the person testifying.

[1] From T. H. Huxley, *American Addresses*, Lecture I, D. Appleton-Century Company, New York. By permission of the publishers.

For the sake of ourselves, therefore, and the causes that we are interested in, we should form the habit of testing witnesses and weighing their evidence.

Various tests for testimonial evidence have been proposed, but for most purposes the four following will serve : —

(1) Is the witness honest and willing to tell the truth?
(2) Is the witness prejudiced against, or biased in favor of, either of the contending sides?
(3) Is the witness in full possession of the facts and well informed on the matter under discussion?
(4) Is the witness's knowledge up-to-date and thoroughly abreast of the times?

The essentials of these four tests may be summed up informally in two simple questions : (1) Is the witness trying to tell the truth, or is he twisting it to suit his own ends? (2) Does he know what he is talking about?

The question as to the witness's honesty and his personal bias is of peculiar importance. Human nature is much the same everywhere, and it is a sad fact that even the least personal interest one way or the other is apt to render a witness's testimony next to valueless. According to the cynical old maxim, "Whose bread I eat, his song I sing"; or, to turn the saying around, "He who pays the piper calls the tune." For example, the president of the Brewers' Association or the owner of a chain of distilleries would not make a good witness on matters connected with prohibition; nor, for the opposite reason, would a paid organizer of the Anti-Saloon League. The owner of an industry protected by a high tariff would not ordinarily be considered a reliable witness in matters affecting tariff reform. No fair-minded citizen would accept at full value the political conclusions of a newspaper owned by a politician or recognized as the organ of special interests or of a certain party.

After the battle is over and the campaign closes, we can usually recognize propaganda for what it is and often have the pleasure of congratulating ourselves that we were not taken in by it. In the heat of the conflict, however, with words flying thick around us from rostrum, radio, newspaper, pamphlet, and magazine, we need a great deal of mental poise, intelligent reflection, and unselfish purpose to keep from being swept off our feet.

To reach a reasoned judgment under these circumstances would be hard *even if everyone were trying to tell the truth, the whole truth, and nothing but the truth.* But with special interests, ambitious leaders and would-be leaders, political parties, and big and little business, each with a special axe to grind, and each aggressively clamoring for the grindstone to be turned his way, the American national headgear should unquestionably be a thinking cap instead of a wishing cap.

THE ROUND TABLE

1. From your personal experience relate a coincidence which was mistaken for cause and effect.

2. From a current newspaper or magazine bring to class the best example you can find of (*a*) circumstantial evidence and (*b*) testimonial evidence.

3. Can you relate from your experience or observation any good instance of circumstantial evidence which later turned out to be (*a*) right or (*b*) wrong?

4. Recalling the section on Definition, pages 128–134, what method does Huxley use in defining Testimonial and Circumstantial Evidence, page 287?

5. Do you know of any instance in college, community, or state life where seemingly valid testimony lost its effectiveness because the witness was shown to be biased or prejudiced?

6. Memory of things seen and heard during excitement is unreliable. To prove this, a professor staged a fake riot to frighten and surprise his class. Four persons rushed into the classroom, fought one another and smashed furniture for thirty seconds, and then rushed out. Questioned, only three of the twenty-nine witnesses even knew how many persons had entered the room.[1]

With this incident compare the results obtained from the sixth exercise in the Round Table under Description, page 507.

7. In spite of what Huxley said concerning the trustworthiness of circumstantial evidence when properly handled (page 288), great care must be taken to avoid making a serious mistake. Very often there is an alternative explanation which accounts for all the facts. Following is a striking example taken from real life.

Two men, A and B, were seen fighting in a field. Soon after, A was found dead. His body showed wounds from a pitchfork. Near him a bloodstained pitchfork was found. It was known to belong to B. And B was known to have taken it from his own toolshed that morning. Also, a standing enmity was known to have existed between A and B. On the strength of these facts, eleven of the jury found B guilty of murder. But one juryman held out, maintaining that the

[1] Freling Foster, "Keeping Up with the World," *Collier's, The National Weekly*, 1937, Crowell Publishing Company, 250 Park Avenue, New York.

evidence did not converge only on that hypothesis.   A fresh jury was sworn in, who promptly found B guilty.   Then the dissenting member of the first jury gave himself up.   He himself, not B, had murdered A.   He had come by after A and B had been fighting; found B's pitchfork; quarreled with A; stabbed him; and got away unsuspected.   Finding, later, that the innocent man had been arrested, he contrived to get on the jury as the only way of saving B without endangering himself.[1]

8. Invent a case (a crime?) where all the circumstances seemed to point clearly to one explanation, but where the real solution was otherwise.

3. Overhasty Generalization

One of the commonest and most useful forms of reasoning is **induction — that is, reasoning from individual facts to a general law**.   The term "induction" comes from the two Latin words, *in*, meaning "into" or "to," and *ducere*, meaning "to lead."   It was so named because it leads (*ducere*) from the particular to (*in*) the general. Its opposite, or rather its complement, is **deduction, or argument from the general to the particular**.   Induction is the approved method of science and experimentation, and when rightly used is as reliable as the multiplication table.

A typical instance, stripped to its essentials for the sake of clearness, is this : —

A was a man, and he died.
B was a man, and he died.
C was a man, and he died.
(And so on through a multitude of instances) Therefore, all **men** die (or are mortal).[2]

Reasoning in this way from a number of observed instances to which no exception has been noted, we have every reason to believe that the

[1] From S. M. Phillips, *Cases of Circumstantial Evidence*.   Quoted in Albury Castell, *A College Logic*, The Macmillan Company, 1935, p. 200.

[2] The deductive form of argument corresponding to this is the following : Note that deduction begins where induction leaves off, namely, with a general law, which is known as the **major, or greater, premise**.   It then applies this general law to a specific instance, which is known as the **minor, or lesser, premise,** and then draws a conclusion from them.   This typical form of deductive reasoning is called a **syllogism** : —

All men are mortal (Major Premise).
X is a man (Minor Premise).
Therefore, X will die (Conclusion).

sun will rise in the east tomorrow, that iron sinks in water, that water freezes at 32° Fahrenheit, that sugar is sweet, that the days are longer in summer than in winter, that if we do not drink water or some other liquid we grow thirsty — and so on through innumerable laws of nature and generalized human experiences ranging from the simplicity of the instances just cited to such imperial scientific generalizations as the law of falling bodies and the law of gravitation, which reveals that every particle of matter in the universe attracts every other particle with a force that varies directly as the mass and inversely as the square of the distances.

The chief, indeed the only, danger that we have to guard against in induction is overhasty generalization or jumping at conclusions. The human mind works on a hair trigger, and frequently the mental gun goes off before it is properly loaded. We observe a few instances and rush headlong into a generalization before we are justified by the facts. This tendency is a holdover from childhood into mentally immature manhood and womanhood. A little girl once suddenly screamed and ran when she saw a black dog, although she was fond of all other kinds of dogs and would pet them with childish eagerness. It developed that a black dog had recently growled and snapped at her, whereupon blackness in a dog became for her an unmistakable danger signal.

The same kind of weakness in inductive reasoning on a slightly more adult scale is seen in such remarks as the following:

1. A college education is useless, since Henry Ford, Thomas Edison, and Abraham Lincoln succeeded without it.
2. I noticed that all the people in town who died last year were attended by physicians. If I get sick, therefore, I shall take care not to call in a doctor.
3. My best friend and his roommate got passing grades in History 99 without doing any work. I must be sure to take that course next year.

The same kind of partial reasoning lies behind such loose popular beliefs as these: —

1. Rich men's sons are usually shiftless.
2. Ministers' children always turn out badly.
3. Fat men are good-natured.
4. Red-headed people have hot tempers.

Such generalizations state at most a mere probability and sometimes not even that.

A similar weakness in overhasty generalization is evident, though not to the same degree, in the following statements, all of which have just enough truth in them to make them dangerous.

1. A college education is a guarantee of success.
2. All ambitious men are selfish.
3. He is energetic because he is a New Englander, and all New Englanders are energetic.
4. Every man has his price.
5. When thieves fall out honest men get their dues.
6. A little learning is a dangerous thing.

Proverbs are based on a still higher degree of probability. Many of them are the result of wide human experience, and, though subject to many and startling exceptions, they will prove true in the main.

1. As the twig is bent the tree is inclined.
2. A bird in the hand is worth two in the bush.
3. In a calm sea every man is a pilot.
4. You never miss the water till the well runs dry.
5. The highest branch is not the safest roost.
6. Too many cooks spoil the broth.
7. You can't judge a horse by his harness.
8. Fine feathers do not make fine birds.
9. The proof of the pudding is in the eating.
10. The more haste, the less speed.

In all cases of inductive reasoning, whether in the form of popular belief, proverbs, or scientific observation, the simple but adequate test is, Have enough typical instances been examined to justify the generalization?

THE ROUND TABLE

1. From your experience or reading describe an example each of (a) valid and (b) faulty induction.
2. Look up "deduction," "syllogism," "enthymeme," in a logic or a small encyclopedia and be prepared to explain and illustrate them in a brief oral report.
3. From past or present experience bring in two examples of overhasty generalization.

4. What, if anything, is wrong with the following statements : —

(1) My fiancé (fiancée) has broken his (her) engagement.   This shows how fickle all men (women) are.

(2) He must be a Swede, for all Swedes have light hair and a ruddy complexion.

(3) A cheerful disposition is a cause of good health.   All the cheerful, good-humored people I know are healthy.

(4) His word is absolutely reliable.   I have never known him to lie.

5. Following is one of the most famous examples of valid inductive reasoning on record.   It is William Harvey's argument for the circulation of blood.   The passage was printed in his "Essay on the Motion of the Heart and the Blood," 1628.   (Previous to the work of William Harvey physiologists believed that the flow of blood in the arteries and veins was from the heart to the rest of the body, and simply carried to the various parts of the body the nutriment supplied by the digestion of food.   Harvey's careful measurements and investigations indicated that there must be actual circulation of the blood through the heart and the body rather than a constant creation of a new supply in the heart.   He reasoned as follows.)

Let us assume either arbitrarily or from experiment, the quantity of blood which the left ventricle of the heart will contain when distended, to be, say, two ounces, three ounces, or one ounce and a half — in the dead body I have found it to hold upwards of two ounces. . . .   Let us suppose as approaching the truth that the fourth, or fifth, or sixth, or even that the eighth part of its charge is thrown into the artery at each contraction ; this would give either half an ounce, or three drachms, or one drachm of blood as propelled by the heart at each pulse into the aorta ; which quantity, by reason of the valves at the root of the vessel, can by no means return into the ventricle. Now, in the course of half an hour, the heart will have made more than one thousand beats, in some as many as two, three, and even four thousand. Multiplying the number of drachms propelled by the number of pulses, we shall have either one thousand half ounces, or one thousand times three drachms, or a like proportional quantity of blood, according to the amount which we assume as propelled with each stroke of the heart, sent from this organ into the artery ; a larger quantity in every case than is contained in the whole body ! . . .   Thus, supposing even the smallest quantity of blood to be passed through the heart and the lungs with each pulsation, a vastly greater amount would still be thrown into the arteries . . . than could by any possibility be supplied by the food consumed.   It could be furnished in no other way than by making a circuit and returning.

(Four years after Harvey died, Marcello Malpighi, an Italian, the founder of microscopic anatomy, examined in 1660 with the microscope the tissues in which the smallest arteries and veins were imbedded.   He discovered the tiny capillaries connecting the arteries with the veins, and was thus able to prove by direct observation that the blood flowed through them from the arteries into the veins and back to the heart.)

4. Faulty Analogy

To an extraordinary extent, intelligent people become convinced of highly improbable things because they have heard them supported by analogies whose unsoundness would be apparent to an imbecile.
— R. H. THOULESS

Analogy means imaginative resemblance: not actual physical likeness, as between two peas in the same pod or two eggs in the same nest; but rather resemblance in functions, effects, and relationships, such as the likeness between sleep and death, the similarity of the human nervous system to a telephone exchange, or the resemblance between the sun's lighting the physical world and learning's enlightening the mental world. To argue from analogy is to describe a situation or a circumstance in one sphere of life and to infer that the same or similar results will follow in the case of a like situation or circumstance in another sphere of life.

An unusually striking analogy is the one by which Henry Clay erased a political blunder and restored himself to favor with the rural voters of Kentucky. Henry Watterson relates the incident thus: —

In 1816 Mr. Clay voted for a new Compensation Act of Congress. It aroused a tornado of popular wrath. Not even the great Commoner could stand against this, and sagaciously resolved to try to weather it. Meeting a staunch supporter who had turned against him, he said: —

"Jack, you have a good flintlock, haven't you?"

"Yes."

"Did it ever flash in the pan?"

"Once it did, but only once."

"What did you do with it? Did you throw it away?"

"No, I picked the flint and tried it again."

"Well," said Mr. Clay, "I have flashed only once, — on this compensation bill, — and you are going to throw me away?"

"No," cried the hunter, touched in his tenderest part; "no, Mr. Clay, I will pick the flint and try you again."

— HENRY WATTERSON: *Oratory of the Stump*

When the two parallel situations are not from different spheres of life, as is the case with Clay's comparison of a man to a rifle, but from the same sphere of life, the term **argument from example** is sometimes used instead of argument from analogy. Here is a familiar instance from the speech of Patrick Henry on the Stamp Act, May 29, 1765. Strictly speaking, it is an argument from example: —

> Tarquin and Caesar each had his Brutus, Charles the First his Cromwell, and George the Third ["Treason!" cried the speaker] — *may profit by their example.* If this be treason, make the most of it.

To repeat: what analogy does is to find a point of resemblance between two otherwise unlike situations, draw a parallel between them, and suggest that similar results will follow in both instances. Analogy is frequently used in the attempt to show that a plan that has worked well — or that has failed to work well — at one time in one place will similarly succeed or fail at another time, in another place. Thus any foreign or domestic policy that may be proposed for the United States is usually certain to be discussed on the basis of its success or failure in other countries which have tried it; any proposed state legislation is put to the same test, the assumption being that if a certain tax or a certain educational policy has succeeded in Michigan, Minnesota, and California, it is worth trying in Pennsylvania, Massachusetts, or Virginia; and, if a new policy in athletics, in college entrance admission, in examination system, or in requirements for a degree, has had gratifying results in the private or denominational colleges it should likewise be given a trial in the state institutions.

The use of analogy, or imaginative resemblance, is not confined to argument. The two commonest figures of speech, metaphor and simile, are both based upon it.[1] Likewise many proverbs owe their appeal to the aptness of the analogy between familiar facts in nature and their corresponding parallels in human experience. Indeed, the proverb "What is sauce for the goose is sauce for the gander" is not only based on analogy, but also suggests exactly what analogy itself is. Other familiar proverbs which owe their probability to experience and their phraseology to analogy are these: —

1. As the twig is bent so the tree is inclined.
2. Don't swap horses in the middle of the stream.
3. There is no use locking the stable door after the horse is stolen.
4. A bird in the hand is worth two in the bush.
5. He that gazes at the moon may fall into the gutter.
6. Barefooted men should not tread upon thorns.
7. People who live in glass houses should not throw stones.

[1] See pages 407–409

The most that can be said for an analogy, however, no matter how striking it may be, is that it illustrates rather than proves, and that it is hence more effective in exposition than in argument. In nearly every argument from analogy the differences far outweigh the resemblances. In either using or listening to an analogy, therefore, we should ask and answer two questions: (1) Is the resemblance between the two cases fundamental and essential or merely superficial and incidental? and (2) Are the essential differences sufficient to outweigh and to nullify the one point of resemblance? As a matter of practical strategy, however, an apt analogy is frequently exceedingly plausible, and sometimes sways an audience where solider and duller arguments leave the listeners cold. As a final word, to borrow Henry Clay's figure of the flintlock rifle, an analogy is usually a brilliant flash in the pan. It has little powder and shot behind it.

THE ROUND TABLE

1. John Stuart Mill, who was a real thinker, considered analogy "as a mere guide-post, pointing out the direction in which more rigorous investigations should be prosecuted."

2. What is the most striking analogy you have ever heard or read? Present it to the class and analyze its weakness and strength.

3. On some current question in international, national, state, community, or college affairs, compose as sound and striking an analogy as you can think of.

4. Here are two typical arguments from analogy: —
    (1) Women as well as men should have a voice in the world's political affairs, for government is nothing but national housekeeping.
    (2) To say that a modern man is not justified in believing in God because primitive man believed exclusively in fetishes, taboos, totems, personification of natural forces, animism, and ancestor worship, is as illogical as to believe that a highly complicated government like that of the United States is to be disregarded because man once had a simple tribal organization.
                                                                    — SHAILER MATTHEWS

5. Analogy not only is employed in metaphor and simile, in proverbs, and in argument, but it is also the basis for fables. Examine several of the most familiar of *Aesop's Fables* and point out the underlying analogy.

6. The following is an interesting object lesson based on analogy.

At a state banquet given by Frederick the Great of Prussia to his courtiers and noblemen, the monarch asked those present to explain why his revenues continued to diminish despite incoming taxes. An old general of the Hussars remarked dryly, "I will show Your Majesty what happens to the money."

Procuring a piece of ice, he lifted it high for inspection; then he handed it to his neighbor and requested that it be passed on from hand to hand to the King. By the time it reached Frederick, it was about the size of a pea.

— *Christian Science Monitor*

7. Here is an example of an anecdote based on analogy that was used effectively in a campaign speech. The first speaker had just concluded his appeal to the voters, closing with a series of protestations of affection and promises of service. Whereupon his opponent opened his speech in this fashion: "In listening to my distinguished friend's declarations of good will and his undying desire to serve you, I am reminded of the heroic deed of an old colored acquaintance. He and a little colored boy were fishing together on the bank of a deep river when suddenly the little boy fell in. Instantly Uncle Henry jumped in after him, and after a hard struggle, in which he almost lost his own life, he succeeded in pulling the little boy out. As both of them lay on the ground gasping for breath, a white man who had seen the incident from a distance came up and complimented Uncle Henry on his bravery.

"'Is the little boy your grandson?' he asked.

"'Naw, sir! He ain't no kin to me.'

"'You must be very fond of him, then, to risk your life to save him.'

"'Naw, sir. I don't care nothin' about him, nothin' at all.'

"'Then why in the world did you jump in after him?'

"'De little rascal had de bait can in his pocket.'

"And I can't help wondering," the speaker continued, "what would be my opponent's attitude toward *you*, if you didn't have the vote in your pocket."

5. Ignoring the Question, or Evading the Issue

Like the fallacy of overhasty generalization, ignoring the question, or evading the issue, is another childish device which every adult ought to put away along with other childish things. Says little sister, "Your face is dirty. Go wash it." Retorts little brother, "And your hair is mussy. Go comb it." He runs out, whistling, perfectly satisfied over having won the argument.

Another amusing case of the same kind of logic was recently related in the *New Yorker's* column, "The Talk of the Town."

A moving-picture magnate of Hollywood was arguing with a dramatist whose play was being produced. The man of the pen was resisting a certain change in the script, and he argued his point valiantly and at length. Finally the big movie man said, "Come here," and led him over to a window. "What do you see?" he asked. What the author saw was an expanse of parked cars, and he said so. "Which one did you come in?" he was asked. The author pointed out a modest Ford, a year or two old. "See that new Cadillac V-16?" said the producer. "I came in that. . . . And you argue!"

Obvious as these examples are, they are no more extreme than many another that passes muster as serious argument on the forum of public discussion "anywhere in America."

ARGUMENTUM AD HOMINEM

A prevailing form of arguing beside the point is known in logic as *argumentum ad hominem* — that is, argument against the person. The debater guilty of this fallacy turns aside from the point at issue and assails the character, past record, former beliefs, or personal weakness of his opponent. He deals in personalities instead of in principles. In so doing he usually employs vehement earnestness effectively tinctured with invective, sarcasm, and ridicule. Either openly or subtly he appeals to the passions and prejudices of the audience instead of to their intelligence and powers of reason. A classic example of such strategy is cited by W. S. Jevons from the English courts. The attorney for the defense is said to have handed to the barrister his brief in a certain case marked, "No case; abuse the plaintiff's attorney."

These tactics are the rule rather than the exception in political campaigns, and are all too often resorted to in heated arguments on other subjects no matter how serious and weighty. Could we only realize it, this form of dodging the issue is always a conscious or unconscious confession of weakness on the part of the person who resorts to it. In effect it is equivalent to saying: "My opponent's cause and his arguments are too strong for me, but I can throw so much mud on him that you will be ashamed to be seen in his company."

Probably the most brilliant answer to an *argumentum ad hominem* in literature is the way Macaulay revealed the weakness of the attempt of the followers of Charles I of England to answer the official charges against him as king by praising his private virtues.

The advocates of Charles, like the advocates of other malefactors against whom overwhelming evidence is produced, generally decline all controversy about the facts, and content themselves with calling testimony to character. He had so many private virtues! . . .

We charge him with having broken his coronation oath; and we are told that he kept his marriage vow! We accuse him of having given up his people to the merciless inflictions of the most hot-headed and hard-hearted of prelates; and the defence is, that he took his little son on his knees and kissed him! We censure him for having violated the articles of the Petition of Rights, after having, for good and valuable consideration, promised to obey them; and we are informed that he was accustomed to hear prayers at six o'clock in the morning! It is to such considerations as these, together with his Vandyke dress, his handsome face, and his peaked beard, that he owes, we verily believe, most of his popularity with the present generation.

This striking passage illustrates the proper way to deal with *argumentum ad hominem* — namely, to strip the charges to their simplest terms and show that they have no actual bearing on the matter under discussion. If we can do this fairly and effectively, the faulty argument will of itself recoil upon its author, and he will be singed in the fire of his own kindling.

THE ROUND TABLE

1. Can you name an experience from childhood which would serve as an example of ignoring the question?

2. From experience or observation describe a case of evading the issue (*argumentum ad hominem*) in national, state, county, community, or college politics.

3. In your reading have you come across any article or editorial that evades the real issue and introduces irrelevant matter?

4. Would these arguments carry weight with you?

   (1) At a church heresy trial the defendant maintained that his accuser was not wholly orthodox himself.

   (2) This man's arguments are worthless, for he is notoriously dishonest.

5. Following are two well-written pieces of informal argument. "The Profits of Parenthood" delightfully illustrates, and "Education and Business" ably exposes, the weakness of leaving out of account certain vital issues in the question under discussion. Discuss these arguments in class. Remember, of course, that "The Profits of Parenthood" is humorous.

1. The Profits of Parenthood [1]

A generation sophisticated, civilized, and whatever are the other past-participial adjectives, will welcome the latest application of the debunking process to the greatly overrated industry of parenthood.

What would be the present market price of a non-interest-bearing bond maturing in eighteen years and at the end of that time worth nothing? Yet that, according to official figures, is the sort of investing the American people are practising on a huge scale.

A baby is born to a family enjoying, more or less, an income of $2500 a year. At the age of 18 years that baby will represent a parental expenditure of $10,000, not including the valuable but unpaid services of the mother. At eighteen that baby will be worth $29,000, this being its future net earnings during life expectancy. Of this net profit the return to the investing parent is precisely zero. From the age of eighteen to twenty-four the "investment" will spend his earnings on life and haberdashery. About the age of twenty-four he will put on his hat and say, "So long, Ma and Pop; I've found a girl."

Once upon a time the farmer could depend upon his multitudinous brood to supply his farm hands and run the farm for him when he became too old to plow. Now his children spend their youth in school and leave the old farm for the city immediately upon graduation. And urban children, instead of supporting their parents in their old age, acquire a family of their own and seek their fortunes in parts too remote to remember their debt to their parents.

2. Education and Business [2]

Some time ago I read in the daily papers the news of an interesting statistical survey among the graduates of a noted university. The report showed that the earnings of the graduates who were members of the Phi Beta Kappa Society were considerably less than those of most of the other graduates. The papers drew what to them seemed the clear moral of the tale: it is a mistake to concentrate on the things of the mind while in college. Was this really the moral? The reply suggests itself that the Phi Beta Kappa men had been successful in the light of what they had sought in education, which was a knowledge not of how to make money, but of how to make something of themselves. Is the function of college to equip the young for a specific occupation or for life? Many students incline towards the former of the two alternatives, and while in college choose their courses accordingly; if they intend to enter business, they concentrate on courses in economics; if medicine, they study chemistry and biology, and so forth. And these same youths, when well on their way to a business or professional career,

[1] Homer A. Watt and Oscar Cargill, *Highways in College Composition*, Prentice-Hall, Inc., 1930, p. 710.
[2] *The Yale Review*, July, 1926, pp. 725–726. By permission of the publishers.

find that, once through with their work, they have nothing to fall back upon; they have formed no habits of reading, and cannot keep their minds long enough on an open book; they lack any cultural interests with which to refresh the mind, and so resort to the "movies" or the radio to fill their spare time; and what is more important still, they have no general philosophy of life, with which to face the world and see their own occupation in its proper perspective. So, gradually their work engulfs them; whether in or out of the office, their minds are never off its problems, till business, ceasing to be mere business, becomes life itself. . . .

College is a preparation for life, and life is infinitely wider than work. Life is also leisure and thought and family relationships; it is play and art and religion; it is sleep and waking and death itself. Not only is life wider than work, it is the only thing that justifies work. If you absorb life into work, you find that there is nothing to work for. Work must always lead beyond itself to a life of the mind by which the fruits of work may be enjoyed. To work is to make a tool of oneself; and man should be not only a tool, but also the craftsman behind the tool. All too often, the calls of actions are so insistent that one has no time for the repose and thoughtfulness that enter into the building up of an inner life; one comes to live altogether outside oneself. And here is the opportunity of education. Colleges should fill, to some extent, the rôle of the medieval monasteries in which man may take an inventory of his vital resources, away from the bustle of the world, and determine his place in the general scheme of things. It is impossible to complete this task in college, but it is possible to begin it. Education should be the process of forming a personality which may function in the world of work and yet be free of it, of cultivating those intellectual and spiritual interests by reference to which only has work or life any importance.

— RAPHAEL DEMOS

6. Begging the Question : Calling Names

Begging the question means assuming the truth of something that needs to be proved. The most insidious form of this fallacy, and one of the greatest weaknesses that the reasoning animal called man is heir to, is the influence of the effective epithet, or, in other words, calling names.

In the proscription scene that opens the fourth act of Shakespeare's *Julius Caesar*, Antony, Octavius, and Lepidus are seated around a table condemning their enemies to death. Concerning his own nephew, as he marks him for slaughter, Antony says: —

"He shall not live; look, with a spot I damn him."

Substitute "name" for "spot," and you have the subtlest and most successful form of begging the question.

On this foundation stone rises one of the greatest of human industries — propaganda.

(1) UNMASKING PROPAGANDA

Propaganda has been well defined as the "expression of opinion or action by individuals or groups deliberately designed to influence opinions or actions of other individuals or groups with reference to predetermined ends." No one likes to be made use of in this way, either unconsciously or consciously; but to be used unconsciously is much the worse of the two. As a defense mechanism against the propagandists' pet device of the unfair term has been proposed a former advertising slogan, "It's fun to be fooled but it's more fun to know." Here, truly, knowledge is power.

A recent writer assails this practice under the suggestive title, "Oily Words." "All oily words," he says, "can be divided readily into two classes — good oil and bad oil. They serve either to make something look better than it really is or to make it look worse. . . . In political as well as in national warfare, we find a great many of these words employed. We say our candidate is a 'statesman' and has 'vision' and 'ideas.' How do we express these facts about the opposing candidate? We say he is a 'politician,' a 'visionary,' and that he has 'theories.'" [1]

Thus goes the war of words with men and movements. The choice between good names and bad names as applied to exactly the same object is only too often a question of whose interests are to be served, or, in the Biblical phrase, whose ox is being gored. "Orthodoxy is *my* doxy; heterodoxy is *your* doxy."

Consider the following parallel columns. Their difference is mainly one of mood or emotional point of view. Which one of any contrasting pair would be used would depend upon whether the speaker were on the affirmative or the negative side.

Pro	*Con*
1. brave, courageous	rash, reckless
2. determined, strong-willed	stubborn, obstinate

[1] Frederick Adams Woods, "Oily Words," *Century Magazine*, September, 1927, pp. 556–563.

	Pro	*Con*
3.	idealist, man of vision	impractical visionary, well-meaning sentimentalist
4.	realistic, practical	materialistic, pessimistic
5.	well-deserved praise	fulsome flattery
6.	frank, outspoken	rude, blunt, impolite
7.	tactful, pleasant	deceitful, not to be trusted
8.	saving, economical	stingy, close-fisted
9.	avoid entangling alliances	change our policy of selfish isolation

(2) THE FAVORABLE SIDE

To damn with a phrase is only one side of the picture, the side of unfriendly propaganda. The other side is represented by **advertising,** especially in the form of the complimentary slogan and the alluring trade name. Upon them is largely based the tremendous industry of advertising, in all of its many phases. Producers and merchants know that what a thing is called not only makes a difference, but makes a critical difference — often, in fact, the difference between success and failure.

Consider the following instance, which was taken from a recent article in *Nation's Business:* —

Name experts are important vertebrae of the business backbone. . . . Anybody can mark down a shelf of left-over rubbers to thirty-nine cents and dispose of them. It takes sales intuition to name them *Rainbeaus* and watch them sell at a profit. . . . Three times more men purchased a gray felt hat called *Tyrolia* than when it was unnamed. A piece of furniture becomes irresistible when called *Snuggle Sofa*. One big electric concern increased sales to the saturation point for clocks by calling them *Morning Star*. Customers wishing cathedral-like doorbells ask for *Mello-Chimes*. . . . A diplomatic hosiery company calls its short-legged lengths *Brev*, long-legged ones *Duchess*, while the stoutish lady unembarrassedly asks for *Classical* and feels understood.[1]

The chapter on The Power of Words in this book contains a section dealing with Connotation, or the Suggestive Power of Words, pages 393–396. Glance briefly through it at this point, and apply it here to the use of question-begging terms, for it is the **connotation,** or indefinable emotional suggestiveness of words, that performs the lion's

[1] See the *Reader's Digest*, July, 1935, p. 48.

share of the invisible work in propaganda and advertising. It is this hidden field of operation, therefore, that we must watch closely. A small amount of propaganda and a large amount of advertising are based on facts and tell the truth. It is a wise man who can tell the difference. We must be constantly on our guard, however, against rising to the lure of a brilliant phrase like a trout striking at an artificial fly. The purpose in both transactions is the same, and so, alas, are the results. The best guarantee of straight thinking and sound judgment is always to ring the coins of language on the hard counter of common sense and experience and thus separate the true from the false.

THE ROUND TABLE

1. Bring to class the most effective or most obvious instance you have encountered of begging the question by calling names.

2. Do you know of any case where a person or a cause was either hurt or helped by the use of an effective phrase?

3. Write two brief emotional paragraphs about the same proposal or measure, one favoring and praising, the other opposing and condemning. Ask the instructor to have the two or three best on each side read aloud in contrasting pairs.

4. It is said that the phrase that has probably had the greatest influence on American history is Washington's "avoid entangling alliances."

5. An excellent example of the attractiveness of a good phrase is the substitution of "social security" for "old-age pensions."

6. If you are interested in examples of effective sales sentences, see Elmer Wheeler's book, *Tested Selling Sentences* (John Murphy Company, Baltimore, Md.)

7. The article on "Oily Words" referred to on page 303 closes in this fashion. The article is well worth reading in its entirety.

> Only a small percentage of all the oily words contained in the English language has been given here. A complete collection would make a small book which might be called, "The Handy Book for Lawyers, Orators, Historians, Diplomats — and Others Who Wish to Pervert the Truth."

8. A recent best seller in the field of practical psychology is Dale Carnegie's *How to Win Friends and Influence People* (Simon and Schuster, Inc.). Glance through it for suggestions.

9. This whole matter of clear reasoning and straight thinking is so important for everyone that we need all the light we can get. Here is an excerpt from an unusually helpful article on the subject. Read and discuss the whole article. It is entitled "How to Detect Propaganda," and appeared

in the *Bulletin of the American Association of University Professors*, January, 1938, pp. 49–55. It was quoted there from *Propaganda Analysis*, Vol. I, No. 2, Institute for Propaganda Analysis, 132 Morningside Drive, New York City. This excerpt is quoted here by permission of both publications.

How to Detect Propaganda

We are fooled by propaganda chiefly because we don't recognize it when we see it. It may be fun to be fooled but, as the cigarette ads used to say, it is more fun to know. We can more easily recognize propaganda when we see it if we are familiar with the seven common propaganda devices. These are : —

> (1) The Name-Calling Device
> (2) The Glittering-Generalities Device
> (3) The Transfer Device
> (4) The Testimonial Device
> (5) The Plain-Folks Device
> (6) The Card-Stacking Device
> (7) The Band-Wagon Device

[Here follow six pages explaining and exemplifying the seven propaganda devices mentioned. The article closes as follows.]

Propaganda and Emotion

Observe that in all these devices our emotion is the stuff with which propagandists work. Without it they are helpless; with it, harnessing it to their purposes, they can make us glow with pride or burn with hatred, they can make us zealots in behalf of the program they espouse. As we said in our first letter, propaganda as generally understood is expression of opinion or action by individuals or groups with reference to predetermined ends. Without the appeal to our emotion — to our fears and to our courage, to our selfishness and unselfishness, to our loves and to our hates — propagandists would influence few opinions and few actions.

To say this is not to condemn emotion, an essential part of life, or to assert that all predetermined ends of propagandists are "bad." What we mean is that the intelligent citizen does not want propagandists to utilize his emotions, even to the attainment of "good" ends, without knowing what is going on. He does not want to be "used" in the attainment of ends he may later consider "bad." He does not want to be gullible. He does not want to be fooled. He does not want to be duped, even in a "good" cause. He wants to know the facts and among these is included the fact of the utilization of his emotions. . . .

10. Another good article on detecting propaganda is Hadley Cantril's "Propaganda Analysis," *The English Journal*, March, 1938, pp. 217–221. Read and report on it in class.

GENERAL ROUND TABLE

Here are a number of interesting matters drawn from the field of logic and argumentation. Some of them are examples of fallacies, or errors in reasoning; some are not. Glance through them and bring up in class those which you would like to see discussed or those which the instructor assigns.

1. Jot down at random several of your strongest beliefs. Upon what evidence is each based?

2. Examine one, or several, of the volumes in Erich A. Walter's *Essay Annual* series (Scott, Foresman and Company, since 1933) for current arguments and argumentative essays. Make a brief, interesting report to the class on the one which you found most significant, either confirming or rebutting the arguments presented.

3. Should one argue on the side he doesn't believe in?

4. Cite the discovery of the causes of malaria and of yellow fever as instances of valid reasoning by cause and effect.

5. Describe (*a*) the phlogiston theory of combustion and (*b*) the Ptolemaic system of astronomy as seemingly logical but invalid instances of reasoning by cause and effect.

Fallacies

6. A fallacy is any argument that seems convincing to the normal mind but that proves, upon examination, not to establish the alleged conclusion.

— RALPH M. EATON, *General Logic*

7. Can you refute satisfactorily (wittily?) the two irritating mock-excuses : —

(1) The better the day, the better the deed.

(2) When in Rome do as the Romans do.

8. Any business which fails to show a profit at the end of the year may fairly be called unsuccessful. Most colleges and churches, therefore, must be considered failures.

9. This man is a good golf player, and hence will write a good account of the match.

10. (*a*) I have a disagreeable task to do. I shall therefore postpone it as long as possible; for if I do, something may happen to make it unnecessary for me to do it at all.

(*b*) I have a distasteful task to do. I shall therefore do it as soon as possible, so as to have it off my mind.

11. I will not do this act because it is unjust; I know it is unjust because my conscience tells me so, and my conscience tells me so because the act is wrong.

12. All fish are cold-blooded; no whales are cold-blooded; therefore, no whales are fish.

13. A man deposited $50 in a bank and then withdrew that amount in small sums from time to time as follows: —

First	$20, leaving a balance of	$30
Second	15, leaving a balance of	15
Third	9, leaving a balance of	6
Fourth	6, leaving a balance of	0
	$50	$51

Account for the extra dollar. — *The Literary Digest*, March 5, 1927

14. There is no rule without exceptions;
     This statement is itself a rule,
     ∴ This statement has exceptions, or
     There are rules without exceptions.
(Handle in the same way, "Epimenides the Cretan said that all Cretans are liars.")

15. "Have you stopped lying yet?" "I will answer that one if you will answer this one: Have you stopped beating your wife yet?"

16. If intoxication follows from consuming whiskey and soda, brandy and soda, rum and soda, gin and soda, may it not be argued that soda causes intoxication?

17. Pat was trying to induce Mike to take a drink of beer. "Didn't Paul write to Timothy telling him to take a little wine for his stomach's sake?" he urged. To which Mike answered: "In the first place, my name's not Timothy; in the second place, that is not wine; in the third place, there is nothing wrong with my stomach." Of which fallacy was Mike reproving Pat?

18. To say that political economy is a dismal science because it shows that certain laws may have unfortunate results is as absurd as it would be to call physics a dismal science because lightning kills.

19. Is the boy friend a gentleman? Yes, because gentlemen prefer blondes and he prefers me, and I am a blonde.

20. Every fourth child born into the world is a Chinese. Therefore, if you are a member of a large family you have Chinese brothers and sisters.

Dilemmas

21. The dilemma is an interesting form of argument which was much more in favor in ancient times than it is at present. "A dilemma is an argument setting forth a forced choice between two alternatives entailing equally unwelcome consequences." — ALBURY CASTELL, *A College Logic*

If accurately framed, a dilemma is devastating, not to say annihilating. It is, however, a tricky expedient and gives opportunity for much mere verbal cleverness and logic chopping. The two best ways of refuting it are either (1) to turn it around and point the two alternatives ("horns") in the opposite direction, or (2) to show that there is a third, or even a fourth, possibility of action which the dilemma does not take into consideration. If a person can find a third valid possibility of action, he is said to escape between the horns of the dilemma. The following are examples of turning the dilemma around : —

(1) An Athenian mother tried to dissuade her son from entering public life by this argument: "If you say what is just men will hate you; and if you say what is unjust the gods will hate you; but you must say either the one or the other; therefore you will be hated." The son answered, "If I say what is just, the gods will love me, and if I say what is unjust men will love me; but I must say either; therefore I shall be loved."

— P. COFFEY, The Science of Logic [1]

(2) The teaching of evolution is either a matter of science or a matter of religion. If it is a matter of religion, the legislature has no business to deal with it; and if it is a matter of science, the legislature has no business to deal with it. Therefore, the legislature has no business to deal with the teaching of evolution. — St. Paul newspaper, March 5, 1927

(3) If a wife be beautiful, she excites jealousy;
      If she is ugly, she excites disgust;
      Therefore, it is best not to marry.
Refute by turning the argument around as in number (1) above.

(4) A classical example of a dilemma and its rebuttal is the famous *Litigiosus*. Protagoras the sophist is said to have made an agreement to teach Euathlus the art of pleading for a fee, one half of which was to be paid to him when the course of instruction was completed, and the other half when he won his first case in court. Euathlus put off beginning his practice, and Protagoras finally brought suit for the other half of his fee. Protagoras offered the following argument in his own behalf : —

"If Euathlus loses this case, he must pay me, by the judgment of the court; and if he wins it, he must pay me in accordance with the terms of his contract, for he will then have won his first case. But he must either lose it or win it, therefore he must pay me in any case."

Euathlus then offered the following rebuttal : —

"If I win the case, I ought not to pay, by the judgment of the court; and if I lose it, I ought not to pay, by the terms of the contract, for I shall then not have won my first case. But I must either win it or lose it, therefore I ought not to pay."

Specimens of Argumentation

Here are two excellent short arguments for freedom of speech. Contrast them for any differences in tone, method of reasoning, and so forth. Which do you find more effective?

(If you are cynically or humorously inclined you will relish Mark Twain's comment on freedom of thought and speech in America: "In our country we have those three unspeakably precious things: freedom of thought, freedom of speech, and the prudence never to practice either.")

1. THE PROMOTION OF IGNORANCE [1]

WILLIAM ALLISON SHIMER

The only force strong enough to prevent the established order from petrifying the intellect and paralyzing progress is freedom of expression. The conservative or radical who is not obliged to prove the superiority of his ideas in order to win and maintain a majority will promote ignorance rather than education. This is the basic argument for freedom of speech — freedom to learn is the other side of the shield. The silly ass who denies to others the right of expression, by the same act plucks out his own tongue and punctures his own ears. It is the height not only of bigotry but also of obtuseness to suppose that one's present understanding is the last word on any subject, or that one can afford to disregard the thoughts of others, even that which proceedeth out of the mouths of babes and sucklings. And it is the height of cowardice or lethargy to refuse to enter the lists with an idea. It is good for a person or a people to have to fight even foolish and criminal ideas.

The only armor impregnable to such ideas is education — education for thinking, education in background, materials, and methods of thinking rather than in what to think. Political and economic theory, sex, color, race, and religion must be banished from the definition of scholarship. The true scholar or thinker must be free to maintain a disinterested, scientific attitude toward the discovery and expression of fact and theory. And the true thinker cannot be free unless all persons are free, for the true thinker must discover and prove himself by testing his thoughts in the crucible of public mentality. Only stupidity or moral thievery would rob a nation or humanity of this lone means to greater knowledge, happiness, and creativity.

2. TO AN ANXIOUS FRIEND [2]

WILLIAM ALLEN WHITE

You tell me that law is above freedom of utterance. And I reply that you can have no wise laws nor free enforcement of wise laws unless there is free expression of the wisdom of the people — and, alas, their folly with it. But if there is freedom, folly will die of its own poison, and the wisdom will survive. That is the history of the race. It is the proof of man's kinship with God. You say that freedom of utterance is not for time of stress, and

[1] From *The American Scholar*, autumn, 1935. By permission of the author.
[2] Pulitzer prize editorial. Reprinted by permission of The Macmillan Company from *The Editor and His People*.

I reply with the sad truth that only in time of stress is freedom of utterance in danger. No one questions it in calm days, because it is not needed. And the reverse is true also; only when free utterance is suppressed is it needed, and when it is needed, it is most vital to justice. Peace is good. But if you are interested in peace through force and without free discussion — that is to say, free utterance decently and in order — your interest in justice is slight. And peace without justice is tyranny, no matter how you may sugar-coat it with expediency. This state today is in more danger from suppression than from violence, because, in the end, suppression leads to violence. Violence, indeed, is the child of suppression. Whoever pleads for justice helps to keep the peace; and whoever tramples upon the plea for justice temperately made in the name of peace only outrages peace and kills something fine in the heart of man which God put there when we got our manhood. When that is killed, brute meets brute on each side of the line.

So, dear friend, put fear out of your heart. This nation will survive, this state will prosper, the orderly business of life will go forward if only men can speak in whatever way given them to utter what their hearts hold — by voice, by posted card, by letter or by press. Reason never has failed men. Only force and repression have made the wrecks in the world.

Pro and Con, or the Two Sides of the Question

More and more it is becoming customary today to present not one side alone of an argument, but both sides, as is done in the pro-and-con debate on intercollegiate football, pages 312–316.

Other pro-and-con presentations of important questions will be found in current magazines — for example, the following. Suggest in class other good two-sided arguments from your contemporary reading : —

The Reader's Digest

Are We Going Communist?	February, 1937
A Compulsory Syphilis Test before Marriage?	November, 1937
Execution by Lethal Gas?	December, 1937
Should We Boycott Japan?	February, 1938
Should We Curtail Those Who Would Destroy Us?	April, 1938
Sterilize the Feeble-Minded?	May, 1938

The Forum

Congressional Digest (The Pro and Con Monthly)

Of the large literature that has grown up around argumentation and debating the three following contain good source material on both sides of many vital questions. Your college library will have others:

Phelps, Edith M., Ed., *University Debaters' Annual:* Constructive and Rebuttal Speeches Delivered in Debates of American Colleges and Universities, H. W. Wilson Company, an annual series from 1914–1915 on.

The Reference Shelf: Debates, Collections of Articles, Briefs, Bibliographies, and Study Outlines on Timely Subjects for Public Discussion, H. W. Wilson Company, a continuing series in eleven volumes and many parts.

Shurter, Edwin DuBois, *Both Sides of 100 Public Questions Briefly Debated*, with Affirmative and Negative References, Noble and Noble.

PRO AND CON

Abolish Intercollegiate Football? [1]

In the following debate Mr. Pro and Mr. Con thresh out this issue with no holds barred. All attitudes treated are derived from acknowledged experts and all facts have been gathered by a skilled investigator.

So, when the smoke has cleared away, what do you think?

[1] *Reader's Digest*, January, 1938. By permission of the editors.

Yes, says Mr. Pro:

"American football is a splendid game. That is why some of us would like to see the game given back to the boys before the over-enthusiastic public squeezes it to death. Here is evidence of the impending suffocation:

"Thanksgiving Day used to end the season. Now, the big intersectional post-season games are played on New Year's Day. Spring practice begins in another four months. Many college players spend their summers at manual labor conditioning for the September opening of the season. That adds up to seven or eight months a year. College football isn't a game any longer — it's a job.

"The University of Texas recently hired a first-flight football coach on a 10-year contract at $15,000 a year. How many college presidents receive as much?

"Radio advertisers paid college athletic associations some $400,000 this season for exclusive rights to broadcast their football games.

"The ultimate comment on football's absurdities was made when Elbert Hubbard wrote that 'football bears the same relation to education that bull-fighting does to agriculture.'

"Francis Wallace, realistic and intelligent friend of the game, summarizes the situation:

"'The colleges enter the open market and bid against one another for the year's crop of athletes. They pay these boys and masquerade the payments. They present these athletes in great outdoor stadia and charge all that the traffic will bear. Football, as now conducted by most of our great universities, is, at best, semi-professional — as much show-business as Broadway.'

"*Colleges do not need football profits to pay for the rest of their athletic programs.* Stevens Institute of Technology abolished intercollegiate football in 1924. Since then it has maintained intercollegiate competition in full schedules of all other standard sports and provided an intramural program which takes in all undergraduates. Exclusive of maintenance on buildings and grounds, the annual cost to the college is around $10 per undergraduate.

"On that basis, the salaries of a high-powered football coaching staff (say $30,000) plus graduate manager and press agent (say $10,000) would pay for such a program for a male student body of 4000.

"Massachusetts Institute of Technology, rid of intercollegiate football these 30 years, finances an extensive athletic program at much the same figure as Stevens from a student tax ($5.80 a year) and general college funds. This includes crew, the most expensive of college sports. Neither alumni nor students ever agitate for the return of intercollegiate football.

"*Football victories are not necessary for keeping alumni and public in a financially generous frame of mind.* An expert survey of representative colleges between 1921 and 1930 showed that those conspicuous for football success had increased their asset values by 117 per cent, their endowments by 125 per cent. Those going light on football did just a trifle better: assets were up 125 per cent, endowments 126 per cent.

"*The publicity values of football have little to do with stimulating enrollment.*
The curve of increasing enrollment of male undergraduates at Columbia
forged steadily upward both in the period when football was abolished
(1905–15) and since it has been restored.   The curve dropped after the de-
pression, in spite of the college's developing football success.

"The enrollment of Reed College, without intercollegiate football, has
grown steadily since the war.   Its proportion of male students has increased
and the student body compares favorably in height and weight with Pacific
Coast students in general.

"*Subsidizing of football players handicaps intelligent boys lacking conspicuous athletic ability, and loads colleges with a dead weight of the less intelligent.*
When athletes of Pennsylvania colleges, large and small, were given tests
measuring intelligence and information, football players rated lowest.
Football-playing Phi Beta Kappas are always rare enough to get publicity.
The rank and file of paid football letter-men are crammed and bullied into
passing grades, or passed by professors who know better than to hold them
to usual standards.

"Most of the scholarships that disguise subsidizing were really intended
to help intelligent boys without money to get an education useful to society.
A fast-running but slow-thinking halfback may be keeping out of college a
bright lad who isn't so good at snagging passes.

"Many college jobs, usually the easiest ones, are reserved for athletes.
The non-athletic poor boy gets what is left.   Athletes are often paid far more
than non-athletes for certain jobs.

"Francis Wallace wrote that he stopped scouting talent for big-time football colleges because too many of the football boys he had wangled into
college graduated only to be too good for hard work and not quite good
enough for the easy jobs they had expected.

"The days when a star end could count on a soft berth in a broker's office
died with 1929.   Professional football will pay a player only some $1200 a
season for the few years he lasts — provided he measures up to professional
standards, which are terrific.   Radio stations were mobbed this season by
bewildered gridiron heroes hoping for soft work as football announcers.
Most of them would have been better off if they'd never had the financial
chance to die for alma mater.

"Guesses on how much went into football pools in 1937 range between
$50,000,000 and $75,000,000.   Nobody knows exactly.   But everybody
knows that the whole huge total, along with other large sums bet on individual games, is handled by the lowest type of racketeers.

"A boy who is living a lie learns a lot about cutting corners.   Now put
these facts together : big money staked every week — chiseling gangsters —
players made cynical by a dishonest system.   Those are the makings of what
might be the nastiest athletic scandal since the Black Sox.

"Many admirers of football deny heatedly that the college game could be fixed. According to highly responsible authority, it is already being fixed right along in at least one football-crazy section of the country. When some such scandal does break wide open, the public will have finished its job of wrecking.

"The colleges will do much better to beat fate to the draw by performing the indicated surgery while there is yet time. All the college color in the country could hardly make up for the disillusioning spectacle of alma mater's young heroes pulling the kind of fast ones that class them with crooked jockeys.

"Football would still survive as a lusty game played, as at Emory University, for fun among intramural teams.

"Or, for the athletic connoisseur, it would survive in the professional leagues which are drawing more money and attention every season.

"But it would no longer pervert the atmosphere of higher education, warp the athletic programs of colleges and set a flagrant example of chicanery for American youth."

No, says Mr. Con:

"This agitation is old stuff. Way back in the day of bone-crushing mass plays, several important colleges bowed to public opinion and dropped football. Most of them have since restored it, as the game, opened and speeded up, became far less brutal.

"The public has responded to the change by filling huge stadia at high prices. The same public is discovering — and not minding much — the fact that one way or another colleges subsidize many of their players. It is learning to take them cordially for what they are — husky kids, using athletic skill to pay for education — and to honor them for their grit, skill and perseverance.

"It also knows that, since dumb beef long since went out of football, the modern college player must be as quick on the uptake as he is on the charge.

"There is no way to repeal this popular enthusiasm for the spectacle of game youngsters fighting a wholesome, thrilling, mimic warfare because they enjoy it and because it helps some of them to an education.

"If intercollegiate football were abolished, the public would seek spontaneous color and drama in some other intercollegiate sport — and find it. The net effect would be merely the elimination of the most colorful and characteristic American spectacle.

"Professional croakers charge that 'college football has turned into big business.' So it has. And a darn good thing too for the American college and the American student.

"For receipts from football buy equipment, pay transportation, hire coaches and build facilities for basketball, baseball, track, hockey, swimming, lacrosse, tennis, squash, boxing, wrestling, fencing, rowing and everything else.

"Every football player who is subsidized is only getting back a fraction of what he contributes in cash and inspiration to the physical good of the whole college community.

"Without football, college athletic associations owing large debts on new stadia would have to default on their bonds, which would outrage the sports-minded alumni who bought those bonds out of devotion to alma mater.

"Conversely, each football victory ties the alumnus closer to alma mater, and makes things far simpler for the college president when he needs funds for new dormitories.   Where colleges are dependent on state funds, it works the same way on state legislators.

"College presidents know that live youngsters, recognizing successful football teams as signs of energy and enterprise and of that electric comrade-ship known as college spirit, are attracted to bigtime football colleges.

"Football is the keystone of college sport.   Its glories foster a vigorous athletic psychology inspiring every youth, dub or not, to play some game as best he can, building up a healthy habit of strenuous play that will pay him dividends the rest of his life.

"Since football demands a maximum of courage, discipline and persever-ance, it is superlative training for later life.   Many a famous college tackle, now a success in his chosen career, testifies that the moral training he got from Coach So-and-So was more valuable to him than all the rest of his college education put together.

"Now that the cuss-and-bully type of coach is passing out of the picture, that factor is still more important.   The modern coach is usually intelligent, smart with boys, soft-spoken, shrewd—perfect for leading and training youth.

"The healthiest thing that ever happened to intercollegiate football is the present tendency to admit subsidization and ask, with all the logic on one side: 'Why shouldn't needy boys be paid for their grueling battles in the interests of the whole college?'

"In a few years most colleges will have candidly brought things into the open.   Already the members of one large conference have an agreement defining and limiting the amounts and number of athletic scholarships. All over the country various mutual agreements on talent-scouting and maximum rates of pay are gradually building up a code of ethics that will eventually either correct the worst abuses of intercollegiate football or put colleges that refuse to observe the code off the schedules of institutions that play fair in scouting and paying players.

"Stringent financial pressure on college athletic associations that are still paying off on boom-time stadia and other buildings is already lessening as the bonds are retired.

"By applying honest and realistic regulation to the present situation, the game can still be saved for the old grad, the student and the public, with all its pageantry and excitement and its nation-wide fostering of a healthy atti-tude toward physical courage and hard knocks.   To abolish the game on account of its present minor extravagances would be to burn the house down to roast the pig."

PART THREE

WORD STUDY AND
VOCABULARY BUILDING

CHAPTER XVII

The Word

I learn immediately from any speaker how much he has already lived,
through the poverty or splendor of his speech.

— RALPH WALDO EMERSON

As was stated on page 3, we think in sentences and speak in sentences. Sentences, however, are made up of ideas, or rather of the relationships between ideas. Each idea in turn is conveyed by a word, so that with the word we reach the starting point of both speech and writing. In the last analysis our powers of both thought and expression depend upon the number, exactness, and effectiveness of the words we have at our command, or rather upon the number, exactness, and effectiveness of the ideas behind our words.

The English language is almost incredibly large. The latest complete dictionary [1] contains 600,000 words. Of this tremendous number even an educated person probably will never come in contact with more than 4 per cent, about 24,000 words in all, and most people meet only a third or a sixth of that number. Estimates of the size of the vocabulary of different people, the actual number of words they know the meaning of, vary so much that not much dependence can be placed upon them. It is supposed that the average child of six or seven uses between 500 and 1200 words; the high-school graduate between 3000 and 5000; and the college senior adds between 1000 and 2000 more, possessing a vocabulary of between 4000 and 5000 as a lower limit and between 7000 and possibly 10,000 as an upper limit. In nothing do people vary more than in their store of mental ideas and the words that express them.

As J. W. Linn has well said, learning to write is learning to grow up. It is equally true that learning to appreciate good literature is

---

[1] The Merriam-Webster, Second Edition, 1935.

learning to grow up. A vital element in thus growing up is increasing one's vocabulary. Increasing one's vocabulary is more than a phrase; it is a basic mental process. To increase one's vocabulary is to deepen and enrich one's inner life. Our whole mental life is based on thinking, and in order to express our thoughts and feelings we must have words. One's word hoard bounds and encloses his mental stature as his skin bounds and encloses his body. If we lead narrow lives we shall need only a small vocabulary, but if we feel keenly and think deeply, we shall need an ever-increasing store of words. As Emerson well said, "I learn immediately from any speaker how much he has already lived, through the poverty or splendor of his speech." One measure of a man is his vocabulary.

1. Our Three Vocabularies

We do not actually use more than a small proportion of the words we know. Every person has three vocabularies, one within the other, like wheels within wheels. First there is our active, or *speaking vocabulary*. This consists of the relatively small number of words we

OUR THREE VOCABULARIES

habitually employ from day to day in the ordinary course of business and pleasure. Second comes our *writing vocabulary*. This is made up of additional words of a more thoughtful and dignified type, for if we are writing an essay on a literary subject, such as a play of Shakespeare, a novel of Dickens, or on a technical subject like the radio or the airplane, we call in a number of words we should ordinarily have no occasion to use. Third comes our *reading* or *recognition vocabulary*, much the largest of the three. By means of it we

read and understand the various books and magazines that we turn
to for information or pleasure as the months and years go by. If we
like to read, and if we read widely enough and long enough, we may
acquire an unusually large and rich reading vocabulary.

The relative size and relationship of these three vocabularies may
be suggested by the arrangement of three concentric circles on the
opposite page.

2. Increasing One's Vocabulary

The chief difficulty does not lie in getting new words into our outermost circle. If we read a good deal and have a fair degree of mental
curiosity, we can't keep new words out. The main trouble comes in
getting a new word first from the outermost circle into our writing
vocabulary and then from our writing vocabulary into our active,
speaking vocabulary. This is no mean achievement, and requires
considerable effort and some independence. George Herbert Palmer,
in his suggestive essay on language, *Self-Cultivation in English*, urges
us (1) to learn and (2) to learn how to use two new words every week.
"I know," he continues, "that when we use a word for the first time
we are startled, as if a firecracker went off in our neighborhood. We
look about hastily to see if anyone has noticed. But finding that no
one has, we may be emboldened. A word used three times slips off
the tongue with entire naturalness. Then it is ours forever, and
with it some phase of life which had been lacking hitherto. For each
word presents its own point of view, discloses a special aspect of things,
reports some little importance not otherwise conveyed, and so contributes its small emancipation to our tied-up minds and tongues."

(1) WAYS TO INCREASE ONE'S VOCABULARY

If we are mentally alert and lead wide-awake lives, each new idea,
each fresh experience, each additional fact, each unknown thing we
come in contact with, adds new words. Our bodies stop growing while
we are still in college, but our minds, unless we put them to sleep with
the drug of routine, keep on developing as long as we live.

In detail, however, there are many ways in which we may re-enforce
and stimulate this important process of acquiring new words. Seven
of these are as follows: —

1. Wide, intelligent reading.

2. Intelligent listening, especially to speeches, sermons, oral reports, addresses by visiting speakers, and class lectures.

3. Careful, idiomatic translating from whatever foreign language we are studying, with special reference to Latin.

4. Paraphrasing.

5. Verse writing.

6. Developing an active interest, if possible a passion, for new words, and collecting them eagerly. Let no unknown word you meet, whether in reading or in listening, pass out of the circle of your mind once it has entered it. Keep the word fast and make it your own.

7. Habitual and friendly use of word books, with special reference to the dictionary.

The last two of these belong together, and call for further attention. Each is of critical importance. It will not do us much good to meet new words either by way of the ear or by way of the eye, unless we look them up in a good dictionary and thus master them thoroughly. Nearly everybody has a hobby of collecting something — possibly stamps, autographs, picture postcards of interesting places and people, pressed flowers, walking sticks, or the like. Let us treat words the same way, and carry over into this undertaking all the enthusiasm and possessiveness of the true collector's zeal. The origin and habits of words form one of the most fascinating studies in the world. To cultivate it as a hobby is to add a constant and increasing source of pleasure to our lives and, what is even more important, to broaden our minds and continue to add to our knowledge and culture as long as life lasts.

(2) WORD BOOKS

Special books on the study of words exist in large numbers. Many of them are interesting, and all of them are useful. Best for your purposes at present are these : —

I. FOR YOUR OWN LIBRARY AND CONSTANT PERSONAL USE

(To Be within Reaching Distance at All Times As You Read and Study)

1. A good, recent dictionary of the size and completeness of Webster's *Collegiate Dictionary*, fifth edition, Funk and Wagnalls' *College*

Standard Dictionary, Winston's *Simplified Dictionary,* or Macmillan's *Modern Dictionary.*

2. A small book of synonyms like Putnam's *Word Book.*

II. For Frequent Consultation in the Reference Room of the Library[1]

1. The latest complete dictionary, such as the Merriam-Webster *New International,* second edition, Funk and Wagnalls' *New Standard Dictionary,* the *New English* or *Oxford Dictionary,* or the *Century Dictionary and Cyclopedia.*
2. Crabb's *English Synonyms.*[2]
3. Roget's *Thesaurus of English Words and Phrases.*[2]
4. Hartrampf's *Vocabularies: Synonyms, Antonyms, Relatives.*[2]
5. John Matthews Manly and Edith Rickert, *The Writer's Index of Good Form and Good English,* Henry Holt and Company.
6. Brewer, E. Cobham, *Dictionary of Phrase and Fable,* rev. ed., J. B. Lippincott Company.

III. For Proper Names

(To Be Available for Consultation When Needed)

7. Lippincott's *Biographical Dictionary.*
8. Lippincott's *Gazetteer.*
9. *Century Dictionary and Cyclopedia:* Proper Names, vol. 9, D. Appleton-Century Co.
10. Gayley, C. M., ed., *Classic Myths in English Literature* (both classic and Old Norse mythology), Ginn and Company.
11. Bulfinch, Thomas, *The Age of Fable,* T. Y. Crowell and Company.

By all means buy a good, recent dictionary for your own individual, personal use. A dictionary should be indispensable in the study of English. Since whatever dictionary you get will serve through all four years of college, the cost per year is less than that of nearly any other book you buy. And see to it that your dictionary is always within reaching distance as you read and write. This may sound like a trivial direction. It is not. It is essential. People are so constituted that when a new or a doubtful word is met, there is a fleeting impulse to look it up. If, IF the dictionary is within three feet at that very moment, we will obey the impulse and look it up. But if the dictionary is in the library, or upstairs, or in the next room,

---

[1] See The Library, pages 256–259.
[2] Now available in inexpensive, revised editions published by Grosset and Dunlap.

or *even across the room we are sitting in*, the odds are that we shall never look that word up at all.   Human nature is that way.

THE ROUND TABLE

1. List ten words that you know the meaning of, but which you have never used in either writing or speaking.

2. A week from today, bring to class a list of all the new words you have come in contact with during that week.   Keep a careful account, look up all the new words, and be prepared to explain them to the class — spelling, pronunciation, meanings, and derivation.   It will be interesting to compare the size and quality of the different lists.

3. Looking back upon the list of new words prepared in accordance with the preceding directions, think of the boundless opportunities life and college are offering to you to increase your vocabulary, if you will do your part fairly by looking up new words.   Reflect upon the chances offered during an entire school year or during your whole college course.

4. Set apart a definite part of your English notebook for new words. Let not one escape you.   Indicate by a check mark or a star any particularly vivid words or interesting, unexpected, or tricky pronunciations or spellings, and interesting derivations.

5. Call for class suggestions about the best ways of getting words from your reading vocabulary into your writing and speaking vocabularies.

6. Which of the ways of increasing your vocabulary listed on page 322 are you individually strong in?   Which are you weakest in?

7. By a show of hands, find out what foreign languages are being studied by the class.   So far as learning English is concerned, those studying Latin are the lucky ones.

8. Which of the word books listed on pages 322 and 323 have you ever used?   Which are available in the college library and which at home?

9. What dictionary do you use?   What is its date?

10. How near to you is the nearest dictionary (*a*) when you are studying in college and (*b*) when you are studying at home?

11. If no dictionary is near at hand as you study and read, what means, if any, do you take to investigate unknown words as you meet them?   If a dictionary is not within reaching distance, the next best thing is to have a small notebook and a pencil at your elbow, and jot down all new or doubtful words as you meet them.   Some such plan is the only way.   Otherwise you will never do anything about it, and will miss many chances of enlarging your mental horizon.

12. Following are some of the most useful vocabulary tests.   They can be secured direct from the publishers.

(1) *Holley Sentence Vocabulary Test, Grades VII to XII*.   Public School Publishing Company, Bloomington, Ill.

(2) *Markham English Vocabulary Tests for High-School and College Students.* Public School Publishing Company, Bloomington, Ill.

(3) *The Inglis Test of English Vocabulary.* Ginn and Company, Boston, Mass.

(4) *Terman Vocabulary Test.* Houghton Mifflin Company, Boston, Mass.

13. Books about words are numerous and highly interesting. Here are some of the best. Glance through as many of them as you can find in the library, and ask your instructor to allow you credit on your English parallel for any that you read.

Anderson, Jessie Macmillan, *A New Study of English Words*, American Book Company.

Fernald, James C., *Historic English*, Grosset and Dunlap.

Greenough, James B., and Kittredge, George Lyman, *Words and Their Ways in English Speech*, The Macmillan Company.

Greever, Garland, and Bachelor, Joseph M., *The Century Vocabulary Builder*, D. Appleton-Century Company.

Holt, Alfred H., *You Don't Say !*, Thomas Y. Crowell Company.

McKnight, George H., *English Words and Their Backgrounds*, D. Appleton-Century Company.

————, *Modern English in the Making*, D. Appleton-Century Company.

Mencken, H. L., *The American Language*, Fourth Edition, Alfred A. Knopf.

O'Connor, Johnson, "Vocabulary and Success," *Atlantic Monthly*, February, 1934.

Palmer, George H., *Self-Cultivation in English*, Houghton Mifflin Company.

Partridge, Eric, *Slang Today and Yesterday*, The Macmillan Company.

Picturesque Word Origins, G. and C. Merriam Company.

Robertson, Stuart, *The Development of Modern English*, Prentice-Hall, Inc.

Robinson, Henry Morton, "What's the Good Word?" *American Magazine*, March, 1938.

Smith, Logan Pearsall, *The English Language*, Henry Holt and Company.

Weekley, Ernest, *The Romance of Words*, E. P. Dutton and Company.

14. Here are two periodicals dealing with words. Look them up if they are available: —

Words: A periodical devoted to the study of the origin, history, and etymology of English words, 808 South Vermont Ave., Los Angeles, Calif.

Word Study, G. and C. Merriam Company, Springfield, Mass.

CHAPTER XVIII

Spelling

In preparation for the channel crossing Caesar built 18 new ~~vesuls~~
~~vessils vesles~~ botes. — *Boners*

1. Using the Dictionary

Three essential pieces of information about every word are (1) its spelling, (2) its pronunciation, and (3) its meanings. A fourth item, sometimes necessary, usually interesting, always helpful, is its derivation or origin. Only the first two, spelling and pronunciation, can be taken up in this book. The dictionary gives all four.

(1) SPELLING

Correct spelling is of fundamental importance both in college and after graduation. Of all the errors in high-school and college themes approximately 20 per cent, or about one in five, are mistakes in spelling. Furthermore, it is usually mistakes in spelling that instructors watch for most carefully and penalize most severely. Almost any other kind of mistake has a better chance of passing unnoticed than has a misspelled word. In the world of business bad spelling is even more relentlessly penalized. In college, it is your grades that suffer; in the world, it is your chance of a job that pays the price of ignorance. When notice is given of an opening, every business house receives a flood of written applications. On the average, three fourths of these are thrown into the wastebasket on the score of bad handwriting and poor spelling. Only the good spellers have the chance of a personal interview. Promotion likewise usually goes to those who are best trained in the spoken and written word. No business concern wants an ignorant executive or department head. You can stay on the bottom and not know your native tongue, but you will have a back-breaking time getting to the top if you are ignorant of how educated people spell and pronounce.

(2) SPELLING DEMONS AND TROUBLE SPOTS

Long experience has shown that most of our spelling ills come not from difficult words but from a relatively small number of fairly easy words, not over several hundred in all, that give trouble to everybody alike. Believe it or not, the three words most commonly misspelled by college freshmen are *too*, *its*, and *their*. A well-known teacher and writer says: Dictate to every ninth-year class in American high schools this sentence, "The next grammar lesson would be too long for one day, but it is all right for two days." [1] You will get these results from every thousand pupils : —

grammer, 238 times   *alright*, 342 times
to for *too*, 261 times   all other misspellings, 47 times

The ten words most often misspelled in the official College Entrance Examinations over a period of almost a decade were these, the number in parentheses after each word indicating the number of times it was misspelled : —

1. too (167)	6. principal (63)
2. its (160)	7. committee (62)
3. believe (77)	8. therefore (61)
4. together (73)	9. separate (61)
5. their (66)	10. pleasant (59)

Many words have a particular trouble spot, and are usually misspelled in only one way. Examples are *goverment* for *government*, *truely* for *truly*, *discription* for *description*, *supprise* for *surprise*, *finaly* for *finally*, *fourty* for *forty*, and *indefinate* for *indefinite*.

The practical lessons for all of us in the light of such facts as these are, first, to find our own particular trouble makers in the general list of spelling demons given on pages 344–347 ; and secondly, to find our own particular trouble spots in the different words we misspell and to cure these spots by emphasizing them in some striking way. For instance, on our personal list of misspellings that we are directed on page 342, question 2, to keep, we might underline twice in red the offending letter or draw a red ring around it. One student taught himself to spell *separate* by writing the first A in red pencil about four times as tall as the other letters — sepArate. Another student

[1] C. H. Ward, *What Is English?*, p. 51.

permanently untangled *until* and *till* by saying over and over whenever he thought of the words, "If you have it in front you can't have it behind" (meaning that if you have the *un-* you won't also have the second *l*); "and if you have it behind you won't have it in front" (meaning that if you have the double *l* you won't also have the *un-*). Any device is a good one — the more absurd the better — that fixes your attention unwaveringly on a trouble spot and helps you to avoid it henceforth and forevermore.

2. Four Useful Rules

(1) DROPPING FINAL *E*

Words ending in a final *e* drop the *e* before suffixes beginning with a vowel, but retain the *e* before suffixes beginning with a consonant.

COMMON SUFFIXES BEGINNING WITH A VOWEL

-able	-ian
-al	-ible
-ation	-ic
-ed	-ing
-er	-ous

COMMON SUFFIXES BEGINNING WITH A CONSONANT

-ful
-less
-ment
-sion, -tion
-some

Examples

come + ing = coming
fame + ous = famous
sale + able = salable
guide + ing = guiding;   + ance = guidance
hope + ing = hoping;   + ful = hopeful
shame + ful = shameful;   + less = shameless
move + ing = moving;   + ment = movement

Exceptions

Words ending in -*ce* or -*ge* before suffixes beginning with *a* or *o* keep the final *e* in order to preserve the soft sound of the *c* and *g*.

change + able = changeable   peace + able = peaceable
courage + ous = courageous   manage + able = manageable

THE ROUND TABLE

1. Find and copy (*a*) five words in the spelling list on pages 344–347 which illustrate this rule when a suffix beginning with a vowel is added; and (*b*) five words when a suffix beginning with a consonant is added; (*c*) three words when the *e* is retained to keep *c* or *g* soft.

2. Using as many of the common vowel and consonant suffixes listed on page 328 as possible, form derivatives from the following words, retaining or omitting the final silent *e* according to the rule : —

1. adore	6. hope	10. notice
2. desire	7. like	11. outrage
3. fascinate	8. love	12. rescue
4. force	9. move	13. service
5. grieve		

(2) DOUBLING A FINAL CONSONANT

(*a*) **Words of one syllable ending in a single consonant preceded by a single vowel, and (*b*) words of more than one syllable which are accented on the last syllable, when ending in a single consonant preceded by a single vowel, double the final consonant when adding a suffix beginning with a vowel.**

Examples

stop (word of one syllable) + *ed* (suffix beginning with a vowel) = *stopped* (final consonant doubled)
slap (word of one syllable) + *ing* (suffix beginning with a vowel) = *slapping* (final consonant doubled)
begin (word accented on last syllable) + *ing* (suffix beginning with a vowel = *beginning* (final consonant doubled)
occur (word accented on last syllable) + *ed* (suffix beginning with a vowel) = *occurred* (final consonant doubled)

(*c*) **Words of more than one syllable ending in a single consonant preceded by a single vowel which do not accent the last syllable *do not* double the final consonant.**

Examples

travel (word not accented on last syllable) + *ed* = *traveled* (final consonant not doubled); + *ing* = *traveling:* + *er* = *traveler*
enter (word not accented on last syllable) + *ed* = *entered* (final consonant not doubled); + *ing* = *entering*

This rule of when and when not to double a final consonant before a suffix is one of the most useful in the entire range of spelling. It applies to more than three thousand words. Best of all, it can be relied on to work regularly and uniformly. Even in the case of words which are spelled in two ways, American usage gives preference to that spelling which is in accordance with the rule, as the following table shows : —

	Preferred	Allowable
bus	busses	buses
cancel	canceled	cancelled
travel	traveled	travelled
worship	worshiper	worshipper

THE ROUND TABLE

1. Find and copy from the spelling list given on pages 344–347 seven words which illustrate the three different classes of words that come under this rule : (a) words of one syllable; (b) words of more than one syllable accented on the last syllable; (c) words of more than one syllable not accented on the last syllable.

2. Add *-ed* and *-ing* to the following words and either double or do not double the final consonant according to the rule : —

1. jab	5. merit	9. omit	13. refer
2. pin	6. equip	10. offer	14. profit
3. cut	7. enter	11. control	15. remit
4. suffer	8. forget	12. differ	16. occur

3. Add *-ing* to the following words : —
pin, pine; tap, tape; feel; help; rout; differ; shin, shine; prefer; camp; look

4. Explain and justify by the rule the following spellings : —
sloping; hating; grinning; planning and planing; canned and caned; ceiling; equaling; referring, reference; developing; offered; forgetting

5. The only exception to this rule of doubling a final consonant is *chagrin'*, *chagrined, chagrining.* Can you suggest a reason?

(3) *IE* OR *EI?* (*POLICE!*)

When *ei* and *ie* have the sound of long *ee*, call the police; that is, *e* follows *c* and *i* follows *l* (and the other letters).

Examples

e after c	*i after l* (*and other letters*)
deceive	believe
receipt	relieve
perceive	pierce
ceiling	yield

Exceptions

There are seven exceptions to this rule: *either, neither, financier, *leisure, *seize, species,* and *weird.* Only the three starred words are likely to be misspelled. If, then, we learn these, — *leisure, seize,* and *weird,* — the police will take care of the rest.

THE ROUND TABLE

1. In the spelling list given on pages 344–347 find and copy the fourteen *ie, ei* words that come under the working of this rule. Do not confuse other *ei* words in which *ei* is not pronounced *ee*.

2. Insert correct form (*ie* or *ei*) in the following words: —

1. ach ve	7. f nd	13. bel f
2. conc ve	8. l sure	14. p ce
3. gr f	9. hyg ne	15. br f
4. dec t	10. s ze	16. c ling
5. ch f	11. th f	17. y ld
6. n ce	12. w rd	18. dec tful

(4) *Y* TO *I* BEFORE *ES*

Words ending in *-y* preceded by a consonant change the *-y* to *-i* before adding *-es.* This rule applies to forming both (*a*) the plural of nouns ending in *-y* and (*b*) the third person singular of verbs ending in *-y.* In both cases, if the *-y* is preceded by a vowel instead of a consonant, simply add *-s.*

Examples

Nouns ending in *-y* preceded by a consonant: —

ally + es = allies	lady + es = ladies
berry + es = berries	fly + es = flies

Verbs ending in -*y* preceded by a consonant : —

$$\begin{aligned} \text{try} \quad + \text{ es} &= \text{tries} \\ \text{deny} \quad + \text{ es} &= \text{denies} \\ \text{marry} + \text{ es} &= \text{marries} \end{aligned}$$

y preceded by a vowel : —

$$\begin{aligned} \text{chimney} + \text{s} &= \text{chimneys} \\ \text{monkey} + \text{s} &= \text{monkeys} \\ \text{allay} \quad + \text{s} &= \text{allays} \\ \text{valley} \quad + \text{s} &= \text{valleys} \end{aligned}$$

THE ROUND TABLE

1. Find and copy one example of this rule in the spelling list given on pages 344–347.

2. Apply the rule in adding -*es* to the following nouns and verbs ending in -*y:* —

Nouns

1. boy	4. hobby	7. melody
2. essay	5. journey	8. mercy
3. fairy	6. key	9. attorney

Verbs

1. carry	3. defy	5. employ	7. satisfy
2. buy	4. delay	6. hurry	8. say

3. Note that *day* + *ly* = *daily;* and that *gay* + *ety* = *gaiety* (preferred over *gayety*).

3. The Division of Words (Syllabication)

In addition to getting all the letters in a word right, there are two other matters we need to know about spelling : (1) how a word is divided — in other words, its syllabication ; and (2) whether a compound word is hyphenated or not.

All words except monosyllables are divided into two or more syllables. Thus words have natural joints, as it were, and can be properly divided only at a joint. When we come to the end of a line in writing, having started on a word of several syllables, the impulse is to continue to write up to the half-inch margin at the end of the line, and then to divide the word exactly at that point, regardless of whether or not a syllable division occurs there. This sometimes leads to just as actual mistakes as if the word had been misspelled. Thus, although a word of one syllable cannot be divided at all, a student who was trying especially hard to get his margins right made the mistake of writing *on-* at the end of one line, and *ce* at the beginning of the next; and another student wrongly divided *month* into *mo-* and *-nth*.

The dictionary, in spelling a word, indicates either by the accent or by spacing and by a very short dash or a centered period where the syllables come. Whenever we divide a word, we must be sure we are doing so correctly. *Combination*, for example, divides itself into *com-bi-na-tion*, and we can divide it at any of these places. *Filling* is divided *fill-ing*, but *fillet* and *filly* are *fil-let* and *fil-ly*. Other tricky divisions are *sign-ing* (but *sig-na-ture* and *sig-nal*), *ful-fill*, *car-ry*, *pen-ny*, *dis-charge*, *sing-ing*, *sin-gle*, *na-tion*, *shad-ow*.

A syllable formed by a single letter, whether at the beginning or the end of a word, should never be separated from the rest of the word, as in *alone*, *about*, *busy*, *many*.

It is best never to divide a proper noun, especially if it is the name of a person.

Do not divide a hyphenated word except at the hyphen.

THE ROUND TABLE

Write the following words in list form, dividing them into syllables as you think they should be divided. Verify your divisions from the dictionary, correcting any mistakes and learning the correct forms: —

1. referring	7. reluctant	13. forever
2. interference	8. terribly	14. galloping
3. solving	9. interrupt	15. forcibly
4. salvation	10. trickling	16. telling
5. bodily	11. processes	17. helping
6. abiding	12. recitation	18. chemical

4. Compound Words
(1) THE USE OF THE HYPHEN

Another troublesome problem in spelling is when and when not to hyphenate. When two words are often used together, there are three possibilities: (1) the words may remain separate and distinct, as is the case with *Red Cross, red pepper,* and *red tape;* (2) the words may be hyphenated, as *red-handed, red-hot,* and *red-letter;* (3) or they may have become one word and thus be written solid, as *redbird, redcap,* and *redhead.* Nearly all compound words go through these three stages. The oftener compound words are used the closer does the union become. Moreover, the growing tendency today is for compound words to be written solid. These three stages shift with time and use, and there is no way of telling in advance which stage a word is in. Many good spellers, who rarely have to go to the dictionary for any other reason, have to consult it constantly to settle this matter of compound words.

Here are some common compound words which illustrate the three stages of union. It is important that you know them.

1. Two Separate Words	*2. Hyphenated*	*3. One Word*
all right	high-strung	highway
high school	so-called	classroom
class day	first-class	textbook
post office	left-handed	schoolmate
school bus	self-denial	bookmark
school year	self-reliance	today
no one	self-respect	tomorrow
per cent	good-bye	tonight
will power	well-bred	drugstore
good night	old-fashioned	baseball
et cetera		football
mind reader		handbag
air mail		cannot
air pump		daylight
day laborer		typewriter
night latch		oneself
night letter		streetcar
		airplane

(2) COMPOUND WORDS USED AS ADJECTIVES

When two words are used together as an adjective preceding the noun they modify, they regularly take the hyphen. Thus, *well known, high school, worth while, post office, class day,* when used as adjectives, all take the hyphen; as, a *well-known* man, a *high-school* game, a *worth-while* book, *post-office* regulation, *class-day* exercises, and so forth.

Notice, also, that most of the hyphenated words in column two on the preceding page are adjectives.

FRACTIONS

Write fractions with the hyphen when used as compound adjectives.

NUMBERS

All numbers from 21 (twenty-one) to 99 (ninety-nine) are hyphenated: —

thirty-six, forty-four, fifty-five, eighty-seven

THE ROUND TABLE

Copy the following sentences and with the aid of the latest dictionary write the italicized compound words correctly.

1. The crow is a large *black bird*, much larger than the regular *black bird*.
2. Please go to the *post office* and send this package to the *book keeper* by *parcel post*.
3. My father sent me a *night letter* on my *birth day*.
4. Please show *common sense* in the use of the *semi colon*.
5. At *mid night*, with his *cut out* wide open, a drunken driver ran into a *street car* and bent his *mud guard*.
6. Please bring me my *walking stick* from the *bed room*.
7. What *wave length* does your local *radio station* use?
8. How many men are on the *rail road's pay roll*?
9. Have you ever seen a *touch down* made from the *kick off*?
10. *Never the less* most *tax payers* dislike to pay taxes on *real estate*.

5. Homonyms or Doublets

One particular source of trouble in English is the large number of homonyms or doublets that our language contains. The word *homonym* comes from two Greek words, *homos*, *homo*, meaning "the same," and *onoma* meaning a "name." **Homonyms, therefore, are words having the same pronunciation but differing in origin, meaning, and usually in spelling.** It is estimated that probably about one in twelve of all our mistakes in spelling comes from these troublesome homonyms or doublets.

Doublets

1. break (Can you break it?)	brake (To put on brakes)
2. coarse (A load of coarse gravel)	course (He took the proper course)
3. fair (Fair play)	fare (Good fare)
4. great (A great man)	grate (Put coal on the grate)
5. ascent (The ascent was steep)	assent (He gave his assent)
6. bolder (Bolder than his brother)	boulder (A very large boulder)
7. heal (To heal one's wounds)	heel (He bruised his heel)
8. missed (Sorry to have missed you)	mist (Fog and mist)
9. pain (To suffer pain)	pane (Broke the windowpane)
10. week (Twice a week)	weak (A weak voice)

The method of treating homonyms varies. On the whole it seems best, however, to realize that there are many troublesome doublets, to couple them together frankly at the outset, and try to distinguish them in spelling, in meaning, and in use. Unless a student learns the difference between them from the beginning, he will certainly confuse them later when, having had the first homonym earlier, he meets its mate.

THE ROUND TABLE

1. Distinguish the following homonyms by using them correctly in phrases or short sentences : —

(1) alter	(8) cereal	(15) lie
altar	serial	lye
(2) bare	(9) complement	(16) red
bear	compliment	read
(3) base	(10) desert	(17) stake
bass	dessert	steak
(4) berry	(11) feet	(18) stationary
bury	feat	stationery
(5) berth	(12) flea	(19) sun
birth	flee	son
(6) bread	(13) formally	(20) there
bred	formerly	their
(7) canvas	(14) here	(21) who's
canvass	hear	whose

2. Give the other doublet for the following homonyms, and distinguish each from the other : —

(1) ate	(8) heard	(15) principal
(2) be	(9) hour	(16) rap
(3) beat	(10) lesson	(17) sail
(4) blue	(11) mail	(18) some
(5) capital	(12) new	(19) stair
(6) council	(13) ode	(20) threw
(7) forth	(14) peace	(21) way

3. Distinguish the following triple homonyms by using them in phrases or short sentences: —

(1) rode	(3) sow	(5) to
road	sew	too
rowed	so	two
(2) seas	(4) site	
sees	cite	
seize	sight	

4. Give the other two members of the following triple homonyms, and distinguish them from one another: —

(1) buy	(2) rain	(3) right
(4) meat	(5) praise	

5. Puns, which have been called the lowest form of wit, are made possible by the existence of so many homonyms or doublets in our language. Here are some old verses which illustrate the possibilities for better and for worse.

Cautionary Verses to Youth of Both Sexes

For instance, ale may make you ail, your aunt an ant may kill;
You in a vale may buy a veil, and Bill may pay the bill.
Or if to France your barque you steer, at Dover, it may be,
A peer appears upon the pier, who, blind, still goes to sea.

A fat man's gait may make us smile, who has no gate to close;
The farmer sitting on his stile no stylish person knows;
Perfumers men of scents must be; some Scilly men are bright;
A brown man oft deep read we see, a black a wicked wight.

Then now you see, my little dears, the way to make a pun,
A trick which you, through coming years, should sedulously shun:
The fault admits of no defense, for wheresoe'er 'tis found,
You sacrifice the sound for sense: the sense is never sound.

So let your words and actions too one single meaning prove,
And, just in all you say or do, you'll gain esteem and love;
In mirth and play no harm you'll know, when duty's task is done,
But parents ne'er should let you go unpunished for a pun.

— THEODORE E. HOOK (1788–1841)

6. What is the best pun you ever heard? One of the few triple puns on record is the following: A rich cattle owner set his sons up in business. He gave them a large ranch on the railroad and named it *Focus*. When asked the reason for the name he replied, "Because there the *sun's rays meet*."

6. The Apostrophe

The apostrophe has three very definite and important uses: (1) to mark the omission of a letter or a syllable; (2) to help form the plural of letters, figures, and words used without reference to their meaning; and (3) to help form the possessive case of nouns and indefinite pronouns.

(1) APOSTROPHE TO MARK OMITTED LETTERS

In the constant effort to take short cuts in speech, we often leave out a letter in certain words, and thus contract them from two syllables into one. Thus instead of saying *are not*, we leave out the *o* and say *aren't;* or instead of *they are* we say *they're;* and for *it is*, we say *it's*. **In all such cases the apostrophe must be used to mark the place of the omitted letter.**

Here are some of the commoner contractions. The three most troublesome ones are starred.

can't	I'll	wasn't
couldn't	I've	weren't
doesn't	isn't	*who's
don't	*it's	won't
hasn't	o'clock	wouldn't
haven't	shan't	you're
he's	*they're	we're

Notice in each contraction that the apostrophe comes not over a letter but exactly between the letters at the spot where the missing letter has been omitted. To write *are'nt* instead of *aren't*, or *does'nt* instead of *doesn't*, in order to indicate a missing *o*, is like putting a spoonful of oatmeal into your ear instead of into your mouth.

Note particularly the three starred forms. They give trouble because they are easily confused with resembling forms. *It's* is the contraction for *it is*, and not the possessive of *it*. (*It's* late; *it's* never too late to mend, etc.; but, The dog came back without *its* collar; This tree has lost *its* leaves.) Similarly, *who's* is the contraction for *who is*, and must not be confused with *whose*, the possessive of *who*. (*Who's* there? *Who's* that at the phone? But *whose* hat is this? I've just seen the man *whose* car was wrecked yesterday.) Likewise *they're* is the contraction for *they are*, and must be distinguished from the possessive *their*. (*They're* here, but *their* baggage did not come.)

(2) APOSTROPHE TO FORM THE PLURAL OF LETTERS AND FIGURES

For the sake of clearness and convenience, apostrophe *s* (*'s*), instead of simply *s*, is usually added to form the plural of letters, figures, and words used without regard to their meaning.

Examples

1. The most troublesome figures to write clearly are *5*'s and *7*'s.
2. Unless you dot your *i*'s and cross your *t*'s, your *i*'s will look like *e*'s and your *t*'s will look like *l*'s.
3. The reason you got the wrong answer is that you mixed up your +'s and —'s.

(3) APOSTROPHE TO FORM POSSESSIVE (*'s* and *s'*)

The possessive case of nouns is formed in the following ways: —

SINGULAR POSSESSIVE

1. If the noun is in the singular number, add apostrophe *s* (*'s*).

The man's hat; a boy's book; father's watch; a lady's fan.

This is the simple, invariable rule in forming the possessive singular, and present usage applies it even when the noun ends in an *s* sound: —

Keats's life; Burns's poems; Jones's wife; Dickens's novels; James's sister.

Only in extreme cases, where there is a multiplication of hissing *s*'s, is the apostrophe alone without the *s* used to form the possessive singular: Ulysses' wanderings; Sophocles' dramas; Edgar Lee Masters' poetry; for goodness' sake.

Hence, ninety-nine times out of a hundred, to form the possessive singular, add *'s*.

Note, however, that this part of the rule applies only to the singular number. The plural number is a different story.

Plural Possessive

2. If the noun in the plural number ends in *-s* or *-es*, to form the possessive simply add the apostrophe.

Take, for example, the s-plurals *sailors*, *trees*, *foxes*, *boys*.
The s-ending is a part of the plural number.
To form the possessive, simply add the apostrophe.

sailors' togs; trees' leaves; foxes' holes; boys' clothes.

3. If the noun in the plural does not end in *-s* or *-es*, to form the possessive add apostrophe *s* (*'s*).[1]

men's failures; women's work; mice's nests; brethren's society; children's games; oxen's horns; deer's enemies; heathen's idols; seraphim's wings; alumni's choice; alumnae's wishes.

To repeat and sum up, then, there are three rules for forming the possessive case: —

1. If the noun is singular, whether it ends in *-s* or not, add apostrophe *s* (*'s*).

2. If the noun is plural, if it ends in *-s* or *-es*, add simply the apostrophe.

3. If the noun is plural and does not end in *s*, add the apostrophe *s* (*'s*).

These three rules are so simple that it hardly seems necessary to restate them. The experience of everyone, however, proves that it is hard to apply them correctly. Remember that of all misspellings about one in twelve is due to the wrong use of the apostrophe.

The Possessive Case of Pronouns

The apostrophe is never used, in any circumstances, to form the possessive of personal, relative, or interrogative pronouns: —

yours	ours
his, hers, its	theirs
whose	whose?

[1] For other examples of foreign plurals, see the Review of Grammar, page 27.

Recall from pages 338 and 339 that *it's* and *who's* are not possessives but contractions for *it is* and *who is*.

The indefinite pronouns, however, many of which end in *one*, *body*, *else*, form the possessive by adding apostrophe *s* (*'s*).

no one's business; everybody's belief; one's wish; another's work; someone's hat; nobody's land; everyone else's opinion; somebody else's seat.

THE ROUND TABLE

1. Using very short sentences, or even phrases, form the possessive case of the following nouns: —

(1) cat	(5) foot	(11) Holmes
cats	feet	(12) alumnus
(2) gentleman	(6) Tom	(13) alumna
gentlemen	Thomas	(14) sister
(3) woman	(7) Daisy	sisters
women	(8) father-in-law	(15) professor
(4) brother	(9) somebody	professors
brothers	(10) nobody else	(16) city
brethren	everyone else	cities

(17) Little, Brown and Company

2. Copy the following sentences and insert apostrophes wherever needed. Do not write in your book.

(1) "Whos there?" a mans voice called. "I wont open the door till Im certain you arent a thief."

(2) If were to be there by four oclock, wed better be starting now.

(3) Why didnt you let me know you couldnt come? Its too late to borrow anyone elses car now.

(4) It wont be long now. Theyre about ready to start.

(5) Your *n*s and your *u*s look exactly alike.

(6) Whose hat is that on the table?

(7) This paper is ours, not theirs.

(8) Its no use to complain. Anybodys guess is as good as anybody elses.

(9) It is hard to observe correctly all the Thou-shalts and the Thou-shalt-nots of social usage.

3. Turn the following italicized phrases into the possessive case: —

(Example: The book of Mary = Mary's book)

(1) The hats of *the children* are in the room *belonging to their father*.

(2) The store on the corner sells clothing *of boys* and *of men*.

(3) The room *of your boy* is in the dormitory *belonging to the boys*.

(4) This paper advertises shoes *of women and girls*.

(5) You saw the tracks *of one deer*, but I saw the tracks *of three deer*.
(6) The dog *of my brother-in-law* had a running fit, and tore up the flower beds *of his neighbors*.
(7) The seven lean cows ate the corn *of the seven fat kine*.
(8) The skin *of one silver fox* is worth the skins *of fifty ordinary foxes*.

7. A Final Word

In all of your efforts to improve your spelling, never forget that you must be your own doctor, nurse, and druggist. Each one must diagnose and prescribe for himself — and then faithfully take his own medicine. No two people are troubled by exactly the same words.

It follows from this that while books and teachers can point the way, you alone can cure your spelling ills. Study your own case as eagerly and constantly as if you were a doctor with a millionaire patient. Analyze your own strong and weak points. Scrutinize the spelling lists on pages 343 and 344–347 for any words you may misspell. Keep a list in your English notebook of your own personal misspellings gleaned from themes, dictation, reports, quiz papers, or from any source whatsoever. This list, together with a similar list of your mispronunciations, should be unfailingly kept up to date and frequently reviewed. If you make these lists complete and study them faithfully, they may possibly prove in later life to be the most directly practical and helpful thing you got from college this year.

THE ROUND TABLE

1. You may be interested to know that it has been estimated that the five leading causes of mistakes in spelling are these : —
   (1) Compounding words (use of hyphen) 15.9%
   (2) Wrong use of prefixes or suffixes 15.4%
   (3) Confusing words alike in sound or appearance (homonyms) 13.3%
   (4) Mispronunciation 12%
   (5) Wrong use of apostrophe, usually in forming the possessive
       case 8.2%
Which of these five do you find most trouble with? And which consequently calls for most care and study on your part to overcome?

2. In your English notebook keep a personal list of all words which you misspell, either from ignorance or from carelessness. One good way is to divide your notepaper into two columns, one headed "My Way" and the other headed "The Right Way." A sample list might look like this : —

Stop! Look!! Listen!!!

My Way (*Never Again!*)	*The Right Way*
fourty	forty
embarass	embarrass
loose	lose
developement	development

3. Select two captains, and let each captain choose in turn a member of the class until the whole class is divided into two sides. On four different days, with or without notice, let the instructor choose and dictate fifty of the words from the list of demons given on pages 344–347. After the dictation let the sides exchange papers and correct them in class. Announce the winning side and the best two spellers.

4. Try this spelling test either privately or in class: —

pronunciation	accidentally	February
dining	therefore	anniversary
perhaps	movable	referring
affect	already	writing
description	altogether	beautiful
definite	describe	conscience
separate	occurring	constitution
running	twenty-four	led

5. Here is a good test list of twenty-five fairly difficult words. It is said that without previous study 50 per cent of college freshmen fail on it. Try the list once without studying it and then after studying it. Each misspelled word will count off four points.

accommodate	professor	inferred
dissipate	stopped	noticeable
disappoint	precede	lovable
laboratory	harass	Thackeray
embarrassment	companies	Macaulay
athletics	equipped	proceed
lose	development	acknowledgment
courtesy	occurred	permissible
	interfered	

6. Here is a list of fifty-five simple, familiar words. Theoretically you knew them all before entering high school. Look at them carefully and suspiciously. Do not scorn them because they are short and deceptively simple. Read again what is said on pages 327–328 about spelling demons. Are you willing to look on these words as forming a special group of Inexcusables, and to agree with the instructor (1) that one misspelled word from this list will reduce any theme to a C grade, and (2) that two or more misspellings from it will automatically give a theme a failing grade?

Inexcusables

1. across	12. does	23. meant	34. studied	45. used to
2. almost	13. doesn't	24. minute	35. studying	46. usually
3. already	14. etc.	25. ninth	36. sure	47. whether
4. all right	15. forty	26. o'clock	37. surprise	48. which
5. always	16. fourth	27. off	38. tell	49. wholly
6. among	17. having	28. quite	39. their	50. who's
7. around	18. hoping	29. really	40. together	51. whose
8. before	19. isn't	30. seems	41. too	52. woven
9. busy	20. its	31. sense	42. tries	53. writer
10. coming	21. itself	32. speech	43. truly	54. writing
11. divide	22. led	33. stopped	44. until	55. yours

7. Here are nine freakish but correct spellings. Learn them; and then, considering accent and make-up, indicate how we might have expected them to be spelled: —

(1) Cincinnati
(2) daily
(3) gaiety (preferred over gayety)
(4) ninth
(5) truly

(6) argument
(7) judgment
(8) acknowledgment
(9) desiccated

8. Why is it that words ending in *c* add a *k* before a suffix beginning with a vowel? For example: —

frolic	frolicked	picnic	picnicking
panic	panicky	mimic	mimicked

Words Easily Misspelled

(CORRECT FORMS TO BE ESTABLISHED)

(*Arranged in Groups of Ten*)

I	II	III
1. absence	11. altar	21. apiece
2. accidentally	12. alter	22. apparatus
3. accommodate	13. alumna (ae)	23. apparent
4. account	14. alumnus (i)	24. argument
5. across	15. always	25. ate (not ĕt)
6. address	16. amateur	26. athletics
7. advice (*noun*)	17. among	27. attendance
8. advise (*verb*)	18. amount	28. author
9. adviser	19. anybody	29. automobile
10. all right	20. anyone	30. bade

IV

31. balance
32. ballad
33. banana
34. baring
35. barring
36. becoming
37. before
38. beginning
39. believe
40. benefited

V

41. biscuit
42. bouquet
43. breeches
44. buoy
45. buoyant
46. bus
47. busses
48. business
49. cafeteria
50. candidate

VI

51. cannot
52. capital   (*adj.*,
       chief;   *noun*,
       wealth, city)
53. capitol   (state-
       house building)
54. ceiling
55. cemetery
56. changeable
57. changing
58. chaperon
59. chauffeur
60. chief

VII

61. column
62. combated
63. coming
64. commit
65. comrade
66. conscience
67. conscious
68. controlled
69. courteous
70. courtier

VIII

71. criticize
72. cupola
73. deceive
74. decided
75. decision
76. definite
77. dependent
78. desert
79. desirable
80. dessert

IX

81. develop
82. development
83. decent
84. descent
85. describe
86. description
87. dilapidated
88. dining
89. disagreeable
90. disappear

X

91. disappoint
92. dissipate
93. divide
94. divine
95. doctor
96. does
97. doesn't
98. don't
99. eighth
100. embarrass

XI

101. envelop (*verb*)
102. envelope (*noun*)
103. environment
104. equipped
105. etc.
106. everybody
107. everyone
108. everything
109. everywhere
110. existence

XII

111. expense
112. extraordinary
113. fascinating
114. finally
115. foreign
116. forehead
117. formerly (not for-
       mally)
118. forty
119. fourth
120. friend

XIII

121. fulfill
122. gaiety
123. generally
124. government
125. governor
126. grammar
127. grandeur
128. granite
129. grievous
130. harass

XIV

131. having
132. height
133. hoping
134. humble
135. humor
136. hypocrisy
137. incidentally
138. indispensable
139. infinitive
140. intelligible

XV

141. isn't
142. isolate
143. it's (contraction)
144. its (possessive)
145. itself
146. judgment
147. knew
148. laboratory
149. laid
150. led

XVI

151. legend
152. leisure
153. lightening
154. lightning
155. loose
156. lose
157. lovable
158. maintenance
159. mattress
160. meanness

XVII

161. medicine
162. mileage
163. misspell
164. mosquito
165. necessary
166. nickel
167. niece
168. ninety
169. ninth
170. nobody

XVIII

171. nothing
172. no one
173. noticeable
174. occasion
175. o'clock
176. occurred
177. off
178. oneself
179. paid
180. parallel

XIX

181. pastime
182. pastoral
183. peaceable
184. permissible
185. picnic
186. picnicking
187. piece
188. pleasant
189. possess
190. practice (*noun*)

XX

191. practise (*verb*)
192. precede
193. preparation
194. prevalence
195. principal (*adj.*, most impor-tant; *noun*, head, chief, capital wealth)
196. principle (*noun*, guiding rule)
197. privilege
198. probably
199. procedure
200. proceed

XXI

201. prodigy
202. professor
203. quiet (still)
204. quite (entirely)
205. quiz
206. quizzes
207. really
208. receive
209. recognize
210. recommend

XXII

211. relieve
212. religious
213. renaissance
214. renascence
215. repetition
216. restaurant
217. rhyme (or rime)
218. rhythm
219. sacrifice
220. salary

XXIII

221. scarcely
222. seize
223. sense
224. separate
225. siege
226. skillful
227. somebody
228. someone
229. sophomore
230. speech (but speak)

XXIV

231. stationary (not moving)
232. stationery (writing supplies)
233. stopped
234. studying
235. superintendent
236. sure
237. surprise
238. syllable
239. there
240. their

XXV

241. theirs (not their's)
242. they're
243. till (but until)
244. together
245. too
246. tragedy
247. tries
248. truly
249. tyranny
250. until (but till)

XXVI

251. using
252. usually
253. valet
254. verify
255. village
256. villain
257. weather
258. weird
259. welfare
260. whether

XXVII

261. who's (who is)
262. whose (belonging to whom?)
263. won't
264. writer
265. writing
266. written
267. yield
268. yours (not your's)

PROPER NAMES

I

1. Baptist
2. Britain (the empire)
3. Briton (a native of Great Britain)
4. Chautauqua
5. Christian
6. Cincinnati
7. De Quincey
8. Eliot, George
9. February
10. Iliad
11. Johnson, Dr. Samuel

II

12. Jonson, Ben
13. Latin
14. Macaulay
15. Macbeth
16. Mississippi
17. Odyssey
18. Philippines
19. Shelley
20. Thackeray
21. Waverley
22. Wednesday

CHAPTER XIX

Pronunciation

Pronunciation is to the spoken word what spelling is to the written word — a sure proof either of knowledge or of ignorance. There is no way to cover up a mistake in pronunciation. It is obvious to everybody, and is usually greeted with an inward smile of amusement, surprise, or pity, according to circumstances. Not what you say but how you say it goes far toward fixing your standing, for better or for worse, in the minds of those you come in contact with. In sheer self-defense we must learn to speak correctly.

Mistakes in pronunciation are due to three causes: (1) slovenly enunciation; (2) wrong placing of the stress or accent; (3) wrong sounding of a letter, either vowel or consonant.

Besetting Sins

As is the case with spelling — and note this fact well — the words most often mispronounced are not long hard ones like *apotheosis* (*à* pŏth′ ē ō′ sĭs), *acclimated* (*ă* klī′ mĭ tĕd), or *Eurydice* (ŭ rĭd′ ĭ sē), but short familiar ones. For example, *was, of,* and *what* are easily the most mispronounced words in English. Many people habitually say *wŭz, ŭv,* and *whŭt* instead of the correct *wŏz, ŏv,* and *whŏt. Kĕtch* instead of *catch* (kătch) is another troublemaker. Pronouncing *put* to rhyme with *but* [1] instead of with *foot* is another bad mistake. *Ruther* for *rather, vurry* for *very, fur* for *for,* and *Amurrican* for *American* are four other common errors. Descending to the bottom of the scale in seriousness, we find almost inexcusable blunders like *ellum* for *elm, fillum* for *film, athaletics* for *athletics, deef* for *deaf, mischeevous* for *mischievous, attacted* for *attacked,* and *drownded* for *drowned.*

Surely, "thy speech bewrayeth thee."

---

[1] Except in golf, when it is spelled *putt*.

1. Slovenly Enunciation

Careless, hasty enunciation is responsible for a good many of our mispronunciations. Instead of giving each word its individual, rightful place, we run them all into each other like a collapsing telescope.

The following anecdote is an amusing illustration of how easy it is to misunderstand indistinct enunciation. Three ladies were talking about a conversation they had overheard between a man and his wife.

"They must have been to the circus," said Mrs. S., "because I heard her mention 'a trained deer.'"

"No, they were talking about going away," answered Mrs. B., "for she said, 'Find out about the train, dear.'"

"Both of you are wrong," exclaimed Mrs. C. "They were discussing music, for she spoke of 'a trained ear' as distinctly as could be."

Just then the woman herself appeared, and they appealed to her to settle it.

"I spent last night in the country," she explained with a smile, "and simply asked my husband if it had rained here last night."

As an exercise in enunciation, try reading this incident aloud, bringing out unmistakably what each of the ladies said.

THE ROUND TABLE

1. For good practice in enunciation read the following sentences aloud clearly and slowly, bringing out the meanings distinctly : —

    (1) She has lost her earring. — She has lost her hearing.
    (2) He lives in a nice house. — He lives in an ice house.
    (3) Let all men bend low. — Let tall men bend low.
    (4) He saw two beggars steal. — He sought to beg or steal.
    (5) This hand is clean. — This sand is clean.
    (6) He would pay nobody. — He would pain nobody.
    (7) That lasts till night. — That last still night.

2. For further practice in enunciation, try the following tongue-twisters. Some are old and familiar ; some are new.

    (1) The sea ceaseth, and it sufficeth us.
    (2) Strange strategic statistics.
    (3) Sarah in a shawl shoveled soft snow slowly.
    (4) She sells sea shells.
    (5) The Leith police dismisseth us.

(6) Surly Shirley sold silly shilly-shally Sally shiny satin slippers.

(7) Shook's snapshot shop shall show some sharp snapshots soon.

(8) Does Daisy's daily dozen delay Daisy's lazy dozing, or does Daisy's lazy dozing delay Daisy's daily dozen?

(9) When wicked witches whisk switches, which witch whisks switches swiftest?

(10) Are our oars here?

(11) Many a wit is not a whit wittier than Whittier.

(12) His suit showed spots of suet and soot.

2. Wrong Accent

The accent is a very important part of English pronunciation. We may sound each letter and syllable in a word correctly, and yet put the stress or voice emphasis on the wrong syllable.

Probably the most sinned-against word in our language in this respect is *exquisite*. It should be strongly accented on *ex*, the first syllable, not on *quis*, the middle syllable. *Ex'quisite* is a beautiful word; *exquis'ite* is both ugly and wrong. Although the wrong pronunciation is frequently heard, in the name of good English avoid it, and help keep *ex'quisite* on its rightful throne.[1]

Other common examples of wrong accent are these. Study the two columns and fix the right accents firmly in your mind by saying the words in the first column over aloud several times with unusually strong stress on the accented syllable.

Right	*Wrong*
1. in'teresting	interest'ing
2. research'	re'search
3. mis'chievous	mischie'vous
4. mustache'	mus'tache
5. the'ater	thea'ter
6. address'	ad'dress
7. adult'	a'dult
8. ally'	al'ly
9. ide'a	i'dea
10. inqui'ry	in'quiry

Sometimes the same word is accented differently if it is used as different parts of speech. Thus, as a noun, *survey* has the accent on

---

[1] Even now it is tottering. The latest Webster adds this note: "Occasionally, especially by way of emphasis, ĕks-kwĭz'ĭt."

the first syllable, *sur'vey;* as a verb, it has the accent on the last syllable, *survey'.* The word *accent* is used similarly: *ac'cent* is the noun; *accent',* the verb. *Expert* as a noun is *ex'pert;* as an adjective it is *expert'.* *Absent* as an adjective is *ab'sent;* as a verb it is *absent'.*

THE ROUND TABLE

1. Read the following sentences aloud, accenting strongly the correct syllables: —

(1) If you *absent* yourself from class, you will be marked *absent.*

(2) If we wish to *progress,* we shall have to make better *progress* than we are doing now.

(3) Please *record* this statement in the *record.*

(4) I *object* to being made the *object* of ridicule.

(5) The loser said he would *contest* the judges' decision in the last *contest.*

(6) The foreman said it was not his habit to *increase* wages if the workman demanded an *increase.*

(7) She disliked to *perfume* her handkerchief with even the most delicate *perfume.*

(8) Please *accent* the syllable on which the *accent* belongs.

(9) If you wish *expert* advice, you had better go to an *expert.*

(10) If you *extract* the flavor of the vanilla bean, it is called vanilla *extract.*

2. We are likely to get the accent wrong in the following words. How should they be accented?

(1) pianist	(7) resources
(2) alternate	(8) Newfoundland
(3) museum	(9) entire
(4) hospitable	(10) recess
(5) finance	(11) detour
(6) lamentable	(12) vehement

3. Letter Sounds

In order to pronounce correctly, not only must the accent be in the proper place, but the letters and syllables must also be given the right sound. To do this in English is not a light matter, for English spelling and consequently English pronunciation are both exceedingly tricky and illogical. It may seem to us that Latin (or maybe French) is a hard language, but imagine the state of mind of a foreigner who is

trying to learn to speak English on having been told that *Sioux* spells
soo, and that the vowel sounds in *herd*, *bird*, *word*, and *curd* are pronounced exactly alike. Then imagine his further stupefaction if
given the following classic lines and asked to learn them for the next
lesson : —

> 'Tis not an easy task to show
> How *o*, *u*, *g*, *h* sound ; since *though*
> And Irish *lough* and English *slough*,
> And *cough*, and *hiccough*, all allow,
> Differ as much as *tough* and *through*,
> There seems no reason why they do.

(1) DIACRITICAL MARKS

(*Key to the Symbols Used in Pronunciation*)

At the bottom of each page of the dictionary is a running list of
common words with appropriate marks showing how the various
letters — vowels, consonants, and diphthongs — are sounded. These
are called diacritical marks, and to become thoroughly familiar
with them is the first thing to learn about your dictionary, for the
pronunciation of a word is given in parentheses immediately following
each word.

THE ROUND TABLE

1. Do you pronounce *was*, *of*, and *what* correctly ? If you are in earnest
about pronunciation, you will make an immediate start on these three
words. They look easy, but it will take all your care and effort to conquer
them.

2. Probably the most variously pronounced word in English is *quinine*.
One dictionary gives five pronunciations. Look them up. Which is the
favored pronunciation in your community ?

3. What eighth sound of *ough* can be added to the seven given in the
verses above ?

4. What is the difference in your dictionary between the dash and the
hyphen marking the division of syllables ?

5. What is the difference in your dictionary between the primary (or
chief) accent in a long word and the secondary (or light) accent ?

6. If two pronunciations are listed as allowable, how can you tell which
is preferred ?

7. Who of all the people you know pronounces most correctly ?

8. In a pamphlet by Professor Thomas Henry Briggs of Teachers College, Columbia University, the following are given as good words to practice your pronunciation on. Try them first without and then with the dictionary.

alias	ally	decade	how
suite	won't	discern	Arctic
mauve	Asia	cents	elm
spavin	ere	Italian	library
tirade	bade	umbrella	

4. Disputed Pronunciations

Although there is usually only one way to pronounce a word correctly, a good many words have two accepted pronunciations, either of which is permissible. In such cases we may use either the pronunciation preferred in the dictionary or the pronunciation preferred in our section or community.

Here is a list of forty-two important common words which have two correct pronunciations. Look them over carefully and see whether you follow the dictionary's first or second choice.

On a percentage basis, counting each word as 2.4, grade yourself on the number of preferred pronunciations you use.

Word	*First Choice*	*Second Choice*
advertisement	ăd vûr′tĭz mĕnt	ăd′vēr tīz′mĕnt (U.S.)
aerial	â ēr′ĭ ăl	âr′ĭ ăl
alma mater	ăl′mȧ mā′tēr	äl′mȧ mä′tēr
almond	ä′mŭnd	ăm′ŭnd
alternate (*adj.*)	ôl′(or ăl′)tēr nĭt	ôl (or ăl) tûr′nĭt
amateur	ăm ȧ tûr′	ăm′ȧ tŭr
automobile	ô tŏ mŏ bēl′	ô tŏ mō′bĭl (or bēl)
azure	ăzh′ēr	ā′zhēr
bestial	bĕs′ty ăl	bĕs′chȧl
bouquet	bōō kā′	bō kā′
cabaret	kăb′ȧ rĕt	kăb ȧ rā′
chauffeur	shŏ fûr′	shō′fēr
civilization	sĭv ĭ lĭ zā′shŭn	sĭv ĭ lī zā′shŭn
courtesy	kûr′tĕ sĭ	kôr′tĕ sĭ
detour	dĕ tōōr′	dē′tōōr
drama	drä mȧ	drăm′ȧ
economic	ē kŏ nŏm′ĭk	ĕk ŏ nŏm′ĭk
ego	ē′gō	ĕg′ŏ
envelope (*noun*)	ĕn′vĕ lōp	ŏn′vĕ lōp

Word	First Choice	Second Choice
falcon	fôl′kŭn	fô kŭn
fetish	fē′tĭsh	fĕt′ĭsh
fortnight	fôrt′nīt	fôrt′nĭt
garage	gȧ räzh′	găr′ĭj
grease (verb)	grēs	grēz (in the South)
humor	hū′mēr	ū′mēr
inquiry	ĭn kwīr′ĭ	ĭn′kwĭ rĭ
isolated	ī′sô lāt ēd	ĭs′ô lāt ĕd
leisure	lē′zhēr	lĕzh′ēr
lever	lē′vēr	lĕv′ēr
medieval	mē dĭ ē′văl	mĕd ĭ ē′văl
menu	mĕn′ū	mā′nū
patriot	pā′trĭ ŭt	păt′rĭ ŭt
prelude	prĕl′ūd	prē′lūd
prestige	prĕs tēzh′	prĕs′tĭj
robot	rō′bŏt	rŏb′ŏt
route	rōōt	rout (in military circles, among railroad men, and colloquially of a delivery route)
scenic	sē′nĭk	sĕn′ĭk
shone	shōn	shŏn
trio	trē′ō	trī′ō
vaudeville	vōd′vĭl	vô′dĕ vĭl
virile	vĭr′ĭl	vī′rĭl
zenith	zē′nĭth	zĕn′ĭth

In cases like these it is sometimes hard to decide how far to follow the dictionary pronunciation. Though the dictionary gives preference to *rā′tion* and *adver′tisement*, most Americans say *ră′tion* and *advertize′ment*. Likewise the dictionary gives the pronunciation *sĭr′ŭp*, with no choice. Most people, however, say "please pass the *surrup*." Whether you say *sĭr′ŭp* or *surrup* is for you personally to decide. Pronunciation is not only a dictionary matter, but a community and family matter also, involving not only knowledge but courage, tact, and common sense as well.

5. Proper Names

In both pronunciation and meaning proper nouns stand in a class by themselves and need special attention. There are many curious quirks in human nature, but none more curious than our almost universal tendency to neglect to look up strange proper names. Explain it as you will, the same person who will go to the dictionary at once if he meets a rare word like *fingan* or *zarf* will pass serenely by words like *Aphrodite* and *Erebus*, though their pronunciation and meaning alike are unknown.

Proper names from foreign languages, especially Greek, Latin, French, German, Italian, and Spanish, follow the laws of their own language unless they have been in common use in English long enough to become Anglicized. We must be extremely careful, therefore, to be sure we pronounce such names correctly. Except to a very hard-hearted person it is very embarrassing to hear someone mention a foreign place or person, and utterly miss the pronunciation. Here, again, eternal vigilance is the price of safety.

Following are thirty-five proper names which are more or less commonly mispronounced. For convenience they are divided into three lists.

(1) PROPER NAMES

Dante (dăn'tĕ; Italian pron., dän'tȧ)

Don Juan (dŏn jŭ'ȧn; Sp., dŏn hwän')

Don Quixote (dŏn kwĭk'sŏt; Sp., dŏn kĕ-hō'tä

Goethe (gû'tĕ)

Himalaya (hĭ-mä'lȧ-yȧ; less correctly, hĭm'ȧ-lā'yȧ)

Iowa (ī'ŏ-wȧ; not wä)

Italian (ĭ-tăl'; not ī-tăl')

Los Angeles (lōs ăng'gĕl-ĕs or lŏs ăn'-jĕl-ĕs or ēz)

Louisiana (lōō-ē'zĭ-ăn'ȧ)

Louisville (lōō'ĭs- or lōō'ĭ-vĭl)

Newfoundland (accent either first or last syllable, not the second syllable; but Newfound'land dog)

New Orleans (ôr'lĕ-ȧnz)

(2) FAMOUS PEOPLE

Beethoven (bā'tō-vĕn)

Chopin (shŏ'păɴ')·

Gandhi (gän'dĕ)

Leif Ericson (lāf)

Machiavelli (mä'kyä-vĕl'lĕ)

Nobel (nŏ-bĕl')

Paderewski (pȧ'dĕ-rĕf'skĕ or rĕs'kĕ)

Rabelais (rȧ'b'lĕ')

(3) CLASSICAL NAMES

Achilles (à-kĭl'ēz)

Aeolus (ē'ŏ-lŭs)

Ceres (sē'rēz)

Circe (sûr'sĕ)

Erebus (ĕr'ĕ-bŭs)

Hades (hā'dēz)

Hebe (hē'bĕ)

Lethe (lē'thē)

Niobe (nī'ŏ-bĕ)

Penelope (pĕ-nĕl'ŏ-pĕ)

Pleiades (plē'yà-dēz or plī'à-dēz)

Psyche (sī'kĕ)

Satyr (săt'ēr or sā'tēr; distinguish from satire, săt'īr)

Ulysses (ū-lĭs'sēz)

Zeus (zūs' or zōōs')

THE ROUND TABLE

1. Make full use of the correct pronunciations given on pages 357 and 358. These words are among the commonest and most uniformly mispronounced in English. If you find listed a pronunciation new to you, verify it and learn it.

2. Have you noticed in yourself the tendency referred to in the first paragraph on page 355, that of not looking up a proper name even though you do not know either its pronunciation or its meaning?

3. What is the most amusing blunder you have made (or heard) recently in the pronunciation of a proper name?

4. What is meant by saying that a word or pronunciation has been *Anglicized?*

5. Look carefully through the three lists of proper names on pages 355 and 356 and check your knowledge of them in the following particulars: —

How many of the thirty-five (a) did you know both the pronunciation and the meaning of? (b) were you doubtful about? (c) were altogether unknown to you?

6. Glance through the "Names in the News" feature of almost any newspaper, and bring to class any interesting or unusual pronunciations you find in the names of people now in the public eye.

7. *An Experience Curriculum in English* advises the following commonsense attitude in this difficult matter of correct pronunciation: "Minor variations in sounds or stresses grow up through adaptations to different physical or mental environments. . . . Such differences are desirable. They indicate life. Dictionaries should be followed with a judicious ear turned toward the habits of speech of the cultured people of the section concerned."

8. On a percentage basis, counting each word as 1.4, grade yourself carefully on the following list of words often mispronounced. Learn the pronunciations you were doubtful or mistaken about.

Words Often Mispronounced

(Arranged in Groups of Ten)

Test yourself carefully on this list and master it thoroughly.

I

1. accessory (accent second syllable)
2. address (address′)
3. adult (adult′)
4. alias (ā′lĭ-ăs)
5. ally (ally′)
6. Appalachian (lăch′ or lā′)
7. apparatus (rā′ or răt′)
8. Arab (ăr′ăb)
9. auxiliary (ôg-zĭl′yȧ-rĭ)
10. aye, ay (ever, ā)

II

11. aye, ay (yes, ī)
12. bade (băd)
13. bicycle (sĭk′l, but motor sīk′l)
14. column (kŏl′ŭm, not yŭm)
15. coupon (kōō′, not kū)
16. creek (kreek, not krĭk)
17. data (dā′ or dä′)
18. demonstrate (accent first syllable)
19. desert (waste of sand, dez′ert)
20. desert (worthiness, dezert′)

III

21. dessert (sweets, dezert′)
22. diphtheria (dĭf-, not dĭp-)
23. draught (dråft)
24. encore (äng-kōr′ as interjection; äng′kōr as noun)
25. entire (accent last syllable)
26. exquisite (accent first syllable)
27. forehead (fŏr′ĕd)
28. genuine (jĕn′ŭ-ĭn)
29. gratis (grā′)
30. hearth (härth ; hûrth, poetic)

IV

31. height (not heighth)
32. hospitable (accent first syllable, not second)
33. humble (sound the h)
34. idea (accent the e, not the i)
35. infamous (ĭn′fȧ-mŭs)
36. interesting (accent the first syllable, not the third)
37. joust (jŭst or jōōst)
38. lamentable (accent first syllable, not the second)
39. lenient (lē′, not lĕn′)
40. literature (lĭt′ēr-ȧ-tûr, not -choor, -chĕr, or -toor)

V

41. longitude (lŏn′jĭ-tūd)
42. long-lived (līvd, not lĭvd)
43. mineralogy (răl′, not rŏl′)
44. mischievous (accent the first, not the second syllable)
45. motorcycle (sīk′l, but bicycle, sĭk′l)
46. museum (mū-zē′ŭm)
47. nape (nāp preferred to colloquial U. S. năp)
48. neither (nē′ther preferred to English nī′ther)
49. often (do not sound the t)
50. parent (pâr′ĕnt)

VI

51. parliament (pär′lĭ-mĕnt)
52. partner (not pardner)
53. perfume (*verb*, perfūm′)
54. perfume (*noun*, per′fūm)
55. pretty (prĭt′ĭ)
56. quoit (kwoit)
57. recess (accent second syllable, except for school intermission)
58. research (accent second syllable)
59. short-lived (līvd, not lĭvd)
60. sirup (sĭr′ŭp)

VII

61. sleek (rhyme with leak)
62. soften (do not sound the *t*)
63. status (stā′)
64. subtle (sŭt′l)
65. theater (accent the first, not the second syllable)
66. usually (sound the *a*)
67. vehement (accent the first, not the second syllable)
68. wont (accustomed, wŭnt)
69. wound (injury, woōnd or wound)
70. yolk (yōk or yōlk)

VIII

71. zoölogy (zô-ŏl′ô-jĭ, not zoō-ŏl′ô-jĭ)

CHAPTER XX

The Standing of Words

1. Speech Levels or Degrees of Dignity

A teacher of composition in correcting a student's expository theme once changed "had a hunch" to "had an idea." In explaining the reason afterwards, and in discussing the choice of words in general, the teacher gave this illustration: "*Father, papa,* and *dad* are equally correct. So are a dress suit, a baseball uniform, and a pair of pajamas. It all depends."

This illustration emphasizes clearly one all-important principle in usage — namely that, like our clothes, our words are adapted to different purposes, and that what is proper for one occasion would be altogether unsuited to another. Imagine a man's wearing a baseball uniform to church or overalls to a formal dance; or an automobile mechanic's changing engine oil in a dress suit. There are similar variations or different speech levels in our vocabulary. The chatty, familiar, slangy language of the street, of the athletic field, and of the summer camp is as out of place in the pulpit, on the public platform, and in the serious essay as the sonorous and dignified language of the Declaration of Independence would be at the family breakfast table or in the nursery.

Consider the difference between saying "to act unwisely" and "to play the fool"; "to lose one's mind" and "to go bughouse"; "I can't agree with you" and "Oh, yeah?" or "Aw, nertz!"; "Dinner is served" and "Come and get it or I'll throw it away"; "The burglars dynamited the safe, stole all the money, and escaped from town before the police discovered the theft" and "The mob cracked the keister, swiped all the kale, and blew from town before the cops found out what it was all about."

These expressions show a fundamental difference both in motive and in purpose, and this difference is double-edged. It extends behind the words, from within the mind of the speaker, and it also projects in front of the words, into the mind of the hearer.

Whether, therefore, any particular expression is suitable depends upon the purpose and occasion it is used for.   In the complicated business of communicating our ideas to others, we need different

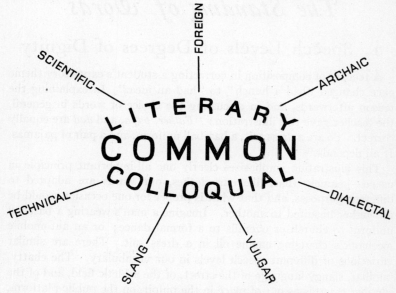

THE MAKE-UP OF THE ENGLISH VOCABULARY [1]

varieties of speech.   Good writers and speakers are careful not to mix up these varieties.   You shouldn't talk to a mule as you would to the Supreme Court, and by the same token you shouldn't talk to the Supreme Court as you would to a mule!

The dictionary recognizes five prevailing classes of words: (1) Standard or current speech (indicated by an absence of any of the four following labels); (2) Colloquial, abbreviated *Colloq.;* (3) Dialect, abbreviated *Dial.;* (4) Obsolete, abbreviated *Obs.;* (5) and *Slang.*

For our immediate purpose in this chapter, we need to familiarize ourselves with only three basic varieties of speech: (1) literary and

[1] Through the courtesy of the *Shorter Oxford Dictionary.*

formal; (2) familiar, informal, colloquial; (3) dialect, slang, and illiterate. We should, however, not only know these groups passively in theory, but also be able to distinguish them actively in our speaking and writing.

Consider the following examples of these three speech levels: —

Permissible		Not Permissible [1]
1. Literary, Formal	*2. Familiar, Informal, Colloquial*	*3. Dialect, Slang, Illiterate*
abundance	plenty of, a great deal of	heaps, lots
father	papa, daddy	pop, pap, the old man
weary, fatigued	tired, worn out	all in, petered out
banquet	meal	grub, eats, a feed
masticate	chew	chaw
oration	speech, talk	spiel, bull, hot air
appropriate, seemly	fit	O. K.
impecunious	poor	broke
pusillanimous	cowardly	yellow
is not, are not	isn't, aren't	ain't
mendicant	beggar	bum
courage	nerve	guts

Although these three standards of usage cannot always be kept clearly apart, and although there are many words which could possibly be ranked either as formal or familiar on the one hand, or as colloquial or slangy or dialect on the other, yet the three standards are fairly definite and distinct, and should be kept apart in our writing. **As a practical point, we should be on our guard in two particulars: (1) we should not use stiff, formal language when easier, shorter words would serve.** At all costs we must avoid trite expressions (see below, pages 418–421) and tall writing (see below, pages 421–424). One of the best rules ever framed is the old familiar one, "Use the simplest words the subject will bear." **(2) On the other hand, we should not fall into the opposite and commoner error of writing beneath the dignity of our subject or of our readers.** We wish to be easy and natural in our writing as in our speech, but we should avoid the over-

[1] Except in unusual circumstances, such as a dialect story.

use of slang, of abbreviated words, of colloquial, and of dialect words. Our everyday speech is full of them — often too full — but we should keep the worst of them out of our written work, especially out of our serious explanatory themes.   Few of us ever want to "talk like a book," but many of us will be helped by trying sometimes to write like a book.

THE ROUND TABLE

Degrees of Dignity: Up and Down in Formality

1. Divide a sheet of paper into three columns as is done on page 361 and head them: I. Literary, Formal; II. Familiar, Informal, Colloquial; III. Dialect, Slang, Illiterate.

Put each of the following words either into column one or into column three, and underline the word.

2. If the word belongs in column one, fill in columns two and three with appropriate synonyms coming down in dignity.   If the word belongs in column three, fill in columns two and one with appropriate synonyms going up in formality.   If you cannot fill in both columns, fill in at least one column.

(1) demise	(6) duds	(11) rube	(16) disremember
(2) slumber	(7) residence	(12) erudite	(17) draught
(3) swipe	(8) pay check	(13) skinny	(18) conflict
(4) doc	(9) inebriated	(14) beat it	
(5) simpleton	(10) stuck-up	(15) frugal	

2. Standard Usage

(Good Use)

"Good English is that form of speech which is appropriate to the purpose of the speaker, true to the language as it is, and comfortable to speaker and listener.   It is the product of custom, neither cramped by rule nor freed from all restraint; it is never fixed, but changes with the organic life of the language." (*An Experience Curriculum in English*, page 242)

The sole test of a word is usage.   If the best writers and speakers spell a given word in a certain way, pronounce it in a certain way, and attach certain meanings to it, then that spelling, that pronunciation, and those meanings are correct for that word, and all other spellings, pronunciations, and meanings are wrong.

Standard usage, or, as it usually is called, Good Use, has three requirements. It must be (1) reputable, (2) national, and (3) present. Or, to express it differently, **Standard usage is the practice of *reputable* speakers and writers, of *national* renown, at the *present* time.** Note that the requirements are three and that each one is necessary. In this respect words are like three-legged stools: it takes all three supports to keep them from falling over.

(1) REPUTABLE USAGE

The first requirement is that a word shall be employed by reputable speakers and writers. This is not only the first but is also the fairest standard. It is the great body of trained speakers and writers, those who know language best and love it most, who mold fashions and set standards in speech. We others are glad to follow their example and do our part toward keeping our mother tongue strong, beautiful, and undefiled.

There are three prevailing ways in which we are in danger of violating reputable usage, and we should guard against each of them consciously and carefully. These violations are: (1) Illiteracies; (2) Colloquialisms; and (3) Slang.

1. ILLITERACIES

On the lowest level of all, far beneath the surface of respectable speech, come what have been conveniently called **illiteracies.** These consist of flagrant mistakes in grammar, and the use of wrong and wholly unauthorized words and turns of expression. Examples are such words as *disremember, anywheres, nowheres, complected, learn* for *teach* (as, "He learned me arithmetic"), and the convenient but impossible *ain't;* such expressions as *between you and I, that there, hadn't ought, this here, this a way, that a way, them books, these kind,* had *of* come, couldn't *of* gone; double negatives like *didn't have no, won't never, can't hardly;* such verb blunders as *drownded* for *drowned,* "I *give* him the book" (past tense), "He *come, done, seen, run*" (for *came, did, saw, ran*), "They *have went, have came, have did, have saw*" (for *have gone, have come, have done, have seen*). Such mistakes as these are among the gravest and most regrettable sins against reputable usage. Happily, few of us would be guilty of them. Their presence in the speech of anyone usually points back to a deplorable lack of opportunity in early training.   If they do occur, every possible effort must be continuously made to root them out forever.

2. COLLOQUIALISMS

The word *colloquial* comes from two Latin words meaning "to talk with." Colloquial, therefore, means about the same thing as does "chatty" or "conversational." It suggests the informal, free-and-easy conversation between friends when they are off their dignity. **A colloquialism, therefore, is a word or turn of expression suitable for informal conversation, but hardly dignified or formal enough for a serious speech or essay.** The dictionary marks such words as this *Colloq.* as a sign to us to be careful how we use them for literary purposes.

Examples of easy colloquial speech are such words as *folks; a raise* (for an advance in salary); *he don't* or *it don't* (for *doesn't*); Stop the car, please, I *want out; wait on;* He comes *of a Sunday;* This is *all the farther* the road goes; It was hard *to get going; Wait a bit; Well, why not?;* *mighty* and *awfully* in the sense of *very, exceedingly; feeling so-so; so long* (for *good-bye*); *carryings-on; to take back* (*recall*); all such abbreviations and clipped forms as *Jap, auto, movie, knickers, math, photo, prof, cap, ad, exam, phone, isn't, aren't, I'd, don't, won't, shan't.* Their name is legion.

Other instances of colloquialisms will be found in the middle column of the three levels of speech described on page 361. Refer to this list and compare it with the examples given in the preceding paragraph. Remember, too, as is explained in the section on Levels in Speech, that although colloquial words are not suitable for formal purposes, like sermons and essays, they are entirely fitting in conversation and informal writing — personal letters, for example. Moreover, the general tendency today, even on the part of the best writers and speakers, is toward a much easier and more familiar style than used to be considered proper. To call a word *colloquial*, therefore, does not necessarily condemn it, but simply puts us on notice to be careful in our use of it and not to employ it on serious, dignified occasions.

For *localisms*, a term sometimes confused with *colloquialisms*, see page 370 below.

3. SLANG

Our slang's piquant as catsup; I decry it
Not as a condiment but an entire diet.
— WILLIAM LYON PHELPS

If you know the meaning of *piquant, decry,* and *condiment,* and will ponder the meaning of the quotation from William Lyon Phelps, you will need little further direction on the subject of slang.

Slang is one of the commonest and most striking forms of language activity. It has been suggestively called "language on a picnic." Its aptness is almost irresistible, and for a short time the latest slang is in everybody's mouth. Like a new coat of paint, however, first it is fresh and then it cracks.

Slang is violently figurative, usually in metaphor (see page 409). It consists either in coining new words or in taking a common word or expression and by a sudden twist giving it an unexpected meaning and thus applying it figuratively to a new situation. Often slang exhibits considerable humor and ingenuity. Everyone can recognize the force and the fun in instances like the following: *to gumshoe, to pussyfoot, bonehead, yellow streak, to bark up the wrong tree, to talk through one's hat, to bring home the bacon, a sucker list, to get cold feet, to face the music, a roughneck, joy ride, to make whoopee.* Many of these expressions are both useful and suggestive, and are still current in colloquial usage.

Just as often as not, however, slang is tame and objectionable. Poor slang has nothing in its favor but its newness, and when its novelty wears off there is nothing at all left to recommend it, not even a pleasant memory. How stale and flat seem now such expressions as the following, each of which at one time had its day — with the emphasis, fortunately, on the past tense: *skiddoo; Oh you kid!; Oh yeah?; Are you telling me?; hooey; hotcha; So's your old man; nertz.* In looking back over such expressions as those, one wonders how they ever gained a temporary foothold even in the slums of speech.

There is no denying that clever slang is fresh and piquant. If skillfully used, it adds zest and humor to informal speech. Under the gradual letting down of the bars and the steady loosening of standards, slang has become increasingly common on a level of both speech and writing where it would have been outlawed a generation ago. Slang is being used by millions and millions of people, and will continue to be used as long as language lives and people have a sense of humor. You have only to read the baseball, football, and boxing columns in any newspaper to have daily proof of humanity's fondness for racy metaphors and fresh slang.

Nor is there any use in abusing slang and trying to abolish it. It is here and it is here to stay. It is one sign that language is not dead but still alive and putting out new buds and leaves. The thing to do is to take a reasonable attitude toward it and to form the habit of using only the best and cleverest slang — and not to overuse that. Too much pepper and mustard spoil even the best food, and too lavish a mixture of slang spoils what would otherwise be bright conversation and good writing. At bottom the problem is not one of correct usage but one of good taste.

Probably the greatest objection to slang is the practical one that it tends to become a "verbicide" or word-killer. We fall into the habit of letting a convenient slang term express a dozen different meanings or shades of meaning, instead of trying to say what we mean in other and more exact words. Thus we both limit the number of words we use, or ought to use, and also weaken the skill and precision of the words we do use. To do this habitually while we are still in school, and ought to be increasing our grasp and mastery of words, is a dangerous and deadening thing.

To sum up, slang is a good servant but a bad master. Keep two rules concerning it constantly in mind. **(1) Discriminate. Use only the best and cleverest slang.** Choose your slang with at least as much care as your hats. They are equally conspicuous. **(2) Don't overdo the matter,** for two reasons: (*a*) Good taste demands moderation. A touch of artistic make-up may render an attractive face more attractive. Too much make-up spoils even the attractiveness that was there originally.

(*b*) Don't let your use of slang starve your growing vocabulary. Again, like strychnine, a little stimulates; a great deal kills.

THE ROUND TABLE

1. What are the two smartest and cleverest slang expressions you ever heard? The two worst and most objectionable?

2. Of all the more or less current slang of the day, do you think any has a chance of being taken permanently into the language? If so, which?

3. Bring to class the slangiest write-up you can find describing a sports contest — baseball, football, or any game.

4. Read aloud in class what Holmes's *Autocrat of the Breakfast Table* says about slang. The passage is found in Chapter XI and occupies one full page immediately following "The Deacon's Masterpiece." It begins: "I have known several genteel idiots whose whole vocabulary had deliquesced into some half dozen expressions."

5. What (*a*) boy and (*b*) girl of all your acquaintance uses the most slang? Apart from slang is his (her) conversation particularly varied or intelligent?

6. Which of the three following opinions of slang comes nearest to expressing your view? Be prepared to argue further for your viewpoint.

(1) Against Slang

(*a*) "Slang is an expression of weakness and ignorance. It shows that you are not willing to take the time or make the effort to find out a proper method of expressing yourself, or else that you are blind to the possibilities of language." — *Life*

(*b*) "The habitual use of slang is a sign of low breeding, or of affected rowdiness." — c. h. ward, *What Is English?* (p. 391)

(2) In Favor of Slang

(*c*) "Pedants, prigs, purists, precisians, and all dry-witted and thin-witted persons naturally hate slang, because it is alive. But men of rich natures love slang. It is the wild game of language. It abounds in imagination, humor, strength, comes warm from the lips of the people, and is the fresh product of the creative impulse by which all language was originally made."

7. In his book on slang (see number 8 below) Mr. Eric Partridge says four features are present in slang of whatever period or country: (1) the search for novelty, (2) volatility and lightheartedness as well as lightheadedness, (3) ephemerality, and (4) the sway of fashion. Discuss those traits in class.

8. Most books on language contain a discussion of slang. See the list in Round Table, question number 13, page 325. Following are three particularly interesting treatments: —

Eric Partridge, *Slang Today and Yesterday*, The Macmillan Company.

Greenough, James B., and Kittredge, George Lyman, *Words and Their Ways in English Speech*, The Macmillan Company, pp. 55–79.

H. L. Mencken, *The American Language*, Fourth Edition, Alfred A. Knopf.

(2) NATIONAL USAGE

The second requirement of standard usage is that a word shall be *national*, that is, in good use throughout the country as a whole — north, east, south, and west. To be thoroughly national a word must (1) not primarily belong to another language, (2) not be peculiar to any particular trade or class, or (3) not be peculiar to any particular section or part of the country. Violations of these three requirements are (1) Foreign Words, (2) Technical Terms, and (3) Localisms, Provincialisms, or Dialect Words.

1. FOREIGN WORDS

Some writers have the fad of flavoring their style with an occasional expression from a foreign language — usually Latin or French. **The best practice is not to use a foreign word when an English word can be found to do the work.** This tendency toward foreign words is not likely to be a besetting sin among college writers, for rarely do they have sufficient knowledge of a foreign language to tempt them to use foreign terms.

Convenient foreign expressions, which most people would understand, whether or not they would use them in their own writing, are these: *ad infinitum, quid pro quo, per se, prima facie, entre nous, esprit de corps, élan, cortège, un fait accompli, motif, politesse, savoir faire, raison d'être, tout ensemble.*

BRITICISMS

An interesting variety of usage that is not entirely national occurs in the case of Briticisms, or words and expressions that are peculiar to Great Britain or to the British. American and British usage is the same in most cases, but differs in a few important details of spelling, pronunciation, and vocabulary. Incidentally, Americanisms are making much more headway in England than Briticisms are in America.

There are five chief differences between British and American spelling, as follows: —

British	American
1. *-re*	*-er*
centre, metre, theatre	center, meter, theater
2. *-our*	*-or*
favour, labour, honour	favor, labor, honor
3. *-ise*	*-ize*
civilise, patronise, criticise	civilize, patronize, criticize
4. *-exion*	*-ection*
connexion, inflexion, reflexion	connection, inflection, reflection
5. *ll*	*l*
travelling, travelled, labelling, labelled	traveling, traveled, labeling, labeled

In vocabulary, likewise, there are a few important differences between England and America. Across the sea they say *luggage* where we would say *baggage; lift* for *elevator; reel of cotton* for *spool of thread; lorry* for *truck; cinema* for *moving pictures; petrol* for *gasoline; guard* for *conductor; bowler* for *derby; different to* for *different from.* English colloquial usage has also practically adopted the convenient *aren't I?* for our less convenient but still necessary *am I not?* British slang is not nearly so vivid or picturesque as ours, but three suggestive bits which we might well have thought of first are *to get the wind up, to get a bit of one's own back,* and *to go off the deep end.*

The presence of any of the Briticisms noted above, whether in spelling or in vocabulary, usually stamps a book as having been written by an Englishman rather than by an American. Watch for these differences in your reading.

2. TECHNICAL TERMS

Most trades, professions, classes, and ranks of society, as well as fads, games, and sports, have developed their own particular vocabulary of technical terms which the members or devotees use when talking to each other. Doctors and lawyers discuss professional matters in terms that mean little to the man in the street. A ship captain and a music teacher would have a hard time explaining their callings to each other. A golfer and a contract bridge player could not each describe these games so that the other could see and applaud the fine points. Except when a writer wishes to add color and flavor and reality to an incident or to a character, it is puzzling to know how far he should go in using technical expressions.

Examples of words that would require definition and explanation before they would be clear to the average man are, in football, *a safety, a touchback, eligible to receive a pass;* in baseball, *an infield fly, a squeeze play, a sacrifice hit;* in tennis, *a foot fault, a let, a cross-court volley;* in golf, *a birdie, a chip shot, a slice,* or *a pull;* in the stock market, *a bull, a bear, a stop order.*

3. LOCALISMS, PROVINCIALISMS, DIALECT WORDS

The third violation of the requirement that words should be national is the use of words and expressions that are peculiar to a certain part or section of the country. The United States covers a great deal of territory — 3,026,789 square miles in all — and is cut up by rivers, mountain ranges, and climate into a number of areas or sections, each almost a country in itself. There are, for example, the East or New England, the South, the Middle West, and the Far West. It is inevitable that the people living in these different sections should develop words, pronunciations, and turns of expression peculiar to their section and differing from the usage of other sections. Such words are known as localisms or provincialisms, and are marked by the dictionary as *Dialect* (abbreviated to *Dial.*). They might fairly be called sectionalisms.

Examples in New England are *clever* in the sense of *good-natured, kind, calculate* for *think* or *expect, to home* for *at home,* and *visit with* for *to go to see* or *to pay a call on;* in the West, *loco* for *crazy, two bits* for *a quarter, wrangle* for *to herd* or *round up livestock, pack* for *carry,* and *make a bed down* for *make up a bed;* in the South, *guess so* and *reckon so* for *think* or *suppose, evening* for *afternoon,* and *you all* in the sense of a group plural for *you.*

All such expressions, while primarily local in origin and use, are apt to spread beyond the boundaries of their particular section and to be used anywhere in informal or conversational talk. They thus give a colloquial,[1] racy tang to both speech and writing that is meant to mirror the local color of the different sections.

---

[1] See page 364.

THE ROUND TABLE

1. Do you know all of the foreign words listed on page 368? They are all rather common, and you should look up those that are unfamiliar to you.

2. What are the two most convenient foreign expressions you know or have come into contact with most frequently in your reading?

3. Name (a) five words peculiar to your father's trade or profession; (b) five words peculiar to whatever science you are studying; (c) five words peculiar to your favorite sport.

4. Name five technical terms connected with cooking, hunting, fishing, gymnasium, boxing, swimming, scouting, moving pictures, the radio.

5. *You all* is probably the most interesting and important of all localisms. It is a group plural for *you*, and means "you and the group with which you are associated in the speaker's mind." Though *you all* is often addressed to one person, it never, if correctly used, means one person, but always "you and your group."

6. Name several of the most characteristic localisms of your community or county.

7. Judging by the American-British spellings listed on page 369, have you recently read any book by an Englishman? Without reference to the author prove that the book you are now reading as class parallel is by an American (or Englishman).

8. For an interesting and amusing account of American and British differences, see *Britannia Waives the Rules*, by F. and Lecoq Douglas, published by E. P. Dutton and Company, Inc.

9. Localisms sometimes cause amusing misunderstandings. A popular Northern girl, who was visiting in a Southern city, was receiving a great deal of attention. One of her admirers phoned asking for permission to call on "Friday evening." She consented. Friday afternoon he went to the house only to find that she was downtown shopping. That night she stayed at home, expecting him in vain, after having refused several other engagements. Both had a good laugh later when they found that the Southern *evening* in the sense of *afternoon* was to blame.

(3) PRESENT USAGE

The third requirement of standard usage is that a word shall be in use at the present time. It is the accepted usage of today that counts, not that of the past or of the future. It is thus possible to err in two ways: (1) to use words that have passed out of active service and are now archaic or obsolete, and (2) to use newly coined words (neologisms) that have not yet made a place for themselves in the language. This process of dropping off words that have outlasted their usefulness and

of taking on new words as the rapid changes of modern life create a
demand for them is one of the signs that language is still a live and
growing function of human society.   As Edwin Arlington Robinson
expressed it : —

> A word has its use,
> Or, like a man, it will soon have a grave.

1. Archaic or Obsolete Words

Archaic means "antiquated, old-fashioned," and *obsolete* means "no
longer in use, outworn."   The terms are thus synonyms, although
obsolete is the stronger of the two and suggests the quality of being
not merely old-fashioned but of being both old-fashioned and laid
aside.   Neither term is a synonym for *old*.   Most archaic and obsolete
words are old, but age alone does not make a word either archaic or
obsolete.   Many of the oldest words in the language are still as vigorous and as necessary as they were a thousand years ago.   Examples
are the words for family relationship like *father, mother, husband, wife,
son, daughter, sister, brother,* and so on ; the numerals *one, two, three,*
and so on ; the pronouns *I, you, he, who, which,* and so on ; the prepositions *for, from, by, with, in, at, to,* and so forth ; the articles *a, an,*
and *the ;* and many of the big-little words that we *have* to use in common speech every day of our lives.   Such words can never become
obsolete or even archaic.

Many other words, however, do outwear their usefulness, and after
a longer or shorter period of increasing neglect are cast up like bits
of driftwood on the banks of time as the great living stream of language flows on through fresh fields and pastures new.   Among the
more interesting and significant of these are the following.   We should
know the meaning of each of them, for they not only have had a long
and honored history, but are still used to add a quaint flavor to poetry
and stories of the long ago.   Such are *yclept* (called, named) ; *dight*
(clad) ; the two old -*n* plurals, *shoon* (shoes) and *kine* (cows) ; various
exclamations and interjections with which people of several hundred
years ago used to flavor their conversation, such as *haply, mayhap,
in sooth* (truth), *forsooth, peradventure, prithee, perchance,* and *anon;
eke* (also) ; the two old words for think or suppose, *ween* and *wot ; eld*
and *yore* (age, time long past) ; *swain* and *wight* in the sense of person ; the two old impersonal verbs which formerly took the dative

case, *meseems* and *methinks*, both meaning *it seems to me; quoth* (said); and the old third person singular verb ending *-eth*, which Coleridge makes such effective use of in "The Rime of the Ancient Mariner," as witness the famous stanza,

> He prayeth best who loveth best
> All things both great and small;
> For the dear God who loveth us
> He made and loveth all.

2. New Words (Neologisms)

Every new invention, every fresh discovery, every advance of science, and every great crisis in world history and world thought calls new words into being. Think of the many word changes that came about when gunpowder took the place of the bow and arrow, and practically abolished hand-to-hand fighting in war. Consider, too, the host of new words made necessary when electricity displaced steam as our major labor-saving power. The World War created a separate vocabulary of its own. The amazing popular spread of four great recent inventions, the automobile, moving pictures, radio, and airplanes, causes us to speak a language that would be absolutely unintelligible to our great-grandfathers. Watch, too, for the new words that television will introduce when it becomes an accomplished fact. In the words of the humorous old saying, "The world do move."

Three Doors for New Words

1. SLANG

New words are constantly knocking at the door of our word house. Sometimes they are admitted, and sometimes not, depending on whether they fill a real need. Much of our slang springs up like mushrooms almost overnight, flourishes vigorously for a brief while, and then goes quickly out of fashion. Occasionally, however, a good wholesome slang word sticks, and eventually becomes entirely respectable. *Highbrow* is a case in point.

2. SHORT CUTS

We are always looking for the shortest way of expressing our thoughts, and uniformly prefer a word of one or two syllables to a word of three or four syllables. That explains how *cab* and *bus* and *pants* came into the language, and also why *phone* and *taxi* give every evidence of replacing the longer *telephone* and *taxicab*. That is also the reason that a number of new verbs, coined from existing nouns, are waiting around on the outside of standard usage, watching only for a chance to slip in. Examples are *to suicide* and *to burgle* or *to burglarize* for *to commit suicide* and *to commit burglary; to railroad* in the sense of *to put through in great haste* or *wrongly; to enthuse; to wire* meaning *to telegraph;* and *to picturize* meaning *to make a moving picture out of a play or a novel.* The best of these is *to wire*, and is almost sure of becoming standard. Probably the most objectionable is *to enthuse* for the longer *to become enthusiastic.* One hates to think of ever adopting *enthuse* into the family, but the saving pull of two syllables over seven syllables may some day bring it about.

3. NEW WORDS FOR NEW THINGS

Entirely different from the various kinds of tramp words, upstarts, and camp followers, which constantly hang around the outskirts of language, are the hundreds of words that are called into being to supply a real need and that thus become a permanent part of the nation's vocabulary. For example, the third edition of Webster's *Collegiate Dictionary* (1927) has six full pages of new words, approximately 350 in all, which had recently come into favor by the year 1927. Among the commonest and most useful of these new words, all of which now seem like old friends, are these: —

(1) Recognized by the Dictionary in 1927

1. ace	8. no man's land	15. soviet
2. airdrome	9. novocaine	16. static
3. to camouflage	10. profiteer	17. swagger stick
4. a close-up	11. reel (in moving pictures)	18. tank
5. decode	12. Rotarian	19. tune in
6. jazz	13. Schick test	20. wheel base
7. middy blouse	14. slacker	

Even more interesting than this group, which was admitted into the language about the time some of you were in the second or third grade in school, are the following words. They are among the new words, about 450 in all, which were given recognition in the fourth edition of the Merriam-Webster *Collegiate Dictionary*, issued in 1934.

They are thus mere infants in official age, but are already behaving like veteran members of the word family: —

(2) Recognized by the Dictionary in 1934

1.	aerial (in radio)	16.	insulin
2.	Armistice Day	17.	intelligence test
3.	balloon tire	18.	jaywalker
4.	beauty shop	19.	League of Nations
5.	blood pressure	20.	mercurochrome
6.	community chest	21.	racketeer
7.	a complex	22.	rayon
8.	contract bridge	23.	Rhodes scholarship
9.	crossword puzzle	24.	shell shock
10.	daylight saving	25.	smoke screen
11.	Diesel engine	26.	spiritual (Negro hymn)
12.	flu	27.	tail spin
13.	free verse	28.	thermos bottle
14.	girl scout	29.	Volstead Act
15.	highbrow	30.	zero hour

The words on these two lists are both significant and typical. Some of them show the direct influence of the World War; some reflect great new industries like the airplane, radio, and the automobile; several important ones are concerned with mankind's constant efforts to fight disease and to prolong life; others name new inventions or improvements in existing inventions; two are from new games; others mirror experiences from science, gangdom, music, and prohibition. It is not too much to say that a complete account of the origin and development of these words, together with that of the other new words in the latest dictionary, would be a fairly comprehensive history of American civilization for the last decade.

THE ROUND TABLE

1. To the examples given in the third paragraph on page 372 add two other archaic or obsolete words you have met in your reading.

2. Think of three words that became obsolete and three words that came into use when gunpowder practically abolished armor and hand-to-hand fighting.

3. List as many new words as you can that have come into the language through the World War, the automobile, moving pictures, radio, the airplane, advances in preventive medicine. Compare lists in class.

4. In this connection name five words you know and use that you would have to explain to your great-grandfather.

5. How many of the words in the two lists on pages 374 and 375 are unknown to you? Discuss this matter in class.

6. In addition to the new words classified in the middle paragraph on page 375 find in the first list, page 374: (a) a word naming a new article of dress; (b) a word naming a social-service club; (c) a health word of particular significance to children; (d) a word for something most officers are very fond of; and in the second list, page 375: (e) a new holiday; (f) a word for financing combined organized charity; (g) the feminine counterpart of a famous boys' organization; (h) a new kind of examination; (i) a new antiseptic; (j) an article almost indispensable on auto trips and picnics.

7. What is the meaning of the four following interesting new words: *capital ship*, *Cheka*, *Doberman pinscher*, *stratosphere?*

8. There is an old proverb, "Give him an inch and he'll take an ell." What kind of word is *ell* and what does it mean?

9. Bring to class two obsolete words, two provincialisms, two colloquialisms, two slang words, and two bookish words. Discuss the lists in class.

10. What are the last two new words you have heard? Where did you hear them and what do they mean? Exchange experiences in class.

11. List five new words learned in the study of (a) this text; (b) a foreign language; (c) a science.

12. From your reading of one of Shakespeare's plays find (a) five obsolete words and (b) five words which have changed their meaning since Shakespeare's day.

13. List ten words familiar to you which would have puzzled Dr. Samuel Johnson, the compiler of the first English dictionary (1755).

14. After you finish this chapter, your vocabulary should be larger by a dozen or so new terms, if you did not know them before. They are as follows. Be prepared (a) to define them and (b) to give two examples of each: —

Standard Usage or Good Use	Localisms or Provincialisms
National	Dialect Words
Reputable	Archaic
Present	Obsolete
Foreign Words	Neologisms
Technical Terms	

Trouble Spots in Current Usage
CORRECT FORMS TO BE ESTABLISHED

Affect, effect. As a verb *affect* means "to influence," and *effect* means "to accomplish, to bring about."

> The mercury in a thermometer is affected by both heat and cold.
> His unusual determination enabled him to effect his purpose.
> If the troops effect an entrance into the fort, it will affect the result of the entire war.

As a noun, *effect* means result. *Affect* is not used as a noun.

Aggravate. Means "to increase, to make worse."

> Right: His illness was aggravated by an improper diet.

Aggravate in the convenient sense of "annoy, vex, exasperate" has not yet become standard English, and should be avoided in careful writing and speaking.

> Colloquial: His constant teasing aggravated me.
> Better: His constant teasing annoyed me.

Ain't. Still a vulgarism or an illiteracy, in spite of our need for such a contraction. The British colloquialism is *aren't I?*

All-around. Wrongly used for *all-round.*

> Right: He is a good all-round athlete.

Alright. There is no such word. The correct phrase is *all right*, two separate words. Compare its antonym, *all wrong.* Contrast *although* and *always*, which are written as one word.

Alumnus, alumni (*a*-lŭm'nī) ; **alumna, alumnae** (*a*-lŭm'nē). *Alumnus* is masculine singular; *alumni* is masculine plural. *Alumna* is feminine singular; *alumnae* is feminine plural. Note the pronunciation of the plural forms.

Among, between. *Among* is used in referring to more than two, *between* in referring to two.

> Wrong: The property was shared equally between the five children.
> Right: The property was shared equally among the five children.
> Right: There is little to choose between the two men.

Anybody, anyone, everybody, everyone. Remember that each of these words is preferably followed by a singular pronoun (*he* or *she*) rather than by the plural (*they*). See page 203.

Aye (ay), pronounced (1) ā and (2) ī. These are really two different words, though they are spelled alike. 1. *Aye* (ā) is poetic and archaic. It means "ever, always, continually."

> Right: Forever and aye (ā); aye-lasting; For aye unsought-for.

2. *Aye* (pronounced ī) means "yes, yea." It is used in voting by word of mouth and by sailors in reply to an order by the mate or the captain.

> Right: Those in favor make it known by saying aye (ī). The ayes have it. "All hands on deck." "Aye, aye, sir."

Beside, besides. *Beside* means "by or at the side of"; *besides* means "in addition to, moreover."

> Right: He laid the second book beside the first.
> Right: He receives his traveling expenses besides his regular salary.

Bursted, busted, bust. All three are wrong. The verb is *burst*, and its principal parts are *burst, burst, burst.*

But what. Often used carelessly for *but that.*

> Wrong: I don't know but what you are right.
> Right: I don't know but that you are right.

Curious. Means "showing curiosity, or anxious to learn." It should not be loosely used for "strange, odd."

> Right: I am curious to know the meaning of his absence.
> Colloquial: I saw a curious automobile accident yesterday.
> Better: I saw an unusual automobile accident yesterday.

Differ with, differ from. Unlike things *differ from* each other. People who do not agree *differ with* (or *from*) each other.

> Right: A tennis ball differs from a baseball.
> Right: Father and mother differ with each other on the subject of dancing.
> Right: I differ with you in your belief that the twins differ from each other in looks.

Different from. *Different from* is preferred in American usage, although *different than* and *different to* are permissible in British usage.

Right: The future will be different from the past.
Right: The trip was different from what I had expected.

Due to. *Due to* is not to be used instead of *because of* or *on account of* to introduce a phrase modifying a verb.

Wrong: Due to lack of study he failed to pass.
Right: Because of lack of study he failed to pass.
Also Right: His failure was due to lack of study.
Wrong: We reached home after dark due to a flat tire.
Right: We reached home after dark on account of a flat tire.

Due to, however, as a prepositional phrase equivalent to *because of* seems to be slowly gaining ground. *Owing to* is traveling in the same direction.

Enthuse. We need *enthuse* in the language, but it is distinctly not a respectable word yet. We must still say "to become enthusiastic" or "to be enthusiastic about." See page 374, lines 12–14.

Etc. This is an abbreviation of two Latin words, *et cetera*, meaning "and other (things), and the like." Since *etc.* is an abbreviation, it must be followed by a period. Since *etc.* means "and others," it is wrong to say *and etc.* The word is never to be spelled *ect.* Someone has suggestively defined it as "a little word we use to make others think we know more than we do."

Everybody, everyone, anybody, anyone. Remember that each of these words is preferably followed by a singular pronoun (*he* or *she*) rather than by the plural (*they*). See page 203.

Farther, further. *Farther* and *further* are in most cases interchangeable, but very careful writers like to make the following distinction: *farther* applies to actual, physical distance and *further* to quantity or degree. In other words, *farther* applies to movements of the body and *further* to movements of the mind, though in common usage both *farther* and *further* may refer to distance.

Right: The farther north you travel, the colder it gets.
Right: We can go further into the plan next week.

Fewer, less. Although carelessly used as synonyms, in careful usage *fewer* refers to number and *less* to amount or quantity.

> Right: There are fewer people in town in summer than in winter.
> Right: He has less money than his brother.

First. *First* comes first when it is used with other numerals. "The first two," "the first ten," "the first hundred," etc.

Firstly. *First* is itself an adverb as well as an adjective, so that there is no need for *firstly* at all, and although it is recognized by the dictionary most careful writers and speakers prefer not to use it.

> Right: First, secondly, thirdly, etc.

Formally, formerly. These are two entirely different words and should not be confused. *Formally* means "in a formal manner, in set form." *Formerly* means "at a former time, in time past."

> Right: The motion was then formally put and carried. It had formerly been twice voted down.

Funny. Means "laughable, humorous." It should not be loosely used for "strange, odd, queer."

> Colloquial: I saw a funny automobile accident yesterday.
> Better: I saw an unusual automobile accident yesterday.

Gotten. *Got* is the preferred past participle of *get*, but *gotten* is correct, particularly in America, where it is still in good use.

Hardly, scarcely. No negative should be used with these words. *Hardly* means "with difficulty," and *scarcely* means "barely, only just."

> Wrong: I couldn't hardly hear him.
> Wrong: The car couldn't scarcely climb the hill.
> Right: I could hardly hear him.
> Right: The car could scarcely climb the hill.

Healthy, healthful. *Healthy* means "in good health, well and strong"; *healthful* means "causing health, good for the health."

> Right: A healthy family; a healthy animal; healthful food; healthful surroundings.

Ingenious, ingenuous. *Ingenious* (ĭn-jēn′yŭs) means "talented, intelligent, clever"; *ingenuous* (ĭn-jĕn′ŭ-ŭs) means "frank, sincere, outspoken."

Right: It takes an ingenious man to make a good inventor; it takes an ingenuous man to be honest and straightforward at all times.

Is when, is where. These convenient but slipshod expressions should not be used in defining nouns.

Wrong: Camouflage is when you make something look like something else.
Wrong: Botany is where you study about flowers.
Right: Camouflage is the act of making something look like something else.
Right: Botany is the study which teaches us about flowers (or, is the science dealing with plants).

Its, it's. *Its* is the possessive case of *it*. *It's* is the shortened form of *it is.*

Right: The puppy is chasing its tail. The tree is losing its leaves. This sauce has lost its flavor.
Right: It's time to go. It's too late now. It's too high a price. It's my fault, not yours.

Kind of (a), sort of (a). There are three different errors we may fall into in using *kind of* and *sort of.*
(1) Using *kind of a* and *sort of a* instead of *kind of* and *sort of.*

Wrong: I do not like that kind (sort) of a car.
Right: I do not like that kind (sort) of car.

(2) Using *kind of* and *sort of* (then usually pronounced *kinder* and *sorter*) as adverbs meaning "somewhat, in a way, rather."

Colloquial: He was feeling kind of bad.
I can't help kind of liking him.
Better: He was feeling rather bad.
I can't help liking him somewhat.

(3) Using *these kind* and *these sort* for either *this kind* (*this sort*) or *these kinds* (*these sorts*).

Wrong: She does not care for these kind of books.
Better: She does not care for this kind of books.
Wrong: These kind of flowers do not smell sweet.
Better: This kind of flowers does not smell sweet.
Also Better: These kinds of flowers do not smell sweet.

Lay, lie. *Lay* is a transitive verb, taking an object, and means "to put, to place." Its principal parts are *lay, laid, laid. Lie* is an intransitive verb, and means "to rest, to recline, to remain in a flat position." Its principal parts are *lie, lay, lain.*

> Right: If you lay the mattress on the porch, it will lie in the sun and dry out.
> Right: Lay your book on the table. I laid mine there as soon as I came in yesterday. It has lain there ever since.

Like. Except in very informal colloquial speech, *like* should not be used for "as, as if," with a subject and a verb. *Like* is a preposition, not a conjunction, and should be followed by a noun or pronoun in the objective case.

> Colloquial: It looks like it will rain.
> Right: It looks as if it will rain.
> Colloquial: Do like I do.
> Right: Do as I do.
> Right (*like* followed by a noun): She plays bridge like an expert.
> Right (*like* followed by a noun): He handles his horse like a professional.

May, can. *May* implies permission to do a certain thing, while *can* implies power or ability. Careful speakers and writers keep these uses apart.

> Right: He always does the best he can.
> Right: A fast airplane can fly faster than two hundred miles an hour.
> Right: May I borrow your pencil?
> Right: May I come to see you tomorrow?

Might of. Slovenly, illiterate pronunciation and spelling for *might have.*

Much, very. *Very* is used with adjectives, as "very sick," "very tired," "very rich," and so forth; *much* or *very much* is used with past participles and participial adjectives: —

> He was very much disappointed. He was much depressed. They were very much surprised.

Myself. Myself has two standard uses: (1) to emphasize *I* as a subject, as in the expressions, "I saw him myself; I myself will guarantee this"; (2) to serve as reflexive object in such sentences

as "I fell down and hurt myself; I overslept myself this morning."
It is best, however, not to use *myself* simply as a substitute for *I* or *me*.

Colloquial: My brother and myself went hunting yesterday.
Better: My brother and I went hunting yesterday.
Colloquial: Will there be room for Alice and myself?
Better: Will there be room for Alice and me?

O, oh. A good working rule for keeping these troublesome words apart is this: *O* (1) is generally used in calling or speaking to someone directly (nominative of address); (2) is never followed by any mark of punctuation; (3) is always capitalized.

Oh (1) is an exclamation used by itself; (2) is not capitalized unless it begins a sentence or a line of poetry or a direct quotation; (3) is usually followed by either a comma or an exclamation point.

Right: This is the truth, O King.
Right: To your tents, O Israel.
Right: Oh! What a beauty (or Oh, what a beauty!).
Right: Oh, for the wings of a dove!

Off of. The *of* is unnecessary. Say *off*, not *off of*.

Wrong: Take the dishes off of the table.
Right: Take the dishes off the table.

Party. Means "a group, body, or association of persons," not "an individual or a single person." Its use in the latter sense is particularly objectionable.

Right: A party of sailors boarded the train.
Wrong: The party I went to see this morning had already left his office.
Wrong: Did you succeed in selling your party an automobile?
Right: Telegram to conductor: "Hold connecting train for a large party." (Twenty-five people arrive.)
Wrong: Telegram to conductor: "Hold connecting train for a large party." (One very fat man arrives.)

In law it is correct to refer to one person as "a party" in the sense of "a party to the suit, the party of the first part," and so forth; but except in a legal document do not use *party* for *person*.

Possessive before infinitive in -ing (gerund). Infinitives in *-ing* (gerunds), like *being, falling, losing, jumping*, and so forth, are verbal nouns. See page 49. When preceded by a pronoun or a noun, therefore, the pronoun should always and the noun should usually be in the possessive case, showing possession of the action named in the infinitive in *-ing* (gerund).

With Pronouns

Wrong : You can depend upon him being there.
Right : You can depend upon his being there.
Wrong : They insisted on me staying.
Right : They insisted on my staying.
Wrong : We all regretted you being sick.
Right : We all regretted your being sick.

With Nouns

Loose :   The mother was afraid of the baby falling. (A mother afraid of a baby under any circumstances!)
Preferable :   The mother was afraid of the baby's falling.
Loose :   I never heard of a man losing his temper as often as you do.
Better :   I never heard of a man's losing his temper as often as you do.
Loose :   I was sure of the greyhound jumping the fence.
Better :   I was sure of the greyhound's jumping the fence.

Principal, principle.   *Principal* is either an adjective or a noun, most often an adjective.   As an adjective it means "first in importance, leading, main."

Right : The principal thing is to be clear.
Right : The principal parts of a verb are the present infinitive, the past tense, and the perfect participle.

As a noun, *principal* has two important uses : (1) to mean "leader, directing head," as, "the principal of the school" ; (2) to mean "a capital sum placed at interest or owed as a debt," as, "We should invest our principal safely and try to live off the interest."

Principle is never an adjective but always a noun, and means "a fundamental rule, a general truth," as "the principle of gravitation" ; "He is a man of the highest principles."

Quite.   Means "entirely, wholly, altogether."

Right : I am not quite sure.   You are quite right.
Right : Have you entirely recovered from your cold?   No, not quite.
Loose : I felt quite sick last night.
Loose   She is quite pretty, isn't she?

Quite a (an) is loosely used to mean "somewhat, very, of considerable size, extent, number, etc." This expression, however, is very convenient, and is gaining ground in conversational usage.

Colloquial: quite a lot, quite a few, quite a number, quite sick, quite a little, quite a long time. Do not overuse these expressions.

Raise, rise. *Raise* is a transitive verb and means "to lift up, to cause to rise." Its principal parts are *raise, raised, raised*. *Rise* is an intransitive verb and means "to get up." Its principal parts are *rise, rose, risen*. In some sections, particularly the South, *raise* is commonly applied to the rearing or bringing up of children.

Right: He rose early and ate breakfast alone.

As nouns : —

Right: a rise in prices; a raise in wages.

Reverend, honorable. Both of these titles, except in the address of a letter, are (*a*) to be preceded by *the* and (*b*) to be followed by a given name, with initials or with another title.

Right: The Reverend T. M. Wilson; the Honorable John T. Davis; the Reverend Mr. White; the Honorable Mr. Pierce.
Wrong: Reverend Wilson; Honorable Davis

Scarcely, hardly. See **Hardly, scarcely.**

Set, sit. *Set* is a transitive verb and means "to put, to place, to cause to sit." Its principal parts are *set, set, set*.

Right: Please set this vase on the mantelpiece.
Right: Set the pitcher on the table.

Sit is an intransitive verb and means "to be seated, to rest, to remain in repose." Its principal parts are *sit, sat, sat*.

Set, however, in an intransitive sense, instead of *sit*, is correct in two special cases: (1) The sun sets; the setting sun; and (2) The hen sets; the setting hen (in the sense of "brooding over eggs").

Right: The hen is setting on her nest.
Right: The hen is sitting on her perch.

Shall, will. The proper use of *shall* and *will* marks the difference between the most careful and the less careful users of English. It is usually the last of the finer points of usage to be mastered. The difference is easy to explain, but hard to put into practice.

I. SIMPLE FUTURITY

1. In the first person *shall* denotes simple futurity.
2. In the second and third persons *will* denotes simple futurity.

II. DETERMINATION OR WILLINGNESS

3. In the first person *will* denotes willingness or determination.
4. In the second and third persons *shall* denotes determination.

There is really only one trouble spot — *shall* in the first person to express simple futurity. The other three uses take care of themselves. We should learn, therefore, to say "*I shall*" unless we mean "I am willing" or "I am determined."

(1) I Will

1. I will go in spite of what you say. (Determination)
2. I will give him a chance to get even. (Willingness)
3. If it takes all afternoon, I will not stop before I work this example. (Determination)
4. I will swap you my knife for it. (Willingness)
5. I am in earnest — I will not equivocate — I will not excuse — I will not retreat a single inch — *and I will be heard.* — WILLIAM LLOYD GARRISON (Determination)

(2) I Shall

All of the following sentences are correct. Consider them carefully and read them aloud several times in order to get used to hearing yourself say *I shall*. In no sentence could you substitute "I am willing" or "I am determined" for *I shall*.

1. I shall be sorry to see you go.
2. I shall expect you, then, at nine in the morning.
3. I shall be glad to hear from him at any time.
4. I shall be very much disappointed if it rains Saturday.
5. I'm not sure that I shall be able to go.
6. I'm afraid that I shall fail in math.
7. We shall never get there in time if we don't go faster than this.

So. Remember that *so* as a conjunction should be used with caution and not allowed to displace other and more exact connectives. See pages 161 and 213–215.

Species (specie). *Species* in the sense of "sort, kind, variety" is both singular and plural.

> Right: This species, that species, these species, those species.
> Wrong: I never saw this specie of bird before.
> Wrong: This is a very rare specie of animal.

Specie is not the singular of *species*, but is another word meaning "coin in bulk, usually of gold or silver."

> Right: The express car was carrying a valuable shipment of gold specie.
> Right: Large sums are more conveniently paid by check or in paper money than in specie.

Transpire. *Transpire* comes from two Latin words, *trans* (through) and *spirare* (to breathe). Its strict meaning is "to become known, to leak out." Many people use it in the looser, colloquial sense of "to happen, to occur, to take place." Avoid this use so far as you can.

> Right: What happened that night never transpired.
> Right: It transpired that there had been a secret treaty between the two countries all the time.
> Loose: A peculiar accident transpired yesterday.
> Better: A peculiar accident happened yesterday.
> Loose: An interesting event transpired at the races last week.
> Better: An interesting event took place at the races last week.

Try to (and). *Try to* is standard usage; *try and* is informal and colloquial.

> Right: I shall try to come.
> Colloquial: I shall try and come.
> Right: Try to do better if you possibly can.
> Colloquial: Try and do better if you possibly can.

The same situation exists in regard to *sure to* and *sure and*.

Unique. Unique means "single, sole, without a like or an equal." It should not be loosely and weakly used for "very unusual, notable, rare." It should not be compared, as *more unique, most unique*.

> Loose and weak: I had a most unique experience the other day.
> Loose: She is a unique person, but not so unique as her sister is.
> Loose: This is the most unique novel I ever read.
> Right: The Egyptian sphinx is unique.

Right: The Grand Canyon is unique; there is no other like it.

Very. Often used with *much* when it modifies a past participle or a participial adjective, as, " He was very much elated. He was very much displeased." See *Much*.

Without. *Without* is a preposition and cannot be used in the sense of "unless, if not."

Wrong: I cannot go without you give me the money.
Right: I cannot go unless you give me the money.
Wrong: She does not wish to play without you play too.
Right: She does not wish to play if you do not play too.

THE ROUND TABLE

Using the method of the preceding section, Trouble Spots in Current Usage, distinguish the following words, first by explaining or defining them, and secondly by using them correctly in sentences: —

1. Ability, capacity
2. Accept, except
3. All ready, already
4. All together, altogether
5. Character, reputation
6. Council, counsel, consul
7. Credible, creditable, credulous
8. Disinterested, uninterested
9. Imaginary, imaginative
10. Last, latest
11. Lose, loose
12. Practical, practicable
13. Stationary, stationery
14. Statue, stature, statute
15. Verbal, oral

CHAPTER XXI

The Power of Words

Style is the use of words for their melody, power, and charm.

— JOHN MACY

Effective Words

We may write correctly so far as the laws of grammar and good use go, and yet express ourselves so feebly and uninterestingly that no one wants to read what we write. **To write effectively, then, — clearly, strongly, vividly, — is our second, and chief, aim.**

Like correctness, power or effectiveness of language is a highly complex quality, and results from fulfilling many other requirements. We shall consider here only the four leading ones, as follows: —

1. The Exact Word: Synonyms
2. Connotation, or the Suggestive Power of Words
3. The Specific Word
4. Idioms

The next chapter will deal with three others: —

1. Figurative Language
2. The Avoidance of Trite, Hackneyed Language
3. The Avoidance of Tall Writing

1. Exactness

(Synonyms)

People sometimes say of a good writer, "He clothes his thought in fitting words." This figure of clothing thought in words is a true one. A thought is formless and bare as it lies idle in the mind. It is not ready to appear in public till it has been given suitable dress in language.

Our words should fit our thoughts as a glove fits the hand or as the skin fits the body. To express it differently, we must use words that are neither too large nor too small, and neither too weak nor too strong. The search for exactly the right word is a task worthy of our best efforts. And the price of success is neither luck nor talent. It is eternal vigilance, and the infinite capacity for taking pains.

Take, for example, the two common words *large* and *small*. They are in almost constant use. Let us consider their possibilities.

(1) LARGE

When we wish to convey the idea of size or bigness, most of us are content to rely on two old stand-bys, *big* and *large*. To add to the idea of size, instead of using a stronger word, we merely add modifiers, and say *very large* or *great big* or *truly big*. There are, however, a half-dozen other words existing for this exact purpose and waiting to be called into service : *extensive, huge, vast, gigantic, immense,* and *tremendous*. Think of the relatively weak muscle of *big* or *large* as compared with *immense* or *tremendous*.

The mere size denoted by the word, however, is only half. The other half is the suitability of the word for its idea — that is, what it suggests to the imagination. Thus if, in addition to size, we wish to convey the suggestion of solidity and immovableness, we can use the word *massive;* or if we want to suggest clumsiness or awkwardness, we may employ *bulky* or *unwieldy*. If we are concerned with bigness of soul, we may need a word like *liberal, generous, munificent,* or *princely*. If it is internal bigness instead of external bigness we are thinking of, we need a word like *roomy, spacious, capacious,* or *commodious.* Incidentally, the word *great* itself is now rarely used to refer to physical bigness. It suggests rather strength of mood or impression, like *great wonder, great surprise,* or *great arrogance;* or, figuratively, it calls to mind importance, eminence, distinction, as a *great leader,* a *great poet,* a *great orator*. Thinking of this sense of *great,* Lowell could correctly write, "There is the same confusion of what is *big* with what is *great*."

Thus instead of the two words *big* and *large,* we can at need call upon any of a score of others to do our bidding and express our idea exactly and forcibly.

(2) SMALL

There is an even larger group of words available to convey the idea of smallness. First there are *small*, the opposite of *great*, and *little*, the opposite of *big*. Then, increasing in force, we have *diminutive*, *minute*, *tiny*, *wee*, *miniature*, *microscopic*, and *infinitesimal*. This group of seven concern the idea of size alone.

If to the idea of smallness we wish to add the suggestion of lack of power because small, we have *weak* and *feeble* to choose between. Or, if we wish to suggest that the smallness is due to lack of growth or development, we have a whole group of synonyms at our disposal — *slight*, *undersized*, *undeveloped*, *weazened*, *puny*, *stunted*, *dwarfed*, and *runty*. If the matter under discussion is of small importance, we can call it *trivial* or *trifling*. And finally, if it is a question of a person of small nature and a little soul, or the deeds done by such a one, we can avail ourselves of *mean*, *petty*, *illiberal*, *ungenerous*, or *sordid*.

The general situation in regard to synonyms is well illustrated by the two foregoing groups. Sometimes synonyms may be very close, and their meanings may be almost identical, only a small fraction of each word differing in meaning or in suggestion from the other. *Weak* and *feeble* are cases in point. Again, synonyms may be fairly distinct, and only a small proportion of the meanings may be the same. *Miniature* and *stunted* are examples. These differences may be suggested objectively as follows, the shaded parts of the circles indicating what the words have in common and the unshaded parts what they have separate.

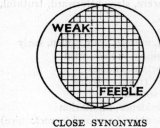 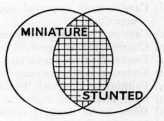

CLOSE SYNONYMS   DISTANT SYNONYMS

THE ROUND TABLE

1. As directed by the instructor, give two synonyms for each of the following words: —

(1) correct (*adj.*)
(2) pale
(3) kill
(4) error
(5) gain
(6) clear (*adj.*)
(7) pretty

(8) ugly
(9) occupation
(10) gay
(11) fix (*verb*)
(12) shine
(13) kind (*adj.*)
(14) allow

(15) courage
(16) frighten
(17) funny
(18) love
(19) mysterious
(20) obtain

2. What is the difference between a *facsimile* and a *copy?*

3. Show that you understand the following words by completing the phrase: —

(1) Flock of ____
(2) Bevy of ____
(3) Brood of ____
(4) Covey of ____

(5) Drove of ____
(6) Herd of ____
(7) Litter of ____
(8) Pack of ____

4. As directed by the instructor, study the following groups of synonyms until you feel that you understand the differences between them in both meaning and suggestion. Then (1) indicate which of them you have ever used in writing or in speaking; and (2) write a sentence containing one of the words in each group that you have never used before.

(1) Abhor, detest, dislike, hate, loathe
(2) Aged, ancient, antique, old, venerable
(3) Air, bearing, carriage, demeanor, mien
(4) Akin, alike, identical, similar, same
(5) Answer, rejoinder, repartee, reply, response, retort
(6) Attempt, endeavor, strive, try, undertake
(7) Baffle, balk, bar, check, fail, frustrate, hamper, hinder, impede, prevent, retard, thwart
(8) Candid, frank, impartial, open, sincere, straightforward, truthful, unprejudiced
(9) Caution, discretion, prudence, care
(10) Churlish, gloomy, gruff, ill-natured, morose, sour, sullen, surly
(11) Empty, fruitless, futile, idle, unavailing, useless, vain
(12) Enduring, lasting, permanent, perpetual, endless
(13) Faithful, loyal, stanch, trustworthy, trusty, reliable
(14) Grief, melancholy, regret, sadness, sorrow
(15) Home, house, dwelling, domicile, residence, habitation
(16) Pleasant, agreeable, delightful, enjoyable (*Loose and inexact:* nice)
(17) Polite, courteous, civil, gentlemanly
(18) Put out, vexed, annoyed, exasperated, provoked, irritable, angry, mad (*Incorrect:* aggravated; *slang,* sore)

(19) Quarrel, disagreement, dispute, wrangle, broil, row, fuss, feud
(20) Raise, lift, heave, hoist, rear, elevate, exalt
(21) Reprove, rebuke, reprimand, admonish, chide, upbraid, reproach, scold, berate (*Slang:* get after, jump on, bawl out)
(22) Smell, odor, scent, fragrance, aroma, perfume, stench, tang
(23) Stay, tarry, linger, stop, sojourn, remain, abide, live, reside, dwell, lodge
(24) Throw, pitch, hurl, fling, cast, toss, flip, sling, heave, launch, propel
(25) Wise, learned, erudite, sagacious, sapient, sage, prudent, discreet

5. As directed by the instructor, learn the difference between the following pairs of tricky words until you are able to use them correctly in sentences : —

(1) Apparently, evidently
(2) Avocation, vocation
(3) Childlike, childish
(4) Contemptible, contemptuous
(5) Continual, continuous
(6) Credible, creditable
(7) Custom, habit
(8) Drive, ride
(9) Healthy, healthful
(10) Human, humane
(11) Ingenious, ingenuous

(12) Invent, discover
(13) Last, latest
(14) Learn, teach
(15) Official, officious
(16) Oral, verbal
(17) Practical, practicable
(18) Pride, vanity
(19) Right, privilege
(20) Sin, crime
(21) Womanly, womanish

6. In a descriptive or narrative theme that you have already written, underline every adjective and adverb. In the margin give two synonyms for each. See whether a synonym or your original choice is the better.

7. Follow the plan explained above in connection with each of your verbs.

2. Connotation, or the Suggestive Power of Words

There are two parts to a word just as there are two parts to a man ; namely, body and soul. The body of the word is the core or kernel of it, its bare, literal, root meaning. This in rhetoric and logic is called **denotation.** The second part of a word, its soul, is composed of the emotional fringe or halo, all the associations and suggestions with which time and use have surrounded it. This is called **connotation.** It is from this second element, connotation or suggestiveness, that words get their richness and flavor. Denotation fixes the basic meaning ; connotation adds power and appeal. It is from connotation, too, that each word derives its own individuality, its distinct personality, as it were, so that its place cannot be taken by any other word.

There is the classic example of *fist*. *Fist* means "the closed hand," or "the hand doubled up." Then, "The lady held a white lily in her delicate fist" ought to be a perfectly correct use of words. We smile, however, at the incongruous suggestion of *lady*, *lily*, *white*, and *delicate* on the one hand, and of *fist* on the other. The denotation of *fist* is correct, but its connotation makes it an impossible word for that sentence.

Boy, someone has said, means merely "boy," but *lad* means "a boy with a man's hand on his shoulder."

Numbers certainly appear prosaic enough, and the 1, 2, 3, 4, 5 of arithmetic seem entirely bare of outside suggestiveness. Two particular numbers, however, have acquired definite associations: 13 is the unlucky number and 23 is the skiddoo numeral. And Fifth Avenue in New York means more than the avenue lying between Fourth and Sixth avenues. It suggests wealth, brownstone fronts, costly automobiles, sable furs, and diamonds — the world of fashion and society.

In fact all language, except the cold, clear, technical language of science, is tinged either faintly or decidedly with characteristic and often unexpected connotations and suggestions. Here are seven groups of familiar words which show interesting variations in connotation: —

1. COMMONPLACE AND PROSAIC

fried fish, dust pan, coal scuttle, suspenders, biscuits, kitchen sink, toothbrush, pig pen

2. COARSE AND UNREFINED

nertz, gents, booze, nigger, sloppy, wench, victuals, swig, bloke, duds, galluses, bughouse, cockeyed, moniker, leery

3. BOOKISH AND OVERLEARNED

meticulous, peruse, mendacity, expeditious, surreptitious, deleterious, adventitious, minutiae

4. CHILDISH

naughty, fairy princess, once upon a time, moo cow, birdie, doggie, kitty, dolly

5. ARCHAIC

oft, ne'er, forspent, surcease, frore, dight, wot, methinks, forsooth, eke, eld, yore

6. ROMANTIC

the Spanish Main, buried treasure, bourgeon, manor, castle, the East, doubloons, gypsy, Arabian, galleon, pearl lagoon, knight in armor

7. POETIC

dell, glade, vale, glen, isle, skylark, evening star, nightingale, blithe, steed, maiden

All writers, of course, avail themselves of the word-magic latent in the connotation of words. Read aloud the two following passages and taste the difference. They form striking contrasts in connotation.

1. THE WITCHES' BREW

(The three weird sisters in *Macbeth* mix their sinister brew on the blasted heath.)

> Round about the cauldron go;
> In the poison'd entrails throw.
> Toad, that under cold stone
> Days and nights has thirty-one
> Swelt'red venom sleeping got,
> Boil thou first i' the charmèd pot. . . .
> Scale of dragon, tooth of wolf,
> Witches' mummy, maw and gulf
> Of the ravin'd salt-sea shark.
> Root of hemlock digg'd i' the dark,
> Liver of blaspheming Jew,
> Gall of goat, and slips of yew
> Sliver'd in the moon's eclipse,
> Nose of Turk and Tartar's lips . . .
> Make the gruel thick and slab . . .
> Cool it with a baboon's blood,
> Then the charm is firm and good.
>   — *Macbeth*, IV. i

2. THE LOVER'S FEAST

(Porphyro prepares the table for his sleeping sweetheart, Madeline.)

And still she slept an azure-lidded sleep,
In blanchèd linen, smooth and lavendered,
While he from forth the closet brought a heap
Of candied apple, quince, and plum, and gourd;
With jellies soother than the creamy curd,
And lucent syrops, tinct with cinnamon;
Manna and dates, in argosy transferred
From Fez; and spiced dainties, every one,
From silken Samarcand to cedared Lebanon.
— KEATS, "The Eve of St. Agnes"

As further examples of the power of connotation, read again the three columns of words on page 361 illustrating the literary, the colloquial, and the slangy levels of speech.

THE ROUND TABLE

1. List what you consider the five most beautiful words in the language. Try to decide what it is that appeals to you in them, whether (1) meaning, (2) suggestion (connotation), (3) sound — or all three.

2. From the individual lists make a class list of the ten most beautiful words, and if there are other sections of your same English class, ask the instructor to compare lists with the other composition sections.

3. What two (or three) words do you dislike most? Can you tell why you dislike them?

4. Among most people, the word *meticulous* is almost universally disliked. Has this word come within your experience?

5. What to you is the most musical word in English? Arnold Bennett said it is *pavement;* Lew Sarett, *vermilion;* Rabbi Stephen S. Wise, *nobility;* George Balch Nevin, *lovely;* Elias Lieberman, *nevermore;* Charles Swain Thomas, *melody;* H. L. Mencken, *cellar door;* William McFee, *harbors of memory;* Irvin S. Cobb, *Chattanooga;* Bess Streeter Aldrich, *gracious;* Lowell Thomas, *home.*

For another striking contrast in connotation, read aloud and compare the speeches of Brutus and of Antony on the death of Caesar, *Julius Caesar,* II. i. 162–183 and V. i. 39–43.

6. A well-known columnist once composed a poem on the basis of the mere sound and suggestiveness of words. Here are four stanzas. Read them aloud for pleasure and, using words of your own choice, compose another stanza like them. Since the stanzas in the poem need not be connected, choose the six or eight best stanzas composed by the members of the class and put them together into a poem like this one.

The Ballad of Beautiful Words

Amethyst, airy, drifting, dell,
    Oriole, lark, alone,
Columbine, kestrel, temple, bell,
    Madrigal, calm, condone.

Emerald, swallow, tawny, dawn,
    Silvery, starling, lane,
Radiance, rosary, garland, fawn,
    Pastoral, valley, vane.

Smouldering, somber, tumbrel, tomb,
    Indigo, ember, shorn,
Sonorous, sorrow, cloven, doom,
    Pendulum, dirge, forlorn.

Charity, gloaming, garnering, grain,
    Curfew, candle, loam,
Benison, mother, lassie, swain,
    Children, evening, home.
            — JOHN T. McCUTCHEON in the *Chicago Tribune*

7. Read again Frederick A. Woods's article "Oily Words" (see page 303) and discuss it in class from the viewpoint of connotation. It is found in the *Century Magazine*, September, 1927, pages 556–563.

8. On the subject of choosing the one word that will fit an idea precisely, the Scottish novelist Barrie tells a striking incident in his novel *Sentimental Tommy*. Tommy and a rival schoolboy, Lauchlan McLauchlan, had been chosen to contest for the prize for essay writing, which carried with it a college scholarship. The subject that year was "A Day in Church." Tommy started off briskly, but stuck in the middle of his second page for want of just the right word to express his meaning. He lost the prize, and none of the judges except Mr. Ogilvy could appreciate Tommy's real talent and flair for writing.

In the story as Barrie tells it, Tommy thought of and then discarded in turn five Scottish words for crowd — namely, *puckle, manzy, mask, flow,* and *curran*. Finally, when too late, he hit upon *hantle*, the exact word that he wanted. Read the account carefully. It is in the last part of Chapter 36.[1] Following are twenty-one English synonyms for crowd. Select the six that you think would best represent the six words mentioned by Tommy, and retell the incident as an oral report, giving it an American setting, and substituting the English for the Scottish words : —

[1] James M. Barrie, *Sentimental Tommy*, Houghton Mifflin Company.

(1) assembly	(8) handful	(15) press
(2) audience	(9) horde	(16) rabble
(3) concourse	(10) host	(17) scattering
(4) congregation	(11) meeting	(18) sprinkling
(5) gang	(12) mob	(19) throng
(6) gathering	(13) multitude	(20) tribe
(7) group	(14) party	(21) troop

3. Specific Words

All of our contacts with the world around us come through the five doors that open inward on our consciousness — the eye, the ear, the tongue, the nose, and the touch. There is no other way in which we can be aware of what is going on around us. Every waking moment is crowded with a series of tiny, definite sensations, with the emphasis on *definite*. Conversely, when we wish to tell anyone else about our experiences, whether we are relating an incident or are describing a scene, the only way we can do it successfully is to reproduce in words the particular sensation and the definite detail just as they came to us through the eye or the ear. Or, to express it differently, **to write vividly, we must feel vividly, and use concrete, specific words.** In the last analysis, that is the secret of all good writing.

(1) GENERAL WORDS

All of our experiences are definite and concrete. Man, however, is not only an animal that sees and feels, but also an animal that thinks. And when we think, we need not only specific, concrete words, but general, abstract words as well. We thus have thousands of general words, which, instead of naming a particular, individual thing, name a group, or class, or species. For example, take *animal*, *vegetable*, *automobile*, *flower*, *house*, *book*, *bird*, *child*, *tool*, and *tree*. Each of these words names a class, not an individual or particular object. Hence general words cannot call up pictures or images in the mind. While riding along in an automobile, someone may exclaim, "Isn't that a beautiful tree?" What he really sees, and what you see when you look where he points, is not a tree in general, but one particular tree — a towering pine, a moss-covered oak, or a graceful elm. Your companion *says tree*, but your eye *sees the picture made by the pine, oak, or elm*. But when you are writing, and hence cannot point to the tree you mean, you cannot say *tree*, but must name a definite specific kind of tree, or your reader sees nothing. If the word *tool* is spoken, you cannot image in the mind a tool in general, but you can and do image the definite sort of tool that you are most familiar with, probably a hammer, a saw, or a pair of pliers. What does the word *dog* suggest to you? If your father likes hunting, it will probably call up the image of a red Irish setter with soft brown eyes and a plumy tail, or maybe a white-and-liver pointer, while to the student next to you it may suggest a graceful collie, an alert fox terrier, or a powerful German police dog with a sharp muzzle and pointed ears. **We must translate a general word into a specific one before we can see (or suggest) a picture.**

(2) ABSTRACT WORDS

When we come to abstract words, still less than general words do they call up images or paint pictures. Abstract words name nothing that you can see, hear, smell, taste, or touch. **Abstract words name only the qualities, actions, and conditions that exist in the thoughts of man.** Read over the following list of abstract nouns. Not one of them suggests an image or paints a picture.

existence	beginning	influence
knowledge	repetition	falsehood
certainty	frequency	vigor
agreement	newness	obscurity
equality	weakness	happiness

All of these words are both familiar and important. We use them almost every day. The point here is, however, that in spite of their familiarity and usefulness they are abstract nouns, and hence pale and colorless. They are concerned with thought, not with feeling, and are useful in an essay of explanation but not in a story or a description. In stories and descriptions abstract words, like general words, must be avoided at all cost. It takes a concrete, specific word to bring the feeling to a focus, as it were, and to penetrate to the center of feeling. General and abstract words are broad and blunt, and glance off without making any impression. Consider the difference in effectiveness between the most general and the most specific words in the following diagrams : —

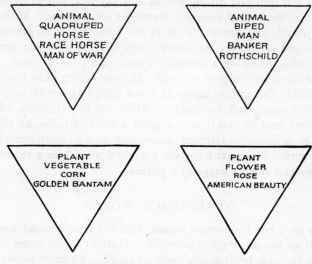

BRINGING IDEAS TO A SPECIFIC FOCUS

Compare, too, the following examples, and notice how as the word becomes more and more specific the idea becomes correspondingly sharper and more vivid : —

1. Bird, songbird, canary
2. Bird, game bird, partridge
3. Utensil, kitchen utensil, frying pan
4. Color, red, crimson
5. Knife, pocket knife, a two-bladed Barlow
6. Furniture, parlor furniture, gate-legged table

Take the ever-interesting topic of the weather. Two of the commonest remarks in the language are, "It's a warm day today," and the opposite, "It's a cold day today." In describing the weather in a story, however, it isn't enough to call it warm or cold. We must specify, and specify exactly and vividly, if we wish our readers to swelter or to shiver with us. There are more than a score of highly specific, hence highly descriptive words for each of the two sensations.

Hot: heated, warm, mild, genial, tepid, lukewarm, ardent, aglow, sunny, torrid, tropical, close, sultry, stifling, stuffy, suffocating, oppressive, fiery, glowing, blazing, smoking.

Cold: cool, chill, chilly, frigid, fresh, keen, bleak, raw, inclement, bitter, biting, cutting, nipping, piercing, pinching, shivering, frosty, icy, glacial, freezing, wintry, arctic, polar.

We must translate the general word into a specific word if we wish to avoid creating a vague and hazy sensation in our readers' minds. They will never know exactly what we mean unless we tell them definitely in specific words.

Verbs are even better instances of the effectiveness of being specific than are nouns and adjectives, for, with the exception of a few useful but colorless verbs like *be* and *seem,* most verbs denote action. When, therefore, you take action and movement and make it highly specific, you flash a vivid picture on the minds of your readers. Take the sentence, "'No,' she said, and left the room." The idea that these words convey is both simple and clear. It is also absolutely colorless, for *say* and *leave* are among the most general verbs in the language. Short of being actually ungrammatical, no worse way of putting it could be found than "'No,' she said, and left the room."

Let us look at some of the specific synonyms for *say* and *leave,* and put a picture into the sentence.

SPECIFIC WAYS OF "SAYING"

bawl	grunt	scream	squeal
bellow	howl	screech	stammer
bleat	jabber	shout	stutter
blubber	jeer	shriek	tease
blurt	lisp	shrill	thunder
croak	moan	smile	titter
cry out	mumble	snap	twitter
drawl	murmur	snarl	whine
falter	mutter	snort	whisper
groan	plead	sob	whoop
growl	rant	sputter	yell
grumble	roar	squall	

SPECIFIC WAYS OF "LEAVING"

bolt	limp	run	steal
bounce	lunge	rush	stumble
crawl	lurch	scamper	tiptoe
creep	march	scoot	toddle
dart	mince	scramble	totter
dash	plod	scuffle	tramp
flash	plunge	shoot	trip
glide	poke	shuffle	trot
hobble	potter	sidle	wabble
hop	prance	skip	waddle
hurry	race	slip	waltz
jerk	recoil	sneak	wander
jump	reel	sprint	whirl
leap	romp	stagger	wriggle

Think of how definite and vivid is the action described by these words, and contrast them in this respect with the entirely colorless word *leave* or with some of its pale synonyms like *advance, depart, go, journey, move, proceed, wend*. There is not a picture in a carload of words like these.

Looking back over the two lists of specific synonyms, let us take the original sentence and add life, movement, and color to it. In short, let us put a picture in it. Here are ten of the possibilities in the case.

1. "No," she groaned, and tottered from the room.
2. "No," she jeered, and marched from the room.
3. "No," she lisped, and sidled from the room.
4. "No," she moaned, and crept from the room.
5. "No," she shrieked, and dashed from the room.
6. "No," she sobbed, and stumbled from the room.
7. "No," she tittered, and minced from the room.
8. "No," she whispered, and tiptoed from the room.
9. "No," she blurted, and bolted from the room.
10. "No," she teased, and tripped from the room.

The images now called up by the sentences are distinct and various. When read aloud the effect is humorous, owing to the rapidity and strong contrasts of the successive pictures. In commenting on this exercise one student wrote: "The difference between '"No," she said, and left the room' and '"No," she snapped, and marched from the room,' is that you can see the second old girl as she slams the door."

THE ROUND TABLE

1. Name five group or class nouns like those mentioned in the last paragraph on page 398. Then name a highly specific or individual example of each class.

2. Give five abstract nouns like those listed on page 399.

3. Choosing among the specific words for *hot* and *cold* given on page 401, describe a day (*a*) pleasantly warm; (*b*) disagreeably hot; (*c*) pleasantly cool; and (*d*) disagreeably cold. Have a definite day in mind each time and make the descriptive phrases as pointed and vivid as possible.

4. Using specific words in place of *say* and *leave*, make up five definitely picture-making sentences like those on page 402.

5. Choose one of your themes which received a low grade. Strike out every adjective and adverb. Draw a ring around every verb and underline every noun. Go back through the theme, substituting as highly specific verbs and nouns as you can find for the ones you first used. Compare the two versions. (This is a variation of numbers 6 and 7 in the Round Table on page 393 above.)

6. Give two specific synonyms for each of the following general, class nouns: —

(1) College	(8) Sport	(15) Weapon
(2) Student activity	(9) Vehicle	(16) Drink
(3) Food	(10) Storm	(17) Moisture
(4) Dwelling place	(11) China	(18) Clothing
(5) Exercise	(12) Fuel	(19) Profession
(6) Waterfowl	(13) Precious stone	(20) Trade
(7) Writer	(14) Insect	(21) Fish

7. Give three specific synonyms for each of the following general verbs: —

(1) Injure	(5) See	(9) Go up
(2) Take	(6) Ask	(10) Go down
(3) Think	(7) Carry	(11) Help
(4) Want	(8) Fasten	(12) Prepare

8. Compose specific picturesque phrases for the following general, colorless phrases: —

(1) An impressive tree	(6) A cheerful noise
(2) An expensive automobile	(7) A melancholy noise
(3) A dark night	(8) An attractive odor
(4) A bad storm	(9) A threatening sound
(5) A melodious sound	(10) A disagreeable odor

9. Bring to class, from either prose or poetry, the best illustration you have ever seen of the force and effectiveness of specific words in painting pictures.

4. Idioms

An idiom is a word or turn of expression peculiar to a language. Usually there is something odd about either the meaning or the grammar of an idiom that marks it off from regular and expected usage and makes it practically untranslatable into any other language. An interesting example is the English idiom *a friend of mine*, or *a friend of John's*, in which the possessive instead of the objective follows the preposition. In translating *a friend of mine* into French we can only say *un de mes amis* (one of my friends); and so with all other languages as well. Another familiar idiom is "How do you do?" colloquially shortened to "Howdy?" For this the French idiom is *Comment vous portez-vous?* (How do you carry yourself?) and the German idiom, *Wie befinden Sie sich?* (How do you find yourself?).

As a general thing idioms are among the most racy and distinctive forms of expression possible to a language. To borrow a phrase from John Galsworthy, they possess an unusual amount of sheer stingo. They make for a strong, homely, vivid style, and should be habitually used except on the most dignified and solemn occasions.

IDIOMS

at arm's length	to fall asleep
bad blood	to fall flat
by and by	to gain ground
to make a clean breast of	to get used to
to beat about the bush	to get wind of
to cap the climax	to give out
to carry on	to give in
to catch cold	had rather
to cast in one's teeth	from hand to mouth
child's play	on hand
a clean sweep	to take heart
to come off	out of one's head
well-to-do	to hit upon
to lay at one's door	out of keeping
ill at ease	a labor of love
to make both ends meet	to make light of
in the nick of time	not to mince matters
odds and ends	by all means
once for all	to show one's hand

to keep pace with
to play safe
to make a point of
to pull through
to put off
rank and file
without rhyme or reason
to run riot
to run amok

on the sly
at swords' points
to take back
to take to heart
touch and go
through thick and thin
it stands to reason
tit for tat
to turn the tables

In writing on "Our Anglo-Saxon Tongue" a poet pays the following tribute to the short, homely, vigorous elements of our language which are discussed in this section. The vigor of the poem is worthy of the vigor of its subject.

OUR ANGLO-SAXON TONGUE

Good is the Saxon speech! clear, short, and strong
Its clean-cut words, fit both for prayer and song;
Good is this tongue for all the needs of life;
Good for sweet words with friend, or child, or wife.
Seax [1] — short sword — and like a sword its sway
Hews out a path 'mid all the forms of speech,
For in itself it hath the power to teach
Itself, while many tongues slow fade away.
'Tis good for laws; for vows of youth and maid;
Good for the preacher; or shrewd folk in trade;
Good for sea-calls when loud the rush of spray;
Good for war-cries where men meet hilt to hilt,
And man's best blood like new-trod wine is spilt —
Good for all times, and good for what thou wilt!

— JAMES BARRON HOPE

THE ROUND TABLE

1. Which ten of the idioms on pages 404–405 seem to you strongest and most original?

2. List two other interesting English idioms and be prepared to explain them if called on.

3. If you are studying a foreign language, can you mention and explain a few of the most peculiar idioms from that language?

[1] Pronounced in two syllables, with short *e* and broad *a*, *sĕ' äx.*

CHAPTER XXII

Figurative Language

God wove a web of loveliness
Of clouds and stars and birds,
But made not anything at all
So beautiful as words.
— ANNA HEMPSTEAD BRANCH

Even when we stop to think about it, it is hard to realize how prevailingly figurative language is. So habitually do we use even the commonest words in a figurative, analogical, tropical, or transferred sense that we are not even aware when we do it. We feel no difference, for example, between saying *a black board* (literal) and *a black look* (figurative); *warm hands* (literal) and *a warm heart* (figurative); *to break one's arm* (literal) and *to break one's word* or *to break one's heart* (figurative); *to extend a hand* (literal) and *to extend an invitation* (figurative); *the dog howled* (literal) and *the wind howled* (figurative); *a weeping girl* (literal) and *gray, weeping skies* (figurative).

One dictionary gives nine uses of the word *head;* only one is literal, the other eight being figurative. Similarly, *hand, foot,* and *palm* were noted as having, respectively, nine, eight, and ten uses, only one of which in each case is literal, the others being figurative. That is, of the thirty-six combined uses of these four common words, four are literal and thirty-two figurative. This ratio of one literal meaning to eight figurative meanings is extreme, for most words do not have as many uses as these four, but it is safe to say that even in our daily speech we use words more often figuratively than literally. Much of language is metaphor; indeed, language has been called "frozen metaphor." This fact is what led George Eliot to say whimsically, "We cannot say what anything is except as we call it something it isn't."

By using words in a figurative instead of a literal sense, we increase the number of uses to which they can be put threefold or even four-fold. And we do more than that: we increase their force and suggestiveness tenfold or even a hundredfold. This increase in vividness through the imaginative use of words is the peculiar province of figures of speech.

The older rhetorics recognized more than twenty figures of speech [1] and devoted much space to defining and illustrating them. Of these we need consider only the leading five: Metaphor, Simile, Metonymy, Personification, and Onomatopoeia.

1. Figures Based on Imaginative Resemblance

1. Simile   2. Metaphor   3. Personification

Metaphor and simile are the two basic figures. Both depend upon the fundamental principle of imaginative resemblance, or analogy — that is, the resemblance of qualities, relations, or functions.

(1) SIMILE

Simile is directly expressed comparison, the point of resemblance being stated by means of *like* or *as* or *as if.*

Thy soul was like a star, and dwelt apart.

The Assyrian came down like the wolf on the fold.

When she had passed, it seemed like the ceasing of exquisite music.

In "To a Skylark" the poet Shelley is seeking for beautiful things to which to compare the bird's singing. He asks: —

> What thou art we know not,
> What is most like thee?

[1] See the Round Table, No. 1, p. 417.

Then he answers the question in a succession of beautiful similes : —

> Like a poet hidden
> In the light of thought —
>
> Like a high-born maiden
> In a palace tower —
>
> Like a glow-worm golden
> In a dell of dew —
>
> Like a rose embowered
> In its own green leaves.

Similes, however, like metaphors, are of course not limited to poetry. They are used constantly in prose, particularly in description. Many a vivid touch in a story owes its power to a striking simile. Recent writers, particularly, have vied with each other in coining pat, unexpected, whimsical similes. Here are a few of the best : —

> Harmless as a rubber rabbit.
> Her hair was like an exploded can of tomato soup.
> Her mind is like a sundial; it records only pleasantness.
> Knocked him so flat you could play him on a victrola.
> Easy to bite as a dentist.
> About as exciting as a stone camel.
> So thin she could fall through a flute and never strike a note.
> So dumb he thought italics were people who lived in Italy.
> A face that looked as if it had worn out four bodies.
> Expressionless as the grin on a letter box.
> Eyes like wise, smiling old buttonholes. — FANNIE HURST

(2) METAPHOR

Metaphor is implied comparison, or imaginative identification. There are no words of comparison such as *like* or *as*. The two things that are compared are fused into one by the energy of the imagination and the intensity of the emotion.

> Thine eyes are stars of morning,
> Thy lips are crimson flowers.
>
> Gem of the crimson-colored Even.   (" To the Evening Star ")
>
> Thy partner in the torch-race, though nearer to the goal.

One generation blows bubbles, and the next breaks them.

Silently, one by one, in the infinite meadows of heaven
Blossomed the lovely stars, the forget-me-nots of the angels.

The pages of poetry are full of beautiful metaphors like these; so, too, are the pages of prose and our everyday conversation. As has been noted on page 365, slang itself usually consists of a violent metaphor. Nor is metaphor always complimentary. We can refer to a girl not only as a peach but also as a lemon; and we can call a man not only a prince but a hog (either the table, end-seat, or road-hog variety), or a fox or a snake in the grass. The possibilities are limitless. A popular magazine in lighter vein gathered the following descriptive metaphors taken from various stories: —

His voice broke			
His heart sank			he pulled himself together.
His face fell			he kept a stiff upper lip.
His hair rose	and yet		he did not show a yellow streak.
His eyes blazed			he put his best foot foremost.
His words burned			he did not show the white feather.
His blood froze			

The actual effect of both simile (stated comparison) and metaphor (implied comparison) is the same. Whether we say "He fought like a tiger" (simile) or "He was a tiger in the fight" (metaphor), what actually happens in the mind is this: the suggestiveness of the second term (*tiger*) is instantly transferred to the first term (*man*). All the tigerish qualities of a fighting tiger — rage, quickness, fierceness, formidableness — are in an instant cut away like a garment from the term *tiger* and applied to the term *man*, who is spoken of as so fighting. Or, to express it differently, the denotation [1] of the first word, by virtue of the simile or metaphor, acquires the connotation [1] of the second word. This principle offers boundless opportunity for increased vividness and suggestiveness. By a skillful trope the temperature, color, aura, or personality of any word can be transferred to any other word. The literatures of all races and ages witness how abundantly writers have availed themselves of this opportunity. Call to mind your favorite quotation, and the chances are that most of its appeal will be found to come from the beauty and vividness of its figurative language.

[1] For a discussion of denotation and connotation, see pages 393–396.

(3) PERSONIFICATION

Personification is a variety of metaphor, and, like metaphor, is based on imaginative resemblance. The word *personify* comes from two Latin words, *persona*, " a person," and *facere*, " do or make." Personification thus means the process of "making a person," and that is exactly what this figure of speech does. It makes a person out of abstract ideas and things without life, or out of the lower animals, and thus attributes to them the thoughts, feelings, and characteristics of human beings.

> Virtue smiles: cry holiday,
> Dimples on her cheeks do dwell.
> — THOMAS DEKKER

> Sport that wrinkled Care derides,
> And Laughter, holding both his sides . . .
> And in thy right hand lead with thee
> The mountain nymph, sweet Liberty.
> — MILTON

> Blow, winds, and crack your cheeks.
> — SHAKESPEARE

> To him who in the love of Nature holds
> Communion with the visible forms
> She speaks a various language.
> — BRYANT

Occasionally a poet will start with a personification, and build a whole poem around it. Sir Philip Sidney does this in his beautiful sonnet: —

> With how sad steps, O Moon, thou climb'st the skies!
> How silently, and with how wan a face!

Shelley, too, uses the same figure in his even more beautiful lines to the moon: —

> Art thou pale for weariness
> Of climbing heaven, and gazing on the earth,
> Wandering companionless
> Among the stars that have a different birth —
> And ever-changing, like a joyless eye
> That finds no object worth its constancy?

Other well-known poems built around personifications are Shelley's "To Night," "Ode to the West Wind," and "To a Skylark"; Lanier's "Song of the Chattahoochee"; John James Ingalls's sonnet "Opportunity"; Dante Gabriel Rossetti's "A Superscription"; William Blake's "To the Evening Star"; Joyce Kilmer's "Trees"; Carl Sandburg's "Fog."

2. Figures Based on Association

(1) METONYMY (SYNECDOCHE)

Associates are persons, or things, that are so often found together that every time we see one we expect to see the other. To illustrate by using algebraic symbols, X and Y usually occur together. When, therefore, X is mentioned we think at once of Y; or when Y is mentioned we think at once of X. *Lily*, for example, suggests purity and grace; a rose calls to mind beauty and fragrance; an onion, its strong characteristic odor; a hog, greediness; a fox, shrewdness and trickery; an eagle, mastery of the air and kingship among the birds; a lion, strength, courage, and kingship among the beasts; bluebells and honeysuckle, spring; ice and snow, winter; turkey and football, Thanksgiving; mistletoe and holly, Christmas.

Among figures of speech, metonymy is based on this principle of the association of ideas. Formerly metonymy and synecdoche were treated as separate figures. The line dividing them, however, is shifting and shadowy at best, and now both are commonly considered together as one figure under the name "metonymy." **Metonymy, then, consists in mentioning one of two things or ideas that are so closely associated that the mention of the first immediately suggests the second.**

Some of the important varieties of association on which metonymy may be based are the following: —

1. *A significant part for the whole:* He employs three hundred hands; A fleet of thirty sail; He was an old hand at the game.
2. *Cause for effect, or effect for cause:* Wrinkles and gray hairs (for old age); The bright death quivered at the victim's throat (for dagger).
3. *The container for the thing contained:* The kettle is boiling; He loves the bottle; A man in his cups; Fond of his pipe.

4. *The material for the object made of it:* She has beautiful household linen; She wears silks and satins.
5. *An author for his works:* Are you fond of Dickens? Do you ever read Sandburg?
6. *The instrument for the agent:* A troop of a thousand bayonets.
7. *The concrete for the abstract or the abstract for the concrete:* The pen is mightier than the sword.

3. A Figure Based on Suggestiveness of Sound

(1) ONOMATOPOEIA

Onomatopoeia is made up of two Greek words, *onoma,* meaning "name," and *poiein,* "do or make." That is, **onomatopoeia is an imitative figure, in which the sound that is imitated makes, or suggests, the word.** Our vocabulary is full of onomatopoetic words. Examples are *click, clank, clack, cluck, cackle, hiss, pop, boom, whiz, siss, splash, murmur, tinkle, buzz, crash, roar, swish, plunk, zip, sizzle.* Even a foreigner who did not know a word of English could gather the meaning of most of these words if they were read aloud to him.

The poets have availed themselves fully of the principle of onomatopoeia in their verses, and by this means gain some of their most skillful results. Read the following passages aloud and consider their imitative effects : —

1. And, whan he rood, men mighte his brydel here
   Ginglen in a whistling wind as clere,
   And eek as loude as dooth the chapel-bell.
   — CHAUCER
2. And the silken, sad, uncertain rustling of each purple curtain.
   — POE
3. Bang-whang-whang goes the drum, tootle-te-tootle the fife.
   — BROWNING
4. Brushed with the hiss of rustling wings.
5. (An avaricious farmer talking about a trotting horse)
   "Property, property, property," that's what I 'ears 'im say.
   — TENNYSON
6. (Imitating the slow gathering and breaking of a big wave at sea)
   Where the huge Atlantic swings heavy water seaward.

7. Strike for the King and die! and if thou diest,
The King is King, and ever wills the highest.
Clang, battle-axe, and clash brand! Let the King reign.
— TENNYSON, "The Wedding of Arthur"

8. Elephints a-pilin' teak
In the sludgy, squdgy creek.
— KIPLING

9. Booth led boldly, with his big bass drum.
Loons with bazoos blowing blare, blare, blare . . .
The banjos rattled, and the tambourines
Jing-jing-jingled in the hands of queens!
— VACHEL LINDSAY: "General William Booth
Enters into Heaven"

10. Here is a stanza built of onomatopoetic words. It is from Elisabeth Scott Stam's attractive poem, "A Jingle of Words." [1]

Don't you love the noisy words —
Clatter, *pop*, and *bang;*
Scrape and *creak* and *snarl* and *snort,*
Crash and *clash* and *clang;*
Crackle, *cackle*, *yowl*, and *yap,*
Snicker, *snare*, and *sneeze;*
Screech and *bellow*, *slash* and *howl;*
Whistle, *whine*, and *wheeze?*

Sometimes the poet goes further than to use onomatopoeia in a line or in a short passage, and builds a whole poem out of it. Southey's "Cataract of Lodore" and Poe's "Bells" are probably the most familiar and obvious examples. Other good instances are Poe's "Ulalume," Tennyson's "Blow, Bugles, Blow," Browning's "How They Brought the Good News from Ghent to Aix," Vachel Lindsay's "Congo" and "Santa Fé Trail," Masefield's "Cargoes," and both of E. E. Cummings's "Chansons Innocentes" from *Tulips and Chimneys.*

THE ROUND TABLE

1. Add five onomatopoetic words to those listed in the first paragraph on page 412.
2. Can you think of any bird that is named after the sound it makes? Any animal?

---

[1] "A Jingle of Words" from *The Triumph of John and Betty Stam* by Mrs. Howard Taylor, copyright 1935. By permission of the China Inland Mission. If the book is available, read the whole poem.

3. Invent two imitation words and see if the class can guess the meaning from the sound.

4. Try to find two lines or short passages from either prose or poetry which get their effect through onomatopoeia, like the quotations given on pages 412–413.

5. Describe the onomatopoetic effects produced by Tennyson, Kipling, and Lindsay in numbers 5, 7, 8, and 9 on pages 412–413.

6. As the instructor directs, bring to class and read aloud some of the ten onomatopoetic poems (or typical selections from them) named above. Each of these will repay careful study. Better than that, each poem is enjoyable for its own sake, especially Masefield's "Cargoes" and E. E. Cummings's two "Chansons Innocentes."

BEAUTIFUL FIGURES OF SPEECH

First and foremost, read the following figures of speech for the pleasure afforded by their aptness, suggestiveness, and beauty. Then, as directed by the instructor, name the kind of figure and tell upon which principle each is based.

1. Haply I think on thee, and then my state,
   Like to the lark at break of day arising
   From sullen earth sings hymns at heaven's gate.
   — SHAKESPEARE

2. Thick as autumnal leaves that strow the brooks
   In Vallombrosa.
   — MILTON

3. That chastity of honor, which felt a stain like a wound.
   — EDMUND BURKE

4. I saw Eternity the other night,
   Like a great ring of pure and endless light,
   All calm as it was bright.
   — HENRY VAUGHAN

5. As some tall cliff that lifts its awful form,
   Swells from the vale, and midway leaves the storm,
   Tho' round its breast the rolling clouds are spread.
   Eternal sunshine settles on its head.
   — OLIVER GOLDSMITH

6. The countless gold of a merry heart,
      The rubies and pearls of a loving eye,
   The idle man never can bring to the mart,
      Nor the cunning hoard up in his treasury.
   — WILLIAM BLAKE

7. The sentinel stars set their watch in the sky.
   — CAMPBELL

8. But pleasures are like poppies spread,
   You seize the flow'r, its bloom is shed,
   Or like the snow falls in the river,
   A moment white, then gone forever —
   Or like the rainbow's lovely form
   Evanishing amid the storm.
   — ROBERT BURNS

9. . . . The sounding cataract
   Haunted me like a passion; the tall rock,
   The mountain, and the deep and gloomy wood,
   Their colours and their forms, were then to me
   An appetite.
   — WORDSWORTH

10. Stern Daughter of the Voice of God!
    O Duty!
    — WORDSWORTH, "To Duty"

11. It is a beauteous evening, calm and free,
    The holy time is quiet as a Nun
    Breathless with adoration.
    — WORDSWORTH

12. . . . With this key
    Shakespeare unlocked his heart: the melody
    Of this small lute gave ease to Petrarch's wound.
    — WORDSWORTH, "To the Sonnet"

13. Still as a slave before his lord,
    The ocean hath no blast.
    — COLERIDGE

14. My only books
    Were woman's looks,
    And folly's all they've taught me.
    — THOMAS MOORE

15. Time writes no wrinkle on thine azure brow —
    Such as creation's dawn beheld, thou rollest now.
    — BYRON, "To the Ocean"

16. Then felt I like some watcher of the skies
    When a new planet swims into his ken.
    — KEATS

17. I warmed both hands before the fire of life,
    It sinks, and I am ready to depart.
    — LANDOR, "On His Seventy-Fifth Birthday"

18. Love took up the harp of Life, and smote on all the chords with
    might,
    Smote the chord of Self, that, trembling, pass'd in music out of
    sight.
    — TENNYSON

19. The chimleys shudder in the gale
    That lulls.   Then sudden takes to flappin'
    Like a shot hawk.
                                         — LOWELL

20. Forlorn! the very word is like a bell
    To toll me back from thee to my sole self!
                                         — KEATS

21. From you, Ianthe, little troubles pass
    Like little ripples down a sunny river;
    Your pleasures are like daisies in the grass,
    Cut down, and up again as blithe as ever.
                                         — LANDOR

22. Love wakes men once a life-time each;
       They lift their heavy lids and look;
    And, lo, what one sweet page can teach,
       They read with joy, then shut the book.
                                  — COVENTRY PATMORE

23. Look in my face; my name is Might-have-been;
    I am also called No-more, Too-late, Fare-well.
                            — DANTE GABRIEL ROSSETTI

24. When the blue hills grow tender, when they pull the twilight close
       with gesture beautiful.
                              — GRACE HAZARD CONKLING

25. When the soft, gray-breasted Evening like a carrier-dove goes
       freed.
                              — WILLIAM ROSE BENÉT

26. These laid the world away; poured out the red
    Sweet wine of youth.
                        — RUPERT BROOKE, "The Dead"

27. As a white candle
       In a holy place,
    So is the beauty
       Of an aged face.
          — JOSEPH CAMPBELL

28. The mountains they are silent folk.
                              — HAMLIN GARLAND

29. The wind is sewing with needles of rain,
    With silent needles of rain.
                                    — HAZEL HALL

30. You are beautiful and faded,
    Like an old opera tune
    Played upon a harpsichord.
          — AMY LOWELL, "A Lady"

31. Grant this my only prayer — Oh, keep
    My soul from turning gray.
                              — JOHN G. NEIHARDT

32. With beauty like a tightened bow.
    — WILLIAM BUTLER YEATS
33. He felt like the symptoms on a medicine bottle.
34. Dumb as the man who thought a football coach has four wheels.
35. His heart knocked like a Ford trying to climb the roof of the Methodist Church.
36. A good man is like a tennis ball; the harder you hit him, the higher he bounces.
37. Developed like a bottle, from the neck down.
38. Hard to catch as an eel in a bucket of oil.

THE ROUND TABLE

1. Here is a list of the formal figures of speech as given in the older rhetorics. Look up the definition and get two examples of any of them that the instructor assigns : —

Simile
Metaphor
Personification
Metonymy
Synecdoche
Allegory
Onomatopoeia
Irony
Hyperbole (Overstatement)
Antithesis
Climax
Interrogation (Rhetorical Question)

Epigram
Exclamation
Understatement (Litotes)
Vision
Historical Present
Anacoluthon
Antonomasia
Asyndeton
Euphemism
Innuendo
Parrhesia

2. Make up and bring to class one serious and one humorous simile like those listed on page 408.

3. The inventing (and discovering) of apt similes has almost become a national hobby. "Picturesque Speech" in the *Reader's Digest* usually contains an excellent selection. Two books of similes are Frank J. Wilstach's *Dictionary of Similes* and Grenville Kleiser's *Similes and Their Use*, both published by Grosset and Dunlap.

4. What is your favorite quotation? Does it contain a figure of speech? If so, what figure?

5. As directed by the instructor, look up any of the nine poems mentioned in the last paragraph of page 411, and see how aptly and beautifully the personifications are carried out in detail. Be prepared to bring to class and read aloud the one you think most beautiful and most suggestive.

6. What is alliteration? (a) Find and bring to class two good examples. (b) On the following page is an interesting old illustration of the acme of alliteration :

The Siege of Belgrade

An Austrian army, awfully arrayed,
Boldly, by battery, besieged Belgrade;
Cossack commanders cannonading come —
Dealing destruction's devastating doom;
Every endeavor, engineers essay,
For fame, for fortune — fighting furious fray : —
Generals 'gainst generals grapple — gracious God!
How honors Heaven, heroic hardihood!
Infuriate, — indiscriminate in ill,
Kindred kill kinsmen, — kinsmen kindred kill!
Labor low levels loftiest longest lines —
Men march 'mid mounds, 'mid moles, 'mid murderous mines :
Now noisy, noxious numbers notice naught
Of outward obstacles opposing ought :
Poor patriots, partly purchased, partly pressed :
Quite quailing, quaking, quickly quarter quest.
Reason returns, religious right redounds,
Suwarrow stops such sanguinary sounds.
Truce to thee, Turkey — triumph to thy train!
Unjust, unwise, unmerciful Ukraine!
Vanish vain victory, vanish victory vain!
Why wish we warfare? Wherefore welcome were
Xerxes, Ximenes, Xanthus, Xaviere?
Yield! ye youths! ye yeomen, yield your yell!
Zeno's, Zarpatus', Zoroaster's zeal,
All, all arouse! all against arms appeal!

4. The Avoidance of Trite, Hackneyed Language

As was pointed out on pages 398 and following, two kinds of words
that should be avoided at all costs are abstract and general words.
To these must now be added a third class, namely, stale, commonplace, worn-out words, phrases, and figures of speech. Words become
stale with unbelievable quickness. This has been strikingly expressed
in the following modern free-verse poem, " The Word."

THE WORD

The first time the emperor Han heard a certain Word he said, "It is strange." The second time he said, "It is divine." The third time he said, "Let the speaker be put to death."[1]

The pity of it is that it is usually the cleverest expression and the catchiest phrase that wear out first. Their very popularity ruins them. This, among other reasons, is why slang is so short-lived.

In avoiding triteness we must be on the watch against two varieties in particular: (1) trite comparisons (usually similes), and (2) trite quotations and phrases.

(1) TRITE COMPARISONS

It is appallingly easy to fall into stale, commonplace comparisons either from hurry or from sheer laziness. Take a column of such common descriptive words as the following, and try to complete the comparison : —

1. black as _____	6. light as _____
2. white as _____	7. cold as _____
3. quick as _____	8. hot as _____
4. busy as _____	9. green as _____
5. heavy as _____	10. hard as _____

When we read over this list, instantly into the minds of four out of five people come the following comparisons — all of them the essence of triteness : —

1. ink or night	6. a feather
2. snow or milk	7. ice
3. a flash or lightning	8. fire
4. a bee	9. grass
5. lead	10. a rock

The very fact that the second half of such comparisons slips so easily into the mind is a danger sign. It means that nearly everyone else would use the same simile. And this, in turn, is exactly what constitutes triteness.

By way of contrast, glance back over the original, vivid similes given on pages 407–408 and the beautiful figures of speech quoted on pages 414–417. There we have true originality and suggestiveness.

---

[1] Allen Upward, "The Word," from *Scented Leaves from a Chinese Jar*.

(2) TRITE PHRASES

In the second place, make the acquaintance of a number of rubber-stamp words and expressions like those given below, and cross them definitely out of your vocabulary. All of them went on the retired list before you entered college. So convenient are they, however, that one still meets them here and there in the sentences of unskilled or lazy writers. Such expressions bear the same relation to real writing that a rubber stamp does to a signature.

RUBBER-STAMP EXPRESSIONS

reach one's destination	all too soon
tired but happy	last but not least
no sooner said than done	sigh of relief
wended our way	a few well-chosen words
favor with a selection	sadder but wiser
reigned supreme	proud possessor
all nature seemed	fond parent
goodly number	fair sex
doomed to disappointment	finny tribe
delightful feature	downy couch
beggars description	wee, small hours
partake of refreshments	sands of time
old Sol	sea of life
among those present	psychological moment
beat a hasty retreat	voice the sentiments of

The ease with which we use such expressions as these has been cleverly parodied in the following bit of anonymous newspaper verse.

THE LITERARY HACK

He was a writer, and he learned
    The art "in all its phases"
Of using well-known synonyms,
    And penning hackneyed phrases.
"Conspicuous by his absence" was
    Another stand-by, too,
A maiden had "a willowy form,"
    And "hair of golden hue."
He followed on "with bated breath,"
    "So near and yet so far,"
"An eagle glance," "magnetic gaze,"
    "The moaning of the bar";

"A sight to make the angels weep,"
"The human form divine,"
"Dilating nostrils," "flowing locks,"
"And all the muses nine."
"The inner man," "last but not least,"
"A few well-chosen words,"
"The mellow moon" and "twinkling stars,"
And "little twittering birds,"
"Arch smile," and "lips of rosy tint,"
"A dainty gloved hand,"
And "succulent bivalve," of course,
Was always in demand.

THE ROUND TABLE

1. Which, if any, of the trite (*a*) comparisons or (*b*) expressions do you remember having ever used in your writing?

2. Choose five of the similes listed on page 419 and complete the comparison as originally and vividly as you can.

3. Can you add any examples to the rubber-stamp expressions listed on page 420?

4. O. Henry has an amusing story called "Calloway's Code," in which a war correspondent in Mexico got a forbidden dispatch through the censor by the clever expedient of using the first half of certain well-known, hackneyed expressions. The editor of the paper was shrewd enough to take the second half of the expressions and make a story of them which scooped all the other papers. Read the story and explain how Calloway worked it.

5. Using as many as possible of the rubber-stamp expressions given on page 420, write a burlesque paragraph (or poem) like that quoted above.

5. The Avoidance of Tall Writing

Many inexperienced writers have a strange tendency to use big words and indirect methods of expression whenever they begin to write. They may talk simply and interestingly, but give them paper and pencil and they seem hypnotized out of their true selves. Naturalness and ease fly away, and in the effort to measure up to the situation they try to be too dignified, and end by becoming stiff, stilted, and wooden.

Too often in freshman themes, for example, the writer does not get ready to leave, but "spends much time in preparing to depart";

he does not "go on," but "wends his way" or "proceeds on his journey"; he never gets to where he is going, but always "arrives at his destination"; he does not eat, but "enjoys a delicious repast." And so it goes throughout most of the theme : inflated words and rubber-stamp expressions where simple words and specific expressions are needed.

The best illustration of this point is what Oliver Goldsmith once said to Dr. Samuel Johnson. You will remember that Dr. Johnson was a very influential and admirable man of letters, but sadly given to using pompous language and involved sentences in his writing. On one occasion Goldsmith, who stammered slightly, sidled up to the great doctor and innocently remarked, "You couldn't write a f-f-f-fable about little f-f-f-fishes, could you, doctor?"

"Why not, sir?" thundered Dr. Johnson. "I could write a fable about little fishes as well as any man going."

"No, doctor," replied Goldsmith. "You'd make them all t-t-t-talk like wh-wh-wh-whales."

The tendency toward "tall writing" or "fine writing" is of course not limited either to Dr. Samuel Johnson or to freshman themes. It has always been the bane of all writers, both amateur and professional, who have the urge to make their little fishes talk like whales. As long ago as the Civil War James Russell Lowell satirized it in comparing what he called the "old style" and the "new style" of writing. It does not take much thought to determine which style is better.

Old Style	New Style
A great crowd came to see	A vast concourse was assembled to witness
Was hanged	Was launched into eternity
Great fire	Disastrous conflagration
The fire spread	The conflagration extended its devastating career
House burned	Edifice was consumed
Man fell	Individual was precipitated
The frightened horse	The infuriated animal
Sent for the doctor	Called into requisition the services of the family physician
I shall say a few words	I shall, with your permission, beg leave to offer some brief observations
Began his answer	Commenced his rejoinder
Asked him to dine	Tendered him a banquet

The bad taste of using inflated language to express commonplace ideas is clear. There is even an element of unconscious humor in it, like a man on stilts trying to mow the lawn and dig around the flower beds.

As the final word on the whole matter of style, therefore, **always use the simplest words the subject will bear,** and never make little fishes talk like whales.

THE ROUND TABLE

1. Look back over some of your themes to see whether you have a tendency toward tall writing. Ask your instructor's opinion on this point.

2. Translate the following high-flown lines back into their simple original: —

> Here stalks the impetuous Cow with crumpled horn,
> Whereon the exacerbating hound was torn,
> Who bayed the feline slaughter-beast that slew
> The Rat predacious, whose keen fangs ran through
> The textile fibers that involved the grain
> Which lay in Hans' inviolate domain.

3. Read aloud in class Aesop's fable about "The Frog Who Tried to Make Himself As Large As an Ox." The application here is obvious.

4. One of the best take-offs on fine writing is the following, which was suggested by a similar sentence of H. L. Mencken's : —

> If you think a flea is as large as a Newfoundland dog, as beautiful as the Queen of Sheba, and as dignified as the Archbishop of Canterbury, then say "A conflagration destroyed the edifice"; otherwise say, "The house burned down."

5. Turn the following balloons [1] back into wheelbarrows: —

> (1) "Refrain from resorting to mathematical calculations relative to your gallinaceous, feathered vertebrates preceding their evolution from the embryonic status."
>
> (2) "A calculous substance which is subject to lateral rotation accumulates no cryptogamous substance."
>
> (3) "A feathered vertebrate reposing within the confines of the extremity of a human upper limb has a value equal to twice the number inhabiting a scrubby growth."
>
> (4) "Those of the human family who are domiciled in vitreous places of abode are admonished against hurling petrified substances."
>
> (5) "A measure of duration and the ebbing and flowing of an expanse of colorless, inodorous, transparent saline fluid grant stay in expectation to no member of the non-divine kind."

[1] Through the courtesy of *Life Magazine, Inc.*, June, 1935, p. 42.

6. Imitating the style above, paraphrase two familiar proverbs into the most polysyllabic and magniloquent English you are capable of. Discuss results in class, and put the two or three most inflated specimens on the board.

7. If you will remember the sentence on the flea (number 4 above), together with Aesop's fable about the frog and Goldsmith's remark to Dr. Johnson about little fishes, you will never let yourself fall into the habit of tall writing.

PART FOUR

IMAGINATIVE WRITING

But all the fun's in how you say a thing.
— EDWIN ARLINGTON ROBINSON

CHAPTER XXIII

Incident

1. The Love of Stories

The world has always kept the warmest spot in its heart for its story-tellers. We cheer our orators; we admire our essayists and our scientific writers; we applaud our dramatists; we honor our poets; but we love our novelists and story writers. The names that stand highest in our affection are such names as Dickens, Scott, Thackeray, Stevenson, Dumas, Hugo, Mark Twain, Bret Harte, Poe, Kipling, and O. Henry. How could we help being warmly drawn to those who gave us *A Tale of Two Cities, Ivanhoe, Treasure Island, The Three Guardsmen, Huckleberry Finn*, and *Soldiers Three?* If you want the key to the world's heart and to its bank vault as well, tell the world absorbing stories, and make it laugh and weep and thrill over your characters.

2. Kinds of Narrative

There are many different kinds of stories, or rather types of literature which have a narrative backbone. Merely to name these over makes a significant display. We may divide the entire field into (*a*) fact and (*b*) fiction, and list the various types as follows: —

Fact	Fiction
Personal Anecdote	Epic (poetry)
News Stories	Ballad (poetry)
History	Drama
Letters	Tale
Diary	Fable
Memoirs	Novel
Biography	Short Story
Autobiography	
Travelogues	

These various kinds of narrative writing are not hard-and-fast divisions, for some of them shade almost imperceptibly into each other, and sometimes it would be puzzling to say whether a given incident should be classed as a personal anecdote, a news story, a tale, or a short story.   In general, however, the types are clearly recognizable. Together they offer impressive testimony to the far-flung scope of narration and the tremendous place it occupies in the literature of the world.

Important as these various narrative types are, only two of them concern us this year in the composition course.   These are the simple incident and the story.   The present chapter, as its title implies, is devoted to the incident and the next chapter to the story.

3. Simple Incident

Most of your narrative writing this year will be concerned with what is usually called simple incident.   **Simple incident** might also be accurately termed "single incident."   **An incident is a single episode,** describing a man or woman in a predicament which in the main is unrelated to the past or the future.   It appears unexpectedly, disturbs the tranquillity of the moment, and disappears.   It just happens, as it were, out of a clear sky.   You may have walked by a certain corner for years without seeing anything worth telling about, but one day something exciting takes place as you pass — a runaway, an automobile wreck, a fight, a fire, a mad-dog scare, any of the dozen things that find their way into the newspaper and that people talk about for several days afterward to their family and friends.   Or you may have been fishing many times in a certain river or pond with only average luck, when suddenly after a long struggle you land a record-breaking trout or bass; or your boat turns over and you and your companion have a hard time getting to shore; or you witness a duel to the death between a water moccasin and a king snake.   Or you may be spending a few days at a quiet place on the coast, and have the luck to see a fishing crew bring in to shore a giant ray or devilfish that plays havoc with the net; or witness an eagle harry a fishing hawk till the hawk, screaming with rage, drops its fish, which the eagle dives down and seizes before it hits the ground; or go gigging at night for flounders with an iron basket of lightwood flaring over the water and revealing the big flat fish like dark shadows on the bottom.

Things like these happen now and then to all of us — and then we have material for an incident. The incident may be thrilling, but it does not have to be. It can be funny, sad, typical, or even common-place, if only we observe it with seeing eyes and relate it accurately and minutely.

Of course the incident does not have to be actually and literally true. You may have invented it in whole or in part. Often it is a combination of fact and fancy. Something that we have seen or heard or read gives us a hint, and our imagination pieces it out, adds to it here, takes away from it there, heightens the interest, focuses the attention, and trims it to the desired length and proportion. All that is demanded of us is that the incident seem true as we tell it.

Read the incidents related by students given on pages 453–457. What makes them interesting is not any inherent thrill in the happening itself, but the skillful way in which the given details make the incident live again in our imagination as we read. After all, the chief thing in narrating, as in all forms of writing, is the detail.

Here are two simple incidents as told by college freshmen.

Wise Guy [1]

WILLIAM FARIS

(*University of Illinois*)

The three boys sauntered into Prehn's with a carefully studied sophistication. They leaned nonchalantly against the cigarette counter and indifferently surveyed the crowd of students. The tall blond was named Robert but was known as Ace, a name which, though he brushed it aside casually, was a source of great pride to him. He lit a cigarette and, through the cloud of smoke, spoke to his companions without turning his head or looking at them; he moved his lips as little as possible.

"There's Beachman over there with a rather smooth-looking filly. Think I'll ankle over and show our little pledge how it's done."

He swaggered over to young Beachman's table and raised one hand slightly in greeting.

"Hi, pledge," he drawled slowly, and, pulling out a chair, he sprawled carelessly in a very good imitation of Noel Coward.

[1] From *Green Caldron*, A Magazine of Freshman Writing.

"Oh, hello, Ace. I'd like to have you meet —" Beachman stopped, confused and a little embarrassed because Ace had completely ignored him and was talking to the girl.

"Seems to me I'd recognize you if I'd ever seen you before. Are you visiting?" Ace regarded the girl lazily through a cloud of blue smoke.

"I came down this afternoon from Chicago. I wanted to see the campus and —" The girl leaned back in her chair and ran a hand over her soft blonde hair, hoping fervently that she looked a little like Carole Lombard. She lowered her head a little and smiled wanly up at him through her lashes.

"Then how about seeing the campus this evening with me? We could take in Katsinas' and the Park, and if you're here tomorrow night we could go slumming. You'll find me rated among the best as a guide."

"Grand. It sounds like a lot of fun to me. You'll find me at the Delta Gamma house this evening about nine o'clock."

"Be seeing you then." Ace rose lazily, smiled at the girl, and flicked a finger at Beachman.

He joined the boys, who had been watching in awe at the cigarette counter.

"Don't know her name, but I've dated her for tonight and tomorrow night. Is Beachman burned up!"

"Not bad!" breathed his public.

That evening at the fraternity house Beachman came up rather timidly.

"Well?" asked Ace coolly.

"I just wanted to thank you for being so nice to my sister, sir."

DEATH PASSES [1]

IRVING STRADER

(*University of Illinois*)

It dipped crazily out of sight behind some buildings about three miles away. Then it shot high into the air, trailed by a weird twisting snake of wood. I had no idea at the moment what it was, but turned and ran into the store. I took about three steps and reached the candy counter. Then it happened! I thought the world was coming to an end. There was an ungodly shriek; there was a thunderous roar that eclipsed all other sound. It was ear-splitting; it was terrifying! There was a thin straining whine; it rose in pitch; it shrilled to a high, wild crescendo. There was a mighty crash of glass. Several boxes of Post Toasties — or were they Corn Flakes? — were flying drunkenly through the air. I must not forget to pick them up. Then it became almost pitch dark. I crouched and instinctively ran behind the counter to the rear of the store. I almost reached the door. Open it came, and back I was hurled against the meat block. I was careful to keep my hands from the top of the block where the meat was cut. Then the sound and darkness were gone.

[1] From *Green Caldron*, A Magazine of Freshman Writing.

I found myself staring dumbly at a cut of round steak — fresh, juicy — resting on the scales. Except for the drip, drip of rain from the jagged fragments of plate glass that still remained in the show windows, all was deathly quiet. I tiptoed slowly to the front of the store. The baker's truck was sprawled incongruously on its side across the streetcar tracks. There was a long line of buns and biscuits twisting down the street. I was bewildered. All was topsy-turvy; all was distorted. The house across the street was completely overturned. I wondered vaguely why there was no water flowing from the bathtub that jutted forth so nakedly from the ruins. The houses on the other two corners seemed to have taken wings and flown from their foundations; they were squatting in the middle of the street. A woman's shriek broke the silence with a nerve-jangling suddenness. Men were pouring forth from the factory, a block away. Some looked fearful; some looked dazed; one was laughing hysterically. I glanced down at the candy counter where I had stood about thirty seconds before. Huge pieces of plate glass were imbedded in the side of the counter. I idly wondered how they had all missed me. I left the store and started for home. I picked my way around the snake-like roots of a fallen tree; I stepped high over fallen electric wires; I absently noted a group of people pulling an inert form from under a garage roof. I climbed up the steps — there were four, and the bottom step was cracked — onto the porch of our home, which was not damaged. Suddenly my knees grew weak, and I sank onto the swing, feeling very ill. The tornado had passed.

4. Details

Three fourths of being interesting consists in giving definite details. The other fourth doesn't matter.

The art of telling a story is the art of going into details. There are two requirements: first, we must give enough details; and secondly, the given details must be tiny and definite, so that the reader can get the picture and visualize the action; or, to state it more accurately, so that the reader can from the given details create the action for himself and visualize the scene. Without details the reader is helpless. The writer may be quivering with excitement — or shaking with indignation — or bursting with laughter — or choking back the tears — but unless he gives us the actual, specific details which so moved him, he leaves us cold and blank. It is as if he took us into a closed room to show us a wonderful picture and then failed to turn on the light.

This principle is fundamental. Every writer must realize it and train himself to write in accordance with it before any solid progress can be made. Glance again at the descriptive paragraph on "An Untidy Room," page 7 above. It is built up exclusively from details. Read the first version of "An Unsuccessful Night Hunt," page 8 above, and compare it again with the other version on page 9. The advance in interest and narrative effectiveness comes solely from (a) more and (b) better details. It is Swift's skillful handling of details that makes *Gulliver's Travels*, impossible as much of it is, a convincing story as well as one of the world's great books. It is Defoe's realistic use of details that for more than two hundred years has made *Robinson Crusoe* one of the most widely read books in English and that has caused it to be translated into nearly all languages. Similarly it is the wealth of details that makes Pepys's *Diary* and Boswell's *Life of Johnson* the two greatest books in their respective fields. Again, it is by details that the famous French story writer de Maupassant has created his masterpieces of succinct narration, particularly "A Piece of String" and "The Necklace," which are as popular in America as they are in France. The way of details is the way of all successful writers.

Here is an obvious example of the power of details to make a scene come alive before our eyes. The two following passages were written by the same person and deal with a minor crisis in the lives of a newly married couple.[1] The only difference between the versions is that the first does not go into detail and the second does, but this makes all the difference between poor writing and good.

First Version

Bob and Audrey were sitting at the dinner table when one of Bob's friends called up to see if he could play golf in the morning. Audrey had been dreading this, for she hated the idea of being a golf widow.

Second Version

The telephone pealed. . . . Simultaneously they knew that the fatal moment had come.

Bob took the telephone. "Oh, hello, Tom. How are you?"

[1] Ruth Herrick Myers, "Improve by Re-Writing," *Writer's Digest*, November, 1934, p. 18.

Audrey, sitting on one foot, a childish trick she had never outgrown, traced the outline of her shoe round and round through her skirt.

"Oh, it is? Chuck and I were saying yesterday that it ought to be open pretty soon. Why — wait a minute. Audrey?"

Audrey looked up smiling. "Yes?"

"Care if I play golf tomorrow?"

Here is another striking illustration of the power of the concrete detail to arouse interest and to create an impression of reality. In it the details are neither grouped nor selected, but just set down one after the other as they happened. It is part of a letter from an English clergyman to an old friend written about a hundred and fifty years ago.[1] It gives the commonplace, routine experiences in a most uneventful day, but it gives them so concretely and definitely that we cannot help being interested in spite of the lack of either a unifying principle of selection or a climax : —

Went to the ploughs — set the foot a little higher; went to the other plough — picked up some wool and tied over the traces — mended a horse-tree, tied a thong to the plough-hammer — went to see which lands want ploughing first — sat down under a bush — wondered how any man could be so silly as to call me *reverend* — read two verses and thought of His loving kindness in the midst of His temple — gave out "Come, all harmonious tongues" and set Mount Ephraim tune — rose up — whistled — the dogs wagged their tails, and on we went — got home — dinner ready — filled the pipe — drank some milk, and fell asleep — woke by the carpenter for some slats, which the sawyer must cut. The Reverend Messrs. A____ in a coat, B____ in a gown of black, and C____ in one of purple, came to drink tea, and to settle whether Gomer was the father of the Celts and Gauls and Britons, or only the uncle — proof sheet from Mr. Archdeacon — corrected it — washed — dressed — went to meeting and preached from, "*The end of all things is at hand; be ye sober and watch unto prayer*" — found a dear brother *reverence* there, who went home with me, and edified us all out of Solomon's Song with a dish of tripe out of Leviticus and a golden candlestick out of Exodus.

Not an exciting day, you'll agree. But suppose Mr. Robinson had written it this way : —

Nothing interesting has happened lately. Yesterday I went out to the farm and attended to several matters. Three brother clergymen, the Reverend Messrs. A____, B____, and C____, dropped in for a cup of tea,

---

[1] Robert Robinson to an "Old Friend," Chesterton, May 26, 1784. (E. V. Lucas, *The Gentlest Art*, p. 277.)

and we discussed the Celtic question. After church another clergyman came home with me and expressed himself at length on certain parts of the Old Testament.

This is a summary or synopsis of what took place, not the things themselves. A few general statements are given us, but not enough details for us to enter imaginatively into the writer's experiences and share them with him. **The summary or synopsis style is sure death to all interest and effectiveness.** It is the bane of story writing, and must be avoided at all costs. Our aim should be, "Always the details, never the general statement, never the synopsis or summary."

Added light is thrown upon the all-importance of going into detail by the way a story is put into shape for the moving pictures. The first step is to make from the original story a "treatment," as it is called, showing the details of the plot.

In satirical vein an experienced motion-picture writer describes as follows how a typical treatment begins: "Treatments are not just synopses. They do not begin, 'Alfred Ogle, having fallen in love with Abigail Dillwater, followed her to the house party in the Pocono Hills, where he posed as an African big-game hunter.'" [1]

On the contrary, into the treatment a little of the motion-picture magic begins to creep. Let us run our eyes over the opening paragraph : —

As the credit titles fade we see Abigail Dillwater stepping into a large, sleek roadster in front of a New York apartment. She is a typical Park Avenue deb, blonde and hot. Talking to her are three or four young people of her set. Her suitcases are in the back. We get a close-up of her as she drives off waving, and then we see from her angle, standing unobtrusively in the shadows of the buildings and looking hungrily after her, Alfred Ogle. Ogle is a tall, handsome, rich man's son, whose father, to punish him for his reckless living, has cut him off temporarily and forced him to become a janitor of the building in which the gal lives.

We find this out as we follow Ogle in a series of travel shots through the ornate upper corridors of the building down to the cellar, pick him up stoking the furnaces, and develop his condition as he talks to the Swede assistant. The Swede assistant is the comic in the picture and later becomes Ogle's valet.

In the cellar the Swede says to Ogle, "I can tell by the way you handle that shovel that you haven't swung one all your life."

Whereupon Ogle briefly outlines his predicament.

[1] Philip Wylie, "Writing for the Movies," *Harper's Magazine*, November, 1933.

This is a parody on a very uninspired type of moving picture. Although it is very hackneyed, its insistence upon details almost redeems it. Even the poorest plot can be made interesting by a skillful use of details.

THE ROUND TABLE

As an exercise in observing and recording details, work out the four following assignments. Remember that your purpose is to get as many tiny, accurate, definite details as possible. Proceed somewhat along the lines of the Reverend Mr. Robinson's letter on page 433.

1. Watch someone unobtrusively but closely, for five minutes. Notice and record anything he (or she) does within that length of time — every movement, every expression, every gesture, every act — even if it is as simple and homely a one as coughing or scratching his nose.

2. Listen closely to a conversation in a public place such as a street corner, a bus, a store, a grandstand, or the like. Try to reproduce exactly what was said, and also to describe how it was said — whether fast or slowly, with or without a pause, in what tone of voice, accompanied by what gesture, movement, or facial expression, and so forth.

Thus far for the observing of facts and actual details.

3. Run through the accumulation of details gained in Exercises 1 and 2 and see if you can work each of them into a readable account. Leave out both the altogether trivial and the conflicting details. Touch up and heighten the others, trying to unify them into a character sketch or the impression of a mood. In other words, turn yourself from an observer of facts into a writer of fiction.

4. Hand in both the first and the second draft of both assignments and ask the instructor to read aloud several of the best and to discuss them with the class.

5. Vivid Verbs

Any discussion of details brings up at once the necessity likewise for specific, concrete words. Details cannot be pictured in general terms. Review again the sections on specific, concrete words, pages 398–403 above. Remember, as was pointed out on pages 398 and 399, that we cannot see *a tree, a tool, a dog;* what we see is *a big live oak, an old pair of pliers, a graceful collie.* Remember, too, that no picture was ever suggested by a sentence like " 'No,' she said, and left the room." To give the picture we must use specific action words like those listed on pages 401–402. **A definite detail can be suggested only in definite words.**

This principle holds true of four parts of speech in particular : adjectives, adverbs, nouns, and verbs. Adjectives and adverbs are, by definition, the parts of speech that exist for the purpose of describing. For example, the words *a big fat man* suggest something very different from the words *a little thin man;* and *to run fast and straight* is not *to run slowly and waveringly.* Glance again at the synonyms for *large* and *small* given on pages 390–391 above. Properly used, adjectives can be highly descriptive.

Along with adjectives and adverbs, however, concrete, specific nouns also have the power to describe and to suggest pictures. Few adjectives are able to call up images more vividly than such highly specific nouns as the following synonyms for *light: flare, flash, flicker, glare, gleam, glimmer, glitter, glow, shimmer, sparkle.*

Few readers would be interested in a statement by an Englishman who lived during the time of Charles II that on April 4, 1663, he "enjoyed an unusually big dinner with many different kinds of meat and fish." With astonishment and growing admiration, however, we read the following entry from Pepys's *Diary* for that date : —

Very merry at, before, and after dinner, and the more for that my dinner was great, and most neatly dressed by our owne only maid. We had a fricasse of rabbits and chickens, a leg of mutton boiled, three carps in a dish, a great dish of a side of a lamb, a dish of roasted pigeons, a dish of four lobsters, three tarts, a lamprey pie (a most rare pie), a dish of anchovies, a good wine of several sorts, and all things mighty noble and to my great content.

Great is the power of details and specific words!

The most vivid of all words, however, are not adjectives, adverbs, or nouns, but verbs. The verb is truly the king of words in suggestive power. Adjectives, adverbs, and nouns are in general quiet and stationary. They depict life sitting down. The verb denotes action, and depicts life in motion. It combines action and description, the action vivifying the description and the description vivifying the action. Many concrete verbs really carry their own adverbs on their back, both naming and describing the action at the same time. *To leap* means to jump quickly, and is a much better way of expressing the same idea. Likewise *to drawl* means to say slowly ; *to whisper,* to say softly ; *to gleam,* to shine brightly ; *to crawl,* to move very slowly ; *to dart* or *to dash,* to move very fast ; *to adore,* to love devotedly; *to dawdle,* to waste time idly; *to hound,* to pursue unrelentingly; *to collapse,* to break down utterly; *to swarm,* to throng together in crowds.   Consider the picture in such words as *dodged, glared, limped, shoved, winked, squatted,* and *lounged,* and the similar concrete specific verbs on pages 401 and 402.

Nearly all effective narration and much effective description depend alike upon vivid, picture-making verbs.   Here is a sentence that endeavors to suggest the idea of a fast train as it rushes along the track : "The needle of the speed indicator moved quickly to and fro, the cinders fell upon the roof, and a whirl of dust followed the whirling wheels."   But somehow the idea of speed is not vividly suggested. Change the colorless verbs *moved, fell,* and *followed* back to the verbs that Kipling originally used, and the train picks up speed before our very eyes : "The needle of the speed indicator flicked and wagged to and fro, the cinders rattled on the roof, and a whirl of dust sucked after the whirling wheels."

Read the following paragraph from Kipling's *Captains Courageous* [1] describing how the little schooner *We're Here* was almost run down by an ocean liner in a fog.   Read it first for the picture as a whole.

A jaunty little feather of water curled in front of it, and as it lifted it showed a long ladder of Roman numerals — XV, XVI, XVII, XVIII, and so forth — on a salmon-colored gleaming side.   It tilted forward and downward with a heart-stilling "Sssooo"; the ladder disappeared; a line of brass-rimmed portholes flashed past; a jet of steam puffed in Harvey's helplessly uplifted hands; a spout of hot water roared along the rail of the *We're Here,* and the little schooner staggered and shook in a rush of screw-torn water as a liner's stern vanished in the fog.

Now reread it analytically with special reference to the verbs and participles.   The passage contains twelve descriptive adjectives, four adverbs, twenty-eight nouns, and eleven verbs.   Its effectiveness, however, depends mainly upon its specific, picture-making verbs — *curled, tilted, flashed, roared, staggered, shook.*   In counting the verbs, the four participial adjectives *gleaming, heart-stilling, uplifted,* and *screw-torn* should probably be added, for they all denote action.   If this is done, it would change the totals to eight adjectives and fifteen verbs.

[1] Copyright 1896, 1897, 1925.   Reprinted by permission of Doubleday, Doran & Company, Inc.

Here, again, is a newspaper account of the start of a yacht's race: —

A gun boomed. The fleet leaped to life. Sails tautened. Anchor chains squealed. Moorings were cast off and the schooners and yawls, first to cross, jockeyed around the basin, maneuvering for a start.[1]

Its verbs give it life, color, movement.

Adjectives, adverbs, nouns, and verbs — in telling a story or describing a scene we must watch them all, but chiefly we must watch the verbs. Like Atlas, they bear the burden on their shoulders.

Here is a take-off on the subject under discussion — the effect of vivid, concrete verbs. By its clever satire on their overuse it drives the point home.

THE BRICKLAYER'S BRIDE [2]

JAMES J. MONTAGUE

"Don't kiss me," she insincered, as he gathered her in his arms.

"Why not?" he curiosed.

"Because," she uneasied, "my husband might find it out."

"Husband?" he amazed. "Have you a husband?"

"Yes," she regretted. "I suppose I should have mentioned him before."

"Then," he tentatived, "there is no hope for me?"

"None," she corroborated, "none whatever, unless —"

"Unless what?" he excited. "Unless what?"

"He is a bricklayer," she disdained. "A bricklayer! My father, a poor, but moderately honest professor of applied lepidoptery, forced me to wed him. We needed money. He had it. His attentions were unwelcome. But what could I do? However —"

"However —?" he eagered.

"You are young and strong," she obvioused. "Seek a position as his hod carrier. It will bring you money — power. Pretend sometime that you have forgotten what floor he is working on. Carry your hod to the floor above. Stumble, clutch for support. Drop the hod. The bricks will fall on his head, and then — and then —"

"And then I'll get locked up," he yellowed.

"Not at all," she disgusted. "The world will hold it an accident. I shall be free. And with his money — do you know what bricklayers are making nowadays?"

"But," he delayed.

"Are you afraid?" she increduloused. "Are you afraid to do this little thing for me?"

[1] The *Chicago Tribune*, July 29, 1923.
[2] By permission of The Bell Syndicate, Inc.

"I am not afraid exactly," he stalled, "but murder, you know —"

"Very well," she chagrined. "Go."

"No," he fierced suddenly. "I will do anything for you. Anything. Wait till I come back."

"Stay," she terrored. "What is it you would do?"

"Kill him," he savaged. "Kill him for the dog he is."

"Ah," she enthusiasticated. "You may kiss me now. But look —"

"Look where?" he agitated, studying her pallor.

"There," she alarmed. "He's coming now." Then, brightening, "You can do it here," she joyed, "and save all that long weary climb up the ladder."

"But I have no bricks," he unhappied, looking about him.

"With your fists then," she inhumaned, her eyes flashing. But the bricklayer was already upon them.

"Who's yer friend?" he suspected, eying the youth angrily.

"Just an old school chum, dear," ineffectualled the woman.

"I don't like his face," honested the husband.

"It's all the face I have —" uncomfortabled the young man.

"This'll improve it," enraged the bricklayer, leaning his fist smartly against one corner of the objectionable chin.

"Oh! Ethellred," happied the bride. "You're so brave and strong."

"I'll say I am," bromided the bricklayer, as he kicked aside the lifeless form of defeat and with his arm around his bride walked out of the story.

6. Three Don't's

In writing narratives there are three constructions to be avoided: (1) beginning a sentence with " There is " or " There are "; (2) the use of the passive voice; and (3) ending a sentence with a participial phrase. Each of these constructions weakens the narrative impetus and slows up the movement. The first two are highly useful in explaining, but not in telling a story.

(1) BEGINNING A SENTENCE WITH "THERE IS" OR "THERE ARE"

Weak: 1. There is no reason for us to fear a storm at this time of the year.

Better: 1. We have no reason to fear a storm at this time of the year.

Weak: 2. There are many people who have never had a chance to watch an automobile race.

Better: 2. Many people have never had a chance to watch an automobile race.

(2) THE PASSIVE VOICE

Weak: 1. The sound of the crash was heard by everyone in church.

Better: 1. Everyone in church heard the sound of the crash.

Weak: 2. As the car approached the hairpin curve at a high rate of speed, it was seen by the horrified crowd to leave the track and crash into the fence.

Better: 2. As the car approached the hairpin curve, the horrified crowd saw it leave the track and crash into the fence.

(3) PARTICIPIAL CLOSE

Weak: 1. He played on the scrub team faithfully for three years, making his letter his last season.

Better: 1. He played on the scrub team faithfully for three years and made his letter his last season.

Also Better: 1. After three years of faithful playing on the scrub team, he made his letter his last season.

Weak: 2. At the sound of the shot the hawk darted aside and then fluttered toward the ground, seeming about to fall.

Better: 2. At the sound of the shot the hawk darted aside and then fluttered toward the ground. It seemed about to fall.

Also Better: 2. The hawk, darting aside at the sound of the shot and then fluttering toward the ground, seemed about to fall.

THE ROUND TABLE

1. After reading the simple narratives and the stories by students on pages 453-457 and 484-497 once for pleasure, read them again more critically to see how the writers gain their effects.   In particular, if any story or part of a story seems especially real and vivid, skim through it again, picking out the verbs and noting those that are highly specific and suggestive.

2. In your own work try again an experiment already advised on page 403, no. 5, above. After you have written the first draft of a simple incident, run through it and draw a ring around every verb and underline every adverb. Try to substitute the most specific and vivid verb possible in each instance. After doing this, see if all the adverbs are still needed.   Omit any that may now seem useless.

3. If the second draft still seems dull and lifeless, run through it again, underlining all nouns and adjectives. For these try to substitute more specific and striking synonyms.   Then compare the versions.

4. From the sports column of a good newspaper select a paragraph describing a football, baseball, golf, tennis, wrestling, or boxing contest. For all the slang and specially coined verbs substitute verbs that are recognized in standard usage. Consider the marked evaporation of speed and flavor.

7. Dialogue

Description requires attention; dialogue rivets attention.
— WALTER BESANT

The English novelist Wilkie Collins once gave this advice on writing a story: "Make 'em laugh; make 'em cry; make 'em wait." He was thinking of the readers, and thus stressed the value of humor, pathos, and suspense as the means of getting and holding their interest.

To these three let us add a fourth, "Make 'em talk." And the *them* in this case refers to the characters in the story, not the readers.

Dialogue is of great service in narrative. It quickens and livens it up, and makes it easier to read. Good dialogue serves three distinct purposes: (1) it explains the situation, (2) it advances the action, and (3) it reveals character and thus makes the people in the story more real and vivid. A story with a good deal of conversation in it is apt to be an interesting story. City librarians say that many readers, before they will take out a book, run hurriedly through it to find out how much conversation it contains. They will not choose a book that is printed too solidly. Incidentally, if entertainment is the sole object, this plan is by no means the worst way of selecting what to read.

Skillful dialogue often serves both to strike the right tone at the beginning and to put the reader into instant touch with the characters. O. Henry, a master of dialogue, in his story "The Day Resurgent," introduces one of his characters in this way: —

"'Tis Easter Day," said Mrs. McCree.
"Scramble mine," said Danny.

These two remarks introduce Danny to us better than a page of explanation could do. We know his mood from that moment.

The opening dialogue in Stevenson's *Markheim* [1] between Markheim and the old curio dealer is remarkable for the light it throws upon the characters of the two men and their past dealings (antecedent action).

[1] By permission of the publishers, Charles Scribner's Sons.

So skillfully does it accomplish this that it will repay several readings : —

"Yes," said the dealer, "our windfalls are of various kinds. Some customers are ignorant, and then I touch a dividend on my superior knowledge. Some are dishonest," and here he held up the candle, so that the light fell strongly on his visitor, "and in that case," he continued, "I profit by my virtue."

Markheim had but just entered from the daylight streets, and his eyes had not yet grown familiar with the mingled shine and darkness in the shop. At these pointed words, and before the near presence of the flame, he blinked painfully and looked aside.

The dealer chuckled. "You come to me on Christmas Day," he resumed, "when you know that I am alone in my house, put up my shutters, and make a point of refusing business. Well, you will have to pay for that; you will have to pay for my loss of time, when I should be balancing my books; you will have to pay, besides, for a kind of manner that I remark in you today very strongly. I am the essence of discretion, and ask no awkward questions; but when a customer cannot look me in the eye, he has to pay for it." The dealer once more chuckled; and then, changing to his usual business voice, though still with a note of irony, "You can give, as usual, a clear account of how you came into the possession of the object?" he continued. "Still your uncle's cabinet? A remarkable collector, sir!"

And the little pale, round-shouldered dealer stood almost on tiptoe, looking over the top of his gold spectacles, and nodding his head with every mark of disbelief. Markheim returned his gaze with one of infinite pity, and a touch of horror.

In lighter vein, the opening dialogue in Katharine Brush's attractive college story, "Young Man Looking for Trouble," strikes the keynote of the story, introduces the main male character, and starts the action off with a rush — and does it all most interestingly.

At seven o'clock on an evening in June, Mr. Anthony Porter and Mr. Pebble Stone, classmates, roommates, intimates, emerged from the dining room of Zeta Kappa House, proceeded with rapid and businesslike gait along the hall to the telephone closet and simultaneously squeezed themselves in. Mr. Stone switched on the light. Mr. Porter seated himself before the instrument and laid six nickels in a row on the shelf below it.

"Who first?" he queried.

"Margery?" suggested Mr. Stone.

Mr. Porter considered; nodded; plucked the receiver from the hook and said "Main 348" to the transmitter.

Mr. Stone shut the glass door and put his back against it.

They waited.

It seems a good time to look them over. Beginning, if you please, with Mr. Stone. Mr. Stone is sunburned and snub-nosed, with cheerful red hair. He has a lettered sweater and a sweetheart at home and he plays the banjo-mandolin. In a week he will graduate and in a year he will have a wife and a very new, noisy baby and a radio set with which he will get Cuba now and then.

Shift your glance. Look, if you please, at Mr. Porter; look well, for he is the hero of this tale. Note the breadth of him and the lounging length of him. Note the wet-seal hair and the gay blue eyes and the Barrymore profile. Hearken to the line: —

"Hello. Hello, Main 348? This you, Marge? The Rev. Elmer Gantry speaking. . . . Good guess! . . . Say, listen, gorgeous: how's to don the duster and the goggles and come for a little spin in the kiddie car? There's a moon and all that. . . . Oh, you would have! Who with? . . . But how *infra dig!* Why, madam, Toby Tate is a sophomore! At your age . . . Eighteen? Really? Ah, well. What a child it is, to be sure. Just a bud. Just a babe in arms. But that the arms should be those of *Toby Tate.* . . . I mean, was it for this I reached the eve of graduation, *magna cum lousy,* that I should be tossed aside for a mere . . . Oh, well. Say no more, woman, say no more. This is the end. And may all your children be substitute coxswains. . . . Wait a second, here's Pebble, wants to bicker a bit. . . ."

Pebble, who did not, perforce accepted the telephone. Anthony produced from his vest pocket a small tattered notebook and began to thumb its pages energetically over. "Cut it short," he mumbled. "We'll try Eloise."

They tried Eloise. Eloise was sorry, she was desolate, but she had promised Gordon Gale to go to the movies.

"Why," she cried heartbrokenly, for Anthony was handsome and his roadster was long and lean and brisk, "didn't you call me sooner? You can't expect to get anybody at this hour, can you? Even you can't."

"'Hope springs eternal' —" began Anthony, and Pebble beside him suddenly said, "There's a thought. What's Hope Stanley's number?"

But Hope Stanley's number did not answer.

By this time there had congregated outside the plate-glass door a horde of brethren eager to call numbers of their own. They were to be seen making gestures, indicative of despair. They were to be seen swooning on one another's shoulders every time Anthony lifted up the receiver anew. They were to be heard remonstrating, threatening, and rapping sharply on the glass with nickels.

"We'd better evacuate," Pebble remarked. "We'll get murdered."

Anthony heeded him not. "Buzz Mary what's-her-name then," he said resignedly. "Any doll in a dearth." [1]

---

[1] Collegiate World Publishing Company (*College Humor*). By permission of the author.

In Joel Chandler Harris's pathetic Negro dialect story, "Free Joe and the Rest of the World," the following bit of dialogue between Free Joe and Spite Calderwood, who owns Free Joe's wife, Lucinda, does two things and does them supremely well: it advances the action by telling us that Joe will no longer be allowed to visit Lucinda, and it reveals Calderwood's brutal nature as if by a lightning flash. We know about him all that we need to know, and hate him from that moment.

One Sunday he was sitting in front of Lucinda's cabin, when Calderwood happened to pass that way.

"Howdy, marster?" said Free Joe, taking off his hat.

"Who are you?" exclaimed Calderwood abruptly, halting and staring at the Negro.

"I'm name' Joe, marster. I'm Lucindy's ole man."

"Who do you belong to?"

"Marse John Evans is my gyardeen, marster."

"Big name — gyardeen. Show your pass."

Free Joe produced that document, and Calderwood read it aloud slowly, as if he found it difficult to get at the meaning: "To whom it may concern: This is to certify that the boy Joe Frampton has my permission to visit his wife Lucinda."

This was dated at Hillsborough and signed "John W. Evans."

Calderwood read it twice, and then looked at Free Joe, elevating his eyebrows, and showing his discolored teeth.

"Some mighty big words in that there. Evans owns this place, I reckon. When's he comin' down to take hold?"

Free Joe fumbled with his hat. He was badly frightened.

"Lucindy say she speck you wouldn't min' my comin', long ez I behave, marster."

Calderwood tore the pass in pieces and flung it away.

"Don't want no free niggers 'round here," he exclaimed. "There's the big road. It'll carry you to town. Don't let me catch you here no more. Now, mind what I tell you."[1]

(1) THE DIFFICULTY OF DIALOGUE

Authentic, natural dialogue is very hard to write, and always gives inexperienced writers a great deal of trouble. Try as we may, our characters at first will always insist upon talking in a stilted, artificial, unnatural way. Someone once remarked concerning the many uninteresting people he came into contact with in real life: "I am really amazed at the way people can talk and talk without ever showing

---

[1] By permission of the publishers, Charles Scribner's Sons.

that they have lived, consciously, in this world. I want to stick a pin in them, to get one genuine reaction." After writing a story, that is the way we are apt to feel toward our characters: they just won't talk like real human beings.

To remedy this situation we must **avoid long speeches and too many complete, dignified sentences.** Conversation is not a series of speeches which the characters address to each in turn. It is more like a verbal game of tennis, with short, quick returns and unexpected volleys and rallies. Real speech is brief, broken, incomplete, pieced out and made intelligible by gestures, tones of voice, and facial expressions. If you have ever tried to copy down a conversation from real life, you must have been struck by the large number of exclamations, interruptions, changes of subject, and fragmentary sentences. Remember what was said on page 3 above to the effect that an actual shorthand report of most conversations would read like a parody or a burlesque.

In writing dialogue we must try to give this impression of quickness, incompleteness, and lifelikeness. Without going to an extreme, feel free to use colloquial and abbreviated expressions, exclamations, and slang whenever and wherever they are needed. An excellent way to write dialogue (as well as to revise it) is to repeat it aloud in emphatic and animated tones. Often the sound of your voice itself will call forth exactly the right word or turn of expression; and, what is equally important, tell you when it is time for one character to stop talking and another to answer him. Only first-class dialogue can stand the test of being read aloud.

Notice, too, how the successful writers manage dialogue. Take any of your favorite chapters from Dickens or Thackeray, or stories by Kipling, Stevenson, or O. Henry, or passages from more recent writers like John Galsworthy, Irving Cobb, Willa Cather, Sinclair Lewis, Katharine Brush, or Ernest Hemingway, and see how their characters talk. Watch for such things as the length of the speeches, exclamations, interruptions, questions, echoes, and so forth. Intelligent analysis of this kind will prove very helpful in your own writing.

Incidentally dialect is much harder than straight dialogue. When well done it is exceedingly effective. Do not, however, attempt it in any extended way unless you know intimately the dialect you are using and are willing to revise and rewrite carefully and often.

(2) "STAGE DIRECTIONS" IN DIALOGUE

It is not enough to give *what* was said; we must also give *how* it was said. The reader must know not only which person is speaking, but also in what manner and in what mood: whether his voice is soft, loud, bored, angry, affectionate, anxious, timid, pleased, doubtful, or what. We must hear the very tones themselves. Likewise, what look, action, or gesture accompanies each remark? What is the character doing while he is speaking? And, of equal importance, what is the person he is speaking to doing, and how is he reacting to the speech? Finally, at what rate of speed is the conversation taking place? Real conversation goes by fits and starts, now fast, now slow. Where do the breaks and pauses come as the characters talk to each other? All of these accompaniments of conversation are called "stage directions." They are of paramount importance in lending an air of reality and vividness to dialogue. Careful attention must be given them both in writing and in revising.

The following examples will illustrate their value.

WITHOUT STAGE DIRECTIONS

"No, no, silly," she said. "That's not the way to do it. Let me show you."

WITH STAGE DIRECTIONS (1)

"No, no, silly. That's not the way to do it," and in her voice was all the affectionate impatience of big-sister-aged-ten for little-brother-aged-five. "Let me show you," and she took the crayon from his chubby fingers and drew the head of a black cat with big, staring eyes.

WITH STAGE DIRECTIONS (2)

"No, no, silly. That's not the way to do it," and turning from the stove she smiled affectionately at her tall brother home from college for the holidays. "Let me show you," and she took the big wooden spoon from his strong but inexperienced fingers and began expertly to beat up the eggs for the omelet.

In an article on William Dean Howells, Mark Twain praised his book, *The Undiscovered Country*, and quoted approvingly the following stage directions which accompanied certain of the speeches: —

. . . and she laid her arms with a beseeching gesture on her father's shoulders.

. . . she answered, following his gesture with a glance.
. . . she said, laughing nervously.
. . . she asked, turning swiftly upon him that strange, searching glance.
. . . she answered, vaguely.
. . . she reluctantly admitted.
. . . but her voice died wearily away and she stood looking into his face with puzzled entreaty.[1]

Here is a final bit from a current mystery story: —

"How many were here tonight when this happened?"
Mills brought the toe of his shoe forward, balanced himself, and studied it, another trick of his. "That, obviously, I cannot say with certainty. I will tell you what I know." He rocked back and forth. "At the conclusion of dinner, at seven-thirty, Dr. Grimaud came up here to work. . . ."[2]

(3) SYNONYMS FOR *SAY*

In order to get away from the monotonous repetition of "he said" and "she said," various specific synonyms should be used as needed. By actual count there are between two hundred and three hundred of them. Some of the more usual and useful ones are these: —

acquiesced	faltered	put in
agreed	grinned	remarked
assented	hesitated	retorted
besought	implored	roared
breathed	laughed	shouted
burst out	maintained	sighed
coaxed	mimicked	smiled
continued	murmured	sobbed
denied	nodded	stammered
echoed	pleaded	warned
exclaimed	promised	whispered

Review again the various ways of expressing, "'No,' she said, and left the room." See pages 401–402 above.

(4) THE PUNCTUATION OF DIALOGUE

Both while writing and while revising dialogue there are **four definite items of punctuation to watch for.**

1. A new paragraph is made every time the speaker changes.
2. Each speech begins with a capital letter.

---

[1] "William Dean Howells," *Harper's Magazine*, Vol. 113, 1906, p. 224. By permission of the publishers.
[2] John Dickson Carr, *The Three Coffins*, Harper & Brothers, p. 34.

3. Each speech is enclosed in quotation marks. Note particularly that each part of a divided speech is enclosed in its own set of quotation marks.

4. A comma is used to separate *say* or its equivalent from the speech, whether *say* comes first or last.

All of these uses are explained and illustrated in the chapter on punctuation, pages 88–124 above. Unless you are thoroughly familiar with them, review them briefly at this time.

(5) ONE–ACT PLAYS

It is not hard to make a one-act play out of an incident that offers a good chance for dialogue. Probably a "one-scene" play would be a better term than a one-act play. There are **three steps from incident to play.**

1. Choose an incident or a situation with humorous, thrilling, or unexpected possibilities, and write it out as a straightforward story.

2. After these stories have been corrected and criticized, retell your story entirely by means of dialogue without the aid of any impersonal narrative at all.

3. Arrange this dialogue in dramatic form, with stage settings and directions in the place of the descriptions of the first step, and put the names of the characters before the speeches.

After a little practice, if any student shows a liking for the dramatic form, the first two steps can be dispensed with and the plot be put directly into play form.

THE ROUND TABLE

1. Who is your favorite writer of fiction? Glance through one of his (her) books and examine the use of dialogue.

2. Bring to class any particularly bright and interesting bit of dialogue you have come across recently.

3. Let the instructor write on the board a line or two of conversation, and let each member of the class copy it, supplying full stage directions as is done in the example given on page 446. Read aloud for interesting variations!

4. Familiarize yourself with some of the synonyms for *say* listed on page 447, and make use of them as needed in your next bit of dialogue.

5. Select any two interesting or strongly contrasted people, imagine a situation, and write a page or so of the resulting dialogue. Here are a few suggestions. Ask the instructor to read aloud to the class several of the best dialogues.

    (1) A tramp knocks at the door of a suspicious housewife.

    (2) A college athletic idol meets a gushing girl admirer.

    (3) A boy explains to his father why his grades are so much lower this semester than last (or a girl explains to her mother).

    (4) A boy takes a girl to her first football game.

    (5) A book agent tries to sell a book to a busy housewife.

    (6) A farmer shows the farm to a girl who has never been in the country before.

    (7) A small boy goes on his first train trip with his father or older brother.

    (8) Two girls who have lost a pocketbook and are looking for it find you with it in your hand.

    (9) Two car owners (two men? two women? a man and a woman?) have scraped fenders in trying to park in the same place on Main Street.

    (10) A green clerk and a quick-tempered shopper.

6. As directed by the instructor, let the whole class take the following skeleton plot and write it out in full, furnishing characters, setting, description, dialogue, details, and so forth, in three steps or stages : —

    (1) Told as an incident, with only the necessary amount of dialogue.

    (2) Told entirely in dialogue.

    (3) Turned into a one-scene play.

The Plot

A man (boy, girl, woman, tramp, Negro, Irishman, Jew, Swede, Italian, sailor, autoist) went into a store, and asked for a dime's worth of bananas. The storekeeper gave them to him, whereupon he asked if he could exchange them for a dime's worth of apples instead. The storekeeper agreed and gave him the apples. The man took them and started out of the store. The storekeeper asked him for the money.

"The money for what?" he asked.

"The money for the apples," said the storekeeper.

"But I gave you the bananas for the apples," answered the man.

"Well, then, the money for the bananas."

"But you've still got the bananas."

Whereupon the man walked out, leaving the storekeeper to figure it out as best he could.

7. Select one of your back narrative themes and retell it almost entirely in dialogue form. Compare the two versions.

8. If you have written an unusually interesting narrative theme, or have a suitable plot in mind, try turning it into a one-act play.

9. On page 447 are quoted stage directions for dialogue of which Mark Twain approved. If you have access to the bound volumes of *Harper's Magazine*, read to the class his humorous take-off on stereotyped stage directions. It follows immediately the quoted passages, page 224, Vol. 113, 1906.

10. Invent a dialogue between two famous characters in literature or history such as Samson and Hercules, Helen of Troy and Cleopatra, Alexander and Caesar, Enoch Arden and Sidney Carton, D'Artagnan and Cyrano de Bergerac, Robin Hood and Davy Crockett, Queen Elizabeth and Queen Victoria, Benjamin Franklin and Thomas A. Edison.

11. Record a conversation between a dog and a cat revealing their mutual distrust and dislike (either realistic or humorous).

12. Convicted on false circumstantial evidence (discuss in class for unusual instances and review pages 287-291).

13. A polite little girl tries to entertain a caller while mama is dressing.

14. A daughter who has just completed a business course argues with her father about taking a position in an office or a store.

15. If you are familiar with any dialect or peculiar manner of speech, try to reproduce it in a page or less of dialogue.

8. Paragraphing a Story

In telling an incident the paragraph is managed differently from the way it is managed in explaining. In exposition, paragraphing serves the following purposes: each paragraph is devoted to explaining a single topic idea, and a new paragraph indicates a new idea; this idea is usually stated in the topic sentence; successive paragraphs are linked with each other by means of transition words and phrases; the development of the thought is orderly and logical, and we pass from one topic to the next as we go from one room to another in a house, or climb a ladder rung by rung. This type of paragraph is explained at length in the chapter on Chain Paragraphs and Jointed Subjects, pages 141-177.

In narration, however, no such logical or clear-cut use of the paragraph is possible. **The narrative paragraph is a much looser, and generally a shorter subdivision than the expository paragraph.** In dialogue, for example, which plays an important part in narratives, a new paragraph is made every time the speaker changes. This is done if only one sentence or a phrase or even a single word is spoken.

This device helps the reader to follow the conversation intelligently, and is a great aid to clearness.

In the story itself, when the characters are not talking, a new paragraph is used to introduce any new stage of the incident, or a bit of description inserted in the narrative, or a piece of explanation or characterization, or a comment or reflection, or any decided break or change in the continuity of the story. These reasons for paragraphing obviously differ from one another, so that in the last analysis much depends upon the exact impression the writer is trying to convey. If given the same story to paragraph, several trained writers would, within certain limits, paragraph it differently, and none would be clearly wrong, though one arrangement would certainly be superior to the others.

In your own work, on the one hand, avoid paragraphing each sentence by itself; and, on the other, examine any long stretch of over half a page to see whether it should not be divided.

As assigned by the instructor, note carefully the paragraphing in several of the stories given on pages 453–457 and 484–497. If you do not understand the paragraphing, or think it could be improved, mention the fact for discussion in class.

THE ROUND TABLE

1. Relate from experience (or invent) a concrete illustration of the truth of some familiar proverb.

2. Relate from experience (or invent) an incident, with dialogue, illustrating some single trait of character or motive such as unselfishness, greed, stinginess, ignorance, courage, good nature, true friendship, loyalty, etc.

3. Choose one of Aesop's fables and transfer the scene to modern times, giving ample details, dialogue, characterization, etc.

4. Relate an incident in your life that had an important influence on your character, ambitions, or future.

5. Give an instance of everybody's natural desire to be someone else.

6. Relate an incident or a situation that made you very angry.

7. A false report has gotten out that a distant relative has died and left you $5,000. What do your friends do and say?

8. Relate an unsuccessful mouse hunt from the point of view of (a) the cat; (b) the mouse.

9.   Situations Suggesting Incidents [1]

(1) A child; a swift millrace; a large dog.
(2) Two young girls alone in a farmhouse at night; footsteps; a knock at the door.
(3) Girl; pile of unwashed dishes; telephone.
(4) Handsomely dressed woman; powder puff; monkey.
(5) Girl; umbrella; windstorm.
(6) Pretty girl; snake; man.
(7) Child; toothache; dentist.
(8) Ragged little girl; window of toys; well-dressed man.
(9) A small child on the porch roof; a slip; a scream; a man runs up and catches her like a ball.

10.   Titles for Incidents

(1) How I Came to Admire —— (some friend)
(2) An Experience with Hypnotism (actual or observed)
(3) Absent-Mindedness Was to Blame
(4) Believe It or Not ——
(5) A Mad-Dog Scare
(6) The Most Exciting Thing I Ever Saw (Heard)
(7) A Resolve to Tell the Truth to Everyone for One Whole Day and What Came of It
(8) I Argue with My Family about —— (anything, such as a larger allowance, changing colleges, not taking a certain college subject, the way to dress, hitch hiking, etc.)
(9) An Interesting Legend of My Locality
(10) How I Broke Myself of —— (any bad habit)
(11) The Reverie of a Park Bench
(12) Hiving a Swarm of Bees
(13) How I Caught and Tamed —— (a curious pet)
(14) Locked Out
(15) The Autobiography of a Counterfeit Dime
(16) Down to My Last Quarter in a Strange Town
(17) The Bravest Act I Ever Saw
(18) The Narrowest Escape I Ever Saw
(19) The Meanest Thing I Ever Saw
(20) The Meanest Man I Ever Knew (narration through incidents, not merely description)
(21) The Cleverest Trick I Ever Saw Played
(22) Why I Almost Believe in Ghosts
(23) Was My Face Red?
(24) The Meanest Thing I Ever Did

[1] Thomas C. Blaisdell, *Ways to Teach English*, Doubleday, Doran and Co., pp. 521-524.

(25) The Worst Break I Ever Made
(26) I Would Have Been a Hero If ——
(27) My Most Exciting Plunge
(28) A Pause That Did Not Refresh

Student Incidents

I. MY FIRST SOLO [1]

GLENN L. BROWN

(University of Illinois)

The last, lingering rays of the setting sun were fading out as we settled slowly in for our dozenth landing on this warm August evening. As usual, after the plane had come to a stop, I taxied it back into position for the next take-off and was beginning to open the throttle, when my instructor, Ted, held up his hand and turning around with a rather queer look on his face said, "Hold it a minute."

"What now?" said I to myself. "That last landing wasn't perfect, but it wasn't so bad, either."

As I glanced up again, Ted was crawling out of the front cockpit, and as I realized what was coming, my heart did a couple of flops and lodged somewhere in the vicinity of my mouth. At last it was here — the day I had been longing for and looking forward to for weeks — and now that the time had come, I was not at all sure that the experience was going to be such a lark as I had anticipated.

My reverie was interrupted by the calm, matter-of-fact voice of Ted saying, "You can take her around alone now. Fly the same course we have been using; if she quits running, put her down into the wind, and most important of all, *keep plenty of flying speed*. All right, take her away!"

With what I fondly hoped was a convincing "Okay," I turned my face forward, and, with a definite sinking sensation in the pit of my stomach, opened the throttle wide. The tail came up with a rush as the ship sped down the field and, much before I expected it, the lightened load enabled me to take off.

As the ground fell rapidly away, my feet increased their nervous tattoo against the rudder pedals and the perspiration streamed from every pore in my body.

However, I mechanically followed the course we had been flying in the past hour, and before long found myself at the point where I must begin my descent. This was the critical moment. The take-off of a training plane is a relatively simple matter, but the landing is something entirely different. Across my mind flashed memories of "hangar yarns" of student fliers who

[1] From *Green Caldron*, A Magazine of Freshman Writing.

had tried to stretch their glide, and as a result had fallen into a deadly stall at a low altitude, and of others who had overshot the field and crashed into the fence at the far end. A glance at the altimeter did nothing to reassure me as I realized that I had climbed a couple of hundred feet higher than I had been accustomed to do. Would I be able to hit the field? Finally, with the thought that I might as well get it over with, I closed the throttle and nosed down into my glide. If only that front seat were not so empty! The sight of Ted's broad shoulders and wind-bronzed face would have been very welcome at that moment.

Then I said to myself, "Snap out of it! You've landed with Ted along, so there is no reason why you can't land without him. Look out! Watch that tree! Pull the nose up, pull it up! Now down with her — not too much or you'll run her nose into the ground. Careful there now; take it easy. Pull the stick back — more, more; not too much; now, all the way back with it!"

With a faint rumble the wheels and tail-skid struck the ground in a nice three-point landing, and as the ship rolled to a stop, Ted came striding over with a broad grin on his leathery face and shouted, "Hyah, Pilot!"

My "big day" was complete.

2. ENTER MILES [1]

RICHARD ALAN

(University of Illinois)

"For look!" cried Priscilla with an arch wiggle of her eyebrows. "Yonder comes Miles Standish."

(Enter Miles right, dragging antiquated piece of ordnance, some six feet in length. Upon his head rocks a tin helmet of questionable period. Hung from his shoulders are paired "back-and-breast," replicas of what the well-dressed-man-about-Plymouth wore in 1621, although the same armor had been used by Hector, Caesar, and King Philip, and gave every indication in appearance of having also done duty as a Chinese gong. Dragging behind, for all the world like the leeboard of a canoe on the weather reach, is a huge English cavalry saber. Miles' crepe-whiskered face takes on a semblance of ferocity as he turns toward the cowering women.)

"Be not afraid," I said reassuringly, "'tis only I, Miles Standish." And, with a nonchalant gesture, I hung my helmet upon the nearest chair. I had but turned around, when I heard a shattering metallic clangor behind me. Priscilla giggled, and, out of the corner of my eye, I saw my recalcitrant headgear clattering about the cabin floor in the most unnerving manner imaginable. My histrionic instinct bade me ignore the incident; so I turned to Priscilla, who was still tittering, and glowered with genuine dislike. She countered with a charming saccharine smile and we spoke at length.

[1] From *Green Caldron*, A Magazine of Freshman Writing.

Upon the word "calumny," young John Alden, long, blond, and quite the Puritan macaroni, entered airily. His high Pilgrim's hat was perched jauntily over one eye and his hands wandered vaguely up and down the seam of his flimsy trousers, searching for pockets which some crafty costumer had failed to put in. Very calmly and with an air of great unconcern, he stooped and picked up my battered helmet. Time and cue held no terrors for young John, for he very carefully hung the thing on a chair amid a tense silence. Then he turned and began to spout his lines, but his first words were marred by a triumphant clatter from behind. We flinched as we saw the devilish thing roll gleefully about on the floor; even Priscilla was deeply moved, for she did not laugh; she sat, pensively chewing her gum, at the old spinning wheel, which had not been spun for almost a century. John was visibly shaken, but he went on with his lines like the seasoned trouper that he was.

All too suddenly, I found myself trying to pick up the now truly battle-scarred helmet. My unyielding armor squeaked, buckled, pinched, and bent, as I leaned toward the floor. I was still dazed. I didn't remember a single moment of action after the second crash, but I must have gone through my lines, for the stage manager was well on the way to apoplexy over my hampered efforts to get off. At last the armor gave way with an audible crack like that of a carelessly bowed, starched shirt-front. I set the thing on my head as I turned to go off, and it settled down over my ears with a faint demoniac chortle. For the first time I heard the comments of the small children on the first row. I saw John standing beside the ancient mahogany spinning wheel, absent-mindedly kicking it a foot to the left and then back again. Priscilla stood in the wings with tears in her eyes and a handkerchief in her mouth.

Slowly I walked toward the right exit. "Clonk!" rang the helmet on my forehead; "Clunk!" on the nape of my neck. Heavy ordnance and cutlery made a barely audible sarcastic rasping noise as they followed me along the boards.

(*Exit Miles right.*)

3. TOO CLOSE [1]

JOE DALY

(*University of Illinois*)

It was a perfect afternoon, grand fishing weather, and Mack and I had had splendid luck in the morning, each having caught four fine bass. Now the sun was just touching the top of the east wall of Apple River Canyon, which is not really a canyon although the natives call it that. It was late afternoon, and I do not believe I ever saw the fast-running water sparkle more, or the rocks of the canyon reflect their reds and blues more brilliantly. Just above the rapids Mack was slowly "whipping" his fly on the surface of a

[1] From *Green Caldron*, A Magazine of Freshman Writing.

quiet, deep pond that was nestled close against the steep rock wall. I was tired of fishing; so, in order to enjoy the west rays of the sun, I clambered up the wall toward a small shelf that hung out over the water. After carefully laying down my rod, I stretched out to rest before we started the long walk back to camp.

I had dozed for a few minutes, when that silent sixth sense which all people who sleep in the wilderness have, made me wake up suddenly, but without moving. I lay thus for a very short time; then I heard the voice of Mack, who apparently was below and to the left of me.

"Listen, Joe," he cautioned quietly, "don't be alarmed at what I am going to say, and under no circumstances must you move a muscle of your body, or ask me why you must not."

He spoke quietly, reassuringly, but what he said was as sharp and as cold as ice-water. It was something like being told that an executioner's squad you were facing had only blank bullets in its guns. Obeying this tone in his voice, I remained perfectly motionless, and he spoke again.

"Now listen carefully, and again, don't move," he warned. "There is a rattlesnake about a foot from you, and slowly approaching you. You will be perfectly safe if you won't move. Perhaps he will crawl around you, but he will not strike if you do not move. I shall not speak again, because it might frighten him."

My muscles tensed; the blood rushed to my face; I wanted to jump and run, anything to get out of there. The thought flashed through my mind that perhaps my companion was joking, but almost the minute it entered, I knew that no one, speaking the way he did, could be joking. Lord! what could I do! If I could only see the snake, perhaps I could kill it, but I dared not move. Thus I waited, unable to analyze my feelings, almost sure of certain death if I moved. I closed my eyes and waited. Suddenly I felt something on the biceps of my right arm — a queer, light touch, clinging for an instant — and then the smooth glide of an oily body. I could feel the muscles of the snake's body slowly contract, then relax as it slid smoothly, oh, how smoothly, across my naked arm. Again and again that body contracted, and again and again it relaxed. At last I saw a flat, V-shaped head, with two glistening, black, protruding buttons. A thin, pointed, sickening-yellow tongue slipped out, then in, accompanied by a sound like that of escaping steam. Slowly, slowly it advanced, the rounded spots on its back and sides drawing together and then stretching to their length as it moved slowly forward. When it was about in the middle of my chest, it paused, slowly turned its head toward me, and fixed its cold, boring eyes in my direction. Now I could not have moved had I wished; I was fascinated. So he remained, darting his tongue out and in. Finally he slowly, very slowly, turned his head, and again moved forward. Once more I had to see and feel the slow contraction, relaxation, contraction, relaxation. The body began to narrow, the spots grew smaller, the cracks on his revolting greenish-white stomach grew closer together and more minute. At last the slender, whipping tail appeared on my chest, and then slowly slid along until . . .

My head felt so queer; up and down, up and down it went. Why, my face was all wet! I weakly shoved at the bronzed arm that shook me, and asked, "What's the matter?"

"God! and only a couple of minutes!" I heard a voice filter into my brain. "Wonderful! I don't think I could have let a rattler crawl across me. Lord! but you're clammy, and look at your muscles and veins, all swollen and red, while your face looks like a dead man's."

CHAPTER XXIV

The Story

The story differs from the simple incident in several ways. For one thing, it is apt to be much longer. An incident may run anywhere from a page or two up to five or six pages. A story is apt to run anywhere from five or six pages up to ten, twelve, fifteen, or even twenty. Along with this increased length goes more emphasis on both the characters and the plot. The characters are presented more in detail, and thus there is more opportunity for dialogue. The plot is more complicated, and is usually so planned as to lead up to an intense or surprising final scene, called the climax. The climax brings events to a focus and thus ends the story, and ends it quickly at the point of highest interest.

A good formal definition of the short story is the following: "**A short story is a brief imaginative narrative, unfolding a single predominating incident and a single chief character; it contains a plot, the details of which are so compressed, and the whole treatment so organized, as to produce a single impression.**" [1]

1. The Three Elements of a Story

Every story has three elements or ingredients: (1) plot or action, (2) characters, and (3) setting. They may be defined very simply as follows: —

1. Plot or Action = the events that happen
2. Characters = the persons to whom the events happen
3. Setting = (a) the place where and
   (b) the time when the events happen

[1] J. Berg Esenwein, *Writing the Short-Story*. The Home Correspondence School, Springfield, Mass.

All narratives, whether short stories, novels, or dramas, have these three elements, though one of the three is apt to be more important than the other two in any given case. Indeed stories usually suggest themselves to writers primarily as either a story of action, or a story of characterization, or a story of setting. As Robert Louis Stevenson expressed it : "There are, so far as I know, three ways, and three ways only, of writing a story. You may take a plot and fit characters to it, or you may take a character and choose incidents and situations to develop it, or lastly . . . you may take a certain atmosphere and get action and persons to express and realize it." [1]

To stories of plot, character, and atmosphere, a fourth kind should be added — stories of theme. **Theme may be defined as an inevitable inference of a cardinal principle of life, or, more simply, as a governing motive of action or a philosophy of life.** It is the central idea that the writer endeavors to set forth and illustrate in his story. Among the leading themes of fiction and drama are love, jealousy, hate, devotion to an ideal, love of country, courage, fear, and revenge. Whenever a writer chooses to exemplify one of these themes he invents incidents and imagines characters in accordance with his purpose. In other words, the central theme is the creative force in the story, and both plot and characters are so molded as to illustrate it. For example, the theme of Hawthorne's story "The Great Stone Face" is the unconscious influence of a high ideal, and everything in the story is planned to bring out this idea. The theme of Hawthorne's "The Ambitious Guest" is the futility of ambition. Stevenson's *Dr. Jekyll and Mr. Hyde* is built around the moral law that if a man's worst side is indulged too often at the expense of his best side, the worst side will gradually gain the upper hand. The theme of O. Henry's "Roads of Destiny" is the impossibility of escaping one's fate. Edward Everett Hale's *The Man without a Country* portrays an unusual and tragic instance of loyalty to one's country. In a different way Shakespeare's *Macbeth* shows the evil influence of ruthless ambition on the human heart, and *Julius Caesar* portrays in Brutus the ruinous effect of misguided patriotism on a noble nature.

When the theme story is well written and not too obviously told for the sake of the moral, it is very impressive. The theme, however, should never be argued about or obtruded on the reader's notice. It

[1] Graham Balfour, *Life of Robert Louis Stevenson*, II, 168, 169.

should control the action of the story quietly and invisibly, as gravitation and magnetism operate in the physical world. If the story is
sincere and successful, the reader will feel the force of the theme all
the more strongly because it has not been thrust upon his notice.

(1) THE PLOT OR ACTION

The plot or action of a story consists of events, happenings, incidents.
It is the plot that makes a story move or, to use larger words, that gives
it narrative momentum. Most readers prefer stories with swiftly
moving plots to stories which are concerned mainly with portraying
character or depicting setting. As we grow older we become more
interested in quieter stories, but in the first third of life we crave action.
Call to mind the three or four stories you like best and the odds are
that they will be plot stories. Practically all adventure, mystery, and
detective stories, which together form such a large part of current
fiction, are chiefly stories of plot.

When it comes to writing the short story in college, strange as it
may seem it is easier to handle successfully a short, simple plot than
a crowded, unusual one. Many stories by students fail because they
are overloaded by a long, complicated plot which would require fifty
pages instead of ten or twenty to develop properly. If you are hesitating between a complicated and a simple plot, choose the simple plot
and go into many and minute details. Remember that the section on
Details, pages 431–435, applies as forcibly to the story as to the incident. Not even Kipling or Stevenson could take a lengthy, complicated plot and treat it successfully in ten or fifteen pages of your
handwriting. What they would probably do would be either to make
a novelette of it, as Stevenson does in *The Strange Case of Dr. Jekyll
and Mr. Hyde*, which runs to about seventy-five printed pages, or to
throw away three fourths of the plot, select a single episode or situation,
and unfold it in detail. One of the most unprofitable exercises in the
entire narrative field is to try to put into short-story form the plot of
an interesting moving picture we happened to see. All that can be
done within our limits of time and length is to give an unconvincing
summary or synopsis of the action. Many English students have tried
to do this, but it is not on record that any has succeeded. If you wish
to use something from a moving picture or an action-crammed plot

from some other source, choose a single scene or situation and concentrate on that.

1. DIVIDE THE PLOT INTO PARTS OR STAGES

Very few plots are suited to being told straight through from beginning to end in one narrative rush or surge. Most plots profit greatly by being planned as a series of scenes or stages, usually three, four, or five in number. Then each scene or stage is worked on as an individual unit or step in the story, and developed in sufficient detail to be interesting and convincing. All the stages lead up to the final stage or climax, and thus when put together form a continuous narrative road, with steadily increasing interest, up to the climax and conclusion.

Take the two following skeleton plots as examples. Neither is original, but both are good illustrations of the principle under discussion.

A. FOR THE HONOR OF THE NAME

A young man, whose forefathers since the American Revolution have an unbroken record for gallantry of war, enlists at the first declaration of war. His friends and family expect great things of him. He goes to the front, and at the first call volunteers for spy duty inside the enemy's lines. He is captured and condemned to be shot. Faced with the certainty of death he loses his nerve and breaks down utterly. His mother, who has managed to get permission to visit him the night before his execution, sees with horror his tears and cowardice. He will disgrace the family name on the morrow. Knowing that there is absolutely no hope of reprieve, she tells him that she has overheard the commanding officer say that an exchange of prisoners has been arranged and hence order all the cartridges to be loaded with blanks. The boy takes heart, and goes to his death next morning at sunrise with a smile on his face.

The scenes or stages into which this plot may be conveniently divided for ease of handling are these : —

1. The family tradition
2. War and enlistment
3. Spy duty and capture
4. Condemnation and breakdown
5. The mother's visit in prison : the good (!) news
6. Bravery (!) and execution

Other divisions than these might be proposed according to the way in which a writer might wish to vary the proportions or the emphasis of the plot. The six stages suggested above, however, are the obvious ones. Numbers one and three could be very much condensed or even combined respectively with numbers two and four.

The thing to be determined at the outset is whether it is the boy's story or the mother's. It could be told from either his or her viewpoint. If it is the mother's story, number five is the climax and number six should be condensed into a few striking sentences, closing with a tribute from the officer in charge of the firing squad. If it is the boy's story, number six is the climax and should be related in greater detail. In either case, however, the most dramatic situation is the prison scene. Most students agree that it is the mother's story.

B. THE AMERICAN BIRD

While the American fleet was anchored in Cuban waters cockfighting was frequently engaged in, and betting and rivalry were keen between the marines and the Cubans. Because of the prowess of one particularly powerful Cuban bird the marines lost steadily. It became almost a point of national honor to find some way to beat the big Cuban rooster. Finally a plan was made and a special fight arranged for July 4, and a contract duly drawn up and signed by both sides to the effect that the Cuban bird should be matched against the American bird with a forfeit of ten thousand dollars in case either side tried to withdraw from the fight, which sum was to go to the winner. On the appointed day huge holiday crowds of Cubans and Americans gathered. The American bird was brought in in a big crocus sack, to the great amusement of the crowd. When the judges called time the sack was opened, and out tumbled a big bald eagle, "the American bird"! In spite of vigorous protests from the Cubans, the fight had to go on or the forfeit money would be lost. The gamecock was game and picked and spurred the sleepy eagle until, finally aroused, it stretched out a claw and wrung the gamecock's head off. Then the eagle went back to sleep. Pandemonium!

This plot, which is fairly complicated, could be divided into the following convenient stages: —

1. The American fleet in Cuban waters: the rivalry between the marines and the Cubans.
2. The unbroken string of victories for the Cuban gamecock.
3. Desperate situations require desperate remedies: the plan (not revealed till the climax).

4. The holiday contest and the big wager.

5. The fight and its unexpected conclusion.

Again, though other divisions are possible, the five suggested ones are probably the best. As in the case of "For the Honor of the Name," the plot is somewhat complicated. Either story, if written out from the beginning in the usual way, would prove too long and cumbersome for inexperienced writers.

The best way to handle these and most other plots is, first, to divide them into stages, and secondly, to follow the plan explained in the next section.

2. Do Not Begin at the Beginning

The way to pick up a story is the way to pick up a puppy — a little in front of the middle.

— C. N. GREENOUGH AND F. W. C. HERSEY

As has just been stated in the previous section, one fault of inexperienced writers is trying to crowd too much plot into one story. The other chief weakness is beginning the story at the beginning instead of in the middle or just before the end. One of the best directions ever given amateur story writers is that quoted above: the way to pick up a story is the way to pick up a puppy — a little in front of the middle.

In order to hold the reader's attention a story should not waste time warming up, but should begin swiftly and keep moving from the start. Above all it must grow more interesting and intense the further it goes, leading up to the final scene of highest interest which forms both climax and conclusion. In fact, the technique of the short story may be likened to a skyrocket, which is touched off quickly, soars upward with a rush to the top of its flight, and then bursts into a brilliant display of stars that are instantly quenched by darkness through which the supporting stick falls unseen.

That is the ideal — but it cannot be attained by accident or without careful planning and practice. Time, space, and human nature being what they are, if we rush into the actual writing of the story too soon and begin at the beginning, what happens only too often is this: we start writing with considerable enthusiasm, and do fairly well for the first few pages. Then we get tired and begin to slow up. The minutes slip by, and the story seems to stretch out longer and longer, with the end not much closer than it was at the outset.   Finally, having covered the required number of pages with writing, tired-out from the extended effort to do our best, we bring the story to a hurried and inadequate close.

A story written in this way exactly reverses the correct procedure, and almost always results in a weak climax and a lame ending.   Instead of the story's getting better as it goes along, it gets steadily worse until it just runs out of breath, gasps a few times, and curls up and quits.   Such narratives remind one of a stream flowing from a spring into a sandy country.   At first it moves promisingly and sparkles bravely.   Then it begins to get smaller and slower, and at last dries up, leaving only a damp spot in the sand.

The remedy for this situation is fairly simple and easy.   It is to plan the story as a series of scenes or stages and think it through from beginning to end in the mind, but *actually to start writing only on the last scene or the next to the last.*   Into this scene put all the time, energy, dialogue, and detailed vividness that you have at your command.

For example, in writing the spy story outlined in the preceding section, leave the first four stages untouched for the moment and begin with the mother's visit to her son in prison.   Do all in your power to enter fully into that situation; try to put yourself into her place and into his.   How did each feel?   How did each look?   How did each act?   What did each say?   Extend yourself to the limit of your possibilities for dramatic feeling.   Make your readers see and feel all that went on in the hearts of the grief-stricken mother and her unfortunate son.   Relate the execution briefly but as suggestively as you can. Then stop.

The next day, or the next night, read over what you have written, and tighten and improve it in all the ways suggested in the sections on revising on pages 181–184 above and pages 478–479 below.   Then run back in your mind through the first four stages of the story and write them out in only enough detail to make your climax and conclusion clear and probable.   It is surprising, if the story is written in this way, how little time and space have to be given to the first half of the plot. Its complications and difficulties seem to vanish into thin air, the path to the climax is short and easy, and the climax itself stands out vividly in all its details and impressiveness.

In the story of "The American Bird" follow the same plan.   Begin with the climax, that is, with the fight and its unexpected conclusion. The opening sentence might well be, "The day of the fight dawned hot and clear," or, "As the hour for the contest approached an increasing throng of excited, gesticulating Cubans and blue-clad marines began to push their way through the narrow streets that led to the arena." Then relate the events of the fight with all the detail, color, life, move-ment, excitement, and surprise you can muster. Take as much time and paper as you need to go into full narrative and descriptive details. Then lay the manuscript aside, and at a later time write the first part of the story. If this is done, instead of the preliminaries taking three fourths of the total space, and the climax being crowded into what is left, the climax will have three fourths, and the action leading up to it will adjust itself easily and pleasantly into its rightful place.

The plan suggested for these two plots is an excellent one for inex-perienced story writers to follow. It is a great aid to securing propor-tion, emphasis, and climax. It is not adapted to all plots and all narrative purposes, but wherever you can apply it it will increase your chances of success. All you have to do is to imagine that you wrote the first part of the story yesterday and put it safely away in the table drawer. Then write the second part.

To repeat the opening quotation: "The way to pick up a story is the way to pick up a puppy — a little in front of the middle." Or, as the same authors have said elsewhere: "A story is read from the begin-ning to the end, but it is planned from the end to the beginning." [1]

THE ROUND TABLE

1. (a) As a narrative exercise discuss the division into stages of the two specimen plots. Choose the one you prefer, begin at the climax, and finish the story. Next day write the opening paragraph. Ask the instructor to read aloud the two best climaxes and the two best opening paragraphs.

(b) Rather than using either of the suggested specimen plots, take a plot of your own or one assigned by the instructor, divide it into scenes or stages, and, following the plan suggested in this section, indicate where you would begin the story. Write out the opening and closing paragraphs.

2. Read how Poe says that he wrote "The Raven," as described in his suggestive essay, "The Philosophy of Composition." He tells us that he first put pen to paper at the third stanza from the end. The whole essay

[1] C. N. Greenough, F. W. C. Hersey, and H. L. Bruce, *Writing Well*, The Mac-millan Company, 1932, p. 336.

is a masterly description of writing "from the end to the beginning." It will repay class discussion.

3. "It would interest nobody to know that I always write the last paragraph first, and then work directly up to that, avoiding all digressions and side issues."— THOMAS BAILEY ALDRICH

4. In planning your plot try to visualize definitely what will be the final word, gesture, and look of the characters in the last scene.

2. Characters

The second important element in a story is the characters, the people to whom the events happen.

To depict character is harder than to narrate events. Even in a plot story, however, the characters should be made as real and lifelike as possible. If we can *see* and *hear* the actors in the plot, the action itself will of course be more interesting and vivid.

(1) IMAGINING A CHARACTER

Most professional writers take their characters from real life, or rather take hints and suggestions for their characters from real people they have come into contact with. They will meet a person with some outstanding or unusual trait, perhaps mental alertness, or good nature, or extreme slowness of thought and speech, or irritability, or quickness in repartee, or courage, or marked charm, or the habit of exaggeration, or fondness for gossip, or boastfulness — any of the thousand and one physical, mental, and moral characteristics that individualize people and make them different from one another. Then, with this trait as a starting point, the writer will mold and build up the rest of the character in accordance with it, adding here and taking away there until the character fits the plot and the part in it he is supposed to play. This was the way both Scott and Dickens conceived their characters. And Stevenson tells us that Long John Silver in *Treasure Island* was modeled in part after his friend the English poet William Ernest Henley, though Stevenson altered the portraiture so greatly to fit the needs of the story that no one except himself could have identified the source. Eden Phillpotts, the novelist, said: "My characters are composite and I never transfer a living person to a story, though I seldom meet a living person who does not offer me something to be recorded. Thus my puppets are built on live men and women." [1]

The way a figure from real life can be adapted and molded beyond recognition can be seen from the following account of the origin of an amusing hunting sketch. A party of hunters in a Southern state were once going on a dove hunt. In the winter the wild dove is a wary and speedy bird, very hard to hit. While stopping at a combined store and filling station the hunters heard the sound of a gun, and saw a man sitting under a tall tree in a large field shooting doves as they came to light in the tree. The filling-station attendant said the man was the proprietor of the store and regularly sat under the tree and killed six or eight doves every day. He had even taken an old chair to sit in.

That was the start of the story, but as the hunters drove on, they began to talk about the man, and to invent detail after detail. They made the man very slow and fat — weighing three hundred pounds. The chair became an old office swivel chair so that he could turn around to face in any direction without getting up. They added a brown cocker-spaniel retriever which would lie at his master's feet and run out every time he shot a dove and bring it to him. As a final touch they invented a little Negro boy to keep the flies and gnats off him, to call attention to the doves as they flew in, and to run to the store to bring him drinks and sandwiches.

When they got home that night one of the hunters wrote out the sketch, and it was published in the newspaper under the title, "Dove Hunting de Luxe." It aroused considerable amusement in the community, and one sporting magazine wrote in offering to reprint the article provided a picture of the hunter sitting in the chair under the tree with doves, dog, and boy at his feet, could be procured!

This incident illustrates the process by which many a character and many a story has originated and grown to more serious and constructive (!) proportions.

(2) DEPICTING CHARACTER

There are six ways of depicting character: (1) By direct description; (2) by direct explanation; (3) (*a*) by what the character does

[1] Quoted in C. N. Greenough, F. W. C. Hersey, and H. L. Bruce, *Writing Well*, The Macmillan Company, p. 285.

and (b) how he does it; (4) (a) by what the character says and (b) how he says it; (5) by what he makes the other characters do; (6) by what the other characters say about him (which is really one form of number 2, direct explanation).

Of these six ways, the first four will be considered in detail.

1. DIRECT DESCRIPTION

Properly to realize a character we must know how that character looks — the details of his dress, bearing, stature, gestures, the expression of his face, and any tricks or mannerisms in speech or bearing. As has been well said, "Of all the things you wear, the most important is your expression." This is the field of direct description, and every story writer gives his best efforts to portraying the physical appearance of his characters. Before he can do this successfully, the writer must first see and realize his characters in his own mind in the minutest detail. This in itself is no easy thing to do. It is said that the Russian novelist Turgenev studied his characters as if they were living persons, and wrote out an account of everything that had happened to them before the story began. Whether or not a writer studies his characters in this way, he must settle on the prevailing impression which he wishes the character to make upon his readers — whether of calmness, strength, courage, unselfishness, charm, weakness, meanness, cowardice, spitefulness, lovableness, hatefulness, greed, treachery, loyalty, or what, depending upon the needs of the plot and the part that character plays in it. Then the writer must single out and focus the physical and mental details which serve to emphasize this impression and bring out this effect.

These details can either be given together in one paragraph of preliminary description, or distributed bit by bit through the story at opportune times during the action. The first is the easier way; the latter the better way.

Following are well-written descriptions which not only help us see the physical appearance of the person described but also suggest his mental and moral traits. They are models of their kind.

A DANGEROUS CREOLE DANDY [1]

Manuel Mazaro, whose small, restless eyes were as black and bright as those of a mouse, whose light talk became his dark girlish face, and whose redundant locks curled so prettily and so wonderfully black under the fine white brim of his jaunty Panama. He had the hands of a woman, save that the nails were stained with the smoke of cigarettes. He could play the guitar delightfully, and wore his knife down behind his coat collar.

— GEORGE WASHINGTON CABLE, "Café des Exilés"

A NEW ENGLAND MOTHER [2]

There she stood waiting. She was a small woman, short and straight-waisted like a child in her brown cotton gown. Her forehead was mild and benevolent between the smooth curves of gray hair; there were meek downward lines about her nose and mouth; but her eyes, fixed upon the old man, looked as if the meekness had been the result of her own will, never of the will of another.

— MARY E. WILKINS FREEMAN

HUCK FINN'S DADDY [3]

He was most fifty, and he looked it. His hair was long and tangled and greasy, and hung down, and you could see his eyes shining through like he was behind vines. It was all black, no gray; so was his long, mixed-up whiskers. There warn't no color in his face, where his face showed; it was white; not like another man's white, but a white to make a body sick, a white to make a body's flesh crawl — a tree-toad white, a fish-belly white. As for his clothes — just rags, that was all. He had one ankle resting on 'tother knee; the boot on that foot was busted, and two of his toes stuck through, and he worked them now and then. His hat was laying on the floor; an old black slouch with the top caved in, like a lid.

— MARK TWAIN

She sat down, crossing her knees self-consciously; self-consciously she allowed the scarf to slip halfway down her arms. It was curious, the way she had of looking at him; as if she would like to eat him — curious and disturbing. She reminded him of the wolf grandmother in "Little Red Riding Hood." She was always smiling at him in this odd, greedy manner — showing her sharp, faultless teeth, her eyes incredibly and hungrily bright. It was her way — wasn't it? — of letting him know that she took an interest, a deep interest in him. And why on earth shouldn't she, as the widow of his best friend?

— CONRAD AIKEN, *Spider, Spider* [4]

[1] *Old Creole Days*, Charles Scribner's Sons. By permission of the publishers.
[2] "The Revolt of Mother," Harper & Brothers. By permission of the publishers.
[3] *The Adventures of Huckleberry Finn*, Harper & Brothers. By permission of the publishers.
[4] Charles Scribner's Sons. By permission of the publishers.

Descriptive paragraphs like these are excellent means of making characters real and of helping the reader to see and understand them. The important thing in such description is not simply to give a list or catalogue of physical traits, but so to select and group those details that they tend to make one definite and unified impression.

THE SINGLE STRIKING DETAIL

The other method of describing is to distribute the description through the story, giving one striking detail at a time — a picture in a phrase, as it were. This method calls for all our ingenuity and art, for the single detail must be carefully selected and admirably expressed. Here are examples : —

In came Mrs. Fezziwig, one vast substantial smile. — CHARLES DICKENS

A lanky boy whose bolts needed tightening. — CHARLES BROOKS

The smiler with the knife under his cloak. — CHAUCER

"I am Lord Tilbury," said his Lordship, looking like a man unveiling a statue of himself. — P. G. WODEHOUSE

A stiff man, starched with self-esteem. — BULWER-LYTTON

Around her eyes were the dry beds of old smiles.
— GERTRUDE ATHERTON

A little bladder of a man inflated with words. — WARWICK DEEPING

Her beauty caused a crisis in my vocabulary. — LOUIS ADAMIC

She wasn't exactly cross-eyed — one of her eyes just ignored the other.
— *The Reader's Digest*

She was off down the street with the grim purposefulness of a battleship going into action — one could almost see the smoke pouring from her smokestacks. — I. A. R. WYLIE

R. S. V. P. eyes. — ALMA WHITAKER

Parenthetical legs. — CHARLES DICKENS

She said with fingernails in her voice, "Thank you!"

A New England spinster grim with respectability.
— PRINCESS ALEXANDRA KROPOTKIN

Looking as though she'd hiss if a drop of water touched her.
— VICKI BAUM

His breakfast is an affair of a hand groping out from behind a paper.
— HELEN HULL

The possessions of Christopher Alexander Pellett were these: his name, which he was always careful to retain intact; a suit of ducks, no longer intact, in which he lived and slept, a continuous thirst for liquor, and a set of red whiskers. Also he had a friend.
— JOHN RUSSELL, "The Price of the Head "[1]

She was built in terraces. — DOROTHY PARKER

With these striking descriptive expressions compare the descriptive similes given on pages 407–408 above, and the single descriptive touches quoted on pages 518–519 below.

2. DIRECT EXPLANATION

The second method of characterizing is briefly to inform the reader exactly the kind of person you are writing about. You analyze the character in your own mind and then tell the reader plainly that he is large, strong, courageous, and calm; or mean, cruel, and stingy; or that she is beautiful, affectionate, and unselfish; or fat, friendly, and full of humor; or old, gossipy, and malicious. Whatever impression of your character you have, you pass it on to the reader in direct, literal statements. In other words, instead of, or rather in addition to, writing a paragraph of description about your character, you also write a paragraph of exposition.

Direct explanation should be used as sparingly as possible. It is usually an evidence of either haste or weakness. There is about the same difference between describing a character and explaining him as there is between a picture and a map. The characters should make themselves known by what they do and say in the story, not have to be explained by the writer as if they were a laboratory experiment or a sum in algebra. An occasional line of explanation is useful and may even be necessary. As a rule, however, it should be avoided whenever possible. If on rereading your incident or story you find that you are prone to explain your characters, mark out every explanatory sentence and see whether you cannot give your reader this same information by means of something you make your character do or say. That is the effective, impressive way.

Here is an excellent explanatory paragraph by William H. Prescott on the character of Pizarro, the Spanish conqueror of Peru. Remem-

[1] *Where the Pavement Ends*, Alfred A. Knopf, Inc.

ber, however, that Prescott was writing history, not prose fiction, and the historian is primarily an expositor rather than a narrator.

"He was temperate in eating, drank sparingly, and usually rose an hour before dawn. He was punctual in attendance to business and shrank from no toil. He had, indeed, great powers of patient perseverance. Like most of his nation he was fond of play, and cared little for the quality of those with whom he played; though, when his antagonist could not afford to lose, he would allow himself, it is said, to be the loser, a mode of conferring an obligation much commended by a Castilian writer for its delicacy.[1]

A modern Spanish story writer introduces his characters in one of his stories in this way: —

She was capricious, capricious and extravagant, like all women of the world.
He was superstitious, superstitious and valiant, like all the men of his time.
Her name was Maria Antunez.
His name was Pedro Alfonso de Orellana.[2]

3. BY WHAT THE CHARACTER DOES AND HOW HE DOES IT

What you do makes so much noise I can't hear what you are saying.
— EMERSON

Emerson's striking words are true in both literature and life. To explain your characters is sometimes necessary; to describe them is better, but to let your reader see what they do and how they do it is best of all. "By their deeds shall ye know them."

In the third chapter of *Silas Marner* George Eliot first describes Dunstan Cass as follows: "To be sure the neighbors said, it was no matter what became of Dunsey — a spiteful jeering fellow, who seemed to enjoy his drink the more when other people went dry." A page further on he is again referred to: "The door opened, and a thick-set, heavy-looking young man entered, with the flushed face and the gratuitously elated bearing which mark the first stage of intoxication. It was Dunsey, and at the sight of him Godfrey's face parted with some of its gloom to take on the more active expression of hatred.

[1] Chapter V, Book IV, *The Conquest of Peru*, J. B. Lippincott Company.
[2] Gustav Adolf Becquer, "Our Lady's Bracelet," O'Brien's *Best Short Stories of 1925*, Dodd, Mead and Company.

The handsome brown spaniel that lay on the hearth retreated under the chimney-corner."

The touch about how the dog acted when Dunstan came in is more suggestive than all the rest of the description.

In *Vanity Fair*, when Thackeray wishes to let us know Becky Sharp's frame of mind upon leaving Miss Pinkerton's school, he does not tell us how she felt, but reveals it by means of one significant act : —

"Stop!" cried Miss Jemima, rushing to the gate with a parcel.

"It's some sandwiches, my dear," said she to Amelia. "You may be hungry, you know ; and Becky, Becky Sharp, here's a book for you that my sister — that is, I — Johnson's Dixonary, you know ; you mustn't leave us without that. Good-by. Drive on, coachman. God bless you!"

And the kind creature retreated into the garden, overcome with emotion.

But, lo! and just as the coach drove off, Miss Sharp put her pale face out of the window, and actually flung the book back into the garden.

In *Dr. Jekyll and Mr. Hyde*, Stevenson's problem was to arouse in his readers a strong feeling of utter repulsion toward the horrible little monster, Mr. Hyde. He did this in several ways — for instance, by direct description and by stressing the abhorrence that all the other characters felt for him. Chiefly, however, Stevenson revealed him to us by means of his horrible deeds, two of the most inhuman of which were these : —

(1) MR. HYDE AND THE CHILD [1]

All at once, I saw two figures : one a little man who was stumping along eastward at a good walk, and the other a girl of eight or ten who was running as hard as she was able down a cross street. Well, sir, the two ran into one another naturally enough at the corner ; and then came the horrible part of the thing ; for the man trampled calmly over the child's body and left her screaming on the ground. It sounds nothing to hear, but it was hellish to see.

(2) MR. HYDE AND THE OLD GENTLEMAN [1]

When they had come within speech (which was just under the maid's eyes) the older man bowed and accosted the other with a very pretty manner of politeness. It did not seem as if the subject of his address were of great importance ; indeed, from his pointing, it sometimes appeared as if he were only inquiring his way ; but the moon shone on his face as he spoke, and the girl was pleased to watch it, it seemed to breathe such an innocent and old-world kindness of disposition, yet with something high too, as of a well-

---

[1] *Dr. Jekyll and Mr. Hyde*, Charles Scribner's Sons. By permission of the publishers.

founded self-content. Presently her eye wandered to the other, and she was surprised to recognize in him a certain Mr. Hyde, who had once visited her mother and for whom she had conceived a dislike. He had in his hand a heavy cane, with which he was trifling; but he answered never a word, and seemed to listen with ill-contained impatience. And then all of a sudden he broke out in a great flame of anger, stamping with his foot, brandishing the cane, and carrying on (as the maid described it) like a madman. The old gentleman took a step back, with the air of one very much surprised and a trifle hurt; and at that Mr. Hyde broke out of all bounds, and clubbed him to the earth. The next moment, with ape-like fury, he was trampling his victim underfoot and hailing down a storm of blows, under which the bones were audibly shattered and the body jumped upon the roadway. At the horror of those sights and sounds, the maid fainted.

No description or denunciation of Mr. Hyde on Stevenson's part could impress us half so horribly as letting us see him perform these two inhuman deeds.

In all these cases consider what a definite and vivid impression we get successively of Dunstan Cass, Becky Sharp, and Mr. Hyde. It is because we do not see them through the author's eyes, as he describes or explains them, but through the eyes of our own imagination as we watch them reveal themselves through their deeds. Direct revelation of character through action is the story writer's highest art.

4. By What the Character Says and How He Says It

Along with what a character does, as a direct revelation of the kind of person he is, go what he says and the way he says it. "Thy speech bewrayeth thee." Glance again through the section on Dialogue, pages 441-448 above. It deals with the function of dialogue both in advancing the action and in revealing character. It applies even more to the story than to the simple incident, and should be fitted here into your approach to writing the short story. Note particularly what is said of the stage directions of dialogue, pages 446-447.

THE ROUND TABLE

1. Can you think of instances from your own reading in which character is revealed by direct action?

2. In your reading for the rest of the year be on the lookout for this kind of direct revelation of character. If you come across a particularly good instance, bring it to class and read it aloud.

3. Choose an incident or a single stage in the plot of a short story, and by means of what the character does (and how) and what the character says (and how) reveal him (or her) directly to us. Use little or no description and no explanation at all. For instance, try one of the following situations: —

(1) A conceited athlete and an admiring girl.
(2) A beautiful, selfish girl and a male admirer.
(3) An angry motorist comes home after a minor collision.
(4) A very selfish boy or girl on a picnic.
(5) A timid child is sent upstairs in the dark to get mother's glasses or father's slippers.
(6) A lazy tramp and a positive housewife.
(7) A tired mother and a fractious child in a railroad-station waiting room.
(8) A deaf old lady and a taxi driver.
(9) The baby loses his temper over his building blocks.
(10) A boy (or girl) who knows more than his (her) parents argues with them at the table.
(11) A cat and a dog meet each other in a narrow alley.
(12) A messenger boy tries to deliver a telegram in a yard guarded by a large dog.
(13) The census taker tries to get information from an ignorant (suspicious) householder.
(14) A college boy during vacation tries to sell an encyclopedia to a farmer's wife.
(15) A sophomore sells a freshman a desirable seat in chapel.
(16) An automobile agent demonstrates a new car to a middle-aged man (or woman) who has just come into a great deal of money.
(17) A hard-to-please patron in a restaurant.
(18) A prim little girl on the way to school is teased by a Huck Finn type of boy.
(19) A ticket agent tries to explain the difference between Eastern and Central or Mountain and Pacific time to a nervous woman not used to traveling.

4. Imagine a character (man, woman, or child) who exemplifies one of the following traits and invent an incident, with dialogue, to depict him: hate, love, greed, timidity, boldness, fear, anxiety, ill temper, conceit, good nature, lonesomeness, loyalty, suspicion.

Use no explanation. Read aloud the incident and let the class name the trait it illustrates.

3. Setting

The third element of a story is the setting — the place where and the time when the events happen.

In some stories the scene is of no great importance, and the action could be set in one place as well as in another; that is, the plot would fit almost any section or locality. In other stories, however, on account of some peculiarity in the characters or the unusual nature of the plot, the action definitely calls for some particular time or some particular place. To remove Mrs. Mary E. Wilkins Freeman's stories, "The Revolt of Mother" and "A New England Nun," from New England would destroy half of their appeal and probability; Poe's "The Cask of Amontillado" could hardly have happened outside of Italy; George Washington Cable's Creole stories could be laid only in New Orleans, Bret Harte's stories only in the West, and Thomas Nelson Page's Negro stories only in Virginia; Robert Louis Stevenson's "A Lodging for the Night" of necessity occurs in Paris during the lifetime of François Villon; to think of Kipling is to think of India; and to call the names of Jack London and Rex Beach is to bring to mind Alaska and the frozen North.

Stories like these are called local-color stories because in them the setting plays an actual part in molding the action and influencing the characters. Instead of being merely a suitable or convenient place for the story to take place, it is necessary to both plot and characterization, neither of which would seem so logical and probable anywhere else.

Certain localities and certain surroundings undoubtedly suit certain types of stories better than they do others. As Stevenson expressed it : —

One thing in life calls for another; there is a fitness in events and places. The sight of a pleasant arbor puts it in our mind to sit there. One place suggests work, another idleness, a third early rising and long rambles in the dew. . . . Some places speak distinctly. Certain dank gardens cry aloud for a murder; certain old houses demand to be haunted; certain coasts are set apart for shipwreck.[1]

[1] R. L. Stevenson in "A Gossip on Romance," *Memories and Portraits*, Charles Scribner's Sons. By permission of the publishers.

When you choose a plot, therefore, and fit characters into it, or when you conceive a character and invent action to reveal him, consider carefully where (and when) both plot and character seem most naturally to belong. For example, in Wilbur Daniel Steele's "Footfalls," the author chose a difficult character to portray, and made him seem probable by putting him in the right setting, which the author explained as follows : —

He lives in one of those old Puritan sea towns where the strain has come down austere and moribund, so that his act would not be quite unbelievable. Except that the town is no longer Puritan and Yankee. It has been betrayed; it has become an outpost of the Portuguese islands.

(1) STAY CLOSE AT HOME

In choosing a setting you should make use of the time and the place that you know best. Of course that time is the present and that place is your own college or community. You can write more convincingly of the here and the now than of anything else. This is contrary to the inclination of most of us. It is said that everyone has a desire to be somebody else. Certain it is that everyone wants to write about something else than his own daily life. Most inexperienced writers wish to write a story laid in the time of the crusades or of the Spanish Armada or of Napoleon. Or they are attracted by such picturesque and adventurous regions as the valley of the Amazon River, the jungles of Africa, the Desert of Sahara, or the South Sea Islands. Very occasionally a young writer may succeed with a tale of the long ago and the far away. The odds, however, are heavily against it. It takes actual first-hand knowledge of your place and people to make them seem real. The great romancers of the world have studied their fields as long and arduously as a university graduate student does his specialty. Think of the tremendous familiarity of Sir Walter Scott with legend, folklore, and history that made the *Waverley Novels* possible. Sir A. Conan Doyle is said to have read three hundred books in the British Museum as a preparation for writing his unexcelled historical romance, *The White Company*. Even Edgar Wallace, the most popular and prolific mystery-story writer of the last decade, said of his book *The Devil Man*, which dealt with the life and times of the notorious English murderer, Peace: "It took me four years to collect my facts, four months to construct the book, and four days to write it."

The writers mentioned in the second paragraph on page 476 — Mrs. Wilkins Freeman, Cable, Bret Harte, Page, Kipling, Jack London — all had lived in the localities of which they wrote and knew them intimately and at first hand.   Someone commenting on Caesar's famous message, "I came, I saw, I conquered," said that even Caesar had to *see* before he could *conquer*.   We must know whereof we speak.

Our own home neighborhood may seem very tame and humdrum to us, but it may be very novel and interesting to those who do not live there.   A palm tree is a commonplace in Florida, but would be a curiosity in Maine.   The people and places you see every day and are apt to consider hopeless as story material may furnish a story of absorbing human interest if you have eyes to see and the eagerness to record patiently, faithfully, and minutely.   Once in a college class Sandburg's *Chicago Poems* was being studied.   A girl remarked somewhat impatiently, "I've lived in Chicago all my life, and I never saw anything like that."   "Ah," said another, "and that's one reason you can't write like Sandburg!"

Owing to the unexpected places in which pay ore was sometimes discovered, in the old West there grew up the saying, "Gold is where you find it."   This is peculiarly true of the story writer's material. Gold is where you find it — even in your own back yard.

4. Revising

It goes without saying that a story needs revising before it is submitted either to an editor or to the instructor.   Glance through the chapter on Revising, pages 178–187, slowly turning the pages and noting again the section headings and the examples.

In revising your own narrative writing, train yourself to look for the following items: —

1. Does your story begin and end effectively?   If you had not written it and did not have to read it, would the first few paragraphs make you want to go on with it, or would you feel inclined to yawn and toss it into the wastebasket?

2. Is the ending definite, pointed, and clear-cut, and does it bring the incident to a focus and a climax?

3. Are you making general statements and giving a summary of events instead of furnishing your reader with details, details, details?

4. Are your adjectives, adverbs, and nouns specific enough, or are you rocking your reader to sleep with general words?

5. Is there enough dialogue, or could you heighten the interest by making your characters talk more? In passing, is the dialogue that you have included paragraphed and punctuated correctly?

6. Run through your verbs and see to it that you use the strongest, most specific verbs possible. In this connection avoid "there is," the passive voice, and the participial close.

7. How are the paragraphs running? Too long or too short? Divide or combine them as seems advisable.

8. Always remember that the title is an integral part of the story. It is your invitation to the reader. It should be interesting, suitable to the story, and not too long. It should not tell too much.

5. Writing a Story in College

Writing a story is a formidable matter, and calls for extended effort. It is the longest and hardest piece of writing which this book deals with.

Some such plan as the following will be found helpful for beginners. The instructor will of course adapt it to the needs of each class.

1. Choose a plot either from those given in this chapter, pages 482–483, or assigned by the instructor, or suggested and discussed in class. Feel free to change or adapt this plot to your particular purpose.

2. As the first assignment, (a) divide the plot into scenes or stages according to the plan suggested on pages 461–463 and 463–466.

(b) Settle on the exact stage at which you are actually going to begin writing.

(c) In two or three sentences each, describe the appearance and disposition of the one, two, or three leading persons in the story.

(d) In a half-dozen sentences describe the setting.

Submit (a), (b), (c), and (d) to the instructor for criticism and suggestions.

3. As the second assignment, run through in your mind your plot, characters, and setting to see whether any changes or improvements occur to you, and begin the actual writing of the story at or near the middle (end?).

4. As the third assignment, read over and touch up what was previously written, and continue writing the story.

5. The fourth assignment continues the third, and is devoted to revising what has already been written, and completing the writing of the story.

6. The final assignment is to revise the whole story according to the suggestions made on pages 478–479, and to copy it neatly by hand or in type.

IN CONCLUSION

If in spite of your best efforts your plot seems to lag and drag, and your characters insist on talking like wooden dolls, do not feel permanently discouraged. Read again the chapter on Revising and Rewriting, pages 178–187 above. There is no way to improve except by the try-try-again method. Ray Long, who for twenty years was a successful and influential magazine editor, once said that the receipt for success in writing stories is simple: "Think better and work harder than your competitors."

Both ingredients are essential to success.

THE ROUND TABLE

1. Name your two favorite novels and your two favorite short stories. Are they concerned primarily with plot, character, or setting; or is the interest balanced between two or three of these elements?

2. On the subject of unity of impression, or preconceived totality of effect, read Poe's "Critique on Hawthorne's *Twice-Told Tales*," particularly the famous paragraph beginning, "A skilful literary artist has constructed a tale. . . ." That paragraph and Poe's "Philosophy of Composition" leave nothing more to be said concerning the technique of the impressionistic story.

3. O. Henry gave the following advice about beginning a story swiftly: "Begin abruptly without any philosophizing. I know of one magazine office where they take out the first paragraph of at least a third of the articles that are accepted for the simple reason that they do not add anything to the story. These first paragraphs bear the same relation to progress in the story as cranking an automobile does to progress on the road. They are merely to get the engine running."[1]

[1] Arthur W. Page, "Little Pictures of O. Henry," *The Bookman*, August, 1913, Dodd, Mead and Company.

4. In two stories that you like read again carefully the opening and the closing pages, and see whether you think the end is implied in the beginning.

5. Have you noticed an incident or a person this week that might contain the material for a story? Be on the lookout for such a suggestion for the next twenty-four hours and jot down in synopsis form any ideas that occur to you.

6. Is there a historical or folk legend of your county or state that would make an interesting narrative?

7. Do you know an exciting situation or happening that you have heard the older members of your family tell which might be turned into a story?

8. Try giving each story that you write three titles, and then select the best.

9. Name a list of places in your county suitable for different kinds of stories. Discuss the lists in class.

10. In choosing a plot and characters, think carefully before deciding on a love story. Love stories are pitfalls for the unwary writer, and are apt to be either oversentimental or unintentionally humorous.

11. Let each member of the class submit in tabloid form the best plot he can think of. From these plots the instructor will select several to be read to the class and discussed for further possibilities.

12. Let the instructor select the one or two best stories written on each assignment and (*a*) have them read aloud to the class and (*b*) filed for use in the class magazine.

13. Invent one plot for a mystery or horror story. Discuss the plots in class and agree on the best, whether or not the story is written out.

14. Invent one story of fantasy, full of fanciful or impossible incidents, with a surprise ending.

15. In telling a story or writing a news item we should be brief and pointed, but not too brief.

> "Get the dope on this accident," said the editor of the college paper to the cub reporter. "And when you write the story, remember that brevity is the soul of the newspaper. Never use two words where one will do. Now get going." A few hours later the reporter handed in his copy. "Professor Stapleton struck a match to see if there was any gasoline in his tank," the story read. "Age 55." — *Reserve Red Cat*

16. ### Suggestions for Stories

(1) Try to find in the day's news a suggestion for an unusual or human-interest story. In this connection read Robert Benchley's light essay, "News from Home."

(2) Here are two suggestions from Hawthorne's notebook: —

(*a*) "A person or family long desires some particular good. At last it comes in such profusion as to be the great pest of their lives."

(b) "A person to be in the possession of something as perfect as mortal man has a right to demand; he tries to make it better and ruins it entirely." (See Hawthorne's story, "The Birthmark.")

(3) A strayed (or stolen) dog (or cat) returns home after great hardships, only to find the house locked and empty. The family in the meantime had moved to another part of town. They are finally reunited.

(4) On the streets of a large city, a beggar, who ran away from home as a boy, strikes a man for a dime to get a sandwich and recognizes his father, who has been searching for him for ten years.

17.   Plots for Stories [1]

(1) A boaster has built up a tissue of exaggerations about the things he has seen and the people he has met in another city. Traveling with friends, he is unexpectedly compelled to stay for some hours in that city. One by one his falsehoods find him out, and he has to put up the price of a dinner for the party.

(2) A freshman at college is making a fool of himself in all the ways a freshman can. His father, who never went to college, and is trying to make something of the boy, seems harsh and unreasonable. They have violent scenes. The father is a man who cannot express his tragic disappointment in any other way than by sarcasm and bitterness. An old physician, who knew the boy's mother and her unfulfilled hopes, has a talk with the freshman and opens his eyes.

(3) A very bright attractive girl had become egotistical and dictatorial. Her opinions had always been accepted by her parents and younger sisters as conclusive. At college Dorothy continued her habit of giving advice. Some of her classmates, becoming weary of her dictation, decided to cure her. Within the space of two or three days every one of them asked her opinion about dress or entertainment or college activities. Not until more than a dozen, both boys and girls, had humbly consulted her did she begin to suspect a plot. When her friends confessed, she was at first furiously angry but ultimately accepted the device as a very just criticism and changed her ways.

(4) One day when John was driving with his sister on a lonely road, he needed gas. His sister pointed out a filling station half a mile away. When John reached the place a beautiful blonde girl came out and gave him the gas. The next day John

[1] The first two plots are taken, by permission, from J. K. Slater's *Freshman Rhetoric*, D. C. Heath and Company; the next three are taken, by permission, from Virginia J. Craig's *Teaching of High School English*, Longmans, Green, and Company.

purchased a new suit and a new tie. Two days later when he was wearing these and had brought out his carefully cleaned car, his sister asked if she might accompany him. He gave a grudging assent. After all kinds of difficulty on a rocky road a slovenly woman weighing three hundred pounds appeared. John asked her how long she had had the filling station. "Bought it two days ago," she answered. John never again traveled that remote road to get gas.

(5) Mr. and Mrs. Jones were a young couple who had been married for several years. Mrs. Jones was considered the best housekeeper in the town. As a result of a car collision she had a fall and broke her leg. After a few days, the nurse was called away. Mr. Jones told her that she need not worry, for he had watched her and could do the work exactly as she had done it. The result was that he put every kitchen utensil to some incorrect use. He put dozens of household articles in peculiar and unusual places. On the day when Mrs. Jones could first walk around, she made many startling discoveries. These discoveries should be arranged in climactic order.

(6) Here is a famous old plot from the East. Chaucer used it in "The Pardoner's Tale," changing the poisoned bread to poisoned wine. It has been given a modern setting several times. Adapt it in any way you please, omitting or touching very lightly on the moral.

THE DOUBLE PLOT

(*Excerpt from Persian Poetry*)

Three hungry travelers found a bag of gold;
One ran into the town where bread was sold.

He thought, "I will poison the bread I buy,
And seize the treasure when my comrades die."

But they too thought, "When back his feet have hied,
We will destroy him, and the gold divide."

They killed him; and, partaking of the bread,
In a few moments all were lying dead.

O world! behold what ill thy goods have done;
Thy gold thus poisoned two, and murdered one.

18.   ## Mr. Fothergill's Plot

A man gets into correspondence with a woman whom he doesn't know and he finds romance in it. Then he sees a girl, falls in love with her in the ordinary way, marries her, and drops the academic correspondence. Happi-

ness, then friction.   He writes again to the unknown woman and finds con-
solation, till by an accident it is discovered that the married couple are
writing to each other.

Try this plot if you like, though it is a difficult one to handle.

Incidentally, fourteen living English writers were asked to use this same
plot — among them G. K. Chesterton, Frank Swinnerton, Sheila Kaye-
Smith, and A. E. Coppard.   Their stories are published in John Milton
Berdan's *Fourteen Stories from One Plot*, Oxford University Press, $1.35.
The book is interesting reading in the technique of story writing.

Stories by Students

Here are four stories by college students.   One is by a girl and
three are by boys.   The states represented are Illinois, Nebraska,
California, and Montana.

The first two belong to the recent development of narrative art
known as the short short story or more familiarly as the "short short."
Its usual length is from three to five ordinary book-sized pages, or,
say, from a thousand to two thousand words.   Its reading time is
seldom more than five or six minutes.   Because of the modern fondness
for speed and dash, the short short has become a popular form of light
fiction and is a regular feature of a score or more of weekly and monthly
magazines.   It is hard to write but easy to read.   If the short story is
narrative art stripped to the skin, the short short is narrative art
stripped to the bone.

The first story, "Nothing on the Printers," is on the border line
between simple incident and the short short story, and might equally
well be considered one as the other.   The close connection of the
related happening with the past life of the main character, however,
and its implications for the future, make it rather a short short than a
simple incident.   In these respects compare it with the unconnected
casualness of the equally well-told simple incidents, "Death Passes,"
page 430, "My First Solo," page 453, and "Too Close," page 455.
"Grid Incident," while only a trifle longer than "Nothing on Printers,"
is definitely a short short.

The other two stories, "The Bird Is Free" and "Carnival," are good
examples of what can be expected of college writers at their best.   Read
them once for the interest and pleasure that are the birthright of the
short-story art.   Then read them critically as one craftsman examines

the work of another craftsman, noting such features as their beginnings and endings, the handling of dialogue, the use of description, the interplay of character on action and vice versa, the leading up to the climax or focus, and any especially strong or significant elements. Finally, discuss the stories in class with the instructor, and determine which two are liked best.

1. Nothing on Printers [1]

ERNEST TUCKER

(University of Illinois)

Doc Potter sat on the rim of the copy-desk, in the seat that he had occupied for twenty years, and dreamed. His eyes hurt, and he shut them. He was nearly through with another day's work; half an hour would see him waiting for the streetcar that would take him back to his little hole-in-the-wall apartment on the near north side. Things were quiet now, and the "slot man" in charge of the desk had gone downstairs for a cup of coffee. Doc was the only one left on the rim. He blinked his eyes to ease their aching, and looked at the clock. . . . Ten more minutes. He would make a last check of any possible news stories, and go home.

"Boy!" he called. "Check the printers!"

The copy boy ambled toward the little room where the news teletypes rattle out their stories twenty-four hours a day. He was in no hurry; it was late, and the news was coming in slowly. Doc Potter closed his eyes and resumed his dreaming. He had Chuck's last letter in his pocket. Chuck, his boy, coming home! It had been nearly a year since Doc had seen him; nearly a year since Chuck had proudly sat here at the desk and written the headline announcing his own graduation from Harvard and his sailing on a protracted European cruise. And now he was coming home!

Twenty years on the copy-desk. Twenty years, since Chuck's mother died, of saving, planning, hoping, dreaming for Chuck. He had been afraid, before, to let himself be carried away by his dreams; but tonight he let his heart lead him. How many times had they talked it over together, about the wonderful things Chuck was going to do when he graduated; joking about it when each knew the other was not joking. The list of Chuck's undergraduate achievements almost frightened him. That one boy-man could do so much! He was bound for success; no, he was fated for success. He could not avoid it. And as for Doc, he forgot the years on the copy-desk — years of writing about people being born, marrying, dying, fighting — the same old stories year after year, writing the same headlines to fit each one. People are all so alike — except Chuck — so wearily monotonous, doing the same things in the same way as long as he could remember.

[1] From *Green Caldron*, A Magazine of Freshman Writing.

He was through with this, through; now would come happy years that they had both looked forward to so long, when Chuck would have a good job — he could not help getting one — and Doc would sit back a bit, and light a cigar, and look around at some of the things he had missed these twenty years. He had not seen Chuck for eleven months. And now he was coming home.

Tommy, the copy boy, stood watching the printers. One story coming in; he would wait until that finished, and then take it to Doc. The clacking of the teletype stopped. Tommy ripped the paper from the machine, and began to read it, idly. He caught his breath, and the paper trembled in his hand.

NEW YORK NY JAN 6 — (AP) — CHARLES POTTER, 23, OF CHICAGO, WAS KILLED TODAY AS HE TRIED TO SAVE A CHILD FROM AN AUTOMOBILE

That was all. Tommy blinked his eyes. Damn this cigarette smoke! Just like Chuck . . . he'd been a swell kid. And poor Doc! Writing the obit headline on his own son! And then Tommy did something he had never done before and has never done since. He deliberately tore live copy in two and crumpled up the pieces. Doc would find out soon enough anyway.

He walked down the narrow, paper-littered aisle between the desks. Doc was putting on his overcoat. "Nothing on the printers, Tommy?"

Tommy bent his head to light a cigarette. "No, Doc," he said. "Nothing on the printers."

2. GRID INCIDENT [1]

D. LINDGREN

(*Nebraska State Teachers College*)

The rain pounded and clattered like stones in a rolling pail; and suddenly Hutch began to cry; so we sat there on a stone, like soaked kittens, while Hutch sobbed, and I miserably watched the kid have it out. Then he stopped, and we began walking again, leaving splotchy pools of water, and me trying to humor him, mentioning something about how salty the water would be now. But Hutch begins to sniffle again, so I shuts up.

We tramped all afternoon, following the muddy car tracks, with Hutch feeling a little cheerier as we went along, but saying nothing. Finally he asks the first question he'd popped all afternoon.

"How much d'ya get for pickin' apples in Yakima?"

"Well," I says, glad that the kid is feeling more chipper — "for a youngster your size, I'd say you could earn close to four dollars a day."

"I'd save three," says the kid, and was silent again. 'Long toward evenin' with the curtains clearin' away, and the sun lookin' as colorful as a

[1] From *The Antler*.

tomato-can wrapper, we stopped at a little town called Drummondsville, and I boiled some coffee I had along. Hutch drinks a little, and stares around the countryside with all the enthusiasm of a sleepy turtle, and when I speaks to him, he looks at me as if I was a ghost.

We stayed there that night, and when the fire warmed him up, as I expected, young Hutch began to snap out of it. I knew, as we talked, that the kid would open up, and tell me what I was wondering.

"You say," says I, gentle as I can, "that your pop is dead?"

The kid chokes, "Executed this morning at six-thirty," as if he'd read it in the papers. "I — I couldn't stay back there."

Then I knew the whole story — his father had been Munstermann, convicted of murder in a hold-up. His mother would have to support Hutch and herself — I saw it then. "You'd like to make some money yourself, and help with the family budget. Is that it, fella?"

"Well, I'm fourteen," was all he said.

"And where are you going now?" Not daring to say more.

The kid's lips barely moved. "Money first, for my mom; then I've got to have an education. Mom always said she wanted to have me go to Dartmouth — then." And young Hutch's face beamed. "I want to be a professional football player."

"Do you think this will help your mom, laddie?"

The boy looked up in misery. "It's got to," he said.

"Why the football, kid?" says I.

The boy brightened — "You can make lots of money playing football. I'm going to be a halfback like Jacksie Jordan." And believe it or not, he pulled out a bunch of clippings a mile long, telling how Jordan runs eighty-five yards against Green Bay, and seventy-three yards against Boston. Another, where he is given the most-valuable-player award, and then one big headline — JORDAN SAID TO HAVE THROWN CHICAGO GAME, STAR'S WHEREABOUTS UNKNOWN.

Hutch was silent on that one, then says, "He didn't do it, mister. He wasn't that kind — b-but he shouldn't have run away."

"You're running away," I says. "Jacksie Jordan probably felt the same way you do about it."

I thought the kid would say, "That's different" — but he didn't. He sat there and thought a long time. Finally, "I s'pose Mom would like to see me back. She needs me now — don't she?"

"More than ever, sonny," says I. Then I tells him, "We'll hook a freight in the morning, and I'll go back with you."

"You're swell, mister," says the kid. "I'll send you passes to the games when I get to playin' for New York."

So the next day, we reached the kid's home town about dark, and Hutch kisses his mother. She smiles, I bet, for the first time in a year. They both wave good-bye, and I starts back the same way I came, then turning and legging it for the station as hard as I can; all the time wondering how

Hutch is goin' to make it, how the sports writers will act when I come back, and how the good ol' pigskin will feel in my hands when the returned Jacksie Jordan runs wild against Brooklyn.

3. THE BIRD IS FREE [1]

WINIFRED JEAN SMITH

(Leland Stanford University)

When I entered the lower hallway, I closed the door softly and stood there a minute before I went to the stairs. The house was dark and as cold as the clear autumn day outside. The stale, sweet odor of flowers filled the hall and the unnatural silence of the late afternoon eddied slowly around me as I leaned against the door.

I hate funerals. I hate the unnecessary, awkward clutter of people and phrases, the stiff politeness and embarrassment. I wondered why I had been fool enough to say I'd come back to the house and help Ellen pack. But I went up the spacious, graceful stairs to Ellen's room and knocked on the door.

"Come in," she called and I saw her heavy shoulders bent over a suitcase. "I'm nearly through, Ann, but it's good of you to come."

Some boxes huddled together with an old Gladstone bag near the edge of the bare floor by the door, but otherwise the bedroom was immaculately clear. It was cold and I went toward the window to shut it.

"Don't," said Ellen. "I hate the smell of those flowers. Put on my coat if you're cold."

"Have you had the flowers taken away?" I asked.

"Yes." She turned a bureau drawer out onto the white bed. She started to collect hairpins from the folds of the counterpane, putting them carefully into a little gray box. "The cook took them to her family when she left. I told her."

I watched her put a rubber band around the box of hairpins and pack it, together with a pile of white handkerchiefs. The room seemed even colder because of its barrenness. The rugs were rolled up in one corner, the curtains lay folded neatly on a chair. The desk and bureau top and walls were bare, reflecting the white sunlight and pale naked-branched shadows from the garden outside.

Ellen Chilton was a homely woman. In this narrow, icy room she looked taller and more thick-waisted than ever. Her face was heavy and the two deep wrinkles that drooped from her nose to the corner of her mouth made her look old and dull and tired. The coat to her navy-blue suit hung on her closet door. I put it around myself and sat on the bed where I could see the plain-faced alarm clock.

"What time does your train go, Ellen?"

[1] From Stanford Writing.

"Five twenty-two." She didn't look up. "I had the electricity and water turned off this afternoon, and the telephone disconnected tonight. You can give the key to Harmless Porter if he wants to act as agent." She shut the suitcase with two sharp clicks, and carried it into the hall. "Help me with this bedding, will you, Ann?"

We took off the plain cotton coverlet and the faded lamb's-wool quilt. Together we folded them, Ellen's square, dry-fingered hands white against the patterned material. I picked up the sheets and tied them into a loose bundle.

"You could take them downstairs to the back porch," said Ellen. "The laundryman will stop for them tomorrow."

I dropped the laundry on the step and walked back into the kitchen thinking about Elizabeth, who had always been the one I had come to see. Ellen was only a cousin of Elizabeth's who had come back with her to Custer after Jock died. But Elizabeth I grew up with. We'd played together and she'd bossed me since before we started school. None of the rest of us had married so well and Jock had left her such a lot of money it seemed natural that we should have envied Elizabeth her clothes and jewelry and furs, her perfumes and cars. We loved to drop in to see her in the house that was such a graceful background for her. She had been more vividly alive, more witty than any of us.

We didn't pay much attention to Ellen. She sat lumped in a chair while Elizabeth told us about life in Paris or on the Riviera; or she served tea while Elizabeth sat drinking hers from a pale-blue cup in swift, tiny sips; or she went into the post office with Elizabeth's little square, white envelopes when Elizabeth was giving a party. I thought she was rather stupid. But Elizabeth was always very sweet with her — bringing her to all the lunches, and teasing Ellen about how quiet she was, or including her in the conversation by asking her the name of someone they had met somewhere. Often I wondered how a person like Elizabeth could have stood Ellen's dourness. Elizabeth, with her flowers and slim wrists and high, silky laugh! Elizabeth, with her pet birds and her naughty child's sense of humor!

I walked around the cold, darkening kitchen with its empty drawers and gaunt, dim cupboards, thinking about those two. I wondered what Ellen would do with the money Elizabeth must have left her. It had been sixteen years since she had come to Custer. She should have caught something of Elizabeth's gaiety — but Ellen had so little imagination! It was natural that Elizabeth would want someone in her family to have the money, but what would Ellen do with it? She might travel, but not Elizabeth's kind of travel. I had a vision of her, flat-footed and spectacled, doing her duty by Fontainebleau as quietly as she had washed Elizabeth's Sèvres china.

Or, probably Ellen would buy a small house somewhere and have a garden; and every Wednesday and Saturday go to the public library for a book. It was queer to think of Elizabeth's money turning into trowels and water bills and cakes of soap and serviceable underwear and aprons.

I heard Ellen coming down the stairs, so I went into the dining room through the swinging door. There, on the floor, was a tumbled heap of bright clothes: a lively tangle of colors, with a froth of underclothing decorating the top. Ellen came into the room with some striped suitboxes in her arms.

"We'll have to fold these." She plumped down by the pile. "They can go to the Salvation Army."

I knelt beside her on the polished floor, now devoid of its thick carpets, and began to put the fragile things into the boxes. I hated to let them go, for I'd seen Elizabeth wear them with such jaunty charm. I said as much to Ellen and she smiled her slow, unamused smile.

"What should she have done with them?" she asked.

"She might have left them to someone," I answered.

"She did," said Ellen. "She left them to me."

I looked at Ellen quickly. She wasn't laughing and she'd never made a joke in her life, so it must have been one of Elizabeth's. Ellen was a good two sizes bigger than Elizabeth had been.

"But you couldn't possibly use them." I stared at Ellen's heavy face bent over the gay clothes.

"Exactly," said Ellen. Her voice was soft and expressionless; it was lost among the shadows of the ceiling. I sat quite still with the slippery, worthless silks in my lap, remembering what Elizabeth had been like. It was so dark now, I couldn't see Ellen.

We finished packing the clothes finally. I put them in the back of my car and followed Ellen up the twilit stairs to her room for the suitcases. Ellen put her coat on; buttoned it, her white, thick fingers working quickly. She walked over to the mirror, stooping a little to put on the dark-blue hat. Elizabeth had always joked about the matronly hats Ellen wore and the way she wore them. She said that if Ellen had the latest thing in millinery she would put it on as if it belonged to a middle-aged missionary. It wasn't very kind, I suppose, but it had been funny at the time; even Ellen had smiled because it was so true.

I went to the window to pull it down slowly, watching Ellen's blurred, dark face in the mirror. I was a little afraid to ask what I wanted to know.

"Ellen," I said, "what did Elizabeth leave you, beside those clothes you can't wear?"

She caught some strands of her straight, black hair back under her hat and looked hard in the glass. It was difficult to see without a light.

"You were here sixteen years. It's almost a lifetime. You ought to be able to do a lot of things you've always wanted to, now." I wondered what she did want. Nobody had ever bothered to ask her.

"Yes." Ellen turned. "I should. I'm going to my brother's house for a while."

"And afterward, what?"

"And afterward I'm going to look for a job to live on." She looked at me steadily. "Elizabeth left her money to the Juilliard Music School."

"What did she leave you?" I was obstinate, thinking of Elizabeth's laughter.

"She left me her clothes and her pet parakeet as a souvenir," said Ellen. "You remember — the one that always hung in her window."

There was nothing more to say or do. The light had gone and the far whistle of the five twenty-two train re-echoed in the cold emptiness of the dark house. Ellen picked up her suitcases and pushed open the door.

"Let's get out," she said.

I turned to the window to fasten the catch.

"There's something in the garden," I said, looking down. "It looks like a cat."

"It probably is." Ellen's voice was flat and cool. "The neighbor's cat. I wrung the parakeet's neck and threw it out the window."

4. CARNIVAL [1]

ROWE MORRELL

(State University of Montana)

The shrill notes of the merry-go-round mingled with hoarse cries of barkers in front of gaudy booths. The soft evening air was full of sound of women's high-pitched laughter, and the pad of many feet in the white dust. Axel, from the silence of the gloomy Oregon mountains, from the deadly monotony of the lumber camps, liked the sounds. He liked the smells in his nostrils, smell of hot dogs, cheap whiskey, popcorn, and the livestock from the great barns. And the people! The men, in their tight-fitting, clumsy suits; the women, exciting in bright colors. He gazed with awe at the rickety ferris wheel, but was afraid to ride on it. He tried to win a little painted doll by tossing baseballs into a wooden bucket, and laughed uproariously when the third ball bounced out.

County Fair! The lumber camps of his nineteen years of life had been full of tales of it. Yes, here he was, and here was the fair, and the crowds of people. He wandered aimlessly between the booths, liking the feel of so many shoulders rubbing against his. He smiled, and was smiled at in return, a gigantic man — with simple blue eyes, a mop of tousled yellow hair, and size fourteen shoes.

On a platform a man was beating a bass drum, a crowd was collecting. Axel stopped. Another man stepped out on the platform, and some people wrapped in old cloaks and overcoats followed him and stood there. The man spoke in a loud voice, pointing first to one of the people on the platform, and then another. One man, he said, was a sword swallower, and Axel laughed.

[1] From Warren Bower, *The College Writer*, W. W. Norton & Company, Inc.

"And last but not least, we have the *greatest* exponent of the famous hula-hula dance in the entire world! Beautiful Tessie! Folks, for the *ridiculous* price of one thin dime, you can see all these wonders! And *don't* forget, folks, the little lady shakes! Shake for the folks, Tessie, shake for 'em!'"

The girl threw off her cloak, and the man beat the bass drum; another man played a cornet. She was almost naked, and moved her hips only. Axel watched greedily, with the blood throbbing hot against his temples. Then with a few of the crowd he paid his dime, and followed the performers into the tent.

He came out and moved slowly up the narrow street, confused. The man had swallowed the sword. The dancing girl was vivid in his mind, he felt restless, queer. He wanted to touch her, get close to her. In the tent she had danced up against him, her eyes had looked into his, and her painted lips had smiled at him. He, Axel, out of all the men in the tent! His face had gone suddenly scarlet; the other men had laughed, and he had grinned sheepishly.

Up toward the end of the street there was the biggest crowd he had seen yet. A man was beating on a gong, yelling.

"Right dis way — right dis way!" he yelled. "Evyboddy dis way to de mammot athaletic stadium!"

People moved leisurely towards where the man yelled and the gong rang; Axel drifted with them absently, perplexed by strange, powerful emotions. He was still in the tent of the dancing girl, watching her sinuous body, wanting to crush her to him. Unfulfilled desire tormented him. The crowd halted in front of the platform, and Axel looked up. The man on the platform wore a derby hat cocked over his eyes. He was thin and hawk-nosed, and his harsh voice was curiously like a slap in the face. Axel didn't like him.

The hum of voices in the crowd stilled as the man spoke. Here there was a sense of excitement, expectancy.

"Gents," the man said, "it gives me great pleasure t' introdooce th' worl's champeen heavyweight rassler. Professor Nick Atlantis! In ten long years of competition all over the world, gents, Professor Atlantis has yet to meet defeat!" He waved his hand in a sweeping gesture, a pair of dirty curtains parted behind him and a huge bulk of a man stepped out. He was wrapped in a dingy blue bathrobe, and there was dark stubble on his chin. Axel watched the man with awe. Once, a long time ago, he had sent to a magazine for a course called "How to Wrestle, in Ten Easy Lessons." The bull cook had put him up to it, and with the combined learning of the whole lumber camp, they had managed to decipher the first two lessons. After that they had quit, but Axel had thrown every man in the camp with ease. Now the professor clasped both hands overhead and waved, someone beat frantically on the gong, and the man in the derby hat bowed deep. There were a few handclaps in the crowd, but a little fellow wearing a checkered cap nudged Axel and made a sound with his tongue and lips. Others took it up, it grew louder and drowned out the brazen voice of the gong.

The man in the derby hat was visibly angry. He shouted until he made himself heard, sneered as he spoke. "Awright, awright, smart guys," he said. "You got any local boys dat wanna take on d' professor? No? — C'mon, step up, who'll take 'im on? You? — You? Well, I'll tell ya wat d' professor is willin' t' do. If any a you smart guys can stay twen'y-fi' minits wit d' professor, he gits twen'y-fi' bucks cash money! Think it over, smart guys, twen'y-fi' bucks! Who wants it? Whooo wants it?"

Axel's slow mind fumbling — trying to rid himself of confusion. Twenty-five dollars — the professor leering down from the platform — the dancing girl — twenty-five dollars — twenty-five dollars and the dancing girl.

No sound from the crowd; the men shifted uneasily, looked at one and another. The voice from the platform grated. "Watsa matter, watsa matter? You guys all yellow?" The men growled sullenly, but no one stepped out.

Then the little fellow in the checkered cap scrambled to the platform. "Listen," he said, "you ain't gonna let these mugs get away with this, are ya? One a you huskies step up here an' take a fall outa this ape! Watsa matter, ain't ya got any shame? Ain't ya got no guts? Ya ain't gonna let 'em call ya yella an' get away with it, are ya?"

A hoarse roar from the crowd, but still no one stepped forward. A big man in greasy overalls left hurriedly. Axel was still in a study, hesitating. He could throw the professor, he was sure of it. Hadn't he learned all about how to wrestle? He wanted to get back to the tent of the dancing girl, but twenty-five dollars is a lot of money. Most of his had gone over a gambling table. Maybe with twenty-five dollars in his pocket, the dancing girl might —

"Hey, you! Hey, big boy, wot about it?" Axel started, the man in the checkered cap was shouting at him.

"Hah?" His china-blue eyes regarded the man dazedly.

"*You* ain't afraid of this mug are ya, big boy? C'mon up here an' lessee wot ya look like. C'mon, Swede, don't be bashful. Get 'im started there, some a you guys!" No one touched him, but they looked at him; he was embarrassed by so many eyes. Violently he decided, and shouldered his ponderous way through the crowd. Then he was up there in front of them, bewildered. He stood stupidly, and fidgeted with his great knotted hands.

"Here he is, boys," the little man shouted exultantly. "How d'ya like 'is looks, professor?" The professor snarled ferociously, and threw off his bathrobe, displaying enormous bulging muscles, matted hair on a barrel chest. He strutted up and down the platform, and the crowd jeered and whistled.

"You ever rassle, son?" It was the man in the derby.

"Yah, sure."

"Ya wanna make twen'y-fi' bucks, don'tcha?"

"Yah."

"Geez!" The man sighed, and looked at Axel with pity. "Well, O.K. then. C'mon, I'll fix ya up wit' some duds." Axel followed him into a tiny room that was blue with stale smoke, and smelled raw of rubbing alcohol. On a rough table there was a pint of whiskey. Outside the gong clanged raucously, feet scraped past the door, as people went into the tent. The man in the derby sat on the table, spatted feet swinging free. He looked at Axel sharply.

"Here," he said. "Wanna drink?" Axel gulped and coughed, the whiskey burned all the way down. "So you're a rassler," the man observed, sneering. "Take off them clothes." He reached into a cubbyhole and tossed Axel a pair of short woolen trunks and some tennis shoes. Axel didn't want to take off his clothes in front of the man. He reached for the whiskey bottle and took a huge swallow; it made him feel better. Win the twenty-five dollars and *then* go back to the girl, that's it! His pulses leaped at the thought. "Get goin'! We ain't got all night, Buddy!"

Axel undressed methodically, self-consciously, feeling the man's eyes on him. His head spun a little from the whiskey. Then the little man with the checkered cap came in.

"Geez!" he exclaimed softly. "Wot a man!" He whistled a long low whistle of admiration. Then he talked, without taking the cigarette from his mouth. "I'm gonna be th' referee, big guy, an' ya wanna do just like I tell ya. All ya gotta do is keep 'im from puttin' ya on yer back, see? Ya don't wanna get rough, just don't let 'im get ya on yer back!" As Axel bent over his shoes, the little man winked at the man in the derby. Axel was putting on the trunks; they were stiff, and smelled of sweat. He couldn't get the tennis shoes on. The man in the derby told him he could get along barefooted, because that was all the shoes they had. Axel didn't care, the cool night air felt good on his feet.

"Well, Swede, ya all set? Have another drink before we beat it!" The little man handed the butt of his cigarette to the man in the derby, who took a couple of puffs and pressed the light out against the wall. Then he put the butt in his pocket.

Axel drank deep. "Yah, I'm ready now."

"Ya ain't scared, are ya?"

"Naw."

Both men slapped him on the back, then they all had a drink. They left most of it for Axel, and he drained the bottle.

"Le's go!" said the man in the checkered cap.

He followed the two into the tent. There was a ring, the floor covered with dirty white canvas. Electric bulbs shed yellow, dim light. The men sitting in the flimsy seats around the ring cast huge black shadows against the wall of the tent. As Axel clambered through the ropes they roared.

He blushed scarlet, feeling naked before all these eyes; his whole body was hot with the sting of rushing blood. Across the ring the professor sat in his bathrobe, glaring. Axel ventured a grin in his direction, and the professor turned his head, and spat on the floor.

Checkered cap in the center of the ring, talking again. "This match will be twen'y-fi' minit contes' between Professor Nick Atlantis, champeen heavyweight rassler of th' world; in this corner" — he paused, and there were boos and catcalls. "An' in this corner — the local wil'cat! If th' local boy stays twen'y-fi' minits with th' professor, he wins *twen'y-fi' bucks* cash money!" Roars from the crowd, a bull voice rising above the others, dinning in Axel's ears.

"Go get 'em, Swede!" He looked into the crowd. The voice belonged to a man sitting near the ring: a man smoking a stumpy cigar. There was a shiny badge on his vest.

For an instant Axel was in the center of the ring, close to the professor and the man in the cap. The man was giving them instructions in a low voice, but Axel didn't hear. The whiskey made his mind wander, it was pleasant. The hips of the dancing girl — he would go back to her — he felt happy, confident that she would be waiting for him. "Wrestling in Ten Easy Lessons" — Axel could not remember much about it. First you got down on the floor on your hands and knees — and then you — and then you — It was vague; a long time ago; he didn't remember very well. Now back into his corner; a gong rang deafeningly in his ears.

No one in the ring but himself and the professor — and the man in the checkered cap. Axel saw him standing still as a statue in a far corner, leaning against the ropes. The professor was coming towards him, feet slipping over the canvas with a rasping sound; he was crouched, menacing, snarling; Axel watched his approach, fascinated. A terrific flying tackle, something new to Axel. He crashed down hard, the wind butted out of him by the professor's hard head. Little puffs of powdered rosin flew into the air as he struck. The professor was quick as a cat. His weight crushed Axel down; lightning-like, his hands slapped here and there, seeking a hold. There were red, livid spots on the fair skin where his hands slapped, and Axel lay face down, his fuddled brain racing helplessly. The professor's sinewy hands gripped a bare foot, fingers curled around the toes, and Axel's leg bent slowly backward up over his buttocks. The men in the seats sighed — so soon! This toe hold; this painful, deadly toe hold — they didn't get out of that! Backward — backward — and the leg moved no further, the breaking point! The professor set himself to his task, he put his whole body into it! Now the leg, bent so grotesquely, was corded with muscle, pushing gallantly downward, bursting with pain. The ox-like face was a horrible grimace. Then unbelievably the straining hands began to slip. Imperceptibly the leg went down and the hands loosened little by little. Axel tore himself free and scrambled to his feet, sweating, wild-eyed. The crowd shrieked and howled like demons. The professor rose grimly; the brute strength of this rube baffled him.

Axel watched the professor coming at him again. He stood, feeling helpless, not knowing what to do. This wasn't fair, he was being cheated, cheated out of his chance to try. He wished the professor would get down on the floor, then it would be something different! Time after time he was smashed brutally to the canvas. Clumsily he attempted his favorite hold — headlock it was called. You put one arm around your enemy's neck and pulled down on your wrist with the other hand. The boys at the lumber camp had been helpless against it, but Axel couldn't get a hold on the professor. The man was greased and slippery, and Axel was terrified of his skill. The memory of that racking toe would send him scrambling to his feet through sheer, brute force — he was safe on his feet.

Every time he rose his body was more leaden, duller; his red thighs were quivering with the repeated blows. Desperation was in the face of the professor. He came in again, and a savage knee drove into Axel's groin, a hard heel ground into his bare foot.

That was too much. Axel rose with little dancing lights in front of his eyes. Again; almost blind with the pain; red rage creeping into his brain. Again — again — each time the knee driven — Axel rising sickly; weaving upon his feet — the red rage giving way to sullen, cold lust to kill.

Once more? Axel sees him advancing with his sliding, crouching gait. The man dances up and down in the wavering, blood-red haze.

This time the crowd is silent, tragedy hangs in the air. This will be the last time; human flesh and blood can stand no more. No sound save the gasping breath of the men in the ring, the slithering of feet over the canvas. Outside the merry-go-round pipes its stale melody faintly, someone draws deep, hissing breaths. The man with the badge on his vest drops his cigar; his clenched fingers bite the flesh.

Axel goes down. He doesn't rise this time. Neither does the professor. Straining, they lie there. Then inch by inch a great blond arm encircles the bull neck. The pink muscles stand out as if possessed of individual intelligence. One knotted hand grasps at the wrist of that arm — misses — grasps again — catches. Feebly the professor struggles to wrench himself free. The arm holds. The professor's grasp loosens — his arms and legs straighten out on the canvas — his breath gurgles horribly. Tighter straining — the arm closing down like a vise. No sound from the crowd. The professor's hand twitches futilely in defeat.

The little man in the checkered cap leaps to the center of the ring. He is tapping on Axel's shoulder. No movement but the arm bearing down a fraction more. The little man pounds; then he shouts.

"Get up, buddy, that's enough! Let 'im up!" He tears ineffectually at the steel arm, then frantically. "Let go of 'im, ya big sap!" He bends low, and looks straight into the face of the professor, and springs up as if jerked by a giant hand. His blank, terror-stricken eyes stare into the crowd.

"For Christ's sake, somebody stop 'im! He's killing 'im!"

As the echoes of his words die away, there is a sharp, unmistakable crack. The professor rolls free, and lies still. Axel lies on his face, panting. The man with the badge is turned to stone, halfway between the seats and the ring.

Axel rode away in the back seat of a car beside the man with the badge. Their wrists were fastened together by a steel bracelet. The car honked importantly, and slid down between the rows of gaudy booths. The people lined both sides of the narrow street and stared at Axel as he passed. On her platform looking down at him was the dancing girl — she looked directly into his eyes for an instant — she smiled.

SHORT-STORY READING LISTS

I. INDIVIDUAL STORIES

The Arabian Nights	*Ali Baba and the Forty Thieves*
Aldrich, Thomas Bailey . . .	*Marjorie Daw*
Crane, Stephen	*The Open Boat*
Hawthorne, Nathaniel	*Dr. Heidigger's Experiment*
	The Great Stone Face
	The Ambitious Guest
	David Swan
	Ethan Brand
Henry, O.	*A Retrieved Reformation*
	The Last Leaf
	The Gift of the Magi
	A Municipal Report
	The Furnished Room
	Roads of Destiny
Irving, Washington	*Rip Van Winkle*
	The Legend of Sleepy Hollow
	The Stout Gentleman
Moffett, Cleveland	*The Mysterious Card* (in Carolyn Wells's
	American Mystery Stories)
O'Brien, Fitz James	*What Was It? A Mystery*
Poe, Edgar Allan	*The Gold Bug*
	The Murders in the Rue Morgue
	The Purloined Letter
	The Masque of the Red Death
	The Fall of the House of Usher
	The Cask of Amontillado
	Ligeia
Stockton, Frank P.	*The Lady or the Tiger?*

LOCAL-COLOR STORIES

Cable, George Washington . . *"Posson Jone"*
Jean-ah Poquelin
Madame Delphine
Edwards, Harry Stillwell . . . *Eneas Africanus*
The Woodhaven Goat
Freeman, Mary E. Wilkins . . *The Revolt of Mother*
A New England Nun
Garland, Hamlin . . . . . *Up the Coolly*
Under the Lion's Paw
The Return of the Private
Harris, Joel Chandler . . . . *Six Uncle Remus Stories*
Free Joe and the Rest of the World
Harte, Bret . . . . *The Luck of Roaring Camp*
Tennessee's Partner
The Outcasts of Poker Flat
Colonel Starbottle for the Plaintiff
Jewett, Sarah Orne . . . . . *Marsh Rosemary*
A White Heron
London, Jack . . . . *All-Gold Canyon*
To Build a Fire (in *Lost Face;* also *Century Magazine*, LXXVI, 524)
Page, Thomas Nelson . . . . *Marse Chan*
Twain, Mark . . . . *The Celebrated Jumping Frog of Calaveras County*
Baker's Blue-Jay Yarn (*A Tramp Abroad*, Chapter III)
A Delicately Improper Tale (*Following the Equator*, Chapter II)

ENGLISH STORIES

Brown, John . . . . *Rab and His Friends*
Conrad, Joseph . . . . . *Youth*
The Heart of Darkness
The Lagoon
Dickens, Charles . . . . . . *A Christmas Carol*
Galsworthy, John . . . . . *Quality* (in *Inn of Tranquillity;* also *Scribner's Magazine*, LI, 292)
Hardy, Thomas . . . . . . *The Three Strangers*
Kipling, Rudyard . . . . . *The Man Who Would Be King*
Rikki-Tikki-Tavi
The Man Who Was
Without Benefit of Clergy
On Greenhow Hill

Kipling, Rudyard . . . . . *They*
An Habitation Enforced
Stevenson, Robert Louis . . . *A Lodging for a Night*
Will o' the Mill
The Sire de Malêtroit's Door
Markheim
The Strange Case of Dr. Jekyll and Mr.
Hyde
Wells, H. G. . . . . *The Stolen Bacillus* (in *The Stolen*
Bacillus and Other Incidents)
The Man Who Could Work Miracles
Wilde, Oscar . . . . *The Birthday of the Infanta*

FOREIGN STORIES

Daudet, Alphonse . . . . . *The Death of the Dauphin*
de Maupassant, Guy . . . . *The Necklace*
The Piece of String
Pushkin, Alexander . . . . . *The Shot*
Turgenev, Ivan . . . . *Mumu*

RECENT AMERICAN STORIES

Adams, Bill, "Home Is the Sailor" (*O. Henry Award*, 1928; *Good Reading for High Schools*, ed. Cross, T. P., Smith, R., and Stauffer, E. C., Vol. II, *Achievement*).

Adams, Frank R., "3000 Miles Away" (*Redbook Magazine*, October, 1918; Ray Long, ed., *Twenty Best Stories*).

Boyle, Jack, "Boston Blackie's Mary" (*Redbook Magazine*, November, 1917; Ray Long, ed., *Twenty Best Stories*).

Brush, Katharine, "Night Club" (*O. Henry Award*, 1927).

Canfield, Dorothy, "Portrait of a Philosopher" (in *Hillsboro People;* Robinson, K. A., *Contemporary Short Stories*).

Cather, Willa, "Paul's Case" (in *Youth and the Bright Medusa; McClure's Magazine*, XXV, 74; *Golden Book*, May, 1927; Robinson, K. A., *Contemporary Short Stories*).

Cobb, Irvin S., "The Smart Aleck" (in *Local Color;* Robinson, K. A., *Contemporary Short Stories*).

Daniels, Roger, "Bulldog" (*Saturday Evening Post*, Nov. 13, 1926; *O. Henry Award*, 1927).

Derieux, Samuel A., "The Trial in Tom Belcher's Store" (in *Frank of Freedom Hill*).

Dreiser, Theodore, "The Second Choice" (in *Free and Other Stories;* Robinson, K. A., *Contemporary Short Stories*).

Edmonds, Walter D., "Death of Red Peril" (*Atlantic Monthly*, November, 1928; O'Brien, 1929).

Ferber, Edna, "The Gay Old Dog" (in *Cheerful, by Request;* O'Brien's *Best Stories of 1917;* Robinson, K. A., *Contemporary Short Stories*).

Hemingway, Ernest, "The Killers" (*O. Henry Award,* 1927; O'Brien, 1927).

Heyward, DuBose, "The Half Pint Flask" (O'Brien, 1927).

Hurst, Fannie, "Humoresque" (in *Humoresque; Cosmopolitan Magazine,* March, 1919; *O. Henry Award,* 1919).

Kyne, Peter B., "Point" (*My Story I Like Best*).

March, William, "Fifteen Men from Co. K" (*O. Henry Award,* 1931).

Milburn, George, "Heel, Toe, and a 1, 2, 3, 4" (O'Brien, 1932).

Paine, Ralph D., "The Freshman Fullback" (in *College Years; Good Reading for High Schools,* ed. Cross, T. P., Smith, R., and Stauffer, E. C., Vol. I, *Adventure*).

Parker, Dorothy, "Big Blonde" (*O. Henry Award,* 1927).

Patterson, Pernet, "Buttin' Blood" (*Atlantic Monthly,* Sept., 1928; *O. Henry Award,* 1929; O'Brien's *Best Stories of 1929*).

Paul, Louis, "No More Trouble for Jedwick" (*O. Henry Award,* 1934).

Rutledge, Archibald, "Then Gabriel Blew His Horn" (*Good Reading for High Schools,* ed. Cross, T. P., Smith, R., and Stauffer, E. C., Vol. III, *American Writers*).

Saroyan, William, "The Daring Young Man on the Flying Trapeze" (*O. Henry Award,* 1934).

Stallings, Laurence, "Vale of Tears" (*Cosmopolitan Magazine,* May, 1931; Ray Long, ed., *Twenty Best Stories*).

Stringer, Arthur, "The Juggler" (Ray Long, ed., *Twenty Best Short Stories*).

Tarkington, Booth, "The Big Fat Lummox" (in *Seventeen; Metropolitan Magazine,* Nov. 18, 1915; Robinson, K. A., *Contemporary Short Stories; Good Reading for High Schools,* ed. Cross, T. P., Smith, R., and Stauffer, E. C., Vol. III, *American Writers*).

Terhune, Albert Payson, "The Day of Battle" (in *Lad: a Dog;* Ray Long, ed., *Twenty Best Stories*).

Wharton, Edith, "Xingu" (in *Xingu and Other Stories;* Robinson, K. A., *Contemporary Short Stories*).

II. GENERAL COLLECTIONS

THREE ANNUAL SERIES

O'Brien, Edward J., *Best Stories of 19—,* etc., Dodd, Mead & Company.

O. Henry Memorial Award Prize Stories (1919 on), Doubleday, Doran & Company.

The (N. Y.) *World's Best Short Stories of 19—,* etc., Doubleday, Doran & Company.

GOOD ONE-VOLUME COLLECTIONS

Ashmun, Margaret, *Modern Short Stories,* Macmillan Company.

Becker, M. L., *Under Twenty,* Harcourt, Brace and Company.

Bercovici, Conrad, *Best Short Stories of the World*, Stratford Company.

Boas, Ralph P., and Hahn, B. M., *Short Stories for Class Reading*, Henry Holt and Company.

Bower, Warren, *The College Writer* (stories by college students, pp. 293–455), W. W. Norton and Company, Inc.

Brewster, Dorothy, *A Book of Contemporary Short Stories*, Macmillan Company.

Brown, Leonard, *Modern American and British Short Stories*, Harcourt, Brace and Company.

Cody, Sherwin, *The World's Greatest Short Stories*, A. C. McClurg & Company.

Conrad, Joseph, *Selected Stories*, Doubleday, Doran & Company.

Cross, E. A., *A Book of the Short Story*, American Book Company.

Ellis, Amanda M., *Representative Short Stories*, Thomas Nelson and Sons.

Fuess, Claude M., *Selected Short Stories*, Charles E. Merrill Company.

Hale, E. E., Jr., and Dawson, F. T., *The Elements of the Short Story*, Henry Holt and Company.

Harte, Bret, *Selections from Poems and Stories*, ed. C. S. Thomas, Houghton Mifflin Company.

Hastings, W. T., Clough, B. C., and Mason, K. A., *Short Stories*, Houghton Mifflin Company.

Herzberg, Max J., *Stories of Adventure*, Allyn and Bacon.

Heydrick, Benjamin A., *Types of the Short Story*, Scott, Foresman and Company.

Jessup, Alexander, *Representative American Short Stories*, Allyn and Bacon.

Johnson, R. I., Cowan, E. M., and Peacock, M. S., *Study and Appreciation of the Short Story, with Representative Readings*, Silver, Burdett and Company.

Kipling, Rudyard, *Selected Stories*, ed. W. L. Phelps, Doubleday, Doran & Company.

Long, Ray, *Twenty Best Short Stories*, Ray Long and Richard R. Smith, Inc.

Mabie, H. W., *Stories New and Old, American and English*, Macmillan Company.

MacMinn, George R., and Eagleson, Harvey, *College Readings in the Modern Short Story*, Ginn and Company.

Matthews, Brander, *The Short Story*, American Book Company.

Merrielies, Edith, *Significant Contemporary Stories*, Doubleday, Doran & Company.

Mikels, Rosa M. R., *Short Stories for English Courses*, Charles Scribner's Sons.

My Best Story (twenty-one contemporary writers give their own favorite), Bobbs-Merrill Company.

My Story I Like Best, ed. Ray Long (Edna Ferber, Irvin Cobb, Peter B. Kyne, James Oliver Curwood, Meredith Nicholson, and H. C. Witwer select and explain their own best stories), International Magazine Company, New York.

Nettleton, G. H., *Specimens of the Short Story*, Henry Holt and Company.

O'Brien, Edward J., *The Twenty-Five Finest Short Stories*, Ray Long and Richard R. Smith, Inc.

O. Henry, *Selected Stories*, ed. C. A. Smith, Doubleday, Doran & Company.

Pence, R. W., *Short Stories of Today*, Macmillan Company.

Pendleton, M., and Wilkins, D. S., *Recent Short Stories*, D. Appleton-Century Company.

Pittenger, L. A., *A Collection of Short Stories*, Macmillan Company.

Pugh, Cynthia A., *A Book of Short Stories*, Macmillan Company.

Ramsay, R. L., *Short Stories of America*, Houghton Mifflin Company.

Robinson, Kenneth Allan, *Contemporary Short Stories*, Houghton Mifflin Company.

Royster, James F., *American Short Stories*, Scott, Foresman and Company.

Schweikert, H. C., *Short Stories*, Harcourt, Brace and Company.

Seely, H. F., and Roling, Margaret, *Recent Stories for Enjoyment*, Silver Burdett Company.

Sherman, Stuart P., *A Book of Short Stories*, Henry Holt and Company.

Smith, C. Alphonso, *Short Stories, Old and New*, Ginn and Company.

Stevenson, Robert Louis, *Selections*, ed. H. S. Canby and F. E. Pierce, Charles Scribner's Sons.

Thomas, C. S., *Modern Atlantic Stories*, Little, Brown and Company.

Trent, W. P., *Best American Tales*, Thomas Y. Crowell Company.

Waite, A. V., and Taylor, E. M., *Modern Masterpieces of Short Prose Fiction*, D. Appleton-Century Company.

Williams, Blanche Colton, ed., *Short Stories for College Classes*, D. Appleton-Century Company.

CHAPTER XXV

Description

My senses five are five great Cups
Wherefrom I drink delight!
For them to God a grace I sing
At morning and at night,
For five fair loving cups are they
That feed me with delight.
— RACHEL ANNAND TAYLOR,
"A Child of Joy"

1. What Description Is

Description is that form of writing the purpose of which is to portray a sense impression (usually a picture) or to suggest a mood. It seeks in the main to portray the outside world as it is revealed to us by means of our five senses — sight, smell, hearing, taste, and touch. During every waking moment we are receiving impressions through the eye, the nose, the ear, the tongue, and the skin; and whenever we try to tell anyone else how something looks, smells, sounds, tastes, or feels, we are describing. Description deals with places, things, scenes, persons, and animals. We can also try to depict an interesting or curious character or to portray our own moods and feelings. What we say or write under these circumstances is description too.

Description rarely extends to the length of a book or even to that of a chapter. Except for guidebooks, which are mainly exposition, and travel books, which are mainly narrative, it would be practically impossible to name a solid book of description. If there were such a book, few would ever read it. Description is at its best when it comes in little spurts and sparkles and flashes, to lend reality and vividness to stories and to plays.

The more varieties of sense impressions that can be called on, the more vivid will the description be. It is a mistake to limit description to how an object looks. Ear, nose, tongue, and touch must all be called upon to contribute their fair share. Sight is our king sense, but not our only one. Then, too, one of the greatest aids to description is to tell how the object acts or works; in other words, to describe it in motion. At first this would seem to be included in portraying how an object looks, but in reality it is not. Movement, gesture, the doing of deeds and the performing of acts, introduces a new world from that of rest, quiet, and the static description of landscape and still life.

The point is further stressed and exemplified in the section on Variety of Sense Appeals, pages 508–512 below.

2. The First Requisite: Close Observation

Talent is long patience. — GUSTAVE FLAUBERT

To repeat an important point made several times before, you can't build a brick wall without bricks or erect a stone house without stones. No more can you write an incident or a description without details. With details it is easy; without details it is impossible.

The gathering of details depends solely upon close observation, the noticing and the noting of the separate items in the unending stream of consciousness that flows in upon us every waking moment and, through our dreams, even in our sleep. Five avenues of entrance we have for receiving outside impressions: sight, hearing, touch, taste, and smell. Through each of these channels a host of stimuli come crowding in upon us day after day, week after week, and month after month, as long as we live. Upon the number and vividness of these sense impressions depend both our intenseness in living and our success in writing.

(1) LACK OF OBSERVATION

One reason why it is hard for us to give enough details in writing is that we do not observe closely enough in life. We have not trained ourselves to look carefully and steadily at things around us. Eyes we have, but they see not. For instance, there is the familiar question as to which way the figure six on the dial of a watch is turned, up or down? Or take any well-known public building that you pass frequently. How many stories, columns, and outside steps has it? If there is a monument on the town square, how accurately can you sketch it, giving its dimensions, material, design, and inscription? Has it ever fallen within your experience to take a walk in the country with a forestry expert, a botanist, a biologist, an experienced hunter, or an old woodsman? If so, you can faintly realize the thousand and one details of earth, sky, and water that most of us miss entirely as we pass from place to place and go from year to year. This is a textbook in English, not in science or psychology. We should endeavor, however, to form the habit not only of looking at things, but of really seeing what we look at. Without that ability, we can never narrate or describe successfully. With it, we can not only improve our writing but also enlarge our experience and increase our zest for living.

Listen to what Helen Keller has to say about intense observation. With two of her chief avenues closed from early childhood, — sight and hearing, — she trained and intensified the sense of touch till it became miraculously delicate and responsive. She says to us: —

I who am blind can give one hint to those who see — one admonition to those who would make full use of the gift of sight: Use your eyes as if tomorrow you would be stricken blind. And the same method can be applied to the other senses. Hear the music of voices, the song of a bird, the mighty strains of an orchestra, as if you would be stricken deaf tomorrow. Touch each object you want to touch as if tomorrow your tactile sense would fail. Smell the perfume of flowers, taste with relish each morsel, as if tomorrow you could never smell and taste again. Make the most of every sense; glory in all the facets of pleasure and beauty which the world reveals to you through the several means of contact which Nature provides. But of all the senses, I am sure that sight must be the most delightful.[1]

With Helen Keller's challenge to use our eyes as if tomorrow we would be stricken blind, compare the instructions that the great French novelist Flaubert gave his nephew, the even greater short-story writer, de Maupassant, when de Maupassant was trying to become a writer: —

. . . *Talent is long patience.* It is a question of looking at whatever one wishes to express long enough and attentively enough to discover a side

[1] "Three Days to See," from *Atlantic Monthly*, January, 1933. By permission of Famous Features Syndicate.

which no one has seen and which has been expressed by none. . . . The smallest thing has in it a grain of the unknown. Discover it. In order to describe a fire that flames or a tree in the plain, we must remain face to face with that fire or that tree until for us they no longer resemble any other tree or any other fire. This is the way to become original.

. . . When you pass a grocer seated in his doorway, a concierge smoking his pipe, a row of cabs, show me this grocer and this concierge, their attitude, all their physical appearance; suggest by the skill of your image all their moral nature, so that I shall not confound them with any other grocer or any other concierge; make me see, by a single word, wherein a cab horse differs from the fifty others that follow or precede him.

This advice of Flaubert's is high and hard, but, as he told de Maupassant, it is the way to become original. It is the way that all the masters of description have followed. It is the way to attain the highest success.

Along with close, patient, and accurate observation goes the importance of recording in our notes or in our memory what we have seen. Both the painter and the sculptor work directly from models, with eyes fixed on what they are trying to reproduce. Otherwise they would be lost. The writer, however, in describing either a scene or a person, unless he has taken notes, is working from memory alone, and only highly trained memories can call up details distinctly. The mental pictures of most of us resemble an old photograph, or even a photographic negative, which has darkened and faded with time, and is more like a blur than a likeness.

THE ROUND TABLE

1. From memory make a list of descriptive details of a familiar building, monument, or your own front or back yard. Then compare the list with the actual scene itself.

2. From memory make a list of what can be seen from your bedroom window. Then look out of the window to see how complete and accurate the list is.

3. Offhand try to tell how your pet dog or pet cat or horse differs from all other dogs, cats, or horses. Then study the animal to see what additional differences you can discover.

4. With a friend walk slowly by a crowded store window and observe its contents. Make lists and compare them (a) with each other and (b) with the window itself.

5. Devote a recitation period, or a special night meeting of the class, to an Observation Game of the Five Senses. Try several or all of them.

(1) Sight

Prepare a table with a number of miscellaneous objects laid out upon it, such as several kinds of knives, pieces of different-colored chalk, several different fountain pens, a bunch of keys, a small notebook, a large notebook, several small dolls, several china figurines, a top, marbles, fishing line, several kinds of fruits and flowers, doll dishes, pocketbooks, a bottle of ink, and so forth.

Let the class in sections walk slowly around the table once, and then list from memory what was on it. Compare the lists with each other and with the official list.

(2) Smell

Arrange containers all alike, such as small glasses or butter plates. Upon them put a number of familiar objects with a distinctive odor. One set might be these: a slice of banana; kitchen soap; a slice of lemon; a geranium leaf; a spoonful of lard; a spoonful of Listerine; clover (or grass); leather; a flower; turpentine; rubbing alcohol; tobacco; tea; coffee; a mothball.

Blindfold all but two of the class, and let these two, one carrying the containers and the other a scoring pad, go down the line recording the answers after each person has taken a smell.

(3) Touch, (4) Taste, and (5) Hearing

These tests are made after the same fashion as that of smell.

Getting up the "exhibits" will entail some trouble, but if a different committee is appointed from the class to prepare and administer each test, the work will be divided up fairly, each committee will be interested in making a good showing, and no little interest and entertainment will result.

6. It is a matter of common knowledge that eyewitnesses who are honestly trying to tell the truth will give utterly unlike accounts of the same accident or incident. As an instance, try this experiment. Let the instructor select someone outside the class to pay it an unexpected visit. Let him be dressed in some unusual or outlandish costume and wear a false face. Let him carry certain objects such as a clock and a walking stick, or a sofa cushion and an umbrella, or a small baseball bat and a bunch of flowers. Let him walk around the room and speak two unrelated sentences such as "Caesar conquered Gaul, but time and tide wait for no man," or "The weather has been unusually rainy thus far this year; however, the British navy is still sailing the seven seas." Let him do certain definite things with the objects he is carrying, when he gets to the table or desk in the front of the room. If desired, the instructor can remonstrate with him, and seem to try to persuade him to leave the room. (Of course, if this experiment is tried, it need not follow exactly these directions.)

Then, either toward the end of the period, or the next day, ask the class to write out a full and accurate account of exactly what happened, including a full description of the visitor.

Compare versions in class, and have the visitor describe his costume and tell what he did and said.

With the results of the experiment suggested in number 6, compare what is said of the unreliability of human evidence, pages 287–291.

3. Details in Description

The preceding section on Close Observation points directly to the paramount importance of details. All that description is, in the last analysis, is the grouping of a few — or many — specific details in order to arouse an image or to suggest an impression.

Recall the constant emphasis that has been put upon details throughout this book. Glance again at pages 6–8 dealing with "An Untidy Room" and "An Unsuccessful Night Hunt," pages 8–10. Everything that has been said in all of these passages applies with peculiar force to description. Let us paraphrase one of the opening statements of this book, which by this time should be entirely familiar, and make it read, "Three fourths of describing consists in giving definite details. The other fourth doesn't matter."

When you have a descriptive paragraph to write, or a descriptive passage in a story, try some such plan as this in order to gather the material — that is, the necessary details. **Settle, first, on the exact moment or circumstances under which you are viewing the scene or object you are describing.** This may concern the time of day, as early morning, noon, twilight, or night; it may be the season of the year, as winter, summer, spring, or autumn; or it may be a particular moment in an important incident or accident. Whatever it is, fix it definitely in your mind. **Determine, secondly, the prevailing mood or impression you wish to arouse,** whether of confusion, peacefulness, alarm, beauty, ugliness, decay, pleasure, danger, heat, or cold. **Thirdly, list all the details you can think of,** using as many of the five senses as possible, with particular reference to movement and action.

1. VARIETY OF SENSE APPEAL

To insure thoroughness at first and to gain practice, use some such diagram as the following, which can be conveniently drawn on regular theme paper by turning the sheet lengthwise and writing along the red margin line.

1. *Subject:* ____   2. *Time:* ____   3. *Mood or Impression:* ____

Sight	Hearing	Smell	Taste	Touch	Movement

As illustrations of the relation between the separate details and the description itself, take the following analysis of two descriptive paragraphs.

I

A. The Material (Details) of the Picture

1. Subject: Westminster Abbey   2. Time: Twilight
3. Mood or Impression: Increasing darkness and gloom

Sight	*Sound*
Last beams of sun streaming through high, colored windows.	Distant footfall of a verger has a dreary sound.
Lower parts of Abbey in obscurity.	On leaving, the door jars shut and fills the building with echoes.
Chapels and aisles getting darker.	
Statues of kings and figures on the monuments fading uncertainly.	
Evening breeze cold as from a grave.	

B. The Picture

TWILIGHT IN WESTMINSTER ABBEY

WASHINGTON IRVING

The last beams of day were now faintly streaming through the painted windows in the high vaults above me; the lower parts of the Abbey were already wrapped in the obscurity of twilight.   The chapels and aisles grew darker and darker.   The effigies of the kings faded into shadows; the marble figures of the monuments assumed strange shapes in the uncertain light; the evening breeze crept through the aisles like the cold breath of the grave; and even the distant footfall of a verger, traversing the Poets'

Corner, had something strange and dreary in its sound. I slowly retraced my morning's walk, and as I passed out at the portal of the cloisters, the door, closing with a jarring noise behind me, filled the whole building with echoes.

II

A. The Material (Details) of the Picture

1. Subject: A compound yard in India   2. Time: Afternoon
3. Mood or Impression: Silence, seclusion, and tranquillity

Sight	*Sound* (here, absence of sound)
Inn cow poking about.	Country seclusion emphasized.
Dog asleep stretched out in the sun.	Place tranquil and restful.
Servants in white coming and going.	Crows not there.
Elephant rocking in shade of a large tree, begging with trunk and playing with brown children.	Servants barefooted and making no sound.
Camels here and there.	Camels on padded feet and fitting in with the silence and serenity.

B. The Picture

THE COMPOUND YARD IN JEYPORE, RAJPUTNA, INDIA [1]

MARK TWAIN

The inn cow poked about the compound and emphasized the secluded and country air of the place, and there was a dog of no particular breed, who was always present in the compound, and always asleep, always stretched out baking in the sun and adding to the deep tranquillity and reposefulness of the place, when the crows were away on business. White-draperied servants were coming and going all the time, but they seemed only spirits, for their feet were bare and made no sound. Down the lane a piece lived an elephant in the shade of a noble tree, and rocked and rocked, and reached about with his trunk, begging of his brown mistress or fumbling the children playing at his feet. And there were camels about, but they go on velvet feet, and were proper to the silence and serenity of the surroundings.

Turning to our own writing, suppose we have to write a description of a city cafeteria at lunch time. Using the suggested form of analysis, we might get some such results as the following: —

[1] By permission of the publishers, Harper and Brothers.

(1) DETAILS FOR DESCRIPTION

1. Subject: A city cafeteria   2. Time: The noon rush hour
3. Mood or Impression: Hurry, bustle, confusion

Sight	*Sound*	*Smell*	*Movement*
A number of white-topped tables, some seating two, others seating four.	Noise of chairs being pushed back on floor.	The heavy moist odor of food and crowded humanity as one first enters the door.	Assistants hurrying to and fro among the tables balancing heavy trays on their hands.
Most of the seats occupied by busy men, women, and children, eating, facing various ways.	Rattle of china and of knives and forks on the hard-topped tables.	Then specialized smells of cabbage, string beans, boiled beets, vegetable soup, fried beefsteak, cigarette smoke, coffee, as one passes down the line near the tables and past the food counter.	Other assistants clearing off dishes and wiping tables for waiting customers.
Walls colored a light green with an interlaced border of darker green outlined in pink.	An occasional louder crash as an assistant stacks dishes hurriedly in large piles in clearing the table.		Those who have finished leisurely gathering their hats and wraps and strolling toward the door.
The male assistants clothed in white.	The buzz and murmur of conversation from all over the room.		A long row of waiting diners standing in line.
The serving girls clothed in green trimmed with pink.	The whir of the cash register and the sharp ting of the bell as the cashier rings up a sale and makes change.	A whiff of whiskey on one man's breath.	Another line slowly pushing their trays along the white metal rails, pausing at the counters to get soup, meat, bread, salad, a drink, and a dessert.
Steam rising from the meat counter and the huge polished coffee urn.	The click of the ice-water cooler as the glasses are filled.	An odor of cheap violet cologne on a heavily rouged girl.	
The evident embarrassment of a big sister aged fourteen over little brother's loud talking and acrobatic stunts on the heavy steel rail along the serving counter.	A child's shrill voice protesting at being made to leave the sugar dish alone and finish his spinach.		Fumbling for change in purse or pocket to pay the cashier.
The smiles and side glances of the serving girls at the good-looking young men in line.	The crash of a feeble old man's half-filled tray as he pushes it uncertainly along the rails and tilts it over the edge.		Then following the assistants with the trays, looking anxiously all over the room for a vacant table.
These glances returned with interest by the fat middle-aged men who want extra large helpings or choice portions.	The consequent titter of some of the diners.		A small boy running back and forth to refill water glasses for his table.
The disapproval of the obviously efficient businesswoman whose usual twenty-five-cent luncheon creates no interest on the part of the cashier.	The loud objection of the small boy whose sister made him stop playing on the steel rail.		A little girl with an air of great importance exchanging a special order slip for a dish of chocolate ice cream.
Fussy old woman who can't decide what she wants — chooses fish — rejects it in favor of chicken pie — serving girl looks very bored as the old lady finally decides she'll have soup instead of a meat.			

Here then, in list form, is the material (details) for a description of a cafeteria during the rush hour.   In writing out the description it will not be necessary to use all the details, but only the most suggestive ones, particularly those that contribute to the special mood, impression, or purpose of the writer. If, for example, you do not object to cafeterias, but rather like their democratic air, choosing your own dishes, and the absence of tipping, your choice and grouping of details would be entirely different from that of a person who frankly dislikes cafeterias and prefers a quiet café or tea shop. And whether you are describing the cafeteria in a complimentary or an uncomplimentary mood, the details will not be separated according to the different senses, as in the analysis, but will be given in the order in which they most naturally came to us. We do not first see and then hear and then smell, but frequently do all three at the same time. Which of the three impressions we shall present first — whether of eye or ear or nose — will depend upon which impression seemed strongest at the time and which we want our reader to realize first. The chief value of this exercise is that it insures an abundant supply of eye-ear-nose-touch-and-motion details, which can be selected and grouped as needed.

Closer to the actual process of writing is the way the following details of a storm in the country are listed — that is, not according to the different senses but according to the time order in which they were perceived.

(2) MORE DETAILS FOR DESCRIPTION [1]

A STORM IN THE COUNTRY

1. Simpson's farm. Hot afternoon; corn droops. (Make it very hot.)
2. Old mule asleep. He stands with his weight on three legs; a straw sticks from his mouth; his lower lip wiggles as if he had something to say, but couldn't remember what it was.
3. Thunderheads on horizon; then darker, nearer.
4. Storm about to break. Wind in trees, windmill clanks wildly; horses race along pasture fence; air cool; farmer's wife rushes to drive a brood of little chicks under shelter; shutters drawn; thunder and lightning.
5. Rain pours. Big drops first, then sheets. Old mule still asleep.
6. Attitudes of animals. Chickens under corncrib, rooster on one leg. On porch, cat curled up in a ball, disgusted; dog licking his paws.

---

[1] *Ideas for Narration*, Bulletin of the Illinois Association of Teachers of English, 1929.

7. Cow in barnyard, pleasantly chewing cud, eyes half closed; water runs off her in little rivers.
8. Pigs in pen. Ducks active.
9. Frogs start a chorus; sound of rain on shingles. Old mule all this while asleep.
10. Comedy: Little girls rush up — have been on picnic — soaked.
11. Chattering crowd of kids on porch. Scrape off mud. What's the use?
12. Tragedy: Little girls take out wet lunch; try to eat it.
13. Charity: Farmer's wife helps out.
14. Merry sound of talk and laughter louder than beat of rain.
15. Appearance of flooded road and field.
16. Heroism: Farmer, with boots and rubber coat, goes out to rescue a drowning hen.
17. Storm slackens; birds in eaves begin to tune up.
18. Little girls depart with thanks and more chattering.
19. One little girl stuck in mud. Rest all shriek and laugh.
20. Sunshine. Old mule suddenly wakes up, shakes one ear, and looks surprised.

SPECIMENS OF DESCRIPTION

Following are six examples of good description, three by students and three by trained authors. Read them critically, paying close heed to (1) the number and grouping of the details, (2) the sense or senses appealed to, and (3) the writer's prevailing mood or the impression the description is intended to make on the reader.

Student Descriptions

(1) DETAILS OF SIGHT AND SOUND

A RIDE THROUGH THE COUNTRY IN HORSE-AND-BUGGY DAYS

RUTH DYER

(University of Arkansas)

Sometimes the road grew rough and rocky, and the horses would slow down to a careful walk. Little hills were common, and we often drove through shady woods where ferns grew among mossy rocks and grapevines fell in tangled masses from the tree-tops. Birds flew about everywhere, spilling their songs like sunshine through the branches overhead. We found swift little brooks in which the water splashed cheerily over the rocks, and occasionally father drove into the middle of a wider stream and stopped to let the horses drink. Never shall I forget the clear chug-chug of their feet as they slowly pulled out upon the bank to start afresh. The road led between tree-covered hills to fields beyond where men plowed corn; children followed with hoes; and at the end of a freshly turned furrow a dog wallowed in the earth and stuck out its pink tongue to cool.

(2) DETAILS OF SIGHT, SOUND, AND SMELL
DAYBREAK ON A SLOOP AT ANCHOR

DORIS VIVIAN

(University of New Hampshire)

. . . The dull, gray, breathless stillness that comes just before the world awakes, covered the sloop and sea like a soft enveloping blanket. Each tiny sound was magnified; the creaking and rubbing of the ropes, the *pap-pat* of sneaker-clad feet on the deck, the bump and scrape of the tender riding alongside, the rasping protest of the anchor chain as the long ground swell lifted and dropped the bow with almost clocklike regularity. Below decks, the muffled clink of silver, the peculiar *thuck* of coffee mugs on a linoleum-covered table, the smell of fresh, steaming coffee, sizzling mackerel, and smoking johnnybread mingled and drifted tantalizingly up to the watch on deck. Through the open hatch the yellow light of a lantern made a square of living gold in the dull, gray dawn. Eight bells chimed out softly from the ship's clock, the watch stretched, and dropped swiftly down the companionway. The clink of silver and the *thuck* of coffee mugs became more audible. . . .

(3) DETAILS OF SIGHT, SOUND, AND MOTION
SKIPPY

DALLAS ACHENBACK

(University of Illinois)

Half of a graham cracker is balanced on the edge of the window sill, likely to topple over onto the slanting porch roof. On the limb of an adjacent maple, with his hind claws pricking the rough bark, his gray, plump body and expanded tail in rhythm with the soft motion of the branches, sits Skippy, sawing through a walnut. The inquiring eyes lift; they jerk toward the porch roof and then to the window sill. The nut bangs on the porch roof and thuds to the ground. Skippy makes a hurried head-first descent to the roof with a four-point landing. Here his bravado deserts him. Nostrils quiver and eyes blink in indecision. He sits down on his haunches, forepaws suspended, and makes a jerky survey of the roof. Courage returns with a forward scratch of nails over the shingles toward the cracker. The white curtain in the window flutters, but Skippy does not wait to investigate. A blur shoots through the air like the swoop of a bat and disappears on the other side of the maple. A sleek, protruding head peers through the forks. Temptation overcomes fear. With an occasional spasmodic retreat the would-be thief slinks toward the window sill. Reaching the window, he stretches out his neck in an attitude of careful watchfulness and stands petrified. His furry body jerks fitfully, but, instead of scurrying away, he bounces to the window sill. Sharp needle teeth snatch the cracker. Gray bounds across the roof onto the tree; gray streaks up a slender limb. Bits of crumbs sprinkle the ground beneath.

Author Descriptions

(4) DETAILS OF SMELL

REMEMBERED ODORS [1]

THOMAS WOLFE

Yes, and the smell of hot daisy-fields in the morning; of melted puddling-iron in a foundry; the winter smell of horse-warm stables; of old oak and walnut; and the butcher's smell of meat, of strong slaughtered lamb, and of brown sugar melted with slivered bitter chocolate; and of crushed mint leaves, and of a wet lilac bush; of magnolia beneath the heavy moon, of dogwood and laurel; of an old caked pipe and Bourbon rye, aged in kegs of charred oak; the sharp smell of tobacco; of carbolic and nitric acids; the coarse true smell of a dog; of old imprisoned books, and the cool fern-smell near springs; of vanilla in cake-dough; and of cloven ponderous cheeses.

(5) DETAILS OF MOVEMENT, SIGHT, AND SOUND

THE LITTLE SCHOONER "WE'RE HERE" AT SEA

RUDYARD KIPLING

The low-sided schooner was naturally on most intimate terms with her surroundings. They saw little of the horizon save when she topped a swell; and usually she was elbowing, fidgeting, and coaxing her steadfast way, through gray-blue or black hollows laced across and across with streaks of shivering foam; or rubbing herself caressingly along the flank of some bigger water-hill. . . . Harvey began to comprehend and enjoy the dry

---

[1] *Look Homeward, Angel*, Charles Scribner's Sons. By permission of the publishers.

chorus of wave-tops turning over with a sound of incessant tearing; the hurry of the winds working across open spaces and herding the purple-blue cloud shadows; the splendid upheaval of the red sunrise; the folding and packing away of the morning mists, wall after wall withdrawn across the white floors; the salty glare and blaze of noon; the kiss of rain falling over thousands of dead, flat square miles; the chilly blackening of everything at the day's end; and the million wrinkles of the sea under moonlight, when the jib-boom solemnly poked at the low stars, and Harvey went down to get a doughnut from the cook.[1]

(6) DETAILS OF SIGHT, SOUND, SMELL, TASTE, FEEL

CHILDHOOD MEMORIES [2]

MARK TWAIN

I can call back the solemn twilight and mystery of the deep woods, the earthy smells, the faint odors of the wild flowers, the sheen of rain-washed foliage, the rattling clatter of drops when the wind shook the trees, the far-off hammering of woodpeckers and the muffled drumming of wood pheasants in the remoteness of the forest, the snapshot glimpses of disturbed wild creatures scurrying through the grass — I can call it all back and make it as real as it ever was and as blessed. I can call back the prairie, and its loneliness and peace, and a vast hawk hanging motionless in the sky, with his wings spread wide and the blue of the vault showing through the fringe of their end feathers. I can see the woods in their autumn dress, the oaks purple, the hickories washed with gold, the maples and the sumachs luminous with crimson fires, and I can hear the rustle made by the fallen leaves as we plowed through them. I can see the blue clusters of wild grapes hanging among the foliage of the saplings, and I remember the taste of them and the smell. I know how the wild blackberries looked, and how they tasted, and . . . the pawpaws, the hazelnuts, and the persimmons; and I can feel the thumping rain, upon my head, of hickory nuts and walnuts when we were out in the frosty dawn to scramble for them with the pigs.

THE ROUND TABLE

1. Using the details of the cafeteria scene given on page 511, and adding or substituting others of your own if you wish, write a descriptive paragraph either in class or on assignment as the instructor directs. Ask the instructor to read aloud several of the best paragraphs to show what different results can be obtained from the same material.

---

[1] From *Captains Courageous*, by Rudyard Kipling. Copyright 1896, 1897, 1925. Reprinted by permission of Doubleday, Doran and Company, Inc.
[2] From Mark Twain's *Autobiography*, Harper and Brothers. By permission of the publishers.

2. Suggest in class other subjects rich in sense impressions, and from them or from the subjects given below (a) choose one and analyze it according to the diagram on page 509, giving as many definite details under each sense as you can; (b) take another subject in class and, with the instructor at the board, work together, suggesting all possible details.

Suggested Subjects

An Early Morning Walk in the Woods (City)
A Noon Walk in the Woods (City)
A Late Afternoon Walk in the Woods (City)
The Railroad Station Just before the Train Comes In
The Railroad Station Just after the Train Has Left
A City (or Town) Street on Saturday Afternoon
A City (or Town) Street on Sunday Afternoon
Running from an Unexpected Shower
The Big Parade Passes
A Fashionable Church Wedding
The Grandstand Just before the Kickoff
The Grandstand between Halves
A Classroom Just before the Bell Rings
A Classroom Just after the Bell Rings

3. Without using the diagram given on page 509, but jotting down the details as they occur to you without reference to whether they come through the eye, ear, nose, and so forth, list all the sense impressions (details) you can think of in connection with one of the subjects given below, pages 534–536. (a) Analyze one subject individually and (b), with the instructor at the board, let the class analyze another subject.

4. (a) Which of the three student descriptions and (b) which of the three author descriptions quoted on pages 513–516 seems most vivid to you? Try to explain why.

5. (a) Following the method of Thomas Wolfe's "Remembered Odors," page 515, write a short paragraph detailing the odors that you can call to mind most vividly. (b) Follow the same method with a paragraph of taste details. (c) Follow the same method with a paragraph of touch details or "feels," both pleasant and unpleasant.

6. After the model of Mark Twain's "Childhood Memories," page 516, recount your most vivid childhood impressions and recollections. Go into minute detail, and appeal to as many senses as possible.

4. The Suggestive Power of the Single Detail

Long descriptions are hard to write and tiresome to read. Not without reason will you occasionally find a public library book with the penciled comment on the flyleaf: "No good. Too much description." The way recent writers manage description differs from the way of the older writers. A present-day story may contain as much description as one written fifty years ago; but the description, instead of being given solidly all at once at the beginning of the story, is distributed bit by bit throughout the narrative. In this way the reader gets as definite an impression of the scenes and the characters as formerly, but he gets it gradually, and is rarely confronted with more than two or three descriptive sentences at one time. Instead, therefore, of writing your description in one solid block, break it up into bits and distribute it throughout the story.

Often, too, the writer tries to make his impression not by giving a number of details, but by selecting only one or two and expressing them as suggestively and vividly as possible. Run through also the striking descriptive similes quoted on pages 407 and 408 and the single, striking details in characterization, pages 470–471. If you thus rely on a single detail, naturally the detail must be chosen carefully and phrased strikingly. Here are some good examples: —

The cat poured itself through the fence. — ANNE PARRISH

The velvet hum of bees. — H. G. WELLS

Puddles puckered with raindrops. — BEVERLEY NICHOLS

Her voice stamped its foot just a little. — *Cosmopolitan Magazine*

He received the news with his eyebrows. — JOHN GALSWORTHY

The softness of a kitten's feet — like raspberries held in the hand.
— ANNE DOUGLAS SEDGWICK

He stands at bay with his little red eyes sizzling and his great fore-trotters extended, tusks down and spine up.
— HENRY MORTON ROBINSON, "The Wild Boar"

Breezes honed on icebergs. — *Reader's Digest*

The day was fine, but not convincingly fine. A long line of woolly yet possibly wicked little clouds were putting their heads together.
— P. G. WODEHOUSE

The tails of little birds trying to roost were blown inside out like umbrellas. — THOMAS HARDY

It was the kind of day October loves to serve, soft and warm in the middle but crisp about the edges. — MARY BADGER

Henrietta threw down the suet. It landed with a thump on the paper. Sammie drew back startled and outraged, but under encouragement consented to sniff at it with his pink nose. Then, giving his white-mittened paw one delicate utterly decisive shake, he turned his back and walked away. It described the suet perfectly.

— RUTH SUCKOW, "Spinster and Cat" [1]

BROTHER AND SISTER [2]

WILLIS BALLANCE

One brother was undeniably elephantine; when he walked he rippled, and I had the impression that should he sit down suddenly, he'd splash. He had a good-looking daughter, but she gazed at me in a calm and detached manner as if I were a train she didn't have to catch.

COUPLE [2]

BETTY BETZ

Susie was a minister's daughter with wild red hair and a dead fish expression. Harry was just a smile between two ears; he wore old football jerseys to school.

THE ROUND TABLE

1. Try to phrase several unusually vivid details of some scene or action or character like those quoted above. Ask the instructor to read aloud some of the best in class.

5. Mood or Impression in Description

There are two factors that fix the character of any piece of description. Obviously the first is the kind of person or scene described, and the second is the mood of the writer and the impression he wishes to convey to the reader. As to the scene itself, there is almost as much personality in places as there is in people. A scene is prevailingly

---

[1] *Harper's Magazine*, June, 1928.
[2] From *Green Caldron*.

beautiful, ugly, quiet, noisy, squalid, heated, cool, confusing, restful, attractive, or unattractive. This definiteness of impression that a scene makes is sometimes called "dominant tone." It is what Stevenson had in mind when he said: "There is a fitness in events and places. . . . Some places speak distinctly. Certain dank gardens cry aloud for a murder; certain old houses demand to be haunted; certain coasts are set apart for shipwreck." Consider, for example, the difference between the block of handsomest residences in your town

Courtesy of Collier's Weekly and Charles Dana Gibson

TWO STRIKES AND THE BASES FULL

and the row of tumbledown shacks in a back alley or lining the railroad tracks. Or compare the prettiest woodland pool you know of with an old pond in a deserted brickyard or a mud puddle in an automobile graveyard. In the words of Sir Thomas Browne, "The difference is very great and very strange."

The nature of the scene itself, therefore, is obviously one of the determining factors in description. More important than this, however, is the mood of the person viewing it. Our feelings are like bits of colored glass through which everything we see is transformed. Look

through a piece of red glass, and everything appears rosy. Change
the glass to blue or green or yellow or black, and the landscape changes
with it. When we feel well and happy, every person and thing we
see seems pleasant and likable. But if we are tired or disappointed
or grieving or angry, we look out upon a different world. A touch of
flu or malaria will make any future look dark, and an attack of pto-
maine poisoning will for several days cause any life to seem a failure.
As Scrooge says to Marley's ghost in Dickens's *Christmas Carol,*
"There's more of gravy than of grave about you."

Courtesy of Collier's Weekly and Charles Dana Gibson

FANNED OUT

Much of the description in a story is thus colored by the moods and
the emotions of the characters. The practical point in this connection is the need of giving not all the possible details of the scene but
only those which match the mood and will hence produce a similar
impression on the reader.

If you will glance again at the descriptions of "Twilight in Westminster Abbey," pages 509–510, and "The Compound Yard in India,"
page 510, you will find that both are alike in this particular: they do
not try to give a complete, general description of the respective scenes,
but a special kind of description resulting from a particular mood in
the writer and designed to produce a particular impression on the

reader. In the first, Washington Irving is not so much concerned with Westminster Abbey as with the increasing gloom, both physical and mental, of the twilight moment; in the second, Mark Twain is interested mainly in producing an impression of sleepy silence and restfulness. In each case the writer selects only those details that will suggest the desired mood and make the desired impression, and omits all others. In the picture of Westminster Abbey, for instance, the setting sun is spoken of as throwing its beams through the colored windows. There was probably reflected, therefore, somewhere in the interior a bright cheerful spot of yellow or blue or red light. Irving does not mention it because it does not accord with the prevailing mood of his description. Similarly, in the Indian Compound Yard picture, one of the little brown children must have tumbled down sometime or quarreled with a little brown sister or brother and therefore let out a howl, but if so Mark Twain does not record it, for it would have disturbed the impression of peace and serenity he was striving to convey.

This is the method of all descriptions that proceed by mood and impression. The writer is highly selective: he gives only those details that chime in with his mood and that minister to his impression, and he rejects all others. It is conceivable, for instance, that a description of a town by a person who likes and admires it would not have a single detail in common with a description by someone who dislikes and scorns it. Similarly, an enemy and a friend would describe the same person in entirely different terms.

Read the following descriptions with special regard to their mood. Notice that the details match one another perfectly and are so grouped as to produce one definite impression. The conflicting details in each picture that are omitted are almost as significant as the details that are presented.

(1) STUDENT DESCRIPTIONS BY MOODS

1. To Walk Like a Cat

(English A, Harvard University)

Have you ever seen a cat walk? Treading daintily with an easy grace, running fast with a long bounding lope, or, when it's wet, tasting the pavement with her soft, pink-padded feet as she picks her way. A cat never walks carelessly; she has eyes and ears in her paws and she walks to a kind of soft jazz, a fox-trot or a waltz or a tango, all in perfect time and rhythm, always in absolute harmony with her environment.

2. Parlor [1]

FREDERICK G. FAUST

Aunt Emma lived in a high square house in town with shutters for summer heat and storms. There was a parlor where little boys were not allowed, and chairs remained in fixed places, and Great-grandfather glared with righteous indignation from his picture on the wall. There were crystal candlesticks on the mantel. Aunt Emma's hand-painted wooden shovel and wicker easel stood in the corner.

3. "Ole Man" Poor [1]

DOROTHY DEAL

He moved onto the poorest farm in the neighborhood, his sorry horses breasting the keen March wind with stolid pertinacity and dragging the clumsy wagon heavily through the deep-cut ruts that sucked with hungry mouths at the worn steel rims of its wheels. The crate of dispirited fowls on the top of the swaying load of household goods seemed ready to cascade to the ground at any moment. On the wagon seat, huddled together in their drab wraps, were a small woman and several little children; as the wagon jolted onward, they were jerked passively with its motion. A figure bowed against the fury of the wind and awkward in a shabby sheepskin jacket, "Ole Man" Poor trudged stubbornly by his team, clucking sympathetically to them.

A year later the same team pulled the same load down the same road in the opposite direction. "Ole Man" Poor was moving out. This time there was one more on the high wagon seat, for the frail woman held a small bundle close to her old brown coat with hands that were encased in too large shucking gloves. The wagon wheels whined complainingly, and I looked up from an ice-coated pump to see the burdened wagon with its owner at its side out-

[1] From *Green Caldron*.

lined in a red-gold halo against a cold sunset. Involuntarily my eyes followed the plodding man and the plodding horses until all I could see was a large black object in the distance with a small black object persistently beside it. "Ole Man" Poor was running, with dust in his eyes, trying to catch up with life.

4. WINTER, 1935

RICHARD FLEBBE

(State Teachers College of Nebraska)

Straggling bunches of stock are digging cornstalks from under the snow. The hay crop burned in the drouth of last summer and every spear of edible grass has long since gone from the pastures. Two underfed calves with dirty, ragged hides are trying to obtain milk from starving mothers. When they move one sees that their ears and tails have been frozen off and that they cannot possibly live through the next cold spell. The cows wander aimlessly, pausing occasionally to lip up a stray bit of forage. A bony old horse, his shaggy coat covered with filth, noses his mate, who is down in the snow. He will never rise; he has done his last work. A summer of exhausting labor followed by a winter of starvation and cold have finished him. Tonight he will die and in two or three days only a pile of bones surrounded by a circle of snow packed by the feet of coyotes will remain. It is with relief that one enters the limits of the town, where only the people are hungry.

(2) AUTHOR DESCRIPTIONS BY MOODS

1. THE EAST [1]

JOSEPH CONRAD

And this is how I see the East. I have seen its secret places and have looked into its very soul; but now I see it always from a small boat, a high outline of mountains, blue and afar in the morning; like faint mist at noon; a jagged wall of purple at sunset. I have the feel of the oar in my hand, the vision of the scorching blue sea in my eyes. And I see a bay, a wide bay, smooth as glass and polished like ice, shimmering in the dark. A red light burns far off upon the gloom of the land, and the night is soft and warm. We drag at the oars with aching arms, and suddenly a puff of wind, a puff faint and tepid and laden with strange odors of blossoms, of aromatic wood, comes out of the still night — the first sigh of the East on my face. That I can never forget. It was impalpable and enslaving, like a charm, like a whispered promise of mysterious delight.

[1] By permission of Doubleday, Doran and Company.

2. ALL GOLD CAÑON [1]

JACK LONDON

It was the green heart of the cañon, where the walls swerved back from
the rigid plain and relieved their harshness of line by making a little sheltered nook and filling it to the brim with sweetness and roundness and
softness. Here all things rested. Even the narrow stream ceased its
turbulent downrush long enough to form a quiet pool. Knee-deep in the
water, with drooping head and half-shut eyes, drowsed a red-coated, many-
antlered buck.

3. A YOUNG MOUNTAINEER IN PRISON [2]

F. HOPKINSON SMITH

There was no question about his strength. As he stood in the glare of
the overhead light I could trace the muscles through his rough homespun
— for he was a mountaineer, pure and simple, and not a city-bred thief
in ready-made clothes. I saw that the bulging muscles of his calves had
driven the wrinkles of his butternut trousers close up under the knee joint,
and that those of his thighs had rounded out the coarse cloth from the knee
to the hip. The spread of his shoulders had performed a like service for
his shirt, which was stretched out of shape over the chest and back. This
was crossed by but one suspender, and was open at the throat — a tree-
trunk of a throat, with all the cords supporting the head firmly planted in
the shoulders. The arms were long and had the curved movement of the
tentacles of a devilfish. The hands were big and bony, the fingers knotted
together with knuckles of iron. He wore no collar nor any coat; nor did
he bring one with him, so the Warden said.

4. STOP! GO! [3]

JOHN DOS PASSOS

Red light. Bell.
A block deep, four ranks of cars wait at the grade crossing, fenders in
taillights, mudguards scraping mudguards, motors purring hot, exhausts
reeking, cars from Babylon and Jamaica, cars from Montauk, Port Jefferson, Patchogue, limousines from Long Beach, Far Rockaway, roadsters

[1] Opening paragraph of "All Gold Cañon." By permission of Mrs. Eliza
London Shepard.
[2] "Bud Tilden, Mail Thief," from *The Under Dog*, Charles Scribner's Sons.
By permission of the publishers.
[3] *Manhattan Transfer*, Harcourt, Brace and Company. By permission of the
author and the publishers.

from Great Neck . . . cars full of asters and wet bathing suits, sun-singed necks, mouths sticky from sodas and hotdawgs . . . cars dusted with pollen of ragweed and goldenrod.

Green light.   Motors race, gears screech into first.   The cars space out, flow in a long ribbon along the ghostly cement road, between black-windowed blocks of concrete factories, between bright slabbed colors of signboards towards the glow over the city that stands up incredibly into the night sky like the glow of a great lit tent, like the yellow tall bulk of a tent show.

5. THE LANDLADY'S DAUGHTER

OLIVER WENDELL HOLMES

Tender-eyed blonde.   Long ringlets.   Cameo pin.   Gold pencil-case on a chain. Locket. Bracelet. Album. Autograph book. Accordion. Reads Byron, Tupper, and Sylvanus Cobb, Junior, while her mother makes the puddings.   Says "Yes?" when you tell her anything.

THE ROUND TABLE

1. Is there any house, street, or scene in your community or county that seems to have a marked personality or "dominant tone"? If so, name it and describe its effect in a single sentence.

2. Can you give an example from your own experience when your own mood colored or influenced strongly your feeling toward a particular place or person?

3. Try to put into a single sentence the mood (or impression) of the descriptive paragraphs quoted on pages 523–526.

4. Following the method of John Dos Passos in "Stop! Go!", above, describe two contrasting pictures of the same scene, as Before and After, Night and Morning, Summer and Winter, etc.

5. Following the method of Oliver Wendell Holmes in "The Landlady's Daughter," above, give a thumbnail sketch of some person or type you know.

6. In a few sentences describe the following: —

   (1) A baby as seen by (a) its mother, (b) a bachelor friend of the family, and (c) a nervous old man who lives in the flat above.

   (2) An automobile as it seems to (a) the man who owns it, (b) a man who drives a much finer car, and (c) a man too poor to afford a car.

   (3) A football game as seen by (a) a younger brother of one of the players and (b) a trustee opposed to football.

   (4) A dinner table as seen by (a) a hungry boy and (b) a dyspeptic old man.

(5) A student theme as seen by
  (a) the student who wrote it,   (c) the class, and
  (b) his instructor,   (d) the writer's mother.

7. Write a descriptive paragraph for a letter about the college campus by (a) one who likes it and (b) one who dislikes it.

8. Describe some acquaintance as if you (a) liked him very much and (b) disliked him extremely.

9. Describe some person in two of the following moods, letting him (her) reveal himself (herself) by what he (she) does or says: —

  (1) Blue   (4) Stubborn   (6) Vexed
  (2) Merry   (5) Exhausted   (7) Disgusted
  (3) Quarrelsome

10. Describe a scene trying to convey an impression of heat, cold, restfulness, confusion, fear, horror, nervousness, untidiness, desolation, or haste. Open with a topic sentence something like one of these: —

  It was a terrifically hot day.
  It was the coldest day of winter.
  The scene was extremely restful.

Then read the paragraph aloud, omitting the topic sentence, and see whether your choice and grouping of details convey the desired impression to the class.

11. A student gets a letter or note at school. Describe what he does or says or how he looks so that we can tell whether he is pleased, grieved, angered, surprised, annoyed, delighted, or puzzled.

12. Write a descriptive paragraph on one of the following: —

   (1) Rain! Rain! Rain!
   (2) I Hate the Place
   (3) Description of My Room for My Mother
   (4) Description of My Room for My Chum
   (5) A Haunted House
   (6) An Abandoned Water Mill
   (7) A Sickroom
   (8) The Most and Least Attractive Parts of Town
   (9) Before and After Dinner
   (10) Piano Lessons As Viewed by Father, Mother, and Young Son
   (11) A View on a Clear and a Rainy Day

13. Look carefully at the two Gibson drawings on pages 520 and 521. Describe the contrast as vividly as you can.

6. Revising Description

In revising description, look carefully to the following five points: —

1. Maintain the physical point of view accurately, and keep the reader informed whether it is stationary or changing.

2. Be sure to give enough definite details to enable the reader to realize the object described and your feeling toward it. See Details in Description, page 508.

3. Appeal to as many of the five senses as possible — sight, smell, sound, taste, feel, and motion. See Variety of Sense Appeal, pages 508–512.

4. Try to sharpen and focus each detail so that it will be as vivid and suggestive as you can make it. See "The Suggestive Power of the Single Detail," pages 518–519.

5. Adhere strictly to the mood or impression and follow and reinforce it throughout. See Mood or Impression in Description, pages 519–526.

Specimens of Description

(1) STUDENT DESCRIPTIONS

1. Scenes from Childhood : Practice Hour [1]

BERNARDINE PENDERGAST

She sets the alarm clock on top of the piano in the most inconspicuous corner, and reluctantly places two pillows upon the piano bench. The cookies, which up to this time have been very carefully concealed beneath her printed apron, are put at the right end of the keyboard. After a few prolonged minutes which she uses in giving an additional pat to the pillows and in searching for the already obvious music — all of this time carefully counted on the practice hour — a few faint, unsure notes become audible. Slowly, up and down the keys her little fingers feel out the notes of the "C" scale. She continues this for perhaps two or three minutes, but with every second her look of boredom is increased. Finally the monotony of the scales ends with a diligent bang, and she eagerly reaches for a cooky, which she eats with such careful mastication that even a doctor would nod his head in approval.

[1] From *Green Caldron*.

2. EVENING ON THE RIVER

DORIS L. TOWNE

(*State University of Iowa*)

Many evenings after supper at the cottage we rowed up the river to set the trotlines. Before we pushed off the point, the sun had slipped behind the pines, leaving the western sky brilliantly washed in red, the hills and trees outlined with fire, and the whole scene glowingly mirrored in the water. We rowed by the sand bar where a long-legged heron stood on one foot in a shallow pool, through the pond where the water lilies grew, their pale petals flushed from the sunset and their big leaves swaying with a sudden motion, to Catfish Channel, where the fish flopped above the surface, rippling the flaming water. We strung the long line across the river. Grandpa baited the hooks with shining minnows (we called them "minnies" then), which darted and flopped on the end of their line. Then we floated downstream in the slowly changing light. The brilliancy of the sky softened to limpid gold and faded away. The long pointed shadows of the pines leaned farther into the river, pushing the red and gold still lingering on the water deep into its black depths. The birds hushed their songs to twitters, except the thrushes, who began their antiphonal evening chants as the woods lapsed into darkness. The sound of our oars dipping and dripping rhythmically and the faint purling sound of the spring rose liquid in the evening quiet. When our boat struck the rocks on the point Grandmother spoke from the shadows where she awaited us. "Is that you, John?" With her we sat on the rocks as the night mist fumed on the river and watched as the water brimmed with wavering, twinkling stars and the fireflies wheeled in the woods about us. Then Grandmother slapped at a mosquito and declared that it was bedtime.

3. AN EXPERT AXMAN [1]

NATHAN OSER

Leisurely he picked up his axe, looked at it critically, took a stone out of his pocket, and honed the edge of the axe in places where it looked a little dull. Then he walked placidly up to a tree, surveyed it, shifted the quid of tobacco to the other cheek, spat a stream of black juice, and moved around to that side of the tree which seemed most advantageous to start on. He raised his axe, and with all the strength he could muster, struck it into the tree. But the instant the blow was struck, he was once more calm, relaxed, placid. Almost gently the axe was pulled loose, a careful glance told him where it would be most advantageous to strike next, the axe was raised, and once more a blow was driven home. And so, methodically, slowly, but steadily, without a blow wasted, without a blow misplaced, chip by chip, the

[1] From *Green Caldron.*

tree was undermined, until it fell with a crash, precisely in the spot he had picked for it. He surveyed the prostrate tree, again shifted his quid, leisurely mopped his brow, and started trimming. After the huge oak he had felled had been turned into a pile of cordwood, there was only one difference that could be noticed in him — his quid was in the left, instead of the right cheek. But he was not one whit more fatigued, not one whit less ready to start on another tree. He had the genuine article — endurance.

4. NIGHT-RIDE

(English A, Harvard University)

It was very dark. There was no moon, and the bright scatter of stars didn't help much. My horse's head moved up and down in silhouette against the road, which wound away in front of us in a pale stream. The trees along the roadside were smudged in indistinctly, except for an occasional birch, whose slim trunk shone with a faint, pearly glow. Branches formed a gnarled fretwork through which one could see a vague sweep of fields, and two pricks of light on the horizon.

The sharp klopping of hoofs on the hard road made distinct, dead sounds, cut off from one another; now and then, pebbles rattled into the ditch with a frightened, scurrying rush. Except for these sounds, and the occasional, tiny thread of our voices, there was silence. And yet, there seemed to be vast, whispering waves of sound moving over us, that we did not hear; perhaps it was wind in the trees.

Like spring water, the air was chill and clear; it began to penetrate my clothes, and I noticed uncomfortably how my breath misted on the air. The sides of my horse were warm against my legs, but I grew steadily colder. Perhaps, we decided, a race would bring the old circulation back. A jolting trot, hoofs drumming faster, then suddenly, we were galloping. The rhythmic lift and leap of the horse conveyed a feeling of swift, powerful flight; every time the muscles in his shoulders rolled, we went up, and my stomach seemed to float inside me with a pleasant lightness.

The road billowed in front of us with a sort of fluid undulation. Then suddenly, it spilled over a hill. Down we went, with a swoop that lifted me out of the saddle. The darkness seemed to have silted more thickly in the little valley; I could see almost nothing except for the occasional sparks from the horses' hoofs. Then, a breath of moss and reeds — a gleam of twisted water — the hollow ring of a wooden bridge — and as suddenly, upward again, and on a level with our eyes, an ebony hillcrest set with stars. Surging over its top, we swept through a farm in a breathless flash, catching briefly the sharp warning of a watchdog. Through several others we galloped, their barns and houses close up to either side of the road. In one barn, a lantern shone where a man curried his horse without looking up; in the doorway of another, a man held his lantern aloft to see who rode abroad so madly at that hour. Between these farms, as ever, stretched the timeless, winding road, and the trees. The night seemed to stretch in a dark, smooth, endless curve ahead of us.

It didn't. It ended at our barn door, under the flat glare of an electric bulb. And when I turned to take one last look behind me, the countryside had dropped behind an impenetrable veil of darkness.

(2) AUTHOR DESCRIPTIONS

1. The Deserted Beach [1]

CHRISTOPHER MORLEY

The sands are lonely in the fall. On those broad New Jersey beaches, where the rollers sprawl inward in ridges of crumbling snow, the ocean looks almost wistfully for its former playmates. The children are gone, the small brown legs, the toy shovels and the red tin pails. The familiar figures of the summer season have vanished: the stout ladies who sat in awninged chairs and wrestled desperately to unfurl their newspapers in the wind, the handsome mahogany-tanned life-savers, the vamperinos incessantly drying their tawny hair, the corpulent males of dark complexion wearing ladies' bathing caps, the young men playing a degenerate baseball with a rubber sphere and a bit of shingle. All that life and excitement, fed upon hot dogs and vanilla cones, anointed with cold cream and citronella, has vanished for another year.

2. On a Local Train [2]

IRVIN S. COBB

The train continued on its course — not hurriedly, but with reasonable steadfastness and singleness of purpose. After much the same fashion the sun went down. The bride repeatedly whisked away cindery deposits off her cashmered lap; the large-faced man, being awakened by one of his own snores, put on his shoes and indulged in fine-cut tobacco, internally applied; but the youngest passenger now slept all curled up in a moist little bundle, showing an expanse of plump neck much mottled by heat-rash, and clutching in one greased and gritted fist the denuded shank-bone of a chicken with a frieze of gnawed tendons adhering to its larger joint.

[1] From *Travels in Philadelphia*, David McKay Company. By permission of the author.
[2] From "The Smart Alec," from *Local Color*, by Irvin S. Cobb, copyright 1916 by Doubleday, Doran and Company, Inc. By permission of the publishers.

3. Run Down by a Mississippi Steamboat [1]

MARK TWAIN

We could hear her pounding along, but we didn't see her good till she was close. She aimed right for us. Often they do that and try to see how close they can come without touching; sometimes the wheel bites off a sweep, and then the pilot sticks his head out and laughs, and thinks he's mighty smart. Well, here she oomes, and we said she was going to try to shave us; but she didn't seem to be sheering off a bit. She was a big one, and she was coming in a hurry, too, looking like a black cloud with rows of glow-worms around it; but all of a sudden she bulged out, big and scary, with a long row of wide-open furnace doors shining like red-hot teeth, and her monstrous bows and guards hanging right over us. There was a yell at us, and a jingling of bells to stop the engines, a pow-wow of cussing, and whistling of steam — and as Jim went overboard on one side and I on the other, she come smashing straight through the raft.

4. The Storm [1]

MARK TWAIN

The door of the cavern was big enough to roll a hogshead in, and on one side of the door the floor stuck out a little bit and was flat and a good place to build a fire on. So we built it there and cooked dinner.

We spread the blankets inside for a carpet, and eat our dinner in there. We put all the other things handy at the back of the cavern. Pretty soon it darkened up and begun to thunder and lighten; so the birds was right about it. Directly it begun to rain, and it rained like all fury, too, and I never see the wind blow so. It was one of these regular summer storms. It would get so dark that it looked all blue-black outside, and lovely; and the rain would thrash along by so thick that the trees off a little ways looked dim and spider-webby; and here would come a blast of wind that would bend the trees down and turn up the pale underside of the leaves; and then a perfect ripper of a gust would follow along and set the branches to tossing their arms as if they was just wild; and next, when it was just about the bluest and blackest — fst! it was as bright as glory and you'd have a little glimpse of tree-tops a-plunging about, away off yonder in the storm, hundreds of yards further than you could see before; dark as sin again in a second, and now you'd hear the thunder let go with an awful crash and then go rumbling, grumbling, tumbling down the sky towards the under side of the world, like rolling empty barrels down stairs, where it's long stairs and they bounce a good deal, you know.

[1] From *The Adventures of Huckleberry Finn*, Harper and Brothers. By permission of the publishers.

"Jim, this is nice," I says. "I wouldn't want to be nowhere else but here. Pass me along another hunk of fish and some hot corn-bread."

5. Autumn Twilight in a Small, Medieval French Town [1]

ROBERT LOUIS STEVENSON

It was September, 1429; the weather had fallen sharp; a flighty piping wind, laden with showers, beat about the township; and the dead leaves ran riot along the streets. Here and there a window was already lighted up; and the noise of men-at-arms making merry over supper within, came forth in fits and was swallowed up and carried away by the wind. The night fell swiftly; the flag of England, fluttering on the spire-top, grew ever fainter and fainter against the flying clouds — a black speck like a swallow in the tumultuous, leaded chaos of the sky. As the night fell the wind rose, and began to hoot under archways and roar amid the tree-tops in the valley below the town.

[1] From "The Sire de Malétroit's Door," Charles Scribner's Sons. By permission of the publishers.

THE ROUND TABLE

1. Describe, in one sentence each, any five of the following (five sentences in all): an animal, a bird, a boy, a girl, a man, a voice, a flower, a pair of eyes, someone's hair, a laugh.

2. Bring to class and be prepared to read aloud one of the following:—
    (1) The best description of a storm you ever read
    (2) The best description of a scene you ever read
    (3) The best description of a person you ever read
    (4) The best description of a dog you ever read
    (5) The best description of a horse you ever read

3. Describe your most vivid childhood memory.

4. In what imitative (onomatopoetic) words would you suggest the sound of a typewriter, a sewing machine, a vacuum cleaner, a lawnmower, an airplane, sawing wood, frying, boiling, thunder, surf, a rifle, a shotgun?

5. Try to describe in a sentence any two of the following: the feel of silk, worsted, velvet, sandpaper, a just-caught fish, a cat's fur, a dog's nose, diving, riding rapidly with the windshield open, caught in a sudden shower of rain.

6. Try to describe in a sentence any two of the following: the smell of a salt marsh at low tide, a bed of sweet peas, hay, an old attic, a cellar, burning leaves, burning paper, cigar smoke, wood smoke, coal smoke.

7. Try to describe in a sentence any two of the following tastes: bacon, bananas, oranges, apples, orange marmalade, cheese, green apples, honey, coffee, vinegar.

8. Describe two of the following birds that are most familiar to you: an English sparrow (cock or hen), a redbird (cardinal), a mocking bird, a robin, a wren, a crow, a bluejay, a woodpecker or sapsucker, a pigeon, a lark.

9. List the tastes in food and drink that you (*a*) like and (*b*) dislike. Try to describe one of each in a single sentence (two sentences in all).

10. Describe the scene when a long-winded visitor comes just as the family have packed a picnic lunch and are ready to get into the automobile for a day's outing. Introduce the mother, the father, a grown daughter, and a young son. Use plenty of dialogue.

SUBJECTS FOR DESCRIPTION

1. A Street in the Rain
2. The Spoiled Child
3. A Nervous Mother
4. The Deserted Farm
5. A Snowy Morning
6. The Old Oak
7. Class Dismissed

8. A Crowd Waiting for a Parade
9. The Blue-Ribbon Dog
10. While Waiting for Her to Come Downstairs
11. Pleasing Noises of a Large City (the Country)
12. Disagreeable Noises of a Large City (the Country)
13. Five Members of the Family Discussing What Kind of Dog They Shall Buy
14. My Favorite Picture
15. A Description of a Famous Historical Character (Let the class guess who it is)
16. Having a Group Picture Taken
17. Washing the Dog (Cat)
18. A Blind Date
19. Stage Fright
20. Our Family Doctor
21. A Crowd Waiting for a Parade
22. The Most Beautiful Object I Ever Saw
23. Snapshots of This Human Race
24. A Town Character
25. My Favorite Walk
26. My Little Brother on Christmas Morning
27. Waiting for the Train
28. The Barnyard on a Rainy Day
29. The Street I Live On
30. A Student's Room
31. Our Library Table in the Evening
32. After Church
33. What I Call a Good Dinner
34. Voices I Could Identify
35. When I Thought I Heard a Burglar
36. A Cat Stalking a Sparrow
37. An Old Landmark
38. Feeling Your Way in a Dark Room in Search of the Electric Light Switch
39. Night Sounds in the Woods
40. On the Bus
41. A Dusty Road
42. A Person I've Seen Often but Do Not Know
43. A Hen Protecting Her Chickens
44. A Cat Protecting Her Kittens
45. Getting Out a Book for Parallel Reading
46. At a Bargain Counter
47. A Pawnshop Window
48. A Rainy Day in a Country Hotel
49. Five Minutes to Six in a Five-and-Ten-Cent Store

50. A Dog Investigating a Strange Yard
51. A Dog Fight versus a Cat Fight (first by sight, then by sound)
52. A Cat Washing Its Face
53. A Flirt
54. The Laziest Man in Town
55. The Village Post Office Just before Mail Time
56. The Limited Goes Past
57. A Calm Night
58. A Cold Winter Morning
59. Housecleaning Sounds
60. The Top Pantry Shelf
61. A Night Call for the Doctor
62. When Father Shaves
63. The Oldest Inhabitant
64. A Small Boy (Girl) Taking Medicine
65. After Company Has Gone
66. A Grasshopper (Lizard, Snake) and I Sit Down Together
67. The Playful March Wind

CHAPTER XXVI

The Personal Essay

It is myself I pourtraye. — MONTAIGNE, 1580

A personal essay may be about anything in the heavens above, the earth beneath, or the waters under the earth. Nothing in life is too large or too small, too sad or too funny, too weighty or too trivial, to sparkle for a moment in the white light of the essayist's reason or to glow in the rainbow tints of his imagination. For example, in a handful of informal essays contained in a recent literature text,[1] among the subjects are a pet dog, the power of words, a literary confidence game played upon authors, a satire on schools, the pleasure we get from our vanity, and a charming old romantic love story. In the table of contents of a good recent collection [2] are to be found the following diverse titles: "On *And*," "A Little Debit in Your Tonneau," "The Truth about Women," "He Tries a Cafeteria," "In Praise of a Lawnmower," "Holding a Baby," "Concerning Revolving Doors," "On Wearing a Hat," and "Talkability."

In form, too, the personal essay is varied and elastic. It has no set form, no outward pattern by which it can be recognized. Nor has it any inner quality that can always be looked for and identified, like the story element in a narrative poem. A personal essay is indefinite because its sole purpose is to reflect its writer's mood or to voice his feeling. It is lyric in the same sense that a lyric poem is — because it is subjective and personal. Its aim is not chiefly to inform or to instruct, but is to interest and to entertain, to make the reader see more clearly and to feel more intensely. Truth is its aim, but truth to the spirit rather than to the fact, and always truth presented

---

[1] T. P. Cross, Reed Smith, E. C. Stauffer, *Good Reading, American Writers,* Ginn and Company, pp. 457–478.

[2] Raymond Woodbury Pence, *Essays by Present-Day Writers,* Macmillan Company.

lightly and suggestively, not ponderously, self-consciously, and heavy-footedly.   About all we can say of a personal essay is that if it isn't short it isn't informal; and if it isn't interesting, it is negligible.

Thus the virtue of a personal essay comes not from its subject but from its writer.   In the words of a modern English novelist: "An essayist, indeed, is a kind of autobiographer, one who begins anywhere and is always beginning over again.   Our indifference to his subject is the mark of a real essayist.   We do not care a fig what Lamb writes about, just as we do not care what an old friend talks about; so long as Lamb writes, the old friend talks, that is good enough for us." [1] It is the writer's personality that attracts us, revealing itself in unexpected turns of thought, in new and original ways of looking at things, in flashes of fun and sadness, in cordial sympathy and in simple kindness of judgment.

One person may travel through Europe, and return only to bore us, but another can't take a bus ride or go to the corner drugstore without making us sorry when he stops talking about it.   It is that kind of person who writes good personal essays.

1. Writing the Personal Essay

Because the personal essay is both highly personal and exceedingly varied, no definite pattern or prescription can be given for writing it.   The best plan is to read thoughtfully the personal essays by students quoted on pages 548–559 and in the Suggested Readings in the Essay listed on page 546.   The individuality and the charm of these two groups of light essays will afford far more helpful directions for writing than any textbook could do.   Read them first for enjoyment, and then, more critically, for their individual flavor and effect. Then do your best to equal them.   If, as it well may, the artistry of the essays in the author group makes you feel like saying, "What's the use?" turn back to those which were written by college students. Do you not feel able to write up to the level of "Invocation of the Muse" or "The Cross-Word Puzzle"?

[1] J. B. Priestley, "Test of a Good Novel," *English Journal*, Vol. 18, 1929, p. 330.

(1) SEVEN SUGGESTIONS

In choosing a subject, in settling on your mood and the approach to it, and in writing out the essay, consider the seven following suggestions.

1. **The subject does not matter much.** It is your attitude toward it, your mood, that makes or breaks the essay. Among possible fields for subjects are the manners, morals, and customs of today, either considered by themselves or in contrast to those of former times; interesting animals, persons, or places; authors, books, plays, stories, or poems; your own personal experiences, recollections, opinions, and confessions; the world of nature in any of its varied manifestations — bird, beast, tree, flower, river, lake, or season; a character sketch; your own fads, foibles, hobbies, prejudices, whims, impressions, moods, desires, feelings, fancies gay and fancies grave; in short, anything at all that concerns you personally and that you have strong feelings or decided opinions about. From one of the fields named above you can select a subject that fits you individually as your glove your hand. Further definite subjects (or rather titles) are suggested on pages 543 and 544 below.

2. **Your approach to your subject should be frank and intimate.** Remember that the appeal of your essay to others will come not from the subject but from your attitude toward it, from your own thoughts and feelings concerning it — in short from the way you reveal yourself as you talk about it. Avoid stiffness, formality, dignity. Never try to argue, or to prove anything. **The one imperative in the personal essay is " Be yourself "** — "be yourself," it might be added, at your best, at your highest pitch of wit, individuality, observation, and sympathy. Try to write as you would talk to a close friend sitting in the woods on the bank of a stream as twilight comes down, or as you would do before a leaping log fire in the winter time, with the light turned low and the wind tugging at the windows. Let us see your real self. Never forget the word *personal* in connection with this kind of essay; for as Carl Van Doren has said: "It differs from a letter by being written to more — happily a great many more — than one person. It differs from talk chiefly by being written at all."

3. Because it is personal and frank, **the light personal essay has a casual, informal tone which no other form of writing except the**

friendly letter has. It does not begin with a sentence of enumeration naming over the topics to be discussed and telling us in advance what is coming. It begins suddenly and unexpectedly, with the air of an old friend suddenly joining us in a walk and starting in to tell us an interesting experience or a funny story. Consider how informal — and how attractive — are the opening sentences of the following essays : —

Lo, the Poor Introvert

Who is that frightened biped, teetering unsteadily forward on a tight-rope over Niagara Falls, trying to keep two balls in the air as he goes? He is you — me — our poor race, born with single-track minds into the traffic tangle of the world. — DOROTHY CANFIELD

Column Left

Utopia-making is good fun, and so is sand sculpture at low-tide.
— STUART CHASE

Of Corks, and the Late Diplodocus

Once I met a man whose hobby was collecting corks. In a serious way.
— JOHN PALMER GAVIT

Leafing

Poets, I said, have kept pigs for an escape from their poetry.
— DALLAS LORE SHARP

Syntax for Cynics

The feminine language consists of words placed one after another with extreme rapidity, with intervals for matinées. — CHRISTOPHER MORLEY

A Chair of Nonsense

It is easy to talk sense ! — BURGES JOHNSON

On Wearing a Hat

There is a good deal to be said about wearing a hat.
— ROBERT CORTES HOLLIDAY

On Lying in Bed

Lying in bed would be an altogether perfect and supreme experience if only one had a coloured pencil long enough to draw on the ceiling.
— GILBERT K. CHESTERTON

Not only does the light essay begin casually and informally, but it also proceeds on its way informally and easily. Colloquial language, slang, and exclamations all find a place if needed. The paragraphing is loose and seems done in a happy-go-lucky manner. Even the sentence structure is relaxed, and in order to build up a desired effect words and phrases and clauses are allowed to do the work of sentences. Formal transitions like *first, secondly, in the next place*, are conspicuous by their absence. As we read, we almost feel that most of the laws of composition are temporarily repealed, and that the writer is taking a vacation from serious work. We are also apt to feel that it is no trouble to write a light essay, and that we could toss one off in half the time it takes to write a serious theme.

4. Be not deceived. **Informality is not carelessness, and some of the most attractive strokes and happiest effects result from long, thoughtful effort and frequent revision.** A bright, careless air of ease and naturalness is much harder to achieve than a more serious, explanatory style. It is much easier, for example, to write a perfect sentence of enumeration like those described above on page 157 than it is to start an essay off on exactly the right note through such happy openings as those quoted on the preceding page. As the story-essayist William Saroyan expressed it: "A beginning is always difficult, for it is no simple matter to choose from language the one bright word which shall live forever." The more we study sentences like these the more we realize their artistry. Read thoughtfully, too, the last few lines of the essays quoted below, pages 548–559, in connection with their opening paragraphs, and some of the thought and skill that went into their making will become apparent. Remember that the highest art is to conceal art, and the reason that such work seems easy and spontaneous is that the author toiled long and arduously over it. In your own work, too, do not forget what was said on pages 178–181 about the value of revision. You will probably have to go over your essay not once but several times, in different moods, to make it what you want it.

5. As a matter of fact **what holds the light essay together and keeps it from flying off in fragments into space is the writer's mood.** Like an iridescent soap bubble, it is the mood that gives roundness, perfection of form, and continuity to the shifting shapes and glowing colors that are reflected therein. This mood may be anything —

mock indignation, mock despair, gentle satire, gaiety, whimsical nonsense, sadness, wistfulness, yearning, or sheer nonsense. Whatever
it is, however, it is the essay's reason for being, and holds the essay in
itself as a soap bubble holds its colors and its own shimmer. The
mood gives unity to the whole, and however random and unrelated
the different parts may seem, they all cohere in the central feeling.
The essay may be narrative in tone; or it may be largely descriptive;
but it is not told for the sake of its story or its description. It is
told for the sake of the author's mood; and whether narrative or
descriptive, what chiefly matters is not what the writer saw or what
happened to him, but how he feels about it. The mood, the feeling,
is the thing.

6. Whatever other qualities we may try to write into our light
essays, **we should do all that lies within our power to be whimsical,
humorous, and unusual.** This is not easy on paper. We laugh and
joke and make ourselves very entertaining when among friends, but
we too often put on a long face and pull a stiff wooden overcoat over
our feelings when we take pen in hand. It may be hard to be whimsical
or funny; it is impossible unless we were born that way. The point
here is to encourage any, even the least, spark of fun we may have to
shine forth in our writing. If we can't be funny we can at any rate
try to say witty, unusual, or unexpected things. Say anything except
the expected thing; take any attitude except the usual one. Perpe-
trate a pun or get off a wise-crack — even a stale one — if you can't
do any better. You'll improve with practice — but you've got to
make a start. A familiar essay fairly begs and beseeches you for a
grain of humor. Recall here again one of the sayings that follow the
title page of this book: Learning to write is a serious business, but it
need not be a solemn one.

7. In the last place, **get as bright and attractive a title as you can.**
The title is your invitation to the reader. It is bone-of-the-bone and
flesh-of-the-flesh of what you are writing. Often you can get a better
title after you have written the essay than before. Don't think you
have to write your title across the page first and then begin your
opening paragraph. You must of course have definitely in mind your
subject — that is, what you are going to write about; but your *title*,
or what name you give it, can very well wait till last. Many professional writers write their essays or stories first and then cast about

on all sides, sometimes for days and weeks, for a good title.   Glance
again at the titles listed at the end of the first paragraph on page 537
and at those given on page 540.   Consider, too, the following : —

Practice What You Teach	James Weber Linn
Shavings from Shaw	Robert Benchley
A Herring for My Uncle	Albert Halper
Trained to Take It	Quentin Reynolds
I Don't Like Ladies	Joan Maybury
Myself upon the Earth	William Saroyan
Holidaying in the High Andes	Alicia O'Reardon
The Man Who Went to Pieces Entirely . .	Gilbert Seldes
Lost: The Gentle Reader	Philip Curtis
Tremendous Trifles	Gilbert K. Chesterton

All of these are real invitations : they sound interesting and make
us want to read on.   And that, of course, is what a title is chiefly for.

In conclusion, not everyone is fitted by nature to write light essays.
It may be that you are made of sterner stuff, and do not share your
feelings easily with others.   In this case your field is the expository
essay, and you should put redoubled effort on that.   If, however, you
can write informally, whimsically, and humorously, you will become
an increasing source of pleasure both to yourself and to others.

SUGGESTED TITLES FOR PERSONAL ESSAYS

1. Rain! Rain! Rain!
2. Fashions
3. Fat Men
4. On Spanking Children
5. More about Grapefruit
6. Reminiscences on Seeing My Shoes in a Row
7. The Fun of Being Poor
8. The Disadvantages of Having Ears
9. The Cruelty of Children to Parents
10. The Bad Result of Good Intentions
11. Noses
12. Women Should Propose
13. How Colors Affect Me
14. A Love Letter to My Alarm Clock
15. Brighter Clothes for Men
16. Playing Tennis with a Girl
17. When Books Are Better Friends than Persons
18. The Beauty of Weeds

19. How to Flunk a Course
20. In Defence of Laziness
21. If My Umbrellas Could Get Together
22. When I Expect to Marry
23. What Animal I Should Like to Be for a Day
24. How I Would Dress if I Were a Girl
25. On Getting Up in the Morning
26. On Being Cheerful before Breakfast
27. On Waiting for the Train (Bus or Streetcar)
28. On Being Very Small (or Large or Thin or Fat)
29. On Being an Only Child
30. Back Yards
31. On Cutting Class
32. Rich Uncles
33. Maiden Aunts
34. On the Word "Don't"
35. My First Smoke
36. Socrates at the Thanksgiving Game
37. Just Cats
38. A Woman at the Wheel
39. Hitchhiking — by a Hitchhiker
40. Hitchhiking — by a Car Driver
41. Girls
42. Boys
43. On Developing a Complex [1]
44. On Weighing in Public
45. Suppressed Desires
46. The Attraction of Fresh Paint
47. On Laughing at Myself
48. On Sunday-Night Suppers
49. Why Owls Are Considered Wise
50. Guest Towels
51. What My Dog Must Think of Me
52. The Gentle Art of Purring
53. The Art of Killing Time
54. On Finding One's Name in Print
55. On Seeing a Boy in His First Long Trousers
56. Why Girls Dislike Me
57. On the Uses of a Sister

[1] The last fifteen subjects are taken by permission from William M. Tanner and D. Barrett Tanner, *Modern Familiar Essays*, Little, Brown and Company, 1931.

THE ROUND TABLE

1. Looking back upon your English course this year, about how many explanatory themes have you written as compared with verse, incident, description, or informal essays?

2. If you have not read them, look up Lamb's "Dream Children" and "Dissertation on Roast Pig." They are famous personal essays.

3. Have you come across any personal essays lately whose subjects sounded as interesting as those mentioned on pages 537, 540, and 543? If so, mention a few in class.

4. Taking suggestions from Addison's *Sir Roger de Coverley Papers*, satirize gently some modern fad, foible, custom, or type of person that has fallen under your observation recently.

5. Which of the essays by students, pages 548–559, do you like best?

6. Which, if any, of the personal essays you read previous to starting this chapter could you recommend to the class as interesting?

7. With the opening sentences given on page 540 contrast one of the sentences of enumeration given on page 157 — for example, "The four leading causes of student failure in school are poor preparation in previous years, not knowing how to study, too much indulgence in outside social activities, and downright laziness."

Do not undervalue the sentence of enumeration. It is as effective for its purpose as are the light essay openings for theirs. There is the same difference between them, shall we say, as between a toothbrush and a bracelet, or between a potato and a pansy.

8. Speaking of humor, what is the funniest (*a*) poem, (*b*) story, (*c*) essay or sketch you ever read? Give the class the benefit of it.

9. Have you ever really tried to be funny on paper? It is a serious business, and at first, in the slang sense, is apt to be a sad one. But Rome was not built in a day.

10. For current critical and personal essays, look over several issues of "The Contributors' Club" in the *Atlantic Monthly* and "The Lion's Mouth" in *Harper's Magazine*. Do you find any difference between these departments? Select the essay you like best and either read it aloud to the class or make a brief oral report on it. Be ready to explain why you find it interesting.

11. Some of the best contemporary essays are published each year in Erich A. Walter's anthology, *Essay Annual*, published by Scott, Foresman and Company since 1933. Look up several of the recent volumes.

12. In your approach to writing personal essays you may find suggestive the following list of "Some Points Considered by the Judges in Reading Atlantic Essay Contest Manuscripts."

(1) Is the manuscript really an essay — formal or familiar?

(2) Is the essay interesting in subject matter, point of view, theme, mood, and the like?

(3) As a composition, is it well organized and correctly written?
(4) Is it entertainingly written?
(5) Does the writer evidence considerable originality in thought and in expression?
(6) Is his attitude honest and sincere?
(7) Does he think for himself?
(8) Does he employ his own vocabulary?
(9) Does he affect oversophistication and an intellectual pose?
(10) Does he seek to be iconoclastic?
(11) Does he indulge in literary flourishes?
(12) Is his style, all in all, well adapted to the subject matter, his personality, point of view, theme, mood, and the like?

13. A delightful personal essay on the personal essay is Carl Van Doren's "Note on the Essay." Find this in the college library in both magazine and book form, and read it.

SUGGESTED READINGS IN THE ESSAY

1. Collections by Individual Authors

Burroughs, John, *Birds and Bees*, Houghton Mifflin Company.
Dunne, Peter Finley, *Mr. Dooley in the Hearts of His Countrymen*, Small, Maynard & Company.
Hagedorn, Hermann, *You Are the Hope of the World*, Macmillan Company.
Huxley, Thomas H., *On a Piece of Chalk*, Houghton Mifflin Company.
Leacock, Stephen, *Literary Lapses*, Dodd, Mead & Company.
Lucas, E. V., *Adventures and Enthusiasms*, Doubleday, Doran & Company.
Maeterlinck, Maurice, *Our Friend the Dog*, Dodd, Mead & Company.
Morley, Christopher, *Forty-Four Essays*, Harcourt, Brace and Company.
——— *Essays* (selected by himself from many of his books), Doubleday, Doran & Company.
Palmer, George Herbert, *Self-Cultivation in English*, Houghton Mifflin Company.
Repplier, Agnes, *Essays in Miniature*, Houghton Mifflin Company.
Smith, Logan Pearsall, *All Trivia*, Harcourt, Brace and Company.
Stevenson, Robert Louis, *Virginibus Puerisque*, Charles Scribner's Sons.

2. Collections by Different Authors (Less Advanced)

Chamberlain, Essie, ed., *Essays Old and New*, Harcourt, Brace and Company.
Heydrick, B. A., ed., *Types of the Essay*, Charles Scribner's Sons.
——— *Familiar Essays of Today*, Charles Scribner's Sons.
Law, F. H., ed., *Modern Essays and Stories*, D. Appleton-Century Company.

Leonard, Sterling A., and Pooley, Robert C., eds., *Introducing Essays*, Scott, Foresman and Company.
Mabie, Hamilton Wright, ed., *Essays Every Child Should Know*, Doubleday, Doran & Company.
McClay, Harriet L., and Jackson, Helen, eds., *Story-Essays*, Henry Holt and Company.
Morley, Christopher, ed., *Modern Essays for Schools*, Harcourt, Brace and Company.
Tanner, W. M. and D. B., eds., *Modern Familiar Essays*, Little, Brown and Company.
Ward, Bertha Evans, ed., *Essays of Our Day*, D. Appleton-Century Company.

3. Collections by Different Authors (More Advanced)

Bachelor, Joseph M., and Henry, Ralph L., *Challenging Essays in Modern Thought*, two series, D. Appleton-Century Company.
Brown, Sharon, ed., *Essays of Our Times*, Scott, Foresman and Company.
Cody, Sherwin, ed., *Selections from the Best English Essays*, A. C. McClurg Company.
Hastings, William T., ed., *Contemporary Essays*, Houghton Mifflin Company.
McCullough, B. W., and Burgum, E. B., eds., *A Book of Modern Essays*, Charles Scribner's Sons.
Matthews, J. B., ed., *Oxford Book of American Essays*, Oxford University Press.
Pence, R. W., ed., *Essays by Present-Day Writers*, Macmillan Company.
Pritchard, F. H., ed., *Essays of Today*, Little, Brown and Company.
Robertson, Stuart, *Familiar Essays*, Prentice-Hall, Inc.
Shepard, Odell, *Contemporary Essays*, Charles Scribner's Sons.
Shepard, Odell, and Hillyer, Robert, eds., *Essays of Today*, D. Appleton-Century Company.
Tanner, William M., *Essays and Essay-Writing*, new ed., Little, Brown and Company.
Walter, Erich A., *Essay Annual*, published annually from 1933 by Scott, Foresman and Company.
―――― *Toward Today*, Scott, Foresman and Company, 1938.
Winchester, C. T., ed., *Book of English Essays*, Henry Holt and Company.
Withington, R., *Essays and Characters* (Vol. I, Montaigne to Goldsmith; Vol. II, Lamb to Thompson), Macmillan Company.

Personal Essays by Students

1. Invocation of the Muse [1]

CELIMA ROI LEONARD

Familiar essays are such easy things to write. Just any subject will do, you know — just be clever and a little mad about it, and it will make amusing reading, and be a *lot of fun* to write.

Yes, that is quite right. I have the facts well in hand : easy subject. That makes it easy, doesn't it?

The room in which I am writing must offer a variety of subjects. I shall check them off on my fingers : assorted chairs, a table, an Indian blanket, two Indian baskets, two loving cups on the mantel, and the pictures of my bearded ancestors. Inspiration, I am waiting.

Did you hear me? I said I was waiting.

2. The Cross-Word Puzzle [2]

DORIS MONTAGUE GILL

(*Simmons College*)

Sunday is traditionally a day of rest. In spite of what the other members of the younger generation may say, I am a firm believer in tradition. That is why I protested so hotly against the invasion of the cross-word puzzle. But in truth it was more an insinuation than an invasion. It stole into our home almost unnoticed, and established itself in our household before any-one but myself realized what it was about. As they say of the malady that has lately gained so much publicity through modern advertising, that is the insidious thing about it. You yourself do not know how completely it has you in its thrall until you are powerless to escape.

Sunday morning, in my home, the family used to gather in the living room to read the newspapers. After a few minor disagreements, relative to who should have the front pages, sporting news, or pictorials, the quiet was broken only by the occasional rustle of a paper. With what keen regret do I look back upon that happy scene! It is irrevocably a thing of the past.

It was at just such a time as I have described that my brother asked a fateful question — a question that was to change the whole tenor of our lives.

"What," he inquired, "is the word for Hades, beginning with *P?*" It was a significant introduction to the cross-word puzzle.

I shall always remember with something like pride that I was the first to voice an objection.

"If it's one of those puzzles," I said, "don't start it; because you're sure to wish you hadn't."

---

[1] From Warren Bower, *The College Writer*, W. W. Norton & Company, Inc.
[2] From *Atlantic Prize-Winning Essays*, 1923–1924.

Instead of replying, he asked if I knew the French word for mouse.

I said No, because I didn't wish to encourage him; besides, I was reading. But he was not to be so easily discouraged. And after a few more questions, other members of the family strolled across the room and peered over his shoulder, just to "have a look." Soon a group had formed on the divan, and they were all busily murmuring to themselves, and counting out the letters on their fingers. Occasionally one of them would address me point-blank, and I would drag myself up from the depths of a very absorbing novel long enough to mutter "No, no," and then plunge back again. Finally, after what to me seemed at least the hundredth interruption, I flung down my book in despair.

"Oh, why, why don't you get a dictionary, and leave me in peace?" I cried.

"Don't get sore," said my brother, soothingly, "I only thought you might happen to know a synonym for intelligence."

"I have never given you reason to think so," I answered, as I hoped, crushingly.

He replied, more thoughtfully, that perhaps I hadn't.

By this time, I had definitely relinquished all hope of finishing my book, and I went upstairs to write some letters. On returning, I found that they had adopted my advice. Volumes of the *Encyclopaedia Britannica* were stacked about on the floor beside the couch. A Roget's *Thesaurus*, a French dictionary, and some sort of treatise on electricity were strewn on the table near by. They were in the thick of it now.

At dinner, I tried to reason with them. I brought forward a plan which I had thought out quite carefully, and I considered rather ingenious. What was the sense, I pointed out, of straining every nerve, trying to solve this thing? All they had to do was to wait until next Sunday! Then they would find it all written out for them, and all they would have to do would be to read it. Really, I had quite outdone myself. I was tremendously proud of my scheme, which I fancied had cleared up the matter for good and all. But I did not reckon with my audience. My plan fell on deaf ears. They would not even listen.

Later in the afternoon, I began to notice a certain constraint, which made itself felt in several distinctly unpleasant remarks.

"You've studied geology. Why the devil don't you know another word for the Neolithic Age?" inquired someone, in a voice that was nearly savage.

"Well, you've had the history of religion, and you don't know a Mohammedan division of the year," snapped the person addressed, under the impression that he was justifying himself by this counterattack. They seemed unable to agree on many points, and all accused one another of having become frightfully stupid.

I want to believe that I held out as long as was humanly possible. But I was alone in the house, reading had become an impossibility, and the sight of the absorbed little group beneath the warm glow of the lamp proved too alluring.   And so, when someone chanced to glance up and ask me for some word, I felt my resolution slipping from me.

"What does it have to begin with?" I groaned, and I knew that from that moment I was lost.   Like one of those Great Loves of movie fame, it was stronger than I.

Late that night, a feeble cheer went up from our circle.   We were exhausted, physically and mentally, but we had conquered the Puzzle, or so we imagined.

How it must have laughed to itself!   For now this inexorable tyrant has taken our Sundays for its own.   We begin early in the morning, so as to "get a good start."   Orders are given and executed with a lightning-like rapidity.   There is a scattering of books in every room, besides those in the library, and members of the family are sent out all over the house, scouting for miscellaneous information.   Indeed, I hardly recognize my brothers in these zealous seekers after knowledge.

The day that was once spent in reading, visiting, or writing letters, is now passed in determining the name of a child's marble beginning with *i*; a Hindu symbol of religion; a small knife used in sacrificing; and other equally profitless bits of abstract information.   Gone is the day of quiet pleasures, gone the happy family life that used to characterize our one day together.

I beg, I beseech you, with tears in my eyes, be warned by our terrible fate. Do not, as you value your future happiness, your peace of mind, indeed, perhaps even your sanity — do not allow yourself to fall victim to the horrid fascinations of the Cross-Word Puzzle.

3. EFFIE [1]

RANDALL BROWN

(*Olivet College*)

"Where's another font of twenty-four point chelt extended?"

To this question, and to dozens of others which arose daily in the smalltown print shop where I received my college preparatory education, came the reply from any one of the force of five linotype operators, printers, and devils, "Ask Effie."

"Ask Effie."   I have heard that gentle command until it rings in my ears. It was a wise order, for Effie did know where to find everything from the lost benzine can to a fifty-year-old cut of the first mayor of Reed City, my home town.   If you didn't know how to cut slugs, Effie was there to show you.   If you wanted someone to doctor up the temperamental linotype, your shortest and best way to end your troubles was to call on Effie.   If you were reading proof and wanted to divide "Canada," Effie would tell you every time.

[1] From *Atlantic Prize-Winning Essays*, 1931–1932.

I have never found a teacher or professor from whom I have gained so much genuine knowledge as from Effie.   She was no Doctor of Philosophy ; why, she didn't even have a high-school diploma !   Yet she succeeded in pounding into my spongy brain more than any other person.   Effie taught me how to read proof, how to feed a press, how to cut paper, how to handle a stick, how to operate the linotype, how to set heads, how to lay out ads, how to make up the front page, how to fold and jog paper, and above all how to feel at home in a jungle of presses, type cases, hot lead, and imposing stones amid the sweet odor of printer's ink and musty newsprint.

And it was Effie who saw to it that I was sent comp. copies of the home-town paper (on which I had so assiduously slaved for three years) after I bade the old *Herald* force good-bye and sought further fortune on a college campus.   It's been nearly two years since I left, but I haven't missed a single issue of the "old rag," as we called it.

Yes, Effie had a past.   When she was young she was in love.   I mean visibly so.   Now she smothers her affection for her boyhood sweetheart, who wouldn't marry her because his brothers and sisters insisted that such a relationship would be "unwise."   Effie is (sh-shh, I'll whisper it) an old maid.   And Abe, her old lover, is the town bachelor.   Every day the two pass each other on the street in going to work and the only greeting is a silent nod.

Now Effie is nearly sixty.   Save for a few weeks' illness she has been on the job every morning at seven-thirty for forty years.   How many miles of shiny silver linotype slugs and of sticky ink foundry type she must have set ! How many tons of paper she has folded !   How many barrels of ink she has seen whisked on to auction-sale handbills, school newspapers, supervisors' proceedings, and merchants' stationery !   What a thundering crash all the chugs of the linotypes, all the fierce groans of the presses, and all the *rat-a-tats* of the printer's mallet she has heard would make if combined in one report !

While scanning old files of the *Herald-Clarion* one day I discovered my own birth notice.   I showed the item to Effie.   "Why, I remember setting that," she smiled.   I was amazed.   To think that this good woman, ever since (and long before) the beginning of my frail existence, during the distant days of my babyhood and throughout my grammar schooling, had been setting type day in and day out !   Some indescribable religious respect for her overcame me.

Out of every five phone callers at the office, four would demand to speak to Effie.   "No, it isn't anything you can't take, young man, but I would like to give it to Effie."   Even the Boss had this happen to him.   Effie knew how to place every comma to suit the taste of our "persnickety" customers. We would let Effie talk with all the cranks who came into or telephoned the office and who "knew what they wanted to say, but not how to say it."   Effie always "fixed them up."   And they liked it.   Who wouldn't ?

Effie kept the books.   She was the only one in the shop (Boss included) who knew how.   If you wanted to find out the amount of the six-year-old account of Silas English, Effie would dig it from an ink-smudged, chaotic set of ancient files in less than a minute. She could tell you how much less the shop was earning than a year before, how many copies had fallen off, and how many years John Ruppert was in arrears.

If I ever run a publishing business, Effie will be the first employee I ask to work. But she won't accept. She will turn down higher pay (as she has done dozens of times) to stay in the old home town, where she must care for her aged mother. She will set many more miles of type before . . .

She dies with a stick in her hand.

4. FIDDLES [1]

SUE EMELYN MEYERS

(*University of Missouri*)

How it happened I don't know, but there I was, crowded into one corner of a nine-by-twelve room with a hundred other people crowded into that same nine-by-twelve, and all but the eight dancers were looking at me; and even they cast admiring glances in my direction whenever they could spare a minute from their stomping and whirling. It was the first time they had heard a girl play honest-to-goodness fiddling tunes on an honest-to-goodness fiddle. Oh yes, there was Dewey's oldest girl who went off to school; she learned to play "Turkey in the Straw," but she learned it out of a book. And it sounded like book music, too.

"Wal, by gollys," the guitar picker mused between tobacco spats, "it sounds jest like them guys ye hear on the raddio." That was a real compliment to my fiddling. All I could do was smile to myself and try to manufacture some other excuse for being there than that I was an egoist who was more content to be the idol of a crowd of toothless square dancers than just one of the bunch of college seniors back on the campus.

But fiddler I am. I'm proud of it, too, though I sometimes feel a little ashamed that those few ergs of talent weren't directed to some other line of musical development that would have been of more use to society. Why, I could be teaching grade schoolers to sing the "Star-Spangled Banner"; but I'm not. Instead, I'm sawing off "Chicken Reel" over and over again on a valuable instrument that might be playing "*Salut d'Amour*" or a Kreisler composition. My instrument ranks with my playing: the finest in the fiddle world, but rather subordinate in the world of violins and violinists.

When I was in the sixth grade, my parents put forth every effort to make a violinist of me, but an uncle who loved the old hoe-downs persuaded me to quit practicing scales and learn a real piece, like "Ragtime Annie." What a surprise it was to Mother when she returned from the club one day and found wire strings on my lovely violin, which had begun a metamorphosis into a

[1] From *Atlantic Prize-Winning Essays*, 1935–1936.

regular fiddle. What a surprise, too, when she found, a few weeks later, that I had tightened my bow into a convex curve and had not unwound it; and that I was buying regular fiddler's rosin in the bulk at a hardware store and had given my violinist's rosin (wrapped in chamois skin and packed in an aluminum box) to a chum who was still practicing those silly scales.

I laid aside my leather music case (with my name on it in gold) and folded my hand-written fiddling tunes to fit my violin case, which was rapidly coming to be known as a fiddle box. Nothing Mother could say would convince me that I should give up this "fool idea" and return to the scales. My twelve-year-old determination was further augmented the first time Uncle Harry heard the "Little Brown Jug" from my own nimble fingers.

I soon learned that there was an art to this fiddling and that it wasn't all just "a lot of scratching around," as violinists see it; there was never a doubt about my art among those ninety people packed in the corners of this room in which the floor heaved up and down as the caller patted out the set. Four sweating farmers and four perspiring farmers' wives were having the time of their lives. Onlookers from outside the house were snuffing out any breeze that had a chance to sneak by their heads through the window. I was going over great!

What if some of the kids at school could see me now! Yes, I thought with a sickening glub in my throat, what if they should! With that I missed a note and would have lost time except for the stamping of the dancers' feet. The guitar picker had long since lost all consciousness of the smoke-filled room full of overalled onlookers. Lucky fellow, too, for a fiddler can't go off like that. He can't even chew gum and keep on fiddling. One mix-up on the bowing of a piece and the entire rhythm and melody are lost.

That's why you can't learn to play square dances from a book. Every fiddler has his own particular way of bowing a piece, and though it seems to an observer that he is most concerned with the fingering on the left hand, it is actually the bowing that makes the difference between good fiddling and bad. I was once interrupted in the middle of a square dance, and, though my bowing only stopped for a second, I could not pick up the tune and had to begin the piece again. A fiddler does not play with reckless abandon, but with a skill that no violinist can ever attain.

From the very beginning, a violinist is taught to place his fingers firmly on the strings in the exact tone position. But even the beginning fiddler knows that the way to produce a good rolling tone is by sliding from a lower half-tone into the position of the ultimate note. The fiddler, consequently, cannot leave his fingers on the note until he needs that note again as the violinist does, for he has to raise them to get ready for another slide into position.

So inborn is the art of fiddling that it cannot be taught. I learned by following an Ozarkian fiddler as he played for dances in my home community. I sat by him for hours until I finally got the hang of fiddling and then went home to work it out for myself. A fiddler can't wait till it's convenient for him to practice a new tune. When it first starts running through his head, he has to sit right down and work out the co-ordination between fingers and bow. That's the way it is in learning to play. You have to take one piece and play it over and over until you're good at it before you stop. One fiddler I know will stop his car in the road and get his fiddle out to try over a new tune that has just come to him.

Every chance I got, I would grab a fiddle at intermissions of our dances and pick up a few vital pointers from the guitar pickers. I was surprised when I found out that a fiddler does not stop playing a square dance when he gets tired, but must go on until he breaks a string or until the dance ends (which is practically never).

The climax of my fiddling career came one night when I was in a strange community and was scratching around during intermission. When the real fiddler came back and heard me he said, "Say, why don't you play one and let me and my gal dance?" Before I knew what I was doing, I had agreed. I knew that I could not last till the finish, but I had been hoping for this chance since the first time I played "Little Brown Jug." Six sets were arranged in the hayloft dance hall. The dance began and I played "Golden Slippers" over and over until I thought I should turn into one. No one even dreamed that I was likely to collapse any minute. A cramp crept up my right shoulder blade like a serpent and my bow hand was so numb that I wondered if I wasn't paralyzed. Just at the crucial moment, two Bohemians became entangled over a partner and the dancers stopped to watch the fun. After a five-minute intermission in which the pieces of the Bohemians were lugged outside, the dancing was resumed and I finished the set apparently without struggle. They think I'm a great little fiddler down there; they'll never know that I had never played for a complete square before.

Before I quit playing that night, I noticed a burly, unshaven man watching my every move; I was becoming uneasy under his stare when he ventured to the "orchestra pit" and said, "Sister, you'll never have to work for a living." I knew that I was made!

As if fiddling weren't work! After four hours of fiddling, that ever-recurrent pain strikes my girlish backbone just as it did that night in the hayloft, and settles there for the rest of the evening. Four hours of fiddling is only a start at a real square dance. The farmers collect as soon as the cows are milked and the chickens fed and locked up for the night; they seem never to stop dancing. Not a single Ford is wound up and headed for home until the host has treated with coffee, cake, and sandwiches of country-cured ham. The men drink so much home-brew on the back porch that it's up to the women to get the kids bundled up and persuade their husbands to go home, which is hardly ever before 2.30 A.M.

I often wonder what it would have been like if I had kept up my scales. What would these farmers think of mellow tones produced by a well-haired bow on silver and gut strings instead of the sharp rasping ones produced by a greasy bow on steel? How should I manage to keep my instrument tuned with the ebony pegs that are now replaced with patented metal non-slip ones? How out-of-place those hobnail boots would be on a hardwood dance floor after being accustomed to this splintered nine-by-twelve bedroom! Would "Marmaduke's Hornpipe" carry above the noise of the dancers if my fiddle were tuned down two tones to universal pitch, which violinists use? No, the other fiddlers would think I had gone sissy on them, just as they would if I trimmed my bridge, as violinists do, to where it would be just as easy to reach the farthest strings as the nearer ones.

Not a one would dance, even though I played the same tunes, in the same rhythm, if I held my instrument as violinists do, on my shoulder and collarbone rather than on my upper arm, and if I grasped the bow by the frog rather than midway between the frog and the tip. Suppose my accompanist sat at a Steinway instead of a $3.98 mail-order-house guitar.

In my dreams I raise my bow to caress the silver strings of my valuable violin, but the master of ceremonies interrupts me as he hands me a sweat-stained hat with $38.87 in small change for it — my pay for one night's performance!

5. "QUEEN PIGEON"[1]

JEAN M. HEALY

(*Northwestern University*)

Four o'clock! The last giggle was muffled as the door to the pin shower slammed. Sirkka stood quietly on the curb of the pool, her toes curled over the edge in anticipation — or from habit. Funny little stolid Finn? I recalled what I had first thought of this child. Just three years! Was it possible that this splendid creature, ready to take off in a long, lithe dive, was the same being who had appeared, silent and uncommunicative, while her cousin asked if there was room for one more on the Junior High squad? Sirkka had no smiles then. She looked. Her blue, inscrutable gaze missed nothing. Even then there were depths in her eyes I wanted to understand. Her fists were clenched tightly around a wadded handkerchief. She seemed determined to dig a foothold in the tiled floor with her restless feet. A shaft of late afternoon sun cut obliquely through the skylight and played a moment on the child's hair. Here was an odd situation. Red-bronze hair! It should have been an indiscriminate yellow. Well, what influence could the color of her hair have on her ability to swim? She would come next day. She moved reluctantly toward the door. That evening I was haunted by the rigid intentness of Sirkka's face.

From that time on I saw Sirkka daily. She came regularly to practice. When the last swimmer had departed this silent youngster would come back and ask seriously for one more plunge. In the presence of the other girls

[1] From *Atlantic Prize-Winning Essays*, 1932-1933.

she was still painfully intent, as though she feared she might miss some vital experience. This extra swim was a lark. A smile would break through that reserve and an unmistakable dimple would appear under one of those characteristically heavy cheekbones. Her smile has always been as irresistible as it is rare.

One day there were Junior games and races. Play day is always exciting, but this day there was a note of strained eagerness about the place. "Were the seventh-graders to be permitted to compete?" "Yes, it had been agreed, but only one event for each of the younger girls." Groups gathered in the corners. The excitement grew. In one group there was much dissension. "Was Sirkka to swim on the relay?" She strenuously objected. "Why?" Finally I understood. There was to be a "Queen Pigeon" race. If Sirkka swam in any other event she could not enter this one. This race came at the end of the programme and was clearly an endurance test. In it group after group of swimmers would be eliminated until only the fastest swimmer remained. It would be a real occasion in this Finnish stoic's career. She won her race; she was "Queen Pigeon." From that day her little water monarchy paid loyal and generous allegiance to its queen.

Three years! How little and how greatly she was changed! Praise and success have done much for her. The tension has gone from her manner. The somber, determined glint in her eyes? That's gone, too, and in its place is a gay assurance. Now, when she dashes up the steps to the pool, there is a significant pause in all activity. Her bright expectancy takes one's breath — demands instant recognition. Her blue eyes sweep over the pool with some of the same transparency which marks that water. She is possessive; her domain here, this spot where she holds undisputed sway, excuses her commanding air. But the "Queen" is evident in other ways.

Speed implies power and strength. This child has grown strong and beautiful. Those shoulders, so easily hung, and the muscular rhythm of long sinews under the smart silk suit, betray capacity for both grace and speed. She coquettes for a moment on the edge of the pool. Rippling, feminine, satin muscles appear as she stretches eagerly up on her toes. Slim legs and restless feet have such potential vigor. Yes, Sirkka has changed. She is quite a lady now. She is fourteen years old, and her world is a glorious place.

The Finnish people are not easily spoiled by too much attention. Sirkka is a true daughter of that North country. Life has been kind, but she knows how fickle her world is; competition is continuous, not seasonal, to this girl. Her race knows the meaning of long, hard winters; they have learned passive resistance to mental forces; their endurance is unequaled by any other people. Sirkka's quiet brow, her firm mouth and contemplative gaze, indicate her conditioning for a more strenuous type of competition. One feels that this swimmer will always finish her race.

Fifteen hundred spectators waited to see the great Morrison demonstrate her ability. Stop watches were checked by men in immaculate "white ducks." Swimmers with coldly perspiring palms and flushed faces sat on the white benches. In position before the take-off were four splendid girls, three of them tried competitors, and the fourth, Sirkka. Outwardly she was composed and apparently unconcerned. One might have thought this was Thursday and her ordinary "workout." Her wide eyes suggested a childish awe as if she were thinking, "I'm swimming with the great Morrison! Isn't she wonderful? I must swim well. This is no ordinary meet. I must do . . ."

Her body assumed the habitual position of readiness, arms outstretched, head eagerly forward, heels down to maintain balance. The gun cracked! There was a static moment after the report, then a powerful upward swing of arms and shoulders carrying the swimmers into their flying start; the lightning tension of toes, calves, knees, thighs; the stretching of chest and ribs with that supreme effort for more air, enough to last through the long glide; the lowering of the chin and the locking of rigid arms as the body broke the unrippled surface of the pool.

Then the phenomenon occurred. This was supposed to have been a wildly enthusiastic competition, not for first place, but for second. The crowds began their coaching: "Swim, Pelto!" She *was* swimming, with long, effortless, rhythmical strokes. No hysteria in this. She understood her job. Her orderly mind had caught its rhythm. "Breath-pull-way-back! Breath-pull-way-back!" Her long legs thrashed the accompaniment with a steady four beat, with only an occasional break in the rhythm as she exerted herself more strenuously at the turns. Those well-timed turns! The soft click of feet meeting the wall, and the mechanical doubling up and lightning-like extension of lithe bodies under the surface of the water! On the fifth lap she passed her closest opponent. The crowd registered its noisy approval, for she gradually quickened her pace. The massaging water gently worked the blue bathing cap from her head. The cap floated off in the wake from her feet. Her short hair whipped around and across her face as she turned for each pivotal breath. She rode higher now; her face only flirted with the water; her lovely shoulders and back were well out, and even the calves of her legs left a fine line on the surface of the pool. The last turn! Her slender wrists hooked determinedly into every stroke. The crowd's enthusiasm was uncontrolled. One of the swimmers choked, broke her rhythm, and fought madly to gain what she had lost. Sirkka slid swiftly and smoothly into the finish. Her hand touched the cold tile. Turning in her lane, she saw two swimmers reaching into their last strokes.

The race was Morrison's, of course, but to all of us it was Sirkka's. Hers was the real exhibition of steady, beautiful, effortless, and joyous swimming. After it was over? There was no pretense — she was simply happy to have done her job well. She tried to create alibis for her opponents, though she herself would never have accepted one.

Another picture that persists — moonlight, pines, and shadowed water. A Finnish Sauna on the shore of Long Lake, where slow smoke curls upward as the bath is being heated. If you have never taken a *sauna* (the word means both the bath and the bathhouse), you have a colorful experience in store. The building is made of well-seasoned logs. They are fitted as only Finns can fit logs. There are two rooms, one for dressing and the other for the bath. Along one wall of the dressing room are pegs of curiously shaped cedar. Now the pegs are hung with checked sport shirts and other bright wool garments. Benches line three walls. A door on the inside wall leads into the steam room. There are three tiers of benches in this room — all scrubbed white. There is a stove made from an oil barrel, the sides squared off with sheet metal and the top covered three inches deep with stones. Another oil barrel stands next to the stove, connected by a small pipe to provide hot water. It is all very crude.

There are several girls in the bath. Each has her own tin bucket, a sponge, and soap. Back in the corner, on the top bench, completely shadowed, sits Sirkka. That corner is the hottest spot in the bath. She stretches out at full length and drapes a saturated towel over her face to ease her breathing. The heat is stifling. Languidly she reaches out for her sponge, and a lazy trickle of suds patterns the glow of her skin. When the heat begins to be bearable someone throws another dipper of water on the stone-covered stove, and another cloud of steam ascends. Light flickers into the room from a kerosene lamp which stands on a shelf in the dressing room and shines through a small slit in the dividing wall. Grotesque shadows appear on the wall. An elbow is bent and huge biceps are silhouetted. Sirkka raises one leg, and endless toes project themselves in ludicrous array. "All good swimmers have big feet!" sings out the supine one. The air is heavy with the odor of pine knots, stale steam, strong soaps, and fresh cedar boughs.

There has been enough inactivity. Sirkka rises, a lovely figure, seen though the dimness as though photographed through chiffon, and begins the careful descent. The seats are soapy and "skiddy," not the safest places in the world. The girls throw pails of clean, warm water on each other to rinse off the soap. The plunge in the lake is the cold rinse. They run out on the dock and slide silently into black waters. Trite though it sounds, the sensation is "velvety." When the skin is warm and thoroughly free from oils, water and skin meet with an unusual affection. Phantom shapes move slowly into the path of the moon. Sirkka swims carefully. She knows the dangers of these sudden changes of temperature. A few strokes on her breast, her fair hair catching the moonlight, then she begins to play like some wanton fairy or sprite. She floats for a moment, feeling the silky ripples curl about her young breasts, and suddenly, with an easy elliptical swing, she raises white legs and pointed toes and disappears in a surface dive. She is up again, far out beyond the others, treading and bobbing, joyously blowing the water from her face, then welcoming it into ears, eyes, mouth, and through her hair. I still see her shifting from back to face with long, easy, spiral strokes, a perfect example of unsuppressed youthful exuberance.

There are swimmers and swimmers, but this child has her place in all my water pictures. When I see old Michigan in her glad moods, Sirkka runs down the beach, hair creeping out from under her jaunty bathing cap. When I reread *Peter Pan*, Sirkka has donned a shiny tail and cavorts among the rocks and rushes. Then sometimes, when gayety is too gay and confusion would spoil the picture, I see a little girl with a wadded handkerchief, a child whose direct eyes and determined mouth once promised great achievement. I see strong young feet firmly gripping the edge of a great pool. With the calm assurance of inarticulate Northern lakes, and the purposefulness of clear, swift streams, this daughter of Finland takes the mark for another — greater race.

General Theme Topics

(See also the lists of Jointed Subjects, pages 166–169; Subjects for Description, pages 534–536; and Suggested Titles for Personal Essays, pages 543–544.)

Here are hundreds of suggestions as to what to write about. In order to make topics a little easier to find, the list has been divided, the titles being grouped under headings that represent different phases of life — observations, preferences, reading, thoughts on better citizenship, and so forth.

I. Watching the World

1. Birds I Have Studied
2. Setting a Hen
3. A Dyspeptic in a Restaurant
4. How I Classify People
5. A Freak I Knew Once
6. My Experiences with Goldfish
7. The Most Stupid Kind of Animal I Know
8. The Greeting of a Dog to His Master
9. Birds I Know
10. Trees That Keep Their Leaves Longest
11. The Best Hour's Walk from Here
12. The Study of Insects As a Source of Pleasure
13. Which Trees Put on Leaves First
14. Seeds
15. Intelligence of Horses
16. Tricks of Horses
17. The Flight of Birds
18. Where Salt Comes From
19. The Age of Trees
20. Mimicry in Nature
21. The Firefly's Light
22. Life of Bees
23. The Carrier Pigeon
24. Hibernation
25. How a Bee Makes Honey
26. How a Spider Weaves

27. What Is Ore?
28. Where Iron Comes From
29. Where Silk Comes From
30. Tree Surgery
31. Baby Swallows a Piece of Ice
32. Having a Toothache
33. The First Cold Snap
34. Our Family at the Breakfast Table
35. A Man in the Rain
36. Before the Curtain Rises
37. Before the Examination
38. A Cafeteria
39. Bargain Day
40. The Man Who Never Smiles
41. The Doctor's Office
42. An Old-Fashioned Kitchen
43. The Country Store
44. The Mosquito
45. Temperamental Susie   (Give contrasting moods with her change in appearance.)
46. The Boy in the Back Row
47. The Back-Seat Driver
48. The Two Gigglers
49. Intelligence in Animals (Describe evidences you have seen.)
50. The Questions She Asked at the Game
51. Overheard in a Pullman
52. Overheard in a Day Coach
53. A Squirrel and a Dog on the Campus
54. My Church
55. The Back-Yard Cat
56. The Country Store As a Social Center
57. Memories of an Old Bum
58. A Barber Shop for Women
59. Little Willie Shows Off before Company
60. The Lucky Piece
61. The Romantic Drudge
62. Our Best Bird Friend
63. A Dialogue between a Farmer and His Hired Man
64. When Mother and Father Disagreed
65. A Rough Road
66. Some Local Superstitions
67. Talking to a Deaf Person
68. Souvenirs I Have Collected
69. The Billboard
70. A Poet I Know

71. What I Have Learned from ____ (Tell what you have learned from watching some animal.)
72. A Display in a Store Window (Describe it.)
73. Coming from Church (Describe people coming from church, particularly two or three.)
74. A Description of Some Unfamiliar Animal (Let the class guess it.)
75. The Difference between a Crocodile and an Alligator
76. Animal Tracks
77. My Kid Brother
78. My Distinguished Relative (or Ancestor)
79. What Roots Do
80. What Leaves Do
81. The Wisdom of Cats (Describe evidences you have seen.)
82. Overheard in a Streetcar
83. A Picture
84. College Noises
85. A Parade
86. Barnyard Sounds
87. Chiggers
88. A Distant Relative

II. Money Value

89. How I Could Earn a Living if I Left College Now
90. My Father's Business
91. On Working during Vacation
92. Getting Nothing for Something
93. What Is a Bank?
94. Where Do Taxes Go?
95. How to Get a Patent
96. Wiles of a Book Agent
97. The Use of Advertising Slogans

III. The World Is My Oyster

98. A Man Famous in My Chosen Profession
99. My Future As I See It
100. Why I Am Going to ____ College
101. Chances for Success in My Profession
102. What I Expected College Life to Be
103. What Constitutes Real Success?
104. The Greatest Influence in My Life
105. My Careers (A humorous account of all the careers you have selected and why)
106. What I Should Like to Do for My Life Work
107. Why the Average Man Is Average
108. What I Am Compared with What I Want to Be

IV. Notions and Preferences

109. On Wearing a Hat
110. Queer Names
111. Luck
112. Things I Like to Do on a Rainy Day
113. Things I Would Like to Forget
114. Stamp Collecting
115. Collecting Postcards
116. My Favorite Boyhood Heroes
117. My Favorite Girlhood Heroes
118. Putting Away the Things of a Child
119. White Shoes
120. The Dictionary for Entertainment
121. Wise-cracks
122. Waste Not, Want Not
123. Household Chores I Most Dislike
124. Things I Can Do Without
125. Trials of an Only Daughter (or Son)
126. Football Players Are Not So Dumb
127. The King I Most Admire
128. Things I Wish Our Doctor Wouldn't Do
129. Does My Cat Think?
130. The Last Thing I Expect to Own
131. The Fascination of the Forbidden
132. The Quickest Way to Make Me Furious
133. If Anyone Really Wants to Please Me
134. Radio Announcers
135. People Who Bore Me
136. On Keeping a Secret
137. Hair Cuts
138. Lending Books
139. Borrowing Books
140. Secondhand Books
141. My Nicest Compliment
142. How It Feels to Be Red-Headed
143. How It Feels to Be Left-Handed
144. How It Feels to Be Fat (Thin)
145. My Pet Extravagance
146. My Pet Economy
147. How Many Things Would You Buy before You Buy a Car?
148. Sounds That Keep Me Awake at Night
149. A Dog's Love of Motoring
150. The Thoughts of a Dog on a Running Board
151. Proof That the Earth Is Flat
152. Make 'Em See It Your Way

153. Gossip
154. On Deceiving Children
155. The Blues
156. The Nerve of Some People
157. Matters in Which I Am Forced to Disagree with My Parents
158. A Student's Breakfasts
159. The Most Enjoyable Party I Ever Attended
160. The Most Tiresome Party I Ever Attended
161. My Greatest Fear
162. What My Dog Has Taught Me
163. The Folly of Pet Prejudices in Others
164. How Persons I Dislike Help Me
165. The Importance of Having Someone to Whom to Explode
166. On Lending Money to Fellow Students
167. Have I Enough Curiosity?
168. The Other Fellow's Job Is Always Better than Mine
169. The Value of a Real Sense of Humor
170. What I Have Learned from My Enemies
171. How I Could Start on Curing My Prejudices
172. What Pictures Impress Me
173. Things I Have Lost
174. Queer Names for Domestic Animals
175. Effect of Weather on My Thoughts
176. Do Animals Know When Sunday Comes?
177. How I Intend to Spend Old Age
178. Pictures I Should Like to Paint
179. What Is the Most Monotonous Thing in the World?
180. What to Pile on the Piano
181. The Game I Invented
182. Pies
183. Pride
184. Fairies
185. Secrets
186. How I Feel in a Dentist's Chair
187. Impressions While Sick (Sounds, Tastes, etc.)
188. How Music Affects My Imagination
189. Daydreaming — Examples
190. When I Forgot a Friend's Name
191. At a Function to Which I Didn't Want to Go
192. On Hearing the Alarm Clock Go Off
193. What Sounds and Odors Arouse Memories
194. First Thoughts on Waking
195. Passing a Certain Street Always Brings Up a Certain Idea
196. Feeling, "I Have Had This Idea Before, Somewhere"
197. On First Discovering That the World Is a Big Place

198. On Getting a New Pet
199. On Making a Little Garden
200. The Inconvenience of Owning an Automobile
201. Does Silence Always Give Consent?
202. The Disadvantages of Having Too Many Friends
203. Evil Results of Being Obliging
204. The Danger of Being Too Much Admired
205. The Educational Value of Mistakes
206. The Advertising Value of Being Criticized
207. An Ideal Breakfast
208. What Personal Characteristics Do You Most Admire? (Do you know anyone possessing all of these characteristics? Give a conversation that shows what several people think.)
209. When You Take Up a Newspaper, What Do You Read First? (Give the answers of several people who are talking this over.)
210. What Names Do You Like Best for Boys and for Girls? (Let several people give their preferences in talking.)
211. Who Is the Most Interesting Person You Have Ever Met, and Why? (Report a conversation in which several people take part.)
212. A Very Interesting Dream (Let several persons tell their dreams.)
213. Which Is the Most Beautiful Season of the Year? Which Is the Most Enjoyable? (Give a conversation in which two or three persons exchange opinions.)
214. What Are Some Clever Pieces of Advertising You Have Noticed Lately? (Give the comments of several people in conversation.)
215. I Don't Like It
216. Flies in a Web
217. Nicknames I Have Survived
218. Don't Ever Marry a Doctor (a Lawyer, Minister, Dentist, Policeman, Filling-Station Owner, Traveling Man, etc.)
219. My Major Interest in History
220. My Favorite Musical Instrument
221. My Bugbears among Words
222. My Word Hobbies

V. Fair Field and No Favor — Both Sides of Some Questions and More than One View of Some Topics

223. My Opinion of Coeducation
224. Should Examinations Be Abolished?
225. Is Cheating on Examinations Different from Stealing?
226. The Value of Examinations
227. A Best Seller vs. a Classic
228. Should Grades Be Posted?

229. Should Churches Have Picture Shows on Sunday Nights?
230. Studying on Sunday
231. Why Grades Are Necessary
232. Why Pay Taxes?
233. An Education Outside of the Classroom
234. Talking vs. Silent Pictures
235. Is a Lie Ever Justified?
236. A New Year's Inventory of Myself
237. Should Capital Punishment Be Abolished?
238. Are Moving-Picture Shows Harmful to Children?
239. In Behalf of the English Sparrow
240. Greek Athletics vs. Modern Athletics
241. Speaking vs. Writing
242. Is a Small College Preferable to a University?
243. Biology Is More Useful than ____ (any other school subject)
244. Accounting for My Last Semester's Grades
245. Practice in Balancing Differences between
      Setter and Pointer
      Airedale and Irish Terrier
      Snow and Hail
      Rain and Dew
      Elm and Oak
      Wool and Cotton
      Walking and Running As Exercise
      Jersey Cow and Holstein (or Guernsey)
      High School and College
      Intelligence of Cats and Dogs
246. The Question of Hazing
247. What Should Be Done with Students Who Cheat?
248. Ocean, a Help or a Hindrance?

VI. Sports

249. The Service in Tennis
250. Heroes of the Sports Page
251. A Ping-Pong Game
252. Softball Is Rapidly Becoming Popular
253. Our Athletic Situation
254. Hunting Quail
255. What Is the Best Outdoor Sport?
256. Professional Football
257. On Riding a Horse

Books My Roommate Owned Read

VII. My Nose in a Book

258. Words from Mythology
259. Unfamiliar Words
260. My Seven Wonders of the World
261. Three Books I Want to Own, and Why
262. Unnatural Characters
263. How Literature Misrepresents Life
264. Folk Lore
265. Fabulous Animals

My General Reading

266. If You Were Marooned on a Desert Island, What Book Would You Like to Have with You?
267. What Do You Consider the Best Moving Pictures You Have Ever Seen, and Why?
268. Tom Sawyer and Huckleberry Finn — a Conversation
269. Penrod and Sam — a Conversation
270. Amos and Andy — a Conversation
271. What You Like to Read Outside of School
272. A Character from a Play by Shakespeare (any character)
273. My Hero in History
274. My Hero in Fiction
275. My Heroine in History
276. My Heroine in Fiction
277. The Best Scene I Know — a Description (scene from story, book, or play)
278. The Best Short Story — an Appreciation
279. Four Books Recommended — for a Classmate Who Has Never Been Fond of Reading
280. My Favorite Actor
281. My Favorite Actress
282. A Scene I Remember from the Talking Pictures
283. Prometheus and Fire
284. Pandora
285. Hyacinthus
286. Niobe
287. Midas and the Golden Touch
288. Midas's Ears
289. Actæon

Reading for Pleasure & Profit

290. Cupid and Psyche
291. Atalanta's Race
292. Hero and Leander
293. Orpheus and Eurydice
294. Exploits of Hercules
295. Jason and the Golden Fleece
296. Ulysses and Polyphemus
297. Ulysses and Circe

298. Should a Student Sell His Textbooks?
299. A Bible Story   (Choose any well-known story.)
300. The Most Interesting Animal Story I Ever Read
301. L'Allegro's and Il Penseroso's Day in Your Neighborhood
302. My Favorite Comic Strip

VIII. Thoughts on Making the World Better and More Pleasant — Morals and Manners, Speeches and Customs, Comforts and Conveniences

303. What Is an Educated Man?   A Gentleman?
304. On What Virtues Is Self-Respect Based?
305. The Most Useful Man or Woman in Our Community
306. The Essentials of Good Breeding
307. The Smoke Nuisance
308. Drives to Obtain Funds
309. Slang
      Yesterday's Slang
      Childish Misconceptions of Words
      Why Is Slang Undesirable?
310. Decline in Church Attendance
311. Judging Character by Personal Appearance
312. The Decline of Courtesy toward Women
313. How I Broke Myself of a Bad Habit
314. Modern Inventions Have Revolutionized Home Life
315. Protection of Birds
316. Protection of Forests
317. The Prevention of Noises Is Necessary — What Would You Start in Your Town?
318. Illustrations of
      Patience
      Truthfulness
      Frugality
      Politeness
      Loyalty
      (Write one theme or several for this assignment.)
319. What Is Meant by a Sense of Honor?
320. Modern Conveniences on a Farm
321. Forms of Stinginess
322. The Essentials of a Comfortable Living Room
323. How to Improve the Appearance of This Street
324. How to Improve the Appearance of This Campus
325. Blunt Speech As a Good (Bad) Trait
326. When Not to Laugh
327. Harmful Recent Inventions

328. How to Improve the Appearance of a Vacant Lot
329. Recent Statistics about Education
330. When I See Dumb Animals Abused
331. What I Consider the Greatest Invention
332. What Is a True Sport?
333. Tact
334. By Their Words You Shall Know Them
335. Girl Trouble
336. The Chaperon
337. Blinding Lights
338. The Thermos Bottle

IX. Glorious Adventure — and Some Not So Glorious

339. A Night with the Mosquitoes
340. My Greatest Surprise
341. My Proudest Moment
342. The Most Reckless Thing I Ever Did
343. A Card Trick
344. Catching Up with Father
345. Chased by a Mad Dog
346. A Test of Courage
347. Stuck in the Mud
348. The First Time I Bit on a Joke
349. The Spelling Match
350. My Most Embarrassing Word Experience
351. Why I Didn't Get There on Time
352. Amateur Doctoring
353. Making a Dime Go a Long Way
354. Sleeping in Class
355. The Instructor Fails to Appear
356. Sleeping in a Day Coach
357. Waiting for the Bell When You Think You Are about to Be Called On
358. Stuck in an Elevator
359. The Most Important Bridge I Ever Burned
360. We Ran Out of Gas
361. Santa Claus's Mistake
362. It Hurt
363. When My World Tottered
364. I Give Up
365. Cheated
366. A Get-Rich-Quick Scheme
367. Wise Guy!
368. Getting Acquainted with the Neighbor's Dog
369. Investigating a Bumblebee's Nest
370. Finding a Dollar Bill

371. The First Punishment, and What For
372. That Face!
373. My First Fight
374. A Curious Dream
375. The Plumber Arrives
376. And So They Flunked Me
377. The Early Worm Gets Caught by the Bird
378. What Has Been the Most Thrilling Moment of Your Life?
379. What Is the Bravest Act You Ever Witnessed?
380. Conversing with a Friend with Whom You Have Recently Quarreled
381. Talking with Two People Who Are Not on Good Terms with Each Other
382. Interviewing the Town's Worst Grouch
383. Talking to Some Person You Know but Cannot Place
384. Meeting a Speaker at the Train and Taking Him to a Hotel
385. Visiting a Friend Confined in a Hospital
386. Being Introduced to an Important Personage — the Governor of Your State, a Railway President, a General of the United States Army, a College President
387. Carrying on a Conversation with a Silent Dinner Partner
388. Telephoning to One Who Is Deaf   (Tell an interested but deaf person the results of a football game.)
389. In a Fog
390. A Mysterious Message   (Receive a call from someone who refuses to give his name.)
391. An Accident   (Give the points of view of the driver of the car, the vendor whose pushcart has been hit, and a passer-by.)
392. My Narrowest Escape
393. My First Hero Worship
394. The Time I Tried to Use a New Word
395. When My Intuition Played Me False
396. Guaranteed Hole-Proof
397. My First Dance
398. The Results of Taking the Wrong Dress-Suit Case
399. The Story I See in a Picture
400. Sunday-Night Suppers at Home
401. Every Dog Has His Day
402. A Bird in the Hand
403. It Never Rains but It Pours
404. A Miss Is As Good As a Mile

X. Things Every Student Knows — or Might Know

405. What Is the Greatest Honor a Student Can Win at College?
406. New Fashions in Slang

407. How to Develop a Vocabulary
408. How I Improved My Memory
409. Defects in My High-School Training
410. The Duties of the Manager of _____ (any college activity)
411. How to Distinguish Four Kinds of Birds
412. How to Distinguish Four Kinds of Trees
413. Explanation of the Equinox
414. The Leading Extra-Curricular Activities in My College
415. College Politics
416. College Tradition
417. Staying Out of College a Year
418. What Is College Spirit?
419. Our Grading System
420. How to Write a Theme
421. What Does an Honor System Involve?
422. Teaching a Boy to Swim
423. Colds and How to Avoid Them
424. Snap Courses
425. Library Etiquette
426. Learning to Swim
427. How to Keep an Automobile in Good Condition
428. How to Pack a Trunk
429. How to Generate Hydrogen
430. Managing a Drive for Funds
431. Some Fine Points of Automobile Driving
432. How to Sew on a Button
433. Something I Learned in
      Botany
      Chemistry
      Physics
434. The Cause of the Seasons
435. A Good Paragraph
436. First Aid in Fainting
437. What Sicknesses Boys and Girls Are Subject to, and How They
      Can Be Avoided   (Respiration, digestion, etc., will be explained.)
438. Living by Schedule
439. How the Summer Camp Benefited Me
440. First Aid for Burns
441. The Best Fuel for Your Neighborhood (wood, coal, coke, oil, gas, etc.)
442. How to Prepare Ads
443. Why Days Are Short in Winter
444. What Should Be the Length of Vacations?
445. How to Measure the Height of a Skyscraper or a Tall Tree
446. How to Study
447. How to Teach a Dog Tricks

448. Keeping a Diary
449. How Not to Study
450. How to Get Out of Washing Dishes
451. Patching Tires
452. Ways to Amuse a Baby Sister or Brother
453. Why the Leaves Fall
454. How to Learn to Remember Names
455. How to Measure the Area of a Pond
456. How to Define Words
457. How to Feed and Care for a Bird
458. What's a Volcano?
459. Names of the Months
460. Hallowe'en Customs
461. Variations of the Boiling Point
462. The Causes of Dew
463. Why Do We Have Leap Years?
464. Embarrassed by My Misspellings
465. Embarrassed by My Bad Grammar
466. How to Make a Fire without Matches
467. How to Ring in an Alarm
468. Stage Setting for One Scene in *Macbeth* (or *The Merchant of Venice*, or *Hamlet*, or *Julius Cæsar*)
469. What Would You Do If You Were a Millionaire?   A Policeman?   A Mayor?   A Principal?   A Governor?
470. If You Had an Annual Income for the Rest of Your Life, How Would You Spend Your Time?
471. In the Next Twenty Years We'll See Many Interesting Inventions
472. The Man I Marry Must (or Must Not) Be a Dreamer
473. What I Want to See in France
474. What I Would Do with a Thousand Dollars
475. If I Were Banished, I Would Live in ____
476. Suppose a Horse Were Able to Talk
477. What City, Domestic or Foreign, Should You Like Best to Visit?
478. Is There Anyone in the World with Whom You Would Be Willing to Change Places?
479. In the Days of ____   (If you could live one day in any period of history, which period would you choose?)
480. If I Were
    A Missionary Opening a Barrel Sent by the Ladies' Aid
    A Fat Girl
    A Fat Boy
    A Poet at a Football Game
    An Old College Athlete Soliloquizing
481. The Site of the College a Thousand Years Ago — If I Could See It
482. Three (Four) Reasons Why I Like Dogs

INDEX

INDEX

NOTES ABOUT THE MAKING OF THIS BOOK

The type used in this book is classified as an "old style" face, meaning that there is less variation in weight of stroke than in the so-called "modern" face which shows a greater contrast of thick and thin lines.

The text of the book was set on the monotype machine in a face to which the Lanston Monotype Company has given the Series Number 31 E. It was adapted by Sol. Hess from a face called Bruce Old Style (No. 20), and was originally cut by the George Bruce Foundry as shown in their specimen book of 1869.

In selecting a type for a book, and especially a textbook, a face should be chosen that is easy to read and pleasant to look at. The various headings and subheadings should be of adequate strength to indicate their relative importance. For a book of this length it was necessary to select a type compact and close-fitting as well. The main text is in 10 point, well leaded.

SYMBOL	Grammar	REVIEW PAGE	SYMBOL	Punctuation	REVIEW PAGE
N_1	Collective nouns	26	P	Punctuation table and special trouble spots	94–97
N_2	Nouns in -ics	28			
N_3	Foreign plurals	27			
V_1	Strong verbs	42–43	P_1	Period	97
V_2	Irregular weak verbs	44–45	P_2	Comma	98–107
V_3	Subjunctive mood	47–49		Restrictive clauses	100–02
V_4	Auxiliary verbs	52		Nonrestrictive clauses	102–04
Adv	Adverbs vs. adjectives	58			
$Conj_1$	Co-ordinating conjunctions	63	P_3	Semicolon	108–12
			P_4	Quotation marks	112
$Conj_2$	Subordinating conjunctions	63	P_5	Colon	113
			Ital	Underlining (Italics)	113
			Cap	Capital letters	114–19

SYMBOL	Spelling	REVIEW PAGE	SYMBOL	The Paragraph	REVIEW PAGE
Sp_1	Words easily misspelled	344–47	¶	Paragraph construction	13
Sp_2	Dropping final e	328	$¶_1$	Topic sentence	5
Sp_3	Doubling a final consonant	329	$¶_2$	Details	6–11
Sp_4	ie or ei	331	$¶_3$	End Sentence	12
Sp_5	y to i before es	331			
Sp_6	Inexcusables	344			
S	Division of words (Syllabication)	332		The Theme	
Hy	Compound words (Use of hyphen)	333	Anal	Analyzing the subject	144–46
Apos	Uses of apostrophe	338–41	U	Choosing paragraph ideas (unity)	148–49

SYMBOL	Common Symbols		SYMBOL		REVIEW PAGE
∧	Insert here		Emph	Arranging paragraph ideas (emphasis)	150–52
?	Is this right? Omission?		Cl	Announcing paragraph ideas (clarity)	156–58
ℱ	Take out; delete; omit		Coh	Connecting paragraph ideas (coherence)	159–64
✕	Mechanical error		Rev	Revision	181–84
			Ms	Manuscript form	185